Jimmy Stewart
ON THE AIR

CHARLES AND **ERNA REINHART**

Jimmy Stewart On The Air
© 2012 Charles & Erna Reinhart. All Rights Reserved.

No part of this book may be reproduced in any form or by any means, electronic, mechanical, digital, photocopying or recording, except for the inclusion in a review, without permission in writing from the publisher.

Published in the USA by:
BearManor Media
PO Box 1129
Duncan, Oklahoma 73534-1129
www.bearmanormedia.com

ISBN 978-1-59393-693-8

Printed in the United States of America.
Book design by Brian Pearce | Red Jacket Press.

Table of Contents

FOREWORD BY KELLY STEWART 7
ACKNOWLEDGEMENTS 9
AUTHORS' INTRODUCTION 13
THE SIX SHOOTER 17
GUEST APPEARANCES 79
RECORDINGS MADE FOR RADIO 511
BIBLIOGRAPHY 567
INDEX 571

*For our dear parents,
Charles and Thelma Reinhart
and
George and Leona Weigel*

A heartfelt THANKS for introducing us to radio.

FOREWORD *BY KELLY STEWART*

When I was growing up, I saw my father, Jimmy Stewart, on film, but I never heard him on the air. His radio series, *The Six Shooter*, premiered when I was only two. After that, TV pretty much took over home entertainment, and the radio wasn't on much in our house except for when the Dodgers were playing. In fact, my only awareness of Dad's life on the air came from one memorable story he used to tell. This involved an episode he had done for a thriller series called *Suspense*, during which the actors created the sound of boiling blood by blowing through a straw into a glass of water. What sticks in my mind is not so much the story, but the telling of it. Dad would speak slowly and menacingly, with an evil glint in his eye. It was clear that he'd had terrific fun doing this show.

I heard *The Six Shooter* only after my father died. While my sister and brother and I were sorting through our parents' home, we found, in the back of a cupboard, a set of cassettes with the whole series. I listened to it on my car's tape deck while driving from L.A. to northern California. It was a revelation. Dad was an absolutely wonderful radio actor, with the most compelling and evocative delivery. His character, Britt Ponset, was Mr. Cool — droll, sweet, unflappable, but not to be messed with — a cowboy reminiscent of the hero in the early western, *Destry Rides Again*. For the first time I understood why people mourned the demise of radio.

But Britt Ponset was not my father's only foray into the airwaves, something that became clear when Mr. Reinhart sent me the book, along with some recordings. This exceptional volume documents and describes in impressive detail, Jimmy Stewart's radio days: his numerous dramatic performances, including *The Six Shooter*, his public service announcements, and guest appearances. The book contains some delightful surprises. I never realized, for example, that my dad had ever played a leprechaun ("O'Halloran's Luck"), or could even do an Irish accent, for that matter. Compiling material from numerous sources, this wonderfully illustrated archive will be of value for those interested, not just in my father's career, but in radio in general and its interface with TV, film, and American culture. Britt Ponset may never ride the airwaves again, but the record of his having been there is now here for all to read. Congratulations to Mr. & Mrs. Reinhart on their achievement.

Kelly Stewart
February, 2010

ACKNOWLEDGEMENTS

The authors would like to thank the following people and institutions for their invaluable assistance in the completion of our work: Eileen Akin, Coordinator, Penn State University, Special Collections Library, Audio Visual Collections and Fred Waring's America, 313 W. Pattee Library, University Park, PA 16802; Jeanette Berard, Special Collections Librarian, Thousand Oaks Library System (credits for *Suspense* –"The Rescue"); Michael Cowan of Alotabooksnstuff (Toys for Tots record), Vladimir Dragan, owner-operator of the Book Barn of the Finger Lakes, Dryden, NY (various Stewart and radio books); Mark Fuller (Big Sounds Who Am I Contest and Vote); James Gavin (*Monitor* interviews); J. David Goldin (supplying several rare shows); Timothy Harley, Curator of the Jimmy Stewart Museum, Indiana, PA; Art Harvey (photos and ads); Christine A. Lutz, Princeton University Archives Project Archivist, Seeley G. Mudd Manuscript Library; Janet W. McKee, Reference Librarian, Recorded Sound Reference Center, Library of Congress; Aaron Mintz (United Jewish Appeal radio spot); Jay Rubin (various film interviews and radio spots, photos, providing contact with the Stewart family); James A. Sacckette (*Moonlight, Memories and Miller*); Elizabeth Salome (past curator of The Jimmy Stewart Museum); David Siegel (supplying rare radio show); Richard Weigle, librarian at The Paley Center for Media, New York City.

We would like to offer our special thanks to the Jimmy Stewart Museum and its staff for complete dedication and support of our project.

The Mission of The Jimmy Stewart Museum "is to preserve and interpret the life history and career of stage and screen actor James Maitland Stewart." Since its opening in May 1995, the Museum has become an important tourist destination, annually drawing more than 10,000 visitors from many nations, with significant benefit to the struggling Indiana County economy.

Jimmy Stewart's life embodies professional achievement and service to community and nation. His illustrious career encompassed theater, film, radio, and television from 1930 through 1990 and included important milestones in the histories of those media. He won an Oscar for his role in *The Philadelphia Story* in 1940 and in 1985 was awarded the Lifetime

Achievement Oscar. Mr. Stewart's distinguished military career began with his enlistment as a private in the Army Air Corps in 1941. He flew and commanded 20 combat missions, rose in rank to colonel, received the Distinguished Flying Cross and Croix du Guerre, and attained the rank of Brigadier General in the Air Force Reserves before his military retirement in 1968. In 1985, he was awarded the Presidential Medal of Freedom. During his lifetime, Mr. Stewart actively supported conservation efforts; contributed generously to schools, hospitals, and benevolent community organizations; and sponsored the annual Jimmy Stewart Relay Marathon benefitting St. John's Hospital Child Study Center.

Although he attained critical acclaim and financial success at an early age, Jimmy Stewart maintained an exemplary lifestyle focused on family, community, and country. The Jimmy Stewart Museum interprets his life through exhibits of personal photos and effects; movie posters, stills, and memorabilia; and military photos and memorabilia. Presented chronologically, the collection is supported by text panels that provide an overview of Mr. Stewart's life in context with local and national history and with the history of American theater, film, and broadcasting. The Museum places a high value on understanding Mr. Stewart as a contemporary role model.

The Jimmy Stewart Museum is located on the 3rd and 4th floors of the Indiana Community Center at 835 Philadelphia Street through an arrangement with the Borough of Indiana. In addition to the exhibit galleries, the Museum includes a 50-seat movie theater and a shop selling Stewart film memorabilia.

The Museum is governed by the James M. Stewart Museum Foundation board of directors and has two full-time employees assisted by volunteers and students in the Indiana University of Pennsylvania (IUP) Work-Study Program. Income is generated by Museum admissions, shop sales, memberships, special events, and donations. Admission is affordable to visitors, with discounts to military personnel, seniors, youth 7 to 17 years, and the local university students. Children under 7 are admitted free.

The James M. Stewart Museum Foundation is a 501 (c) 3 not-for-profit corporation.

The Jimmy Stewart Museum
PO Box One — 835 Philadelphia Street
Indiana, PA 15701
Telephone: 800-83-JIMMY (724-349-6112) Fax: 724-349-6140
Email: curator@jimmy.org
Timothy Harley, Executive Director

AUTHORS' INTRODUCTION

Since we began telling people that we were working on *Jimmy Stewart on the Air*, we have gotten nearly the same reaction. That reaction was highlighted by a 70-something gentleman who was volunteering at the Library of Congress; when we told him that we were there doing research for a book on Jimmy Stewart, he smiled and told us that he had always been a fan of Stewart. When we added that it would be about his radio career, he said that he didn't even know that he had one. Actually, as you will discover, Stewart had a long and varied career on the radio, appearing on that medium more times and more often than he did in films or television.

Every effort has been made to document each show listed in our book. Old newspapers were scoured for mentions of Stewart. Many previously unknown radio appearances were discovered in this way. Searches of various library holdings also yielded several new programs and online research revealed even more. Despite this, we are sure that there are shows that have been missed, especially local interviews that may have been done as Stewart traveled the country promoting his many films. We have concentrated on programs originating in the United States, although some foreign interviews may have also been aired.

We have been able to locate and listen to about two-thirds of Stewart's radio material. Some of the rarer material has come to us from great distances. *O'Halloran's Luck* came all the way from Australia. The mention of an NBC *Monitor* interview in an eBay auction led us to the acquisition of four of Stewart's appearances on that program. The casual mention of our project to a customer at a record show brought us another Stewart show that we had not previously been able to locate. Several broadcasting museums, including the Museum of Broadcast Communications in Chicago, have digital listening booths online. Finally, there's the Library of Congress. Many of Stewart's appearances, including about fifteen that we could not locate from any other source, were available there.

But, we have no doubt that some of the items that we have not been able to locate do exist. If you have one (or more) of the shows we haven't heard, we'd love to hear from you. You can contact the publisher or email us at *cfreinhart@comcast.net*.

Unless otherwise noted, all times for nationally broadcast programs listed in our book are for the Eastern Time Zone. Many of the non-network and syndicated programs may have aired on different days and/or times at various radio stations around the country.

COPYRIGHT LAW AND OLD TIME RADIO

Many of the radio programs in this book are easily found for sale on eBay and other such online auction sites. Many have been traded and/or sold on reel-to-reel tape and cassette tapes before becoming available on CD and mp3. Many of the ads selling them will carry a disclaimer saying that the shows are out of copyright and in the public domain. In most cases, this is probably true. But unless you're a lawyer, don't bet on it.

When most of these shows were first broadcast, the copyright laws were different than they are today. If published between 1923 and 1963, as most of Stewart's shows were, they were protected for 28 years and then could be renewed for an additional 47 years (under current law, this 47 years could be extended to 67 years). So, if the copyright on these programs had not been renewed, they would have entered the public domain between 1951 and 1991. However, if the copyright holders had the foresight to renew, those shows would still be protected by copyright. Once a program has entered the public domain, copyright cannot be re-established. Further complicating this whole matter is the fact that many shows contain music. It is possible that the music remains protected by copyright, while the program itself does not.

So what is in public domain and what remains protected by copyright? A check with the Library of Congress copyright records might yield an answer for those willing to spend the time to do rather extensive searching. Going through a copyright lawyer would be a better bet. Relying on the word of the seller is not advised.

That being said, many people still want to purchase the special CD and mp3 sets that are quite readily available today, even though some or all of these shows may still be under copyright protection. The main reasons for buying them are that they are usually cheap and, in the mp3 format, hundreds of shows can be placed on just one disc. We have chosen to list only commercially released sources for shows throughout our book, but let's take a brief look at some of the other items available.

A quick search online yielded the following:

James Stewart The Ultimate Collection of his Radio Work (The Orange Set) — 14 programs on 9 CDs
James Stewart The Ultimate Collection of his Radio Work (The Purple Set) — 14 shows on 9 CDs
James Stewart The Ultimate Collection of his Radio Work (The Blue Set) — 11 programs on 9 CDs
James Stewart The Ultimate Collection of his Radio Work (The Red Set) — 13 shows on 9 CDs
The Six Shooter — all shows on one CD
In the Spotlight…Jimmy Stewart — 13 shows on 10 CDs
Madame X — 1 show on 1 CD
Old Time Radio Salutes James (Jimmy) Stewart — 15 shows on 1 CD
Jimmy Stewart Collection — 87 shows on 2 CDs
Good News — 47 shows on 1 CD; several Stewart shows included
Hollywood Star Playhouse — 6 shows on 1 CD; including the *Six Shooter* audition show
Silver Theatre — 43 shows on 1 CD; including all but one of Stewart's appearances
Suspense — 940 shows on 19 CDs; includes all of Stewart's appearances
Jack Benny — 747 shows on 1 DVD; includes both Stewart shows
Western Roundup — 12 shows on 10 CDs; includes "Winchester '73"
In the Spotlight…Loretta Young — 18 shows on 12 CDs; with "Going My Way"
In the Spotlight…Cary Grant — 13 shows on 10 CDs; with "The Philadelphia Story"
June Allyson Gift Set — 12 shows on 9 CDs; including "The Stratton Story"
Best of Old Time Radio Shows — 15 shows on 8 CDs; includes "Magic Town"
An Old Time Radio Western Anthology — 504 shows on 1 CD; includes the entire *Six Shooter* series
Bill Stern's Colgate Sports Reel — 131 shows on 1 CD; includes one Stewart show
Old Time Radio Westerns — 1041 shows on 10 CDs; includes the entire *Six Shooter* series
Marlene Dietrich — 8 shows on 8 CDs; includes "No Highway in the Sky"
1941…As It Was — 8 CDs; includes *We Hold These Truths*
Bing Crosby — 362 shows on 1 CD; three Stewart shows included

13 Classic Old Time Radio Westerns — 4 CDs; with all episodes of the *Six Shooter*

Norma Shearer on the Air — 8 shows on 4 CDs; includes "No Time for Comedy"

Ann Harding on the Air — 6 shows on 5 CDs; includes "Madame X"

Joan Blondell on the Air — 6 shows on 5 CDs; includes "Destry Rides Again"

Katharine Hepburn on the Air — 7 shows on 5 CDs; including "The Philadelphia Story," both the *Lux* and *Screen Guild versions*

Robert Taylor on the Air — 9 shows on 6 CDs; including *Good News* (2-10-1938)

Christmas Drama — 11 shows on 8 CDs; includes "It's a Wonderful Life"

1937 on the Radio — 11 shows on 8 CDs; includes *Good News* (12/30/1937)

Rosalind Russell on the Air — 11 shows on 9 CDs; includes "Up From Darkness Parts 1 & 2"

Loretta Young on the Air — 14 shows on 10 CDs; includes "The Philadelphia Story" on *Lux Radio Theatre*

Myrna Loy — 13 shows on 10 CDs; includes *Single Crossing* and the "Sweet Mystery" sketch from *Good News*

Joan Crawford on the Air — 17 shows on 10 CDs; including the "Ice Follies of 1939" segment from *Good News*

All these were found in just one quick search. The prices range from under $5 to about $40. Packaging will vary from none at all to elaborate color labels and packaging; some even have extensive notes on the program. Expect the sound quality to vary from excellent to barely listenable. The only way a collector might be able to obtain some of the poorer quality shows is by purchasing these sets. Commercial dealers stay away from the poor sound quality shows, so you're not likely to find them from these sources.

CHAPTER 1
The Six Shooter

When Jimmy Stewart was working for Universal Pictures, he was also under contract to its subsidiary, Revue Productions, for work in radio. Radio was on its last legs at the time, being quickly replaced by television. *The Six Shooter* was an attempt to slow down TV's erosion of radio's listener base. In Stewart's own words from an interview with Joan Blakewell for The *National Film Theatre* in 1972, "I did a radio series years ago called *The Six Shooter*, a Western series. Unfortunately it came out just when radio drama had gone out the window so it wasn't a successful series." This was Stewart's only series for radio, although he appeared in more than two hundred other shows through the years.

Although this series was short-lived, the opening lines are some of the best remembered in radio history:

> *The man in the saddle is angular and long-legged. His skin is sun-dyed brown. The gun in his holster is gray steel and rainbow mother-of-pearl; its handle, unmarked. People called them both, The Six Shooter.*

Jimmy Stewart played the very unusual gunslinger, Britt Ponset. The spelling of his character's name is somewhat in question. Although this is the most common spelling, Library of Congress records show that it was also spelled two other ways — "Poncet" and "Poncett." Whatever the spelling, the character is always the same. Ponset is slow to anger, slower to draw on anyone, and always a homespun philosopher. When he was thinking through a situation, it was common for his line to be simply, "maybe so, maybe so," or just a, "yeah, yeah," said in a slow drawl. For dramatic effect, Stewart whispered much of his narration/dialogue during any suspenseful part of a story. It always had a very powerful effect on the listener, drawing him into the story.

Britt's reputation with a gun appears to keep him out of too much gunplay. In the 39 episodes of the program (the two audition shows were not counted), Britt only fired his gun in 1/3 of them. In 26 shows, he didn't fire his gun at all. In the 13 shows in which he did shoot, once he

Stewart, with script in hand, at the NBC microphone.

fired simply to try to stop a stampede, another time he shot a gun from a man's hand, and once he missed his target completely. In nine shows, Britt wounds someone. In only one show does he actually kill someone. In "The Silver Buckle," Britt shoots and kills outlaw Lex Springer. He also indirectly kills Springer's brother, Kit, when a shot he fires spooks the man's horse. In the final show of the series, Britt also insinuates that he had recently killed Bide Prescott.

Before the beginning of each story, the announcer says:

> ...based on the life of Britt Ponset, the Texas plainsman, who wandered through the western territories leaving behind a trail of still-remembered legends.

And wander he and his horse Scar did. Of the total of 41 shows, all mentioned the name of a town that Britt was either in or heading toward. There were 29 different towns in the shows, some he visited more than once. The towns were:

Adobe Junction ("Blood Relations")
Clay City (Audition 00A, Audition 00, "Ben Scofield," "Hiram's Gold Strike")
Clover Fork ("Thicker Than Water")
Copper Springs ("The Shooting of Wyatt King")
Council City ("When the Shoe Doesn't Fit")
Dawson ("Sheriff Billy")
Easter Creek ("Crisis at Easter Creek")
Elk Point ("The Capture of Stacy Gault")
Halfway Creek ("The Double Seven")
Harness Creek ("Revenge at Harness Creek")
Lead Creek ("Jenny")
Lockwood ("Duel at Lockwood")
Minton ("General Gillford's Widow")
Pearl City ("Silver Threads")
Petersville ("Rink Larkin," "Cora Plummer Quincy")
Powder Creek ("A Pressing Engagement," "Aunt Emma")
Prospect ("Johnny Stringer")
Quiet City ("Quiet City")
Russville ("Apron-Faced Sorrell")
Single Pine ("Cheyenne Express")
Smoke Falls ("Escape from Smoke Falls," "A Friend in Need," "Anna Norquist")
Sunset ("Trail to Sunset")
Temple City ("The Coward")
Thompson's Corner ("Britt Ponset's Christmas Carol")
Tower Rock ("Battle at Tower Rock")
Virtue City ("Silver Annie," "More Than Kin," "The New Sheriff")
Walnut Creek ("Red Lawson's Revenge")
Willow Fork ("Myra Baker")
Yellow Crest ("Gabriel Starbuck," "Helen Bricker")

Ponset seemed to finance his traveling by working on a number of different ranches and even on the railroad. Here are the ranches and/or people for whom Britt worked:

Circle G ("Hiram's Gold Strike")
Dad Foster ("Anna Nordquist")
Dad Morgan ("Battle at Tower Rock")
Dad Sommerset ("Escape from Smoke Falls") (Britt tends his herd as a favor)
Dan Porterfield's Bar Y Ranch ("Aunt Emma")
Dave Engleman ("Sheriff Billy") (Britt's winter job)
Floyd Prince's Crown Ranch ("When the Shoe Doesn't Fit") (headed there for a summer job)
Foster Outfit ("Helen Bricker")
Gid Bascomb's Double Seven Ranch ("The Double Seven") (Britt wants a job there, but never signs on)
Mrs. Pritchard ("The Coward")
Rex Jeffer's Tip Top Ranch ("Duel at Lockwood")
Rocky Mountain Western Railroad ("Silver Annie")
Round Y Ranch ("More Than Kin")
Ryfe & Norman McAdams ("The Stampede")
Sam Griffith's Double G Ranch ("A Pressing Engagement")
Saul Poindexter ("Apron-Faced Sorrel")
Silver Spur ("Revenge at Harness Creek")
Square Moon Ranch ("Gabriel Starbuck")
Tim Parker ("Quiet City") (Britt is headed to Fulton to watch over some land for Parker)
Troxler Ranch ("Crisis at Easter Creek")
Widow Jenkins ("Rink Larkin")
Wilcox Outfit (George Wilcox) ("Blood Relations")

The credits for each show were the same:

Writer .... Frank Burt *(wrote all but one show in the series)*
Director .... Jack Johnstone
Music.. Basil Adlam
Announcer .... Hal Gibney
                (John Wald beginning January 24, 1954)
Sound Effects .... Floyd Caton *(never credited on the show itself)*

Frank Burt was born Augustus Berek, on March 11, 1882, in New York City. Besides creating and writing all but one of *The Six Shooter* shows, Burt also wrote for several other radio programs, including *The City, Hallmark Hall of Fame, The Man Called X, This Is Your F.B.I., The Unexpected* and *The Whistler*. Burt also wrote for quite a few TV series, including *Terry and the Pirates, I Led Three Lives, The Cisco Kid, Noah's Ark, The Restless*

Director Jack Johnstone going over script with Stewart.

Gun, Dragnet, and *Schlitz Playhouse of Stars.* Three of Burt's radio scripts were turned into television programs. See "Silver Annie," "Britt Ponset's Christmas Carol" and "When the Shoe Doesn't Fit" for more details. Burt was also involved in Stewart's 1955 film, *The Man from Laramie.* The story of the film was based on a *Saturday Evening Post* story by Thomas T. Flynn, with the screenplay being written by Burt and Philip Yordan.

The one show not written by Burt, "Red Lawson's Revenge," was written by Les Crutchfield. Crutchfield also wrote for many other radio shows, including *Escape, Fort Laramie, Gunsmoke, The Man Called X, Rogers of the Gazette, Romance, The Story of Doctor Kildare, T-Man* and *Yours Truly, Johnny Dollar*. He was a staff writer for the *Gunsmoke* TV series from 1955 through 1967. In addition, he also wrote for several other TV shows — *The Loner, Rawhide*, and *The Man Called X*. Two of his stories were also turned into the films, *Tarzan's Greatest Adventure* and *Last Train from Gun Hill*.

At the end of each show, Jack Johnstone receives the credit line, "The entire production is under the direction of Jack Johnstone." He has many other radio shows to his credit. He was the director of shows like *Buck Rogers in the 25th Century* (producer-director), *CBS Radio Workshop, The Man Called X, Hollywood Star Time, The Prudential Family Hour of Stars, Richard Diamond, Private Detective* (producer-director), *The Secret Life of Walter Mitty*, and *Somebody Knows* (director-narrator). His biggest success was probably *Yours Truly, Johnny Dollar*. He created the program, acted as its producer and director, and also wrote many of the shows. As a writer, Johnstone also used the pseudonyms John Dawson and John Bundy.

George Basil "Buzz" Adlam was born on the last day of December, 1904, in Chelmsford, England and raised in Canada. He began his musical career as a saxophonist for both the Phil Harris and Ozzie Nelson bands. He later arranged and conducted for the Horace Heidt band. Besides *The Six Shooter*, he also wrote music for *The Amazing Mr. Malone, The Clock, Dangerous Assignment, Dark Venture, A Date with Judy, The Eddie Albert Show, Hollywood Star Playhouse, I Fly Anything, The Man from Homicide, Mr. President, The Opie Cates Show* and *Pat Novak for Hire*. He and his orchestra also supplied the music for the U.S. Treasury Savings Bond series *Guest Star*, for which he also acted as producer, and three different Navy recruiting shows — *Navy Star Time, Stand By for Music* and *Your Star Time*. He also worked on *The Adventures of Ozzie and Harriet* on TV and appears on their 1952 album, *The Adventures of Ozzie and Harriet* (Imperial LP-9049). Adlam also wrote some of the music for the 1942 film *Ship Ahoy*. Among the songs, he has written or co-written are *The House is Haunted, Adventure, My Galveston Gal, Mr. President, Poor Robinson Crusoe* and *With Thee I Swing*.

The show's two announcers were both quite experienced. Gibney also announced for *The Adventures of Charlie Lung, Dragnet* (also for the TV show), *Front and Center, Hello, Mom, Jimmy Fidler, The Man Called X, Music With Wings* (host), *NBC University Theatre* (host), *Pat Novak For Hire, Sealtest Variety Theater*, and *Tales of the Texas Rangers*. Wald was the announcer for several of the most popular programs on the radio — *Fibber McGee and Molly, Frontier Gentleman, The Great Gildersleeve* and many episodes of *Yours Truly, Johnny Dollar*. He also was the announcer for *Confession, Guest Star* (host), *Inheritance* and *Short Story*. Wald also appeared in several films, usually as an announcer or broadcaster. Among these were *Gangway for Tomorrow* (1943), *The Senator Was Indiscreet* (1948), *Canon City* (1948), *Under California Stars* (1948), *Slattery's Hurricane* (1949), *Ma and Pa Kettle* (1949), *Peggy* (1950) and *The Pride of St. Louis* (1952).

Floyd Caton, who worked for NBC in Hollywood, was the sound effects master for *The Six Shooter*. He also worked on several other shows, including *Abbott and Costello, The Great Gildersleeve* (with Virgil Reimer and Monty Fraser), *The Jack Benny Show* and *One Man's Family*.

The show's theme music was *Highland Lament* written by Ralph Vaughan Williams, and although the popularity of the song was mentioned by the announcer in several episodes, the song was not available on record. In fact, columnist Bill Doudna even wrote about the song's unavailability in his column on February 9, 1954:

> *Most radio programs are readily identified by their theme songs, but few themes ever become "stars" in their own right and command both mail and phone calls.*
>
> *NBC Hollywood has such a property on hand, however, in the theme song of James Stewart's Western adventure series, "Six Shooter."*
>
> *Producer Jack Johnstone has explained that "at first it was on occasional card inquiring about our theme — who wrote it, its title, and so forth. But now it's resolved itself into a steady flow of letters and phone calls each week."*
>
> *The tune causing all the excitement is "The Highland Lament" by Ralph Vaughn Willimas.*
>
> *To all the mail requesting information on how to buy the record Johnstone must give the same answer:*
>
> *"It's a special English recording restricted to broadcast use only."*

The first four shows were sponsored by Coleman Heating Products, after which the show became sustaining (no sponsor). In place of sponsors, NBC used the time to promote its own shows. Various public service announcements were also aired. It looked like the show would continue past its June 24, 1954, final show, when a new sponsor was found — Chesterfield cigarettes. But, Stewart refused to work for a tobacco company and the show ended.

Beginning with show #20, "Trail to Sunset," John Wald announces at the end of each program that *The Six Shooter* has been chosen to be broadcast to military personnel overseas via the Armed Forces Radio Services (AFRS). These announcements stopped after show #36, "Silver Threads." According to *The Directory of the Armed Forces Radio Service Series* by Harry MacKenzie, 35 *Six Shooter* programs were issued by the AFRS. The shows were unnumbered and no titles were included. Their matrix numbers all were part of the END 370 series, which stood for ENtertainment, using Domestic network broadcast material. All commercials and public service announcements were stripped from the AFRS shows.

SHOW PROMOTION

The newspaper promotion for *The Six Shooter* varied greatly from one area of the country to another. Radio stations in other cities ran special display ads, with and without Stewart's photo, and sometimes a short synopsis of that night's story. In most locations, ads for the program gradually shrank in size and content as the show neared the end of its run. Some of these other ads will appear with the appropriate show later in this section.

A special promotional disc that is part of the NBC Collection in the Library of Congress was also prepared. The disc is marked #71276 and is dated June 29, 1953. The recording, which runs about ten minutes, featured just three bands, one for each new show NBC was touting. The three were *Second Chance*, *The Six Shooter* and *Cousin Willie*. The disc was issued about two weeks before NBC aired its audition of *The Six Shooter* on July 15. The exact purpose of the disc isn't clear, but it most likely was used to promote these new shows to station managers and possibly potential sponsors.

Stewart's band begins with his explanation of why he was doing the show. It is taken directly from the NBC audition show where it appeared between the first and second acts.

> *Well that ends the first act of The Six Shooter folks…hope you're enjoying the show. Before we get on with it, I'd like to tell you a little bit about how I happen to be doing this program. I…ah…I'm lucky enough to do quite a bit of radio acting before, but I've never had a program of my own. The right thing just didn't seem to come along; at least not until The Six Shooter. You see, I've made several stories of this kind for pictures, that is honest legitimate stories of the West, and I hope that this series can offer the same type of enjoyment, with the same integrity. We think this*

is the sort of program the whole family will enjoy and we think that the character of Brit Ponset typifies some of the greatness that built America. We'd be pleased if you agreed with us.

The second part of the Stewart band is a very dramatic 2:39 segment from near the end of the audition program. The segment is mainly Stewart, with just a few lines from William Conrad as Ed Scofield. The dramatic effect of the scene would be sure to give the listener a very good idea of what to expect from the series.

Stewart also recorded a promo for *The Six Shooter*. The promo highlighted the fact that the show had just made the switch from Sunday to Thursday evenings. Here is a transcript of that promo.

> *Hello there, this is James Stewart. I'd like to take a minute of your time, if I may, to remind you about our weekly program series, The Six Shooter. It's now on Thursday evenings over many of these same NBC stations. You know The Six Shooter is a kind of a different type western program. I think maybe you'd like it. As Britt Ponset, I'm a sort of an easygoing cowpoke, just a sort of a cowpoke. No, now don't get me wrong, you'll hear gunplay now and then and some action, too, on The Six Shooter; even a little fun sometimes. And we like to think of our program as the kind that will please every one of you, and from your letters, well, they've all been very nice. So if you haven't already been listening, why don't you check your local paper for the time The Six Shooter is heard in your part of the country. We sure would like to have you in our audience every week.*

The promo was aired on other NBC programs. Five of the promos are known to exist as part of programs readily available to collectors. These are:

Crime and Peter Chambers: Peter Chambers, a dashing private eye, had been created by author Henry Kane, who wrote more than 60 novels, many with the Chambers character. When the series was taken to radio, Kane became the writer, producer and director for the show. Peter Chambers was played by actor Dane Clark. The 23 shows in the series aired on NBC between April 6 and September 7, 1954. Although Jimmy Stewart was never a guest on the show, his promo for *The Six Shooter* did appear on at least one show in the series. It can be heard at the end of "Abigail Chrisenberry," that aired May 4, 1954.

Fibber McGee & Molly: Jim and Marian Jordan starred as *Fibber McGee & Molly* on radio from 1935 until 1959 and broadcast more than 1600 shows. Although Jimmy Stewart was never a guest on the show, he did appear on two shows promoting his own show, *The Six Shooter.* The promo appeared during the final break in the 15-minute program on the following dates:

Wednesday, April 21, 1954: "Nature Hike" (A.K.A "Back to Nature")
Wednesday, May 5, 1954: "An Orchid for the Doc" (A.K.A "Brother Orchid")
Wednesday, June 1, 1954: "Stranger Could Be a Spy" (A.K.A "I Spy With My Little Eye")
Saturday, June 11, 1954: "Installing the Old Porch Swing" (A.K.A "Those Lazy, Hazy, Crazy Days of Summer")

It is probable that the promo was also used in other shows, but these remain undiscovered or lost.

A special disc was issued by NBC to Coleman dealers to persuade them to sign-up for commercial time on their local radio stations.

GRC 2678: Confidential Message from NBC

The disc is marked with a release date of August 20, 1953. It begins and ends with the "cha-ching" of a cash register. Lou Marks, heating equipment sales manager at Coleman, tells those listening that beginning September 15th, Coleman will be sponsoring three NBC radio shows to help you sell Coleman Heaters during the big bonus sales promotion. He then introduces Ham Fish of NBC who talks about each of the three shows. *Barrie Craig, Confidential Investigator* is up first, then the new *Eddie Cantor Show* and finally, *Six Shooter* (with no "The" given in the title).

Fish presents the Stewart segment by saying, "Jimmy plays a straight shooting cowboy and a hard hitting Coleman salesman, too." For *The Six Shooter* promo, two pieces from the NBC audition show are used. First,

Hal Gibney says, "Presenting one of the screen's favorite stars, Mr. Jimmy Stewart as the Six Shooter, based on the timeless legend of Britt Ponset, the Texas plainsman who brought single-handed justice to the western territories." Stewart's opening lines from the show are then played — "I hadn't figured on goin' through Clay City. It was an hour out of my way and I was already a day late for the Jefferson Ranch where I'd signed on for the round up. But, when Scar started limpin' from a loose shoe, I didn't have no choice. We had to head for the nearest blacksmith shop, so we turned north."

Marks then asks that Coleman dealers tie-in with the promotion by advertising on their local station and they'll be hearing the "cha-ching" of the cash register a lot.

The Coleman bonus sales promotion only ran for four weeks, which explains why its sponsorship of *The Six Shooter* lasted only that period of time.

There were three different Coleman commercials aired during *The Six Shooter*. One began with the sound of a howling wind. As mentioned in the newspaper ad, it also highlights the three bonuses — (1) a new low price, (2) a new low operating cost and (3) a free 32 piece set of Libbey safe-edge glassware worth $14. This spot aired in both "Jenny" and "The Stampede."

The second spot began with no sound effects, but instead asks if your house shrinks during the winter because some rooms cannot be heated and have to be closed off from the rest of the house. The three bonuses are also promoted in this commercial. It was aired just once in "The Coward."

The third spot, which aired in "Silver Annie," is similar to commercial #2, but the three bonuses are not mentioned. Low price and low operating cost are worked into the ad, but the Libbey's glassware offer is not mentioned at all.

SIX SHOOTER TRIVIA

The Six Shooter was popular enough to be imported to Japan. But that presented a problem. Jimmy Stewart didn't speak Japanese, so someone had to be found to dub his voice for the show. The person chosen for that job was actor-comedian Marty Brill. Brill had been a naval interpreter during the Korean War and became so fluent in Japanese that he easily carried out the assignment.

Brill later went on to appear in many television series, including *The New Dick Van Dyke Show*, *Love, American Style*, *All in the Family*, *Three's Company*, and *Seven Brides for Seven Brothers*.

THE SIX SHOOTER'S TV OFFSHOOT

In mid-1955, Stewart investigated the possibility of turning some the *The Six Shooter* scripts into television dramas. Writer Borden Chase was brought in to head the project.

Two years later, the show would come to television, but without Jimmy Stewart in the role of Britt Ponset.

Three years after *The Six Shooter* left radio, it was back again in much the same form as a TV series. The title was changed to *The Restless Gun* and it starred John Payne, not Jimmy Stewart. Payne had been searching for a show he could do for TV when he came across Jimmy Stewart's radio series, and liked what he heard. He bought 36 scripts from the show's writer, Frank Burt. He sold one of the scripts, "Britt Ponset's Christmas Carol," back to Jimmy Stewart, who directed and starred in a TV version for *General Electric Theater*.

The leading character's name was changed to Vint Bonner, but his horse was still named Scar. In the pilot for the show, based on "Red Lawson's Revenge" and broadcast on *Schlitz Playhouse* on March 29, 1959, the character was still know as Britt Ponset and he was still called the Six Shooter.

Many of the first season's episodes were based on shows that had been broadcast on the radio and, since they were given titles for TV, we have what are in all probability, the titles for the radio shows from which they were taken. Among the TV titles are "Duel at Lockwood," "Trail to Sunset," "Revenge at Harness Creek," "Rink," "Jenny," "The Shooting of Jett King" (King's first name had been Wyatt on radio), "General Gillford's Widow," "The New Sheriff," "Cheyenne Express," "Thicker Than Water," "Silver Threads," "The Gold Buckle" (it had been a silver buckle on the radio show), "The Coward," "Friend in Need," "Quiet City," "A Pressing Engagement," "Sheriff Billy," "Crisis at Easter Creek," "Aunt Emma," "The Battle of Tower Rock," "Hiram Grover's Strike" and "More Than Kin." Twenty-two of the first 36 TV shows were taken directly from the radio series. Character names and storylines were somewhat changed for TV, but the basic shows were the same. At least one other show is based on a *Six Shooter* script. "The Lady and the Gun" is based on the final *Six Shooter* show, "Myra Barker." Burt is given story credit for the shows, but the TV scripts were written by other writers.

The Restless Gun aired on NBC-TV on Fridays from 8:00-8:30 p.m., beginning September 23, 1957. The final show was broadcast on June 22, 1959. There were a total of 77 shows (plus the pilot). During its first season, the show was ranked #8 by the Neilsen rating system. The show had a large enough following that Whitman Publishing Company, Racine, Wisconsin, published a 1959 Barlow Meyers book based on the series. Signet Publishing also issued several books based written by Will Hickok which were based on the program.

The shows were produced by David Dortort, who would go on to produce the very popular *Bonanza*. Two future stars of *Bonanza* made guest appearances on *The Restless Gun* — Michael Landon and Dan Blocker. Despite the show's popularity in its own time, it has rarely been shown in syndication and it took until October 30, 2007, for a DVD set of the show to be issued. The 3-DVD set featured a 24-episode sampling of the series, including the pilot program.

THE SIX SHOOTER ON TAPE AND CDS

Episodes of *The Six Shooter* are the easiest of Stewart's radio material to locate. All, with the exception of the NBC audition show, have been commercially released. If you're looking for shows in the .mp3 format, you'll be able to find all 41 shows easily on the Internet and most can be downloaded for no cost. One of the first, and most complete sets of *The Six Shooter* programs was issued by Metacom beginning in 1995. In all, they released three sets encompassing all 39 regular-season episodes broadcast by NBC. You would only be missing the two audition shows.

Metacom RM# 2300027 (1995)
Old-Time Radio Drama
This is one of three six-cassette sets issued by Metacom. Included on this set are:

J411: "Thicker Than Water"/"Duel at Lockwood"
J412: "Marrying off Aunt Em"/"The Widow's Secret"
J413: "Crisis at Easter Creek"/"Tracking Down a Killer"
J414: "Revenge at Harness Creek"/"The Accused"
J415: "The Double Seven"/"Reluctant Hero"
J416: "Bad Blood"/"Silver Threads"

Metacom (Adventures in Cassettes) 9133157/AB157 (1996)
"Gold Strike" Collection
This second set in the series includes:

J496: "A Friend in Need"/"Hiram's Goldstrike"
J497: "The Silver Buckle"/"The Outlaw's Wife"
J498: "Trail to Sunset"/"Apron-Faced Sorrel"
J499: "Quiet City"/"Battle at Tower Rock"
J500: "Cheyenne Express"/"The New Sheriff"
J501: "When the Shoe Doesn't Fit"/"Myra Barker"

Metacom (Adventures in Cassettes) 9133223/AB223 (1997)
"The Stampede" Collection
The final set in the series has fifteen shows rather than twelve like the previous sets. To accomplish this, three of the cassettes have three shows each:

J270: "Jenny"/"The Coward"
J271: "The Stampede"/"Silver Annie"
J272: "Rink Larkin"/"Red Lawson's Revenge"
J273: "Ben Scofield"/"The Capture of Stacy Gault"/"Escape from Smoke Falls"
J274: "Gabriel Starbuck"/"Sheriff Billy"/"A Pressing Engagement"
J275: "More Than Kin"/"Britt's Christmas Carol"/"Cora Plummer Quincy"

Radio Spirits has also been a leader in releasing *Six Shooter* sets, the first coming in 1996.
Radio Spirits 52998
This is a 6-cassette set featuring:

"Helen Bricker"/"Trail to Sunset"/"Apron-Faced Sorrel"
"Quiet City"/"Battle at Tower Rock"/"Cheyenne Express"
"Thicker Than Water"/"The Capture of Stacy Gault"/"Aunt Emma"
"The Wolf"/"The Double Seven"/"Blood Relations"
"Silver Threads"/"Rink Larkin"/"Ben Scofield"
"Duel at Lockwood"/"Crisis at Easter Creek"/"Johnny Stringer"

In 2004, they issued a huge 20-show set:
Radio Spirits 48072 (CDs)/48074 (cassettes)
The 20 episodes of the show that are included on this set are:

"Rink Larkin" (10/18/53)
"Ben Scofield" (11/1/53)
"The Capture of Stacey Gault" (11/8/53)
"Helen Bricker" (1/23/54)
"Trail to Sunset" (1/31/54)
"Apron-Faced Sorrel" (2/7/54)
"Quiet City" (2/14/54)
"Battle at Tower Rock" (2/21/54)
"Cheyenne Express" (3/7/54)
"Thicker Than Water" (3/14/54)
"Duel at Lockwood" (3/21/54)
"Aunt Emma" (4/1/54)
"General Guilford's Widow" (4/8/54)
"Crisis at Easter Creek" (4/15/54)
"Johnny Springer" (4/22/54)
"The Double Seven" (5/13/54)
"Blood Relations" (5/27/54)
"Silver Threads" (6/3/54)
"The New Sheriff" (6/10/54)
"When the Shoe Doesn't Fit" (6/17/54)

Three shows can also be found on this 1999 set:
Old Time Radio's Greatest Westerns
Radio Spirits 4410 (cassettes)

Many great westerns, including shows like *The Cisco Kid, Fort Laramie, Cavalcade of America, Frontier Gentleman, Gunsmoke, Have Gun–Will Travel, Hopalong Cassidy, The Lone Ranger, Luke Slaughter of Tombstone, Red Ryder, Roy Rogers, Screen Directors' Playhouse, Straight Arrow, Suspense, Tales of the Texas Rangers, Wild Bill Hickok,* and *The Six Shooter*. Three *Six Shooters* appear on the set:

"The Stampede" (10/4/53)
"Silver Annie" (10/11/53)
"More Than Kin" (12/13/53)

A further four shows can be found on the following set:
Old-Time Radio's Greatest Westerns
Radio Spirits 4217 (CDs)/4216 (cassettes)

A 20-CD set which features 40 old time radio Westerns, including *Red Ryder, The Lone Ranger, Have Gun–Will Travel, Gunsmoke, The Cisco Kid, Fort Laramie, Frontier Gentleman, Hopalong Cassidy, Tales of the Texas Rangers,* and *The Six Shooter.* Four *Six Shooter* shows are included on the set:

"The Coward" (9/27/53)
"Sheriff Billy" (11/29/53)
"A Pressing Engagement" (12/6/53)
"Cora Plummer Quincy" (12/27/53)

Radio Spirits also made many of *The Six Shooter* programs available through various online services as audiobooks. Twenty-nine of the 39 broadcast shows could be purchased in this manner. The only ones not available were: "Jenny," "A Friend in Need," "The Stampede," "Silver Annie," "Escape from Smoke Falls," "More than Kin," "Britt Ponset's Christmas," "Revenge at Harness Creek," "Anna Nordquist" and "Myra Barker."

"A Pressing Engagement," "Thicker than Water" and "When the Shoe Doesn't Fit" were also issued in 2003. All of the remaining programs were released in 2007.

Radio Spirits and other companies also issued single-cassette/CD versions of several *Six Shooter* shows. All these will be listed with the individual shows in the next section.

THE SIX SHOOTER IN THE DIGITAL AGE

The Six Shooter continues to be one of Stewart's most popular shows. Compilations of the entire series, usually in .mp3 format, abound on eBay. The Old Time Radio Researchers Group (OTRR) has even put together a certified series for the program containing the *Hollywood Playhouse* version, the NBC audition show and all 39 episodes, as well as art work and other information. Also, the series continues to be aired and has even made the jump to satellite radio. SiriusXM's *Radio Classics,* hosted by Greg Bell, broadcast several episodes each week.

THE SIX SHOOTER — THE RADIO SERIES

Only five of the shows have names which were mentioned during the broadcasts — "Revenge at Harness Creek," "Anna Norquist," "Blood Relations," "When the Shoe Doesn't Fit," and "Myra Barker." As a result, most shows are known by several titles. When trying to purchase shows, this can be a problem. Alternate titles are listed for those shows where appropriate. Also, to help identify shows, the first line or two of each is given. These lines are usually delivered by Stewart, but occasionally come from someone else.

00: The Six Shooter........... *Hollywood Star Playhouse*, Sunday, 4/13/1952

FIRST LINE: *This is Jimmy Stewart with a welcome to* The Hollywood Star Playhouse, *brought to you by the Bakers of America.*

What would be the regular opening, "The man in the saddle is angular and long-legged..." for the series is not featured here at all. Instead, there is a short introduction by Wendell Niles, the show's regular announcer. The program's theme song, *Hollywood Star Playhouse*, was written by Basil Adlam, Jay Milton and Henry Russell.

The show begins with the robbery scene that was not present in the NBC audition show (July 15, 1953), but was present when the show was redone as "Ben Scofield" (November 1, 1953).

On his way to the Jefferson Ranch, Britt stops at Clay City to find a blacksmith to have a shoe on his horse replaced. When the blacksmith learns who he is, he assumes he's there to help catch the thief who had robbed the Wells Fargo office the night before, killing Sam Norton, the Deputy Agent, and wounding Fred Wilmer. Britt goes to the Wells Fargo office to do a little investigating. He notices that the horse used in the robbery has one damaged shoe which leaves a very distinctive mark in the ground. When he asks the blacksmith if he has seen a horse recently with a shoe that would leave such a mark, he says he has. It belonged to Ben Scofield, the son of the sheriff.

Britt and Sheriff Ed Scofield pay a visit to Fred, who describes the outlaw to them. During the description, he mentions that the robber looked a lot like Ben. Fred had also gotten a shot off at the bandit and was sure he had hit him. Sheriff Scofield is reluctant to search for the thief, but eventually Britt talks him into going along.

They track the wounded boy to an abandoned cabin, where Britt asks the sheriff about Ben. He first says that he is at the Jefferson Ranch working during the round up, but then admits that they had had a fight. Ben needed money and his father refused to lend it to him. They had hit each other and Ben had left home and had not been back for several days.

The sheriff tries to warn Ben that Britt is closing in on his location. He is shot in the shoulder for his efforts. Britt is luckier and shoots the boy and gets his gun away from him. He rolls the wounded boy over, to see if it is Ben.

The show's announcer, Wendell Niles, and Jimmy have this exchange at the end of the show.

NILES: Jimmy, that's one of the most heartwarming and, at the same time, suspenseful yarns we've heard in a long, long time.

STEWART: Well Wendell, when it comes to that thanks department, let's just be mighty sure we include Parley Baer, Herb Vigran, Bert Holland and Bill Conrad, who played the sheriff. Bye.

After the final commercial, Niles mentions that Stewart can currently be seen in the Universal-International Technicolor production, *Bend of the River*. During this final segment, actress Diana Lynn also makes an appearance to promote the following week's show in which she would star.

Stewart makes an obvious mistake in the show, referring to Fred's last name as Miller. The name had previously been established as Wilmer.

CAST
Bill Conrad.. Ed Scofield
Parley Baer .... Fred Wilmer
Herb Vigran .... George "Heavy" Norton
Bert Holland..young robber

The original audition show can be found on *The Best of Old Time Radio Starring Jimmy Stewart*, released in 2002. Radio Spirits 5035 (CDs)/5034 (cassettes).

This 6-CD/4-cassette set features 10 radio shows starring Jimmy Stewart. This show is on the first cassette (SJSC1) or the first CD (SJSD1)

00A: **NBC Audition Show** .... Wednesday, 7/15/1953
(A.K.A.: "Horseshoe Clue," "The Sheriff's Son")

FIRST LINE: *I hadn't figured on goin' through Clay City. It was an hour out of my way and I was already a day late for the Jefferson Ranch where I'd signed on for the round up.*

This is the exact same play that was broadcast on the *Hollywood Star Playhouse*, with just one change. The opening robbery scene has been cut, thus eliminating Bert Holland's role in the show. The opening breaks and ending would also be different to reflect the new series.

The opening narration for the show is a little different than it would be for the shows that followed:

> *The man in the saddle is angular and long-legged. His skin is sun-dyed brown. The gun in his holster is gray steel and rainbow mother-of-pearl, the handle, unmarked. **But, the gun has killed and the man has killed.** People called them both, The Six Shooter.*

The highlighted line would be dropped from the opening, because it made Britt sound like a gunfighter. Britt did not look for trouble, but when it found him, he and his gun were ready.

During the first break in the program, James Stewart tells the audience how he came to do the show:

> *Well, that ends the first act of The Six Shooter folks. Hope you're enjoying the show. Before we get on with it, I'd like to tell you a little bit about how I happen to be doing this program. I, ah, I been lucky enough to have done quite a bit of radio acting before, but I've never had a program of my own. The right thing just didn't seem to come along...at least not until The Six Shooter. You see, I've made several stories of this kind for pictures; that is, honest legitimate stories of the West, and I hope that this series can offer the same type of enjoyment, with the same integrity. We think this is the sort of program the whole family will enjoy and we think that the character of Britt Ponset typifies some of the greatness that built America. We'd be pleased if you agreed with us.*

At the end of the show, Stewart again makes a pitch for the program and its sponsor. His remarks are very generic and no actual product names are mentioned because no sponsor had yet been found.

Well that was your first meeting with Britt Ponset. I hope you'd like to meet him again every week. And I also hope you'll try our product, it's something I would use myself and it's never let me down. I don't think it'd let you down either. Maybe I'm not much of a salesman, but this product I don't think needs a lot of selling. As far as I'm concerned, it sells itself. So, I'd appreciate it if you'd buy it this week and give it a try. Let me know how you like it. So long folks, I'll be seeing you.

The show would be produced again as *Ben Scofield* and would be broadcast November 1, 1953.

CAST
Bill Conrad.. Ed Scofield
Parley Baer... Fred Wilmer
Herb Vigran .... George "Heavy" Norton

01: Jenny..Sunday, 9/20/1953
SPONSOR: Coleman Heating Products
(A.K.A.: "Love of a Good Woman," "Jenny Garver")

FIRST LINE: *It was hot that afternoon. A low crawlin' kind of heat that seemed to be following us as we rode along.*

Britt Ponset is headed for Lead Creek. Britt is hoping to get a job with the railroad that is building a spur line to Salt Lake City. Before reaching town, he comes across a wounded young man. The man tells him that his horse threw him and when he hit the ground, his gun went off. Britt takes him to the cabin of a young woman named Jenny Garber. She bandages the young man and tells Britt that she doesn't know the boy. When Britt tells her that he's going on to Lead Creek, she tells him there's no doctor there so he shouldn't look for one to send back. She also asks that he doesn't tell anyone that the boy is with her because the townspeople will make jokes about her. As he's leaving, Britt sees a horse with a half-moon mark on it in Jenny's corral — the boy had described his horse as having the same kind of mark.

On the trail to Lead Creek, Britt is stopped by the posse who think that he is Ned Landy, the young wounded man. Britt tells them where Ned is and he goes back to Jenny's with the posse. Just as Jenny had told him, along the way, the men make many jokes about her plain looks and lack of suitors. As the posse approaches the cabin, shots ring out. Britt goes to the back of the house and rushes the door. As he breaks in he finds Jenny, not Ned, firing the shots. Britt tells her she is protecting a dead man. As the posse enters her home, Britt finds a way to allow Jenny to retain her dignity.

There is a short promo for Stewart's current movie, *Thunder Bay*, at the end of the show.

CAST
Dee J. Thompson..Jenny Garber
Jess Kirkpatrick..Sheriff Jim York
George Neise.. Tom Jackson
Harry Bartell..Ned Landy

This show can be found on the CD set *Legends of Radio: Famous Premiers*. Radio Spirits 48172 (2005) This 10-CD set is part of Radio Spirits' *Legends of Radio* series.

This premiere episode can also be found on the 2-cassette set, *Six Shooter*, released by Audio File of Glenview, IL. It is listed as "Jenny Garver."

Also included on this set are: "Sheriff Billy" (as "The New Sheriff"), "Duel at Lockwood (as "The Young Gunslinger") and "The Shooting of Wyatt King" (as "The Wyoming Kid").

02: The Coward ....Sunday, 9/27/1953
SPONSOR: Coleman Heating Products
(A.K.A.: "Will Fetter," "Gunsling Ranch," "Fetter Is a Coward")

FIRST LINE: *I had a grandstand seat; a rockin' chair on the front porch of the Temple City Hotel.*

Britt is sitting in a rocking chair on the porch of a hotel in Temple City when he thinks he recognizes Will Tekman, a man he has worked with in the past. He sees another man approach Will and overhears an argument between them. The hotel clerk tells Britt that the second man is Noah Temple, whose grandfather had once owned all the land in the area and after whom the town had been named. The grandfather's son had then sold off most of the land. Now Noah was trying to buy it all back. He now owned all of the original land except for a ranch owned by Will and his wife Sarah. During the conversation, Britt mentions Will's last name, Tekman, and the clerk tells him that he must be thinking of someone else, because this Will's last name is Fetter.

Later, as Britt tries to nap, Sarah Fetter knocks on his door. She tells him that Will had also recognized him in town and now they both were afraid that Britt would turn him in as an escaped prisoner. Will had taken part in a bank robbery, been caught, convicted and sentenced to jail. But, with two years remaining in his sentence, he had escaped and come to Temple City. Sarah had made him promise not to carry a gun anymore. All this was a complete surprise to Britt who knew nothing about the entire incident.

After the hotel clerk tells Britt that Will has bought a carbine, Britt heads for the Fetter ranch but finds Will not at home. So, Britt starts for the Temple homestead. When he arrives at the fence between the two ranches, he finds that a hole has been cut through the barbed wire. Several steers and heifers lay dead and Will's horse is tied to the fence. Britt ties Scar to the fence and begins searching for Will. He finds Will with his rifle aimed through a window at Temple and stops him from pulling the trigger. As they start back to their horses, they are ambushed by Temple and three of his men. Britt gives the rifle back to Will, who immediately starts off in Temple's direction. After wounding the other three men, Britt starts after Will. As he watches, Will throws down his gun and takes on Temple in a fistfight and beats him. When asked why he didn't just shoot Temple, Will says that he just couldn't break his promise to Sarah.

The Fetters and Britt decide that he should tell the sheriff about Will. But, as he rides away, Britt decides that the sheriff wouldn't be interested in a law-abiding rancher.

There is a short promo for Stewart's current movie, *Thunder Bay*, at the end of the show.

CAST
Michael Anne Barrett .... *Sarah Fetter*
Herb Ellis .... *Will "Tekman" Fetter*
Howard McNear .... *hotel clerk*
Will Wright .... *Noah Temple*

03: The Stampede ....Sunday, 10/4/1953
SPONSOR: Coleman Heating Products
(A.K.A.: "The McAdams Brothers," "Cattle Drive to Abilene," "Rival Brothers")

FIRST LINE: *There were over 400 head in the McAdam's herd; 400 white-faced Texas cattle and only three of us to shove 'em along the trail to Abilene.*

For a 10% share of the profits, Britt is helping the McAdams brothers drive their cattle to Abilene. When a lightning bolt threatens to start a stampede, Norm McAdams, the younger of the two brothers, heads for higher ground leaving Ryfe McAdams to stop the cattle. As an excuse for his actions, Norm says that his horse had bolted.

Later, Ryfe tells Britt that he has recently married a younger woman, Carrie, and that she is pregnant. Britt finds a letter on the ground and assumes that it must be Ryfe's because it is signed, "Love, Carrie." On learning of the letter, Ryfe becomes agitated because he can't read and Jenny knows it. She wouldn't write to him, so the letter must have been sent to Norm. Ryfe wants Britt to read the letter to him, but Britt balks at doing it. No matter, because Norm shows up and says that the letter is his and that Carrie loves him, not Ryfe. Britt has to stop a fight from starting by reminding them that all three of the men are going to be needed to get the cattle to Abilene.

As the drive continues, Norm takes the lead with Britt in the middle of the herd and Ryfe brings up the rear. When they begin to enter a narrow gorge, Ryfe fires several shots to start a stampede. Since Norm is already in the gorge, Ryfe believes he will be trampled to death. But Norm starts firing and the cattle turn and crush Ryfe. As Ryfe is dying, Norm tells him that he had lied and that Ryfe had no reason to be so jealous. Britt suspects that the story isn't true, but doesn't ask.

There is a short promo for Stewart's current movie, *Thunder Bay*, at the end of the show.

CAST
Lou Merrill .... *Ryfe McAdams*
James McCallion .... *Norm McAdams*

04: **Silver Annie** ....Sunday, 10/11/1953
SPONSOR: Coleman Heating Products
(A.K.A.: "Annie Huxley's Mine")

FIRST LINE: *The trail to Virtue City was over the crest of Bare Neck Mountain and then down the northern slope.*

Britt rides into the slowly dying town of Virtue City. He plans on getting a job with the Rocky Mountain Western Railroad, which is about to start laying new track through the town. But, Doc Cross, the mayor of the town, tells him that is not likely to happen because Annie Huxley won't sell her right of way to the railroad. Silver Annie, as she is known, owns an old, worn-out silver mine, but she refuses to give up hope of finding another rich vein. The mayor has brought her cousin Clyde, a lawyer from Chicago, to town to try to talk her into selling. He is shot at by Annie for his trouble. So, the mayor drafts Britt to talk to her. Annie tells Britt that she is not against the railroad; she just wants them to choose their alternate path which would bypass her mine. Their talk is interrupted when Clyde and the sheriff rush in and arrest Annie.

As the second act begins, Doc Cross tells Britt that Silver Annie won't be charged with any crime. Instead, there will be a sanity hearing. As the judge is about to rule in favor of Clyde, Britt speaks up. He tells the judge that he has taken some ore and has shown it to an assayer. He shows the judge a report that says the ore has enough silver to be worth about $125 a ton. Annie is judged to be sane and Nelson, the railroad man, announces that the railroad will begin building using the alternate route. Only Annie knows that Britt has not told the whole truth.

There is a short promo for Stewart's current movie, *Thunder Bay*, at the end of the show.

CAST

Jeanette Nolan .... "Silver Annie" Huxley
Dan O'Herlihy .... Clyde Huxley
Herb Vigran .... Judge Drayton
Robert Griffin .... Thad Nelson and the sheriff
Parley Baer .... Doc Cross

This was one of the three *Six Shooter* episodes that was turned into a TV vehicle for James Stewart. It was broadcast on the *General Electric Theater* on February 10, 1957, as "The Town With a Past." The story was adapted for TV by Oscar Brodney. Ronald Reagan was the show's host. Stewart starred as Britt, with the other cast members being Beulah Bondi (Annie), Walter Sande (Sheriff), Fredd Wayne (Clyde), and Ted Mapes (Joe). Also appearing were Will Wright, Greg Barton, Reggie Parton, Chuck Robeson, Henry Wills, Dean Williams, Pat O'Malley and Howard Wright. The production crew included James Neilson (Director), William Frye (Associate Producer), Ray Rennahan (Director of Photography), Don Herbert (Progress Reporter), George Patrick (Art Director), James Walters (Set Decorator), Richard G. Wray (Editorial Supervisor), Michael McAdam (Film Editor), Stanley Wilson (Music Supervisor), Earl Crane Jr. (Sound), Jack Barrow (Makeup), Florence Bush (Hair Stylist) and Vincent Dee (Costume Supervisor).

05: **Rink Larkin** ....Sunday, 10/18/1953
(A.K.A.: "The Mine," "Revenge in Petersville," "Sins of the Father")

FIRST LINE: *The wind had died down and it was quiet now. Only thing I could hear was the crick tricklin' away about 20 feet down from where I'd made camp for the night.*

Eleven-year-old Rink Larkin sneaks into Britt's camp at night to steal some food, but gets caught. Britt cooks him some beans and, as they talk, learns that the boy is on his way to Petersville to find his father. Britt is also headed there, so they travel together. Arriving at Sheriff Jay's, Rink asks about his dad, Earl Larkin. The sheriff has to tell him that he had shot and killed his father during a bank robbery and that he had just been buried that morning. Another man named Cliff Trager had also been wounded in the robbery, but had escaped. Rink is very upset and runs away. Later, Britt finds Rink at his father's grave promising revenge on the sheriff.

The following morning Sheriff Jay comes to Britt's hotel room and tells him that someone had stolen a gun and ammunition from the hardware store overnight. They both know it was the work of young Rink. They follow a trail of small boot prints that lead away from the back of the store. Instead of finding Rink, they find Trager who shoots and wounds the sheriff. Trager wants to know what had happened to Larkin and a discussion of the robbery and shooting follows. Rink, who was hiding behind some nearby rocks, hears everything.

After a surprising ending, Britt gets permission from Rink's aunt to take care of the boy for the summer while he watches the Widow Jenkins' house while she is back east.

There is a short promo for Stewart's current movie, *Thunder Bay*, at the end of the show.

CAST
Sammy Ogg.. *Rink Larkin*
Russell Thorsen.. *Sheriff Jay*
Tony Barrett.. *Cliff Trager*

06: **Red Lawson's Revenge**..........................Sunday, 10/25/1953
(A.K.A.: *A Brother's Revenge*)

FIRST LINE: *I hadn't seen Mary and Dan for purt near three years. Not since I left the Panhandle.*

This was the only show in the entire *Six Shooter* series that was not written by Frank Burt, instead being written by Les Crutchfield. Crutchfield wrote for many other radio series, including *Gunsmoke, Fort Laramie, Dr. Kildare*, and *Yours Truly, Johnny Dollar*.

Britt is on his way to Walnut Creek to visit old friends Mary and Dan Maylor. He's about to make camp for the night when he sees a campfire ahead. He rides into the camp of Red Lawson. Lawson tells him that he's also going to Walnut Creek to kill Dan Maylor, the man who had killed his brother four years earlier. Lawson knew that Dan was a friend of Britt's and that Britt would warn him. In fact, he wanted him to do just that.

Britt continues on to the Maylor's farm and receives a warm welcome from them. They have a surprise for Britt — their year-and-a-half-old baby boy named Britt. While Mary puts the baby to bed, Britt tells Dan about Lawson. The next morning, Britt rides to town to talk to the sheriff, but finds that he is out of town for three days. He does, however, find Lawson is in town. Red tells Britt that he knows Dan has a wife and child.

That night, back at the farm, Britt hears something outside and goes to investigate. Lawson fires a shot and Britt fires back, then hears a horse leaving the property. Back in the house, Mary is very upset because one of the shots had come very close to her and the baby. Britt apologizes and rides off to track down Lawson. After a while, he realizes that he is chasing an empty horse and quickly returns to the farm where he finds Dan and Mary locked in the store room of the barn. After freeing them, they realize that Lawson must have the baby. Britt and Dan find Lawson standing with his gun pointed at the baby. He makes Dan drop his gun. Britt and the entire Maylor family escape the desperate situation unharmed. How they do it may surprise you.

There is a short promo for Stewart's current movie, *Thunder Bay*, at the end of the show.

CAST
Shirley Mitchell .... Mary Maylor
Leone Le Doux .... Britt Maylor
Paul Richards .... Red Lawson
Barney Phillips .... Dan Maylor

There are several sources for this show, including:
The World's Greatest Old-Time Radio Shows (The Six Shooter) MediaBay Inc. 80934 (2004)

The Six Shooter tape is also marked with two other numbers — #151 and 2838 — and has two episodes:

"Red Lawson's Revenge"
"Gabriel Starbuck"

The Eddie Cantor Show tape also featured two shows from that series, with Judy Canova and George Raft being the guests. The set also included two old-time radio collector cards — one on *The Six Shooter* and one on Harry Von Zell. *The Six Shooter* card featured information and facts on the series.

These same two shows can also be found on *Old-Time Radio Famous Westerns*.

Radio Spirits 4473 (CDs)/4472 (cassettes) (2001)

This 10-CD/Cassette set features two shows each from *The Lone Ranger*, *The Cisco Kid*, *Frontier Gentleman*, *Frontier Town*, *Gunsmoke*, *Have Gun–Will Travel*, *Hopalong Cassidy*, *Red Ryder*, *Tales of the Texas Rangers*, and *The Six Shooter*. The two *Six Shooters* included are:

"Red Lawson's Revenge"
"Gabriel Starbuck"

In 2011, it was issued in mp3 only format on *Jimmy Stewart the Ultimate Radio Collection Vol. 1* (Master Classics Records).

07: Ben Scofield..Sunday, 11/1/1953
(A.K.A.: "Horseshoe Clue," "The Sheriff's Son,"
"Holdup at Clay City")

FIRST LINE (delivered by William Conrad): *The rain had stopped, but the wind still carried slivers of moisture that cut into the boy's face as he rode along the edge of the creek.*

This is a new production using the same script as was used for both audition shows. The short, extra robbery scene that had appeared in the *Hollywood Star Playhouse* production, but not the NBC audition show, is reinstated here. For this scene, Bill Conrad acts as the narrator and Jimmy McCallion replaces Bert Holland as the young robber. Other than this, the cast is the same as that for the audition shows.

Unlike the audition shows, Stewart gets Fred Wilmer's last name correct during this enactment.

There is a short promo for Stewart's current movie, *Thunder Bay*, at the end of the show.

CAST
Bill Conrad..*narrator, Ed Scofield*
Parley Baer... *Fred Wilmer*
Jimmy McCallion...*young robber*
Herb Vigran .... George "Heavy" Norton

This show can be found on the 4-cassette set, *Old Time Radio Westerns* (HighBridge Audio HBP 89049), which was released in 2002. The title used on the cassette was "Holdup at Clay City." Show #10, "Gabriel Starbuck," is also included on this set. Also see that entry.

08: The Capture of Stacy Gault.................................Sunday, 11/8/1953

FIRST LINE: *I sure couldn't figure it. I'd ridden down the whole main street all the way from Seth Tooley's Bank to Ma Bensen's Rooming House and I had not seen a single, solitary person.*

Britt rides into a seemingly deserted Elk Point. He stops at Ma Benson's Rooming House to find out what's going on. She tells him that a bank robber named Stacy Gault is headed their way. Ed Scott has taken a posse to look for him and the town is unprotected so everyone is staying inside. As Ma and Britt are eating supper, there's a knock at the door. It's Seth, the banker, and he says that he has seen Gault in town and is afraid that he is there to rob the bank. There's another knock and Britt opens the door to find a man standing there. The man is looking for a room. Ma and Seth are convinced that he is Gault, but Britt talks her into giving him a room for the night.

Seth goes after the posse. When the posse arrives back in town, Ed Scott wants to go into Gault's room with guns blazing. Britt wants no part of that and says that he will go up and bring the man down himself. The man puts up no fight and even calls the men crazy after Britt tells him that they think he is Stacy Gault. Turns out he is Amos Foster, and he has an interesting story to tell Britt and the posse.

There is a short promo for Stewart's current movie, *Thunder Bay*, at the end of the show.

CAST

Eleanor Audley	*Sadie "Ma" Benson*
Barney Phillips	*Amos Foster*
Forrest Lewis	*Ed Scott*
Parley Baer	*Seth Tooley*

09: Escape from Smoke Falls .... Sunday 11/15/1953
(A.K.A.: "Love Rivals")

FIRST LINE: *I hadn't expected to stay over in Smoke Falls, but when I stopped off to see ol' Dad Sommerset and found him all crippled up with lumbago…*

Britt stops at Smoke Falls to see Dad Sommerset. Dad's lumbago is very bad, so Britt stays to tend his herd until he feels better. While there, Britt attends a social and witnesses a bidding war for Ellen's picnic basket. Tom Leverett finally wins the basket with a $10 bid, but he's quickly set upon by Spud Hooker, Ellen's boyfriend, and the other bidder. Britt separates them as a man rushes in to say there has been a jailbreak and the sheriff has been wounded.

The sheriff asks Britt to catch Dink Falk, the escapee, himself with maybe just one other man to help. He's afraid that Falk will be able to pick off too many members of the posse before they get him. Britt asks Tom to go with him. This upsets Spud, who rides off on his own to catch Falk. Tom thinks that Falk may be holed up in Giant Cave. Falk is there, and he has Spud as a hostage. Britt and Tom leave the cave first, then Spud and Falk, his gun trained on Spud, come out next. Tom pushes Spud out of the way and takes a bullet himself. Britt draws and shoots Falk. Tom admits that he doesn't like Spud, but he does love Ellen and he didn't want to see her get hurt should anything happen to Spud. Will Ellen find out the truth about what happened at Giant Cave?

There is a short promo for Stewart's current movie, *Thunder Bay*, at the end of the show.

CAST

Jeanette Nolan	*Grace Proudly*
Frank Gerstle	*Spud Hooker*
Robert Griffin	*Sheriff Ray Tinsmith*
Forrest Lewis	*Dink Falk*
Sam Edwards	*Tom Leverett*

10: **Gabriel Starbuck**..Sunday, 11/22/1953
(A.K.A.: "Sheriff Gabe," "Elderly Sheriff,"
"Put Out to Pasture")

FIRST LINE (delivered by Herb Vigran as the town's barber): *How's that, Al? Short enough for ya'? I asked ya' if it was short enough for ya'!*

Gabe Starbuck, the sheriff of Yellow Crest for 40 years, is about to be fired because he's too old to do his job any longer. Alf, Britt and Breezy, the barber, discuss the situation in the barbershop. Britt, being an old friend of Gabe's, agrees to talk to Gabe about the situation. During that talk, it becomes clear to Britt that Gabe has no intention of retiring or giving up his job.

That evening, the town's alarm is sounded. The bank has been robbed — a bag of gold and a bag of cash are missing. Gabe says that he saw the thieves head east. The other men feel that can't be right because the salt flats are to the east and the robbers wouldn't be able to make it through them. They think they must have turned toward the hills. Gabe heads east, while the others head into the hills. Britt follows Gabe at a distance and watches as Gabe "fires shots at the bandits, and gets back the bank's two sacks."

Some townspeople doubt Gabe's story, but Britt backs him up. They decide not to fire Gabe, but instead hire him a deputy.

There is a short promo for Stewart's soon-to-be-released film, *The Glenn Miller Story*, at the end of the show.

CAST
Herb Vigran .... *Breezy*
John Stephenson .... *Alf Crandall*
Lamont Johnson .... *Mark Fawcett*
Dal McKennon .... *Jim Waterby*
Bill Johnstone .... *Gabe Starbuck*

Before signing off, Hal Gibney gives a special salute to NBC affiliated station WGBF, Evansville, IN, on the occasion of their 30th anniversary.

The show can be found on several sets, including:
The World's Greatest Old-Time Radio Shows (*The Six Shooter*) MediaBay Inc. 80934 (2004)
Old-Time Radio Famous Westerns Radio Spirits 4473 (CDs)/4472 (cassettes) (2001)

See 06: "Red Lawson's Revenge" for complete details on these releases, and *Old Time Radio Westerns* HighBridge Audio HMP 89049 (2002). Also see Show 07, "Ben Scofield."

11: **Sheriff Billy**..Sunday, 11/29/1953
(A.K.A.: "Billy Riddle," "New Sheriff,"
"The Sheriff's Old Man," "Man and Boy")

FIRST LINE: *The snow was beginnin' to melt by the time I reached Dawson. You could hear it drippin' from the eves and hittin' the boardwalk on the main street.*

Britt rides into Dawson for his winter job at Dave Engleman's ranch. There's a new sheriff, Billy Riddle, in Dawson. Billy has been hoping that Britt would come to town because he knows Britt has traveled throughout the area and he wants to know if he has ever run into Blake Riddle, Billy's father. Britt says he hasn't, but as they talk shots ring out. Britt recognizes the shooter as Ben Reed who had escaped from the jail at Fort Lyon. When Billy goes to arrest Reed, Britt is sure there will be trouble, so he follows. But, when Ben hears the sheriff's name, he drops his guns and surrenders.

Britt hears that Billy plans on taking Ben back to the jail at Fort Lyon in the middle of a snowstorm and goes to talk to him about it. Billy tells him that Ben is actually his father Blake. He had found a locket among Ben's belongings and, in the locket, was a picture of Billy's mother. Billy plans on taking him out of town and turning him loose. Then he's going back to Georgia himself.

Photo-ad which appeared in the Tucson Daily Citizen, *Tucson, AZ on December 5, 1953.*

Reed tells Britt and Billy that he had taken the locket off a dead man. The man had been a part of a posse that was chasing Reed. Billy believes him and decides to wait until the weather clears and there's a better chance of getting his prisoner to Fort Lyon. But, Britt knows that Reed's story isn't true.

There is a short promo for Stewart's soon-to-be-released film, *The Glenn Miller Story*, at the end of the show.

CAST
James McCallion .... *Billy Riddle*
Ken Christy .... *Ben Reed*
Howard McNear .... *Cotton White*
Alan Reed .... *Milt*

This show is available on the 2-cassette set, Six Shooter as "The New Sheriff." See 01: "Jenny" for more information on this set.

12: **A Pressing Engagement**.........................Sunday, 12/6/1953
(A.K.A.: "The Groom," "Britt is Engaged,"
"Britt Ponset Gets Married")

FIRST LINE: *'Bout the last place I expected to be that Tuesday was the town of Powder Crick.*

Britt is in Powder Creek to close a cattle deal for his boss at the Double G Ranch. He gets an odd reception in town when everyone he meets seems to have been expecting him for about a month. Quint Todd, editor of the weekly newspaper, even seems agitated to see Britt. He tells Britt that he will keep a copy of the next paper for him so he can see his name in print. When Britt doesn't know why, he tells him there is always a story about the groom. Since Britt has no plans to get married, he is stupefied.

Eventually, Britt finds out that Minnie Flint has been telling everybody that he is going to marry her niece Helen. Minnie is surprised when Britt knocks on her door. She explains to Britt what she has done and she and Helen invite him back for supper that evening. Before returning to their home, Britt leaves a note for Quint Todd, asking that he also come to get information for their wedding story. In the end, there really is a wedding in Britt's future.

There is a short promo for Stewart's soon-to-be-released film, *The Glenn Miller Story*, at the end of the show.

CAST

Barbara Eiler	Helen
Virginia Gregg	Minnie Flint
Bill Johnstone	Forrest Trent
Sam Edwards	Quint Todd
Herb Vigran	Checker player

This show is also available on the following cassettes:
Radio Spirits #1435 (1994)
Radio's Greatest Westerns (Prime Time Nostalgia PTN-728) (1992)
This five-cassette set features one take of *The Six Shooter*. Two shows are included on the cassette — this one, under the title *The Silver Belt Buckle*, and *A Pressing Engagement*. See Show #18.

13: More Than Kin .... Sunday, 12/13/1953
(A.K.A.: "The Actors" "Barnum and the Thespians")

FIRST LINE (delivered by Dan O'Herlihy): *Confess thee of thy sin Desdemona or indeed thou art to die.*

The story begins with an acting company delivering a Shakespeare play in Virtue City and the locals are less than impressed and heckle them. Later, in the hotel lobby, as Britt Ponset is looking at pictures through a stereoscope, Mr. Plunkett, one of the actors, comes to check out. Britt recognizes him and calls him Arch. Arch takes Britt back to his room. When Britt had known Arch and his wife Maggie, they were store owners. Now they have given their names a more sophisticated sound and become actors. As the friends talk, a man knocks on their door and tells them that he is sorry they have cancelled their performance of *Hamlet* that evening because he would have liked to have seen it. He gives Arch his card and leaves. Arch can't believe his eyes. The name on the card is P.T. Barnum.

Arch and Maggie decided to "uncancel" their performance for that evening and send Britt to tell Barnum that they will be saving a box for him. When their excitement begins to wear off, they realize that they have a problem and enlist Britt's help to solve it.

There is a short promo for Stewart's soon-to-be-released film, *The Glenn Miller Story*, at the end of the show.

CAST

Michael Anne Barrett	*Maggie Plunkett*
Dan O'Herlihy	*Arch Plunkett*
Ted Bliss	*Sid, heckler*
Marvin Miller	*P.T. Barnum*
Tony Barrett	*Hotel clerk, heckler*

14: Britt Ponset's Christmas Carol .... Sunday, 12/20/1953
(A.K.A.: "A Western Christmas Carol," "Christmas Story")

FIRST LINE (not delivered by Stewart): *There was a nip in the air. Not a freezing, biting, angry nip, but a sort of tingle that made the morning stars shimmer...*

A young boy rides into Britt's camp. Johnny tells Britt that he has run away from his Aunt Millie's in Thompson's Corner. He's been staying with her since his parents were killed eight months ago. Britt can't understand why he would run away so close to Christmas, but finds that Johnny doesn't really believe in Christmas anymore.

Britt tells him the story of Charles Dickens' *A Christmas Carol*, as well as he can remember it, but with a distinct western flair. Ebenezer Scrooge becomes simply Eben.

Johnny likes the story and knows why Britt has told it to him, but he has nothing to give to his aunt. Britt points out a spruce tree that would make a nice Christmas tree and offers Johnny an extra red bonnet he has if Johnny would just show him the way back to Thompson's Corner. Before leaving Aunt Millie's, Britt also gives her his pocket knife — the one gift that Johnny had wanted for Christmas.

There is a short promo for Stewart's soon-to-be-released film, *The Glenn Miller Story*, at the end of the show.

Writer: Frank Burt, in collaboration with Charles Dickens

CAST

Howard McNear	*Eben Scrooge*
Richard Beals	*Johnny Carvel, Tim*
Sam Edwards	*Bob*
	(and various other characters)
Eleanor Audley	*Aunt Millie*
	(and various other characters)

During the middle break in the show, Hal Gibney tells the listening audience that all involved with the show are grateful for the kind words and letters and wishes them a Merry Christmas from the cast and staff. He also announces that the show is moving from Sunday to Thursday beginning on December 31. He reminds listeners of this move again at the end of the show, but the move doesn't go as planned.

In addition to other sources already given, this show can also be found on:

Radio's All Time Greatest Christmas Shows
Dove Audio 81350 (4 cassettes)

The program can also be found on the 6-cassette set, *Great Christmas Show Volume 1*, released by Audio File. The show is incorrectly dated as having been broadcast on December 20, 1950. The set is still available, now on CD, but the date of the show has not been corrected.

Frank Burt's radio play was adapted for TV by Burt and Valentine Davies and broadcast on the *General Electric Theater* as "The Trail to Christmas" on December 15, 1957. This TV version was produced by Revue Productions for General Electric. *The Six Shooter* radio series had also been produced by Revue. Ronald Reagan was the host of the show. Jimmy Stewart made his directing debut on this program. Stewart's character name was changed from Britt to Bart for the production. Also in the cast were Richard Eyer (Johnny Carterville), Hope Summers (Elizabeth), Sam Edwards (Bob Cratchit), John McIntire (Ebenezer Scrooge), Sally Fraser (Belle), Mary Lawrence (Mrs. Cratchit), Dennis Holmes (Tiny Tim), Kevin Hagen (Ghost), and Will Wright (Jake Marley). The show's production credits included: Elmer Bernstein (Music), William Daniels (Director of Photography), John Meeham (Art Direction), George Milo (Set Decorator), Richard G. Wray (Editorial Supervisor), Michael R. McAdam (Film Editor), Stanley Wilson (Music Supervisor), John C. Grubb (Sound), James Nicholson (Assistant Director), Jack Barron (Makeup), Florence Bush (Hair Stylist) and Vincent Dee (Costumes).

15: Cora Plummer Quincy ....Sunday, 12/27/1953
(A.K.A.: "Ned Plummer's Widow")

FIRST LINE: *The rain sure was comin' down that afternoon in Petersville. It had started all of a sudden, too.*

A sudden rainstorm drives Britt under the porch roof of the hotel in Petersville. Twenty-one-year-old Calvin Plummer is there, too. Cal tells Britt that his father had died less than a year ago. He asks Britt if he has ever been to Elk Point, New Mexico, and if he had ever heard of the Quincy ranch. Britt's not sure why such a question has been asked, but tells Cal that he has been to Elk Point, but had not heard of the ranch.

Britt's in town to see Doc Early because he has sprained his wrist. The doctor tells Britt that Cora Plummer has married a man named Oliver Quincy. Quincy is supposed to be a rich man and owns a large ranch near Elk Point, but the people in town aren't sure he's on the up and up. In fact, Sheriff Jay has gone to New Mexico to check out the story.

Later, as Britt is eating, Doc comes in to tell him that Cal has told him that his mother has been shot, but not seriously. He asked that the doctor come to the ranch and bring Britt with him. When they arrive at the ranch, Quincy tells them that his gun had gone off accidentally when he was cleaning it, but the true story comes to light when Cal comes in holding a gun on Quincy. It had been Cal who had shot his gun, with the bullet grazing his mother's shoulder. Cora breaks down and tells them all the story of why she had married Quincy so soon after the death of her first husband.

There is a short promo for Stewart's soon-to-be-released film, *The Glenn Miller Story*, at the end of the show.

CAST
Virginia Gregg .... Cora Plummer Quincy
Jean Tatum .... waitress
Robert Griffin .... Oliver Quincy
Parley Baer .... Doc Early
Bert Holland .... Calvin Plummer

16: A Friend in Need .... Sunday, 1/3/1954
(A.K.A.: "Step Brothers," "Man on the Run,"
"Fifty Yard Canyon")

FIRST LINE: *Fifty Yard Canyon, that's what folks called it. Probably there was another name, more official, written down on a map in the territorial capitol.*

Britt is traveling through Fifty Yard Canyon on his way to Smoke Falls when someone starts shooting at him. Britt gets off a shot that hits the man. The shooter turns out to be Art Hemper, an old friend of Britt's.

Art tells him that his stepbrother Clyde had been shot and killed the day before and that Sheriff Vale thinks that he did it and is after him. After talking to Britt, Art says that he will give himself up at Squirrel Rock at noon.

Britt runs into the posse and tells them what has happened. They tell him that Art had lied to him. George, one of the posse members, had witnessed Art shooting Clyde in the back. As the posse rides on, Britt goes to Squirrel Rock. Art is waiting there and gets the drop on him. He takes Britt's gun and removes all the cartridges. He then gives the gun back to Britt along with instructions to hold that gun on him and pretend he is Britt's prisoner. When they run into one of the men the sheriff has left behind in the canyon, the man wishes he could get a look at Britt's famous gun. Britt tosses it to him and Art takes a shot at Britt. The posse member fires at Art, mortally wounding him. Before he dies, Art apologizes to Britt for lying to him.

During the break between the two acts of today's show, Hal Gibney talks about the show's theme music. Apparently many listeners had written in asking the name of the song and where they could get a recording of it. Gibney says that the theme, *Highland Lament*, was recorded especially for the show and that it was not available for purchase in any record stores. He also announces that there is a story about the Stewarts and their twin daughters, Judy and Kelly, in the current issue of *McCall's* magazine.

There is a short promo for Stewart's soon-to-be-released film, The Glenn Miller Story, at the end of the show.

CAST

Shepard Menken	Sam Bittley
Bill Johnstone	Sheriff Vale
Frank Gerstle	Art Hemper
Howard McNear	George Crump

17: Hiram's Gold Strike .... Sunday, 1/10/1954
(A.K.A.: "The Prospector," "Hiram Grover's Strike")

FIRST LINE: *It must have been about 4 o'clock in the afternoon when I rode out of the Saucer Mountains and hit the flat.*

Britt rides out of the Saucer Mountains on his way to Clay City. Along his way, he runs into Hiram. Hiram has struck gold and is also on his way to Clay City to have the ore assayed.

Later, as Britt tries to go to sleep in his hotel room, Hiram knocks on his door. Hiram is suspicious of the assayer, Enoch Wilson. Wilson had told him he would have to wait at least two days for a report because tomorrow was a holiday — the 4th of July. But later, Hiram sees a light in the assayer's office and looks through the window only to see Wilson working with Hiram's ore. Britt goes back to the office with Hiram. Enoch explains that he saw how anxious Hiram was to get a report so he decided to work on it that night so he could report back as soon as possible. Two robbers enter the office. Hiram tries to keep them from his ore and is shot and seriously wounded. Britt wounds and captures the robbers.

The next day Enoch tells Britt that the strike is real and Hiram is going to be rich. But, when he told Hiram, he hadn't reacted the way he had hoped. He just didn't seem to have the will to live. Enoch was afraid that Hiram hadn't believed him and asks Britt to tell him. Britt does and gets the same response. Hiram tells him that he really didn't care about getting rich. He just wanted to prove to everyone that he had been right about gold being in the Saucer Mountains. Britt uses a little reverse psychology and Hiram is soon back on his feet.

There is a short promo for Stewart's soon-to-be-released film, *The Glenn Miller Story*, at the end of the show.

CAST

Howard McNear .... *Hiram Grover*
Herb Vigran .... *Enoch Wilson*
Bill Johnstone .... *Doc Nibbles*
Barney Phillips .... *Outlaw (Len)*
Tony Barrett .... *Outlaw (Zed)*

This show and the next were released on the following single cassette: *Six Shooter Starring James Stewart* Radio Spirits 2025

18: **The Silver Buckle** ....Sunday, 1/17/1954
(A.K.A.: "The Silver Belt Buckle")

FIRST LINE (Delivered by William Conrad): *The twilight wind carried the sound of the train toward the two figures who waited hidden in the clump of maple trees.*

William Conrad narrates the story's opening as he describes a train robbery. The story then opens with Carl Davis' wife telling the sheriff about the robbery and how and why the bandits shot and killed her husband of 25 years for his belt with the silver buckle. She told him that the buckle wasn't even made of silver, it just looked like silver.

The two robbers, brothers Kit and Lex Springer, ride into Britt's camp, claiming to be part of the posse looking for the robbers. Britt is heading across Miller Pass, a tough mountain trail. The brothers tag along saying that they think the robbers have gone that way and they are anxious to collect a $1500 reward. When Kit sheds his jacket, Britt admires his belt and silver buckle. He also notices that they are are stained with blood. Kit explains that he had cut his hand and must have gotten some blood on the belt.

After camping overnight on the trail, Britt awakens to hear the two brothers talking. Kit is telling Lex to kill Britt. Lex gets a shot off and it hits Britt in the chest. Britt returns the fire and kills Lex. Kit returns with the horses and he and Britt get off a few shots at each other. Britt is getting weaker, but gets off a final shot and Kit goes by him on his horse.

Britt returns to consciousness with Doc Easton and other posse members standing around him. They tell him that even though his last shot had not hit Kit, it still caused his death.

There is a short promo for Stewart's soon-to-be released film, *The Glenn Miller Story*, at the end of the show.

This was Hal Gibney's final week as the show's announcer. Beginning with next week's show, John Wald would take over that role.

CAST
William Conrad .... Narrator
Eleanor Audley .... Mrs. Davis
Forrest Lewis .... Sheriff
Joel Cranston .... Lex Springer
Frank Gerstle .... Kit Springer

This and this next program, "Helen Brinker," can be found on *The History of Radio: Great Western Radio Shows*, released in 2004. Topics Entertainment CA-217 (CD), Topics Entertainment CA-058 (cassettes).

This show, and show #12, under the title "Britt Ponset Gets Married," can also be found on the five-cassette set, *Radio's Greatest Westerns*. Prime Time Nostalgia PTN-728 (1992).

The set was also issued on CD with the same release number. The Stewart shows are on disc 3.

19: Helen Bricker .... Sunday, 1/24/1954
(A.K.A.: "Outlaw's Wife," "Mrs. Billy Stark")

FIRST LINE: *The post office at Yellow Crest was in Jim Pincher's General Store.* (John Wald replaces Hal Gibney as the show's announcer.)

Britt rides into Yellow Crest and heads for the post office that is located in Jim Pincher's general store. There's no mail for him. A woman comes in and asks about mail also. Jim practically ignores her. The woman is Helen Bricker, wife of Billy Stark, a robber and killer. Britt follows her from the store and talks with her. She tells him that the entire town is shunning her, even her father, Strad Bricker. When she drives off, Buck, the deputy sheriff, tells Britt that the townspeople would appreciate it if he didn't act so friendly toward her. They are very upset because Billy had robbed their bank and killed Dave Fletcher. Billy had been tried and convicted and was scheduled to be hanged at 11 that night.

When Britt takes his boot to Seth the shoemaker to have it repaired, he's told that some of the men in town plan to run Helen out of town and burn her cabin that night at about the same time her husband is hanged.

Britt talks with Strad Bricker, but he already knows of the men's plans and won't do anything to stop it. So, he goes to Helen's cabin to try to keep her from shooting at the men. When the men arrive, there is a bad wind. Britt suggests that if they set fire to the cabin, they might just burn down the entire town. Some of the men agree and nothing really happens.

As Helen and Britt are talking, her clock strikes 11:00. Britt thinks that Helen has a relieved expression on her face. As they talk, Britt guesses a secret Helen has been keeping.

There is a short promo for Stewart's soon-to-be-released film, *The Glenn Miller Story*, at the end of the show.

CAST
Lillian Buyeff .... Helen Bricker
                                                                  (Mrs. Billy Stark)
Ken Christy .... Jim Pincher
Herb Vigran .... Buck Thompson (deputy)
Parley Baer .... Seth
Will Wright .... Tim Slater, Strad Bricker

See "The Silver Buckle" (Show #18) for an extra CD source for this show.

20: Trail to Sunset..Sunday, 1/31/1954
(A.K.A.: "The Lynching," "Wrong Man Lynched")

FIRST LINE: *It had snowed during the night. A thick, wet snow that bowed the pine trees and banked over the big boulders turnin' them white.*

Britt wakes up to six inches of snow and wanders over a nearby hill to find some dry firewood. He hears Scar whinny several times and runs to the top of the hill in time to see a man putting a saddle on him. Britt yells for the man to stop, but he jumps onto Scar and starts to ride away. Britt fires three shots, the final one striking the man in the leg and sending him sprawling onto the ground. Britt finds him passed out with not only a bullet in his leg, but also one in his back. The shot in his back was partially bandaged and had not been the result of any of Britt's bullets.

When the man comes to, he tells Britt that he is Ace Tressler. He was a criminal and Britt recognized the name. He admits to robbing the stage depot in Sunset the day before and killing Sam Fletcher who ran the depot. Britt ties Tressler onto Scar's back and the two of them head back to Sunset.

Along the way, they run into five members of the posse — Doc Prince (a dentist), Ty Barstow, Frosty Ender, and two men whom Britt did not know. The two strangers are introduced as Cliff Slawson and Harv North. Britt tells them that it's Ace (by mistake, Stewart calls him Art this time) tied to his horse. They say that they weren't even looking for Tressler. They were after George Revit. They tell Britt that Revit had robbed the stage depot in Sunset and killed Sam Fletcher. They had trailed him to a cabin near Walnut Creek, tried him, and hanged him.

Britt tells them that Ace had confessed to the same robbery and killing. Revit didn't have anything to do with it. Now the men are worried about what will happen to them when Ace tells his story and the town finds out that they had lynched the wrong man. The problem is somewhat relieved when Tressler dies. But, Frosty is afraid that Britt will still tell everyone what happened, so he pulls his gun and tries to force him to head east, away from Sunset. Ty steps in and says that he's going back to town, telling their story and taking whatever punishment might be handed out. The other three agree and they head back to Sunset. Frosty also relents and rides back with Britt.

There is a short promo for Stewart's current film, *The Glenn Miller Story*, at the end of the show.

CAST

Robert Griffin	Frosty Ender
Harry Bartell	Ace Tressler
Lamont Johnson	Ty Barstow
Howard McNear	Doc Prince
Forrest Lewis	Cliff Slawson

21: Apron-Faced Sorrel.. Sunday, 2/7/1954
(A.K.A.: "City Boy," "City Boy at the Ranch")

FIRST LINE: *The 2 p.m. from Chicago wasn't more than, oh, 'bout 45 minutes late. That was practically a record for this time of year.*

Britt meets 16-year-old Clay Fenton who has arrived at Russville on the Chicago train. Britt had been good friends of his mother and father in the Dakota Territory years before. Now his father is dead and his mother has sent Clay to live with Britt for the summer and to learn about the West. Britt is working on Saul Poindexter's ranch and takes Clay there. Saul's son, Jeff, prods Clay into riding the apron-faced sorrel and the horse throws Clay.

The next morning, Britt is awakened at 4:00 by a horse whinny. He sees Clay come in all sweaty and with dark spots on his clothing. Clay undresses and goes back to bed. About an hour later, Saul rushes into the bunkhouse shouting that the sorrel had been badly whipped and blaming Clay for doing it. Clay denies it. Britt suggests that Clay try to ride the sorrel again. He tells Clay that horses are smart and that the sorrel would know the person who had whipped him. When the horse comes after him, Clay runs away.

When Britt finally catches up with him, Clay admits that he is afraid of horses because he and his father had been thrown from a horse when he was just three years old. Clay hadn't been injured badly, but his father had died. Is there any way that Clay can get over his fear of horses?

There is a short promo for Stewart's soon-to-be-released film, *The Glenn Miller Story*, at the end of the show.

CAST

Bill Johnstone	Saul Poindexter
Bert Holland	Jeff Poindexter
Sam Edwards	Clay Fenton

22: Quiet City..Sunday, 2/14/1954
(A.K.A.: "A Town Grows Up," "Sheriff's Son,"
"Sheriff's Son to Study Law")

FIRST LINE: *I sure don't know where the town ever got that name, Quiet City. Every time I came through it was anything but quiet.*

Britt is in Quiet City. He stops in to see Heck, the sheriff. The conversation turns to Buzz, Heck's 20-year-old son. Buzz wants to go east to school to become a lawyer, rather than become his father's deputy. Buzz feels that Quiet City is a civilized place and becoming a lawyer would be a good way to give back to his home town. His father doesn't agree.

The doctor rides by and tells Heck that Jason Norton has been shot. Heck heads for the ranch. At Buzz's urging, Britt follows. He finds Mabel Norton telling the sheriff that Pipe Clamper had shot and killed her husband over some of Pipe's cattle that had roamed onto their range. She tells them that Pipe had ridden toward the canyon and not toward his own ranch.

As they ride toward the canyon, Heck tells Britt that Norton's brother, Abe, and the other townspeople will want to lynch Pipe when they take him back to town and he asks Britt to help him prevent this from happening. Before Britt can give him an answer, shots are fired and the sheriff is hit in the leg. Britt wounds and captures Pipe by himself.

When Heck comes to and finds out that Pipe is alone with the doctor in his office, he's upset. But, when Britt and Buzz tell him what has happened, he changes his mind about the town and Buzz's plan to go to college.

There is a short promo for Stewart's current film, *The Glenn Miller Story*, at the end of the show.

CAST
Virginia Gregg... *Mabel Norton*
Robert Griffin.. *Doc Anderson*
Lamont Johnson..*Buzz*
Will Wright .... *Heck (Sheriff)*

23: Battle at Tower Rock ....Sunday, 2/21/1954
(A.K.A.: "The Blue Ribbon," "Young Gunslinger")

FIRST LINE: *Tower Rock sure was spruced up. Flags on almost every building, a big banner stretched all the way across Main Street...*

The Franklin County Fair is being held in Tower Rock on August 20 and Britt is there a day early. (Although he says Franklin County here at the beginning of the show, Stewart says Foster County near the show's end.) He stops by to see Kermit and Rome who run the local bank. They are married to sisters Thelma and Bessie. They had always been the best of friends, but Britt soon learns that there is something wrong between them. He talks to Otis Spears, the undertaker, hoping to find out what had caused the rift. It seems that Kermit had given Thelma a surrey for her last birthday. When Bessie's birthday came around, Rome gave her an even better surrey and the feud was on. Even the townspeople had taken up sides.

With the fair being the next day, Otis tells Britt that he needs someone to evaluate the preserves and Britt agrees to judge them. Later, Bessie stops by the hotel to take Britt back to her home for supper. Then, Thelma shows up for the same reason. Unfortunately for Britt, he learns that both Thelma and Bessie have strawberry preserves entered at the fair and that theirs are the only two entries. Britt doesn't go to supper with either of them, but he does go to see Otis to tell him that there's no way he'll be judging the preserves. But Otis is a slick talker and manages to calm him down by telling him that the townspeople respect him and will go along with whatever he decides. And, that decision may very well stop the feuding.

After a quick breakfast at Gravy Gibson's, Britt heads for the fair. He tries very hard not to make a decision, even going so far as to drop Bessie's jar, but she has an extra. Luckily, Britt's decision on the best strawberry preserves brings the sisters and their husbands back together again.

There is a short promo for Stewart's current film, *The Glenn Miller Story*, at the end of the show.

CAST
Les Tremayne .... *Rome Madden*
Jess Kirkpatrick .... *Kermit Bingham*
Bill Johnstone .... *Otis Spears*
Virginia Gregg .... *Bessie Madden*
Eleanor Audley .... *Thelma Bingham*

23A: *Show is Pre-Empted* .... Sunday, 2/28/1954

Show is pre-empted by a political program featuring Vice President Nixon at a meeting of the American Association for the United Nations in Washington, DC.

24: Cheyenne Express.. Sunday, 3/7/1954
(A.K.A.: "Wilbur English," "The Gang Falls Out,"
"Back Shooter")

FIRST LINE (not delivered by Stewart): *The fire had almost gone out and the evening chill crept through the chinks in the rough-hewn logs of the cabin walls.*

Wilbur English comes into the cabin to tell Floyd Winters that there are about 15 men in a posse heading to where the two robbers are standing. Floyd gives Wilbur his guns and tells him to load them. Instead, Wilbur shoots him twice in the back, killing him.

Britt rides into a camp at night and a man, calling himself Russ, gets the drop on him. Britt pulls a move on him and shoots him in the hand. The man tells Britt that his name is Warren Jones, but from things the man has said, Britt already figures that he is Wilbur English. He tells Britt that he is convinced Russ Winters, Floyd's brother and another gang member, is still out to kill him.

Britt allows Wilbur to ride along with him to Single Pine. From there, Sheriff Mike Preston will take him to Cheyenne where a pardon and his reward are waiting for him. When they arrive at Single Pine, Deputy Phil Waterman says that the sheriff is out of town on business and the trip to Cheyenne would have to be put off for a day or two. Wilbur is to stay at the hotel and wait for the sheriff.

A note saying "…you don't have much longer to wait" and signed "Russ," is pushed under Wilbur's door. Wilbur goes to Britt and shows him the note. Wilbur wants to catch the Cheyenne Express, but Britt advises him to wait for the sheriff. Wilbur boards the train anyway.

Britt shows the note to Phil, and Phil says that he had seen the McPhearson kids at Wilbur's door and that it was probably them who had put the note there as a joke. The sheriff returns and tells them that he had nearly captured Russ earlier in the day. He would have caught him if Russ hadn't managed to board the Cheyenne Express and get away.

There is a short promo for Stewart's current film, *The Glenn Miller Story*, at the end of the show.

CAST
Frank Gerstle.. *Floyd Winters*
Herb Vigran .... *Phil Waterman*
Barney Phillips .... *Mike Preston*
Paul Richards .... *Wilbur English*

25: Thicker Than Water .... Sunday, 3/14/1954
(A.K.A.: "Gus Proctor," "Gus & Ted Proctor,"
"Gambler's Son")

FIRST LINE: *I could tell he was a big man from the sound of his steps as he plowed through the trees toward where I was squatted by the fire eatin' my lunch.*

Gus Proctor walks into Britt's camp at lunchtime. He is walking because he'd lost his horse in a poker game. He's on his way to Clover Fork to see his wife Janet and son Ted. Britt tells him that Janet had died more than a year ago and that Ted was now living with his Aunt Amy. Gus asks Britt to tell Amy and Ted that he'll be coming to town for a day or two. When Amy hears about it, she's not very happy. She'd told Ted that his father was dead. Hearing this, Gus introduces himself to Ted as George Parker, a friend of his father's. Ted has many questions for him. Later, Gus gets $5 from Britt for his stickpin and then sits in on a game of poker.

During a break in the show, John Wald offers "thanks to the audience from Jimmy Stewart, from our writer Frank Burt, the entire technical crew and our director Jack Johnstone for the warm, friendly letters we receive from you every week. It makes us feel that you are somehow sharing the pleasure that is ours in bringing you *The Six Shooter*. We only wish it were possible to answer them all individually for we appreciate hearing from you more than you may realize."

Gus does well in the poker game, pays back Britt, buys new clothes, and a rifle to take Ted hunting. Returning to town a week later, Britt is surprised to find Gus still there. Ted comes to see Britt and tells him that he is planning on going away with Parker when he leaves Clover Fork. He also plans to become a gambler. He asks Britt to tell Parker what he has decided to do. Gus is happy that Ted wants to go with him, but he's not at all pleased that he wants to be a gambler. Gus doesn't want to be Ted's idol.

Gus hatches a plan to disillusion Ted. With a little help from Britt, the plan works to perfection.

There is a short promo for Stewart's current film, *The Glenn Miller Story*, at the end of the show.

CAST

Shirley Mitchell .... *Aunt Amy*
Dick Beals .... *Ted Proctor*
Barney Phillips .... *Gus Proctor/George Parker*
Robert Griffin .... *Bart Finch*

26: Duel at Lockwood ....Sunday, 3/21/1954
(A.K.A.: "Young Gunslinger," "Wes Singer, Gunfighter," "Target, Britt Ponset")

FIRST LINE (Delivered by Elvia Allman and Sam Edwards): *Whoa, boy, whoa. Wes, Wes! What are ya' hollerin' about Jim Cassidy? I'm lookin' for Wes, Mrs. Singer. You know where I can find him?*

Jim Cassidy is looking for Wes Singer, but Mrs. Singer, his grandmother, says he's not home. Well, he is home and Jim tells him that Britt Ponset is in Lockwood staying at the hotel. He was in town to have 2,000 posters printed by Pete Drum at the Lockwood Clarion. Pete tells him that Lockwood has a new gunfighter — Wes Singer. Britt also stops by to see Sheriff Ben Hittelman. He tells Britt that Wes is looking for a gunfight with him. Singer was due in town at 4 o'clock and the sheriff wants Britt to stay in his hotel room and let him take care of Wes. The sheriff is afraid that the people in the town will lose respect for him if he doesn't deal with Wes.

When he returns to his hotel room, Britt finds Mrs. Singer waiting for him. She's worried about all the men who will die if Wes isn't stopped. She wants Britt to kill him. Britt didn't think that was the answer, but he's not sure what the answer is.

Britt now is faced with several problems. First, how can he keep Wes from killing Sheriff Hettelman? Next, how can he avoid a gunfight with Wes himself? And finally, how can he keep Wes out of Lockwood for good?

There is a short promo for Stewart's current film, *The Glenn Miller Story*, at the end of the show.

CAST

Elvia Allman	Mrs. Singer
Sam Edwards	Jim Cassidy
Will Wright	Sheriff Ben Hittelman
Howard McNear	Pete Drum
Bert Holland	Wes Singer

At both the beginning and the end of this show, John Wald announces that *The Six Shooter* will be moving from Sunday to Thursday nights. The first Thursday night show will be April 1. During "Britt Ponset's Christmas Carol," broadcast on December 20, 1953, Hal Gibney had announced that the show would be moving to Thursdays beginning

December 31. That move did not take place. Now, three months later, the move would finally be made.

This show is available on the 2-cassette set, Six Shooter. See 01: "Jenny" for more information on this set.

27: Aunt Emma .... Thursday 4/1/1954
(A.K.A.: "Marrying Off Aunt Em," "Aunt Em from Kansas")

FIRST LINE: *This was my first trip into Powder Crick for oh, oh three months, I suppose.*

(The show moves from Sunday night to Thursday night where it will remain until the end of the series.)

Britt rides into Powder Creek for the first time in three months. He stops at Ethan Greenriver's General Store to buy some new clothes. There's also a letter there for him from his Aunt Emma in Topeka, Kansas. According to the letter, she's coming to Powder Creek to live and she wants Britt to live with her. Britt wants to wire her and tell her not to come, but Ethan tells him that she's already been in town for a week. She's moved into the old Mack Dennis house and has a room already fixed up for Britt.

Britt tells her that he's signed on at the Bar-Y and really can't stay in town with her. She says that there are other jobs. In fact, she already has one lined up for him at the bank. It's time for him to settle down. Besides, she needs someone to take care of now that all her children are grown and gone.

Within a week, Britt knows that he can't stay on with her much longer. He would just have to find someone else for her to fuss over. But who in Powder Creek would be right for her?

There is a short promo for Stewart's current film, *The Glenn Miller Story*, at the end of the show.

CAST
Eleanor Audley .... *Aunt Emma Bancroft*
William Johnstone .... *Ethan Greenriver*

28: **General Gillford's Widow** .... Thursday 4/8/1954
(A.K.A.: "The Widow's Secret," "The Wolf")

FIRST LINE: *We weren't exactly lost, Scar and me, well not completely anyhow.*

Britt is headed for Minton, but gets somewhat lost. He comes upon a rundown house and knocks at the door. The woman who answers gives him directions. He asks if he can have some water for Scar. As they're getting the water, she tells him that she is Hannah Gillford, General William Gillford's wife. She mentions that the general is napping. This surprises Britt, because he thinks that the general, who is considered a hero, is dead. Before he leaves, Hannah gives him a list of supplies she needs and asks him to take it to Trailor's General Store in Minton and have Trailor deliver the order the following morning.

At first, Trailor is reluctant to fill the order, because he knows that he won't be paid. Hannah orders things specifically for the general, even though everyone in town knows that he is dead. But, he feels sorry for her and starts to pick items for the order. Britt volunteers to take the order out that night. When he arrives back at the house and goes to the door, he hears Hannah talking to her husband. And then...he hears the general talking back. He tells Britt that he wasn't even with his men the night of the fight with the Cheyenne. He didn't feel well and left to find a doctor in Browning. When a wounded corporal catches up to him and tells him of the battle before he dies, the general had gone back only to find all his men dead. Fearing he would be charged with desertion, he has stayed in the house for five years. General Gillford believes that if Britt goes back to town and tells people that he's alive, they will believe him. He doesn't want that to happen, so he holds a gun on Britt and threatens to kill him. Britt turns and walks out, knowing the general won't shoot him. He looks back and sees the general start up the stairs, trip and fall. His gun goes off killing him. Britt is left to decide if he should tell the townspeople what has happened. What happens may surprise you.

There is a short promo for Stewart's current film, *The Glenn Miller Story*, at the end of the show.

CAST
Virginia Gregg .... Hannah Gillford
Parley Baer .... General William Gillford
Robert Griffin .... Mr. Trailor

29: Crisis at Easter Creek .... Thursday, 4/15/1954

FIRST LINE: [church choir singing] *Sowing in the noontide and the dewy eve.* [Britt] *I hadn't attended a Tuesday evenin' choir practice in quite a spell.*

Britt is in John Farley's General Store for the regular Tuesday evening church choir rehearsal (there is not a church in town, yet). We hear Britt singing a bit of *Bringing in the Sheaves*. But, the organ gives out and rehearsal ends. Elvira, the organist, refuses to play the old organ ever again. Reverend Broome knows that a church in Whitefield has just purchased a new organ and is willing to sell their old one for $95. But, there's only $42.50 in the building fund. Britt, against his will, is drafted to raise the other $52.50 they need. After asking everyone in town to contribute, he has raised exactly $11. The sheriff is willing to put in $1 to help him out. Britt tells the sheriff that he has hit the area across the creek east of town. The sheriff tells him that's not a good area at all. Britt has heard there are criminals living there, including "Red Eye" Kirk, the toughest bandit around. The sheriff won't admit to that, however, but says there is a man living there who looks a lot like "Red Eye."

Britt rides to the house, but the man who answers the door says he's Bill Jones, not "Red Eye" Kirk. When Britt tells him he's collecting money to buy a church organ, Jones can't believe it. But Britt says that he doesn't want a contribution from him. Instead, he wants Jones to ride with him to the other houses in that area and help get contributions out of the people who live there. Jones laughs, and then says he thinks it would be fun and agrees to go along.

During the break in the middle of the show, John Wald mentions the story's title.

Their first stop is to see Jack Denton. He contributes two $20 gold pieces. That's enough for Britt. He now has all the money he needs. But Jones, who has now admitted to being "Red Eye," was having too much fun and wants to visit every house and cabin. Britt can't believe the amount of money they collect.

On the way back to town, Britt realizes that someone is following him. It turns out to be Wisconsin Billy, who hadn't been home when Britt and Red Eye had called. He had met Red Eye on the trail and Red Eye had sent him to find Britt and make his contribution.

It turns out that Britt had collected nearly $1,000, enough to buy the organ and build a church. But, there's one more problem to overcome.

On Easter Sunday, the church has its new organ and also some new members in the congregation.

There is a short promo for Stewart's current film, *The Glenn Miller Story*, at the end of the show.

CAST
Virginia Gregg.. Elvira Peebles
Marvin Miller .... Reverend Broome
Ted de Corsia .... Wisconsin Billy
Robert Griffin .... Sheriff Abner Appleton

Bill Conrad (actually John Wald says "and Red Eye Kirk." He doesn't mention Bill Conrad's name.)

30: **Johnny Stringer**... Thursday, 4/22/1954
(A.K.A.: "Tracking Down a Killer")

FIRST LINE: *Well, it sure didn't look like I was goin' to get much sleep that night. The Prospect Hotel was right in the middle of town and from my room I could hear justa bout everything that went on outside.*

Britt is in the Prospect Hotel, but, because of the heat, he's not getting much sleep. He hears a shot and from his window, sees a man ride away from the front of the hotel. He goes to the lobby and finds Sid Tucker has been shot. Doc Prince is called in, but Tucker dies. Before he dies, he says that it was John Stringer who had robbed and shot him.

Britt and Sam, the town's sheriff, ride out to track down Stringer. They find some tracks and the tin box that had held the money taken in the robbery. From the tracks, they know that Stringer's horse is going lame, so they know he can't be far ahead. They see a cabin with smoke coming from the chimney. They sneak up and rush through the back door only to find a young girl named Maria Gonzalez Mendez. Stringer isn't there, but his horse is. Maria tells them that she gave him a new horse and he rode away. She did this because he is her boyfriend and they are going to be married. But, when Britt and the sheriff mention that he is already married, she changes her story and tells them that he is hiding in the loft of the barn.

When they get to the barn, Stringer starts shooting at them. Britt goes to the back of the barn and breaks a small window. He starts some brush on fire and throws it through the window. The smoke soon drives

Stringer from the barn. Maria rushes up to him and he grabs her to use as a shield. This will turn out to be a bad move on Stringer's part.

There is a short promo for Stewart's current film, *The Glenn Miller Story*, at the end of the show.

CAST
Virginia Gregg............................Maria Gonzalez Mendez
Harry Bartell...Johnny Stringer
Parley Baer.. Doc Prince
Joel Cranston... Sid Tucker
Barney Phillips.. Sheriff Sam

31: Revenge at Harness Creek...............Thursday, 4/29/1954
(A.K.A.: "Harcourt Brothers")

FIRST LINE: *I'd known the Harcourt brothers a good many years. First time I passed through Harness Crick, they was just youngsters.*

Britt is in Harness Creek to join the Silver Spur cattle drive. He stops by to see the Harcourt brothers — Cash and Lex — and their Aunt Bessie Petrie. Lex wants to join the Silver Spur drive with Britt, but Cash is against the idea. In the middle of the night, Aunt Bessie knocks on Britt's door and tells him that Lex has been shot. Cash, who is the sheriff, has already gone to town, but she wants Britt to go, too.

Lex is dead, shot by Adam Robie. Cash goes after Robie and Britt goes back to tell Aunt Bessie what has happened. Mrs. Robie, Adam's wife, comes to the Petrie house to talk with Britt. Adam had told her that Lex was spoiling for a fight. Adam wants to give himself up to Britt if Britt will promise to turn him in to the district marshal in Standish Falls. Britt isn't sure he wants to do it, but Aunt Bessie talks him into it.

During the break between the first and second acts, John Wald thanks the listeners for all the letters they have sent. Going into act two, he mentions the title *Revenge at Harness Creek*. It's the first time that a show title was mentioned during the series.

Robie is in a cabin in Moon Canyon. On his way there, Britt runs into Cash, who is heading in the opposite direction. Britt tells him all that has transpired and why he is there. Britt then rides to the cabin. He and Robie set out for Standish Falls, but they run into a little trouble along the way.

There is a short promo for Stewart's current film, *The Glenn Miller Story*, at the end of the show.

CAST

Virginia Gregg	Mrs. Robie
Eleanor Audley	Bessie Petrie
Lamont Johnson	Cash Harcourt
Forrest Lewis	Adam Robie
Bert Holland	Lex Harcourt

32: Anna Nordquist .... Thursday, 5/6/1954
(A.K.A.: "Mail Order Bride," "Swedish Bride," "The Accused")

FIRST LINE: *It was Friday morning when I got to Smoke Falls and my first trip to town in about three months.*

Britt is in Smoke Falls to drive some cattle to auction for Dad Foster. He goes to Windy Knight's Café. Windy tells him about Marshal Burke finding Seth Quincy's body. Pete Kelgrin had been arrested and convicted of the murder and robbery. He is set to be hanged the next Monday.

On his way across town, Britt sees a young woman who looks like she is waiting for someone. Britt asks if he can help her. He finds out that her name is Anna Nordquist and she is there waiting for Peter Kelgrin whom she has come from Sweden to marry. Britt tells her that Pete is in jail. After inviting Britt to the wedding, Anna heads for the jail. After visiting with Pete, Anna is convinced that he didn't commit the murder and asks Britt to prove it.

(For the second week in a row, John Wald says the show's title as they go into act two.)

Britt goes to Seth's house to look around, but finds nothing. As Britt is riding back to town, moonlight reflecting off a metal object catches his attention. Britt stops to investigate and finds a gun nearly hidden under some leaves. Pete's initials are on the gun handle. Britt gives the gun to the sheriff and then goes to tell Anna. She still refuses to believe that Pete is guilty. Britt wonders how he can make Anna believe that Pete is guilty.

There is a short promo for Stewart's current film, *The Glenn Miller Story*, at the end of the show.

CAST

Lillian Buyeff	Anna Nordquist
Bill Johnstone	Windy Knight
Lou Merrill	Marshal Ned Burke
Harry "Killer" Bartell	Peter Kelgrin

This program can be found on *Old Time Radio Westerns*. Radio Spirits 5009 (CDs)/5008 (cassettes) (1996).

Eleven different shows are featured on 4 CDs. Shows include *The Lone Ranger*, *The Cisco Kid*, *Screen Directors' Playhouse*, *Lux Radio Theatre*, *Tales of the Texas Rangers*, *Gunsmoke*, *Hopalong Cassidy*, *Frontier Gentleman*, *Have Gun – Will Travel*, and *The Six Shooter*. Just this one *Six Shooter* included.

33: The Double Seven .... Thursday, 5/13/1954
(A.K.A.: "Ranchers vs. Sodbusters," "Half-Way Creek")

FIRST LINE: *Halfway Crick sure wasn't much of a town. Oh, there was a general store and a café, roomin' house, and a blacksmith shop, that's about all there was to it.*

Britt is in Halfway Creek to try to get a job with the Double Seven Ranch. Gid Babscomb, the owner of the ranch, would be happy to have him, but Britt spots Clint Sutton and turns down the job offer. Gid explains to Britt that he needs a gunfighter working for him. Some sodbusters have been rustling his cattle and someone had even taken a shot at him.

Perry Waudel, one of the sodbusters, talks to Britt and tells him that it wasn't any of the farmers who were causing the trouble. Rufe Lovett, another farmer, shows up and tells the pair that Gid is planning to burn down their farmhouses that night. Since Gid's own ranch house will be unprotected, the farmers plan to burn it down at the same time. Perry gets Britt to go talk to Gid for them.

On his way to Gid's ranch, Britt runs into Gid and his men on their way to burn out the sodbusters. Britt tells him that the sodbusters had talked about burning down the Double Seven. Gid turns his men around and heads back home.

On his way back to Half Creek, Britt is ambushed. Britt wings the man and discovers it is Rufe Lovett. Rufe admits that it was he who had stolen the cattle and taken the shot at Gid. But, his reasons have Britt wondering about the man's sanity.

There is a short promo for Stewart's current film, *The Glenn Miller Story*, at the end of the show.

CAST

Lamont Johnson	Clint Sutton
Gerald Mohr	Gid Babscomb
Bob Griffin	Rufe Lovett
Parley Baer	Perry Wautel
Howard McNear	Christy Ott

34: The Shooting of Wyatt King..........................Thursday, 5/20/1954
(A.K.A.: "The Wyoming Kid," "Reluctant Hero," "Wyatt King")

FIRST LINE (Delivered by Bill Johnstone): [knocking] *Keep your shirt on. Keep your shirt on. Bank don't open 'til 9 a.m. You got five minutes to wait.*

Matt Hawkins knocks on the door of the bank about five minutes before opening time. He tells Ollie, who runs the bank, that Wyatt King, the Wyoming Kid, has been captured. Just the day before, King had robbed the bank of $2500, which Matt says has been recovered. Sheriff Spud Hemphill and the posse hadn't really captured King; instead, they found him along the road shot in the abdomen. No one can figure out who would have had the courage to face up to King. When they learn that Britt Ponset is in Copper Springs, they naturally jump to the conclusion that he was the one who had shot Wyatt. Britt denies it, but they don't believe him.

Britt goes to the jail to talk to the sheriff, but the sheriff is also convinced that Britt was the unknown hero. Why? Because Wyatt told him that he was shot by the Six Shooter. Britt asks to talk to King, but even face to face Wyatt sticks to his story. Britt asks the sheriff to leave and then gets Wyatt to tell him the real story. Wyatt tells him that he will stick to the story because he doesn't want anyone to know that he was really out-drawn by a gray-haired, pot-bellied older man in a suit and tie.

Britt knows that he has to find this other man and he is sure that he has recently seen someone fitting the description. It was Jonas Pilgrim, the teller at the bank. Jonas admits to the shooting, but asks Britt not to tell anyone. He says that Matilda, his wife, would never understand him carrying a gun. He had never told her that in his younger days he was pretty quick on the draw. He wouldn't have even had the gun except the widow Tolliver had given it to him for protection. She had given him money to put in the bank for her because she didn't want it stolen.

Britt knows that he is going to have a problem convincing anyone that it was Jonas, and not he, who had captured Wyatt King. The solution to that problem seems clearer to Britt when Wyatt breaks out of jail.

There is a short promo for Stewart's current film, *The Glenn Miller Story*, at the end of the show.

CAST
Bill Johnstone .... Oliver "Ollie" Rowan
Herb Vigran .... Mack Hawkins
Junius Matthews .... Jonas Pilgrim
Barney Phillips .... Sheriff Spud Hemphill
Joel Cranston .... Wyatt King

The show has been released, as *Wyatt King*, on a cassette. Radio Spirits #700 (1994). Also on the cassette is "Silver Threads." See Show #36.

It can also be found on *Old-Time Radio's 60 All-Time Favorites*. Radio Spirits 4461 (2001).

A 20-cassette set, which features one Jimmy Stewart show from *The Six Shooter* series. "The Shooting of Wyatt King" had originally been broadcast on May 20, 1954.

It is also available as "The Wyoming Kid" on the 20-cassette set, Six Shooter. See 01: "Jenny" for more information on this set.

35: Blood Relations .... Thursday, 5/27/1954
(A.K.A. "Bad Blood")

FIRST LINE: *It was a little over four years since the last time I worked for the Wilcox outfit. But when George Wilcox wrote me about his pa's death....*

Britt shows up at the Wilcox ranch to take a new job. George Wilcox tells Britt that he won't be going along on the drive this year. His sister, Viola, is dating Hunt Coffin, the brother of convicted killer Jud Coffin. Coffin is using the name Hank Wallace, but George knows the truth and he wants to break up the pair. When he confronts Vi, she says that she knows his true identity. He had changed his name because he didn't think people would understand. Vi tells George that she plans to marry Hunt. Britt has to hold George away from Vi.

Next day, George and Britt ride out to see how the round-up is going, returning to the house about lunch time. Vi tells George that she had been in town to see Hunt and that they were planning on coming to get her that night. Britt doesn't want to be there for another fight, so he rides for Adobe Junction. Hunt runs into Britt and thanks him for sticking up for Vi the night before. He also tells Britt that he has bought a gun.

When Britt returns to the ranch, he tells George that Hunt has a gun. George gets a rifle and sits by the window waiting for Hunt to arrive. When Hunt arrives, George warns him to leave. When he doesn't, George aims his rifle and begins to pull the trigger. A shot is fired and George is hit in the shoulder. That shot allows Vi to marry Hunt and Britt to lead the cattle drive.

For the third time during the series, the title of the show is mentioned by John Wald as the second act begins.

There is a short promo for Stewart's current film, *The Glenn Miller Story*, at the end of the show.

CAST
Barbara Eiler.. Viola Wilcox
Herb Ellis.. George Wilcox
Sam Edwards......................... Hank Wallace/Hunt Coffin

36: Silver Threads.. Thursday, 6/3/1954
(A.K.A.: "Silver Threads Among the Gold," "Song and Supper")

FIRST LINE (Delivered by Ben Wright): *We'll be turnin' in here, Michael. Huh? As long as we're goin' into town anyway, we can be seein' whether there might be anything Homer Danfield might be needin'.*

Michael O'Hara and his father Sean are on their way to town. They stop by Homer Danfield's house to see if they can get anything for him. They find Danfield shot, but still clinging to life. Michael rides for the doctor and the sheriff.

Meanwhile, Britt is on his way to Pearl City and is looking for someplace to camp for the night. He comes upon the camp of Toby Yeager, a singing cowboy. Toby gets Britt to sing a bit of *Streets of Laredo* with him (the second time Mr. Stewart has sung in the series). He also tries to teach him how to play a song on the guitar. The song is *Silver Threads Among the Gold*, which Toby says is a new song and not too well known in the west yet. When Britt tries singing a bit of it, the coyotes begin howling.

After breakfast, Britt starts off for Pearl City. When he passes Homer's house, he notices there seems to be a few people there, so he stops by to see if anything has happened. Sean tells him that Homer has been shot and robbed. The sheriff tells him that Homer was able to say that the robber had been singing a song about silver and gold, but no one had heard of such a song, except Britt. Britt tells Sheriff Gentle about Toby and the song. The sheriff and Britt start to track Yeager. They pick up his trail heading toward Saddle Mountain. They hear him singing and ride into his camp. Britt introduces Yeager to Cleat Gentle and tells him that he is the sheriff of Pearl City. They ask Toby how much money he has and he produces $48, which is about what was taken from Homer. Toby tells them it was his railroad pay. They tell him what has happened and ask him to return with them. As they pass Sean's ranch, he tells them that Homer has died. Since Homer will not be able to identify his attacker, they let Yeager go. But, there's a surprising twist to the story.

There is a short promo for Stewart's current film, *The Glenn Miller Story*, at the end of the show.

CAST

Ben Wright .... *Sean O'Hara*
Bert Holland .... *Michael O'Hara*
Will Wright .... *Sheriff Cleat Gentle*
Barney Phillips .... *Toby Yeager*

Bob Bain as the guitarist

The show has been released on a cassette under the title "Song and Supper." See "The Shooting of Wyatt King" (show #34) for complete details on this cassette.

37: The New Sheriff .... Thursday, 6/10/1954
(A.K.A.: "Write-In Candidate," "Virtue City Election,"
"The Election," "Sheriff Ponset")

FIRST LINE: *Well, at first I didn't know what I was gettin' into. The town of Virtue City had never looked like this afore.*

Britt arrives back in Virtue City right in the middle of an election. Doc Cross welcomes him as he is checking into the hotel. Doc tells him that Gus Cotton, a gunfighter, and his brother Roy have moved into Virtue City and taken over the town. They had been in the McGuinness Gang, but now are feuding with them. Sheriff George Davenport had been killed in August and now Roy Cotton is running for sheriff. The other candidate is Ernie Needle, the town blacksmith. Doc asks Britt to come to a meeting for Needle and other candidates, but Britt doesn't want to get involved.

Britt changes his mind when Roy Cotton visits him and tries to run him out of town. He goes to the meeting and Doc tells everybody that Britt backs their candidates. He also tells them that Britt will be at the polling place to make sure everything goes well during the election.

During a break between the two acts, John Wald again thanks the audience for their letters, as he has done several times in the past.

The voting goes smoothly and after the election is over, Britt goes back to his room to get some sleep. But, Doc comes knocking on his door to tell him that, due to a write-in campaign, Britt has been elected sheriff... and mayor. According to town laws, he can't serve in both positions. If he resigns as sheriff, the man with the second most votes will take over the job. That would be Roy Cotton. It looks like there's no way out for Britt, but then he has an idea.

There is a short promo for Stewart's current film, *The Glenn Miller Story*, at the end of the show.

CAST
Carleton Young .... Hotel Clerk, Jeff Perkins
Dal McKennon .... Doc Cross
Paul Richards .... Roy Cotton
Frank Gerstle .... Gus Cotton
Junius Matthews .... Jeff Perkins

The show can be found on the 6-cassette set, *Radio Favorites — Volume Two* (Radio Spirits, 1991). It can be found on tape 6, side A.

On the packaging, the show is called "Sheriff Ponset" and it is marked as having been originally broadcast on November 15, 1953. However, it is actually this show, not "Escape from Smoke Falls," that was broadcast on that date.

38: When the Shoe Doesn't Fit .... Thursday, 6/17/1954
(A.K.A.: "Shades of Cinderella," "Western Cinderella")

FIRST LINE: *It was about 7 o'clock on a Saturday evening, and I was ridin' down the east trail that led from Council City over to Crown Ranch.*

Britt is headed for the Crown Ranch when he passes a house. A girl, Cindy Lou Ames, comes out and asks if he has seen "Friendly" DeWitt and his traveling mercantile. He hasn't, but about five minutes later he runs into him and tells him that the family is waiting for him. DeWitt tells Britt that Monty Prince has just returned home from college and there was going to be a big square dance for him that evening. He has a dress for Fern Ames to wear to the dance. Her mother, Hattie, will be very upset if he doesn't get the dress there on time. Hattie plans on getting Monty to marry Fern. Hattie and Fern's wagon passes them, but neither one sees them because of poor eyesight. Britt wonders why Cindy Lou isn't with them. DeWitt tells him that Cindy Lou is only Hattie's stepdaughter and that Hattie has no time for her.

"Friendly" decides to take the dress to Cindy Lou and get her as pretty as possible for the dance. Britt can be her escort. DeWitt has everything he needs except shoes. The only shoes he has are for another girl's wedding and he must have them to her the next day. "Friendly" figures that if Britt gets Cindy Lou back home by midnight, he will still be able to get the shoes where they belong by eight the next morning. That should be in plenty of time. The shoes turn out to be very tight, but Cindy Lou doesn't seem to mind.

Britt comes into the dance with Cindy Lou, but before long her time is being monopolized by Monty Prince. Britt winds up dancing with Fern. About 11 o'clock, Britt rounds up Cindy Lou and heads for home. Cindy Lou is a little upset because Monty hadn't recognized her. When they get home, Cindy Lou's feet have swollen so much that they can't get the shoes off. As Hattie and Fern arrive, Britt and DeWitt quickly leave.

The next day, Monty visits Britt in his room at the Castle Hotel to ask about the identity of the girl he had brought to the dance the night before. Monty doesn't have a glass slipper to slip on Cindy Lou's foot, but it's still the shoes that lead to her identity.

Between the two acts, John Wald mentions the title of the show.

There is a short promo for Stewart's current film, *The Glenn Miller Story*, at the end of the show.

CAST

Barbara Eiler..Cindy Lou Ames
Eleanor Audley...Hattie Ames
Sandra Gould...Fern Ames
Bill Johnstone.."Friendly" DeWitt
Sam Edwards...Monty Prince

This was the third and final episode of *The Six Shooter* to be turned into a TV show. It was broadcast on December 15, 1959, on *Startime* as "Cindy's Fella." It was adapted for TV by Jameson Brewer with Gower Champion directing and William Frye producing. Gone is Britt Ponset. Instead, Stewart plays the role of Azel Dorsey. The cast included Mark Allen (Swaney Rivers, Duke's buddy), Alice Backes (Esther, an ugly stepsister), James Best (Duke, the rancher's son), Kathie Browne (Phyllis, an ugly stepsister), George Gobel (Drifter), Maurice Kelly (Bartender), George Keymas (Zack Riney, a barroom bully), Lois Smith (Cindy), and Mary Wickes (Myrtle, the widow Parke). Other crew members included John Meehan (Art Director), Richard G. Wray (Editorial Supervisor), Edward Haire (Film Editor), Alex Romeo (Choreographer), Conrad Salinger (Music), Stanley Wilson (Music Supervisor), Earl Craine Sr. (Sound), Jack Barron (Makeup), Florence Bush (Hair Stylist) and Vincent Dee (Costume Supervisor).

In 2011, this program was issued as part of the mp3 only set, *Jimmy Stewart the Ultimate Radio Collection Vol. 3* (Master Classics Records).

39: Myra Barker..Thursday, 6/24/1954
(A.K.A.: "Unpredictable Horse")

FIRST LINE (Stewart and Parley Baer): [dog barking] *Lem. Lem Pruitt. Oh. Where are ya', Lem? This stall here, Britt. I'm currying down one of my mares.*

Without Britt's approval, Lem Pruitt, operator of the livery stable in Willow Fork, rents out Scar to Myra Barker, a visitor from the east. When Britt finds out, he's not very happy and is even afraid that Scar will throw her because he doesn't like anyone riding him except Britt. But Scar seems to really take to Myra and so does Britt.

Myra is staying with Jesse Aldon and his wife Zoey and she invites Britt for supper. Myra knows that Zoey is trying to marry her off, but she tells Britt that she's not interested in getting married. Britt says that some of his friends also try to marry him off from time to time, too. They make a plan to see each other to take the pressure off, but there will be no commitment.

Between acts, John Wald mentions that this is the last show in the series and also gives the show's title.

Before he knows what has happened, Britt asks Myra to marry him. She has to sleep on it before giving her answer. She says yes. John Wald has just informed the listening audience that this was the final show and now Britt is going to settle down and get married. Or…is he?

There is a short promo for Stewart's current film, *The Glenn Miller Story*, at the end of the show.

CAST
Virginia Gregg.. *Myra Barker*
Dee J. Thompson.. *Zoey Aldon*
Howard McNear ....*Jesse Aldon*
Parley Baer..*Lem Pruitt*

John Wald's final announcement is, "It's been good to be with you with *The Six Shooter* each week and I hope that sometime, somehow, we can do it again."

This was one of the first *Six Shooter* shows to be commercially released. It's listed on the cassette as "Unpredictable Horse," instead of this, more familiar, title. Radio Spirits #1435 (1994). The other show on the cassette is "A Pressing Engagement" — see show #12.

CHAPTER 2
Guest Appearances

Beginning in 1933 and continuing until 1990, Jimmy Stewart appeared on over 250 radio shows. His appearances can be grouped into several categories. The earliest programs were simply promos for the play and/or films in which he was currently appearing. Falling into this class is the time he performed in a scene from the play *Yellow Jack* on the *Fleischmann Hour* in 1934 and several appearances on *Leo is on the Air*. Stewart also acted as host or master of ceremonies for several shows. He was often the host of *Good News*, beginning in 1937. He also occasionally served the same role when other famous radio personalities couldn't appear on their own shows, for whatever reason. He has filled in for both Bing Crosby and Fred Waring.

As a dramatic or comedic actor, Stewart made appearances in many original radio plays on programs including *Family Theater*, *Plays for Americans*, *Radio Reader's Digest*, *Screen Guild Theater*, *Silver Theater*, *Suspense* and *Theatre Guild on the Air*.

Stewart also appeared in several radio plays based on short stories by famous authors. The two most famous were Hemmingway's *The Short, Happy Life of Francis Macomber* and Stephen Vincent Benet's *O'Halloran's Luck*.

One of the largest categories of Stewart's appearances involved recreating roles from some of the many films in which he starred. The list is long and includes: *Broken Arrow*, *Call Northside 777*, *Destry Rides Again*, *It's a Wonderful Life*, *Jackpot*, *Made for Each Other*, *Magic Town*, *Next Time We Love*, *No Highway in the Sky*, *No Time for Comedy*, *The Philadelphia Story*, *The Shop Around the Corner*, *The Stratton Story*, *Winchester '73*, *Vivacious Lady* and *You Gotta Stay Happy*.

Stewart frequently did the same radio play on two or more programs. The scripts, of course, were always different. He did "Call Northside 777" for both *Screen Directors' Playhouse* and *Screen Guild Theater*. "It's a Wonderful Life" was done for *Lux Radio Theatre, Screen Directors' Playhouse, Screen Guild Theater* (airing on three separate occasions) and *Stars in the Air*. "Magic Town" was performed on both *Lux Radio Theatre* and *Screen Directors' Playhouse*. Jimmy did "One Sunday Afternoon" for both *Academy Award Theater* and *Theatre Guild on the Air*. The very popular "The Philadelphia Story" was enacted on *Lux Radio Theatre, Screen Guild Theater* and *Theatre Guild on the Air*. Finally, Stewart performed the radio play "Consequence" two times in the series *Suspense*, once in 1946 and once in 1949. The same script was used for both appearances, but different actors appeared in each version.

When a film actor wasn't available to reprise his role for the radio, Jimmy sometimes took on that character for him. On *Lux Radio Theatre*, he took on Robert Montgomery's role of Carey Jackson in "June Bride," Henry Fonda's part of Anthony Amberton in "The Moon's Our Home," and Dan Dailey's character, Bill Kluggs, in "When Willie Comes Marching Home." For *Academy Award Theater* and *Theatre Guild on the Air*, Stewart played the Dennis Morgan role of Biff Grimes in "One Sunday Afternoon." In "The Meanest Man in the World" for *Theatre Guild of the Air*, Jimmy played Jack Benny's character of Richard Clarke.

Many of Stewart's remaining radio appearances were guest appearances on other performers' programs, including Jack Benny, Bob Hope, Edgar Bergen-Charlie McCarthy and also interviews. Whether being interviewed on Barbara Welles, Brickhouse and Hubbard, Bud's Bandwagon, Gisele of Canada, Larry King or Tex and Jinx, the questions almost always centered around Stewart's current film. Few of the interviews reveal much insight into his personal life.

As a subcategory, let's look at Stewart's singing performances on various radio shows. Jimmy's singing was always good for a laugh and was used for such purposes on several shows. But, he could also sing seriously when called upon. If you'd like to hear Stewart's singing voice, here is a list of shows to seek out.

> *Leo Is On the Air — Born to Dance* (1936) — Jimmy and Buddy Ebsen are heard singing *Rollin' Home* from the film *Born to Dance*.
> *Academy Award Theater — One Sunday Afternoon* (August 28, 1946) — Stewart's character, Biff Grimes, harmonizes with Snappy on *In the Good Old Summertime*.
> *Philco Radio Time/Bing Crosby* (March 10, 1948) — Jimmy sings *I'm A Wolf*.

Let's Talk Hollywood (July 4, 1948) — In trying to imitate Al Jolson, Stewart sings a short segment of *April Showers*.
The Chesterfield Show/Bing Crosby (December 14, 1949) — Crosby and Stewart sing a bit of *Baby, It's Cold Outside*.
The Chesterfield Show/Bing Crosby (March 19, 1952) — Crosby, Stewart and Fran Warren sing a few lines from *Mississippi Mud*.
Theatre Guild on the Air — *The Silver Whistle* (April 6, 1952) — Stewart and other members of the cast sing *Mademoiselle from Armentieres*.
The Jack Benny Show (April 27, 1952) — Jimmy, Jack and the Sportsmen Quartet sing *I'm An Indian, Too*.
New York Close-Up (May 19, 1953) — Stewart sings and recites a few lines from the *Princeton Fight Song*.

WHAT MIGHT HAVE BEEN?

For all the appearances that Jimmy Stewart made on radio over the years, there might have been even more. In Erskine Johnson's *In Hollywood* column of February 8, 1949, this small item appeared:

> ...Jimmy Stewart has his agents looking for a comedy radio series

Of course, the agent never did find just the right vehicle for Stewart and no comedy series materialized. Just a little more than a month later, the following item was being circulated by INS (International News Service):

> A dramatic series — title not yet decided. Star not yet picked. CBS tried to get Jimmy Stewart, but he is reported to have declined on the ground that he's already in the upper tax brackets and can't use any more money. Show will describe adventures of a dreamy young man.

There's no mention of the show's title or just what it might have been. Whether or not it ever got on the air is not known. It's doubtful that Jimmy was making too much money, but maybe he was very serious in his commitment to find a comedy series in which to star.

Whatever the reason or reasons for his failure to find a suitable series, the listening public would have to wait another four years before being able to tune in Stewart on a weekly basis when *The Six Shooter* made its debut in 1953.

A&E Biography for Radio

A&E *Biography* is a very well-known show on TV, but there also was a radio version which was hosted by Jack Perkins. The shows were very short, running just 2 minutes, including a 30-second spot. Stewart was the subject of just one show.

(1) Monday, May 5, 2003
NETWORK: Syndicated
SPONSOR: Salvation Army
HOST: Jack Perkins

The main facts presented in the show center around Jimmy's military career. From the fact that he failed his first Army physical because he was under weight, to the fact that he ate pasta and bananas to increase his weight. He flew 20 combat missions and received the Distinguished Flying Cross. After the war, upon his request, his Hollywood contract forbade the studio from mentioning his military service or exploiting his real-life heroism on the screen. Jimmy is heard during the show from the film *It's a Wonderful Life* exclaiming, "Hello, Bedford Falls, Merry Christmas."

Academy Award (Theater)

Although the title of the series is usually given as *Academy Award Theater*, the word *theater* was not used in either the show's opening or closing, where it is referred to as simply *Academy Award*. Most of the radio listings of the time also refer to it as *Academy Award* or the *Academy Award* program, although a few do use *Theater*. The program set out to do what *Lux Radio Theatre* had already been successfully doing for many years. The program took Academy Award-winning or nominated films and actors and performed the stories on radio. One of the big expenses for the show was to pay the Academy of Motion Picture Arts and Sciences $1600 a week for the use of the Academy Award name. Actors were also paid up to $4000 for their appearances. Only 39 episodes were produced and aired between March 3, 1946, and December 18, 1946. Stewart appeared just once on the show.

(1) Wednesday, August 28, 1946 (10:00-10:30 p.m.) — *One Sunday Afternoon*
NETWORK: CBS
SPONSOR: E.R. Squibb & Sons
ANNOUNCER: Hugh Brundage

PRODUCER/DIRECTOR: Dee Englebach
ADAPTATIONS: Frank Wilson
ORIGINAL MUSIC COMPOSED AND CONDUCTED BY: Leith Stevens
SOUND EFFECTS: Berne Surrey

One Sunday Afternoon had originally been done in 1933 with Gary Cooper in the role of Biff Grimes. It had been remade in 1941, under the new title of *The Strawberry Blonde*, with James Cagney as Biff. For this radio version, Jimmy Stewart was cast as Biff. In 1948, the story would be made into a third film, reverting to the original title, this time as a musical starring Dennis Morgan as Biff. (Stewart also gets to sing in the radio show, as he and "Snappy" harmonize on "In the Good Old Summertime" near the beginning of the show.)

Biff Grimes, a dentist, is reminiscing with an old friend when he gets a call asking him to pull the tooth of his nemesis, Hugo Barnstead. As he is putting Hugo under with gas, Biff relives his experiences with Hugo.

Biff, Hugo, Amy Lind and Virginia Brush meet for a date. Biff chooses Virginia to be his date, but she winds up with Hugo, leaving Amy for Biff. When Hugo and Virginia get married, Biff and Amy decide to do likewise. Hugo becomes Biff's boss in the factory. He wants Biff to spy on his fellow employees and inform him which ones are not working as they should so that they can be fired. Biff balks and then quits. Hugo refuses to give Biff his back pay, so Biff returns with a gun. Hugo has him arrested and he spends two years in prison.

Biff returns to the present to find Virginia in his office. He sees that she is not happy in her marriage. She even asks Biff to put Hugo out of his misery. Biff realizes that he had gotten the better woman and that he is very happy with his life and marriage.

At the end of the show it is announced that Jimmy would soon be seen in the Liberty Films/Frank Capra production, *It's a Wonderful Life*.

This show can be found on a 6-cassette set titled *The Academy Awards* (Metacom/Adventures in Cassettes), which was released in 1994. The set features 12 radio shows from *Academy Award Theater*. Metacom was bought by Radio Spirits in 1998.

Academy Awards Presentations

Stewart appeared on a number of Academy Awards shows on the radio. The first was broadcast from Grauman's Chinese Theater, the second from the Shrine Civic Auditorium in Los Angeles, CA, while the remaining three were all held at the RKO Pantages Theatre, Hollywood, CA.

(1) Thursday, March 7, 1946 — The 18th-Annual Academy Awards (11:30 p.m.–12:30 a.m.)

According to another article in The La Crosse Tribute, La Crosse, WI, Stewart would host the first half of the show and Bob Hope the second half.

NETWORK: ABC

MASTER OF CEREMONIES: Jimmy Stewart, Bob Hope

Unfortunately, only Bob Hope's half of the awards show was broadcast by ABC. It was during this hour that the major awards were presented. The show is available and Stewart is nowhere to be heard.

(2) Thursday, March 13, 1947 — The 19th-Annual Academy Awards (11:45 p.m.–2:30 a.m.)

NETWORK: NBC

MASTER OF CEREMONIES: Jack Benny

PRODUCED AND STAGED BY: Mervyn LeRoy

MUSICAL DIRECTOR: Leo Forbstein

Save for this one ad, no other verification that Stewart appeared on this program has been located and the show is not available for listening. He was nominated for an Oscar as Best Actor for his role in *It's a Wonderful Life*, losing to Fredric March (*The Best Years of Our Lives*). Only two of the others listed in the above ad were also nominated — Olivia de Havilland and Jane Wyman, which may indicate that the six mentioned did appear in some capacity on the program.

(3) Thursday, March 23, 1950 — The 22nd-Annual Academy Awards (11 p.m.–12:15 a.m.)

NETWORK: ABC

MASTER OF CEREMONIES: Paul Douglas

ANNOUNCER: Ken Carpenter

ASSISTANT ANNOUNCERS: Eve Arden, Ronald Reagan

GENERAL DIRECTOR: Johnny Green

MUSICAL DIRECTOR: Robert Emmett Dolan

Stewart appeared near the end of the show to present the Academy Award for Best Actress of 1949, saying:

> *Please forgive me for not stopping to acknowledge how honored I am to be here, but I can't wait to see who won it either. So, those nominated for the best performance by an actress are Jeanne Crain in Pinky, 20th Century-Fox; Olivia de Havilland in The Heiress, Paramount; Susan Hayward in My Foolish Heart, Samuel Goldwyn Productions RKO*

Radio; Deborah Kerr in Edward, My Son, Metro-Goldwyn-Mayer; and Loretta Young in Come to the Stable, 20th Century-Fox. Now, if I can have the envelope...Olivia de Havilland.

Other presenters on the show included: Walter Winchell (who introduced *The National Anthem*), Charles Brackett, Patricia Neal, Mark Robson, Anne Baxter, John Hodiak, John Lund, Barbara Hale, Ruth Roman, George Murphy, Peggy Dow, Joanne Dru, Dick Powell, June Allyson, Jose Ferrer, Donald O'Connor, Ginger Rogers, Cole Porter, James Hilton, Ida Lupino, Claire Trevor, Ray Milland, Jane Wyman, and James Cagney.

Performing on the show were:
It's a Great Feeling — Jack Smith
My Foolish Heart — Ann Blyth
Lavender Blue — Gene Autry with the Cass County Boys
Through a Long and Sleepless Night — Dean Martin
Baby, It's Cold Outside — Original cast members Ricardo Montalban, Red Skelton, Betty Garrett and Arlene Dahl (filling in for Esther Williams, who was out of town)

(4) Thursday, March 19, 1953 — The 25th Annual Academy Awards (10:30 p.m.–midnight)

For the first time this year, the awards ceremony was broadcast not only on the radio, but also on television. The presentations took place at the RKO Pantages Theatre (with Bob Hope as the host) and the NBC International Theatre, New York City (with Conrad Nagel as host).

NETWORK: NBC (Simulcast from NBC-TV)
DIRECTOR: William A. Bennington
PRODUCER: Johnny Green
PRODUCER, NBC: Robert L. Welch
MUSICAL DIRECTOR: Adolph Deutsch

Stewart and Joan Fontaine were the co-presenters for the Art Direction-Set Decoration awards. They read the nominees and announced the winner, *The Bad and the Beautiful*. The winners of the black-and-white award were Cedric Gibbons and Edward Carfagno (art direction) and Edwin B. Willis and Keogh Gleason (set decoration). The other nominations were: Matsuyama (art direction) and H. Motsumoto (set decoration) for *Rashomon*; Hal Pereira and Roland Anderson (art direction) and Emile Kuri (set decoration) for *Carrie*; Lyle Wheeler and John DeCuir (art direction) and Walter M. Scott (set decoration) for *My Cousin Rachel*;

and, Lyle Wheeler and Leland Fuller (art direction) and Thomas Little and Claude Carpenter (set decoration) for *Viva Zapata!*

The winners for color film were Paul Sheriff (art direction) and Marcel Vertes (set decoration) for the film *Moulin Rouge*. The other nominees were Richard Day and Clave (art direction) and Howard Bristol (set decoration) for *Hans Christian Andersen*; Cedric Gibbons and Paul Groesse (art direction) and Edwin B. Willis and Arthur Krams (set decoration) for *The Merry Widow*; Frank Hotaling (art direction) and John McCarthy, Jr. and Charles Thompson (set decoration) for *The Quiet Man*; and Lyle Wheeler and John DeCuir (art direction) and Thomas Little and Paul S. Fox (set decoration) for *The Snows of Kilimanjaro*.

Other presenters on the show included Anne Baxter, Charles Brackett, Frank Capra, Ronald Colman, Olivia de Havilland, Walt Disney, Greer Garson, Janet Gaynor, Edmund Gwenn, Jean Hersholt, Fredric March, Ray Milland, Mary Pickford, Luise Rainer, Ginger Rogers, Dore Schary, Claire Trevor, Teresa Wright, Jane Wyman, and Loretta Young.

The performers included:
Billy Daniels — "Because You're Mine" from *Because You're Mine*
Celeste Holm — "Thumbelina" from *Hans Christian Andersen*
Bob Hope — "Am I In Love?" from *Son of Paleface*
Peggy Lee and Johnny Mercer — "Zing a Little Zong" from *Just For You*
Tex Ritter — "High Noon (Don't Forsake Me, Oh My Darlin')" from *High Noon*

Others appearing on the show included Edgar Bergen and Charlie McCarthy, Shirley Booth, Charles Coburn, Broderick Crawford, Joan Crawford, Donald Crisp, Jane Darwell, Cecil B. DeMille, Katherine DeMille, Bobby Driscoll, Gloria Grahame, Dean Jagger, Piper Laurie, Marilyn Maxwell, Victor McLaglen, Paul Muni, George Murphy and John Wayne.

(5) Wednesday, March 26, 1958 — The 30th-Annual Academy Awards (10:30 p.m. –midnight)
NETWORK: NBC (simulcast from NBC-TV)
DIRECTOR: Alan Handley
PRODUCER: Jerry Wald
PRODUCER, NBC: Alan Handley
MUSICAL DIRECTOR: Alfred Newman

There were seven co-hosts for this year's show. Jimmy Stewart was the first to appear. He was followed by David Niven, Jack Lemmon, Rosalind Russell, Donald Duck (via film, of course), and finally Bob Hope.

The presenters included: June Allyson, Fred Astaire, Ernest Borgnine, Cyd Charisse, Joan Collins, Gary Cooper, Wendell Corey, Bette Davis, Doris Day, Anita Ekberg, Clark Gable, Cary Grant, Rock Hudson, Van Johnson, Jennifer Jones, Hope Lange, Sophia Loren, Dorothy Malone, Paul Newman, Gregory Peck, Vincent Price, Anthony Quinn, Ronald Reagan, Robert Ryan, Eva Marie Saint, Lana Turner, John Wayne, Joanne Woodward, and Dana Wynter.

Performing on the show were:

"April Love" — Anna Marie Alberghetti, Ann Blyth, Tab Hunter, Shirley Jones, Jimmie Rodgers, Tommy Sands

"It's Great Not To Be Nominated" — Sammy Cahn, Kirk Douglas, Burt Lancaster

"An Affair to Remember" — Vic Damone

"Baby, It's Cold Outside" — Rock Hudson, Mae West

"All The Way" — Dean Martin

"Wild Is the Wind" — Johnny Mathis

Also appearing on the program were Red Buttons, Maurice Chevalier, David Lean, Kim Novak, Debbie Reynolds, Jean Simmons, Sam Spiegel, and Miyoshi Umeki.

America Salutes the President's Birthday

NETWORK: CBS, NBC, MBS, Blue Network
ANNOUNCER: Dan Seymour
HOST: Conrad Nagel

On the east coast it aired from 11:15 p.m.–12:15 a.m. on January 29, 1944.

This special broadcast was actually associated with the March of Dimes fundraising kickoff for 1944 and was aired the day before President Roosevelt's birthday (although technically the show did end on his birthday in the Eastern Time Zone). Several bands were on the show, including: Axel Stordahl's Orchestra, Paul Whiteman's Orchestra, the U.S. Marine Band, and the Santa Ana Air Force Flying Training Command Band conducted by Major Eddie Dunstedter. Appearing on the program were President Roosevelt, Bob Hope, Frank Sinatra, Frances Langford, Dinah Shore, Garry Moore, Jimmy Durante, Georgia Gibbs, Mary Pickford, Eddie Cantor, Lily Pons and Jerry Colonna. Major Stewart appeared from London, along with Edward R. Murrow and Beatrice Lillie. Also speaking was Basil O'Connor, chairman of the National Foundation for Infantile Paralysis.

Despite the newspaper articles of the time, Stewart's appearance on this program cannot be confirmed. The best source for the program is *60 Greatest Old-Time Radio Shows Starring Frank Sinatra and Friends* (Radio Spirits, 2000). However, the version available only times out at 54:55, and does not contain the London portion of the program. The London segment was broadcast live via shortwave radio and apparently was not preserved. In the introduction to the program, Dan Seymour announces that those appearing from London would be Edward R. Murrow and Major Morton Wilson. He doesn't mention either Stewart or Beatrice Lillie. Stewart has been involved in other March of Dimes projects, so it is not out of the question that he was heard on this program, but without the London portion of this show that fact cannot be established.

Also see March of Dimes section in Chapter 3.

Amos 'n' Andy Music Hall

When the *Amos 'n' Andy* show finally passed into history, the characters remained on this new show. Here Freeman Gosden as Amos and Charles Correll as Andy simply played popular records of the day. In between the music, they did comedy bits and talked with guests. The show was aired weekdays from September 1954 until November 1960. Jimmy Stewart appeared on two shows; unfortunately, neither is available for review.

Monday, September 20, 1954 (9:30-9:55 p.m.)
NETWORK: CBS
ANNOUNCER: Jim Ameche
PRODUCER: Sam Pierce
DIRECTOR: Cliff Howell
EXECUTIVE PRODUCERS: Joe Connelly, Bob Mosher (after radio, this pair went on to create several popular TV shows, including *Leave It to Beaver* and *The Munsters*)
ANNOUNCER: Harlow Wilcox
THEME MUSIC: *Angel's Serenade* (Gaetano Braga)

(2) Friday, September 26, 1958 (6:35-7 p.m.)
NETWORK: CBS

An Incident of War

This program was broadcast over WOR in New York City. It appears to be Stewart's very first radio broadcast, airing on May 28, 1933. It would be easy to miss this broadcast as featuring Stewart because he was not mentioned in the newspaper listing. However, an article in Stewart's hometown paper, the *Indiana Evening Gazette*, the previous day, tells of his upcoming appearance.

Stewart played the role of the chauffeur in *Goodbye Again*, which had its pre-Broadway run in Falmouth., MA, before moving to the Masque Theatre on December 28, 1932. It ran on Broadway for 216 performances. The play was written by Allan Scott and George Haight and was produced by Arthur J. Beckhard.

The radio show is not available for audition.

Army Air Forces Day Celebration

The program, which was broadcast from the Teterboro Airport, Teterboro, NJ, featured Jimmy Stewart, Ronald Reagan, General Jimmy Doolittle, General Carl A. Spaatz, and Representative J. Gordon Canfield. It was broadcast August 1, 1946. In the New York area, WOR broadcast the program at 2:15 p.m. and again that night at 10:30. As seen in the following newspaper ad, in the Chicago area it aired at 11:15 p.m. The show is not available for audition.

Army Day Drama

This program was broadcast on Saturday, April 6, 1946. According to other ads, General Courtney Hodges was also a speaker on the program. It is not available for audition.

Art Baker's Notebook (a.k.a. Art Baker & His Notebook)

Art Baker (born Arthur Shank, January 7, 1898-August 26, 1966) had his own radio show from 1938-1958. The 15-minute show was heard weekdays. Jimmy appeared on his show on Monday, January 20, 1947 (week 20, Program #196). The show was a Cardinal Co. Production.

NETWORK: Syndicated
PRODUCER: John Nelson
SPONSOR: Montgomery Ward & Company
ENGINEER: Joe Garrett

Although this particular show is not available for listening, Baker did offer to send copies of the script to any listener who wrote in and asked for one. As a result, it's not too difficult to find one of these scripts today. Here is a copy of that script, at least the portion featuring Jimmy Stewart, exactly as it was used for the show. From things that are said during the show, it can be assumed that Baker and Stewart sat down a few days before the show and chatted about the things they would talk about on the show. A writer(s) then sat down and typed out a script. This way, the show could be timed to meet restrictions. There apparently was little room left for ad-libbing during the show.

If you read comments on *Art Baker's Notebook*, it is usually called a philosophy or home-spun show. This script bears out that description.

BAKER: (ON CUE) This is Art Baker, from Montgomery Ward. And this, as you may not know, is a red letter day on the Notebook — or its Open House — and we have as our guest one of the up-and-coming young men about Hollywood. Or maybe it would be more truthful to refer to him as "up and *already* come." He started with a stock company in Cape Cod and stuck with the acting business until he'd become one of the top-ranking, Oscar-winning stars of the movie world. Then, at the height of his popularity, he dropped everything to enlist as a Private in the United States Army, back before Pearl Harbor — and he stuck with the soldiering business until he'd become a full-fledged Colonel in the Army Air Corps. Now he's back in Hollywood — but this time he doesn't *have* to start at the bottom. He's the movie star that most people want to see most — and he's just completed Liberty Films' *It's a Wonderful Life*, which critics are acclaiming the outstanding picture of the year. This time, he's starting at the top — and I confidently predict he'll work his way up from there. Who is he? That's silly! There's only one person he could *possibly* be! Jimmy Stewart!

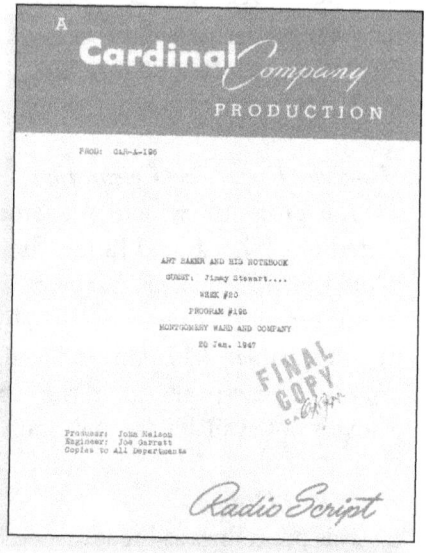

Listeners could receive a copy of the show's script like this one simply by writing and asking for it.

STEWART: You know, Art, I always figured the world lost a great politician when you decided to go into radio. Anybody who can throw words around like you do oughta be a great politician.

BAKER: As a matter of fact, Jimmy, I've often *thought* about it — but there's just one tiny thing that holds me back. Like you, I always like to start at the bottom. But unlike you, I generally manage to *stay* there. However — enough of this trivia. We're met here to talk about that mythical character you've portrayed in so many of your movie roles — the Common Man — or the typical American...whatever you want to call him.

STEWART: And right there, I figure, is the crux of the whole problem. What *do* we want to call him? We talk about the world's little people — or common people...*or ordinary* people. And all those things have a kind of looking-down-the-nose attitude behind them. If they really want to DO something for the Common Man, it seems to me they could give him a better title.

BAKER: You don't go for this theory, then, that a rose by another name would be as sweet?

STEWART: That may be okay — for roses. But we're talking about *people*. And I'm not trying to quibble over words, Art. Basically, it's not a matter of words at all. It's a matter of attitudes. It seems to me there's been too much of this talk about, "Oh he's just a shoe clerk" or "He's just a plumber" — or — "He's just an unimportant, small-town banker." We call 'em little people, and we gradually get to thinking they're not important. But if the people who make up the backbone of a country aren't important — then who in thunderation *is* important?

BAKER: What's your objection to the term, "the common man"? It always seemed to me that it had a kind of dignity about it — especially in recent years.

STEWART: Oh, it's not too bad, I guess. But it seems to me we oughta be able to do better if we tried. It's that word, "common." Generally, you associate it with grades of lumber that aren't so hot. Or like in a movie scene, for example: You want to picture some girl getting told off, so you write dialogue: "Don't be cheap — and common!" So the girl gets red in the face and starts throwing things. The general idea seems to be that common is about the worst thing anybody can possibly be. And then we try to turn right around and talk about the dignity of the common man.

BAKER: I know what you mean, Jimmy, and I'm all with you — a hundred percent. Do you have any suggestions for a better term?

STEWART: Oh, I don't know. Like I say, it's not just a matter of words; anyhow, it's a matter of attitudes. And that's where I think we have a lot of responsibility and a lot of opportunity — those of us who are in pictures, or radio; those who write books and stories...those who make speeches before the Tuesday afternoon bridge club. We've got to counteract this notion that there is any such thing as an "unimportant, small town banker" — or "an unimportant little clerk." People *are* important — no matter where they live or where they work.

BAKER: I'll admit it would be a silly looking world without 'em.

STEWART: We talk about big people, and little people…and that may be okay when it comes to ordering clothes from the store. But when you go beyond that — it's not for us to judge who's big, and who's little — who's important and who's unimportant.

BAKER: A question, Jimmy. Don't you honestly feel that pictures like your *Mr. Smith Goes to Washington* — or your latest one, *It's a Wonderful Life*…don't you feel that stories like those do a lot to counteract this looking-down-the-nose business, at the so-called little people?

STEWART: At least, Art, I like to think so. That's Frank Capra, you know. He directed me in both of them. He also was my director in *You Can't Take It With You*. They're really typical of him, more than they are of me.

BAKER: That point, we could argue, too. Personally, I think they're typical of the two of you, working together — and as typically American as Kate Smith singing *God Bless America!*

STEWART: I still say you should have been a politician, and a professional apple polisher. However, I'll stick to my earlier statement that they're Frank Capra stories, and I think he's earned any bouquets you want to toss him. I'm merely proud of the privilege — to play the characters as he envisioned 'em.

BAKER: I'd like to put in a question about this latest character you've portrayed…

STEWART: Well, I take the part of George Bailey in "It's a Wonderful Life" — just a…what'll I say? Just an ordinary youngster who grows up in an ordinary town and dreams ordinary dreams. The old home town looks pretty drab and common-place, and the youngster dreams of travel — adventure — excitement — seeing big cities — meeting important people. He wants *to be* somebody — wants to *amount* to something. All that sort of thing. But for one reason and another, things don't work out that way. It gets to be a case of settling down to live an ordinary life, as supposedly unimportant small town businessman. It's not easy to put dreams aside. And it can be discouraging, sometimes, speculating on what might have been. It's kinda tough feeling little, and insignificant, and unimportant — when you'd always dreamed of being a big shot. However, thru a switch in the plot, I get a chance to reshape my ideas of what's important in this life. It's the most potent argument I know of — proving that there's no such thing as an unimportant person in all the world.

BAKER: I don't know for sure, of course. But chances are there may be somebody listening to this broadcast right today who feels a little discouraged — a little fed-up with an ordinary, routine, supposedly insignificant life. For a lot of folks have dreams that don't work out, quite the way they'd dreamed 'em. I'd appreciate it, Jimmy, if you'd tell them your philosophy of life, as portrayed in this picture — just the way you told it to me the other afternoon.

STEWART: I'd be glad to try. Maybe you get to feeling you don't amount to much — just one little digit in the census report — just one, insignificant little vote in the nation-wide election returns…and it wouldn't

Listeners who ask for the show's script also received this "autographed" photo of Baker and Stewart.

make much difference to world history whether you lived or died. The world would go along just about the same, either way. You get to feeling you're awfully unimportant in such a big world. But that's where you're WRONG. Did you ever stop to think how different the world would be if you'd never been born? Naturally, none of your children would ever be born then, either. An entire chain of posterity would be snuffed out. Every clean and decent and worthwhile thing you have done in your lifetime would remain undone. Those whom you've befriended in an hour of need would have gone friendless. Did you ever give a word of cheer to someone who was despondent? Did you ever help an elderly lady safely across the street? Did you ever teach a youngster a lesson in sportsmanship? Those are the things that are important in this world — more than bright lights or the temporary possession of dollars. If you think you're not important in this life, just stop and think how very differently all those stories could have been written — except for you. Suppose the despondent friend had received no word of encouragement when he needed it most. How might he have acted then? And what unknown tragedy might have brought grief and heartbreak to others? Suppose you hadn't been there to help the elderly lady safely across the street — and she'd started out alone — at just the wrong time? Suppose you hadn't been on hand to teach that youngster a basic lesson in sportsmanship. How might the lack of that lesson affected him, and how might it have affected others — twenty, thirty — even fifty years from now? There was a supposedly unimportant man who lived many years ago, who never did anything outstanding in his entire life. But once he rendered an insignificant little kindness. He loaned a neighbor youngster a few books, so the kid could learn to read. Shucks, 'twarn't nothing.' Didn't amount to a hill of beans. But the youngster's name was Abraham Lincoln — and history *was* important, that he learned how to read. So you see, it's kinda tough to ever say what *is* important.

BAKER: Pardon me, Jimmy — but I can think of one other man — wasn't very important, either. In fact, he's the little man who really wasn't there. He's the fellow who wasn't on hand, to teach a neighbor youngster the meaning of sportsmanship, and fair play. It probably didn't seem very important at the time — but that youngster was to be known in history as Adolf Hitler — and several million men had to die — because he had not learned the simple basis of justice and fair play.

STEWART: That's the idea. And those are the things that are important in this world — more than money — more than fame — more than being a big frog in a small puddle. And if a picture can have a philosophy — that's the philosophy of "It's a Wonderful Life." Also, Art, if I can infringe on you enough to do a little sincere apple-polishing of my own — from the bottom of my heart — I'd like to pass along a verbal orchid to the other members of the cast. There's Donna Reed who plays the part of my wife, Mary. And Lionel Barrymore, the hard-boiled town banker who's a sort of modern Scrooge. There's Thomas Mitchell, Beulah Bondi, Ward Bond, Henry Travers, and a host of others — all of 'em turning in a marvelous performance. Frank Capra, as I've already mentioned, is the producer-director, for Liberty Films.

BAKER: Just one little addition, Jimmy. There's also a young feller named Jimmy Stewart, and it's his first picture after five years in the Army Air Corps. The Title: "It's a Wonderful Life." And I have a hunch if a few more of us could absorb Jimmy's philosophy, it really would be. Now, doggone it, I see our time is up, and I'm going to ask the announcer to take over with a word for Montgomery Ward, while I usher Jimmy Stewart to the studio door. It's been a thrill to have you, Jimmy — and we hope you'll hurry back.

Arthur Godfrey Time

Arthur Godfrey Time was a radio institution, airing daily from New York City for 27 years from 1945 until 1972. Stewart appeared twice and neither program is available for review.

(1) Wednesday, July 30, 1947 (11-11:30 a.m.)
NETWORK: CBS
ANNOUNCER: Tony Marvin
MUSIC: Archie Bleyer & his Orchestra

(2) Friday, August 24, 1962 (9:30-10:00 a.m.)
The program was broadcast on the AFRTS Far East Network (FEN). It is not known what Stewart may have talked about on the show.

The Barbara Welles Show

It shouldn't really be a big surprise that the woman responsible for *The Barbara Welles Show* was named Florence Pritchett. George, her announcer, calls her by her real name at various points in the show, but Stewart refers to her as Miss Welles. *Time* magazine (June 30, 1947) called her "The newest and youngest of radio's women's home companions...is a bejeweled, baritone-voiced ex-model..." The Welles show was broadcast weekdays from 3:00-3:30 p.m. from WOR in New York City. WOR was part of the Mutual Network, and the show may also have gone out over other Mutual stations. Welles and her announcer, George, would spend the first half of the show giving household hints to their listeners. In the second half of the show, there would be a guest star who was interviewed by Welles.

(1) Monday, July 21, 1947 (3-3:30 p.m.)
During the first half of the show, Welles talks about two World War II veterans who had their land for a gas station taken away by the United Nations. But, the U.N. then gave them $5,000 to buy new property. She also talks about seeing the film *Miracle on 34th Street* and visiting friends, the Berlins, in Purchase, NY, who had turned a 14-car garage into a house, and gives some decorating tips based on what she had seen there. For those who wanted to paint a ceiling, she suggested that they cut a rubber ball in half and push the handle of the paintbrush through one of the halves. That way the ball would catch any paint drippings. Finally, we learn that if you coat a nail with wax and then push it through a stiff piece of paper; you can hammer it into plaster without breaking the plaster or hitting your fingers with the hammer.

Finally, fifteen minutes into the show, Welles introduces her special guest for that day, Jimmy Stewart, "who is currently starring in *Harvey*."

STEWART: Ah…thank you, Miss Welles.
WELLES: You're welcome…anytime at all.
STEWART: I want to take this opportunity to tell you that I think it's just wonderful the way you just keep talking on and on there…and she doesn't have any script. How do you remember all that stuff?
WELLES: I don't know…I just…I've talked most of my life and I find that I just save it all up for this half hour.
STEWART: Well, I thought all you girls in the radio here had it all typed out and everything. I…you just talk, don't you?
WELLES: Um…hum.
STEWART: That's…that's very good. That's amazing the way you can remember. I don't know whether it's amazing or not, but I'm very impressed.
WELLES: Well, I'm glad you're impressed, Mr. Stewart.
STEWART: Maybe everybody can remember stuff like that.
WELLES: Can't you remember things?
STEWART: No…I…I…for a long time I couldn't remember my hat size.
WELLES: You couldn't? What size is it?

STEWART: Oh, you wanna…you wanna bring the thing right to a head.

WELLES: No…right now…before the show's over…I can't remember where Purchase [a town mentioned in the first half of the show] got its name, so it's all right for you to remember…not remember your hat size, but tell me…ah…

Welles and Stewart share a moment at the Stork Club.

STEWART: You didn't even ask anybody about Purchase. Somebody said they told you…go ahead.

WELLES: Well, Jimmy tell me…you came to New York to do a play… *Harvey*…and…ah…in movies you have a script and you do them a scene at a time. Did you have trouble in coming back to do a whole play and memorizing the part?

STEWART: Oh yes…yes. I…I hadn't done it for 13 or 14 years and it's a very difficult thing. It's very hard, especially…ah…in a play that has been going a long time. So you want to get every and, if, and but. That's very hard to do…very, very difficult. And of course you have…you…you always have that fear of opening night of…of…ah…something happening to the line. Of course there's so many things that can happen opening night.

WELLES: Well, like what for example?

STEWART: Well, I was thinking about it. I…I…ah…in those sleepless nights I had here and…before the opening…I…I…I was thinking about all the things that could happen on an opening night. And some that I just…I just remembered when I was on the stage years ago, things that really happened. But there are…and I sort of put them in categories… categories. I…I…I…ah…I…I put them…ah…well, I didn't really put them in categories…but I…I suppose…ah…you could. If you wanted to put them in categories, you could. You could say like…like…ah…you know when you used to make…ah…an outline of something in school, you'd say Roman numeral one…let's call it unfortunate things than can happen…

WELLES: By James Stewart.

STEWART: …opening…opening night, by James Stewart, Roman numeral one.

WELLES: All right, go on…I'm fascinated.

STEWART: Now…ah…this…this would be…ah…this would just say Roman numeral one of the unfortunate things that could happen…ah… hello…ah…Roman numeral one…

WELLES: I think we should say Jimmy is now saying hello to some people who are peaking through doors.

GEORGE: All the girls in the organization.

STEWART: Roman numeral one is non…non…nonfatal…nonfatal happenings.

WELLES: Nonfatal?

STEWART: Yes, nonfatal. The…ah…a small one under Roman numeral one.

WELLES: One A.

STEWART: No, we'll get to "A" later…small one…small one would be I would say…ah…voice flub dubs.

WELLES: What? What in the world is a voice flub dub?

STEWART: Well, a voice flub dubs is just…you have…say you have a line to say and you say, I'm…ah…some people think I'm gonna be on time for the appointment, but I'm gonna be later than most people think. Well, instead of saying most people think, you say most theople pink…and… you don't…you don't notice it, you see. But the person that you're saying it to either faints or laughs or drops the teacup or something, and…ah… it's confusing to the audience. But it…ah…they forget about it pretty soon. What was that? That was one under Roman numeral one.

WELLES: Nonfatal happenings on opening night.

STEWART: Well, then…ah…I'd say small number two under that would be mechanical…ah…things…mechan…or physical, let's go to the physical things first. And that is just coming on…on the stage and tripping and falling down.

WELLES: Yeah, and that wouldn't be very good.

STEWART: I…well, I've done that…and that…that again, especially in a serious play which is the one I did it in…it couldn't be a comedy… but I…I forget…coming in to tell my wife that I'm going to leave her or something and I fell down. I didn't trip on the…well…ah…that was… and there again the audience sort of forgets about it and it isn't too serious and you can overcome that. Then there…then I'd say number…where are we now? Two?

WELLES: We're through one and two in nonfatal.

STEWART: Two. Three, I would say would be prop…ah…misfortunes. Well, a prop is anything…where you go to a door and open the door and the door knob comes off. Or you back into a potted plant and it falls over and all the plant comes out and you have to…or, you want to light a cigarette and the match keeps going out because you're…you're nervous and you're…you're blowing out instead of in and…ah…the cigarette…you can't light the cigarette. I've had that happen. Or,…ah…with teacups… when the teacup…you have the teacup…before they pour the tea into the teacup…the shaking makes the teacup rattle and the teacup usually falls… ah…off the cup…or off the saucer and breaks. And, of course, there aren't any more cups, so you can't have any tea. And that's probably the cup that the poison's in…you know, so it spoils the story. But, even then, you can get…ah…you can get over that. Well that's about…those are the things that…that could happen and, of course, you have the stage manager who can…if you just forget a line. Of course, that's another classification. But I…if you just forget a line, well the stage manager can tell you or somebody else can tell you and, lots of times, the audience can tell you what it is. So, that isn't so hard. But, now that, I think, would take care of that category. Then the other category, Roman numeral two, is the fatal type of…ah…the fatal type. And under that I would say…now I…I want to make it quite clear to you…ah…Miss Welles, that…ah…these are certainly not all the things that can happen to you, but they're just things… the…the…things that come to my mind at the moment. Under Roman numeral two of the…the…ah…fatal type happenings on the stage…ah… is a thing that is known as the dry up.

WELLES: What's that?

STEWART: Well, the dry up…

WELLES: How can you dry up if you're playing the part of an inebriate like Elwood P. Dowd?

STEWART: Well…ah…I'm glad you ask that question.

WELLES: You are?

STEWART: Yeah.

WELLES: You are?

STEWART: It's…ah…it's a very good question.

WELLES: Well, I'm glad you think so.

STEWART: Well, that's all right, Barbara…ah…I'm willing to like a question if it came to me all in good faith.

WELLES: Well, go on.

STEWART: Where were we? We were under Roman numeral…Roman numeral…ah…two. Roman numeral two…ah…the dry up. No…but… Roman numeral two is…is the classification, which is fatal happenings.

WELLES: Yes, so now you're drying up.

STEWART: Well…well you want me to…are you worried about something? You keep looking at the clock all the time.

WELLES: I'm sorry, I can't say very much, you've got me laughing so hard.

STEWART: The dry up is the thing that is known…it's a sort of…ah… it's a sort of a paralysis that comes over you and…ah…you come to a line and suddenly everything stops and you can't move and…and…ah…the stage manager throws the line. Suppose, just suppose…just to illustrate my point, which is Roman numeral two of the fatal kind. Ah…suppose the line is…ah…"Geraldine, I'm going to leave through that door," and, as you say door, you point to the door. You point, but you dry up on door. Everything stops. And the stage manager calls to you and…and says the line, but nothing happens. And all the people on the stage tell you the line, then they open the door and suggest it to you. And then somebody writes it on a piece of paper and says "door" and holds it in front of you. And then somebody goes down in the audience and tells the audience and they get the whole audience to…to…to…say "door" and the audience sort of chants "door." But you can't…you just stand there. And…and the perspiration starts and you start to shake. And finally, they have to lower the curtain…and…and ah…you can do one of two things. You can either go home, or…ah…you can start the act over again. Which…I've seen it happen…I've seen it happen. And that it's really…a very terrifying thing. But, the other night, I…the dry up is a terrible thing. But I finally got through it all right.

WELLES: You got through it beautifully…

STEWART: It's a terrifying…ah…it's a terrifying thing to think that that's possible and it is because I've seen it happen.

WELLES: Well, now you know you didn't do anything the other night that was wrong. You were wonderful. So the opening…you may know all these nonfatal Roman numeral one and two things, but you didn't do any of them.

STEWART: Of, well, yes…yes…you…you didn't…you do them sometimes and they aren't noticed, but there…there were…there were plenty of them…

WELLES: Well, is the…

STEWART: …especially in the first act.

WELLES: If you were so nervous then in the first…you know…in the first few days…

STEWART: It's getting better now.

WELLES: Is it?

STEWART: Yeah. It's getting better now because it's a…it's a pretty tricky part and it's getting a little easier. And another thing…I'm beginning…I'm beginning to eat again.

WELLES: Didn't you eat?

STEWART: No…no, it's ah…when you get nervous…I…I didn't eat. It's a very good habit…

WELLES: Yes, it is.

STEWART: …eating.

WELLES: You're very thin…you don't look like you eat very much anyway.

STEWART: Well, I…I don't. But it is a very good habit and I…I'm glad to be back eating.

WELLES: I'm glad you're glad. How do you like Josephine Hull?

STEWART: Oh well…that…that…that's been one of the wonderful things about…about the ah…about the play. She's really an inspiration. I…I…I watch everything she does, every performance and it's…ah… you can't…as many times as you see it, you can't help but laugh and go right along with her. She's an amazing actress and one of the finest in the country…and in the world. She…ah…here is a very, very difficult part. I'm ah…she's, he…she's done several little things like this. You remember Mrs. Sycamore in *You Can't Take It With You* and *Arsenic and Old Lace*. But I think this is…this is probably…probably the…the…ah…best one she's had for a long time. She can…she does a wonderful thing with the audience.

WELLES: She's wonderful with her face.

STEWART: Yeah…wonderful thing she does with the audience. She can just take…just take them right with it.

WELLES: Jimmy, tell me, I have always heard that everybody sat up all night long to read the reviews. They would wait to…ah…do that. Did you do that?

STEWART: Well, I wanted to…I wanted to. I guess it's a sign of age or something. I…I…I…ah…I got tired and I went to bed.

WELLES: Well, of course, if you'd been eating, it would have helped.

STEWART: I think it would…yeah.

WELLES: What do you eat?

STEWART: What do I eat?

WELLES: Yeah.

STEWART: Oh, various types of things.

WELLES: Have your mother and father come down from Indiana to see the play yet?

STEWART: They were down and saw it Saturday night.

WELLES: How'd they like it?

STEWART: Well, they liked it pretty well. They thought it was fine. They're coming back…ah…they're coming back tonight. They said they missed several things, so they're coming back.

WELLES: Well, there is…

STEWART: They said a lot of people laughed at things and they didn't see it was funny, so they're coming back.

WELLES: To see whether it was funny or not. Well, it was awful funny. I've seen it five times and each time I've seen it, I thought it was funny.

STEWART: Wonderful, wonderful play.

(The interview over, Welles moves on to the show's closing.)

Welles found it difficult to keep from laughing, sometimes to the point of not being able to talk, through the entire interview. She was genuinely entertained by Stewart's attempt at an outline and the stories he used to illustrate his points.

Betty Crocker

Betty Crocker dispensed her cooking wisdom on the radio in one form or another for 29 years. Beginning locally in 1924, the show moved to NBC in 1926. It remained a network feature, moving to CBS and finally ABC, until 1953. Through the years, various actresses played the part of Crocker (Zella Layne, Betty Bucholz and Adelaide Hawley), but all did basically the same thing. All gave housewives information on buying and preparing foods. Stewart appeared on just one show. Hawley was the voice (and her entire persona on TV) of Betty Crocker from 1949 through 1964. And thus would have appeared with Stewart. The show is not available for listening.

Monday, February 25, 1952
NETWORK: ABC
SPONSOR: General Mills
ANNOUNCER: Win Elliot

The 15-minute program was broadcast at 10:30 a.m. on the east coast. The above ad, from a Wisconsin newspaper, shows 9:30 Central time.

Bill of Rights

This 15-minute program was broadcast on KFOX-AM 1280, Long Beach, CA, (and most likely other California stations) on Monday December 12, 1949.

The program is not available for listening and so the extent of Stewart's involvement is unknown.

Bill Stern's Sports Newsreel

NETWORK: NBC
SPONSOR: Colgate
ANNOUNCER: Don Stanley

Bill Stern was born in Rochester, NY, on July 1, 1907. He became the most popular sportscaster of his day and is much emulated, even now. Among his achievements are National Sportscasters and Sportswriters Hall of Fame (1974), American Sportscasters Hall of Fame (1984), Radio Hall of Fame (1988), and the International Jewish Sports Hall of fame (2001). He also has a star in the Hollywood Walk of Fame.

Bill Stern's Sports Newsreel was on NBC from October 1937 until the end of September 1952. From October 1939 until June 1951, the show was sponsored by Colgate and the Colgate name was added to the show's title. It was during these years that Jimmy Stewart appeared on the show. After leaving NBC, the show continued on ABC before finally ending in June of 1956.

Stern had a famous guest on each show and whenever he was on vacation, a famous person would substitute for him. Stern himself had a gift for telling a story. He was afraid to twist the facts or even make up things that would add to an otherwise true story. Long pauses and exaggerated words were his trademark. Stern died in Rye, NY, on November 19, 1971.

Not much information is known about the show until about the middle of 1942. Very few, if any, shows from before this time have survived.

SHOWS FEATURING JIMMY STEWART:

(1) Friday, July 23, 1948 (6:15-6:30 p.m.)
Don Stanley begins the show by telling everyone that Bill Stern is aboard the *S.S. Mauritania* on his way to England to broadcast the London Olympics. He introduces Jimmy, as a former track star, who was a last-minute replacement for the originally scheduled Errol Flynn.

STEWART: Thanks, Don Stanley. Ah…I'd like to sort of qualify that introduction. My name's Stewart all right, but I think maybe you ought to soft pedal that track star business. Unless, of course, you wanna count a little running I did back in my prep school days at Mercersburg Academy and high jumping and hurdles during my freshman year at Princeton. But to tell you the truth, I never broke a single world's record. But track's always been my favorite sport and tonight I've got an Olympic track story I'd like to tell you. I think it packs quite a wallop. However, I'll let you decide that for yourself. But first…

(commercial)

When the show returns, Jimmy tells the following story, complete with organ music and short dramatizations.

STEWART: By this time next week, in London, the Olympic Games will be underway and American athletes will be smashing their way towards new records, new athletic triumphs. But the Olympic story I have to tell you tonight is not one of triumph, but of bitter disappointment. Disappointment for the entire U.S. track team and personal heartbreak for three of the greatest track champions in the history of sports.

In 1936, when the last Olympic Games were held, these three track stars were just kids. One was eight, one 12 and the oldest, barely 17. But for each of them that year, the Olympics became a dream, a goal which one day they might achieve. For 12 years that dream remained alive in the hearts of those three American boys and one by one they began to prove themselves and their names came soaring over the sports horizon into the public eye — Fonville, Dillard and Dodds.

The first of the three boys to be noticed was a young divinity student from Boston, Gil Dodds. A serious-faced fellow who wore his thick lens glasses even on the track. He looked more like a college professor than a champion miler. But for all his dignified appearance, he was a runnin' fool.

(short dramatization)

STEWART: Well, yeah, but they were wrong, 'cause he lasted all right… and won. Won meet after meet. When Gil Dodds was ordained a minister and still continued track, the newspaper boys kidded him. They called him the "Perambulating Parson." But, Gil Dodds didn't kid. He was dead serious about running the mile and wearing the cloth. One day, after a race, a reporter came up to him and asked ("Tell me, Dodds, what's religion got to do winning a race anyhow?" — not said by Stewart). Dodds stopped for a moment and then answered slowly ("Folks who doubt the Bible and tear it apart, take the heart out of the Bible. They tear the Master's training rules before they ever start life's race and they can't possibly win" — not Stewart). Yeah, quite a fella this Gil Dodds. And when one after another of the best milers in the country went down in defeat to Gil Dodds, well the reporters started to change their tune a little bit. Now they called him the "Flying Parson." And this year, he completely shattered the world record for the indoor mile.

(short dramatization)

STEWART: Yes, that's the way things stood for Gil Dodds, America's #1 miler only two weeks ago.

The second man in our story is a shot putter, Chuck Fonville, a 20 year…a 21-year-old Negro lad for the University of Michigan, who this spring at the Kansas Relays, put the heavy shot farther than any man who's ever lived. For 12 years he'd been practicing, strengthening that arm and shoulder. Up until this year's world shot put record, the record had never passed 57 feet one inch. But then one day this spring, in Kansas, Chuck Fonville stepped into the circle in a championship meet and let the heavy iron ball fly in a throw that made every fan in the stadium rise to his feet.

(short dramatization)

STEWART: Uhah…uhah…correction — that's 58 feet ¼ inch–a new world's record. Almost a foot farther than any man has ever put the shot before. Yes sir, it certainly looked like Chuck Fonville was another cinch for the U.S. Olympic team when they started the qualifying trails back on July 9 at Evanston. But, more on that is a moment.

Now, what happened to the third man in our story? He's been doing all right, too. In his 12 years of painstaking practice, he'd managed to turn himself into the fastest high hurdle runner in the world — a winner of 82 consecutive races and the world's record. His name, Harrison Dillard. A little on the skinny side, his friends called him "Bones." Back home at Baldwin-Wallace College, he was quite a hero. He's managed to pick up nine world's records for different distance hurdles. And, earlier this year, he was proclaimed as the greatest high and low hurdler who ever wore spikes.

(short dramatization)

STEWART: Yes, those were the predictions for the three biggest names in American track — Fonville, Dillard and Dodds. But, in sports, there are no sure things. And a series of disasters began to take place in Evanston, Illinois; first, to the champion miler, Gil Dodds. Two days before the trials he strained his Achilles tendon and didn't even get to the meet. Next, Chuck Fonville, the world's record holder in the shot put; he wrenched his back while training. And, though he bettered the old Olympic mark by a good foot, he still failed to get a place on the squad. Last, Harrison Dillard. Well, "Bones," too, had a bad break that day. Here's how Jesse Owens explained it later:

(Short dramatization; Owens says that Dillard wore himself out running in other races during the trials and didn't have enough left to win the hurdles, his best event.)

STEWART: Yeah, "Bones" was tired when he ended that 110-meter high hurdle that day, but he had won that first heat. Then came the finals. Dillard was out in front and then there was a gasp from the crowd. He tripped on the second hurdle and on the fourth, he tripped again. And finally, in front of the seventh hurdle, he just…just drew up helplessly and pushed it down with his hands. "Bones" Dillard was out of the running. And that's our Olympic story for tonight, just six days before the 14th Olympic Games begin. A story of heartbreak and disappointment…of three boys who worked for 12 long years for their crack at the Olympics; who all became far and away the best in their class, but were beaten… beaten out by a cruel twist of fate in the finals. And last week when the Olympic boat sailed for London, Gil Dodds and Chuck Fonville were not aboard and "Bones" Dillard, the only one of the trio to make the boat, was not on the hurdle team where he belonged. But somehow I can't help but feel that next week at Wembley Stadium in London, all three of those great champions will be out on the field in spirit. Somehow, I feel that in the hearts of every member of the U.S. team, a little wish is being made tonight that goes something like this: Please a win for me and one for Fonville and Dillard and Dodds.

Dillard did win two gold medals in the 1948 Olympics (100-yard dash and 400-yard relay team), but had to wait until 1952 to pick up a gold medal for the 110-yard hurdles.

STEWART: But hope and courage are not confined to the field of sports, no sir. You find them in all walks of life, just as in this story which began back in 1926. It was the year an unknown 19-year-old youngster left his native town of Rochester, New York, and landed on the campus of the Pennsylvania Military College in Chester, PA, and there this unknown lad from Rochester became a sports hero, for he proved himself quite an athlete. He became the quarterback of the football team, played baseball and basketball and polo. But, college years must come to an end so this kid from Rochester went out into the world in search of a job. However, the…the love of sports still was first in the heart of this former college athlete. He wanted to be part of the sports world, and then…then a horrible tragedy changed his destiny. The kid from Rochester had an accident. The doctors saved his life, but they had to take off his left leg. For months the injured athlete lingered in the hospital, his spirit was broken. And then one day an important executive of a broadcasting company was making a tour of the hospital and he stopped by the sick boy's bedside and, for want of something better to say, the kind-hearted radio executive made him an offer.

(Short dramatization; he tells the boy that when he gets better, he should come to his office and he'd give him a radio job.)

STEWART: Well, the big radio man left the hospital and soon forgot his promise. He…well, he thought the injured athlete would never recover sufficiently to claim his job. But the former athlete did show up and he became a sports announcer. He began to live a strange, fascinating, marvelous life. He was now under a lucky star. Airplane crashes, boat sinkings and train wrecks, auto accidents…nothing could stop him… nothing could stop him until the kid from Rochester became the most famous sports announcer in America. His name…oh yes, his name is Bill Stern.

I'll be back in just a moment to tell you about next week's show in which Bill Stern will speak to you from London, but first…

(Commercial)

STEWART: Well, it's been a lot of fun for me tonight and if Bill Stern heard this program…I know he's on the *Moratania* borne for England… but, if he heard it, I hope he liked it as much as I liked doing it. Good night.

At the end of the show, Stanley announces that Stewart will shortly be seen in the Alfred Hitchcock film, *Rope*.

(2) Friday, April 22, 1949 (10:30-10:45 p.m.)

This show is currently not available for listening. This is most likely the source of the clip used in the show of October 20, 1950. Stewart had just finished the filming of *The Stratton Story*, which would be released shortly in the US.

(3) Friday, October 20, 1950 (6:15-6:30 p.m.)

It is the 572nd edition of the show and therefore its 12th anniversary. To celebrate, Stern looks at the biggest hit record and the greatest guest star of each of the years the Colgate version of the show has been on the air. It is inferred that Jimmy's contribution is from the year 1940, but it is far more likely that it is from his April 22, 1949 visit to the program. Jimmy's entire contribution is:

> *Well, Bill, we've just finished the picture of his life and I consider it a great honor to be allowed to play the part of this courageous boy.*

He is, of course, referring to the film, *The Stratton Story*.

In 2011, this program was issued on the mp3 only set, *Jimmy Stewart the Ultimate Radio Collection Vol. 3* (Master Classics Records), where it is misidentified as *Sealtest Variety Theater (Part 2)*.

The Bing Crosby Show(s)

Harry Lillis "Bing" Crosby was born in Spokane, WA, on May 3, 1903. He began appearing on radio in February 1929, singing on *Old Gold Presents Paul Whiteman & His Orchestra*. By 1931, he had gone solo and had his own nightly (except Sunday) radio series titled *Presenting 15 Minutes with Bing Crosby*. Fifty-two shows were broadcast from September 2 through October 31, 1931. This was followed by another 15-minute series, *Bing Crosby — Cremo Singer*, sponsored by Cremo Cigars. Next came *Music That Satisfies* (1933) and *Bing Crosby Entertains* (1933-1935). With all this experience behind him, Bing was ready to take over a big-time show in the form of *Kraft Music Hall*.

Several other radio programs followed this, with Stewart appearing on three different incarnations of the show. Bing's final appearance on radio was broadcast by the BBC on December 27, 1977. The show was hosted by Alan Dell and Crosby sang eight songs. The program had been recorded on October 11, 1977, just three days before his death.

In 1998, Bing was inducted into the Radio Hall of Fame.

Kraft Music Hall

The *Kraft Music Hall* was on radio for 16 years, from 1933 until 1949. Bing Crosby was the host who remained with the show for the longest period, from January 2, 1936, through May 9, 1946. Stewart appeared on the show three times in a span of five weeks in 1937, during Bing's 13 weeks off the show for summer vacation. During this period, the show was hosted by Bob Burns. He also appeared once the following summer, with Burns again hosting. Although none of the shows is available for listening, it is probable that Stewart played accordion on these shows.

NETWORK: NBC
SPONSOR: Kraft Foods
HOST: Bob Burns
ANNOUNCER: Ken Carpenter
MUSIC: John Scott Trotter
SINGERS: Paul Taylor Choristers
THEME: *Where the Blue of the Night (Meets the Gold of the Day)* (Fred Ahlert/Roy Turk/Bing Crosby)

(1) Thursday, July 15, 1937 (10-11 p.m.)
Other guests on the show were Bob Burns, Jose Iturbi, Dorothy McNulty [Penny Singleton] and Fortunio Bonanova.

(2) Thursday, August 5, 1937 (10-11 p.m.)

(3) Thursday, August 19, 1937 (10-11 p.m.)
Although several different sources state that Stewart also appeared on this show, it could not be confirmed. Newspaper ads from this period do not list him as a guest. Instead, the guests are listed as George Raft and Lupe Velez. Because of the similarity in dates, it is likely that these sources are referring to the August 18, 1938 date.

(4) Thursday, August 18, 1938 (10-11 p.m.)

Philco Radio Time
The Philco Radio Show was on the air for three seasons (October 16, 1946-June 1, 1949) and Jimmy Stewart appeared during the second and third. These were the first of Bing's shows which were not live. They were issued on 16-inch lacquer-coated aluminum discs. However, for the second season, he began using magnetic tape. His was one of the first shows to use this format. His first tape-recorded show was done in August of 1947 for the new fall radio season beginning in September. Crosby believed that he could produce a better quality show by using tape. Tape could be easily edited to eliminate any mistakes that might occur. Extra bits could be taped and if they didn't work well with the audience, they could be edited out of the finished show. Timing a show to fit the network's required time was also easier to do by using tape. The shows in

which Stewart were involved were transcribed in Hollywood. The shows' credits included:

NETWORK: ABC
SPONSOR: Philco Radios
PRODUCERS: Bill Morrow and Murdo MacKenzie
MUSIC: John Scott Trotter Orchestra
MUSICAL GROUP: Rhythmaires
ANNOUNCER: Ken Carpenter
THEME SONG: *Where the Blue of the Night* (Fred Ahlert/Roy Turk/Bing Crosby)

SHOWS FEATURING JIMMY STEWART:

(1) Wednesday, March 10, 1948 (10-10:30 p.m.) (The show had been transcribed on December 26, 1947)

Bing and Ken Carpenter begin the show with a comedy routine about baseball. Bing follows this with two songs, separated by a commercial for Philco.

"A Hundred and Sixty Acres" (with the Rhythmaires)
"Love Me Or Leave Me"

Bing introduces Jimmy Stewart and their sketch takes up about half of the show's 30 minutes.

CROSBY: Tonight's guest towel has been hung on the rack for the exclusive use of a gangling young man who's a flicker favorite with many successful starring roles to his credit; the bashful bachelor of Beverly Hills, Jimmy Stewart. Hi, Jimmy.
STEWART: Howdy, Bing.
CROSBY: Hey, Jim, just by the way of prying into your personal affairs, tell me, how is it you've managed to remain a bachelor all these years?
STEWART: Ah...huh...is this the Crosby program or Louella Parsons?
CROSBY: No, I'm interested, I really am, Jimmy. How...how have you stayed single?
STEWART: Well, I guess it's because, even though I talk sort of slow, I'm very fast on my feet.
CROSBY: That explains it then. I saw you at a party the other day, surrounded by beautiful girls, and you were wearing track shoes.
STEWART: Yes...yes, I gotta have 'em for a speedy getaway.
CROSBY: Naturally.
STEWART: Of course, I never spike the girls...unless I'm cornered, of course.

CROSBY: Well, do you wear the spiked shoes all the time, Jim?

STEWART: Oh sure. The other night I was thrown out of the Macambo for scratching up the dance floor…and a cigarette girl.

CROSBY: Well, even though I realize that you're one of the few bachelors left in Hollywood, aren't you a little more jittery than usual?

STEWART: Well, you'd be jittery, too, Bing…this is leap year.

CROSBY: Oh, yeah…366 Sadie Hawkins' Days.

STEWART: Ah…you're…you're a married man, aren't you, Bing?

CROSBY: Very.

STEWART: Well, I might consider marriage if somebody could give me one good reason.

CROSBY: Oh, I've got four…oh, I forgot Dixie…five…five.

STEWART: Now…now there's something I haven't thought much about, Bing…kids. Gee, I'm crazy about kids.

CROSBY: Then get busy.

STEWART: I…(more laughter)

CROSBY: I want that third coronet player with us all the time. He laughs more than Milton Berle's mother.

STEWART: You know, Bing, I…I really would like to settle down, take life easy and raise a lot of children.

CROSBY: Well, make up your mind, Jimmy. Do you want to take it easy or raise kids? They're different categories entirely.

STEWART: They are?

CROSBY: Sure.

STEWART: I thought in marriage the wife takes care of the babies.

CROSBY: That's a fallacy, James. Why in my day I've swallowed more safety pins than a busy dressmaker and I include Orry-Kelly, any of the big boys around town.

STEWART: Is that so?

CROSBY: Yeah, but I'll say one thing for Dixie; every time I swallowed a pin she was right there with the magnet.

STEWART: You know, sometimes I wish I wasn't so darn bashful around women.

CROSBY: They really upset you, huh?

STEWART: Mm…hum…mm…hum.

CROSBY: I'll be darned, Jimmy, I've seen you in your new picture, that *Northside 777*. You managed to overcome your embarrassment long enough to kiss that girl. If you can kiss a gal in a movie, why can't you do it with a gal at home?

STEWART: Well, it's a little dangerous, Bing. At home I don't have a director around to yell cut.

CROSBY: Yes, some of them do hang on, as I recall.

STEWART: Oh…even in those days?

CROSBY: Ah…you're just bashful with the fair sex, huh, Jim?

STEWART: It's heredity, I guess, Bing. My father was the same way. He was so bashful that when he was courting my mother, back in the horse and buggy days, mother used to ride in the buggy and Dad rode up with the horses.

CROSBY: Well, my brother, Everett, did something like that when he was courting up in Spokane.

STEWART: What's that, Bing?

CROSBY: Well, he couldn't afford horses so he wouldn't date any girl who wasn't strong enough to pull the buggy.

STEWART: Everett's a big strong fella, why would he let the girl pull the buggy?

CROSBY: Well, he likes to drive.

STEWART: Oh.

CROSBY: But, he was very gallant…he never used a whip.

STEWART: Well, if you get a girl that's willing, you don't really need one.

CROSBY: Well, getting back to your dad, Jim, you say he was more bashful than you?

STEWART: Ah, I guess it's about a toss up, Bing.

CROSBY: Sort of a shy tie, huh?

STEWART: Ah, yeah…yeah…I…you know I won't take a girl to the movies unless the theater's crowded.

CROSBY: Why a crowded theater?

STEWART: Well, so we don't have to sit together, of course…ah…that runs into money.

CROSBY: Runs into money? What do you mean?

STEWART: Two separate bags of popcorn every time.

CROSBY: Well, you ought to sit with your girl at the movies, and besides, just one sack of popcorn is a lot more fun.

STEWART: It is?

CROSBY: Sure, you see, as soon as the girl reaches into the sack for some corn, you sneak in there with her and you hold hands.

STEWART: Oh.

CROSBY: Yes.

STEWART: You used to do that, Bing?

CROSBY: Sure, saved plenty of loot that way, Jim. A sack of popcorn last me three or four months.

STEWART: Well (Jimmy laughs), I...I don't see how two people can get their hands into one little sack of popcorn at the same time.

CROSBY: Well, it's tricky, but after you get a little butter on your hands, they slip in the sack...

STEWART: That might have been okay for you, Bing, but when I go to a movie, I'm there to eat popcorn, not for squeezin' salty fingers.

CROSBY: Ah...yeah, but you don't eat popcorn during your own pictures?

STEWART: Bing...

CROSBY: Humm...

STEWART: Without popcorn, my pictures are nothing.

CROSBY: Well, move over. I don't understand how you ever escaped marriage, track shoes or not. You know what you need, Jim? You need a girl who's shy and retiring just like you are.

STEWART: Well, my type doesn't interest me. You know...you know, Bing, women are getting bolder and bolder every year.

CROSBY: Ah, I wouldn't know. I don't get out of the house much.

STEWART: Oh, you don't? You just take my word for it; they've really got a lot of nerve. Just look at those ankle-length dresses they're wearing now.

CROSBY: You think it takes nerve to wear one of those, huh?

STEWART: Well, would you wear one?

CROSBY: Oh yeah, but I'll wear anything.

STEWART: I know, when it comes to clothes, Bing, you sure are brave.

CROSBY: Well, it's sheer madness, not bravery and, Jimmy, if you adopted a more reckless attitude toward women, you'd be better off.

STEWART: You really think so, huh?

CROSBY: Positive...you oughta get married, Jim. See, at night when you come home, there'll be somebody at the door to throw her arms around you and shower you with affection.

STEWART: Yeah, that's if I come on time, of course.

CROSBY: This boy knows.

STEWART: Sure, my parents were married, you know, Bing. I...ah...I really don't need a wife. When I come home, I just like to sit by the fire all by myself and smoke.

CROSBY: Well, you oughta have a wife to bring you your pipe and tobacco.

STEWART: Oh, I don't use tobacco.

CROSBY: Well, then how do you smoke?

STEWART: Well, I'm absent minded…I always get a little too close to the fire.

CROSBY: Oh yeah, that wouldn't happen if you had a woman around.

STEWART: No, it wouldn't happen if I had a screen in front of the fireplace.

CROSBY: I better get a wife to watch over you, I guess.

STEWART: Oh, now don't bother, Bing. It's…it's nearly spring and I won't be using the fireplace much anymore.

CROSBY: I insist, Jimmy, I'm gonna get you married, I swear, if it's the last thing I do.

STEWART: Oh, now, why don't you lay off me, Bing?

CROSBY: A guy like you oughta be married. Now, let me see, what girl would I pick for you?

STEWART: No, never mind, Bing, now…

CROSBY: Now let's see, Eddie Cantor's got some daughters left over.

STEWART: Cantor always has daughters left over.

CROSBY: Well, you don't worry, I'll find a nice gal for you, Jimmy.

STEWART: What do you mean, don't worry? This whole thing terrifies me.

CROSBY: Nonsense, Jimmy, there's nothing to it. I'll show you how easy it is to get married.

STEWART: Well, just a minute, Bing.

CROSBY: Don't be difficult…now just to get you ready, we'll act the whole thing out. To make things easier for you, I'll be the groom and I'll let you be the bride.

STEWART: Just take it easy…take it easy. I know less about being a bride than I do about being a groom.

CROSBY: Just pretend you're a girl and do what comes naturally and I'll…pay close attention, Jim. Mr. Carpenter?

CARPENTER: What is it, Bing?

CROSBY: Will you take charge?

CARPENTER: Gladly, Bing, I do love a wedding.

CROSBY: Me, too.

STEWART: I love a parade.

CROSBY: Well, right after the wedding, we'll have a parade…now stand still and stop fidgeting, you're the bride.

CARPENTER: And so Harry and Jimima were married.

STEWART: Boo hoo hoo hoo…I'm very happy, darling.

CROSBY: Me, too, sweetheart. Come on, let's jump on the train.

CARPENTER: And so our happy honeymooners take the train to Buffalo, New York…Niagara Falls.

STEWART: Boo hoo hoo hoo hoo.

CROSBY: Oh, Jimima, darling, look at the falls. Aren't they beautiful? Stand over there; I want to take a snapshot of you.

STEWART: Let's check into the hotel.

CROSBY: The fellas at the office gave me this peachy Kodak at my bachelor dinner and if I don't bring back lots of snaps, they'll think I just didn't want to take pictures.

STEWART: Well, the girls in my office gave me a beautiful negligee to wear and I'm dying to try it on.

CROSBY: I know…I know, you run up to the room and put it on and then come on back and I'll take some pictures of you.

STEWART: Let's check into the hotel, Harry.

CROSBY: Okay. Hello room clerk, my name is Harry Crosby and this is my bride.

CARPENTER: Oh, he's lovely.

CROSBY: Yes, we were just married.

CARPENTER: So I noticed. The bride still has track shoes on.

STEWART: Hey, look, this isn't helping any, Bing. I'm not learning any more about marriage.

CROSBY: I'll tell you what let's do. We'll start the whole thing over and, in as much as I'm gonna see to it that you wind up as a groom this year, you be the husband and I'll be the wife.

STEWART: All right, here, you put on this veil.

CROSBY: Carpenter, reset the scene.

CARPENTER: And, so, Jimmy married Harriet.

CROSBY: I'm so happy, sweetheart.

STEWART: I'm scared to death and stop wiping your nose with your veil.

CROSBY: Sorry, come on, Jimmy, let's jump on the train.

CARPENTER: And so the little bride carried her struggling husband aboard the train to Buffalo, New York.

CROSBY: We took a milk train this time.

STEWART: Boo hoo hoo hoo hoo.

CROSBY: Oh, stop crying, I'm the bride. Come on, let's check into the hotel.

STEWART: Well, stop dragging me.

CARPENTER: Well, Well, Well, newlyweds.

STEWART: Yes, yes, I'm Mr. Stewart and this is my bride, Miss Harriet Crosby.

CROSBY: Darling, we're married now.
STEWART: Oh, pardon me, Mrs. Harriet Crosby.
CROSBY: Oh, he's gorgeous.
STEWART: We'd like an ice…we'd like an ice…
CROSBY: With lemon.
STEWART: We'd like an outside room so we can take snapshots.
CARPENTER: Now, just a minute, weren't you two here before?
STEWART: Yes, but I was the bride then.
CARPENTER: Well, let's try this whole thing once again and I'll be the bride.
STEWART: Not very enlightening. It still…still doesn't sway me. I'm gonna stay single.
CROSBY: Now don't be too sure, your spikes may fail you. You're liable to run into a gal who's got track shoes on herself.
STEWART: Well, if I do, I'll resort to my ace in the hole.
CROSBY: You're holding out on me?
STEWART: Yeah, yeah, when I was in the Army I learned that the best defense is an offense.
CROSBY: What have you got?
STEWART: Surefire offense…I sing.
CROSBY: Your singing is an offense?
STEWART: When I sing, it's as offensive as you can get.
CROSBY: Well, what song do you do? Something romantic, I trust.
STEWART: No, I've got a special number that frightens women so much that they never come near me again. It's a sort of a vocal D.D.T.
CROSBY: Don't get any on me, Jimmy, but let's hear it, huh?

"I'm A Wolf" (also known as "The Wolf of Wolf Creek Pass")

CROSBY: Really great…really great. It oughta work out fine, too, because once the girls get to thinkin' you're a wolf, they'll run for cover every time.
STEWART: I certainly hope so, Bing. Just those few minutes we spent at Niagara Falls made a wreck out of me, you know.
CROSBY: I still think you oughta get married, Jim.
STEWART: Well, if I do, Bing, I'll have it transcribed for release at my convenience.
CROSBY: Well, when you pick the girl and the date, Jimmy, give me a call, will ya, because I'm doing a little outside singing these days. I'm available for weddings, barbershop quartets, bar-b-ques and bar mitzvahs.

CARPENTER: And, Jimmy, be sure and let me know if you're going to take the big step.
STEWART: What for, Ken?
CARPENTER: Well, I wanna send you a wedding present. A nice Philco console.
STEWART: Oh, for free?
CARPENTER: Certainly.
CROSBY: This man gives things away.
CARPENTER: (Philco commercial)

"But Beautiful"

CROSBY: ...Many thanks for Jimmy Stewart for coming over tonight. He was stubborn, but charming.
STEWART: Oh, Bing, I'm sorry if I was stubborn, but you know the old saying, once bitten, twice shy.
CROSBY: Jimmy, you've been married before?
STEWART: Oh, gosh, no, nothing like that. You see, Bing, I proposed to a girl and she turned me down.
CROSBY: She turned you down.
STEWART: Yeah, broke my heart.
CROSBY: Ah, I didn't know that, Jimmy, I'm sorry. When did this girl spurn you?
STEWART: Well, I was in the fourth grade.
CROSBY: Fourth grade? Oh well, Jim, you should've pulled out of that by now. She was...she was just a kid.
STEWART: Kid nothing, she was in the eighth grade.
CROSBY: Oh, one of those older girls. Well no matter what happens, Jim, good luck.
STEWART: Thanks, Bing, thanks very much. Say, who's your guest next week?
CROSBY: Miss Margaret O'Brien.
STEWART: Margaret O'Brien, say she's real cute, you know.
CROSBY: Sure is...we're gonna do a great big St. Patrick's Day program.
STEWART: Well, I'll be sure to catch it. Good night, Bing.
CROSBY: Good night, Jimmy and good night, folks, and thank you very much.

The program is available on the mp3 only set, *Jimmy Stewart the Ultimate Radio Collection Vol. 3* (Master Classics Records, 2011).

(2) Wednesday, April 6, 1949 (the 100th show in the series) (10-10:30 p.m.)

After a short talk with Ken Carpenter, Bing opens the show with two songs, separated by a commercial.

"If You Stub Your Toe On the Moon" (with the Rhythmaires)

"Once In Love With Amy"

Bing then talks a little with the show's other guest star, Kay Starr. Kay then sings a song.

"You Broke Your Promise"

Next, Bing and Ken Carpenter do a sort of comedy routine, which serves as a very different kind of introduction for Jimmy Stewart.

CARPENTER: Say, Bing, where's Jimmy Stewart?

CROSBY: Stewart?

CARPENTER: Well, yeah. Gee, I'm sure anxious to see him. He's such a wonderful, sweet, loveable person.

CROSBY: Hmmm…he is, huh? Whatever gave you that impression?

CARPENTER: Well, Bing, haven't you ever seen him in pictures? I saw him the other night and he's such a nice, honest, easygoin' fella.

CROSBY: You're out of your mind, Stewart is a first-class cad.

CARPENTER: Jimmy Stewart?

CROSBY: Yes.

CARPENTER: The Jimmy Stewart I'm so crazy about in pictures?

CROSBY: The Jimmy Stewart everybody's so crazy about in pictures, yes. Sure, on the screen he's a sweet, loveable, honest guy. But in real life, why he'd double cross you quicker than a Mickey Finn.

CARPENTER: Why, Bing, I just can't believe that about Jimmy. Why he wouldn't hurt a fly.

CROSBY: I'm talking about what he does to people.

CARPENTER: But I thought you and Jimmy were great pals.

CROSBY: We were.

CARPENTER: Well, what happened between you two? Jimmy make a record of *White Christmas* or something?

CROSBY: No…no, it's deeper than that. He really pulled a dirty trick on me, that boy. You see, Ken, I was sittin' at home the other evening filing Hope's name off some gold trophies…I won them from him…when the phone rang. (sound of a phone ringing) Hello.

STEWART: Hello, Bing?

CROSBY: Yes.

STEWART: This is Jimmy Stewart.

CROSBY: Well, hello, Jimsy. How's it going?
STEWART: Why just awful, Bing.
CROSBY: What's the matter?
STEWART: Well, Bing, something terrible just happened.
CROSBY: Golly, don't tell me our pyramid has collapsed.
STEWART: No, no, it's even worse than that. It's a catastrophe, Bing. Now you've just got to get over here right away.
CROSBY: Oh but, Jim, I can't go out now, I'm wearing my bedroom slippers and an old bathrobe.
STEWART: Hmmm.
CROSBY: Yes.
STEWART: Well, if you're not going out, what are you all dressed up for?
CROSBY: I'm just eccentric. Jimmy, what's the big emergency anyway?
STEWART: Well, I can't tell you over the phone Bing. This is a party line and I share it with Louella.
CROSBY: Well, Hedda is on mine, we'd both better shut up.
STEWART: Yeah…well hurry right over, Bing, and step on it. I'm in real serious trouble.
CROSBY: I'm on my way, pal, but don't hang up the phone yet — Hedda wants to say something to Louella. I'll see you in a few minutes, Jim.
(Musical interlude as scene changes)
STEWART: Bing! At last! I thought you'd never get here.
CROSBY: Well, I had a little trouble with my car. It's a good thing you just live across the street.
STEWART: Yeah, well, why didn't you walk right in? You didn't have to knock first.
CROSBY: Well, I promised Humphrey Bogart I'd knock on any door.
STEWART: Oh, I see.
CROSBY: Now, what's the big emergency, Jim?
STEWART: Well, here, let me take your bathrobe.
CROSBY: This is my shirt.
STEWART: Oh.
CROSBY: I made a quick change. What's troubling you, Jim?
STEWART: Well, Bing, maybe you'll think I'm crazy, but I'm in an awful jam. You see, Bing, I'm a bachelor.
CROSBY: Well, a lot of single men are bachelors.
STEWART: I know, Bing, and I've been a bachelor all my life. But, tonight, something happened.
CROSBY: Jim, you got a wife?

STEWART: No, a baby.

CROSBY: A baby?

STEWART: Now, don't jump to conclusions, Bing. It's not what you're thinking, if you're thinking what I think you're thinking. Only I don't think you'd think that because it's impossible.

CROSBY: Keep talking, Jim, get yourself out of this.

STEWART: You see…ah…Bing, it's my cousin's baby.

CROSBY: Um…hum.

STEWART: The married one.

CROSBY: Um…hum.

STEWART: Ah, you see, she and her husband left the baby here so they could go to the movies. It's the worst thing that ever happened to me. I…I don't know what to do with a baby. I don't even know how to fold a handkerchief for my jacket.

CROSBY: Me either, I paint mine on.

STEWART: Oh.

CROSBY: Well, Jim, I can't understand your cousins; it's the darndest thing I've ever heard of. Seems to me if they're going to go gallivanting around to the movies all the time, they should have a regular babysitter.

STEWART: Well, they have, but she couldn't work tonight. She's having a baby.

CROSBY: Going into business for herself; that's what I like about America, everybody's got a chance to make good. But, Jim, if you're in trouble with the baby, why call me?

STEWART: Why call you? Bing, you've burped more babies than Dad's Old Fashioned Root Beer.

CROSBY: That's all behind me, Jim. I'm sorry, I've gotta go, I'll see you around. Good luck, Jim.

STEWART: No, you can't walk out on me now, no. I've got a baby in the bedroom.

CROSBY: I don't care if you got a lady in the balcony, I've gotta go…I'm gone.

STEWART: No…I thought we were friends.

CROSBY: I'm your friend, but…

STEWART: I'm scared to death of that kid. I don't know the first thing about handling babies, Bing.

CROSBY: There's nothing to it, they're just like people.

STEWART: Now, please, Bing, no…stop edging toward the door here. Now Geraldine might wake up any minute and, well, darn it, I don't even know which end the talcum powder goes on.

CROSBY: Put a little on both ends. I gotta go.

STEWART: How do I know when she needs talcum?

CROSBY: Well, when she starts yellin' and talkin', you start changin' and talcin'.

STEWART: I see, that's what scares me.

CROSBY: Nonsense, nonsense, I'll be seeing you, Jim. There's nothing to worry about, Jim. There's one thing about babies, once they're asleep, they sleep like babies…it's a cinch.

STEWART: Oh?

(Baby crying. There are many baby sounds heard throughout the remainder of the skit)

STEWART: Hey, what's that?

CROSBY: It's mice, I think…I…

STEWART: Bing.

CROSBY: Good night, Jim.

STEWART: Bing, Bing, don't.

CROSBY: I gotta go, yes.

STEWART: No.

CROSBY: I'll see you, Jim. Good luck, Jim.

STEWART: Bing, Bing, you can't, you can't run away from this, Bing. At Valley Forge, did our forefathers retreat? No. In Cuba, when the Rough Riders charged San Juan Hill, not a man fell back. During the long hard months of World War I, we didn't flinch under fire of enemy's cannon, and in World War…ah…in World War II, through the steaming jungles of the Pacific, across the waste lands of the African deserts, in the freezing Arctic snows, at Iwo Jima and Guam and Okinawa…

CROSBY: Oh, that was a great performance. Now go and try it on the kid.

STEWART: Oh…Crosby…ah…

CROSBY: Huh?

STEWART: Ah, we…ah…we've…ah…

CROSBY: He's tryin' to win the Oscar over there (referring to the person making the baby sounds).

STEWART: A fellow doesn't have a chance. We've gotta get in there. Now, you first.

CROSBY: Me?

STEWART: Don't worry, I'll cover you up from behind.

CROSBY: Never mind me, you cover the baby from behind.

STEWART: Better yet, Bing…

CROSBY: What?

STEWART: You go in and make a reconnaissance tour and report back to me with a full report on the entire problem in triplicate.
CROSBY: The war's over, colonel.
STEWART: Oh…but something's wrong in there, Bing, what is it?
CROSBY: It's nothing serious. It's either pin, pants or pablum.
STEWART: Oh, well, we just can't stand here, Bing. Now let's go in.
CROSBY: Well, I'll…I'll just take a peek…but that's all.
STEWART: I'll snap the lights on.
CROSBY: Okay. Well, just look at that.
STEWART: Be careful, Bing, she's snarling…she's got a tooth, too.
CROSBY: Ah…ah…(baby talk from Bing) isn't she a plump little rascal, huh?
STEWART: Yeah, well, she should be, you know she eats all the time. She's had three bottles in the last hour.
CROSBY: Three bottles of milk?
STEWART: No, this stuff right here…baby oil.
CROSBY: Jimmy, you're supposed to rub it on them.
STEWART: I do, but she keeps lickin' it off.
CROSBY: Jimmy, we're in trouble.
STEWART: What's the matter.
CROSBY: Oh well, just feel under here.
STEWART: I will not.
CROSBY: All this young lady needs is a new diaper. And we're gonna change her.
STEWART: Okay, I'll turn out the lights.
CROSBY: Turn out the lights?
STEWART: Of course.
CROSBY: Okay, snap 'em out. I can do this with the lights out and my eyes closed. This is nuts.
STEWART: Gee whiz, it's pretty dark in here. Where's the baby?
CROSBY: I got her.
STEWART: That's my hand.
CROSBY: I wondered why she was wearing a ring on her ankle.
STEWART: Here, I've got her.
CROSBY: Hang on, hang on now, this will just take a second. First, I put the safety pins in my mouth. (mumbles) Ah…oh…
STEWART: What's the matter?
CROSBY: Hand me some more pins.
STEWART: Here you are.
CROSBY: Hold still now, hold still (baby talk) I'll get it.

STEWART: Bing.

CROSBY: Something seems to be stuck here.

STEWART: Bing, don't pull.

CROSBY: But she's pinned to her shirt.

STEWART: Bing, let go, please.

CROSBY: What's the matter?

STEWART: You've got my necktie.

CROSBY: Here, I got it now. You hold her feet; I'll just slip 'em down like this. Here we go…there we are, all set. Turn the lights on.

STEWART: Okay. Gee, Bing, thanks a lot. Hey…hey, where's the baby? Bing, you covered the wrong end.

CROSBY: I told ya…I told ya, Jim, to hold her feet. Now leave the lights on. I guess I've been away from this thing far too long. I…or something. I couldn't do it by the touch system.

STEWART: Bing, while you're doing that and getting her back to sleep, why don't I go over to the Westwood Theater and get her folks back here?

CROSBY: Well, why don't I run over?

STEWART: No, no, I…you don't know them. Now I'll be back in just a few minutes.

CROSBY: Hey now, wait a minute, hold it.

STEWART: I'll be right back. Now…

CROSBY: Wait a minute.

STEWART: I'm placing you in full charge.

CROSBY: Jim, wait. Well, kid, looks like you and me. Sleep for you and I'm going out and raid the Philco refrigerator. Oh yes, yes they are…they're…they're real beauties. They'll love you in Philadelphia.

(music to show passage of time)

CROSBY: Oh boy, 1:15 a.m. That guy's been gone over three hours. Well, I might as well tune in the Philco and see if any radio stations are still on. Only takes ten minutes to get to the theater from here…oh, maybe he's stayin' for the picture or something. Hope its *Connecticut Yankee*.

(radio music)

DEEJAY: Hi ya, folks, here we are again with the music of Red Nichols and his Five Pennies, comin' at ya from high atop Barney Dean's stylish Ventura Motor Court, overlooking beautiful Sherman Oaks. We've got a lot of celebrities, as usual, here tonight. Let's see, oh, there's Barney Dean himself sittin' with Mr. and Mrs. Bill Gargen. There are the Pat O'Briens, Prince Mike Romanoff and his charming wife, the Groucho Marxs, and over there sittin' in a dark corner with a very charming young lady is that sweet, loveable, shy guy from the movies, Jimmy Stewart.

CROSBY: Jimmy Stewart? And I'm stuck with this baby. What are you laughin' at? Well, that does it — sweet, loveable, shy Jimmy Stewart, huh.
(skit with Stewart ends)
CROSBY: So, Ken, that's...that's what happened.
CARPENTER: Well, Bing, I never would have believed it.
CROSBY: Well, I'd appreciate if you would.
CARPENTER: Have you seen Jimmy since then?
CROSBY: No, but fortunately his cousins came by a little later and rescued me. For all I know, or care, Jimmy Stewart is still sitting in that dimly lit corner overlooking beautiful Sherman Oaks...and, I hope he is.

Bing brings Kay Starr back and the two duet on *You Was*.
"You Was"
Ken Carpenter does a commercial for Philco and then Bing sings his final number.
"While the Angelus Was Ringing" (with the Rhythmaires)
As Bing begins to wrap-up the show, Ken comes back in and says:

CARPENTER: Say, Bing, there's a fella here to see you.
CROSBY: Who's there?
STEWART: It's me, Bing, that loveable, sweet, shy guy of the movies.
CROSBY: Well, if it isn't Peter Lorre.
STEWART: I'm sorry about the other night, Bing. You see...let's see now...at 50 cents an hour for babysitting, I must owe you about $2.25.
CROSBY: According to my time card, it's $3.25 and it said $3.25 on your script, too.
STEWART: Oh, oh, oh yes.
CROSBY: Thanks.
STEWART: There you are.
CROSBY: Yeah.
STEWART: All right then...who's with you next week?
CROSBY: Oh next week, James, we do our Easter show. The Gonzaga University Glee Club is coming down from Spokane and Peggy Lee will be here, too.
STEWART: Gonzaga's your old alma mater, isn't it?
CROSBY: That's right, Jim. Seems like only yesterday I was singing in the glee club, now they're my guests.
STEWART: Ah, time certainly flies, doesn't it?
CROSBY: Yes, especially when you're sitting atop Barney Dean's Ventura Motor Court overlooking beautiful Sherman Oaks.

STEWART: Oh…oh…oh yeah, I have to explain that to you…
CROSBY: Too late…good night Jimmy.
STEWART: Good night, Bing.
CROSBY: Good night, Kay, good night, folks. Thanks a lot.

The Chesterfield Show
Beginning in the 1949 season (September 21, 1949), Bing had a new sponsor and the show also had a new name to reflect this change. He would stay with Chesterfield through June 18, 1952. The show also moved from ABC to CBS. Unless otherwise noted, shows were transcribed from Hollywood. The credits for the Chesterfield Show included:
NETWORK: CBS
SPONSOR: Chesterfield Cigarettes
PRODUCERS: Bill Morrow and Murdo MacKenzie
MUSIC: John Scott Trotter Orchestra
MUSICAL GROUP: Jud Conlon's Rhythmaires
ANNOUNCER: Ken Carpenter
THEME MUSIC: *Where the Blue of the Night* (Fred Ahlert/Roy Turk/Bing Crosby)
SHOWS FEATURING JIMMY STEWART:

(1) Wednesday, December 14, 1949 (9:30-10 p.m.) (Transcribed on December 1, 1949)
Bing opens the show with a couple of songs.
"Rudolph the Red-Nosed Reindeer" (with the Rhythmaires and Gloria Wood as Rudolph)
"A Thousand Violins"
Bing's other guest, Carole Richards, then sings a song.
"I Can Dream, Can't I?"
Next, Bing introduces Jimmy Stewart.

CROSBY: …and now, folks, here's an old friend of ours. He's always been considered a catch, not only in the entertainment world, but also among the pursuing fair sex. However, since he was last with us, his status has changed considerably. In fact, I might even say completely. Because now Hollywood's most famous bachelor has went and did it. And it's with pleasure and congratulations that we welcome ex-bachelor, Jimmy Stewart, to the Chesterfield Show…James, you look wonderful.
STEWART: Well, thanks, Bing. You know all my friends tell me the same thing ever since Gloria and I got married.

CROSBY: It's a fact. I really mean it. Your eyes have real sparkle; you have more zip and zing.

STEWART: Mmm..um. I also snap, sizzle and pop.

CROSBY: Well, you wait till you've been married as long as I have.

STEWART: Ah…no more snap, sizzle and pop.

CROSBY: No, just flap, fizzle and flop. Hey, Jim…Jim, tell me, where'd you and your bride go for your honeymoon?

STEWART: Ah, we went marlin fishing in Sun Valley.

CROSBY: You went marlin…boy, Sun Valley's a thousand miles from the ocean. There's no marlin there.

STEWART: Well, who cares?

CROSBY: I guess you're right, who wants a marlin when you have your darlin'. You know, Jim, I'm sure your marriage made Gloria happy, but I wanna tell you something…it made a lot of other women very unhappy.

STEWART: It did?

CROSBY: Sure. The day you became a groom, Jimmy Stewart fan clubs throughout the nation wore their bobby sox at half mast.

STEWART: Golly.

CROSBY: Yes, and grown-up women all over the world drank a solemn farewell toast to their lover boy. Martinis with black olives in them.

STEWART: Oh, now…now…Ah, Bing…I…I…

CROSBY: It's true, gosh, what a tough year the poor girls have had. Why before their tears had dried over losing you, the next shock came like a bolt out of the blue.

STEWART: What?

CROSBY: Vice President Barkley.

STEWART: Oh.

CROSBY: It's been an awful year, really.

STEWART: Yeah…yeah, *The Missouri Waltz* used to be the theme song of Washington, now it's *St. Louis Woman*.

CROSBY: I just can't get over you. The vice president…especially you. Everybody was betting 20-to-1 that you'd remain single the rest of your life. Did you know that? 20-to-1…what made you decide to get married?

STEWART: Well, Bing, I just couldn't pass up those odds.

CROSBY: Ah, so besides picking up a lovely bride, you also grabbed some lovely loot.

STEWART: Oh, enough to buy a license, pay a minister and rent a tuxedo.

CROSBY: Now, Jimmy, besides making expenses, what other reasons made you forsake bachelordom?

STEWART: Well, to tell you the truth, Bing, I...I wanted to get married a long time ago, but I didn't have a girl.

CROSBY: Well, I guess a girl's a definite must...if you want to get married.

STEWART: Unless you're a girl yourself, then, of course, a man would be necessary.

CROSBY: That's what I like about you, Jimmy, your innate ability to see both sides of a problem.

STEWART: Thanks very much, Bing.

CROSBY: You're incisive in that respect.

STEWART: Well, anyway, I...I finally found the right girl and that's about all there is to my getting married.

CROSBY: What baffles me is how a girl could get used to how bashful you are.

STEWART: Oh well, as a matter of fact, Gloria happens to be very shy herself.

CROSBY: Oh.

STEWART: Yeah, I remember the first time we were introduced. She took one look at me and ran and hid in a closet.

CROSBY: Oh, she is shy.

STEWART: Um...hum. I got so flustered, I...I ran and hid in a closet.

CROSBY: Well, a meeting like that can never lead to romance.

STEWART: Well, it can if you both pick the same closet.

CROSBY: What a pair. Say, James, tell me...ah...how did you ever get up nerve to kiss your bride after your wedding?

STEWART: Oh well, shucks, when it comes to girls, I'm just as aggressive as the next fella. After the ceremony, I just barged over and got in that line like everybody else; went around six times.

CROSBY: What a wolf.

STEWART: And the next time I see one of those lines, she's gonna get kissed again.

CROSBY: Jim, after living alone for so many years and being your own boss, how does married life strike you?

STEWART: Well, I'll tell you, Louella...

CROSBY: Wait'll I get my...

STEWART: I...ah...

CROSBY: Yeah, how do you get...?

STEWART: We get along...we get along wonderfully, but women do funny things. Now like at breakfast this morning, Gloria said, "I had to pay the gardener this morning, so while you were sleeping, I took $20 out of your pants pocket."

CROSBY: Yeah, you can't break them of those habits. But, if you want revenge, do what I do. Now you know when Dixie says to me, "I took $20 out of your pocket," I say that's all right, Honey, I'll still get by today; I have a $10 bill in this other pocket.

STEWART: Oh…what kind of revenge is that?

CROSBY: Oh, Jim, it drives 'em crazy when they think they've missed some. They can't stand it. Jimmy, I don't want to pry into your private life, as if I haven't been, but I think that all of our listeners would really be interested in knowing how you finally got up enough nerve. Now, how did you really…really build yourself up to ask Gloria to marry you? How'd you do that?

STEWART: You mean you wanna know how I proposed?

CROSBY: Yeah…yeah.

STEWART: In front of all these people?

CROSBY: Sure…come on, sure.

STEWART: Well, a fella can't propose all alone, you need a girl.

CROSBY: Well, I'll help out. I'll…I'll be Gloria and we'll reenact exactly what took place the night you popped the question.

STEWART: No…ah…ah…no, Bing, I can't do this.

CROSBY: Why not?

STEWART: Well, suppose I ask you to marry me and you accept… that's bigamy.

CROSBY: Come on, Jimmy, we'll put you in the mood. Come on, John.

CARPENTER: We now take you to the home of Miss Gloria McLean, who will be played by Mr. Crosby. And we find Miss McLean and her suitor seated in the living room.

CROSBY: Oh, Jimmy.

STEWART: Yes, Gloria.

CROSBY: Come over here and sit beside me.

STEWART: Wait'll I cover the bird cage. They keep staring at me.

CROSBY: Jimmy, those are love birds. Notice how they're snuggling together. Why don't we do that?

STEWART: Oh, we could never get in that little cage.

CROSBY: Oh, Jimmy, you're so bashful.

STEWART: No, no, I'm not. Now, as a matter of fact, I have something very important to ask you. Gloria…

CROSBY: Yes, Jimmy.

STEWART: Gloria, have you ever thought of changing your name?

CROSBY: Why, yes. What have you got in mind?

STEWART: Well, Katherine might be a nice…

CROSBY: Oh, Jimmy.

STEWART: No, now what I started to say…I mean…ah…as a matter of fact…I thought perhaps…well, maybe I shouldn't mention it, but I…I just…well, I just got to come right out with it…ah…Gloria…

CROSBY: Yes.

STEWART: You said yes. You said yes.

CROSBY: Jimmy, what are you so excited about?

STEWART: Well, I just proposed to you…you said yes.

CROSBY: I did?

STEWART: Yeah, Honey, you've made me the happiest man in the world…I think.

CROSBY: Jimmy, aren't you going to kiss me?

STEWART: No…no, I gotta go home.

CROSBY: But, Jimmy, we're lovely…we use Pons…we're engaged?

STEWART: No, I'll phone you in the morning, Gloria.

CROSBY: Oh, don't go, it's still early.

STEWART: I really can't stay.

(Jimmy's line leads him and Bing into a short rendition of *Baby, It's Cold Outside*. After the song, Ken Carpenter continues into a commercial.)

CARPENTER: How very romantic, Bing and Jimmy. I'm sure that lovers all over the world will find inspiration in your little offering.

STEWART: Well, thanks very much, Ken.

CARPENTER: Say, Jimmy, you know it's getting pretty close to Christmas and for…ah…the smoker's on your list, this year Chesterfield has something special, the Chesterfield Christmas carton.

CROSBY: Oh, it makes a nice gift, Jimmy.

STEWART: Well, I've got to…

CARPENTER: Yeah, it's really an attractive package. It's in full color with a picture of Chesterfield's Arthur Godfrey as Santa Claus.

STEWART: Arthur Godfrey? Well, what's the matter with you, Bing? Why didn't Chesterfield put your picture on the Christmas carton?

CROSBY: Well, I can't wear a Santa Claus suit, Jimmy, I'm not stout enough to be believable as Santa.

STEWART: Oh, uh…huh.

(Jimmy does not appear in the commercial after this point.)
After the spot is complete, Bing does his last song of the show.
"The Christmas Song" (with Buddy Cole on piano)
After the song, Bing thanks his guests.

CROSBY: ...Well, my thanks to Carole Richards and Jimmy Stewart tonight, too, for joining us this evening

STEWART: Who's with you next week, Bing?

CROSBY: Well, next week, Jimmy, our guest will be Miss Ethel Barrymore.

STEWART: Oh, there's a wonderful lady.

CROSBY: Isn't she? We're especially happy that Miss Barrymore will be with us next week, Jimmy, because it's our Christmas show.

STEWART: Oh, sounds like a real gift for everybody.

CROSBY: In addition to *Jingle Bells*, *White Christmas* and some of the other favorite songs, we'll present a brand-new Christmas play. Thanks again, Jimmy, we'll see you soon.

STEWART: Well, I enjoyed it. Good night, Gloria.

CROSBY: Good night...hum...see you next week for Chesterfield, folks.

At the end of the show, Carpenter announces that Jimmy can currently be seen in *The Stratton Story*.

This show can be found on the 1978 album, *Bing Crosby — The Greatest Christmas Shows* (M.F. Distribution SMF 210). The Stewart show is on the album's B-side. The A-side does not involve Stewart. The album was issued with two slightly different covers. The album with the wide green border says, "Fox American Retrospectives" on the back of its sleeve. The background on the back of the jacket is green and the record number is listed as BMF/210. The album with no border says "Fox American Collectibles" and has a white background on the back of the jacket. The release number is listed as SMF/210.

The entire show can also be found on the 1991 cassette tape, Golden Age Holiday (Metacom GT-220).

Even though it's only a little over 40 seconds in length, Bing and Jimmy's version of *Baby, It's Cold Outside*, from this show, also appears on the cassette *The Christmas Collection: Merry Christmas* (Déjà Vu 5080-4), which was released in 1986 and the CD of the same title released in 1988 (Deja Vu 5080-2). In 1987, it was issued on the CD *The Bing Crosby Christmas Collection* (Déjà Vu DVCD 2080). It was issued again in 1992 on the cassette *The Bing Crosby Gift Collection* (Déjà Vu 5-126-4) and the CD of the same title (Déjà Vu 5-126-2).

(2) Wednesday, January 24, 1951 (9:30-10 p.m.) (Transcribed January 20, 1951)

After a short skit with Bing and Ken Carpenter, Bing's other guest on this show, Toni Arden, opens with a song.

"You're Just In Love" (with the Rhythmaires)

Bing then sings a song, followed by another from Arden.

"Autumn Leaves"

"My Man" (Toni Arden)

Bing introduces Jimmy Stewart and their nearly 10-minute-long sketch begins.

CROSBY: …We have a gangling guest this evening, whose two latest starring vehicles are currently proving that movies are better than ever. As the harried head of a household in *The Jackpot* and as the Pookah's peaceful pal in *Harvey*, his brilliant performances are causing cascades of guffaws, literally cascades of guffaws in popcorn palaces everywhere. We're real happy to uncoil the carpet for James Stewart.

STEWART: Hi, Bing.

CROSBY: Oh, he's a lanky one, isn't he?

STEWART: He's a lumpy one, isn't he?

CROSBY: Well, that's not me, really, I'm breaking in this suit for Everett [Bing's brother]. Where've you been the last few months, Jim, I haven't seen you around.

STEWART: Well, I was in England, Bing, making a movie over there.

CROSBY: Oh, an English movie, huh? Something for television?

STEWART: Ah, no…no…no, not for television. This is an American picture; we made it in spite of television.

CROSBY: Attaboy. That's the fight I like to see. We'll lick 'em yet.

STEWART: Ah, leave it alone. It'll lick itself.

CROSBY: I wished I had some Minute Maid on me; I'd like to drink to that. Anyway, Jim, may I congratulate you on this *Jackpot* picture you made for 20th Century and I want to congratulate you on *Harvey*, too, the picture you made for UI. On this new one, though, the one you went… who…who you workin' for now?

STEWART: Oh, the same old bunch, Bing, the boys down in Washington.

CROSBY: Know them well…Know them well. What's the new picture about?

STEWART: Well, I don't know. I haven't seen it yet.

CROSBY: You read the script, didn't ya?

STEWART: Oh no, I never do that, Bing. If I read the script, it kind of spoils it for me when I see it in the theater.

CROSBY: Well, you got a point there. Course with me, I'm impatient, I…I like to read the script so I can be disappointed from the start.

STEWART: Oh yeah. No, well, you shouldn't be disappointed, Bing, your pictures are wonderful…if you care for singing. Really…really, your pictures are swell, Bing. You're a big favorite in England, you know.

CROSBY: Well, they must like singing, I guess.

STEWART: Oh, they love it, yes. Right now they're having a big celebration. What is it? The Bing Crosby Month; Everett's 20th anniversary as a millionaire.

CROSBY: No kidding, they're really celebrating my anniversary in Europe?

STEWART: Oh…it's…going very big over there, Bing.

CROSBY: Really?

STEWART: After all, you made it possible for America to afford the Marshall Plan.

CROSBY: Oh, is that so? Take the wife over to Europe with you, Jim?

STEWART: Oh yes, Gloria came over with me. Of course, the doctor didn't think much of her making the trip.

CROSBY: Gloria's not sick is she?

STEWART: No…no…no…no, she's not sick. She's more or less under a doctor's care these days.

CROSBY: What's the matter, Jim?

STEWART: Well ah, Bing, in a way, it's all your fault.

CROSBY: My fault? What's my fault? What's wrong? What do you mean?

STEWART: Well, Bing, do you remember back…oh…oh…a couple of years ago I was on your show and you tried to talk me into getting married…to a girl?

CROSBY: I remember, sure. I said a big easygoing guy like you should have been married a long time ago. You were a good catch. If you're afraid to pitch…

STEWART: Yeah…yeah…yeah, well after…after I left you that night, I got to thinking about your advice.

CROSBY: Yeah.

STEWART: And the next thing I knew, I was combing rice outta my hair in a hotel room.

CROSBY: Gloria with ya?

STEWART: Ah, yes, it was her comb.

CROSBY: Nice of you to take her on the honeymoon. That's nice.

STEWART: Yeah, well, I was so excited I didn't know what I was doing, you know. But, as I think back on it, I realize it was the thing to do.

CROSBY: I remember you telling me about your honeymoon, Jim. In fact, don't you remember, we did a broadcast about it.

STEWART: Oh yeah, that's right; seems like I'm on your show every time a major event takes place in my life.

Bing and Jimmy rehearse their lines.

CROSBY: That's right. That's the way it works out, yeah.

STEWART: Yep, that's the way…well, here I am again.

CROSBY: No. Really? Well, put 'er there. Well, congratulations.

STEWART: Thanks, Bing.

CROSBY: So that's why Gloria's under a doctor's care, huh? Tell me, how's she doing?

STEWART: Oh, Gloria's fine, Bing. I don't feel so good.

CROSBY: You'll get over that, I know how it is. Tummy topsy-turvy in the morning?

STEWART: Yeah, yeah.

CROSBY: Middle of the night you wake up sometimes and you think you'll just die if you don't get a strawberry malted milk…

STEWART: And a pickle.

CROSBY: And a pickle, yes, I know, I had the same thing. I had the same with Gary.

STEWART: Did you…did you have terrible heartburn all of the time?

CROSBY: Constantly, everything I ate, heartburn day and night. They say that's a sign the baby's gonna have a lot of hair, you know.

STEWART: Yes, I've heard that.

CROSBY: Last few weeks, I couldn't eat a thing.

STEWART: No…all that I can eat is Tums.

CROSBY: Well, eat a lot of 'em…you're eatin' for two, you know.

STEWART: Well, my…my doctor's quite worried about me.

CROSBY: Your doctor?

STEWART: Yes, I go for a checkup every day. Gloria drives me over.

CROSBY: Oh man, you got it bad.

STEWART: Bing, Bing, we're gonna have to buy all our baby things… I'm just too nervous to knit.

CROSBY: Ah, Jimmsy, now come on, relax.

STEWART: Relax?

CROSBY: Yes.

STEWART: Relax? How can you stand there and…and be so calm about everything?

CROSBY: I've been through it myself several times.

STEWART: Yes, it's awful, Bing. I lay awake nights thinking what'll happen if Gloria suddenly says, "This is it," and I rush out and the car won't start. What…

CROSBY: Oh man, come to think of it, when I was in your predicament, I kept the motor running day and night.

STEWART: Oh, you did?

CROSBY: The car's and mine.

STEWART: Oh, yours…boy, I'll count ten before this happens again.

CROSBY: Oh, now, Jim, don't be so bitter about it.

STEWART: No, when Gloria wakes me up in the middle of the night, I know…I…I still never get me to the hospital in time.

CROSBY: Jim, don't be such a fraidy cat.

STEWART: Well, I can't help it, Bing. I'm the worrying sort, you know. Sometimes I wish I didn't even know about this. You know, why couldn't Gloria have just kept it a secret?

CROSBY: Well, in your case, it might have been more merciful. Just when did Gloria break the news to you anyway?

STEWART: Frankly, Gloria never exactly told me, Bing.

CROSBY: She didn't?

STEWART: No, I read it in Louella's column and…then I got suspicious.

CROSBY: Well, that's ground for suspicion, all right.

STEWART: About a week later, I knew it was true when I went around in back of the garage and I caught Gloria making a playpen.

CROSBY: Ah, Jimmy, you oughta just relax. I'm sure Gloria will take care of everything.

STEWART: Gee, I wish she'd take care of me, I'm a wreck.

CROSBY: Don't be silly. It's just your imagination, Jim. I thought the same thing, but I pulled through.

STEWART: Yeah, look at ya.

CROSBY: Well, you get this way after the baby comes. After he grows up and goes into competition with ya.

STEWART: Yeah, but even…even so, pal; your firstborn was just Gary…just one.

CROSBY: What are you expecting, the Andrews Sisters?

STEWART: Not quite…twins.

CROSBY: Twins! Twins!

STEWART: Um…hum. Two of 'em. The doctor warned me…ah…told me.

CROSBY: Was it your idea to have twins or was it the studio's idea…sort of a stunt for *Jackpot*?

STEWART: Oh no, no, but this is serious.

CROSBY: You're telling me.

STEWART: No, I'm reminding you. I…

CROSBY: The doctor could be wrong, Jim, you know. Do twins…twins, do they run in your family?

STEWART: No. As a matter of fact, children don't even run in my family.

CROSBY: Boy, they're runnin' now.

STEWART: Yes…yeah, Gloria's already redecorated a bedroom in the house in pink wallpaper with little blue bunnies and little chicks on it and she's got stuffed teddy bears and plastic toys and rattles hanging all around and satin bows tied to the bed. Gee, it's just awful.

CROSBY: Awful? What'd ya mean? That's the way a room should be decorated for babies, Jim.

STEWART: No, this is my room, the…the nursery's down the hall.

CROSBY: Now that's foresight on Gloria's part. You see, no matter where you walk the twins at night, the décor will be appropriate.

STEWART: Yeah…yeah, I suppose. Well, Bing, there…there's a lot more things I'd like to discuss, but it'll just have to wait. I…I've been standing on my feet altogether too long for a man in my condition. I…

CROSBY: You poor boy…you poor boy. How inconsiderate of me. You just rest. Now take a seat over there and puff…puff a Chesterfield.

STEWART: Thanks…thanks. I knew you'd understand.

CROSBY: Absolutely. Now if you feel…say, Jim, if you feel…ah…while you're sitting over there, Jim, if you should feel a sudden urge for a pickle, why I think you'll find one in John Scott Trotter's picnic basket.

STEWART: Oh…ah…is John Scott going to a picnic?

CROSBY: No, he's going to a restaurant, but he likes to eat on the way.

STEWART: Oh, I see.

CROSBY: I'll see you later, Jim.

Bing and Ken Carpenter do a commercial for Chesterfield and then Bing then sings one more song.

"May the Good Lord Bless and Keep You"

After this number, Bing invites Jimmy back to the microphone.

CROSBY: …and Jimmy Stewart for joining us this evening.

STEWART: Oh, I enjoyed having that little talk with you, Bing, and I hope you get over your cold real soon.

CROSBY: Thank you, Jim, and I hope you get over your trouble real soon.

STEWART: Ah, oh…oh I will. Who you gonna have next week, Bing?

CROSBY: Next week, Jimmy, we'll have Toni Arden with us again. Also that great jazz band, the Firehouse 5 plus 2, and also that great comedian, Leslie Towne Hope.

STEWART: Huh.

CROSBY: Of course, if he gets arrested on the way to the broadcast, he'll show up as Bing Crosby, I imagine.

STEWART: Oh gosh, two Bing Crosbys. They're sure going all out for you this month.

CROSBY: Aren't they?

STEWART: Good night, Bing.

CROSBY: Good night, Jim…daddy.

STEWART: Good night.

As usual, Ken Carpenter gives the credits and wraps up the show.

(3) Wednesday, November 14, 1951 (9:30-10 p.m.)

Bing and Ken Carpenter begin with a short comedy routine involving Christmas shopping and a new perfume. The perfume comes up again in Bing's sketch with Jimmy Stewart later in the show. Bing then sings two songs, separated by a Chesterfield commercial.

"Bright Eyes" (with the Rhythmaires)
"When the World Was Young"

Bing's other guest for this show was 15-year-old Anna Maria Alberghetti. At this point in the show, she sang a song.

"La Capinera" (*The Wren*) (Phil Shukin plays flute)

Bing introduces Jimmy Stewart and they begin their sketch. Veola Vonn also appears as the salesgirl.

CROSBY: Ah, but now I see a tall, slender, amiable chap ankling our way. That fine fellow, splendid actor, Jimmy Stewart.

STEWART: Now thank you, Bing.

CROSBY: Oh, Jimmy, it's nice to see you. You know this is the first time I've had a chance to talk to you since you became a father.

STEWART: Mm..hum. Well, I had a pretty easy time of it, Bing. I was outta the hospital in seven days.

CROSBY: I suppose the doctor warned you about lifting things.

STEWART: Yes…yes, I still take it easy on the stairs. But only six months, you know.

CROSBY: Must have been a big jolt, huh, Jim? A confirmed bachelor like you having twins right off the bat.

STEWART: Well, I thought Gloria'd be angry, but she didn't seem to mind at all.

CROSBY: Well, wives are very understanding, I'd like to have seen you though, Jim, when you got the news that you were the father of twins. I'll bet you really went wild, huh?

STEWART: I sure did.

CROSBY: What'd you say?

STEWART: Golly.

CROSBY: You had twins…all you said was golly.

STEWART: I said it twice.

CROSBY: Man, you really blew your top. Let's see now, you and Gloria had twin girls, didn't ya?

STEWART: That's right, Bing, twin girls. The first thing I know they'll grow up and then they'll go to school and they'll graduate and they'll start going out on dates and getting married and settle down and have children of their own. By golly, I don't like that.

CROSBY: You don't…you don't like what?

STEWART: Well, being a grandfather at my age.

CROSBY: Wait a minute…time flies, but not that fast. I'll bet you really have a time with those kids though, don't you, Jimmy? Do you help Gloria take care of 'em? Do you bathe 'em and change 'em and such?

STEWART: No, Bing. I'm not much help in that department. I'm just not built that way.

CROSBY: Don't you even feed them?

STEWART: No…umm…same answer. Now when it comes to mixing a formula, I'm a flop.

CROSBY: You can't mix a formula? Why don't you run over to Chasen's and let Dave Chasen stir up a formula for you?

STEWART: Oh no…no…no. Gloria has a much better recipe for pablum than Chasen's.

CROSBY: You'll think of something. Jimmy, you're in for the biggest thrill of your life. You know something; it won't be long now till you'll be spending your first Christmas with your kids.

STEWART: Yeah. I gotta fatten up some if I'm gonna play Santa Claus.

CROSBY: I don't think you'll ever make it with a knife and fork, Jim. You'll have to use pillows for stuffing like the rest of us.

STEWART: Yeah, Bing, speaking of Christmas…ah…

CROSBY: I don't need many pillows, either.

STEWART: Speaking of Christmas, that's why I came down here to see you.

CROSBY: What'd you mean?

STEWART: Well, I wanna buy Gloria a present and…ah…I…I…I thought I might get her something intimate.

CROSBY: Oh well, Jimmy, that's a little out of my line. I don't know anything about…

STEWART: Well, Bing, I always looked upon you as a man of the world and I…ah…thought you might take me shopping. I…I think wives like to get dainty presents. You know, something lacey and sheer.

CROSBY: Of all people, you.

STEWART: Will…will you help me, Bing?

CROSBY: I certainly will and I know just the place to go.

STEWART: Where?

CROSBY: Over at Orbach's. I saw the flimsiest...got a laugh with Orbach's...I saw the flimsiest, sheerest, laciest handkerchiefs there and I'll take you over right now.

STEWART: Oh well, Bing, I'm man enough to walk into a store and buy handkerchiefs alone.

CROSBY: Well, Jimmy, you can't buy anything lacier or sheerer or more attractive than these handkerchiefs I saw.

STEWART: Oh yes you can.

CROSBY: This boy's been looking at the ads in *Harper's Bizaar*.

STEWART: That's right, I have.

CROSBY: Well then, out with it. What do you want to buy Gloria?

STEWART: Well, I don't know what you call 'em, but I'll know 'em when I see 'em.

CROSBY: Hey, this here is real top secret. Okay, Jimmy, I know a very nice lady's shop. It's right here on Vine Street.

STEWART: Oh.

CROSBY: We can run right over now.

STEWART: Oh, now? Well, don't you have to work, Bing?

CROSBY: Oh, this beats workin', Jim. Come on, Let's go.

(short musical interlude to signify the change of scenes)

STEWART: Gosh, Bing, I don't...I've been thinking this over. Maybe... maybe I better get Gloria some kitchenware.

CROSBY: No, no, you...you got a great idea, stick with it. Here's the shop right here — Fifi's Florescent Flimsies, Ltd. Very limited. Let's go in.

STEWART: Well, gee, just looking in the window's frightening. I'm scared...let's walk around the block again and think this over, huh.

CROSBY: We walk by here once more, they'll think we're picketing the joint. Come on, Jim.

VONN: Good afternoon, gentlemen, can I help you?

STEWART: Ah...ah...yes...ah...may my friend and I have a glass of water?

CROSBY: Oh come on, speak up.

STEWART: Bing, this is a girl.

CROSBY: Well, who'd you expect to wait on you, Baron Leoni or somebody?

STEWART: Do you have any gloves, Miss?

CROSBY: Gloves, nothing, show us some florescent flimsies.

STEWART: Bing. Bing.

CROSBY: Come on.

VONN: Very well, would you like to see something in a slip?

STEWART: Well, I'd like to see a slip, but I think it should be empty.

VONN: Here's a very nice imported slip. Are you sure you wouldn't like it modeled?

CROSBY: No, no. My friend's very bashful. You just give it to me, I'll try it on. Well…oh here we are…there we are. What do you think, Jim?

STEWART: Well, I…I…I think it's terrific.

CROSBY: It is beautiful, isn't it?

VONN: Well, it's none of my business, but I don't think it does anything for you.

CROSBY: He's not buying it for me; I'm the technical advisor on this deal.

STEWART: Now, you see, Miss, I'm trying to get a Christmas present for my wife.

VONN: Oh, you're married.

CROSBY: That goes for me, too.

VONN: Well, then, perhaps you would like one of these Malibu bed jackets.

STEWART: Gee, that is nice and fluffy, isn't it? Try that one on, Bing.

CROSBY: Oh…oh, these feathers tickle, Jim. I put one more thing on; I'll get an offer from John Robert Powers here.

VONN: Here's a novelty this year, fancy garters like the French Can-Can dancers wear.

CROSBY: Oh, toss me a couple of those, I need some sleeve holders.

VONN: And here's another new item this season…they're called waist cinchers.

CROSBY: Oh, these are very good.

STEWART: They are?

CROSBY: Yes.

VONN: They're little half corsets; give madam a very slim waist line.

STEWART: No, no, that's not fancy enough.

VONN: Well, then, how about a negligee?

STEWART: Oh, my gosh.

VONN: I know, how about some mules?

STEWART: Ah…no, we got a dog and a cat. I don't think we need…

VONN: Perhaps your wife would like a nice taffeta petticoat.

STEWART: Well, yeah, that might be…oh quick…quick, Bing, duck down behind the counter.

CROSBY: What's the matter? What's the matter?

STEWART: Quick, duck down here.

CROSBY: What's wrong?

STEWART: Boy, that was a close one.
CROSBY: What happened?
STEWART: Louella was looking in the window.
CROSBY: She'll never recognize me with all these fancy duds on.
STEWART: Yeah, I know, but she's liable to think I have a date with Mae West.
CROSBY: Ah…I don't look that good.
VONN: If you gentlemen will get up off the floor, I'd like to show you something I think would make a lovely gift.
STEWART: Well, what's that?
VONN: This is a new perfume from Paris. It's called Good Night Irene.
STEWART: Well, that's…ah…that's fine. I'll take a pint of that.
CROSBY: No…no, wait a minute, whoa. If that's the stuff I think it is, don't even pop the cork, Jim.
STEWART: What's wrong, Bing? Why can't I buy some of this perfume?
CROSBY: It's dynamite, Jim…that stuff's dynamite. One whiff of that and you'd go shopping alone.
STEWART: Humm…well, I think I might take that taffeta petticoat. Will you wrap it as a gift please, Miss?
CROSBY: We can pick it up later, Jim. Let's get to the broadcast, huh.
STEWART: Okay.
VONN: Just a minute, please.
CROSBY: What's wrong?
VONN: Will you please take off that slip, those garters and that bed jacket?
CROSBY: Oh…pardon me…here you are, Miss. I'm really very sorry. I forgot I had this stuff on. Help me off with this slip, will ya, pal?
STEWART: Ah…get out the way you got in.
CROSBY: Well, I'll make it myself then. Here you are. Goodbye, Miss.
VONN: Goodbye…and I'll thank you also to take off that waist cincher.
STEWART: That he came in with.
VONN: Oh, pardon me.
CROSBY: Well, I'll never come here again.

Bing sings the *Sound Off for Chesterfield* song, after which Jimmy says, "Well, you sold me, Bing."

The final song of the show is then sung by Bing and Anna Maria Alberghetti.

"America the Beautiful"

After the song, Bing and Jimmy have one more short discussion.

CROSBY: ...our thanks also to Jimmy Stewart for joining us this evening.

STEWART: Oh, I enjoyed it, Bing. I'm a little worried about my shopping, though. Do you think maybe I should have bought a camisole?

CROSBY: If you wanna send something to Grandma Moses, it'll be nice. Jimmy, will you give my best to Gloria and the kids?

STEWART: I sure will, Bing.

Jimmy and Bing's Christmas shopping is not over. On December 5, four weeks later, Jimmy would again be Bing's guest and the two of them will make a return trip to Fifi's Florescent Flimsies.

In 2011, this show was released in mp3 only format on *Jimmy Stewart the Ultimate Radio Collection Vol.1* (Master Classics Records).

(4) Wednesday, December 5, 1951 (9:30-10 p.m.) (Transcribed November 28, 1951)

Bing and Ken Carpenter open the show with a short comedy routine involving remodeling work at Bob Hope's house, and then Bing performs two numbers, separated by a Chesterfield commercial.

"Over a Bottle of Wine" (with the Rhythmaires)

"Domino" (with the Rhythmaires)

Bing's other guest for the show, Toni Arden, is then introduced and sings her song.

"Once"

Next, Bing introduces Stewart and their skit begins. Veola Vonn also appears as Fifi.

CROSBY: Now, ladies and gentlemen, I'm very happy to present an old friend of mine, the very fine actor, Mr. Jimmy Stewart.

STEWART: Thank you, thank you, Bing.

CROSBY: Well, Jim, how is Gloria and how are the twins?

STEWART: Ah, they're just fine, Bing...they're just fine. I'm a wreck, yeah.

CROSBY: What's wrong?

STEWART: Well, Bing, you remember a couple of weeks ago you went Christmas shopping with me and we bought Gloria a present?

CROSBY: Remember? Huh, I'm glad that's over.

STEWART: Well, it isn't. We gotta go again.

CROSBY: Not we...not we, old boy. I took you to that little French dress shop next door and I helped you select a beautiful petticoat. What's... what's...what's...

STEWART: Yeah, but I found out that Gloria has one exactly like it.

CROSBY: You sure, Jimmy?

STEWART: I'm absolutely sure, yes. The other morning I was peeking in the window…I mean…I…I…the other morning I was peeking in the window of the Bendix. [In less than a year, General Electric would be Bing's new sponsor and Bendix would never stand a chance of being mentioned again.]

CROSBY: Oh, the Bendix.

STEWART: …and I…there it was.

CROSBY: What?

STEWART: Well, just spinning around there, the same darn petticoat.

CROSBY: This is a blow. It's tough luck, Jim. But, I'll tell you, all you gotta do is you take the petticoat, you go back to Fifi's lingerie shop and you exchange it for something else.

STEWART: Yeah, that's just what I've been trying to do since 9 o'clock this morning.

CROSBY: Since 9 o'clock this morning?

STEWART: Yeah, every time I start into Fifi's place, I lose my nerve and wind up in the drugstore next door.

CROSBY: Jimmy, you gotta get a hold of yourself.

STEWART: So far today, I've had 12 cups of Ovaltine and six bacon and tomato sandwiches. And, I was spoken to twice for loitering in the magazine counter.

CROSBY: Buddy, I was in the drugstore earlier today. Funny, I didn't see you.

STEWART: Yeah, well that may have been when the woman was demonstrating the mud pack on me. She came over and…

CROSBY: Oh, what you won't go through to stall. I noticed you were carrying a lot of bundles when you walked in here tonight, too.

STEWART: Yeah, well one of those packages was the petticoat and the rest of the stuff I picked up in the drugstore.

CROSBY: Get any bargains?

STEWART: Yes, yes, I got a nice alarm clock and a canasta shuffler…

CROSBY: I must get one of those.

STEWART: A mahjong set…

CROSBY: Mahjong set, huh?

STEWART: Yes…half a bushel of assorted nuts.

CROSBY: Say, Jim, your Christmas shopping's about done.

STEWART: You know, Bing, I…I…I just think this whole mess I'm in is…is just fate.

CROSBY: What are you getting at?

STEWART: Well, you know, when we talked about the gift originally, my whole idea was to get Gloria something that was daring, something intimate, you know. Well, the petticoat, it…it…the petticoat just doesn't cut the buck.

CROSBY: Well, Jim, come here…well, wait a minute…there's plenty of daring stuff over there in Fifi's shop. You had your chance.

STEWART: Yeah, same thing happened last year. Last year I was gonna give Gloria a sweater.

CROSBY: A sweater?

STEWART: Um…hum, at the last minute I got cold feet.

CROSBY: What happened?

STEWART: I gave her yarn and knitting needles.

CROSBY: I'll bet she's been needling you all year, too, huh?

STEWART: Now this year it's gonna be different.

CROSBY: What are you gonna do?

STEWART: Well, when Gloria opens her present for Christmas this year, she's gonna get the shock of her life.

CROSBY: Now wait a minute, take it easy, Jim.

STEWART: No sir…no sir.

CROSBY: You're going to pop.

STEWART: I'm through with this old-fashioned stuff. I'm gonna take the bull by the horns.

CROSBY: That a boy, Jim. Now you're workin' in there, Jim.

STEWART: I'm gonna take the petticoat right over to Fifi's Florescent Flimsies shop and you're gonna exchange it for something bewitching.

CROSBY: I'm in again, huh? Well, off we go.

(The orchestra plays a bit of The Air Force Song *while the scene changes.)*

CROSBY: Here, Jim, let me take some of those packages, huh.

STEWART: Ah here, you take the petticoat and the canasta shuffler. I can carry the alarm clock and the mahjong set and the assorted nuts.

CROSBY: Okay. Well, here's…here's Fifi's place. After you, Jim.

STEWART: Eh…I…Bing, I…I have an idea, Bing. You go in and exchange the petticoat…I gotta drop into the drugstore.

CROSBY: Oh no, no…come back here.

STEWART: No, no, look, there's a sign there — special, nut crackers, 59 cents.

CROSBY: Well, you get one later. Here we go…here we go again at Fifi's, Now, no stalling this time, you hear me, Jim?

STEWART: Yeah…gosh, the minute I get inside here and see all those thing hangin' around, everything goes black.

CROSBY: There's a lot of black things hangin' around here.

STEWART: Golly, what will they think of next?

CROSBY: I don't know, but I hope I'm not with you when they do.

VONN: (This time playing shop owner, Fifi, and using a very think French accent) Ah, bon jour gentlemen, Entrée s'il vous plais.

STEWART: I'll bet this is Fifi.

CROSBY: Well, it sure ain't Barry Fitzgerald, I'll tell you. Now, no hemming and hawing, Jim, just tell the lady your problem.

VONN: May I help you gentlemen?

STEWART: Eh…I…I…I…I…yes…eh, yes…eh…I wonder if you can tell us how to get to Knott's Berry Farm.

VONN: Knott's? Knott's? They…they have Knott's crackers next door.

CROSBY: We know all about that.

STEWART: You know, Miss, my friend and I were in here a couple of weeks ago and we bought a fancy petticoat.

VONN: Oh, and you are back so soon…oh…oh…you are the playboy from Texas, yes?

STEWART: Oh, oh gosh…oh heck no, you see I bought a petticoat for my wife and…

VONN: Oh, you are married…ah…that is too bad.

STEWART: Why…why's that?

VONN: I am not. Oh, but…

CROSBY: Don't look at me, I'm cooked, too.

VONN: C'est la vie.

CROSBY: …you see, my friend bought this petticoat here for his wife and she has one just like it, so he wants to exchange it.

VONN: Oh, then perhaps you would like a petticoat like this chic one I am wearing…Ah, look at this. Voila.

STEWART: Oh my gosh. (sound effects of nuts falling to the floor) Would anyone care for an English walnut?

CROSBY: There's a hole in that bag, Jim, hold it up.

STEWART: No, Miss, no, I don't want you to get the wrong idea about this thing. I'm married and well I…I thought I might get something more dazzling than a petticoat.

VONN: Oh, I see, something…well, step over here. I have so many attractive things. Oo-la-la, look at these.

STEWART: Hey.

VONN: Oo-la-la, they are beautiful and they come in pale blue, pink and green.

CROSBY: They aren't bad, Jim, just grab one. You can't go wrong with these.

VONN: And the lace is imported.

CROSBY: Got good rubber in them, too.

VONN: Ah, monsieur makes the joke.

CROSBY: Oui, oui, oui, oui.

STEWART: We, we, we, we, gotta go to something else.

VONN: But...but monsieur.

STEWART: I...I think I just better get a nice pair of stockings.

VONN: Stocking...what kind?

STEWART: For the legs, you...

VONN: Oh, you make the joke, too.

STEWART: Oui, oui.

CROSBY: Jim, listen, you gotta go stronger than stockings, come on, live.

VONN: Oh, I know what you can get for madam. It's called the wrap-around.

STEWART: The wrap-around, what is it?

VONN: Well, you see, it's...it's an oversized towel that's shaped and fitted.

CROSBY: Look at that.

VONN: I'll slip it on. See, it buttons up in a wink.

STEWART: Now, ah...what...that garment there...now what...what do you use that thing for?

VONN: Well, if the phone rings when madam is in the bathtub, she can slip on one of these.

CROSBY: I usually slip on the soap.

VONN: Well, here's something else that madam might like. It's the very latest French bathing suit...two pieces.

CROSBY: Oh, itsy bitsy pieces, too.

VONN: And look, it folds up and fits into this little gold locket.

STEWART: Well, I never...look at that.

VONN: You see, when madam wears this bathing suit, she can also wear the little locket around her neck.

CROSBY: She better wear the locket or she'll get arrested.

VONN: Ah-ha, ho-ho-ho-ho, you make another joke.

CROSBY: Joke nothin', I can hear the police wagon now.

VONN: Would you gentlemen like me to model this bathing suit? I can slip in on if you like.

(Jimmy's alarm clock goes off)
CROSBY: Come on, shove it back in the locket. Here comes the cops.
VONN: The cops.
STEWART: I must have hit the button on my alarm clock here.
CROSBY: Come on, Jim, now make up your mind. I'm in a rush. I gotta get back to work.
VONN: Work? Oh, that's the trouble with you Americans. All you think about is business. A Frenchman, he says poof on business, poof on work, a Frenchman says poof on everything but love. That is why all Frenchmen are so…so, oh what is the word?
CROSBY: Poof.
VONN: Oh ho-ho.
CROSBY: All right, Jim, now what'll it be? There are any number of things here. You made up your mind?
STEWART: Well, I've been thinkin' the whole thing over and I think maybe the thing I oughta get is a nice pair of bloomers.
VONN: Bloomers? What is bloomers?
CROSBY: You wouldn't know.
VONN: But bloomers, I do not understand.
STEWART: Well, you see…you see, Miss, they're something like these things here, only they're about three feet longer.
VONN: Oh, you mean the slacks.
STEWART: No, bloomers. No, they're sort of slipcovers for girls.
VONN: Slipcovers?
CROSBY: I…I don't think you'd know about bloomers, Fifi. They go back quite a ways.
STEWART: Bing.
CROSBY: Hum?
STEWART: Look at that girl coming out of the back room there.
CROSBY: Holy Toledo!
VONN: Oh, that is Mimi, my model. And look, she is wearing the new French bathing suit and the little locket.
CROSBY: *(motorcycle sound effects)* So long, Jim.
STEWART: No, No, wait for me. *(Alarm clock goes off again)*
CROSBY: What about…what about the gift for Gloria?
STEWART: She's gonna get the mahjong set.
CROSBY: Okay.

As the applause dies down, Bing comes back with:

CROSBY: Hey, what say we sound off for Chesterfield? You better give me a hand on this, Jimmy, 'cause we got a real great part for you. Now I'll tell you when…I'll just bring my hand down when you come in.
STEWART: Sure, you start, Bing.

(Bing sings "Sound Off for Chesterfield" song)
At the end, after Bing sings "do it," he points to Jimmy who adds "today!"
Bing sings one more song before the end of the show.
"Never Before"
We hear from Jimmy again at the end of the show.

STEWART: Bing, I'm sorry I got you into all that trouble.
CROSBY: Boy, that was some bathing suit, isn't it?
STEWART: Yeah, I only got as far as the locket.
CROSBY: You gotta be quick.
STEWART: Who's gonna be with you next week, Bing?

Bing gives the guests for the following week and ends his part of the show.

(5) Wednesday, March 19, 1952 (9:30-10 p.m.) (Transcribed at the Plaza Theater in Palm Springs, March 6, 1952)
Bing's number to open tonight's show is:
"It Had To Be You" (with Red Nichols on cornet)
After a commercial, Fran Warren, Bing's other guest for this show, sings her number.
"I Hear a Rhapsody"
Bing then introduces Jimmy and their sketch begins. Others in the sketch were Jerry Hausner as Little White Cloud, Viola Vonn as Mabel and Fran Warren as Agnes.

CROSBY: Now ankling in is an old pal of mine. He's one of our most popular and prominent picture actors. As a matter of fact, this tall, lanky gent has been starred in some of the greatest pictures to come out of Hollywood. He's got a darn good Technicolor one out now, a picture called *Bend of the River*. Ladies and gentlemen, here's Jimmy Stewart.
STEWART: Thank you, thank you, Bing.
CROSBY: Jim, it's nice to see you down here. Where are you living in Palm Springs?
STEWART: Well, I'm at a very swanky place.

CROSBY: Oh you are, where are you bivouacked — La Paz, Biltmore, Horace Heidt's Lone Palm?

STEWART: No, I'm staying at…ah…Konky Konkrites Kozy Kactus Kourt.

CROSBY: Spells the whole thing with k's, I'll bet. Where's this place located, Jim? I don't recall it.

STEWART: Oh, it's way out there in the desert.

CROSBY: Oh yeah, they got a swimming pool there?

STEWART: No, but they dug the hole.

CROSBY: Well, why don't they put the water in it?

STEWART: Well, they do…the wind keeps blowing it out.

CROSBY: Well, Jim, the wind is just gonna blow way out there in the desert, not in town, mind you, but out in the desert it's gonna blow.

STEWART: Oh, I…

CROSBY: Well, Jim, if you really want to dunk the body or go for a swim, come over to my place. Drop by, huh?

STEWART: Well, I can't go swimming, Bing.

CROSBY: Why not?

STEWART: Well, I forgot to bring the top piece to my bathing suit.

CROSBY: Get out. No one wears a top piece down here.

STEWART: No one?

CROSBY: No…no

STEWART: I…I've gotta get outta here.

CROSBY: I mean the men don't. Course, that nearly goes for the women, I guess.

STEWART: Well, then I'm not goin' swimmin'.

CROSBY: Oh, Jim, now, you gotta go swimming to enjoy Palm Springs. You gotta take in all the outdoor sports…Listen, how about puttin' on a pair of shorts and we'll have a game of tennis.

STEWART: Golly, isn't there anything you can do in this town with your clothes on?

CROSBY: Jimmy, everybody comes here to soak up some sun.

STEWART: Yeah, I was in the Chi Chi bar last night…that wasn't sun they were soakin' up.

CROSBY: Oh…ha…you were at the Chi Chi. Did you see Sally Rand do her fan dance?

STEWART: No, not me. The minute I saw those ostrich feathers, I ran outside and stuck my head in the sand.

CROSBY: Oh, you're the shyest guy I've ever seen. Have you always been so bashful?

STEWART: No…no, Bing. As a matter of fact, I…ah…I…I wasn't the least bit bashful until I got to be about eight years old. I…

CROSBY: What happened then?

STEWART: Well, I was out in the yard lookin' at the birds and got stung by a bee. And so I started to ask questions.

CROSBY: And you were bitterly disillusioned. Now, look here, Jim, I just got to get you outside in the sun. I gotta get you out in the air…it's wonderful. How about goin' for a horseback ride?

STEWART: Well, I did an awful lot of horseback ridin' in *Bend of the River*.

CROSBY: Oh, what a thrilling picture that was, Jimmy. Gee, that scene where you crawl through the brush and you wipe out all those Indians, boy, that was really something.

STEWART: Yeah.

CROSBY: I never figured you for such a rugged fella.

STEWART: Well, with my clothes on I'm pretty brave.

CROSBY: Hey, what kind of Indians were those you had in the picture, Jim? I wanted to ask you.

STEWART: They were the Shoshoni.

CROSBY: Dagnabit, I thought I recognized them.

STEWART: You did?

CROSBY: Sure, I'm a member of the Shoshoni Piute tribe up in Nevada.

STEWART: Oh really? I didn't know that.

CROSBY: Yeah, my name is Chief Running Deer. I'm very close to those Shoshoni up in Oregon.

STEWART: Yes, I know.

CROSBY: What'a mean?

STEWART: Well, I got shot in the hip with an arrow that had Bing Crosby Enterprises stamped on it.

CROSBY: Well, of course, all the Shoshoni, they do a lot of trading among one another. As a matter of fact, there's no business like Shoshoni business.

STEWART: Well, Bing, I…I (sneezes) excuse me, I'm sorry, excuse me.

CROSBY: Jimmy, what did you do?

STEWART: Well, I didn't do anything. I just sneezed, I'm sorry.

CROSBY: Never…never do that in Palm Springs. Man, that could lead to a jail sentence.

STEWART: Why is that? Why is…

CROSBY: Well, this is a desert resort. It's against the law to have a cold around here.

STEWART: Oh, is that a fact?

CROSBY: Yes, this is very, very serious. You know a fellow sneezed in the racket club a few years ago and Charlie Farrell's hair turned snow white.

STEWART: Now...well...I'm very sorry (another sneeze).

CROSBY: Jimmy, watch it now, will ya. If the Chamber of Commerce hears about this, they'll ride you out of town on a four-way cold tablet.

STEWART: Maybe it's an allergy. Maybe I'm allergic to ostrich feathers.

CROSBY: Yes...no, you've just got a cold, Jim, and you know what I'm gonna do for it?

STEWART: What?

CROSBY: I'm gonna cure it.

STEWART: How's that?

CROSBY: You need the healing waters...a mineral bath. I'm gonna take you over to the Indian hot springs right across the street here. That hot water and that mud'll knock your cold in a jiffy.

STEWART: Are you sure about that, Bing?

CROSBY: Certainly...these baths are sensational and they're only right across the street here, just take a mo...come on, we gotta get outside.

STEWART: I don't know, Bing...

CROSBY: Come on...come on along now...come on...

STEWART: Now every time I go someplace with you, I get into trouble.

CROSBY: How can anyone get in trouble takin' a bath?

STEWART: Well, look what happened to Lili St. Cyr.

CROSBY: That's nothin' like this. Now come on.

STEWART: Okay.

CROSBY: Well, here we are, Jim. Here we are, Jim. Here's the famous Indian baths, the oldest historic spot in Palm Springs. Did you know that? The water in those baths boils from the depths of the Earth at 60 gallons per minute. Boy, this will really take the weight off you, Jim.

STEWART: I have no weight. If I lose anything, it'll have to be skin.

CROSBY: Well, you'll get puckered up. I'll guarantee you that. Oh... oh, there's...her now...her now. Well, there's the Indian. He must be the fella in charge here. Now just let me do the talkin', Jim.

STEWART: Okay, you go ahead. The only Indian words I know are 'how' and 'ugh.' I...

CROSBY: Well, your accent's bad. I'll handle it here. Now, how, me Shoshoni Piute. Me Running Deer.

HAUSNER: Me Little White Cloud.

CROSBY: Well, Chief. I'll tell you what we're going to do. We're gonna step inside…we're gonna step inside and take our baths. Now, if you'll pardon us…

HAUSNER: Okay, you like'um sailboat to play with?

CROSBY: No, no, no, we don't want no sailboat.

STEWART: Okay, let's go in.

CROSBY: Oh, now wait, that's the ladies side.

STEWART: I told you…I told you, you always get me in trouble.

CROSBY: Nothing happened, you never got hurt. Now come on, come on in.

STEWART: Gosh, look at that thing boil.

CROSBY: Course, Jim, that's a natural hot spring. Come on now, peel off your clothes and get in there. Last one in's a rotten egg.

STEWART: You know, it kind of smells like rotten eggs in here.

CROSBY: Oh, that's just the sulfur and the minerals. Soon as I get this off now, I'll be all set.

STEWART: Gee whiz, Bing, you sure are the dude.

CROSBY: What do you mean, a dude?

STEWART: Wearing a money belt with garters.

CROSBY: Well, thanks…thanks for calling it a money belt. Come on, Jim…this is one of the best laughin' bands we've ever had down here…come on, Jim, now help me off with this thing, will ya?

STEWART: Okay.

CROSBY: Well, that feels better.

STEWART: Say, they leave marks, don't they?

CROSBY: They sure do. Jim, what's that mark on your hip there? What is that, a tattoo?

STEWART: No, that's where I got shot with the arrow.

CROSBY: Well, Crosby Enterprises arrows leave fancy marks. Well, I guess I'll jump in.

STEWART: Mud's pretty thick…suppose we get stuck in there?

CROSBY: I belong to the Auto Club. We get stuck, they'll tow us out.

STEWART: Okay, here I go.

CROSBY: I'm right with you. Ah…man…isn't this living, Jim?

STEWART: Oh yeah, this is…holy smoke, Bing, you know what?

CROSBY: What?

STEWART: We forgot to lock the door.

CROSBY: What are you worrying about? We're in mud up to our necks.

STEWART: Oops.

HAUSNER: How.

CROSBY: How he says.

HAUSNER: You like to cook'um hot dogs in mud while you take'um bath?

CROSBY: Ah...no, no, I'm not hungry.

HAUSNER: Me cookin' pot roast in there right now.

CROSBY: Pot roast? You know something...I think I'm sittin' on it.

HAUSNER: Good now you Chief Sitting on Bull.

CROSBY: By golly, White Cloud, that's a crackerjack.

HAUSNER: Ugh. Hey, where big Chief Arrow in Bottom go?

CROSBY: Wait...I'll be darned; I guess he ducked under the mud when you came in. I...

HAUSNER: Okay, me leave.

CROSBY: Goodbye. Now I gotta get...gotta pull Jimmy outta here. Oops, no, that's the pot roast. Wait a minute now, this must be Jimmy. It's either him or somebody threw a golf club in here...one or the other. Up you come, Jimmy...up we go...here we come.

STEWART: Golly, Bing, you know there's a catfish down there a foot long.

CROSBY: I thought I felt something gumming my toe.

STEWART: Bing...

CROSBY: I'll be darn.

STEWART: Bing...I...I...you know...I wish you'd locked the door.

CROSBY: Well, you don't have to duck every time someone comes in here. Now lay back, relax, cure your cold.

STEWART: Okay...okay.

CROSBY: Oh, there he goes again. Now come up outta there, Jim.

STEWART: All clear.

CROSBY: Relax, will ya. Take it easy and relax.

WARREN: Gosh, Mabel, that water looks hot.

VONN: Oh, you'll just love it, Agnes.

STEWART: Gosh, Bing, it's girls.

CROSBY: Yes, but they're on the other side of the wall. We're in the men's side...they're on the women's side.

WARREN: Well as soon as I get this off, I'll be all set.

STEWART: Gosh, do girls wear those, too?

WARREN: Oh boy, that feels good.

CROSBY: Don't I know it, deary.

VONN: Help me with mine, Agnes.

WARREN: Okay.

VONN: Come on, Agnes, let's go.

STEWART: I'm getting' outta here.
CROSBY: Now don't be silly, we've got as much right here as they have.
VONN: Oh my gosh, Agnes, men.
WARREN: Oh, yoo hoo.
VONN: Agnes.
STEWART: Did you hear that, Bing? Did you hear that?
CROSBY: Oh, we're safe…we're safe, Jimmy. Now take it easy, relax, enjoy your bath, cure your cold. This mud is money, boy.
STEWART: Hey, Bing, what…what…what was that…ah…what was that mud song you used to sing all the time?
CROSBY: Mud song? Oh…ah…mmm…

At this point, Bing breaks in "Mississippi Mud," joined by Jimmy and Fran Warren.
"Mississippi Mud" — Bing, Jimmy and Fran
Bing's final song for the evening is:
"Tell Me Why" (with the Rhythmaires)

The General Electric Show
Bing's final 30-minute network shows were sponsored by General Electric and aired from October 9, 1952 until July 2, 1953. The show also made the move from Wednesday to Thursday nights. Unless otherwise noted, all shows were transcribed in Hollywood. The credits for *The General Electric Show* included:
NETWORK: CBS
SPONSOR: General Electric
PRODUCERS: Bill Morrow and Murdo MacKenzie
MUSIC: John Scott Trotter Orchestra
MUSICAL GROUP: Jud Conlon's Rhythmaires
ANNOUNCER: Ken Carpenter
THEME SONG: "Where the Blue of the Night" (Fred Ahlert/Roy Turk/Bing Crosby)
SHOWS FEATURING JIMMY STEWART:

(1) Thursday, October 23, 1952 (9:30-10 p.m.) (Transcribed September 6, 1952)
The show opens with Bing and Ken doing a short comedy routine about National Popcorn Week. Bing follows this up with two songs.
"Feet Up!" *(Pat Him On the Po-Po)* (with the Rhythmaires) (Jimmy Stewart and Bing later get a couple of big laughs by saying "po-po.")

"Wish You Were Here"

After the songs, Bing introduces Jimmy and they proceed into tonight's skit. Veola Vonn plays the part of the salesgirl.

CROSBY: Well sir, guest time is here. Yes sir, it would be tough, I guess, to find a more charming, a more welcome visitor than the lanky lad who is now approaching the microphone. Ladies and gentlemen, here's Mr. Jimmy Stewart.
STEWART: Hi, Bing.
CROSBY: Hi, Jimmy.
STEWART: Hi, Bing, what are you doing back in Hollywood at work? Why, did someone steal your fishing rod?
CROSBY: No, I sneaked into town to buy me a new Lucky Louie lure and General Electric snagged me and put me to work here, Jim.
STEWART: General Electric?
CROSBY: Um...hum.
STEWART: Oh...oh yes, that's the subsidiary of Bing Crosby Enterprises, isn't it?
CROSBY: Well, if it was, I'd still be fishin'. But enough of this fly dialogue, Jim. Whenever you come to see me it seems like you always have a problem...a major problem. I'll bet you have something worrying you now, what is it?
STEWART: Yes, Yes, Bing, I do have a problem.
CROSBY: Well, let's have it. Out with it.
STEWART: Well Gloria and the kids and I rented a place down at the beach and...ah...that...that sea air is awful chilly at night, Bing.
CROSBY: Jim, I'm sorry, but there's nothing I can do about sea air.
STEWART: I know that, but now that you're working for General Electric, I thought maybe you might help me get one of their electric blankets.
CROSBY: Listen, Jim, all you gotta do is go to a G.E. dealer, buy yourself a blanket.
STEWART: Ah...ah...oh...I...I kind of thought maybe you'd like to go with me, Bing. You know you're new with the company; you'd get credit for the sale.
CROSBY: That's an idea...that's nice...that's sweet. Now I've snagged a customer, I'm a cinch for a gold star in my...in my order book after that. I wonder where the closest G.E. dealer is, Jim.
STEWART: Oh well, there's a terrific store right around...right around the corner here on Hollywood Boulevard.

CROSBY: Yeah.

STEWART: Yeah, they've got everything there. I've been there five times this afternoon.

CROSBY: You've been there five times? Well, why didn't you buy the blanket?

STEWART: Well, every time I walked in there, a girl came up to wait on me.

CROSBY: So?

STEWART: And now I own three electric ranges, an all electric kitchen, several automatic washers, but I'll be darn if I'm gonna buy an unmentionable from a girl.

CROSBY: Oh, Jimmy, an un...a blanket isn't an unmentionable.

STEWART: Well, maybe not to a man of the world like you.

CROSBY: Well, Jim, if you feel that way, then I'll go with you. I'll...I'll help you buy the blanket. That way if a scandal develops, I shall share your shame.

STEWART: Yeah, well, thanks...

CROSBY: Come on now, Jim, steel your nerves, let's go.

(short bit of scene changing music from John Scott Trotter)

CROSBY: Well, here we are, Jim, here's the G.E. dealer.

STEWART: Yeah, it's a nice window display, too, isn't it?

CROSBY: Yeah, it's very pretty, but I must speak to the manager. My picture should be in the window there.

STEWART: Oh yeah.

CROSBY: Well, entrée, Jim, in you go now and ask that girl for an electric blanket. Just go right ahead.

STEWART: Ah...yeah...I...

CROSBY: Now, remember, electric blanket. Nothing else...

STEWART: Yeah...I...I...I want an electric blanket, I want an electric blanket, I want an electric blanket.

VONN: Well, what now?

STEWART: Eh...eh...I...would you mind showing me an electric eel?

VONN: An electric eel?

STEWART: (gulp sound effect) Pardon me. Every time I get excited, my Adam's apple pops like that. Bing, are you here?

CROSBY: I'm right beside you, Jim, now be a brave boy.

STEWART: Now, if you'll just wrap up that eel, Miss, I'll get goin' here.

VONN: Say, this is the sixth time you've been in today, have you got a crush on me?

STEWART: (Gulp sound effect)

CROSBY: No…no, he's…ah…he's just a little excited, Miss, what he really wants to buy is an electric blanket.

VONN: Oh, well, then step right in here.

CROSBY: Very well. (crunching sound effect) Hey, Jim, what are you chewin' on? Those pills? What are they…what are those pills you're takin'? What are they?

STEWART: Dramamine, I'm gettin' dizzy.

CROSBY: Oh, what you need's a good pat on your po-po.

VONN: Now, will you gentlemen step in here to the bedroom?

STEWART: The bed…bedroom.

CROSBY: Go…go ahead, Jim, I'm with ya.

VONN: This is a model bedroom we have to show young married couples our blankets and other appliances.

STEWART: Oh…oh.

VONN: That blanket on the bed is ash rose. It also comes in gray-green and blue bonnet.

STEWART: I kinda like that ash rose there.

VONN: There you go, sir.

CROSBY: Should do a lot for you, yes.

VONN: I'll have one of those wrapped for you.

STEWART: Now, just a minute, just a minute. I don't want to get rushed into this thing here. Now, I think maybe I ought to try it out before I buy it.

CROSBY: What are you talk…what's there to try out? You plug it in, you get under it, you set the temperature control and there you are.

STEWART: Never mind…never mind. Is it okay if I try it, Miss?

VONN: Please do. Of course, you can't get into bed with your clothes on.

STEWART: (Gulp sound effect)

CROSBY: Hey…old Adam's apple's gettin' a work out today.

VONN: Now, if you'll just go over there to the dresser, you'll find pajamas. You can change behind that screen.

STEWART: Ah…thank you. Now just one more thing. I'm getting this blanket for two people. Now, how will I know that it works double?

VONN: Well, don't look at me.

STEWART: Eh…you see, Miss, I'm married to a girl. Just a minute here, I've got my marriage license right here somewhere…

CROSBY: Oh, never mind that. Get on your pajamas now and get into bed.

STEWART: Well, what'll I do for a partner?

VONN: Oh yes.

STEWART: Say, Bing.
CROSBY: Oh no…no…no.
VONN: Oh, go ahead, pretend you're his wife.
CROSBY: Well, all right. What I won't do to get a gold star in my order book.
VONN: You'll find sleeping garments there in the dresser.
STEWART: Hey…oh, these look all right. I'll just take this pair of blue pajamas.
VONN: Just a moment, sir, why are you pawing around in that drawer?
CROSBY: I'm looking for more pajamas. All I can find in here are pink nighties.
VONN: Oh, I'm sorry, all we have is one pair of pajamas. Why don't you slip into one of the nighties?
CROSBY: (Gulp sound effect) Now I'm doin' it.
STEWART: Come on, Bing, we'll get behind the screen and change here.
CROSBY: I'm with you. (singing) Take away my undershirt, dear, and there's nothing there but skin.
STEWART: Say, Bing, what's that string tied around your big toe there?
CROSBY: Oh, that, that's to remind me to put on socks.
STEWART: But where are your socks?
CROSBY: Oh, the string's warm enough.
STEWART: Oh gosh, you know these pajamas fit me perfectly.
CROSBY: Oh goody. Say, help me on with my nightie, it's caught on my ears here.
STEWART: Oh, is it? Yeah, yeah…here you go. Gee, Bing, you look like Ray Bolger.
CROSBY: I feel like Rita Hayworth in *Affair in Trinidad*. Let's hit the sack Jack.
STEWART: Okay. Well, no, Bing, no. I always take that side. You… that's…you take Gloria's side here. Say…ah…Miss, how do you work this thing now?
VONN: Tell me, sir, do you sleep on your right side, your left side, or on your tummy?
STEWART: On my po-po.
VONN: Well sir, just get under the blanket. Now, you each have an individual temperature control. Just turn the dial to any temperature you desire.
STEWART: Oh, thank you. Hey, this is all right.
CROSBY: Yes, really comfy, isn't it?

STEWART: Say, Miss, these lights are awfully bright in here, wonder if we could turn 'em out.

VONN: Of course not. Those lights are to show our display.

CROSBY: Close your eyes, Jimmy. Now come on, we'll test the blanket here.

STEWART: Okay, Gloria…ah…Bing.

CROSBY: Call me Gloria if you feel more comfortable.

STEWART: I…I think I'll set my dial here. (tapping sound effects) Pilot to navigator, switch on.

CROSBY: Navigator to pilot, switch on.

STEWART: Contact.

CROSBY: Contact. Say, this is fun.

VONN: Gentlemen, please. You'll never get the right feel of this blanket by playing around with it. Now just pretend you're a young married couple, engage yourself in some chit-chat, and the first thing you know the gentle heat from the blanket will waft you off to dreamland.

CROSBY: Hum…okay, I'll be the missus. Did you have a heavy day at the office, dear?

STEWART: Oh yes. You know we're taking inventory. You know what that means.

CROSBY: How's it going?

STEWART: Mmm…mmm. Up to closing time tonight we were short four paperclips and $12,000 in petty cash.

CROSBY: Well, it'll show up somewhere. Probably in your expense account.

STEWART: Yeah, yeah.

CROSBY: Good night, dear.

STEWART: Good night.

CROSBY: I wish I had a glass of water.

STEWART: I wish you did, too. Good night.

CROSBY: When we were just married, you used to leap out of bed and get me some water.

STEWART: Good night.

CROSBY: Did you put out the cat?

STEWART: What cat?

CROSBY: Meow…that cat.

STEWART: I guess not. Good night.

CROSBY: I think I'll turn my side of the blanket up a little.

STEWART: Must you play with that?

CROSBY: Well, I'm restless; I just don't feel like sleeping.

STEWART: Well, why don't you walk up to Lake Arrowhead and get a glass of water. Meow…and take that cat with you. Good night.

CROSBY: Oh, I have a good notion to tear off my blanket and go home to mother.

STEWART: Well go ahead, rip it off.

VONN: Now gentlemen, gentlemen, please don't tear the blanket.

CROSBY: Oh pardon…pardon, we just got carried away here.

STEWART: Yeah, this blanket is terrific, Miss; I'll take one of these.

VONN: Oh, good, here's one just like the demonstrator all wrapped up for you.

STEWART: Fine, fine. Now how much is it, Miss?

VONN: It's absolutely free.

CROSBY: Free?

VONN: Yes.

STEWART: Hmm.

VONN: And here's one for you, too.

CROSBY: Say, what is this? Why are we getting free blankets?

VONN: Those are your prizes. You boys have just been on television.

STEWART: Oh, my gosh.

After a commercial, Bing sings two more songs, separated by a G.E. spot, to close the show.

"Somebody Loves Me" (with Buddy Clark on piano)

"Auf Wiederseh'n, Sweetheart" (with Loulie Jean Norman)

(2) Thursday, November 6, 1952 (9:30-10 p.m.)

Bing was not on the show that night. Because of the illness and subsequent death of his wife, Dixie Lee (on November 1, 1952), he missed two shows, October 30 and November 6, 1952. Jimmy Stewart acted as the master of ceremonies for this evening's show. The format of the show was very simple, with Jimmy simply introducing musical numbers and talking briefly with the artists. He also helped Ken Carpenter with the G.E. commercial. There were no elaborate sketches. Jimmy is introduced at the beginning of the show and he immediately introduces Rosemary Clooney.

According to newspaper ads of the time, the title of the show was changed to *Music Parade* for this occasion.

CARPENTER: …And now, folks, we bring you a famous and dependable performer, our master of ceremonies for this evening, Mr. Jimmy Stewart.

STEWART: Thank you, thank you, very much, Ken. Good evening, ladies and gentlemen. In Bing's absence this evening, our cast includes Rosemary Clooney, Gordon MacRae, Joe Venuti and John Scott Trotter and his Orchestra. So, we hope you'll enjoy this musical program that will be brought to you by the very fine artists. Here now, to start things off, is the Paramount Pictures star, very popular vocalist, Miss Rosemary Clooney. (Applause) Rosemary come right over here where…where we can hear you.

CLOONEY: Oh, thank you, Jimmy.

STEWART: Now, what's you…what's your opening song?

CLOONEY: "This Can't Be Love."

STEWART: Oh, that's a good one…that's a good one.

CLOONEY: John Scott, will you commence?

"This Can't Be Love"
After her song, Jimmy continues.

STEWART: Well, well, well, that was very good, Rosemary, very…

CLOONEY: Thank you.

CARPENTER: It sure was. Say, Jim, can I ask you a question?

STEWART: Sure, Ken, sure.

CARPENTER: Well, the question is, James, will you love it in December as you did in May?

STEWART: Hmm, well…well, let me see.

CARPENTER: And the answer is yes.

STEWART: It is, huh?

CARPENTER: Yes, Jim. You see, I was referring to food you take from your General Electric food freezer in December. It'll be just as delicious and just as flavorful as when you put it in in May; the stacks of steaks just as juicy and tender, the bushels of fruits and vegetables just as crisp and luscious.

STEWART: Well, that's a lot of food.

CARPENTER: Oh, the G.E. food freezer holds a lot and keeps it for months and months and months. That's why you can store the food in May, eat it in December.

STEWART: Well, what if I get a little hungry long about September?

CARPENTER: Oh well, Jimmy, you can…

STEWART: What happens then?

CARPENTER: …you can delve into your G.E. food freezer, of course. And, Jimmy, you can eat a lot of fine steaks on the money you save when you own a G.E. food freezer. And this new G.E. food freezer costs 13% less to operate than previously.

STEWART: Well, say, that sounds like something we oughta make a big noise about, Ken.

CARPENTER: I'm glad you mentioned noise…

STEWART: Oh?

CARPENTER: …Jimmy, because it's something there just isn't with the G.E. food freezer. The new model is 20% quieter than the previous model and that was a little number often referred to as the silent security national.

STEWART: Security national?

CARPENTER: Um…hum, because you can bank on a G.E. food freezer, you get it?

STEWART: Oh.

CARPENTER: There's G.E. dependability built right in, yet, it costs only about $4.71 a week after down payment. Your G.E. dealer can give you more details and also show you some astonishing style features. So, drop in and ask for a demonstration. Tomorrow might be a good time.

STEWART: That's when I'm going, Ken. And now, folks, here's Rosemary Clooney singing "Half as Much." Ready, Rosemary?

CLOONEY: Right here, Jimmy.

"Half as Much"

STEWART: Rosemary, gee, that was pretty. That was Rosemary Clooney singing "Half as Much," which happens to be a pretty big tune for her right now in the record department. And, now, ladies and gentlemen, I'd like to present our next musical star, the fair-haired boy from Warner Bros. studio, singing star of *The Railroad Hour* and Capitol recording artist, Gordon MacRae. Gordon…

MACRAE: Hi, Jimmy.

STEWART: Hi, Gordon. Gordon, what's your first selection this evening?

MACRAE: Well, sir, it's a Rodgers and Hammerstein song from *South Pacific* called *Cockeyed Optimist*.

"Cockeyed Optimist"

CARPENTER: Ladies, wash day can be a gay day for you, thanks to GEAA.

STEWART: Now, just a minute, now hold on, Ken. I don't like to interrupt, but I feel that if it's something that you have to spell, and can't say just right out, you shouldn't say it at all on a family program. I really…

CARPENTER: Jimmy, no, no, GEAA stands for General Electric activator action.

STEWART: Oh.

CARPENTER: It's exclusive with a General Electric automatic washer, see.

STEWART: Oh, oh, I see.

CARPENTER: Activation action washes your clothes separately and washes them gently, the way a fine hand laundress would, and does it automatically.

STEWART: Well, just so it cleans.

CARPENTER: Clean? Oh-oh with a General Electric automatic washer, you get the cleanest, whitest, brightest wash ever, without any work on your part. And, after the wash is done, the G.E. automatic washer spins them so dry, you can start ironing some pieces immediately. And special features…

STEWART: Well, what about special features?

CARPENTER: Well, a G.E. automatic washer is loaded with 'em. There's the small load selector that saves you lots of hot water on smaller washes, the porcelain wash basket and an interior light that lets you see into the washer. And, remember the most important feature of all, built in General Electric dependability. You can have a G.E. automatic washer for only about $3.94 a month after down payment. Why not stop by your G.E. dealer tomorrow and get the details.

MACRAE: Ladies and gentlemen, here's a wonderful new ballad called *Somewhere Along the Way*. I'd like to give credit to a dear friend of mine, Mr. Dino Martin, who loaned me the arrangement. Thank you, Dino.

"Somewhere Along the Way"

STEWART: Now, ladies and gentlemen, I'd like to present an artist who is sort of a regular on Bing's program. The world's foremost jazz violinist, Mr. Joe Venuti.

VENUTI: Hi, Jimmy.

STEWART: Joe, what are you going to fiddle for us this evening?

VENUTI: Well, for my first number, I'd like to play *Autumn Leaves*. Undoubtedly, it'll be my last.

STEWART: Uh…huh…*Autumn Leaves*, huh?

VENUTI: Incidentally, I'm going to play this with a rake.

STEWART: Well, you're gonna…okay, Joe, start rakin'.

"Autumn Leaves"

STEWART: Thank you, Joe…thank you, Joe Venuti, that was wonderful. And now, folks, Rosemary Clooney and Gordon MacRae return to sing *Walkin' My Way Back Home*.
MACRAE: Well, Jimmy, I can't think of anybody I'd rather stroll with than Rosie.
CLOONEY: That goes for me, too, Gordie.
STEWART: Gee, people sure get acquainted quick around here, don't they?
MACRAE: John Scott, we're ready when you are.

"Walkin' My Baby Back Home" — Gordon MacRae and Rosemary Clooney

STEWART: Thank you. Gee, that was very nice, Rosie and Gordie.
MACRAE: Thank you, Jimmy.
STEWART: Well, now…now, according to my paper, I see that Gordon continues along with Cole Porter's "Begin the Beguine."
MACRAE: That's right, Jim. Mr. Trotter, if you please.

"Begin the Beguine"

CARPENTER: Just picture yourself in the kitchen of tomorrow. Well, open your eyes, lady, you're not dreaming.
STEWART: That's no lady, Ken, that's me. I just closed my eyes…
CARPENTER: Jimmy, I'm talking to the ladies listening.
STEWART: Oh.
CARPENTER: It's no dream, lady. You can have the General Electric kitchen of tomorrow in your home today for only about $47.20 a month after a small down payment.
STEWART: Oh, I see, it's a commercial.
CARPENTER: Yes, Jimmy, a commercial. A G.E. kitchen gives you…
STEWART: Yes, on kitchens.
CARPENTER: Not just on kitchens, on a G.E. all electric kitchen.
STEWART: Ah…huh.
CARPENTER: The kitchen that does everything for you–stores the groceries, cooks them for you, washes the dishes and swirls the food waste away.
STEWART: And that means no garbage.

CARPENTER: Um...hum.

STEWART: I just thought I'd bring that in. I...I...gotta...kind of wanna help you out on the commercial, Ken. I...I wanna do my part, you know.

CARPENTER: That's very nice of you, Jimmy, I appreciate it. Now, ladies, this electric marvel is yours the moment you make a small down payment, with three years to pay the balance. Incidentally, your G.E. kitchen specialist will style your kitchen for you, just the way you want it, and for nothing.

STEWART: And that's mighty little, especially in these days of high prices.

CARPENTER: If you're buying a house, or building one, plan a G.E. all electric kitchen into it. Won't cost you anymore; in most cases you can include the cost right in your long-term mortgage. So see your G.E. dealer tomorrow.

STEWART: Well, no, don't just see him, talk to him, you know. Talk to him about your General Electric all electric kitchen. Okay, Ken?

CARPENTER: Oh, yes sir. Thanks a lot, Jimmy.

STEWART: Oh, I'm glad to do it, glad to do it anytime. And now. folks, here's Rosemary Clooney singing a song which she's recently recorded, titled "Who Kissed Me Last Night?"

"Who Kissed Me Last Night?" — Rosemary Clooney

STEWART: That was Rose Marie [sic]. Well, that's the closing selection for this evening, folks, and now our thanks to Rosemary Clooney, Gordon MacRae, Joe Venuti for a delightful program. Bing'll be back next week and his guest will be Miss Dinah Shore. Well, this is Jimmy Stewart, good night everybody. Thank you.

As Ken Carpenter closes the show, he mentions that Jimmy will soon be seen in the M-G-M production, *The Naked Spur*.

(3) Thursday, March 12, 1953 (9:30-10 p.m.) (Transcribed in Palm Springs)

The show was produced and transcribed from Palm Springs, CA. Bing's life story had just appeared in *The Saturday Evening Post* and he and Ken Carpenter use that as the basis for their opening routine. Bing then sings two numbers, separated by a commercial for General Electric.

"Jeepers Creepers" (with the Rhythmaires)

"'Til I Waltz Again with You"

Bing introduces his other guest, violinist Joe Venuti, who then plays a song.

"Tea for Two"

Next, Bing introduces Jimmy Stewart and they begin the first of two skits. The first involves Jimmy's accommodations in Palm Springs, while the second is basically a long (more than eight-minute) commercial for General Electric washing machines. In the second sketch, Veola Vonn is the salesgirl.

CROSBY: Now, ladies and gentlemen, I'd like to present an always welcome visitor to this program; the two-fisted shy guy who can currently be seen in popcorn palaces around the nation in the Technicolor picture, *The Naked Spur*, Mr. Jimmy Stewart.

STEWART: Hi, Bing.

CROSBY: Hi, Jimmy.

STEWART: Hey, Bing, I was reading your life story in *The Saturday Evening Post* comin' down here on the bus and I…it sure has suspense.

CROSBY: Suspense? What'd you mean?

STEWART: Well, I was reading it over a fella's shoulder and he got off at Pomona.

CROSBY: That's a bad break, Jim. Now let me ask you something. What are you doing in Palm Springs and why did you come down on the bus?

STEWART: Well, a couple of months ago, I was guest on Jack Benny's TV program and he promised me a week in Palm Springs, all expenses paid.

CROSBY: Well…but your wife Gloria…Gloria was on the show, she was very good, too.

STEWART: Yeah…yeah she was.

CROSBY: Well, what about her?

STEWART: I…I couldn't make a deal for her.

CROSBY: So Jack came up with a bus ticket for you, huh?

STEWART: Yeah…yeah, he finally did. At first he wanted to ship me down here on a truck load of tennis balls for the racquet club.

CROSBY: Are you staying at the racquet club, Jimmy?

STEWART: No…no.

CROSBY: Where are you?

STEWART: No, I'm at the El Mirador.

CROSBY: The El Mira…Jack Benny is paying for a room at the El Mirador? That's very deluxe.

STEWART: Eh, no, Bing. I'm not staying at the El Mirador Hotel here in Palm Springs. I'm staying down the road a piece at the El Mirador Enchilada Parlor and Cabins.

CROSBY: And cabins...well, you still...however, you're still in the Spanish motif. But I can't...I don't think I can place it. I don't remember the El Mirador Enchilada Parlor and Cabins. Where is it?

STEWART: Well, perhaps you know this motel by its former name. It used to be called La Cucaracha.

CROSBY: La Cucaracha?

STEWART: Yes, but they changed the name because it was all too true.

CROSBY: Well, that's funny. I...I just can't seem to recall that joint... that place.

STEWART: Ah...no...you must have passed it a million times, Bing,... red and yellow cabins, about a mile on the other side of Cathedral City.

CROSBY: Oh...Oh yeah, I know that spot. The house detective rides a burro.

STEWART: Now, it's...it's not such a bad place, Bing. The beds are quite comfortable and they serve...they serve a lovely continental breakfast.

CROSBY: Continental breakfast?

STEWART: Yeah...yeah, they give you chilled cactus juice, ah...a hot tamale, a big scoop of fried beans and then you have a choice of coffee, tea, milk or Alka Seltzer.

CROSBY: Well, what do you recommend?

STEWART: You take the Alka Seltzer or you won't live till lunch. I...I sort of switched to a room with a wall bed.

CROSBY: Oh, you did?

STEWART: Yeah, so I can hide when the maid brings in the breakfast. She never looks for me in there.

CROSBY: Why go to all that trouble? Why not just hide in the bathroom?

STEWART: Eh...eh...well, to go to the bathroom, I'd have to put on my robe and my slippers and walk across the highway.

CROSBY: Wait a minute. Across the highway?

STEWART: Yes, you see the bathroom is over in the annex...the Mobile Gas Station.

CROSBY: Oh yeah, you know I've often seen people running out of the El Mirador Cabins and across the highway in their bathrobes, but I always thought it was a fire drill or something.

STEWART: Well, sometimes it's one thing and sometimes it's another.

CROSBY: Hey, Jim…say, Jim, now tell me what really is the purpose of your delightful visit? You usually have something on your mind when you come to call.

STEWART: Well, Bing, I have a problem.

CROSBY: My advice to you is move to another hotel.

STEWART: No…no, Bing, it's not that. Now, you see, for some time now I've been thinking of buying Gloria a General Electric automatic washer.

CROSBY: Well, good boy, but why should that be a problem?

STEWART: Ah, well, I thought maybe you might go to the store with me and help me buy it. I…I'm kind of squeamish about that…I…

CROSBY: Oh, but why?

STEWART: Well, I…I…a washing machine's kind of an intimate, personal thing.

CROSBY: Well, I guess so, if you say so.

STEWART: Would…would you go with me, Bing?

CROSBY: We'll go right now. I'll grab my hat. I'll take you over to the G.E. dealer right here on the main drag.

STEWART: Well, can you leave now, right in the middle of the program like this?

CROSBY: I can if it's company business.

STEWART: Oh…Oh yeah.

CROSBY: We may even drop in at the drugstore and have a malted milk. I'll put it on my expense account.

STEWART: Gosh, you sure know how to live.

CROSBY: Well, come on, Jim, let's go get that automatic washer.

STEWART: Okay.

(short musical interlude to mark change of location)

CROSBY: Ah, isn't this a beautiful little town, Jimmy?

STEWART: Ah, it sure is.

MAN: Say, Bud.

CROSBY: Yeah, what's the matter.

MAN: I…ah…I got something here you might be interested in. I got just two boxes left.

CROSBY: Hey, these look like the real thing.

MAN: They're the McCoy, Bud; only a buck and a quarter a box.

CROSBY: I'll take both of 'em.

MAN: Oh boy, what a sport. So long.

CROSBY: So long. Hey, Jimmy.

STEWART: Yeah…yeah, Bing.

CROSBY: Boy, this is our lucky day. That guy just let me have two boxes. These are real tough to get in Palm Springs.

STEWART: Yeah.

CROSBY: Here's yours, Jimmy.

STEWART: Gee, thanks…well, what do you know…dates.

CROSBY: Yes sir, dates. Well, here we are, the G.E. store. Let's come on in, Jim.

STEWART: Okay…okay.

CROSBY: Nice little store isn't it, Jimmy?

STEWART: Sure is. Wonder where the clerk is.

CROSBY: Right there, behind that counter. There's a girl right over there.

STEWART: Oh, you'd think selling automatic washers and things like that, they'd have a man clerk for men.

CROSBY: This girl's probably very broadminded about these things.

STEWART: Think so?

VONN: Can I help you gentlemen?

CROSBY: If you would, please.

STEWART: Say, umm…these are darn good. Would you want a date, Miss?

VONN: Oh sure, but I have to go home and change first.

CROSBY: Now wait…wait, we'd like to see a General Electric automatic washer.

VONN: Oh fine, step right over here. Now here's the G.E. automatic washer right here.

CROSBY: Isn't it a beauty, Jim?

STEWART: Yeah, gee whiz, that's…well, that thing's pretty enough to put in the living room.

CROSBY: It sure is. You know what would really set this off, Jim? A Toby Jug, maybe on top. Maybe a Spanish shawl draped over one corner. Wouldn't that be nice, hmm?

STEWART: Yeah, you know they're having a big sale on Spanish shawls in the gift shop in my motel…there's a sale on shawls and tortillas.

VONN: Well, if we can drop the interior decorating for a moment, I'd like to say that this General Electric automatic washer gives you the whitest, brightest wash in the world. And it does the whole job completely automatically.

STEWART: You mean you don't have to bend over this machine and scrub clothes out by hand, huh?

CROSBY: Where've you been, boy? While the clothes are being washed in this machine, you can drape the Spanish shawl around you and you dance the fandango.

STEWART: Hmmm…the fandango?

CROSBY: Yeah.

STEWART: I don't believe I'm acquainted with that dance.

CROSBY: Well, I'll tell you what I'm gonna do, boy, I'm gonna…if you buy this washer, we'll throw in 12 lessons at Arthur Murray's.

VONN: Say, you're quite a salesman.

CROSBY: I'm with the company, kiddo. Tell my pal here about G.E. activator action, will ya?

VONN: Well, activator action launders clothes gently, piece by piece, individually, just the way a fine hand laundress would.

STEWART: Think of that.

CROSBY: And the G.E. soaks and cleanses, flexes and rinses, deep rinses, each garment. And get this, Jim, in a G.E., the clothes are constantly submerged in detergent water. They're flood washed and they're flood rinsed.

VONN: And the clothes never come out matted or tangled.

STEWART: Well, that's a good point because there's nothing more uncomfortable than tangled laundry.

CROSBY: Ain't it awful? This new G.E. isn't like…this new G.E. isn't like the tumbler-type washers that just dunk your clothes and then wads them up in a ball.

VONN: And the General Electric never drains dirty water back through the freshly laundered clothes.

STEWART: How come?

CROSBY: I guess we better tell him, huh? You see, Jim, when the G.E. wash basket spins, it spins so fast that the dirty, soapy water is literally left out, wafted away, up and over the top. You just can't help getting the cleanest laundry you ever saw.

VONN: And, remember, after washing, a General Electric automatic washer spins your clothes so dry that you can start ironing some pieces immediately, right out of the washer.

CROSBY: And the cost, only $3.90 a week after a small down payment.

VONN: This is the brand-new General Electric automatic washer for 1953. It's built on the solid bedrock of G.E. dependability.

STEWART: Well, that's the machine for me.

CROSBY: This is the machine for everybody.

VONN: Now, your name, please.

STEWART: Oh, now just…just a moment, Miss. I know this is the machine I want, but would you mind demonstrating it for me?

CROSBY: What do you want, a floor show or something? Take the machine.

STEWART: I…I want a demonstration here.

VONN: Well, it would be a pleasure.

STEWART: Oh yeah, I mean with laundry in it.

VONN: Laundry, yet.

STEWART: Yeah…yeah, you don't happen to have some laundry on you, do you, Miss?

VONN: Yes, and I'm going to keep it on.

STEWART: (gulp sound effect) Well, there goes my Adam's apple again. Every time I get nervous, it flips.

CROSBY: Pull yourself together, Jim.

STEWART: I told you this was going to be embarrassing, Bing.

CROSBY: Come on…come on, Jimmy, pay the lady and let's go.

STEWART: No…no…no, now I want a demonstration on it…ah…say…ah, Bing.

CROSBY: No…no…no…oh no, Jim. I'd be glad to toss in my socks, but it so happens I'm not wearing any.

STEWART: Oh gosh.

VONN: This is Palm Springs. You'd be surprised at the things people don't wear down here.

STEWART: (gulp sound effect again)

CROSBY: Now, listen, Jimmy, if you wanna see how this automatic washer works, throw your own laundry in.

STEWART: Well, that seems fair. Yep, that's fair and square. Now, where do I take my clothes off?

VONN: Just step right in there in that little dressing room.

STEWART: Okay.

CROSBY: Well, I'll be doggone. How come you have a dressing room here, Miss?

VONN: Well, the boss always said that someday some lunatic would come in here and wanna do his laundry.

CROSBY: Well, he's here. Come on now, Jimmy, hurry it up. Here, I'll pull the curtain back for you.

STEWART: All right, thanks. Here, hold my dates.

CROSBY: I got 'em. Now get in there…come on, buy. Gee, I hope you'll forgive my buddy, Miss; he's not really off his rocker or anything. He just acts this way.

VONN: Oh, it's all in a day's work. We had an Eskimo come in here one day and he left a chunk of blubber in a G.E. food freezer.

CROSBY: Now what was an Eskimo doing here in all this heat in Palm Springs?

VONN: I don't know, but he muttered something about harpooning his travel agent.

CROSBY: You wouldn't blame him. Hey, Jim, you got your clothes off?

STEWART: Yep.

CROSBY: Well, come on, hurry it up.

STEWART: Now, don't rush me; I'm making out my laundry list.

CROSBY: Well, you can…now you can trust us. Now, hand me those duds.

STEWART: Now wait'll I get my pants and sweater on.

CROSBY: Isn't this awful, this stalling around?

STEWART: Ah…here I am. Here's my laundry.

VONN: Well, now, I'll just toss these things in here and we'll have the demonstration.

CROSBY: Now pay attention to this, Jim, will ya?

(a buzzer is heard)

VONN: Oh, I'm sorry, it's closing time. We'll have to have the demonstration tomorrow morning.

STEWART: Tomorrow morning?

CROSBY: Yeah, now come on, grab your laundry, Jim. Let's…let's hit the trail outta here.

STEWART: Okay, give me my dates. We'll see you tomorrow, Miss.

VONN: It's a date.

CROSBY: Boy, are you in for a thrill, Jimmy. Wait'll you see that General Electric automatic washer tomorrow.

STEWART: Yeah (gulp sound effect), pardon me, Bing.

CROSBY: What's the matter? You still nervous?

STEWART: No, that must have been the continental breakfast.

After the skit, Bing introduces and sings one final number. "Two Shillelagh O'Sullivan" (with the Rhythmaires)

In 2011, it was issued in mp3 only format on *Jimmy Stewart the Ultimate Radio Collection Vol. 1* (Master Classics Records).

Biography in Sound

Biography in Sound was on the air very sporadically for ten years, from October 24, 1954, until October 20, 1964. During that time, the program was broadcast only 97 times, with many of these being repeats. The show did 60-minute biographies of a wide variety of people from many walks of life, including Winston Churchill, Ernest Hemmingway, Eddie Arnold, Leo Durocher, Helen Hayes, George M. Cohan, Franklin D. Roosevelt, and Babe Ruth. Friends and associates were always interviewed so that the listener would get a good perspective of the person.

Thursday, April 10, 1958 — *Captain Eddie: The Iron Eagle* (9:05-10 p.m.)

NETWORK: NBC
SPONSOR: Sustained
GUIDE (HOST): Walter O'Keefe
WRITER & PRODUCER: Don Cameron
SUPERVISED BY: James L. Holton, for NBC News

The biography of Eddie Rickenbacker spotlights his days as a race car driver, his World War I exploits as a member of the 94th Pursuit Squadron and Medal of Honor winner, his failed auto manufacturing company, the rise of Eastern Airlines under his leadership, his survival of a DC3 crash, and the 24 days he spent on a raft in the middle of the Pacific Ocean during World War II. Speaking about Rickenbacker are Arthur Godfrey (a close friend and flying buddy, who appears several times during the program), Tommy Milton (a friend from his car racing days), Reed Chambers, Douglas Campbell, LeRoy Prinz, Colonel Fred Ordway (other members of the 94th), Alfred P. Sloan (President of General Motors), Hugh Nelton (a member of the financial community), Lawrence Rockefeller (a director of Eastern Airlines), Jim Kilgallen (International News Service), Ralph McGill, Adolphe Menjou (actor) and James Reynolds (who was on the raft for 24 days with Eddie).

Jimmy Stewart is not heard until the end of the show when he asks Rickenbacker a question. "Captain Eddie, I'm going to ask you a question. We're sort of making this the anniversary question and we'd appreciate your comments on it. And here's the question: Against the background of Air Force history, what stands out most vividly in your mind and what do you see as the greatest problem ahead?" Rickenbacker's response then ends the show.

Block Party/First Call for the Block Party
NETWORK: Mutual

Stewart appeared on just one show, along with Larry Douglas, Monica Lewis and Teddy Wilson. It was broadcast in the New York City area on August 14, 1947, by WOR. The show is not available for review.

The Bob Hope Show

Bob Hope (born Leslie Townes Hope on May 29, 1903) had a long and distinguished career on radio. Beginning in 1935 with *Intimate Revue*, and continuing with *Family on Tour*, *Ripplin' Rhythm Revue*, *Your Hollywood Parade*, and finally, beginning in 1938, *The Bob Hope Show*. *The Bob Hope Show* was sponsored by Pepsodent Toothpaste from 1938 through June of 1948 and then continued through April of 1955 with a series of sponsors, including Lever Brothers–Swan Soap, Chesterfield Cigarettes, Jell-O, and the American Dairy Association. In all, Hope spent 18 years on the air, all for NBC. Hope died on July 27, 2003, at the age of 100.

SHOWS FEATURING JIMMY STEWART:

(1) Tuesday February 27, 1951 (9:00-9:30 p.m.)
NETWORK: NBC
SPONSOR: Chesterfield Cigarettes
ANNOUNCER: Hy Averback
MUSIC: Les Brown & His Band of Renown
WITH REGULARS Jack Kirkwood, Marilyn Maxwell
THEME SONG: *Thanks for the Memory* (Leo Robin/Ralph Rainger)

This show is not available for listening. It is known that Hope presented the *Look* magazine awards on the show that night. Stewart received an award for his outstanding work in *Harvey*. Hope also presented Bette Davis with an award. A silent film clip of Davis and Stewart receiving their awards from Bob Hope does exist.

(2) Wednesday January 28, 1953 (10:00-10:30 p.m.)
NETWORK: NBC
SPONSOR: Jell-O
PRODUCER: Jack Hope
ANNOUNCER: Bill Goodwin
WITH: Margaret Whiting–vocalist
ORCHESTRA: Les Brown & His Band of Renown
WRITERS: Larry Marks, Norman Sullivan
THEME SONG: "Thanks For the Memory" (Leo Robin/Ralph Rainger)

Bob began the show with his usual comedy routine. Then he and Bill Goodwin did a commercial for Jell-O. Next came a two-part skit with Bob, Bill, Margaret Whiting, and Jimmy Stewart. In the skit, Bob is told that Bing Crosby plans on making a new "Road" picture without him. Margaret suggests that Bob do the same. Bob goes to see Mr. Harkins (sometimes referred to as Harkin; played by Bill Johnstone) at the bank to try to borrow a million dollars to produce the film. Harkins turns him down, telling him that he needs another big name star in the film. When Bob leaves Harkins' office, who should be standing in the bank but Jimmy Stewart.

STEWART: Hello Bob.

HOPE: Oh, Jimmy Stewart. Say, nice to see you Jimmy. What are you doing in the bank?

STEWART: Oh, I came to deposit some money, Bob. My milk bottle's full of pennies again.

HOPE: Well Jimmy, its wonderful bumping into you like this.

STEWART: Well same here, Bob.

HOPE: You know you and Gloria haven't been out to our house in a long time.

STEWART: Well you and Delores haven't been out to our place in a couple of years now.

HOPE: That's right, Jimmy. Why don't we arrange something?

STEWART: What for? We can't improve on the arrangement we have now.

HOPE: I may get a refund on my bottle of Airwick.

STEWART: It's awful nice to see you, Bob. Now what brings you to town today?

HOPE: Oh, I came in to borrow a million dollars.

STEWART: My gosh, a thousand dollars; well that's a lot of money.

HOPE: Now I'm afraid to tell him what I really said. I'm trying to produce my own picture and I want the bank to finance it. If everything works out, I'll amortize a million dollars on short term notes. Am I boring you?

STEWART: Oh no. No, I like to come to town and hear this big talk.

HOPE: Well I've also wired a couple of big money men in the east and they're flying out to have a conference with me and we're gonna survey M-G-M and Paramount and rent a few studios. Have you been doing anything exciting, Jimmy?

STEWART: Oh...oh yeah. Yesterday the washing machine overflowed and I chased my underwear clear down the driveway.

HOPE: You know Jimmy, the bank requires that I have another star in this picture with me.

STEWART: They do, huh?

HOPE: We can't talk about the picture here. Why don't you come over to my radio show tonight and we'll talk about it?

STEWART: Oh fine, Bob.

HOPE: You know making an independent picture's a fine investment. I'm sure we could do alright and, of course, we'll cut off some nice profits.

STEWART: Well, when it comes to business, I'm just a babe in arms, Bob.

HOPE: A babe in arms?

STEWART: Yeah, I'm...I...well for instance, who would get the other fifty percent of the profits?

HOPE: You mean after my half?

STEWART: No, after mine.

HOPE: What did you teethe on, Fort Knox? See you later, Jimmy.

"Keep It A Secret" — Margaret Whiting
Bob and Bill do another commercial for Jell-O
After the commercial, we hear Bob and Jimmy at the radio studio.

HOPE: Say, Jimmy.

STEWART: Yeah, Bob.

HOPE: I just phoned Mr. Harkins, the president of the bank, and ask him to come over. We can do a scene from my road picture for him. It's gonna be a western.

STEWART: Yeah, I don't think I should have come down here tonight, Bob. This is all so different for me.

HOPE: Oh, don't be silly. I've heard you on a lot of radio programs. You've always been great.

STEWART: Yeah, well thanks Bob, but on those programs that you were talking about...

HOPE: Yes?

STEWART: ...I always worked with actors. Oh, Oh, I, I, no offense Bob, but I meant actors doing serious stuff you know.

HOPE: Jimmy, I can be as serious as anybody.

STEWART: Yeah, yeah, you've been doing fine so far.

HOPE: Critic. How can he look like Abraham Lincoln and do lines like Milton Berle? Now Jimmy, in this scene we're going to do, you and I will play the male parts and Margaret Whiting will be the girl. All set Maggie?

WHITING: Sure, Bob. Gee, It's gonna be a pleasure to work with Jimmy. He's made so many wonderful pictures.

STEWART: Well thank you, Maggie. I've had my share of luck.

WHITING: You know it's strange you've been making pictures in Hollywood all these years and yet you've never made one with Bob.

STEWART: I guess I've had more than my share of luck. Of course Bob and I have been friends for a long time. I know when I moved out here to Hollywood, I guess Bob was one of the first people I met.

WHITING: That must have been quite a while ago.

STEWART: Ehh…ehh…yes, yes it was…ahhh…Bob wasn't a star in those days. Bob wasn't a star. He used to come around our neighborhood selling Lily cups *(earlier in the show, Bob had taken some Lily cups from Mr. Harkins' office, so this brought a big laugh from the audience).*

HOPE: Well there wasn't much in it. I hardly made taxi fare from washroom to washroom.

WHITING: Well, I think it's wonderful that two friends like you are finally going to work together in a picture.

STEWART: Well now I haven't made up my mind yet, Maggie. I don't wanna rush into this thing.

HOPE: Well what's the matter, Jimmy?

STEWART: Well you know what can happen to your career in Hollywood if you make a flop picture.

HOPE: Well, what?

STEWART: Well, its goodbye, that's all. Today you're at Ciro's drinking wine, tomorrow you're up at Fresno crushing the grapes.

HOPE: Crushing the grapes. Oh that couldn't possibly happen could it, Maggie?

WHITING: You tell 'em purple foot.

HOPE: Well believe me…believe me, there's nothing to worry about Jimmy, we've both had experience making pictures.

STEWART: That's true, that's true.

HOPE: Have you ever had anything to do with independent productions?

STEWART: Well, in a way…Gloria and I have twins.

HOPE: That makes you NBC's answer to Lucy and Desi, doesn't it? *(knock on the door)* Hey, that must be Mr. Harkins from the bank. Come in.

HARKINS: Hello, Bob. As soon as I got your message, I came right over.

HOPE: Oh fine, Mr. Harkins. This is Maggie Whiting and Jimmy Stewart.

HARKINS: Miss Whiting.

HOPE: Oh how do you do. Glad to see you. Fine, thank you very much. *(Bob's saying this instead of Whiting or Stewart brought a huge laugh from the audience).* See, we're a little short on actors, so I just thought I'd double…boy, we're all set to do a scene from the road picture for you Mr. Harkins.

HARKINS: Oh, splendid, splendid.

HOPE: Oh, just call me purple foot, it's not....Why don't you just take a seat Mr. Harkins and we'll run through the scene for you.

HARKINS: Okay, Bob.

HOPE: Music, Les.

GOODWIN: And now we present a story of two strong men and a girl in the old west — *The Road to Cactus Gulch.*

HOPE: I'm one of the men he mentioned folks; they call me Tex. I'm an outlaw who's been aginst the law. A man like me doesn't have many friends. I only got one buddy in this whole world, my pal Smokey Jim back there in Cactus Gulch.

STEWART: That's me...Smokey Jim. But, I ain't an outlaw no more. When Tex went away, I turned straight. Five years ago, the people of this here town made me their sheriff. I'm so proud of the star they give me; it's never been off my chest since. Of course, I'm getting kind of sick sleeping on my back. I'm a respected citizen in Cactus Gulch, even got myself a gal, Maggie Lou...mighty pretty heifer.

WHITING: You're playing the guitar kind of sad today, Smokey.

STEWART: Well, I got a feeling of foreboding. There's something in the air.

WHITING: What is it?

STEWART: I don't know. I don't know, but everything's so still. The leaves are hangin' down on the trees and look over yonder at the mountains over there, even the Pecos is pooped.

WHITING: Ah, what's the matter with ya, Smokey?

STEWART: I don't know. I don't...it's just a feeling I got. When I come riding over this morning, there was a couple of dead men lying in front of the saloon, door was blown off the bank, the school house was on fire...I just don't know. Can't put my finger on it, but there's something wrong in this town.

HOPE: (A horse comes galloping into town) Whoa.

WHITING: Why look who it is. It's your old buddy.

STEWART: Yeah, that's him. Hello, Tex.

HOPE: Hello, Dopey.

STEWART: That's Smokey.

HOPE: Oh.

STEWART: I'm the sheriff of this here town and I've cleaning up the town.

HOPE: You cleaned up Cactus Gulch?

STEWART: Yeah, I caught the last crook yesterday. I put him in jail and sent his fingers to Washington.

HOPE: You sent his fingers to Washington?

STEWART: I had to…ain't no one around here can take fingerprints.

HOPE: Well, I ain't afraid of no tinhorn sheriff. (Train whistle sound effects)

STEWART: Hey what's that?

HOPE: That's the Super Chief.

STEWART: But there ain't any railroad tracks out in the desert.

HOPE: I know. Those Democrats are really going home.

STEWART: Now Tex, I'm tellin' you once more…get on your horse and git.

WHITING: Yeah, leave us be Tex. Smokey here is trying to go straight, so leave him alone.

HOPE: Well, you're a cute little palomino. You're prettier than a coyote skin hangin' on a bunkhouse wall.

STEWART: This here's my gal, Tex.

WHITING: Yes, Tex (of course, she means Smokey, but her mistake doesn't seem to cause any problems or laughter) and I are fixin' to get married. Old Judge Fisher's gonna let us have a cottage over by the Mill Creek, the other side of Spoon River where Indianhead Mountain juts out and hides the entrance to Moon Valley, down back of the Painted Desert.

STEWART: Yes sir, we're gonna be mighty happy in that house…if we could ever find it.

HOPE: Now looka here Smokey…

HARKINS: Bob, oh Bob.

HOPE: Oh what is it Mr. Harkins.

HARKINS: I think I've heard enough to make my decision, Bob. I'm going to lend you the million dollars for your picture.

HOPE: Yes!

HARKINS: But, there's just one thing.

HOPE: Yeah, what is that?

HARKINS: I don't think we'll need both you and Jimmy Stewart in the picture. From what I've seen tonight, I know now that one of you is a fine, first rate actor and the other is nothing at all. So, the other man is out.

HOPE: Oh gee, poor Jimmy. How am I gonna break the news to him?

HARKINS: It won't be necessary, Bob; you're the one who's out. The picture will star Jimmy Stewart. You're a fine performer Jimmy.

STEWART: Gee, well thank you very much.

HARKINS: Let's go somewhere and discuss the details. So long Bob.

STEWART: Oh, yeah, well I'll see you later, Bob. Gosh, what are you gonna do?

HOPE: Oh, I'll think of something.

STEWART: Well, gee, so long, Bob.

HOPE: Here you are, get your Lily cups here!

At the end of the show, Bill Goodwin announces, "Jimmy Stewart will soon be seen in the M-G-M picture *The Naked Spur*."

An edited version of this program was repeated on the FEN (Far East Network) military network on April 11, 1957 (8:30-8:55 p.m.). The Jimmy Stewart segment of this program was also re-used in the Bob Hope show broadcast on January 27, 1955. See that entry for more details.

This show is available on the 20-cassette/CD set, *Legends of Radio: The Bob Hope Show* (Radio Spirits 40044-cassette/40042CD), which was released in 2002.

Radio Spirits also issued this show as an audiobook, *Bob Hope Show: Guest Star Jimmy Stewart*, in 2007.

The show has also been issued as an mp3 only download as *The Bob Hope Radio Collection Vol. 50* (Radio Library).

(3) Wednesday April 22, 1953 (10-10:30 p.m.)
NETWORK: NBC
SPONSOR: Jell-O
PRODUCER: Jack Hope
ANNOUNCER: Bill Goodwin
WITH: Margaret Whiting–vocalist
ORCHESTRA: Les Brown & His Band of Renown
WRITERS: Larry Marks, Norman Sullivan
THEME SONG: "Thanks For the Memory" (Leo Robin/Ralph Rainger)

This show is not available for listening. However, the sketch described in a newspaper ad was used on a 1955 American Red Cross disc (F-41191 – Program 3). See that entry for more details.

Another segment from this program appears on the 3-record set, *Bob Hope and His Friends*. In this short segment, a small portion of which also appears on the Red Cross disc, Stewart talks on the phone to his wife Gloria about a Bob Hope-Mickey Rooney film they had just seen, *Off Limits*. The joke about the film is cut from the Red Cross program.

These two clips are just over 12 minutes in length and if edited together, make up the entire Stewart skit from this evening's show.

(4) Thursday January 27, 1955 (8:30-9:00 p.m.):
NETWORK: NBC
SPONSOR: American Dairy Association
ANNOUNCER: Bill Goodwin
COMMERCIAL SPOKESMAN: Ed Prentiss
MUSIC: Les Brown & His Band of Renown
WITH: Margaret Whiting — vocalist
WRITERS: Norman Sullivan, Charles Lee
THEME SONG: "Thanks for the Memory" (Leo Robin/Ralph Rainger)

Bob begins the show with his usual comedy routine, touching on topics such as the very cold weather around the country, the size of his nose, the Waldorf Astoria and General Motors. After a commercial delivered by Ed Prentiss, the evening's skit begins.

This night's skit was taken directly from the show of January 29, 1953, and was simply edited into this show. See that show for details on the skit's plot. All the other parts of this show were newly recorded. After the first part of the skit, Margaret Whiting, with Hope and Les Brown & His Band of Renown, performed one song:

"Make Yourself Comfortable"

Next, there is another commercial for the American Dairy Association by Ed Prentiss. Then it's back to the skit. One line has been changed in the second part of the skit. When the train's whistle is heard and Smokey says that there aren't any railroad tracks in the desert, Hope (as Tex) says "I know. The sound effects man had it left over from last week." When the sketch is completed, Prentiss does another spot and then Bob sings "Thanks for the Memories," with specially written lyrics for "Big Brother Week."

At the end of the show Bill Goodwin announces that James Stewart will soon be seen in the film *The Far Country*.

This show is not generally available, but is part of the NBC Collection at the Library of Congress. A highly edited AFRTS version of this show is available. In place of the middle commercial, Hope talks with William B., a member of the audience. William B. wants to know if he should wear his sailor's uniform or a suit when he gets married and, of course, Hope makes many jokes about the question and the impending wedding. More editing has been done to the sketch, with several, non-essential, lines being cut. Hope's comment about the train's whistle is the same as that heard in the regular broadcast version.

This AFRTS version of the show is available as an mp3 download on *The Bob Hope Radio Collection Vol. 68* (Radio Library).

(5) Friday, September 21, 1956 (8-8:30 p.m.)

Although listed in several sources, including *James Stewart A Bio-Biography* by Gerard Molyneaux as a show on which Stewart appeared, newspaper ads from this day only list the Hope regulars.

Because this show is not available for listening, Stewart's appearance has not been confirmed.

(6) Friday, November 9, 1956 (8-8:30 p.m.)

The show is marked as a repeat, but since it is not available for review, it is not possible to identify of which show it is a duplicate or, if like the show of January 27, 1955, it is just a partial repeat with new material added. All Hope's shows from September 21, 1956, through March 21, 1958, were repeats.

Boy Scout Jamboree

These public service programs were broadcast by NBC. Stewart acted as the Master of Ceremonies for five consecutive years. Stewart was a longtime supporter of scouting and would be awarded the Silver Beaver, scouting's highest award. Only two of the four programs are available for listening.

(1) Saturday, February 12, 1949
NETWORK: NBC, from facilities of radio station KFI, Los Angeles, CA
SPONSOR: Public service of NBC
SCRIPT: Jack Hayes
PRODUCTION SUPERVISED BY Warren Lewis
ANNOUNCER: Lyle Bond
The show is introduced by Lyle Bond this way:

> Yes, it's the Annual Boy Scout Jamboree starring James Stewart, Roy Rogers, Verna Felton, the Mitchell Boy Choir, Henry Russell and the NBC Orchestra and radio's own Red Skelton.... From the Shrine Auditorium in Los Angeles, where over 7,000 scouts and cubs are gathered to participate in the annual coast-to-coast Boy Scout birthday broadcast, celebrating the 39th Anniversary of Scouting....

He then introduces Stewart: "And now here in Hollywood is your Master of Ceremonies, Jimmy Stewart."

STEWART: Thank you, Lyle Bond, and a happy birthday to all of you scouts and friends of scouting everywhere. As most of you know, today's great radio tribute marks the official start of the nationwide "Strengthen the Arm of Liberty" program, sponsored by the Boy Scouts of America. And this year we hope to get every single boy in the country interested in scouting. Just think of it, every boy in America a scout, trained for citizenship…why it would be the greatest thing that ever happened. But first, we'll have to get some help from men who know boys, like the fella who's coming up to our microphone right now…America's "King of the Cowboys" — Roy Rogers.

ROGERS: Well, hi, gang, and, hi, everybody. Say, Jimmy, this is quite a get together, isn't it?

STEWART: It sure is, Roy, and you're just the man we've been lookin' for.

ROGERS: I am, Jimmy? Well, what's up?

STEWART: Well, Roy, as you know, we're trying to get every boy in America into the scouts this year. I understand that you've already signed the Boy Scout recruiting card.

ROGERS: And how, Jimmy. I'm already a member of this nationwide round-up. Now, what can I do to help?

STEWART: Well, Roy, how about throwing a big rodeo right here in the old coral? Something to get the boys into the spirit of the round-up.

ROGERS: Sure thing, Jimmy. We'll have ropin', bull doggin' and bronc bustin'. How's that?

STEWART: That's…that's the idea. And while we're lining up the show, let's have Henry Russell and the NBC Orchestra do Morton Gold's *Pavane*.

ROGERS: Good.

"Pavane" — NBC Orchestra

ROGERS: Doggone, say that was wonderful, fellas.

STEWART: It sure was, sure was, Roy. But, say now, who are we gonna get to run our rodeo?

ROGERS: Partner, your troubles are over because here comes the rootinest, tootenist, shootenist cowhand that ever slapped leather.

SKELTON: Whoa…whoa…ah, come on, horse, whoa. If you don't stop, you're gonna wind up on the back of a three-cent stamp. Howdy, folks. I've been listening to your program and I hear you've been lookin' for a real cowpuncher.

STEWART: Are you a real cowpuncher?

SKELTON: Well, I used to be but I give up punching cows.

STEWART: Why?

SKELTON: One of 'em punched back.

ROGERS: Doggone, if it isn't old Deadeye, alias Red Skelton.

SKELTON: Yeah, that's right. Hi ya, fellas. Hi ya, everybody.

ROGERS: So, you're a real cowboy, ha?

SKELTON: Yeah, Texas Deadeye they call me. Good ole Texas they call me.

ROGERS: Where are you from, Tex?

SKELTON: Oklahoma.

ROGERS: Oh…well, I hope you'll pardon me for saying so, but you don't look like a cowboy to me. Most cowboys are bow-legged.

SKELTON: Well, you see, I ride a very thin horse. To prove I'm a cowboy, I'll just light my cigar [mispronounces "cigar" badly] here with…there's a new kind of smoke for ya…I'll light my cigar with my gun.

STEWART: Well, be careful your nose.

SKELTON: Oh, I know what I'm doin'. (shot) Oh well, things didn't smell too good around here anyhow. Say, Roy, who's your tall, skinny friend there?

STEWART: Well, if you mean me, I'm the organizer of this rodeo.

SKELTON: Oh, the organizer, huh. Sure look kind of puny. Yeah, puny. For a second, I thought the word was pony. Say, who are all the strangers out there?

ROGERS: Well, those are boy scouts, Deadeye. And this rodeo is gonna be in their honor. We're gonna try and show 'em some of our American traditions. We kind of figured a presentation of the past would help them visualize their obligation to try and improve the future.

SKELTON: Well, they all look kind of stunted to me. Well, that dad darn frost got everything, didn't it?

STEWART: Say…say, Deadeye, would you like to take a gander at the corral?

SKELTON: Yeah, but you better put some more oil in that smudge pot.

ROGERS: That's not a smudge pot [Roy has trouble saying the word smudge]…it's a barbeque pit.

SKELTON: Yeah, you better give up trying to run this rodeo. Just stick to readin' the script. Trigger could have done a better job on that line.

ROGERS: Well, cowboy, I'm not much on thinkin' of a fast answer, but a song will kind of pull 'em through every time.

SKELTON: Well, sir, then you sing your way out of this one, partner… we'll listen.

ROGERS: Well, if someone will bring me a guitar and a saddle to lay it on, why I might be able to carry on here. We're kind of shorthanded, so bear with me. Anybody got a guitar string they can help me with? Something like this. How 'bout "Down the Trail to San Antoine?"

"Down the Trail to San Antoine" — Roy Rogers

ROGERS: Thank you.
STEWART: Thank you, Roy. That was mighty fine singin', Roy. But now we've got work to do. Hey, Deadeye, wake up.
SKELTON: I ain't asleep.
ROGERS: Well, if you're not, you sure got long eyelids. You know, we need a speaker on this rodeo that can tell us about scouting. Do we have any volunteers in the crowd?

At this point, Red Skelton, as Junior, and Verna Felton, as his mother, perform a routine about scouting. When it ends, Stewart comes back to say the following.

STEWART: Thank you, Junior. As organizer of this scout rodeo, I wanna thank you for that advice. That'll be our opening example of what not to do. But, now, on the plus side of the ledger, here is some honest to goodness advice from that famous Boy Scout group — troop 800X of Hollywood — the Robert Mitchell Boy Choir in a Lincoln's birthday tribute.

After the song, Roy and Red talk more about the ideals of scouting, ending with the following.

ROGERS: Say, Jimmy Stewart, you were a scout back in Indiana. Let's see, what was that troop number, Jimmy?
STEWART: Ah, it was troop 3, Roy. And ever since, I've...I've always had an eye on scouting. Watched its effect on boys. Good scouts become good men. Boys who live fairly, honorably and decently become men who live the same way. Men can outgrow scouting, but they need never outgrow the scout oath and the scout law. They are as important in the adult world as they are in scouting. The things I learned in scouting have stayed with me and, I don't like to think of them as lessons, they were the result of normal American kids doing what normal, average American boys oughta be doing and what they have fun doing. And as we salute scouting on its birthday, it's my hope that every American boy has his chance to be a good scout. And I want to congratulate the Boy Scouts on this crusade to strengthen the arm of liberty.
SKELTON: What was that you said, Jimmy?
STEWART: Strengthen the arm of liberty, Red.
SKELTON: Hey, that's it. By golly, that's it. Instead of having a rodeo for the scouts, why don't we take 'em all, right now, to the Statue of Liberty where a big ceremony is going on back in New York and we'll show them what the arm of liberty really means. Can't we?

ROGERS: That's a swell idea, Red.

STEWART: Sure is, Roy. So stand by scouts all over the country as your scout jamboree takes you now to the Statue of Liberty on Bedloe's Island in New York Harbor.

The show then transfers to New York and reporter Charles Kevy, who introduces Arthur A. Schuck, Chief Scout Executive of the Boy Scouts of America. Schuck then delivers a short speech on the Strengthen the Arm of Liberty crusade. Hannah Shore, as the Spirit of Liberty, then presents Amory Houghton, President of the Boy Scouts of America, a torch as a symbol of liberty and freedom. Houghton makes a short speech and turns the torch over to a local scout master, who in turn, lights a torch held by Eagle Scout Allen Fritz. Fritz leads all the scouts in saying the Scout Oath. With the New York ceremonies complete, Kevy returns the program to the Pacific coast.

Back in California, Lyle Bond makes his final credits and the show comes to an end.

(2) Thursday, February 11, 1950

Appearing with Stewart on the program were William Boyd (Hopalong Cassidy), Hal Peary (radio's Great Gildersleeve), Amory Houghton, and Arthur A. Schuck. This program is not available for listening.

(3) Saturday, February 10, 1951

This show is not available for listening. Stewart and Bob Hope host the show. Roy Rogers and Dale Evans join them.

(4) Saturday, February 9, 1952

This year's show was an hour in length, but it could be played as two separate half-hour shows. The latter is the way it appears to have been aired on many stations. The first half-hour segment appears to be titled *Forward on Liberties Team*, and does not feature Jimmy Stewart. The announcer on this half of the show is Harry Von Zell. Here is a summary of the show's line-up.

"Sippin' Cider Through a Straw" — Sportsmen

Alan Young then talks about the Boy Scouts' new 3-year plan to increase the number of boys in scouting.

"Be a Good Scout" — The Mitchell Choir Boys (all are members of Troup 800, Hollywood)

Harry Babbitt on vocals, with Ben Lasky & the NBC Orchestra, sings a song about all the branches of the armed forces.

Mel Blanc, using his true voice and the voices of Pedro, Bugs Bunny, Tweety Bird, Sylvester and others, performs a skit about scouting.

God Bless America — Harry Babbitt

Next, several athletes talk about scouting. Those participating were:
Glen Davis (football)
Lloyd Mangrum (golf)
Mel Patton (track)
Bill McCall (football)

"Marching Along Together" — Bill Lasky and the NBC Orchestra

The second half-hour of the program, which is titled *Tomorrow's America*, begins with a voice stating that "every 37 seconds, somewhere in America, a boy becomes a scout." After this introduction, Jimmy Stewart begins the program.

STEWART: Good afternoon. The great French philosopher Dennis Diderot once observed…

A voice, with a French accent, says that children are essentially criminals, but their physical strength limits their ability to carry out that criminality.

STEWART: Now, even though Diderot was one of the greatest geniuses of his time, his statement may well be open to argument…conceivably, it is wrong.

A female voice responds, "Wrong, it's ridiculous…"

STEWART: However, we need only look around the world today at Korea, Red China, the Kefauver Commission, race riots, to realize that essentially, criminality in all its forms, is the housing of a childish mind in an adult body. It is, therefore, with the maturing of the children's mind that Americans are concerned.

Next, there is a short skit in which Mr. Calluchi, a businessman, pays two boys $3 each to deliver handbills announcing his sale around the neighborhood. One of the boys wants to just throw the handbills in the garbage, but the other thinks they should follow through on their promise to deliver them. They do throw the handbills in the garbage, saying, "Business is business."

STEWART: Yes, business is business, and our whole world is based on trusting other people. Unless there is trust, our whole machinery of living flies apart and, seems to me, that the future of the entire human race depends, in the ultimate, on each individual member. In the case of Mr. Calluchi and his handbills…

In a continuation of the previous skit, we hear Mr. Calluchi complaining that he has no customers for his sale. He paid $20 to have the handbills printed and a total of $6 to have them delivered, and still no customers.

STEWART: As a matter of fact, Mr. Calluchi went out of business. The sale, which flopped, that was the last straw. And a small part of our economy broke down because two boys couldn't be trusted to do something they'd promised and they'd been paid for in advance. Two boys who will grow up to what? I remember very well quite a long time ago when I was a scout, our scoutmaster was talking to us one evening about being trustworthy. He used an analogy I'll never forget.

We are then treated to the scoutmaster's analogy. He says that when you put a stamp on a letter, you trust the U.S. Mail to deliver it. You know that it will be delivered. He tells the boys that it should be the aim of every scout to be as trustworthy as the U.S. Mail.

STEWART: When we look at our children and think of their future, the closest thing to our heart is that they grow up to become mature, happy, successful citizens. The scout law, which all Boy Scouts pledge themselves to obey, consists of 12 simple words which teach a profound lesson.

We hear a series of boys deliver each word of the scout law…a scout is trustworthy, loyal, helpful, friendly, courteous, kind, obedient, cheerful, thrifty, brave, clean and reverent.

STEWART: The future of a democracy hangs on the character of its citizens. And scouting is very proud of its contribution that it has made over the past 42 years, towards the training of 19 million young citizens. But what is scouting? How do boys learn the real meaning of their oath and law? Well, as a former boy scout myself; I…let me try to tell you parts of the very colorful story.

A short skit emphasizes that a scout is a friend to all and a brother to other scouts.

STEWART: In August of 1951, in a beautiful valley in Austria, 13,000 scouts from India, Ceylon, Greece, Egypt, South Africa, Denmark, England and scores of other countries, joined hands in friendship with the scouts from America. Arm in arm they marched these scouts of the 7th World Jamboree. And there in that valley, at a campfire, each American scout broke a small candle to share with a jamboree friend from another land. And, in the stillness of the night, while he lit his candle, each pledged himself to keep the fires of freedom burning, to build a stronger brotherhood of youth through scouting friendship. There were many other thrilling sights and great moments, but some will never be mentioned because they were single person-to-person incidents, almost too sacred to chronicle.

In the next short skit, two scouts exchange neckerchiefs and find that they have very much in common even though they were from different countries.

As "Auld Lang Syne" plays, Stewart continues.

STEWART: And so boys from all over the world marched back, not just to their homes so widely separated, but also to a destiny that will build for themselves toward a free world of tomorrow for all people.

"Auld Lang Syne" continues and ends.

STEWART: We're all extremely concerned with Korea, well, this is a good thing. We should be concerned. However, I've often felt that when a soldier goes out to fight, he at least knows there's a possibility of his being killed. But when a child starts out to school, or when a family starts out to a picnic, death is the last thing that's even thought of.

We hear the sounds of a car accident and, as Stewart speaks again, we hear the sound of a woman crying.

STEWART: This past December, the one millionth American was killed in a traffic accident. This ghastly figure is almost twice the number of Americans who have been killed in all our wars put together — 35,000 of them every year. A small city obliterated every 12 months. Now it's taken us 50 years to kill our first million, but we're improving, mind you; it will take us only 30 years to kill our second million.

In a short sketch, we are told about the scout's safety week campaign. Scouts will help younger students home from school and make sure that they obey traffic lights.

STEWART: As a part of their public service duties, included in the scout slogan, "Do a good turn daily," scouts across the nation are working hard to lower the ghastly toll of human life taken by the automobile.

Over music, we hear voices saying, "Get out to vote."

STEWART: Physical scientists, those who make the atom bomb possible, are very aware of the fact that what happened to us politically, will determine what happens to us every other way. Our toughest and most elusive problem is how to organize society. Scouts are taught that politics is not a game to be played so that we get whatever we want for ourselves or a game in which men are expected to behave like grownup children. A scout is taught the importance of government and the true significance of democracy. Democracy comes from a Greek word meaning "power of the people." And as a realistic project in participating citizenship, and a significant good turn to the nation, the scouts will help to get out the vote in the 1952 presidential election.

We hear a few scouts placing "Register and Vote" signs in a business.

STEWART: Across the nation, posters encouraging citizens to vote will be placed in store windows, railroad stations, bus depots, post offices, hotel lobbies and churches by the Boy Scouts. And to tell you about this great campaign to get out the vote, I have a very special guest I want you to meet. An old friend and a man whose personal vision is making this magnificent project a reality — the Chief Scout Executive of the Boy Scouts of America, Dr. Arthur A. Schuck.

Dr. Schuck says hello to Jimmy.

STEWART: Chief, we all recognize the significance of this get out the vote campaign. Will you tell us something about it?

Dr. Schuck explains the campaign to the listeners.

STEWART: But, how is this to be done, Chief?

Dr. Schuck continues his explanation of the project. When he completes his speech, we hear a short segment of music. Then we hear boys putting out flyers to vote and explaining to an older woman the importance of voting.

STEWART: As well as providing the right influence in character building and in the struggle towards adult maturity, scouting is a lot of fun.

Dr. Schuck talks of games and skills building teamwork and the ability to follow rules.

STEWART: However, to an 11-year-old boy, games are just plain fun.

We hear a group of scouts playing games.

STEWART: Only one of dozens of active, indoor games played with no equipment by scouts everywhere. Scouting, of course, means different things to different boys.

Some scouting activities are listed in a short skit — tracking animals, cooking, camping, etc.

STEWART: Perhaps the most popular activity in scouting is camping. Every year over a million boys get the opportunity to spend some time sleeping under canvas by a lake or in the forest. The camping and hiking activities are carefully supervised by scoutmasters, camp leaders, along with the ordinary fun of everyday camping and being with the gang. Scouts learn to catch the quick flash of a deer's tail as it disappears into the woods or to see a muskrat before it dives for an opening in its house, or to recognize the squirrel or the song of the wren. Many a present day biologist or physicist, science teacher, got his start as a Boy Scout naturalist on a camping trip. And this thought brings me to the subject of merit badges. All of us here on this Earth are looking, seeking and straining after one thing — it's happiness. The attaining of happiness is, sadly, simple and tragically difficult at the same time. Many millions of Americans, until they reach the age of 35 or 40, are filled with ambition and fire. Many of us realize our dreams were nothing more than just dreams after all and we become depressed and discouraged with the fact that life is leading relentlessly towards anticlimax. Now in scouting, all boys are encouraged to earn merit badges. The choice of subjects is almost limitless.

We hear boys naming the subjects for many merit badges.

STEWART: …and many, many, many, many others. Adults I know who were once scouts, feel that their entire lives were influenced by their merit badge work. Dr. Paul Sipel, who went with Admiral Byrd to the South Pole, first became interested in science through his merit badge work. And there are thousands of doctors, radio engineers, forest rangers, musicians, mechanics or writers whose ambitions were first kindled while they were scouts earning their merit badges. Every scout is given an opportunity to earn merit badges in whatever subjects he feels interested; and also, he's urged to investigate others about which he knows nothing. His merit badge work will remain with him and influence him perhaps all the rest of his life.

Music and a skit follow with an older man using his carpentry skills.

STEWART: I think the most touching story I ever heard about the influence of scouting on a boy came from a scoutmaster in Hollywood. The lad was a tenderfoot scout and after a troop meeting one night, he approached my scoutmaster friend and from the way he behaved, edged around the subject, the scoutmaster knew he was terribly upset and something serious was bothering him.

In a short sketch, the boy tells his scoutmaster that he cheated in school. The scoutmaster tells him to tell his teacher what he had done. He does, and the teacher gives him a second chance.

STEWART: Yes, a boy learns many things from scouting. Many skills may seem unimportant at the moment and require the chemistry of time to bring about their true value. A scoutmaster in Minnesota recently received a rumpled letter, stained with Korean mud, written by one of his former scouts whose tiny campfire tonight is shielded from the eyes of the communist enemy.

In the part of the letter that we hear, the scout tells how he is using his first aid skills as a medic in the military.

STEWART: A scout is obedient. The great men of history have learned to obey when they were young. They learned to discipline themselves before they could give orders to others. Obedience is a manly quality and a scout is taught that. A scout is shown how obedience means self-control, strength of character. One time after George Washington had successfully defeated the British Army, an officer asked the General's mother...

A man's voice asks, "How'd you raise such a brilliant son?"

STEWART: His mother touched on none of Washington's qualities as bravery, honor or character, as she replied...

A woman's voice simply states, "I taught him to obey."

STEWART: Well, we could go on and on, but let's take a look into the future of scouting. Dr. Schuck, I've been hearing rumors about a big three-year program in scouting. Can you tell us something about it?

Schuck outlines the high points of a plan called "Forward on Liberties Team," which will have 13 million boys in scouting by 1954.

STEWART: And the providing of that training is a great challenge to scouting in the coming years isn't it?

Dr. Schuck says that it is and outlines how it will be accomplished.

STEWART: The more than two million current members of the Boy Scouts certainly have a rich experience to look forward to as they go forward on liberties team. Now one of those lads, a brand-new member of troop 187, of Fairfax, Virginia, is standing right here with us now. His name is Richard Lee Hunt and he enjoys a rare distinction — he is the 19 millionth member of the Boy Scouts of America.

Dr. Schuck welcomes the boy and then the two of them, along with all the others present, give the scout oath.

STEWART: Remember, every 37 seconds somewhere in America, a boy becomes a scout. If your son is not a scout, urge him to join. Explain to him the fun and fellowship he'll enjoy, the lessons he will learn and the friends he will make by becoming one of those lucky lads who joins the Boy Scouts of America.

As the show closes, we are told that James Stewart can currently be seen in the Cecil B. DeMille film, *The Greatest Show on Earth*.

The credits for the entire one-hour program are also listed and include:
PRODUCER: Glen Rice
DIRECTOR: Fred Weihe
WRITER: Harry W. Junkin
ANNOUNCER: Bill Rippe

The cast included: Denise Alexander, Ruth Newton, Sylvia Davis, Rich Carvell, David Anderson, Jack Grimes, Bill Quinn, Luis Van Rooten

This show is not generally available to collectors, but is a part of the NBC Collection at the Library of Congress.

(5) Thursday, July 23, 1953

Once again, Stewart was the narrator for the annual Boy Scout Jamboree radio show. The program is not available for listening.

Brickhouse-Hubbard Show

NETWORK: WGN-AM, Chicago, IL (non-network show)
HOSTS: Jack Brickhouse, Eddie Hubbard

Jack Brickhouse (b. January 24, 1916, d. August 6, 1998), a 1998 inductee into the Radio Hall of Fame, and Eddie Hubbard hosted this daily 55-minute talk/interview show for WGN (4:05-5:00 p.m.). In late 1958, Jimmy Stewart was in town to promote his new film, *Bell, Book and Candle*, which was set to open on Christmas Day. He also talked about Method acting, a few of his other movies, and aviation. During the course of the interview, it is also revealed that Stewart had been a guest on the show before, but the date of that appearance has not been established.

In all likelihood, Stewart did many such "local" interviews over the course of his career. Whether in a city to promote a new film, attend some gathering or just a visit, it is likely that he did one or more interviews on local radio. Most of those interviews were never taped or the tapes were lost or reused. A few may still reside with the original owner or a family member. Tracking them down and documenting them is a next to impossible task. Fortunately, this one has survived and can be listened to online at the Museum of Broadcast Communications website (*www.museum.tv*). Here is how that interview unfolded:

HUBBARD: Well, Jack, I think that now's as good a time as any to bring in our guest up to the microphone and since you gave me the courtesy of telling the folks who he was, why don't you go through the introductory period here.

BRICKHOUSE: Well, if you have to introduce this fellow here, that means…if you have to have him introduced to you, that means you must have been living in a cave or something for the last…cough…years.

HUBBARD: Well, my grandmother hasn't seen a movie since Warner Baxter…I mean…ah…you mull that around. Maybe she hasn't seen Mr. Stewart work. That's kind of an incongruous situation though, huh.

STEWART: I remember Warner Baxter very well, you know.

BRICKHOUSE: This is Jimmy Stewart and, brother, here is a man. Jimmy welcome to Chicago.

STEWART: Thank you, thank you, Jack, very happy to be here.

HUBBARD: Last time we had Jim on these microphones, you were busy at a ballpark and weren't able to get here, as I recall.

BRICKHOUSE: That's right…that's right. Jim, you have a particular reason for being here, you might as well tell us what it is.

STEWART: Well, my one reason for being here is just I'm on my way home from Washington. I've been there for about ten days working on a picture, *The FBI Story*. That's the first reason. Then the second reason, I'm sort of here to put in a good word for another picture that is opening here Christmas Day, I think…at the Woods Theater. I'm ah…I did the picture with a local girl you may have heard of…Kim Novak.

HUBBARD: We've heard of her.

BRICKHOUSE: Wow!

HUBBARD: Yes, we have.

STEWART: And…ah…it's a sort of a comedy. As a matter of fact, I use that term not loosely, because we'll find out after Christmas whether it's a comedy or not, but I…I like to believe it is. I hope it is because I think maybe we could use some. I hope this sort of is a part of a trend. I think the movies have been taking themselves too seriously over the last several years and I…I hope we can get some that people can go to the movie theater and come out laughing instead of come out scratching themselves or…ah…or go to a psychiatrist or something.

HUBBARD: I was gonna say, I'm glad you're in a comedy. The last two… ah couple of pictures I saw you in I had to sort of sweat it out there with you. You had your leg broken in one and you were a victim…or you witnessed this murder and that was in *Rear Window*.

STEWART: Um…hum.

HUBBARD: And then the other picture was *Vertigo*…and that was a rough thing.

STEWART: Yeah, well, I'm getting a little tired of that myself.

HUBBARD: Suspense and intrigue.

BRICKHOUSE: Well, a friend of yours was shooting right in front of this building not long ago…Alfred Hitchcock.

STEWART: Yes, well, he was here, I think, with the new Cary Grant picture.

HUBBARD/BRICKHOUSE: Um…hum, that's right.

STEWART: I'm a great Hitchcock fan. I think he has about as much talent as anybody in the business. He's a real exciting man to work for. He seems to have just a bottomless pit of talent. I don't know where he gets his energy and where he gets his imagination and his talent. He's one in a million.

BRICKHOUSE: Jimmy, I remember this fellow if, for no other reason than he cast you as a murderer. And I confess, I would not ever suspect you of being able to get away with the part of a murderer and you did in that one *The Rope*. That was Hitchcock, wasn't it?

STEWART: Yeah, but I was a detective in that one.

BRICKHOUSE: No, no, no, I'm talking about one where you were a murderer. Now which one am I thinking of?

STEWART: Well, that's way, way…boy you're going…

BRICKHOUSE: With Rosalind Russell.

STEWART: No, that was *The Thin Man*.

BRICKHOUSE: Grace Kelly rather, Grace Kelly, no?

STEWART: Yeah, that was a Hitchcock picture, but I caught the murderer in that one. The only time where I've killed anybody…where I wanted to do it was way back years ago in one of *The Thin Man* pictures…*After the Thin Man*…and they finally discovered that I was the real killer.

BRICKHOUSE: That wasn't a Hitchcock movie?

STEWART: No.

BRICKHOUSE: Well, I'm wrong. But, I know that I have this sharp memory…I know I have a sharp memory of your being a murderer, because when you walked into the studio today, it just seemed…ah…here's this pleasant, placid, gentlemanly fellow who, you know is…

HUBBARD: Well, Jack…

STEWART: Well, it's close, but I…that was the picture where I almost got murdered. Maybe that's what you meant.

BRICKHOUSE: Which picture are you referring to…what was the title of this film?

STEWART: *Rear Window*.

BRICKHOUSE: Yeah, you had a broken leg in that one. It's coming back to me now. You had Grace Kelly…

STEWART: And the murderer came and threw me out the window and broke my other leg.

BRICKHOUSE: Well, I'm glad we're nice and confused. It's a good way to get the show started.

HUBBARD: Well you know, that last picture...that *Vertigo*...I was going to ask you...you talked about trends and casting...I know that for awhile William Powell and Myrna Loy were usually linked together in most of their pictures and now this is the second picture you've made with Kim Novak.

STEWART: Um-hum.

HUBBARD: Is this gonna be a sort of a team type thing?

STEWART: I don't know...it's okay with me.

HUBBARD: You don't mind at all.

STEWART: No, don't mind at all. I know this is an entirely different kind of a thing. It's, as I say, kind of a light...light comedy thing. Kim's awful good in it. She's ah...the other thing, the *Vertigo*, this is kind of a tough assignment, you know, it's a dual role and kind of heavy and this is kind of tough stuff to do. But I think Kim learned a lot...an awful lot from Hitchcock and in this thing, *Bell Book and Candle*, she does an awful good job and I think...I think Chicago will be proud of their Kim.

HUBBARD: I remember reading a quote by one of the syndicated Hollywood columnists on you not long ago, Jimmy, in which you, I guess, if you were quoted correctly in this thing, took a pretty good whack at some of the younger generation of actors and actresses who, I guess, your real beef was that they come to Hollywood and then can't wait to get back to New York or keep screaming and hollering that they wanna get out of there. Do you remember the piece?

STEWART: Yeah, I think it was in *The Daily Variety*. A fellow came out, Dave Kauffman, I know very well and it just happened. I was in a talkative mood, I guess, and so he printed it. I don't talk much usually, but I did this day. Yeah, I sort of sounded off about this young crowd and about movies in general. I have very strong feelings about the sort of the Method actors I suppose you'd call them. I'm getting a little bored with all that. I'm getting a little bored with the fact that they seem to feel that they go to this Method school of whatever it is and there's some kind of a high priest and he waves a magic wand over them and touches them and then evidently that means that they're destined for immortality and actually they can do no wrong and they can...there isn't anything, as far as acting is concerned, or writing or directing or raising a family or being in politics, that they can't do. And, ah, it makes it kind of tough for people then, that have to work with them, because you have to sort of wait around for these people to get this message from the...from this spiritual being that they sort of go to; and sometimes it takes hours before they...this comes to them, and this gets a little tiring.

BRICKHOUSE: Meantime, the whole crew is being held up.

STEWART: And then so many times it happens that when they do come out with this inspirational thing that they're going to give to the public who is waiting for them. Ah...you either can't understand what they say or they do it so badly that you have to do it all over again. I...I...I'm...I think that was...

HUBBARD: Jimmy, I would assume that you've worked with some of these people to have adopted this first-hand opinion.

STEWART: No, I haven't worked with very many of them...

HUBBARD: Not many of them are working.

STEWART: ...but I know some of them and I know a lot of directors who have worked with them and, ah, it's pretty tough...it's...it's...it's pretty tough. The thing I object most...most of all is that they seem to insist that the only way to do anything right is to improvise and they have no...they have no basis of skill. They have no...they haven't learned the fundamentals. They haven't learned to walk before they can water ski, you know, they...they...they have nothing to rely on except improvisation. And I think this probably this is sort of a sign of the times. You know, in music today so much of the...so much of the music is improvisation. Now this is fine up to a point. I read a thing the other day about a fellow, a very famous fellow, I suppose there's no use in mentioning his name, who has had a wonderful pianist and had a great jazz band for a long time, and suddenly he announced that he was taking piano lessons. This came as a great shock to everybody, but he...his explanation was that he thought that if he was going to keep on breaking the rules, he might as well learn what the rules are. And this goes into acting, too.

HUBBARD: That's a good comparison there, Jim.

BRICKHOUSE: Now, your early days, for example, were spent in the acting business in the company of some other people who have been... developed a very great reputations in the movie business weren't they?

STEWART: Yeah, I was in a stock company years ago when I first got out of college, up in Massachusetts...ah...Margaret Sullavan, Hank Fonda, Kent Smith, Myron McCormick...oh...Bretaigne Windust, Millie Natwick...ah...these are people that have...that have gone on in the theater and ah...this certainly wasn't a wild crowd of people that... there wasn't any question about improvisation as far as we were concerned; it was a question of learning and learning by experience. We'd all been to college; we all had a sort of basis as far as education is concerned. So many people come up to me and say, well now I want to get into...I want to act. I know I can...I'm just sure...and I just don't want to waste my time in school. Now what do I do? And I say, well, in the first place let's get something straight, you're completely off base as far as wasting your time in school. I think if you wanna act, just go to school and study English and a couple of foreign languages and history and some mathematics, if you can do it, and a little science and then after you get that basis, well then, if you wanna go in the theater, there are plenty of training grounds where you can...where you can start with it. But, get that basis first.

BRICKHOUSE: That makes a lot of sense.

HUBBARD: I wonder if we could hold Jim for another while here. This is the halfway portion, Jimmy. I wonder if we could take sort of an intermission here, have a cigarette along with us, and we'll pause here for a moment and then we'll get back to Jimmy. Okay?

BRICKHOUSE: Hubbard-Brickhouse 4:05 till 5 everyday Monday through Friday on WGN, Chicago. Our guest today is Jimmy Stewart.

HUBBARD: Well, we're enjoying this little chat here with Jimmy very, very much. You know you mentioned a young lady that I always admired and you made quite a few pictures with her, Jimmy, Margaret Sullavan. And I can't...ah...I was trying to think of the picture knowing that you were going to be here today.

BRICKHOUSE: *Shop Around the Corner.*

STEWART: *Show Around the Corner,* yeah.

HUBBARD: That's the one, yeah.

STEWART: Ernst Lubitsch production.

HUBBARD: And I was really digging way back. I was trying to think of some of the early pictures of Jimmy. Remember one you made, it was a naval picture as I recall.

STEWART: *Navy Blue and Gold?*

HUBBARD: Was that with Raymond Walburn? He was a captain, as I recall. Virginia Bruce.

STEWART: Oh no, no, that was a musical. That was one called *Born to Dance.*

HUBBARD: You had a couple of lines in there about...ah...little patter about good morning, Miss, and how are you, how's the captain...

STEWART: Oh, I said much more than that. I...I actually sang...I haven't been ask to sing in a film since. Yeah, I sang a thing...it was a Cole Porter score. I sang a thing called "Hey babe, hi babe, how you doing today babe."

HUBBARD: That was a big hit song, too.

STEWART: Yeah, big hit. I forget who the fellow who made it a hit, I…it sure wasn't me. There were a lot of hits in that thing — *I've Got You Under My Skin* that Virginia Bruce sang; *You'd Be So Easy to Love* that I always say I introduced it. I introduced it, but then when I went to the preview, there was somebody else singing it. I was mouthing it, but somebody else singing it.

BRICKHOUSE: Were you surprised at that?

STEWART: I was pretty surprised. I wasn't sure it wasn't me because I wasn't exactly…I hoped it was.

BRICKHOUSE: Ever find out who it was? Perry Como, maybe.

STEWART: No…now who was it? Bert Eberly? Bert Eberly…

BRICKHOUSE: Bob Eberly.

STEWART: Bob Eberly.

BRICKHOUSE: Bob Eberly was with Jimmy Dorsey — good singer. Well, at least they flattered you or they picked a good one for you.

STEWART: Yeah, they picked a good one.

BRICKHOUSE: Well, now, of course, if you wanna…if you wanna talk to Mr. Stewart and really get him going these days, you talk about aviation. You can really…

HUBBARD: Well, I feel…

BRICKHOUSE: I would like to have been…I would like to have been a mouse in the corner listening to a conversation this full colonel right here in the Army…in the Air Force, Mr., or rather Colonel James Stewart and a fellow who, if they gave commissions in commercial aviation, would probably be a seven-star general, William A. Patterson of United Airlines. You two were together…practically inseparable when Jimmy's in town and I have a hunch that between the two of you settle most of the problems of aviation for the next hundred years, didn't you, Jim?

STEWART: Yeah, I think aviation is a funny thing about this. You can talk almost…almost as much about airplanes and about flying as you can about acting…and you can lie almost as much about it.

BRICKHOUSE: Like golf and fishing, huh?

STEWART: Yeah, and I think that's not only true of people interested in aviation, but if you'll…if you'll think back about conversations of any kind that you've had, everybody…everybody seems to have an airplane story. They have a story about when they were on this airliner and they were going so-and-so, and such-and-such happened and they did so-and-so. I've never been in a group of people yet that everybody didn't have their own little private story about…about flying; which is a good thing, you know.

BRICKHOUSE: What...ah...what is your feeling about aviation we'll say in the next 25 or 30 years?...commercial, as well as, we'll say military.

STEWART: As commercial...commercially, I...I just agree with ah...well, people like Mr. Patterson and C.R. Smith. There's no question about what they believe. They believe that aviation is just starting. And with the jet airplane, this is really gonna open up air travel to not just a few. It's amazing, I think, that 70% of the people in this country have never been up in an airplane. Now 70, that's a lot...that's a big percentage...70%.

BRICKHOUSE: It certainly is.

STEWART: And, ah...these men feel that the jet airplane is going...is going to get some of that 70% and I have no doubt it. I think that flying, as a mode of transportation, is just getting started and is really in the next ten years...ah...I would think that that 70% is going to be cut in half.

BRICKHOUSE: No question about it, Jim. What about the military? How do we stand in your opinion we'll say from what you think you know, or what you maybe do know, with, we'll say, other major powers?

STEWART: Well, militarily, I think as far as aviation is concerned, as far as the air power concept of our military organization, we're second to none...by a million miles, we're the first power in the world. Military aviation, of course, is in a sort of almost a state of flux now because of...because of the importance that is being given to missiles. However, I think as usually happens in a thing like this of new breakthroughs, scientific breakthroughs, people get ahead of themselves. And although people are talking about the intercontinental ballistic missile as though it is a thing in being and something that is operational, the truth of the matter is, it's not operational. It's not operational here and it's not operational in Russia, and it won't be for quite some time. In the meantime, the heavy bomber, I believe, is our first line of defense, and we have the finest heavy bomber force that man has ever devised in the...in the being of the Strategic Air Command. It's a...it's...it's the most amazing military force that has ever been devised by man. It's not only the most powerful force; it actually is a force that speaks for peace more than any...anything that has ever been devised by man. And this...this is quite a combination. I think the Strategic Air Command has kept World War III from becoming a reality. I can't help but feel that it will continue to do so.

HUBBARD: All these things we have to take really seriously because here's a man that we flew from New York to Paris with not too long ago on that long flight as you recall.

BRICKHOUSE: Yes.

HUBBARD: ...on those early planes, so this fellow knows his business about aviation.

BRICKHOUSE: Tell me, where is the Spirit of St. Louis right now, Jim?

STEWART: Well, you know, there's...there were three of them built. And I got so excited about doing the picture and everything; I have a friend, Joe DeBona, who I've...a friend of mine for a long time, flyer... speed raced, as a matter of fact, and we found an old Ryan airplane up in Denver, out in a cow pasture, and I know some other fellows in flying that...that built this thing up and made a replica of the Spirit of St. Louis so this was used in the picture, too. And I rented it to the movie company and then at the end of the picture it reverted back to me. So, I gave it to the Air Force Academy for their museum. Now that was a year and a half ago, but they haven't built the museum yet and in the meantime you just can't sweep an airplane under the rug, so I've been paying rent for this airplane out at a hanger and I...I've never had so much trouble giving a thing away. So if you know anybody who would like to have the Spirit of St. Louis, please contact me.

BRICKHOUSE: Have you talked very much to Lindbergh since the movie was made?

STEWART: No, I just...ah...I remember when it opened in New York; I went to New York a couple of days after the opening and I was sitting in the hotel room with Leland Hayward, the producer, and the phone rang and it was Lindbergh. And, he said a few words, but then he said, "Well, now, we went to see the picture, but I'd like you to speak to my wife." So, Mrs. Lindbergh got on and she said well she liked the picture very much. She said that they went with two of their children that were home. The rest were away, but they went down, bought tickets to the Radio City Music Hall and sat...and one little girl...

BRICKHOUSE: Now wait a minute.

STEWART: Yeah.

BRICKHOUSE: Pardon me for interrupting. Lindbergh had to buy tickets to see this movie?

STEWART: He didn't have to, but he did. That's...this is Lindbergh. He's not gonna go and say well I'd better have...give me some passes. He went to the ticket office and bought 'em. Well, the little girl was... ah...was very interested in it, of course, and...if you'll remember, if you saw the picture, on the way across the ocean I ran into icing conditions on the airplane. I picked up a lot of ice and got closer and closer to the ocean and he started throwing things out and he felt sure that he was gonna crash. And…ah…Mrs. Lindbergh said that the little girl, the little Lindbergh daughter, got farther up on the edge of her seat and farther up on the edge of her seat and got more excited and more excited. And, of course, we were picking up more ice and getting closer to the water. And finally the little girl couldn't stand it any longer and she turned to her mother and she said, "Mother, Daddy did make it, didn't he?" So that…that…that was sort of the Lindbergh appraisal of the picture, which I…I accepted.

HUBBARD: And also a great portrayal by you to…

BRICKHOUSE: Speaking of little girls, you have twin daughters. How old are they, Jim?

STEWART: They're seven…seven and growing up.

BRICKHOUSE: How does it feel to have two rings in your nose instead of just one?

STEWART: Well, it's double trouble, but I love them.

BRICKHOUSE: No question about it. I understand Mrs. Stewart's health is excellent.

STEWART: Yes, absolutely wonderful.

BRICKHOUSE: Jimmy, I wish we could talk everybody in America to see *Bell Book and Candle*. It's gonna open at the Woods Christmas Day. When *The FBI Story* comes out, we'll be certainly watching for that one very, very anxiously. And, I think that for a fellow like you to devote as much time as you have to our little opus here today is pretty wonderful.

STEWART: Well, I've enjoyed it; I always do, and the next time I'm through I hope you'll invite me back.

HUBBARD: Well, it's an open invitation, Jimmy, believe me.

BRICKHOUSE: Absolutely…Jimmy Stewart and thank you very much, Jimmy Stewart.

HUBBARD: Thank you, Jimmy.

Bud's Bandwagon

Bud Widom was the disc jockey for this music show transcribed and distributed by the Armed Forces Radio and Television Service (AFRTS). More than 200 shows were broadcast from 1953 until 1955. The show was designed to air five days a week. Each day Widom would play records and interview someone in the "Celebrity Lounge." In between songs, Widom would dispense his own brand of corny jokes. Widom's only other claim to "fame" is his appearance as General Jonathan B. Thompson in the 1968 film, *The Green Slime*.

SHOWS FEATURING JIMMY STEWART:

(1) Show # 423 (1954)
Widom begins his show by playing the following records:
"Manhattan Mambo" — Henri Rene Orchestra and Chorus
"She Doesn't Laugh Like You" — Johnny Holiday
"The Song Is You" — Dave Brubeck Quartet
"Au Revoir" — Teresa Brewer

At this point in the show, Widom announces that he attended the Hollywood premiere of Alfred Hitchcock's *Rear Window* a few days earlier. While there, he interviewed several people. He plays back bits of interviews with Edith Head and Georgie Jessel. Then, he talks with Jimmy Stewart.

WIDOM: ...Jimmy, first of all, can I tell you this was a swell film and we enjoyed your performance immensely.

STEWART: Well, thank you very much. This is going to the Armed Forces Radio all over...

WIDOM: This is going to the fellows overseas, right, certainly no strangers to you.

STEWART: Well, it's always a pleasure to say hello to them and I do it right now, say hello to...to all the men overseas, wish them the best of luck, and ah...sort of bad to say, I wish you were right here, but ah...you know.

WIDOM: I think they know what you mean. Jimmy, I'd like to ask you something. In your role, you're confined to a wheelchair practically 90% of the time. Did you find this any handicap in portraying the character?

STEWART: Well, no. I don't think so because that's...ah...that's sort of what the fella was...ah...had to put up with. He...he got all busted up because he was a cameraman trying to take a picture of a motor race and he got too close to the car and it hit him and broke his leg. So...

WIDOM: Of course, you never got too close to Grace Kelly, did you?

STEWART: Well, I got as close as I could. She's a very nice girl to get close to.

WIDOM: Jimmy, one more question. We understand that there's a big one that our fellas will especially enjoy that you're in...*Strategic Air Command*. Ah...is that finished now?

STEWART: It's all finished. I imagine that it'll be released about the... after the first of the year. This was sort of a labor of love with me and ah...Bernie Lay, who wrote the story. Ah, we just ran it the other night, ah...I...I...I think the picture has, ah...has a lot of possibilities. I think...

WIDOM: Did you shoot most of it in Omaha?

STEWART: Well, no. We shot a lot of it in MacDill Field, in Florida. Some of it at Carswell Field. This is the story of the Strategic Air Command that a lot of you fellas out there know a great deal about... and...ah...one of the purposes of doing the picture was to acquaint the people back here at home more about the Strategic Air Command because I don't think they, ah...have been able to know too much about it up to this time. I hope that this, in a small way or in a big way, will be able to acquaint the people of America more about the Strategic Air Command and let them know what a great thing it has been and still is and will be in the future to the security of the country.

WIDOM: For General LeMay, may I thank you?

STEWART: Well, for General...to General LeMay, I'd like to say thank you because he...ah...he really gave the facilities of SAC to us from A-to-Z, and...ah...went with us all the way on it. We hope we can deliver for him.

WIDOM: Wonderful. Jimmy, we'll be looking for it and again congratulations on your performance in *Rear Window*.

STEWART: Thanks very much. Bye.

WIDOM: Thanks again, Jimmy Stewart.

Widom then talks to Jerry Lewis and Sara Berner and plays two final records before signing off.

"Candelabra Boogie" — Jerry Lewis
"Slow But Surely" — Gordon Jenkins

(2) Show #542 (1955)

The show begins with its normal theme music and an announcer saying, "That shy guy, Jimmy Stewart, is Bud Widom's guest today." Widom then plays the following records:

"I'm Sitting On Top Of the World" — George Gerard & His New Orleans Five
"I Only Live for You" — Frank Cannon
"Snow Dreams" — Connie Russell
"Mama Inez" — Marco Ritzo
"Can You" — Mickey Marlowe
"Melody of Love" — Four Aces

After these songs, Widom introduces his special guest for the day.

WIDOM: We're very privileged to have with us in the Celebrity Lounge today a gentleman from Hollywood who usually visits this routine by magic lantern. Of course, he's welcome whether he's on the silver screen or in person. And, he's your favorite and mine — Jimmy Stewart. Jimmy, what brings you our way today?

STEWART: Well, I thought that the members of the movie audience all over the country might be interested in hearing a few things about *The Far Country*. It's my new picture which we photographed up in Canada.

WIDOM: Well, we certainly would like to hear about it so start right in, Jimmy. And, as a matter of fact, I'll help you by throwing some questions your way now and then. In fact, suppose you tell us who else is in *The Far Country*.

STEWART: Ruth Roman, Corinne Calvet, Jay C. Flippen, Henry Morgan [later known as Harry Morgan], and Walter Brennan.

WIDOM: That's certainly a real interesting cast and one which can only mean good for us moviegoers. Tell me, Jimmy, was it real rough shooting up in Canada away from the comforts of a Hollywood soundstage?

STEWART: Well, yes. A lot of the picture was shot in the Columbia Ice Field. This is a glacier — a huge glacier up in the Canadian Rockies which actually is the beginning of the Columbia River. In other words, the water from the Columbia River originates in the water that melts off this glacier and a lot of the sequences of the picture took place up in this glacier which is about, I imagine, about 10,000…11,000 feet high.

WIDOM: Sort of sounds like slippery work, Jimmy.

STEWART: Well, of course…sort of like doing a whole picture on a skating rink. It wasn't quite as slick as a skating rink is, but after all a glacier is made of ice so all of us had to wear a sort of rubber shoe with spikes in it…sort of like golf spikes. We had to bring horses up over the glacier and the horses were rigged out with corks which were put into this certain type of shoe that they had to be shod with and then the corks were put in so that the horses could keep their feet. In our case the rubber shoes kind of kept out the damp.

WIDOM: I see. I imagine you had some real rough weather up in Canada, Jimmy. Am I correct?

STEWART: Yeah, we really had a scare one day. This Swiss guide we had, Bruno Engler was his name…wonderful fella and just was invaluable to us during the eight or ten weeks we were up there. He'd been loaned to the company from the provincial government of Alberta. And, it just happened on this one day we were shooting, he'd warned everybody that an avalanche would occur at 3 pm. Well, of course, this seemed a little strange to us, but we'd sort of gotten to have great respect for the fella's decision and also for his judgment and everything. We were working on the glacier that day and he said the avalanche would take place just above where we were working. But the cameras were grinding at 3:05 and that's when we heard the first rumble. And before anyone knew what was happening, the tons of ice crumbled far above us and started moving down toward us with increasing momentum. But the guide had evidently sort of planned this thing ahead of time and he'd put us in a strategic spot so that we were safe from the avalanche which he was sure was going to occur, so that none of us were hurt and none of the equipment was damaged. But, it's a very awesome sight to see tons of ice start down off a mountain…very terrifying sight.

WIDOM: I can imagine. Well, Jimmy, enough of that phase of it for the moment. I notice, as I take mental inventory of what we've discussed so far, you still haven't told us what the picture's about.

STEWART: Yeah, we sort of got off the picture. We can't do that, can we? Better name it again, hadn't we?

WIDOM: Right.

STEWART: *The Far Country*. As a matter of fact, the…sort of the theme for the picture was taken from an actual fact…an actual thing that occurred. Back in about 1870, we didn't put any definite date on it, but around that time. During the start of the gold rush up in Alaska, they say that about 50,000 men invaded the Yukon in the search of gold. They came from all over the world and, of course, gold was the main thing. One thing they sort of forgot about was that in order to mine gold, they have to eat, too. Well, they sort of hunted out the place and after they'd been there for a short time — I don't know exactly how long it was — they found that the food was getting short. Well, this sort of spread all over the country and people heard about it. And, a couple of cowboys down in Wyoming decided they'd try something. And they started to take a herd of cattle from Wyoming to Alaska, and this is sort of the story of what happened. This is quite a formidable feat in the first place cause it has to be partly by boat and of course, if you know anything about cowboys, a cowboy and an ocean going boat don't make much sense together.

WIDOM: Well, they sort of mix like oil and water. But I'm sure in this case they'll be ingredients for some very fine entertainment. Jimmy Stewart, I want to thank you very much for coming to our "Celebrity Lounge" today to discuss your forthcoming Universal International picture, *The Far Country*. Before we say goodbye, tell me one more thing. I suspect it's in Technicolor. Am I right?

STEWART: In Technicolor…widescreen. Technicolor, widescreen.

WIDOM: Good. Thanks again, Jimmy Stewart. We'll all be looking for you, Ruth Roman, Corinne Calvet and Walter Brennan in *The Far Country*. Come back to see us again, will you, because you know you're always welcome.

STEWART: Thank you and goodbye everybody. See you in the movies.

(The interview sounds very much like an open-end interview of the type often used by film studios to help promote new films. Several Stewart interviews of this type — *Shenandoah, Carbine Williams, The Glenn Miller Story, Harvey, The Stratton Story, Rare Breed* — are discussed elsewhere in this book. No official record of an open-end interview being made for *The Far Country* has been encountered. No tape or record of any such interview has been found. However, Stewart does not sound like he is in the studio with Widom. Perhaps this was a special recording made just for Widom's use.)

One more record was played on the show before Widom signed off for the day.

"Funny Thing" — Tony Bennett

(3) Show # 614 (1955)

As usual, the show begins with Widom playing a succession of records, including the following.

"Slewfoot"
"Love Me Or Leave Me" — Billy Eckstine
"Sintoo" — Dolores Sharpe & the Sky Boys
"Enchantment" — Hugo Winterhalter and Henri Rene
"His and Hers" — Gary Crosby & the Paris Sisters

Widom says that he had been at the premiere of *Strategic Air Command* the other evening and had interviewed some of those who attended. He talks to Ann Blyth, Robert Stack and his wife Rosemarie Bowe, Bruce Bennett (who plays General Espy in *Strategic Air Command*), Charlton Heston and his wife Lydia, Arlene Dahl and her husband Fernando Lamas. His final interview was with Jimmy Stewart.

WIDOM: Here comes now the star of *Strategic Air Command*…Jimmy Stewart, wonderful to have you mic-side.

STEWART: Well, thanks very much. I'm sorry I missed you in Omaha. I remember…I remember very well we made sort of a date, but things got a little hectic.

WIDOM: Due to the snow and everything. You know, Jimmy, I didn't have a chance to tell you that I think this is perhaps one of the finest things you've done. I think that it's a wonderful tribute to the Strategic Air Command.

STEWART: Well, we ah…as you and I know, we hope that the picture will be seen by a lot of people because I think in it is sort of the Strategic Air Command and I think it's very important for the people to see what the Strategic Air Command is. And I think it's sort of presented here pretty well.

WIDOM: I think one note of interest…we were talking to General LeMay and we ask him about technical flaws. He said there was only one in the whole picture that he could find and, of course, that was the engine of…getting on fire and viewing it from the wing. He said that was the only thing that wasn't right. He said you can't see the wing actually from a 47.

STEWART: General LeMay hasn't really confided me on this.

WIDOM: I understand now that you've really got a big one coming out on the story of Lindbergh, Jimmy.

STEWART: Well, of course, that doesn't start until the middle of… middle of July. In the meantime, I'm gonna do another one for Alfred Hitchcock in Africa. So I'll be in Africa until July and then I start the Lindbergh story.

WIDOM: Are you gonna shoot it on location?

STEWART: In Africa and London, yes.

WIDOM: Wonderful. Well, we'll be looking forward to them all and for the men of the Strategic Air Command, Jimmy, I'd really like to say thanks for doing the job well.

STEWART: Well, we just ah…all of us just hope that we've done something worthy of the United States Air Force. That's the main thing.

WIDOM: Well, you're pretty busy on the side, too, with your Reserve work too, aren't you, Jimmy?

STEWART: Well, I'm a Reserve officer. I haven't had much time to really be very active. But I hope in the future I can be more active as a Reserve officer.

WIDOM: Thanks again, Jimmy Stewart.

STEWART: Okay, bye.

The final song played on the show this day was the love theme from *Strategic Air Command.*

"The World Is Mine" — Victor Young

Cavalcade of America

When it comes to American history, *Cavalcade of America* was one of the best radio shows ever on the air. All shows were very well researched and written and the acting was always top notch. A historical advisory board was formed to check the authenticity of all facts. At one time or another, the board included Yale University Associate Professor of History Dr. Frank Monaghan, Carl Carmer and Marquis James. Many of the shows were biographies of inventors, authors, artists, playwrights, industrialists and many others. But, there was an ulterior motive on the part of DuPont. The company had made huge profits selling gunpowder during the war years. Many people resented this fact and the show was also produced to help improve the company's public image.

The show was on the air for 18 seasons, from October 9, 1935, until March 31, 1953. There were a total of 781 shows. Jimmy Stewart appeared on just one.

> Monday, November 12, 1945 — *A Guy Who Had To Have a Horse*
> NETWORK: NBC
> SPONSOR: DuPont Chemical
> ANNOUNCER: Tom Collins
> COMMERCIAL SPOKESMAN: Gayne Whitman
> PRODUCER/DIRECTOR: Jack Zoller
> SOUND EFFECTS: Jerry McFee, Art Scott
> MUSIC COMPOSED AND CONDUCTED BY: Robert Armbruster
> SCRIPT WRITERS: Russell Hughes and Bernard Fine
> ORIGINAL STORY: Gretta Palmer
> THEME MUSIC: *March Theme from "Cavalcade of America"* (Harold A. Levey)

The sound effects people working on the program during the NBC years included Al Scott and Jerry McGee.

Joining Jimmy in the cast were: Herbert Vigran (Sammy), Mary Jane Croft (Kathy), Victor Rodman, Horace Murphy, Harry Jackson, Sidney Miller, Eddie Marr, Joseph Julian.

This was show #453 in the series. The show's title is usually given as *A Sailor Who Had to Have a Horse*, but Tom Collins announces the title twice during the broadcast as *A Guy Who Had to Have a Horse*. The original story, as written by Gretta Palmer and appearing in *Reader's Digest*, has the "sailor" in the title. The show was also issued by the Armed Forces Radio Service (AFRS 453).

The show begins with Gayne Whitman doing a commercial for DuPont.

As the play begins, Vance Gorman (Jimmy Stewart) is getting ready to enter the Army and his friends are giving him a party. He'll be a part of the Calvary, which will suit him fine because he is a horseman. Kelly, a friend, tells him that to keep his head and his heart just the way they are now and he should hold on to a dream that he has. That dream, for Vance, is to come back to Montana and raise the finest cow horses in the country. His friends give Vance a new saddle as a gift.

Vance isn't gone long before he's back. He's not going into the Army, he's going into the Navy and he has to report the next day. He still takes the saddle with him because he knows that he will somehow find a horse. He manages to make it all the way to the South Pacific with the saddle still in his possession. On an island there, a young colt in very bad health is found. The Lieutenant wants to shoot it, but Vance talks him into letting him try to nurse it back to health. He names the colt Montana. With the help of his friends Benny and Eddie, Vance does get the colt back on its feet.

But, now Vance runs into another problem. His unit is about to ship back to the U.S. and he will probably have to leave Montana on the island. Vance talks to Kathy, a girl with the U.S.O. troop, and tells her that the show is missing something…it could use a trained horse. Back in the U.S., all the newspapers want to do stories about the sailor with a horse. A movie company has even offered him a lot of money to take Montana to Hollywood. Vance doesn't want any part of it and walks away with Montana.

At the end of the east coast broadcast, Gayne Whitman does another DuPont spot and then introduces Jimmy Stewart, who makes a speech for Victory Bonds which runs about 46 seconds.

WHITMAN: …and now, here is Jimmy Stewart.

STEWART: Thank you very much and…ah…ladies and gentlemen, I'd just like to say a little something about the Victory Loan. The war's been won and that's a great thing, but our victory has brought its responsibilities. There are men who are wounded. There are families who have in their windows or, maybe only in their hearts, a flag with a gold star. We owe a measureless debt to those men and to their families. You can begin to help to pay some of it off by buying Victory Bonds to the limit of your ability. Our victory has been…has made us secure from war, secure in peace and now we've all got a chance to make that security stick. Let's all put every extra dollar in Victory Bonds.

The second performance, the broadcast for the west coast, ran a little long and Stewart had to edit his speech to just:

STEWART: Ladies and gentlemen, I was going to make a little speech about the Victory Loan Drive, but we are running a little short of time. I just want to remind you to buy lots of Victory Bonds. Thanks a lot. Goodnight.

Before the end of the show, Tom Collins mentions that Jimmy Stewart's next picture will be *It's A Wonderful Life* and is to be produced and directed by Frank Capra.

In 2008, this program became available as a part of the 13-show set, *Vintage Radio Collection Jimmy Stewart* (Stardust). This was an mp3 only set.

A second mp3 only set, *Jimmy Stewart Ultimate Radio Collection Vol. 1*, was released in 2001 by Master Classics Records.

Chase & Sanborn 100th Anniversary Show

Chase & Sanborn Coffee had been in business for 100 years and to celebrate, they produced one final radio show with Edgar Bergen and Charlie McCarthy as the hosts. The 1-hour special also featured announcer Jimmy Wallington. The show featured a series of clips from previous Chase & Sanborn shows and was broadcast on November 15, 1964.

NETWORK: NBC
SPONSOR: Chase & Sanborn
ANNOUNCER: Jimmy Wallington
WRITTEN, EDITED AND PRODUCED BY: Carole Carroll and Daniel Sutton

The show began with Edgar Bergen and Charlie McCarthy introducing Maurice Chevalier, who sang;
"Louise"
Next came Eddie Cantor singing his radio theme song when he was sponsored by Chase and Sanborn;
"One Hour With You"
And, finally, Jimmy Durante singing:
"Inka Dinka Doo"
After a short clip of Major Bowes, there were a series of clips of Bergen, McCarthy and a series of guest stars, including Rudy Vallee, W.C. Fields, Rosalind Russell, Caroline O'Connor, Fred Allen, Mae West, Verree Teasdale, Adolphe Menjou, Alec Templeton, Carole Lombard, Clark

Gable, Dorothy Lamour, Nelson Eddy, Don Ameche, Mary Pickford, Charles Laughton, Jimmy Stewart, Margaret O'Brien, Jack Oakie, Ogden Nash, and Ethel Barrymore.

The Jimmy "Zeke" Stewart skit with Mortimer Snerd, is the same one used in the Edgar Bergen Show 16th and 20th anniversary shows, but it is considerably edited here.

BERGEN: Your name, please, sir.

SNERD: Duh...oh, my name, yeah, it's a...well, it's a...it's a, it's a...duh...it's a...well, it always has been, every day of my life, yeah. De dum da de dum...oh, what was the query?

BERGEN: The query? Well, your name...your name is Mortimer Snerd.

SNERD: Yeah, that's right, yeah.

BERGEN: And now for our other expert on the farm panel...ah...your name, please.

STEWART: Well, my name is...ah...my...it's...ah...oh, I know it as well as I know my own name. Ah...what was the query?

BERGEN: Yes, your name, sir.

STEWART: Oh yes, Zeke Stewart.

BERGEN: Gentlemen, greetings and salutations.

SNERD: Well, thank you, I don't mind if I do.

STEWART: I'll go along with that.

SNERD: Mind if I go with you?

STEWART: No...no...come right along.

BERGEN: Gentlemen, gentlemen, please, this is a forum. Now, what is your opinion on agriculture?

STEWART: Well, it's my opinion that no farm should be without it.

SNERD: I'll go along with that.

STEWART: If you get there first, wait for me, huh.

BERGEN: No...no...no...no, we must have some helpful information. Now, Mr. Snerd, what's your idea on increasing milk production?

SNERD: I'm glad you asked me, yes. Ah...first...ah...first...ah...increasing milk production?

BERGEN: Yeah.

SNERD: First, you gotta get a cow. You gotta do that. You'll go along with me on that, won't you, Zeke?

STEWART: Yeah, yeah, should be a female cow.

BERGEN: Perhaps I'll do better if I explain parity. Parity is equality in purchasing power between different kinds of money at a given ratio.

STEWART: Oooooooooooh...no!

SNERD: I'll go along with Zeke's opinion.
BERGEN: Look, gentlemen, in other words, if a bushel of corn costs $2 under present conditions, do you think...
SNERD: Well, I tell you, it's like this.
BERGEN: I haven't asked you the question.
SNERD: Well, I ain't a fella that waits until the last minute.
STEWART: You know now, time's a wastin', and that's for dang sure. I like you Mort. You're nobody's fool.
SNERD: Well, nobody's in particular anyway. And that's for dang sure.
STEWART: Heh-heh-heh-heh. We ought to get along fine...we understand each other.
SNERD: Yeah...ah...who do?
STEWART: You and me.
SNERD: Oh them, yeah.
STEWART: That's who I was talkin' about all...all the time; you and me.
BERGEN: Gentlemen, gentlemen, gentlemen! If a bushel of corn...if a bushel of corn, now get this...
STEWART: I like you, Mort. Let's...let's...let's get together some time, Mort.
SNERD: Okay, where?
STEWART: Well...well, we can decide that when we get there.
BERGEN: If a bushel...one bushel of corn...
STEWART: Anyway, I hope to see you sometime, Mort.
SNERD: Yeah, then some other time, I can see you, yeah. If we change off like that, we won't get so sick of seein' each other.
BERGEN: Now, this bushel of corn...
SNERD: Well, how about comin' over to my farm, Zeke?
STEWART: Okay, where is it?
SNERD: Well. I'll tell you how to get there if you don't mind gettin' lost.
STEWART: Oh, ah...how far is it as the crow flies?
SNERD: Oh, it's about...Well, you ain't comin' by crow are you?
BERGEN: Sorry, gentlemen, but our time is up.

The program has been issued as a single album (RR-4H-5305).

This show is also available commercially as a single cassette titled *Charlie McCarthy Show* (*The Chase and Sanborn 100th Anniversary Show*) (Radio Spirits 1737) released in 1995.

The Chesterfield Show
See *The Bing Crosby Show*.

Christmas 1955

This program was broadcast by Chicago radio station WMAQ on December 23, 1955 (7-8:55 p.m.). In the New York area the show was broadcast by WRCA from 8-9:55 p.m. The theme for the show was, "What Christmas Means to Me." According to the ads for the program, the show featured many stars, including Stewart, Tallulah Bankhead, Ronald Colman, Helen Hayes, Gregory Peck, Fibber McGee and Molly, Roy Rogers and Dale Evans, Alan Young, Dr. Norman Vincent Peale and Frank Sinatra. The program is not available for listening.

This 90-minute special was broadcast by NBC.

Christmas Service from the Hollywood Presbyterian Church

Friday December 24, 1948 (12:30-12:55 a.m.)

This was Stewart's home church when he was in Hollywood. He narrated this particular service which was broadcast by NBC.

At least on the east coast, where the program was broadcast at 12:30 a.m., the air date is actually December 25. Stewart narrated the program. Among the guests were Virginia Mayo, Henry Russell Orchestra, Michael O'Shea, Porter Hall, Colleen Townsend and Dennis Morgan. This show is not available for listening.

Coffee Break

Monday, July 9, 1962 (11:15-11:30 am, and repeated 9:15-9:30 p.m.)

This was a special 15-minute program broadcast on FEN (Far East Network, an Armed Services network).

Stewart's interview had been taped at the 12th International Berlin Film Festival by Walt Sheldon. Stewart was attending the festival because his current film, *Mr. Hobbs Takes a Vacation*, was in the competition. In fact, he won the Silver Bear for best actor. The program is not available for listening, but the interview probably centered on the film and the award.

Command Performance

Command Performance was produced by the Armed Forces Radio Service to provide entertainment for troops, mainly those stationed outside the U.S. The show was developed by Louis Cowan at the request of the War Department. It was shortwaved directly to our troops overseas and was not heard here in the U.S. The shows were a half-hour in length, but there were also one-hour specials. A different star hosted the show each week and both the host and guests were chosen from the requests received by the show. What should have been a very expensive show to produce, actually cost nothing. All the stars donated their time and both CBS and NBC donated their studios for production of the show. Stewart appeared on just one show which is not available for listening.

Sunday April 13, 1947
HOST: Donna Reed
ANNOUNCER: Wendell Niles
DIRECTOR: Glenn Wheaton
PRODUCERS: Vick Knight, Maury Holland, Cal Kuhl

This was show #260 in the series. Besides Stewart, the other guests were The Meltones, Leo DeRogers, jazz vocalist Jeannie McKeon and Danny Thomas.

"Ole Buttermilk Sky" — Meltones
"You Keep Coming Back Like a Song" — Jeannie McKeon

Community Chest — A Salute to Volunteers
Friday, September 26, 1947 (10:30-11 p.m.)

The Community Chest began as Mobilization for Human Needs in 1932 to help local agencies from closing their doors for lack of money. Today, we know it as the United Way. Radio has always been used to raise public awareness of each year's monetary drive. Stewart introduced one of these public service shows, which was broadcast by all four networks — ABC, CBS, Mutual and NBC.

Once thought to be unavailable, two acetate discs (#1, #2, #5, #6) have been located. Together, they contain just less than 16 minutes of the original half-hour program. The premise of this year's program is to have Hollywood stars introducing Community Chest volunteers from around the country and have those people tell how the Community Chest helps in their city. Side one features Jimmy Stewart opening the show with these remarks:

> *Ladies and gentlemen, this is Jimmy Stewart. I think you'll be interested in listening to the program we're about to present. You'll hear the President of the United States and also some people you know out in Hollywood — Dorothy Lamour, Margaret O'Brien, Jack Benny, Edgar Bergen and Charlie McCarthy, Mel Blanc and a young fellow named Robert Hope. They're here to introduce the real stars of this program who are the typical volunteer Community Chest workers from all over America. We hope you'll accept this as a tribute to all the men and women,*

patriotic American citizens, who are giving their time to raise money this year for the Community Chest. We're standing by from coast to coast for this year's annual Community Chest program; the Stars Present a Salute to Volunteers.

Stewart then introduces Bob Hope, who goes into a comedy routine. The routine ends on side two with Hope then introducing John Duncan, a Community Chest volunteer from Springfield, Massachusetts. Duncan talks briefly about the services available in that city through the Community Chest. Next, Edgar Bergen and Charlie McCarthy begin their comedy routine which is still in progress when side two ends.

Side five opens in the middle of Jack Benny dialing the combination on his famous safe. Benny tells his guard, Ed, played by Joseph Kearns, that he is donating money to the Community Chest. Benny then introduces Patrolman Walter Goodlow of the Los Angeles Police Department. Goodlow then talks about the good work done by the Community Chest with the kids of Los Angeles.

Side six begins with Margaret O'Brien talking about how the Community Chest helps children in general. Finally, she introduces President Harry S Truman. Truman begins his speech which has not been concluded by the end of this side.

It is possible that Stewart came back to end the program, but since that portion of the show is not available, it is impossible to say for sure.

Dancing with the Stars with Jimmy Stewart — The '30s

The Mutual Broadcasting System and Westwood One put together this two-hour radio special featuring Jimmy Stewart as your host on a tour of Hollywood's night spots of the 1930s. Original period music is included throughout. Jimmy gets a chance to tell his stories and reminisce. The national sponsors for the show included Manwich, State Farm, Teledisc, and Best Western. The show was scheduled to be broadcast during the week of June 27, 1988, and was delivered to radio stations as four 12-inch vinyl transcription discs (JS 30's).

Many of the songs were not complete, fading early or with Stewart's comments made over them. The show's credits included:

WRITER/PRODUCER: Marsha Richardson
PRODUCTION & ENGINEERING: Fred Lindgren
EXECUTIVE PRODUCER: Norm Pattiz
SPECIAL THANKS TO: John Strauss, Alice Faye, Ed Lewis, Jack Leonard, Jimmy Stewart

Stewart begins the show with the same words that are used for the program's promo:

> *Dancing cheek to cheek, that's the way to do it; twirling around the dance floor to the music of Glenn Miller or Tommy Dorsey or maybe Benny Goodman. Well, we're gonna hear all of your favorite bands in the next two hours and meet a lot of your favorite stars. I'm Jimmy Stewart and I'd like to take you out on the town…my town…Hollywood.*

"Cheek To Cheek" — Fred Astaire

> *First, we'll stop at the Coconut Grove and we'll go dancing at the Trocadera, we'll grab a quick dinner at the Brown Derby and then swing by Earl Carroll's. Do you think you can keep up with me? All right, well put your dancin' shoes on and let's go. We've got a lot of ground to cover before the sun comes up.*

"Chicken Waffles" — Bunny Berigan

> *Hollywood 1935, Roosevelt's in the White House, a brand-new Hudson costs $695 and, if you have a quarter, you can see the latest Fred and Ginger movie, Top Hat. 1935 was the year I made the move from New York to Hollywood. Henry Fonda and I shared a small house that year. One of the first things we tried to do was get to know our neighbors. Of course, when one of your neighbors is Greta Garbo, it can get difficult. Garbo's house didn't exactly invite visitors.*

"Sunny Side of the Street" — Chick Webb

> *There was a big wall around it and we…we just…ah…that…that wasn't very neighborly, we didn't think. Fonda and I have two stories about it, but we've decided to, because of the wall and everything, we decide to dig a trench, underground, and come up inside the wall and just…whether she liked it or not, we'd get to see Greta Garbo. Well, now, Fonda says that we talked about it and…ah…never got around to it. I said that we not only talked about it, but we started to dig a tunnel and the only thing that blocked us was we ran into an enormous pipeline that seemed to stretch right across our road to Greta Garbo. So, after we…we quit after that. Now probably you can take something in between that as fact.*

"All By Myself" — Ella Fitzgerald

Later, much later, I…I wanted to meet her. I was a fan, a real fan, a real Garbo fan. I wanted to meet her and she was at M-G-M and I was at M-G-M and…but, nobody ever saw her. A limousine would come up at the stage where she was working, this is for lunch, and she'd get into the limousine and disappear and then come back and be there exactly on time and then…but I was working right next to her and I knew the soundman on her picture and I just called him and I said some evening, you know, when you know a little ahead of time when they're breaking, ah, some evening when you see she's getting ready to go to the door…ah… give me a call so I can get over and just get a look at her. So one evening he called me up the next day. So I left and I had to make a turn and the door was right here. So, I left and on my way right to go into the door, the door opened, I ran into somebody and kept going and then stopped and I looked back and there was Greta Garbo flat on her ass. I'd knocked her down. I went to pick her up and she said never mind and got into her car.

"Tain't What Cha Do" — Ella Fitzgerald/Chick Webb
At this point, Alice Faye comes in and says:

When I was a little girl in New York, I used to…we had a fire escape — I lived on the west side of New York — and I used to sit up there and dream that was my penthouse. And it all started there and… ah…I used to dream about it…yeah, I loved it.

Then Stewart ends the segment with:

George White Scandals, Poor Little Rich Girl, Alexander's Ragtime Band; *are you ready to take a spin around the dance floor with the star of those movies? Well, I've arranged for Alice Faye to meet us at the Trocadera, so let's get going. We can't keep a pretty lady like Alice waiting. We'll rendezvous in just a couple of minutes, so stayed tuned.*

Jimmy begins the second segment of the show with:

You're dancing with the stars. I'm Jimmy Stewart and I'm pleased to be your host for this evening out on the town in Hollywood.

"Plenty of Money and You" — Dick Powell

Now Hollywood in the '30s, yeah, it was an exciting place. Of course, most actors were too busy workin' to notice. In 1936, I worked in seven pictures, Henry Fonda was in five, Jean Harlow made three, Spencer Tracy showed up in six, Shirley Temple starred in five, Myrna Loy sailed through six motion pictures. Musicals, of course, took a little longer to produce, so Ginger Rogers and Fred Astaire were only able to dance through three movies.

"They Can't Take That Away From Me" — Fred Astaire

This is the way the big studios worked. This is why their…theirs were the real honest way to make movies. 'Cause when you're under contract, you didn't sit at home and wait for them to find a picture for ya. You came to work every day at 8 o'clock and left at 6. If you weren't working on a picture, you were going to a voice class or you were in the gym getting in shape or you were on the road someplace plugging a picture that you weren't even in or you were doing screen tests for people that they were thinking of…of hiring. So you…you…you worked all the time and you did what I think is something that…went on then that is very much missed today. You learned your craft by working at it. You just…this was every day, six days a week, not five days a week, six days a week. And then Saturday night everybody'd meet at the Trocadera and…ah…and sort of have like a big family and have a wonderful time.

"Feelin' High and Happy" — Benny Goodman

After the song, Stewart simply says, "Alice Faye," and then she comes on and talks about how hard they all worked for their studio and how they looked forward to letting off some steam on Saturday night.

"Spreadin' Rhythm Around" — Alice Faye

Well, we're not complaining. We had one night out a week and we made the most of it. The place to go was 8610 Sunset Boulevard, the Trocadera. It was a city block long, filled with music and conversation and a lot of laughter. Dancing began at eight and you could start your evening with a cocktail in Paris. Well, it…it wasn't exactly in Paris, but the walls were painted with French murals to make you think you had crossed the Atlantic. And if you stood at the top of the steps to the dining room, you could see the Eiffel Tower. You also could see the stars…the Hollywood variety. Let's check with one of the three headwaiters here, he knows where all the big celebrities are seated.

We now hear the voice of headwaiter "Johnny Hoy," giving the names of the stars who were there that evening, including George Raft, Carole Lombard, Lupe and Johnny Weissmuller and Connie Bennett.

"Here's the Key to My Heart" — Alice Faye

> *I see David Niven's here. He's working on* The Prisoner of Zenda *right now and Loretta Young, she just finished starring in* Ramona. *Oh, and it looks like Don Ameche's gonna give me a chance to dance with Alice Faye. Who don't you see if Patsy Kelly and Madeleine Carroll are ready for another dance and I'll ask the orchestra to play one of my favorites — 'Body and Soul.'*

"Body and Soul" — Benny Goodman
Stewart ends the show's second segment with:

> *That was Benny Goodman's Orchestra with 'Body and Soul.' You know you never can predict who's gonna show up at the Trocadera on Saturday night. Everybody wants to get in on the fun. In fact, right now it looks like that woman is asking if her daughter can sing with the band. Well, we'll hear about what she sounds like in just a minute.*

Segment three opens with:

> *Dancing with the stars, that's what we're doing. I'm Jimmy Stewart on the Mutual Broadcasting System.*

"Whistle While You Work" — Artie Shaw

> *It's 1936 — you can rent a 6-room, furnished house in the Hollywood Hills for $75 a month; sirloin steak is 22 cents a pound and for $7 you could spend the evening dining and dancing at the Trocadera on Sunset Boulevard.*

"If I Could with Be With You" — Benny Goodman
We hear part of a George Burns-Gracie Allen skit, and then:

> *That was George Burns. And you know what happens when one comedian takes over the bandstand, they all want equal time. Well, this is gonna be interesting. It looks like Bob Hope and Bing Crosby are gonna do a duet.*

"Put It There, Pal" — Bing Crosby and Bob Hope

You know, the only thing that can get Hope and Crosby back to their seats is a pretty girl who can sing louder than both of them and I think they may have met their match. Let's see if I can get close to the bandstand to hear what's happening. A woman sort of went up and asked whoever was leading the orchestra if her daughter could sing a song because she had just been put under contract. And, the guy said, sure, bring her up. And here was Judy in bobby socks and everybody didn't know what to think and her mother stood right there and told the orchestra what to play and what key to play. And Judy sang for an hour. You know, then… this was when she just came under contract to M-G-M and it was just amazing.

"Everybody Sing" — Judy Garland
"Stompin' at the Savoy" — Judy Garland

No, we're not stompin' at the Savoy, we're stompin' at the Trocadera, and that was Judy Garland. Can you believe that she's only 14 years old? She just signed a contract with M-G-M Studios. Oh, I think she's gonna be a big star. And we're gonna give Judy a little advice and information about what life is like when you're under contract. And you stay tuned, too, we have reservations for a late dinner at the Brown Derby and I want to take you over to the Palomar for some more dancing. You're not tired yet are you? Good, good, 'cause I'll be right back.

Segment four begins with "Johnny Hoy," headwaiter at the Trocadera, telling us that he's moved Jimmy Stewart to Alice Faye's table.

"Cocktails for Two" — Tommy Dorsey

When you're as pretty and charming as Alice Faye, you don't need any help in getting a date for Saturday night. But sometimes your home studio would worry. They had their own idea of who you should be seen with. Alice, how'd you handle the publicity people? Were they always suggesting a new blind date or best friend for you?

Alice tells him that they did at first, but that's publicity.

Alice, I…I have to ask you this. How did you feel when they wanted to make you the new Jean Harlow? You know that's quite an assignment to give somebody.

Alice tells him that it was fun and that she actually enjoyed it.

"Jeepers Creepers" — Louis Armstrong

We've all seen her in the movies. The famous Faye stance; right foot up, toes pointed. Alice is that a signal to somebody? Are you saying hello to your mother?

Alice says that that stance was her security blanket and that she doesn't know how it got started.

"I've Got My Love To Keep Me Warm" — Alice Faye

Okay, there are no publicity people around now and no photographers, just you and me and a couple of my friends. Who were some of your favorite dancing partners, Alice? We promise we won't tell Hedda Hopper.

Faye mentions her favorites as including Cesar Romero and Tony Martin. "Stairway to the Stars" — Glenn Miller

That was 'Stairway to the Stars' the great Glenn Miller Orchestra with Ray Eberle singing. That was a #1 song for the Miller band in 1939. This was a big year for Glenn and 1939 was also a big year for the Tommy Dorsey Band. They are gonna make their debut out here on the west coast. And we're goin' over to the Palomar Ballroom to hear them. We'll leave in just a few minutes, so let's have one more dance around the Troc and then go.

All of the music in segment five is by the Tommy Dorsey Orchestra. As the fifth segment opens, Stewart is telling us:

The Palomar, at Vermont and 3rd, in downtown Los Angeles; it's the place to hear great swing music. Now, it is a big place, so let's try and stick together, huh? The Palomar is larger than the Trocadera and a bigger bargain, too. Forty cents admission for the ladies, 68 cents for

the gentlemen. Well, tonight, it would be worth $6 to get in; Tommy Dorsey's band is making his first appearance on the west coast.

"Heaven Can Wait"

1939, the Dorsey band is really riding high. Vocalist Jack Leonard has just been named best vocalist for the second year in a row by both Downbeat and Metronome magazines. That's like winning the Academy Award. I think I can get Jack and get him to come over to our table. I'd like to meet him, how about you?

Leonard says that being with Tommy has been the highlight of his life. He loves musicians and loves being with them; it's very rewarding.

"It's Wonderful"

It was Jack Leonard that gave Tommy Dorsey the nickname Silver Fox. That's because when Tommy hired Jack a few years ago, it was part of a package deal. Dorsey hired a trio from Bert Bloch's band — Jack Leonard, Axel Stordahl and Joe Bowen. So, for the price of three salaries, Tommy picked up five talents; a trio, a soloist, an arranger and two trumpet players.

"Gotta Go To Work Again"

Jack, could you tell me when a tune's gonna be a hit? Was there something you could feel when you first sang it?

Leonard talks about the success of the song, "Marie."
"Marie"

Now, I'm sure Tommy is wondering where you are, but before we let you go back to the bandstand, I have to ask you about one of my favorite singers — Edythe Wright.

Leonard says that she not only sang well, she looked great on the bandstand.
"They All Laughed"

The Tommy Dorsey Orchestra, Jack Leonard and Edythe Wright behind the microphone, making their west coast debut in the summer of

1939. I'm glad we were able to sneak in and see them. Now, I thought we'd swing by Don the Beachcombers. We can't call it a night before we try one of his Zombies. I'm gonna call for a car and then we'll get goin'.

The sixth segment takes place at the Biltmore Bowl, with all songs being performed by the Benny Goodman Band.

"One O'Clock Jump"

I thought we were heading for Don the Beachcombers, but looks like we're gonna have to wait a little longer to sit under the palms and try our first Zombie. But, don't worry; we're taking an amazing detour. Benny Goodman is playing at the Biltmore Bowl. This is a great place to see an orchestra. The room's 140 feet long and no matter where you sit, you have a great view. They built the place with no support poles; the ceiling must be held up by mirrors. And look at that stage. Yes, there's enough velvet in that curtain to cover M-G-M studios. Looks like Goodman's about ready to swing.

"Sent for You Yesterday"

One of the things I like best about the Goodman band is that he always had such wonderful dance teams traveling with him. And yet almost no one was dancin' while Goodman played. We all just sort of stood and watched and we did a little swaying. There's Ed Lewis. It looks like he and his partner, Betty Bliss, are taking a break. Ed, doesn't anybody dance when the Goodman band kicks in? Is... is it always like this?

Lewis says that the band not only sounds good, but it looks good, too, and everybody just loves to watch them play.

"Ti Pi Pin"

You're not ready to leave the Biltmore yet? Okay, well, I'm glad. You havin' a good time, huh? Because it looks like Alice Faye is dancing with Ed Lewis, so why don't we get a little closer to the bandstand and get some the Goodman music.

"Where or When"

After just a few seconds of "Where or When," "Johnny Hoy" closes the segment. Segment seven begins with Jimmy saying:

I'm Jimmy Stewart and you're dancing with the stars. I hope you're having a good time so far. We've been to the Brown Derby, The Trocadera, and right now, we're at the Biltmore Ballroom, one of the great places to dance to the sound of the big bands in the '30s. Benny Goodman's on stage and I can see Paulette Goddard, Martha Raye, Louella Parsons and, oh, that looks like Groucho Marx and Milton Berle are here, too; there, right to your right there.

"This Can't Be Love"

Goodman sure knows how to pick singers, doesn't he? That was Liltin' Martha Tilton. Oh, here's dancer Ed Lewis again. He and Dorothy Lamour are splitin' their seams, they're laughing so hard. What happened yesterday while you were performing? Come on, Ed, you…you have to tell us. Oh, I've never seen Dorothy laugh so hard. Well, I'm guessin' it's about you and your partner, Betty, right? Okay, I think we've got 'em now, folks.

Lewis tells him that he and Betty Bliss, his partner, were dancing on stage. Betty's dress had a bra hooked to the back and neither of them noticed it, but the audience sure did. When Betty finally saw it, she removed it and threw it over her shoulder and it hooked itself right to the front of the bandstand.

"Pick Yourself Up"

Dance teams aren't the ones facing a few embarrassing moments in 1939. Alice, tell me the story again about the Hollywood Cavalcade. *You…you got into a sticky situation, didn't you?*

She tells him that while doing *Hollywood Cavalcade*, Buster Keaton had to throw a lemon meringue pie in her face. They had to do the scene many times and every time she had to have her hair and make-up redone.

"I've Got My Fingers Crossed" — Alice Faye

Well, I didn't have to take any lemon meringue pies in the face this year, but I did have a few hard knocks when I was filming Ice Follies of 1939. *I'll tell you, making that movie gave me new respect for Sonja Henie. We learned how to skate enough to sort of, oh, keep from falling down if we just come up to the camera and the rest of it. But they found that Lew Ayres and I, we were supposed to be a team, ah…sort of an acrobatic team on stage. And they had us in…and the minute they saw* me in tights, and in this sort of fancy thing with gold things all over the place, they said...ah, maybe this team would be better as a skating horse. And...ah...we said okay. And Lew and I flipped a coin to see who would get the back end and I lost. So, that's what...that's figure skating. That's how I wound up on the back end of a horse.

"Get Happy" — Judy Garland

1939 is an amazing year for the motion picture industry — Gone With the Wind, Wuthering Heights, Goodbye, Mr. Chips, Babes in Arms, Stagecoach, Sweethearts, *and now they're all worth 25 cents for admission. And 1939 is when one of my favorite pictures opened* — Mr. Smith Goes to Washington. *Now we'll learn how Mr. Smith was received in the Senate in just a minute. Have...have you seen Alice lately? No, that's funny; I thought she was with you.*

"Johnny Hoy" introduces the eighth segment, and then we hear Stewart saying:

It's the summer of 1939 and we're out on the town in Hollywood. A new Oldsmobile is $777; ladies, you'll have to spend $10 on a new style bustle hat; and a cocktail at the Florentine Gardens on Hollywood Boulevard is 30 cents. 1939, I worked with Frank Capra again on a picture that would be nominated for quite a number of Academy Awards — Mr. Smith Goes to Washington. *Jean Arthur, Claude Rains, Edward Arnold, Guy Kibbee, Thomas Mitchell, Eugene Pallette, it's quite a cast. And, of course, one of the most talented and respected directors in the whole world, Frank Capra.*

"Can't Pull the Wool Over My Eyes" — Benny Goodman

Mr. Smith *was a hit at movie theaters all across the country and...well, almost across the country. You could always get a seat in Washington, DC. It opened in Constitution Hall in Washington and most of the Senate...a lot of the Senate was there. And Frank was there...Frank and his wife Lou were in a box with three Senators and their wives. And Frank could tell after about ten minutes of the thing that things weren't going very well. And about, oh maybe three quarters of an hour, the film broke and Frank knew where the projection room was and he got up and had to go up the fire escape. And, by the time he got up, the operator had fixed it and the film was going all right. But, when he got down to the box, everybody had gone but his wife Lou. And he looked over and people were walking out. You know the press...Tommy Mitchell was always drunk and the, oh...there were a lot of things that were just...at that time there were just questionable as far as the press was concerned and as far as the Senate was concerned.*

"I'll Get By" — Kirk

1939, Mr. Smith Goes to Washington and we all go to Hollywood. Are you still with me? You're...you're not tired yet? Well, should we have one more dance at the Trocadera or try and make it over to Clara Bow's It Club before the sun comes up? Well, you...you think about it and we'll...we'll decide in just a minute.

As *Thanks for the Memories* plays, Jimmy wraps up the show and has one more dance with the stars.

"Thanks for the Memories" (uncredited)

If you check the dictionary, glamour is defined as alluring, attractive, fascinating, and radiant. Originally the word glamour meant a delusion caused by a magic spell. Now, glamorous is a word often used to describe Hollywood in the '30s. Now I don't know about any spells, but it definitely was a magical time. I hope the music and the memories we've listened to over the past couple of hours created a little magic for you. Well, thanks for coming out dancing with me tonight. I...I think I'd like to take one more turn on the dance floor before we head home. The sun's barely peaking over the horizon, so put your shoes back on and let's do a little dancing with the stars.

"Hooray for Hollywood"

A 44-second promo was also included in the discs. It had Stewart saying the following over a bed of "Thanks for the Memories."

Dancing cheek to cheek, that's the way to do it; twirling around the dance floor to the music of Glenn Miller or Tommy Dorsey or maybe Benny Goodman. Well, we're gonna hear all of your favorite bands in the next two hours and meet a lot of your favorite stars. I'm Jimmy Stewart and I'd like to take you out on the town...my town...Hollywood.

You'll notice that these are also the words Stewart uses to begin the program.

Desert Island Discs

Desert Island Discs is a long-running BBC program which was first broadcast January 29, 1942. It was off the air from 1946 until 1951 when it returned to the BBC. In 1967 it was transferred to BBC Radio 4, where it remains today. Stewart appeared on the show two times. Each show was hosted by the show's originator, Roy Plomley.

(1) May 25, 1974

During the program Stewart, like all other castaways, was asked to name the eight records he would like to have with him on the legendary island, as well as a book and a luxury item. His choices, according to the Desert Island Disc website (*http://www.bbc.co.uk/radio4/features/desert-island-discs*) were:

On the Road to Mandalay — Kenneth McKellar
Bye Bye Blues — Guy Lombardo and his Royal Orchestra
I've Got a Crush On You — Betty Grable & Jack Lemmon
I Hadn't Anyone Till You — Ray Noble and His Orchestra
There, I've Said It Again — Vaughan Monroe and His Orchestra
Don't Cry, Joe — Gordon Jenkins and His Orchestra
Moonlight Serenade — The Glenn Miller Orchestra
Dream — The Pied Pipers (Stewart named this song his favorite)

For his book, he chose *Musical Arrangements* by Dave Brubeck and his choice of luxury item was a piano.

(2) December 17, 1983

In the eight-and-a-half years since his first appearance on the program, Stewart made a few changes to the things he would like to have on the island with him. This time his records were:

On the Road to Mandalay — Kenneth McKellar
Moonlight Serenade — The Glenn Miller Orchestra
Rolling Stone — Henry Fonda with James Stewart
Don't Cry, Joe — Gordon Jenkins and His Orchestra
There, I've Said It Again — Vaughan Monroe and His Orchestra
I've Got a Crush On You — Ella Fitzgerald
Ragtime Cowboy Joe — Jo Stafford & the Starlighters
Dream — The Pied Pipers

Stewart chose *Robinson Crusoe* by Daniel Defoe as the book he would take with him and as his luxury item, he chose his family photo album.

To date, the BBC has made 500 Desert Island Disc programs available for listening on their website. Unfortunately neither of the Stewart appearances was among them.

Dinah Shore Show
   NETWORK: NBC
   SPONSOR: Chevrolet
   MUSIC: Frank DeVol
   THEME: *Dinah* (Harry Akst-Sam Lewis-Joe Young)

Jimmy Stewart made an appearance on *The Dinah Shore Show* on June 15, 1953 (7-7:15 p.m. on the west coast).

The show is not available for listening. However, according to a newspaper ad, Stewart would be vocalizing with Shore. At this point in time, Shore's show was heard every week day at 8 p.m. and it was just a 15-minute show.

Don McNeill's Breakfast Club

The show was broadcast by the Blue Network/ABC from Chicago's Merchandise Mart and later from the Terrace Casino of the Morrison Hotel. Very few shows are still in existence — of the literally thousands of shows broadcast, fewer than 50 are available today. Sadly, Stewart's is not among them.

McNeill was inducted into the Radio Hall of Fame in 1989.
Tuesday, November 11, 1958 (9-10 a.m.)

Dorothy Kilgallen Show

Dorothy Kilgallen had gotten her first radio show in 1941, when *Voice of Broadway* went on the air for CBS. The show featured Broadway and Hollywood gossip and remained on the air until 1944. In 1945, she and her husband, Richard Kollmar, were given their own show on New York City's WOR. The show, *Breakfast with Dorothy and Dick*, quickly became a staple of morning radio. Beginning in September of 1947 and continuing through July of 1949, Kilgallen also had her own 15-minute interview show on New York's WJZ and the ABC Network. It was sponsored by the Drackett Company.

The Dorothy Kilgallen Show aired from 10:45 until 11 a.m. on Thursday mornings. Stewart appeared on the show on March 25, 1948. Stewart's next film, *Veritgo*, was set to be released in early May, so it is possible that this was one of the topics discussed on the program. The show is not available for listening.

Edgar Bergen and Charlie McCarthy Show

Edgar Bergen was a popular ventriloquist. Not that it mattered. On radio, even if his lips moved, no one could see them. Bergen was on the radio from 1936 until 1955, beginning on the *Rudy Vallee Show* and then the *Chase and Sanborn Hour*, the *Chase and Sanborn Program*, and *The New Edger Bergen Show*. Several different themes were used during the shows run, including: *The Big Show* (Jerome Kern), *Kingdom Coming* (Henry C. Work), *Happy Days Are Here Again* (Milton Ager-Jack Yellen), and *Mortimer Snerd Theme* (Ray Noble-Edgar Bergen).

Stewart, Bergen and McCarthy are seen in this photo which appeared in the Movie-Radio Guide *(Vol. 11, No. 18, February 7-13, 1942)*.

SHOWS FEATURING JIMMY STEWART:

(1) Sunday January, 18, 1942 — (8:00-8:30 p.m.)
NETWORK: NBC
SPONSOR: Chase and Sanborn
ANNOUNCER: Buddy Twiss
MUSIC: Ray Noble and his Orchestra

This show is currently not available for listening. Bud Abbott and Lou Costello performed a comedy sketch on each week's show during this season. Other guests tonight included actress Janet Blair, Major Linn S. Chaplin and Lt. Francis C. Healey.

On earlier shows this season, Charlie McCarthy had joined the Army Air Corps and then also tried to join the Marines. As a result, McCarthy was to be court-martialed at the Stockton Army Air Corps Advanced

Flying School, Stockton, CA. Lt. James Stewart was brought in to defend Charlie, who was eventually found guilty. Charlie was sentenced to receive half pay for three months by Major Linn S. Chaplin, the court-martial president. But, that didn't set well with Charlie. So, he matched Major Chaplin, double or nothing, and eventually received double pay for three months. In addition, Lt. Francis C. Healey, Training Center Publicity officer, arranged for Charlie to become a flying cadet.

The whole series of shows was designed to promote enlistments in the Armed Forces.

(2) Sunday, September 1, 1946
NETWORK: NBC
SPONSOR: Chase and Sanborn
PRODUCER: Earl Ebb
WRITERS: Zeno Clinker, Alan Smith, Royal Foster
ANNOUNCER: Ken Carpenter
MUSIC: Ray Noble and his Orchestra

Although this show is not in general circulation, it can be found in The Paley Center for Media, 25 West 52nd Street, New York, New York.

The show begins with a typical routine from Bergen and McCarthy. This is followed by a song played by Ray Noble and His Orchestra.

"I've Got the Sun in the Morning" (Irving Berlin)

This is followed with a routine by Bergen and Mortimer Snerd. Anita Gordon, a new regular for this season, then joins Bergen and McCarthy and Charlie announces that he's running for president.

"They Say It's Wonderful" (Irving Berlin)

The show's final skit features Jimmy Stewart, Charlie McCarthy, Edgar Bergen and Ray Noble. Stewart is Charlie's campaign manager and he has his hands full. When Stewart says that he must be "truthful and honest," Charlie says that "there must be an easier way." Stewart adds that boys want a candidate who has made a name for himself in "football, baseball, hookey…" and Charlie quickly corrects him, "hockey, hockey." In the end, Stewart leaves the McCarthy campaign when another candidate offers him a free enchilada.

At the end of the show, announcer Ken Carpenter says that Stewart will soon be seen in Frank Capra's *It's a Wonderful Life*.

(3) Sunday, May 10, 1953 (8:00-8:30 p.m.)
NETWORK: CBS
SPONSOR: Hudnut

This show is currently not available. Since all other Stewart appearances have been documented, this is most likely the source of the Mortimer Snerd-Jimmy Stewart sketch rebroadcast in the June 20, 1954, May 6, 1956, and November 15, 1964 (*Chase and Sanborn 100th Anniversary Show*) shows.

(4) Sunday, June 20, 1954 (9:30-10:00 p.m.)
NETWORK: CBS
SPONSOR: Lanolin Plus
WRITERS: Norman Paul, Sy Rose, Zeno Clinker
PRODUCER: Sam Pierce
ANNOUNCER: Bill Baldwin
MUSIC: Ray Noble & his Orchestra

This was the final show of the 16th season and the guest was Nelson Eddy. In TV terms, this was a clip show. Several recorded bits from past shows were played. First up was a clip of Bergen asking Rudy Vallee if he could be on his show. Next came a sketch featuring Charlie McCarthy and W.C. Fields. A sketch with John Barrymore was up next, followed by one with Don Ameche. Then it was time for a song.

"The Happy Wanderer" — Nelson Eddy with the Ray Noble Orchestra

Next came the longest clip used, just over 5 minutes. This one featured Jimmy Stewart and Mortimer Snerd.

BERGEN: Tonight's discussion will concern itself with the various phases of farm problems and our guests are two of the most prominent farmers in the country. I would like to introduce them to you right now. First, your name please, sir.

SNERD: Duh…oh…my name, yeah, it's a…well, it's a…it's a…it's a… duh…it's a…well, it always has been, every day of my life, yeah. De dum da de dum…oh, what was the query?

BERGEN: The query? Well, you're name…your name is Mortimer Snerd.

SNERD: Yeah, that's right, yeah.

BERGEN: And now for our other expert on the farm panel…ah…your name please.

STEWART: Well, my name is…ah…my…it's…ah…oh, I know it as well as I know my own name. Ah…what was the query?

BERGEN: Yes, your name, sir.

STEWART: Oh yes, Zeke Stewart.

BERGEN: Yes, I see. Thank you. Thank you. Gentlemen, greetings and salutations.

SNERD: Well, thank you, I don't mind if I do.
STEWART: I'll go along with that.
SNERD: Mind if I go with you?
STEWART: No...no...come right along.
BERGEN: Gentlemen, gentlemen, please, this is a forum. Now, what is your opinion on agriculture?

STEWART: Well, it's my opinion that no farm should be without it.
SNERD: I'll go along with that.
STEWART: If you get there first, wait for me, huh.
BERGEN: No...no...no...no, we must have some helpful information. Now, Mr. Snerd, what's your idea on increasing milk production?
SNERD: I'm glad you asked me, yes. Ah...first...ah...first...ah... increasing milk production?
BERGEN: Yeah.
SNERD: First, you gotta get a cow. You gotta do that. You'll go along with me on that, won't you, Zeke?
STEWART: Yeah, yeah, should be a female cow.
SNERD: Now this morning I milked two gallons of milk in 10 minutes.
BERGEN: I see. Well, you must have been in great form.
SNERD: Yes sir, I was really hittin' on all four.
BERGEN: Perhaps I'll do better if I explain parity. Parity is equality in purchasing power between different kinds of money at a given ratio.

STEWART: Ooooooooooh…no!

SNERD: I'll go along with Zeke's opinion.

BERGEN: Look gentlemen, in other words, if a bushel of corn costs $2 under present conditions, do you think…

SNERD: Well, I tell you, it's like this.

BERGEN: I haven't asked you the question.

SNERD: Well, I ain't a fella that waits until the last minute.

STEWART: You know now, time's a wastin', and that's for dang sure. I like you, Mort. You're nobody's fool.

SNERD: Well, nobody's in particular anyway. And that's for dang sure.

STEWART: Heh-heh-heh-heh. We ought to get along fine…we understand each other.

SNERD: Yeah…ah…who do?

STEWART: You and me.

SNERD: Oh them, yeah.

STEWART: That's who I was talkin' about all…all the time; you and me.

BERGEN: Gentlemen, gentlemen, gentlemen! If a bushel of corn…if a bushel of corn, now get this…

STEWART: I like you, Mort. Let's…let's…let's get together some time, Mort.

SNERD: Okay, where?

STEWART: Well…well, we can decide that when we get there.

BERGEN: If a bushel…one bushel of corn…

STEWART: Anyway, I hope to see you sometime, Mort.

SNERD: Yeah, then some other time, I can see you, yeah. If we change off like that, we won't get so sick of seein' each other.

BERGEN: Now, this bushel of corn…

SNERD: Well, how about comin' over to my farm, Zeke?

STEWART: Okay, where is it?

SNERD: Well. I'll tell you how to get there if you don't mind gettin' lost.

STEWART: Oh, ah…how far is it as the crow flies?

SNERD: Oh, it's about…Well, you ain't comin' by crow are you?

BERGEN: Should a bushel of corn be sustained by supply and demand? That is, should the price of that bushel of corn be sustained by supply and demand or by Government subsidy?

STEWART: Where'd you say that place of yours' was, Mort?

SNERD: Well, you see, Mr. Stewart, you go down the road 'til you come to a crossroad and then you make a U-turn straight ahead.

STEWART: Is that there a small 'u' or a capital 'U?'

SNERD: Well, that's your problem, ain't it?

STEWART: Oh, yeah.

BERGEN: Gentlemen, why do refuse to answer my questions about a bushel of corn?

SNERD: Because we raises rutabagas.

BERGEN: I see.

SNERD: City slicker.

BERGEN: Well, let's go on to the question box.

SNERD: Well, all right, let's just go.

BERGEN: No…no…no. Here, here's the first question. How do you treat potato bugs?

STEWART: With contempt.

BERGEN: Oh, sorry, gentlemen, but our time is up.

STEWART: Well, I recon that's as good a direction as any.

BERGEN: Ladies and gentlemen, if you want a printed copy of this discussion, don't write us, write your psychiatrist…you're nuts!

STEWART: I'll go along with that.

SNERD: Yeah, me too.

A clip with Marilyn Monroe and one with Nelson Eddy finish out the show.

Thanked at the end of the show was "our staff:" Kenny McManus, Pat Walsh, Ross Murray, Helen Drill, Jack Kirkwood and the rest of our wonderful cast

This anniversary show can be found on *The History of Radio: Great Comedy Radio Shows* (Topics Entertainment CA-046), which was issued in 2001.

(5) Sunday, May 6, 1956 (7:05-8:00 p.m.)
NETWORK: CBS
SPONSOR: Viceroy Cigarettes, CBS TV Sets
SCRIPT BY: Sy Rose, Zeno Clinker, Hilda Rose
PRODUCER: Sam Pierce
ANNOUNCER: John Hiestand
MUSIC: Ray Noble & his Orchestra

The show is now known as *The New Edgar Bergen Show*. This is a special show, marking the 20th anniversary of Bergen and McCarthy being on the radio. This is basically the same show as the May 10, 1953, show which ended the 16th season of the show. The clips used from past shows are the same as that show, except they are longer, anywhere from a few seconds to several minutes, here (this show was 25 minutes longer than the earlier program). Even much of the dialogue and introductions are the same as those in the earlier show. The remaining time is padded out with several songs and two skits — one featuring Jack Kirkwood and one bird watcher, Mrs. Grace Harvard Philips.

The program begins with:

Edgar Bergen and Charlie McCarthy, with Mortimer Snerd, Carole Richards, Ray Noble, Jack Kirkwood, Rudy Wissler, The Mellomen, Dave Barry, our guests from the past, yours truly John Hiestand and our special guest Neslon Eddy.

The musical numbers, done especially for this show, were:

Carole Richards — "When You're In Love"

Nelson Eddy with Ray Noble Orchestra — "I'm On My Way"

Rudy Wissler — "Without You"

The Jimmy Stewart clip, which ends the first half of the show, is the same clip used on the 16th anniversary show broadcast on June 20, 1954. Also see *Chase and Sanborn 100th Anniversary Show*.

Family Theater
   NETWORK: Mutual Broadcasting System
   SPONSOR: Sustaining
   HOST: Carl Princie
   ANNOUNCER: Tony La Franco
   CREATOR/PRODUCER: Father Patrick Peyton
   PRODUCER: Bob Longenecker
   WRITER: True Broadman

Family Theater (also many times spelled Theatre) was created by Father Patrick Peyton as a way of promoting prayer and strengthening family values. The show's unofficial theme was "The family that prays together, stays together." The Mutual Network donated time for the show as long as four criteria were met: *1. The show must be of top quality, 2. It must be nonsectarian, 3. A major film star must be involved each week, and 4. Father Peyton pay production costs himself.* The show was on the air from February 13, 1947, until September 11, 1957, and there were a total of 540 shows. Jimmy Stewart appeared on two of them.

(1) Thursday, February 13, 1947 — *Flight From Home*

Jimmy Stewart was the host of the very first show to be broadcast. He gave a long speech at both the beginning and end of the show. In the beginning, he told the listeners:

> *Good evening, this is Jimmy Stewart. Tonight the* Family Theater *stars Loretta Young and Don Ameche. You know since this is our first program, maybe we oughta have a dedication. So right now, let's dedicate the Family Theater to your family with the hope that families everywhere will always be together and that your home will be a happy one with the conviction that prayer, simple prayer, will help to keep it that way. Now maybe you're thinking this is sort of an odd way to start a series of radio programs, programs from Hollywood with movie stars, actors and musicians. And maybe you're wondering what it's all about. Well, why don't you just sit back and listen. Listen to the music of Meredith Willson's Orchestra and listen to our story. It's called "Flight from Home," a story written by True Broadman and starring Don Ameche and Loretta Young.*

After the show, Jimmy has more to say. Anyone who still didn't have an idea of what the show was all about would certainly know when he was finished.

> *Thank you, Loretta Young and Don Ameche. You know, I thought maybe you folks would like to know why we call this program Family Theater. Well, I'll tell you—because it's the most important thing in the world. Our most precious possession is our family. We all want our family to be happy. Sure, but well, sometimes the going gets pretty tough — sickness, bills, accidents — which make it almost too much for a man and his wife to handle. You ever feel that way? You know, you don't know where to turn for help. And, because you're upset and worried, you get irritable and wango, your whole family seems to sort of fall apart. And you're positive there's nothing you can do to prevent it. But just stop and think a minute. Maybe you're overlooking something. Maybe there's a way you can get help, the most powerful help a man could ask for. But, you've got to ask for it. And how do you ask for it? Well, you just pray. Yes, you ask almighty God for His help. He wants you to pray. But you and your family will never know how much God can help you unless you ask. Deep down in your heart you know He'll help you. Now, before saying good night, I'm sure that Loretta Young and Don Ameche join me in expressing our pleasure in having had a part in dedicating this first program of the Family Theater. Thanks to everyone who helped make the Family Theater possible. And, you might be interested to know that Richard Sandville directed our play and True Broadman wrote it. Now next week our stars on the Family Theater will be Walter Brennan and Beulah*

Bondi in an original story "No Night Too Dark" by Charles Tazewell. This is Jimmy Stewart saying good night. Good night, everybody.

(2) Wednesday, April 4, 1951 — *Suzie's Prayer Ball*
NETWORK: Mutual Broadcasting System
SPONSOR: Sustaining
HOST: Gene Kelly
ANNOUNCER: Tony La Franco
CREATOR/PRODUCER: Father Patrick Peyton
SCRIPT WRITTEN BY: Kelly Curtis and Dick Stenger
MUSIC COMPOSED AND CONDUCTED BY: Harry Zimmerman
DIRECTED BY: Joseph F. Mansfield

Red, Helen and their daughter Suzie are in St. Petersburg, Florida, for baseball spring training. Red hasn't been able to pitch yet because he won't sign his contract. The team wants him to take a 25% pay cut. He's past his prime and didn't win as many games last season as he has in the past.

Suzie is headed for the beach to try to find her glove and ball that she left there the day before. But, she isn't gone long before she comes home crying. Tommy, one of her friends, says that his dad says that Red has lost his fastball and isn't the pitcher he used to be.

At practice, Red agrees to sign his contract for a 10% pay cut. He pitches that day against a minor league team and really gets hit around. When he arrives home, Suzie shows him a map of the beach. She's marked the area that was searched that day and where she plans on searching the next day. Before going to bed, she prays that she finds her glove and ball tomorrow and that her dad finds his fastball. Red's catcher, Mike, also stops by and warns Red that the team is going to sell his contract to St. Louis.

The next day, Charlie, the locker room attendant, gives Red a brand-new glove and ball that he says someone left behind. The glove is just the right size for Suzie. Red puts them in her bedroom so that she will find them when she wakes up. Suzie asks Red to play catch with her before he leaves for his game. While having to throw the ball more slowly to Suzie than he would in a game, he notices that when he puts spin on the ball it will, according to Suzie, do tricks.

In the game, he uses his fastball against the Braves in the first inning and they hit the ball well. Then he tries the pitch he had worked on with Suzie. He tells Mike it's called "Suzie's prayer ball." He not only finishes the game, he wins it.

The cast included: Jean Bates, Ann Whitfield, Herb Rollinson, Ralph Moody, Charles Seel, Ray Hite, Howard Culver, Bill Kline

In 2011, the show was released on the mp3 only set, *Jimmy Stewart the Ultimate Radio Collection Vol. 3* (Master Classics Records).

First Call for the Block Party
See Block Party.

Fleischmann Yeast Hour (The Rudy Vallee Show)
   NETWORK: NBC
   SPONSOR: Fleischmann Yeast
   ANNOUNCER: Graham McNamee
   FLEISCHMANN SPOKESMAN: Dr. R.E. Lee
   MUSIC: Rudy Vallee's Connecticut Yankees
   THEMES: *Down the Road to Sunshine* and *My Time Is Your Time* (Eric Little-Leo Dance)

This show, broadcast May 3, 1934 (8-9 p.m.), is not available for listening. The show featured a scene from the Broadway play *Yellow Jack* in which Jimmy Stewart played the role of Private O'Hara. The show had opened at the Martin Beck Theatre on March 6, 1934, and ran for 79 performances. The show was written and staged by Guthrie McClintic and written by Sidney Howard in collaboration with Paul De Kruif. The other cast members included:

Edward Acuff	*Private McClelland*
Wylie Adams	*Kraemer of the Rockefeller Foundation, and a Commissary Sergeant*
Jack Carr	*Chambang, a native Lab Assistant*
Eduardo Ciannelli	*Aristides Agramonte, Member of the American Yellow Fever Commission*
Francis Compton	*Royal Air Force Major*
Charles Gerard	*Adrian Stokes, of the West African Yellow Fever Commission*
Lloyd Gough	*Lab Assistant, and an Army Chaplain*
Harold Hoffat	*Roger P. Ames, Assistant Surgeon*
Colin Hunter	*Kenya Government Official*
Bernard Jukes	*Lab Assistant*
Whitford Kane	*Dr. Carlos*
Robert Keith	*Jesse W. Lazear, Member of the American Yellow Fever Commission*
Geoffrey Kerr	*Slackpoole*
Kim	*Kim*
Samuel Levene	*Private Busch*

Richie Ling..Colonel Tory, of the
Marine Hospital Corp.
Barton MacLane.............................James Carroll Finlay,
Member of the American Yellow Fever Commission
Myron McCormick............................. Private Brinkerhof
John Miltern.......................................Major Walter Reed
Millard Mitchell...................... Private William H. Dean
Jock Munro... Lab Assistant
George Nash.................. Major William Crawford Gorgas
Robert Shayne......................Harkness, Major Cartwright
Frank Stringfellow .... Orderly
Clyde Wallers .... Orderly
Katherine Wilson...................... Miss Blake, Special Nurse
in Charge of the Yellow Fever Ward

It is not known which of the other characters may have appeared in the scene presented on the program. Unfortunately, the publicity didn't help the play. It closed late in the month of May.

Focus on Youth

Focus on Youth, Inc. was a radio production company run by students at Princeton University. It billed itself as "America's Student Produced Press Conference of the Air." The founder (in 1974), moderator, and executive producer was Garth R. Ancier. He also acted as the host of the *Focus on Youth*, a weekly half-hour syndicated program. It was the most widely syndicated radio interview show of its time, airing on over 300 stations and reaching an estimated 2.3 million listeners each week (*Variety*, January 8, 1979). Among those interviewed on the program were Jesse Jackson, Tom Brokaw, Alexander Haig, Rosalynn Carter, Norman Mailer, Ted Kennedy, Nelson Rockefeller, Gloria Steinem, Art Buchwald, Barbara Walters, Billie Jean King, Admiral Elmo Zumwalt, Chevy Chase and Jimmy Stewart. According to Ancier, "We try to make the guest look like he is, not something he isn't. We challenge our guests, but we don't trap them." After graduating from Princeton in 1979, Ancier remained in the communication industry where he has been head of programming for the FOX Network, President of Entertainment at NBC, and President and CEO of the Warner Bros. Television Network (The WB).

The President and CEO of Focus on Youth, Inc. and Stewart interviewer was Mitch Semel. Like Ancier, after his 1981 graduation from

Princeton, Semel remained in the communication field. Among his credits are Director of Current Comedy Programs (NBC), President of UBU Productions, Senior Vice President of Programming at Comedy Central, Senior Vice President for Original Programming for Nick at Nite and TV Land and Senior Executive Producer of Program Development for CNN.

Stewart was interviewed for the special 6th-anniversary edition of the program. The interview was broadcast in two parts over two consecutive weeks. Although the programs are not in general circulation, they are available at The Paley Center for Media in New York City.

Both shows share the same credits:

NETWORK: Syndicated
EXECUTIVE PRODUCER AND HOST: Garth R. Ancier
PRODUCER: Mitch Semel
ASSOCIATE PRODUCER: Seth Lerner
DIRECTOR: Eric Linder
EXECUTIVE VICE PRESIDENT IN CHARGE OF FUNDING: Daniel Case
SPONSOR: Shell Oil Company

(1) Sunday, April 13, 1980 — Part 1

The show opens with Ancier reviewing Stewart's achievements, including his college days, Broadway and Hollywood careers, World War II service and his awards. Mitch Semel then conducts an in-depth interview with Stewart. A summary of the interview questions and Stewart's answers follows.

Semel asks if roles in Broadway plays came easily to Stewart. Stewart replies that there were so many plays on Broadway in those days that it was, in fact, easy to land parts.

Semel remarks that in Josh Logan's recent book (*Movie Stars, Real People and Me*, Delacorte, 1978), he says that Stewart wanted to be an architect and that he wasn't really taking his acting seriously. Stewart admits that acting was a "lark" for him at first, but that he found it so exhilarating that he soon became hooked.

Mitch asks about the University Players. Stewart tells him that they were a very special and very talented group of actors.

When asked if he had any sense that he would go into acting, Stewart says, "No, not me. Not until that summer after my Princeton graduation."

Semel next asks if there could ever be a repertoire company for film. Although Stewart thinks that it would be a great idea, he doesn't think that it will ever happen again like the early days of film when it was a great training ground for actors.

When asked what it was like to move to Hollywood in the 1930s, Stewart replies that it was a "big bunch of excitement."

Semel asks if filmmaking was still an experiment industry in the '30s. Stewart didn't think that it was, except for the sound part of filmmaking. Soundmen often controlled the films in those days according to him.

Semel next asks what it was like making the transition from civilian to military life. Stewart relates that he was about 10 years older than all the other recruits and that the officers didn't really know what to do with him. For several months, he was actually assigned to lead daily calisthenics.

When asked if he was ever scared during his missions over Germany, Stewart says, "I was scared all the time."

Was he given special treatment in the military was Semel's next question. Stewart replied that he couldn't be "one of the boys" because of his film and famous stature, but that when he started combat training all that changed and everyone became equal.

Semel asks next if Stewart's attitude toward war had changed because of his experiences in World War II. Stewart replied, "No, it didn't. It was a wonderful experience. It helped me…it broadened me. It helped me to mature in a way that I'll always be grateful for." He added that it taught him the importance of duty to country and the importance of transmitting that feeling to others.

Why do you feel many people in our generation don't have that attitude today, was Semel's next question. After a quick, "I can't answer that question," Stewart says that he believes there is much more patriotism in the country today than people realize. He also states that he thinks a lack of discipline has led to a lack of interest in the military.

Semel says that President Carter has asked for the responsible use of energy and inquires if the lack of discipline could also play a part in that problem. Stewart seems to be caught off guard by the question and simply responds, "Could be."

During a commercial break in the program, Ancier for the first time announces that this will be a two-part interview and promotes the fact that next week Stewart will answer questions about the movie industry, Harvey the invisible rabbit and the Academy Awards. The program then ends with one final question for Stewart.

Stewart is asked why he thinks the country is not willing to accept rationing the way that they did during World War II. Stewart lays the blame partly at the feet of the Senate and Congress for passing laws that hurt oil production in the United States.

(2) Sunday, April 20, 1980 — Part 2

To begin the second part of the Stewart interview show, Ancier again outlines Stewart's history. Although the second part of the interview is mostly conducted by Mitch Semel, Dave Weems also asks a few of the questions.

Semel begins by asking Stewart if he has any techniques for the very different forms of acting needed for film and stage. Stewart replies that it's a very difficult question to answer, but that if anyone can answer it, it would be Hank Fonda (Semel had mentioned Fonda when asking the question).

Dave now asks if it had been difficult to be Elwood Dowd on stage, film and TV. Stewart says that he "always thought it was only suitable for stage."

Mitch adds that Stewart seems to be permanently identified with the Dowd character and asks why. Stewart says that you have to act in a way that it doesn't look like you're acting at all and that you have to be both Dowd and the rabbit.

Semel continues, asking if after doing *Harvey* for a while on stage, if he actually began to see him. Jimmy says that he did and adds that "he's become a very good friend." He says that lots of times when he's alone, he talks to Harvey.

Dave asks if Harvey is in the room with them right now. Stewart says, "He's not here, he's at home."

Semel asks if when he returned to Broadway in 1970, it had changed. Stewart replies that there was not as much excitement and activity as there had been in the 1930s. But added that he thinks some of that is returning now.

Semel now wanted to know if Stewart thought commercialism had changed the Broadway theater, to which Stewart replies, "I think it's changed as much as it's had to change."

Dave then asks if there is enough theater around today for actors to gain experience. Stewart's answer, "No, there can never be enough."

Mitch asks if awards are important to actors. "They are a pat on the back from fellow performers," says Stewart.

Dave says that competition for awards has created immense egos in the industry and wants to know if Stewart thinks those egos take away from the art of acting. Jimmy says that he thinks a certain amount of competition is a good thing.

Semel asks if there was any one thing professionally that Stewart enjoyed so much that he'd want to go back and do it again. Stewart gives a long, "Hmmmmm…no." But then adds that maybe he'd want to redo the flops.

Finally, Semel asks if there were any roles that he regrets never having gotten to play. And, with Stewart's simple, "I don't think so," the interview is completed.

Forest Lawn Memorial Park Easter Sunrise Service
Sunday, April 21, 1946 (8:15-8:30 a.m.)
According to the following newspaper article of the time, Stewart read *A Prayer for Peace* during the nationally broadcast service.
The program is not available for listening.

The Fred Waring Show
This musical variety show featured Waring, his orchestra and chorus, The Pennsylvanians. Stewart appeared on the show three times. Although only a few of Waring's radio shows are in general circulation, all can be heard at Fred Waring's America, The Pennsylvania State University, 313 Pattee Library, University Park, PA. Among the 25,000 recordings in the special collection, are all of Waring's radio broadcasts. These broadcasts, originally on wire, transcription discs and tape, have been transferred to digital audio tape. Many scripts from these shows, including the three Stewart appearances, are also available. Much of Waring's memorabilia, including several Waring blenders, is also on display.
ASSISTANT CONDUCTOR: Fred Culley
CHORAL LEADER: Robert Shaw
OPENING THEME: "I Hear Music" (Roy Ringwald/Fred Waring/John M. Dolph)
CLOSING THEME: "Sleep" (Earl Lebieg)

(1) Friday, January 24, 1947 (Show #447) (11-11:30 a.m.)
NETWORK: NBC
ANNOUNCER: Clyde Catrell
Broadcast from Radio City, New York City
Several musical numbers are performed at the beginning of the show with Waring introducing each.
"Magic Is the Moonlight" (Charles Pasquale/Maria Grever)
"If I Forget You" (Irving Caesar) — Jane Wilson and Glee Club
"MabelMabel" (Irvin Drake/Jimmy Shirl/Henry Katzman) — Swingerettes
"Willow Road" (Mel Torme/Robert Wells) — Joe Marine
"Managua Nicaragua" (Albert Gamse/Irving Fields) — Gordonairs
"Liza" (George Gershwin/Gus Kahn/Ira Gershwin) — Orchestra

As Waring is giving an outro for *Liza*, he suddenly says:

WARING: ...Just a minute, hold it, hold it, hold the music. I think I see somebody in the audience. I see somebody — Jimmy Stewart! Is that Jimmy Stewart down there in the front row? Jimmy Stewart! Jimmy come up here and let me see...You know...greetings, Mr. Smith.
STEWART: Thank you, Fred. Thanks very much.
WARING: This is really the James Stewart of the movies and also of Pennsylvania.
STEWART: Of Pennsylvania.
WARING: Indiana.
STEWART: Indiana, Pennsylvania. How's Tyrone?
WARING: Tyrone is all right, Jimmy, and if I'm right in my recollections, you used to...uh...sort of climb on a barrel and listen in as we used to play dances around there, didn't you?
STEWART: Yeah, yeah. You know, Dutch Campbell there, remember?
WARING: Poor old Delux.
STEWART: Poor old Delux.
WARING: He was here a couple of weeks ago...had his banjo. Nice to see you. What prompted you to come to our show?
STEWART: Well, I'm just a fan of your and you...your outfit, Fred. Uh, I uh, I've been enjoying it for a long time. Come a little different time out at the coast; 'bout eight o'clock.
WARING: Just about the right time for the...
STEWART: Right uh right time on my way to work and it's a wonderful day to start uh...wonderful way to start the day off.
WARING: That wasn't a cue for us to mention *A Wonderful Life* was it?
STEWART: Uh well...just uh thought, thought I'd throw a wonderful...
WARING: Wonderful is a wonderful word to use in uh...
STEWART: Liberty Films.
WARING: In connection with a picture called *Wonderful Life*, and it is a wonderful picture.
STEWART: Thank you, Fred.
WARING: Congratulations.
STEWART: Thank you.
WARING: Uh...how's your golf?
STEWART: Golf is terrible. As a matter of fact, that's why I came east.
WARING: It is?
STEWART: It's snowing here and you can't play.

WARING: Well, you, uh...girls come over here. I want you to meet Jimmy Stewart. I think it would be a very nice...this is Jane Wilson...Jimmy Stewart.

STEWART: Jane, how do you do?

WARING: Jane is our star soprano.

STEWART: I've enjoyed you very much for a long time.

WILSON: Thank you.

WARING: And this is Joanne Wheatley...Jimmy Stewart.

WHEATLEY: How do you do?

STEWART: And there again.

WARING: And this is Gloria...uh...Gloria...uh...what is your name lately?

MUDELL: Mudell.

WARING: Gloria Mudell. And this is Penny Perry.

PERRY: Hello, Mr. Stewart.

STEWART: Hello.

WARING: I have to meet the girls myself occasionally, you know. Jimmy Stewart this is...and that's Ferne over there.

STEWART: Hello, Ferne.

WARING: And Betty Reynolds back of the piano. And uh, boys, this is Jimmy Stewart.

BOYS: Hi.

WARING: Isn't he nice, though, really, and nice of you to come up here. I suppose you came up expecting to just enjoy the show and here you're helping all of our listeners enjoy your presence.

STEWART: Well, uh, I, uh it's, it's wonderful to meet you all. That's, that's, that's what gives me the real kick.

WARING: Well, that's fine, Jimmy.

STEWART: I've certainly enjoyed it for a long time.

WARING: How's sis?

STEWART: Wonderful show...wonderful...saw her yesterday.

WARING: Going back to Indiana?

STEWART: Going tomorrow.

WARING: Will you say hello to the whole gang out there?

STEWART: Sure will.

WARING: Wonder if they all exist?

STEWART: Yeah...

WARING: You know that that's a wonderful live wide-awake town, but they, they live at such a pace. You...

STEWART: Yeah, I know. Well, Dutch has a little girl that, that she plays the piano. I don't know whether you've heard her play the piano.

WARING: Haven't heard her, but he told me, a couple of weeks ago he was here he, he told me all about her.

STEWART: Yeah, uh, fine. Reads music you know, uh...

WARING: She does? Well, she's a little too good for our group then.

STEWART: Well, uh, I remember Dutch had a little trouble, always.

WARING: Yes, he had, uh, we always played his key.

STEWART: I see.

WARING: Stubborn fellow he was...very stubborn.

STEWART: No black keys, all white keys.

WARING: That's right. Uh, Jimmy, is there anything in particular you'd like to hear from our organization? We'd be very glad to change the program for you. (Aside) Give me that program there and we'll tell you what's coming up and uh. That's "Liza" you heard there and now let's see. Behind time at the present time, let's see, uh, let's see, we could do, uh, oh, we could do one chorus of "Wyoming," couldn't we? Let's do one chorus of "Wyoming." That's, uh, out near Indiana, uh, Pennsylvania. Or we could do "Who Is Sylvia" or we could do, uh, "Sometimes I Feel Like a Motherless Child." The part up here we've already done, you see.

STEWART: Uh, huh, yes.

WARING: And so you, you name it and we, we'll be very glad to...to... uh. Name anyone of these last four and we'll be glad to do them...

STEWART: Who, "Who is Sylvia?"

WARING: Who is she?

STEWART: Yeah.

WARING: We'll be glad to find out for you. "Who is Sylvia?" I...I probably have an announcer. Let's see...uh...it says here. Well, you read it. Bill Bivens isn't here.

STEWART: The question was asked by Shakespeare hundreds of years ago, and the orchestra, Stuart Churchill and the Twin Trios are still asking is..."Who is Sylvia?" The music is by Franz Shubert.

WARING: Doesn't give the answer, though, does it?

STEWART: No, no.

WARING: Well, suppose we play it and sing it and then if there's no answer why, we'll just forget it.

STEWART: All right, but I won't forget the way it's going to be sung.

WARING: All right. Would you like to start the number "Who is Sylvia?" You lift your hand this way and then bring it down. You ready?

"Who Is Sylvia" (William Shakespeare/Franz Shubert) — Stuart Churchill & Twin Trios

WARING: (Over opening of song) Congratulations, Jimmy. He really did start the number. That's a cue for this violin.

After the song, Waring adds:

WARING: That was "Who Is Sylvia" and that is the answer, and, believe it or not, it was conducted by James Stewart of the movies. Good Jimmy Stewart of Indiana, Pennsylvania, who dropped in on us most unexpectedly and we imposed upon him and he's still smiling. I, uh, I think he was a little nervous, weren't you, Jim?

There's no answer from Stewart. To close the show, one final number is performed.
"Sometimes I Feel Like a Motherless Child" (Roy Ringwald, arranger) — Glee Club, Leon Kranendonk soloist

(2) Wednesday, September 3, 1947 (11-11:30 a.m.)
NETWORK: NBC (Show #616)
ANNOUNCER: Bill Bivens
Broadcast from Radio City, New York City
As usual, the show opens with several songs introduced by Waring.
"Girl Who Came from Peru" (Charles Tobias/Carlos Maduro) — The Gang
"September Song" (Kurt Weill/Maxwell Anderson) — Walter Scheff (a former Pennsylvanian, now a solo artist)
"Liza" (George Gershwin/Gus Kahn/Ira Gershwin)
Just a very short segment of "Liza" is played and then Stewart is introduced in a very novel way by Waring and Daisy.

DAISY: Fred, Fred, aren't they ever gonna bring Jimmy Stewart on? What's the orchestra playing "Liza" for?
WARING: Well, I guess it is about time. But why are you so concerned?
DAISY: Because I have a wonderful plot for his next picture.
WARING: A plot for Jimmy Stewart's picture? What is it?
DAISY: Well, first "The Murder Man" steals the "Pot of Gold" from "The Shop Around the Corner." Then, "After the Thin Man" says "You Can't Take it with You," "Mr. Smith Goes to Washington," where he

meets a "Gorgeous Hussy" named "Rose Marie" who says you were "Born to Dance." "Come Live with Me" in "Seventh Heaven." We were "Made for Each Other." But he says "No Time for Comedy." Just then "Destry Rides Again" with the "Ziegfeld Girl" and after "The Mortal Storm," "It's a Wonderful Life" in a "Magic Town"…and that's "The Philadelphia Story."

STEWART: Ah, you left out "Shopworn Angel."

DAISY: Ah, Jimmy.

WARING: Ah, Jimmy. You know we've all been excited about your visit, Jimmy. It's really great to see you again.

STEWART: Well, Fred, thanks very much. I certainly enjoyed myself the last time I was here.

WARING: Well, I did, too! You know, Jimmy, it's pretty wonderful what a great motion picture celebrity would do…that he would even bother to take the time to drop in on an old friend…just for friendship's sake.

STEWART: Oh, well, Fred…for friendship's sake…well…ah…I know that's wonderful and I feel the same. You see…I…I think I should explain a little.

WARING: You know fellows…pardon me…pardon me, Jimmy. Fellows from the great Commonwealth of Pennsylvania…fellows in the busy world of the theater…it's nice that's what it is.

STEWART: It is nice. That's what it is. It's nice. There's one thing, Fred. I was talking to the man over at…over at…ah…

WARING: So many stars won't pay any attention to anyone unless they want something. They think of nothing but their own little firmament…now, I could tell you…yes it is…

STEWART: Fred…

WARING: Yeah, I could tell you of an instance…what?

STEWART: Fred, don't say any more…ah…things like that, would ya, please? Don't say any more things…

WARING: Like what?

STEWART: Like…you know…that I am such a nice guy because I came over here just because I…it's so much fun and…well, you know, Pennsylvania fellows together, and I might as well…ah…just confess to you right now.

WARING: Right here? Right here?

STEWART: Yes, you see, I tried to tell you before. But I was talking to the man over at…well, it's…to a man over where I work…at RKO.

WARING: Oh? Mmm.

STEWART: …and that man thought it would be a sort of a nice idea if I came…

WARING: If you came on our show and plugged your new picture! Isn't that it?

STEWART: Well, that's...It wasn't my idea, Fred. You see, it's that man over at RKO...

WARING: OK, OK, RKO. Now what's an illusion or two in this crass world? Name please...

STEWART: James Stewart.

WARING: No, no! The name of the...uh...

STEWART: Robert...Robert Riskin...producer...

WARING: No, no, no, no! That's the name of the man at RKO...the name of the picture.

STEWART: It's opening about the end of this month...

WARING: The name of the picture, please.

STEWART: You sit there and eat popcorn...

WARING: The name of the picture, please.

STEWART: Oh, *Magic Town*.

WARING: More magic? First it's *Second Class Angels*, then all summer it's invisible rabbits, *Magic Town*...

STEWART: Well, it's...it's a very nice picture. I play a sort of a research man in it.

WARING: Research man!

STEWART: Yeah. I study the public's reactions, sort of...

WARING: You study the public's reactions! That'll be something new. They've been studying yours for years, you know.

STEWART: Well, now...now, you're just being complicated, Fred. It's really a very simple type of thing...

WARING: It could be worse, after all, you know...

STEWART: What? The picture?

WARING: No...no...this situation. You're using our program to exploit your...this...uh...Robert Riskin's *Magic Town*...the picture might have a song in it...

STEWART: A song? Uh...hmmm.

WARING: Song! We have trouble with song-pluggers on my station...

STEWART: A song! Uh-ha. As a matter of fact, Fred, that reminds me. I just happen to...

WARING: You mean...uh...uh...

STEWART: No! I just happen to have a copy of it here in my pocket. It's a uh...

WARING: Oh, Jimmy, I give up...here, Joanne, you know Jimmy Stewart, don't you?

STEWART: Hello, Joanne

WARING: Well, uh…here's a song from Mr. Stewart's new picture *Magic Town*. It's called…let's see…it's called…ah…

STEWART: Ah…from the picture…"Magic Town," from the picture of the same name.

WARING: The name of the song? Oh, I see.

STEWART: "Magic Town."

WARING: Well, Joanne, will you run it over with Charley? We might use it sometime.

STEWART: Well, that's swell, Fred…only…ah…

WARING: Only what? Only what? Only what?

(Joanne begins to sing the song)

STEWART: Well…ah…that man said…ah…hey, that's the song…da da da da…Magic Town…Yeah, that's the song…

WARING: Ah, that's it, huh?

STEWART: Ah-huh.

WARING: Just the way it goes, isn't it?

STEWART: Just a simple little song.

WARING: The man said something, did he?

STEWART: Yeah, ah…he said that also I should just happen to have about…

WARING: Thank you, Joanne…thank you very much, Joanne…we'll learn it and we'll work it up then…

STEWART: He said that maybe I should also have about 32 other copies, so maybe you'd…

WARING: Ooooh…that…package under your arm…I see, uh-huh…package under your arm, is it your…

STEWART: No, well, it's not my lunch.

WARING: OK, all right, pass 'em out. Maybe we'll have the glee club do it sometime. Now, Mr. Jimmy "Song-Plugger" Stewart, are you satisfied?

STEWART: Well…in a way…yes, Fred…but I…the man said…

WARING: I know…don't tell me. The man wants us to sing it not someday, but today…is that it?

STEWART: I'm very much afraid that's what he said, Fred.

WARING: Well, don't be too afraid, Jimmy. Ah, I'll tell you, I'm not usually of a suspicious nature, but when we heard you were coming over, we just happened to run through your song a couple of times today.

STEWART: You did!

WARING: Yeah.

STEWART: Well, isn't that wonderful.

WARING: Show him how it sounds now. This is your song, "Magic Town," which probably never we'll hear again.

"Magic Town" (Mel Torme/Bob Wells) — Glee Club
When the song is over, we hear Jimmy again.

STEWART: Thank you, Fred.

Waring invites Stewart back anytime he has another picture or song to promote. He then introduces the next songs.

"Cecilia" (Herman Ruby/Dave Dreyer) — Joe Marine, orchestra, Daisy Bernier & her Dandylions, Boy Meets Girl and some rhythm antics from the whole gang

Fred introduces Hugh "Uncle Lumpy" Brannum, who tells the story of *Little Orley and the Cricket*. (This Uncle Lumpy story can also be found on Decca 88014, 10-inch 78 RPM and the album *More Adventures of Little Orley*, Vocalion VL-73780.) Uncle Lumpy was a regular feature on the Fred Waring Show and Brannum would later portray Mr. Green Jeans on TV's *Captain Kangaroo*. Brannum also played bass for the Pennsylvanians. The story completed, a final song is performed.

"Sometimes I Feel Like a Motherless Child" (Roy Ringwald, arranger) — Glee Club, Walter Scheff soloist

(3) Monday, March 22, 1948 (10-10:30 a.m.) (Show #788)
SPONSOR: General Electric
ANNOUNCER: Bill Bivens
COMMERCIAL ANNOUNCER: Bob Considine

Among the items found at Penn State's Fred Waring's America special collection is a news release prepared for this program.

Stewart is introduced by Bill Bivens and begins the show with this short speech.

STEWART: Hello, everybody, and thanks for letting me come along with the gang for their weekly visit in your home. You know when the man said something about being the Pennsylvanians'"Number One Fan," I don't know whether he was referring to antiquity or enthusiasm. In either case I qualify pretty well because for years now, I've been one of the Waring faithful. You know, when Fred called me up and suggested I be here tonight, he didn't say what I was to do. He just said to "take over"…

ah…so…let's see how it should go here. This is Jimmy Stewart and his Pennsylvanians, opening the show with something bearing the amazing title of "Toolie Oolie Doolie"…in which, I understand, people yodel.

"Toolie Oolie Doolie" (Arthur Beul) — Gang

STEWART: You know, one of the nice things that happens to you when you…ah…sort of take over The Pennsylvanians, is to discover that the beautiful voices you've heard turn out to be very beautiful people. Ah, in this instance…Joanne Wheatley. Good evening, Joanne.

WHEATLEY: Good evening, Jimmy. Perhaps I should have said Mr. Stewart.

STEWART: Ah, perhaps you should have. Yeah, but…ah…let's, ah…perhaps we could talk about that a little later, huh?

WHEATLEY: All right.

STEWART: What are you doing after the show? Anyway, right now you're going to sing. What's the…what's the song?

WHEATLEY: It's a Simeone-styling of "For Every Man There's a Woman."

STEWART: "For Every Man There's a Woman." Well, that's a hopeful thought, isn't it!

"For Every Man There's a Woman" (Leo Robin/Harold Arlen) — Joanne Wheatley, Glee Club, orchestra

STEWART: One of the features I look forward to on the Fred Waring Show is Bob Considine and his reports of the interesting things going on at General Electric. Here he is…

At this point in the show, Bob Considine does a spot for G.E.'s Educational Assistance program and a short musical interlude moves them into the next segment of the show.

STEWART: Now, if I haven't got my notes mixed up here, it's time for some wonderful stuff to happen…Jane Wilson and all…look…ah….look here, Jane, does Fred carry this stuff around in his hands all the time in the studio?

WILSON: Always, Jimmy…but he practically never looks at them.

STEWART: Well, then, I won't either, Jane. As a matter of fact, I made up this announcement on the way east.

WILSON: Oh?
STEWART: Yes, yes. It's…ah…something quite special.
WILSON: Oh?
STEWART: Um-hum…yeah, it's pretty fancy.
WILSON: Oh?
STEWART: Yeah, here it is: Now, a lady and a song…each of infinite charm…the lady, Jane Wilson…the song…Of course, I couldn't…get that because I didn't know what the song was. So, what's your song, Jane?
WILSON: Oh! The song…"It's Spring."
(The orchestra begins the song and over the music we hear Jimmy ask.)
STEWART: You care to dance?
WILSON: Thank you. I'd love to.

It's Spring (Clay Boland/Moe Jaffe/Darrell Smith) — Jane Wilson, orchestra

STEWART: Thank you, thank you, thank you, Jane. Well, if it wasn't spring before, it sure is now.
WILSON: You're very nice.
STEWART: Well, I'm very happy! You know, this is wonderful…I'm having the time of my life. I don't have to act…I don't have to sing, like I had to on Bing Crosby's program the other night…I don't have to talk about motion pictures…
WILSON: Oh…but, you see, we do!
STEWART: We do…do what?
WILSON: We have to talk about motion pictures…they've said especially to tell everybody about your current picture…
STEWART: Oh…oh, I know what you mean…oh that…oh…that's those "James Stewart may now be seen currently" things! Yeah, well, you don't have to worry about that…just throw those in at the end of the program, it's all right.
GIRLS: Not on this show!

Call Northside 777 (Arranger: Harry Simeone/Hawley Ades) — Glee Club, orchestra

STEWART: Well…ah…well sir, wasn't it…wasn't it just a little…over arranged or something?
WILSON: We had it Waringized.
DAISY: Now, will you tell us about *Harvey*? [Daisy is Daisy Bernier.]

STEWART: Well, Daisy, I'm going back into *Harvey* beginning Monday. And ah…say, don't tell me you've had *Harvey* Waringized too!

WILSON: Oh no, we wouldn't do that.

STEWART: Oh no, of course not…not with all those fanfares and everything…no, *Harvey*'s really very simple. It's a play about a man and a rabbit…a large white rabbit. I was introduced to the rabbit last summer and we spent some time together and we parted friends and all that, but he hasn't written for several months and I got concerned and so I'm going to spend the next four weeks with him and get him straightened out.

DAISY: Well, can we come and see you?

STEWART: Oh, sure, sure. We'll be right over here at the Forty-Eighth Street Theater — it's right up the street here, you know — eight-forty curtain…matinee…and…you know, just like it was an ordinary play.

GIRLS: We'll be there.

STEWART: Okay, thanks…wonderful. Well, now, may I introduce Virginia Morley and Livingston Gearhart…they're the good young… young people over there…Liv and Virginia play their own idea of cradle songs…"Baby Boogie."

"Baby Boogie" (Livingston Gearhart)

STEWART: Now, during the last minute of "Baby Boogie" things have been going all over the place. People trading places…grouping at microphones…reaching for instruments…looks like this one is going to be a Waring super-duper…Stuart Churchill's arrangement for the orchestra and Glee Club of "Caprice Espagnol." Fred Culley conducts.

"Caprice Espagnol" (Rimsky-Korsakov) — Orchestra, Glee Club

STEWART: And, now, Bob Considine…with another story about educational opportunities at General Electric.

Considine reads his commercial and music moves the program into its next segment.

STEWART: One of the very pleasant things about the Pennsylvanians… and about the programs Fred Waring presents…is that they can change their mood, and yours, from the gay to the serious in such a sincere and natural way. And, we do that, now, because this is the Monday of Holy

Week. The Glee Club, with Virginia Morley and Livingston Gearhart at the pianos, sings Bach's "Jesu, Joy of Man's Desiring." Don Craig conducts.

"Jesu, Joy of Man's Desiring" (J.S. Bach/English lyrics — Joy Scott)

STEWART: Well, this is James Stewart. It's been an especially happy privilege to be a part of the Pennsylvanians tonight…and to help one of the finest guys I know, enjoy a rest. They tell me that Richard Rodgers and Oscar Hammerstein are taking over next week. Well, that should mean a lot of beautiful music and, come to think of it, twice as many pieces of paper to lose as we had tonight. Well, so long.

BIVENS: Thank you, James Stewart…(into a promo for Easter Seals and a promo for next week's show).

Freedom Under God
Sunday, July 1, 1951 (9:30-10 p.m.)
NETWORK: CBS
The program begins with a recording of "My Country 'Tis of Thee." Coming in under the song is the voice of the host, Jimmy Stewart.

STEWART: Happy Birthday Americans. This is Jimmy Stewart in Hollywood speaking for the Committee to Proclaim Liberty. Next Wednesday, July 4, will be the 175th birthday of the United States. Now it's only right for us to celebrate Independence Day with all the usual American trimmings — ballgames, picnics and good, clean fun. But the Committee to Proclaim Liberty asks you to take time out from the festivities to do three things. First, stop a moment and say thank you to almighty God for our heritage of freedom. Second, read over again — and I'll bet a lot of you haven't read it since you were in school — read once more the Declaration of Independence. That's what this 4th of July celebration is all about…independence. And third, rededicate yourself to freedom under God. Without him, the freedom you have now may not last you all your life. We've been a little careless over the years about giving up some of our freedom without getting anything really worthwhile in return. Make a 4th of July resolution that from now on nobody is going to chisel away any more of your God-given rights so long as you have only to exercise your vote to prevent it. Wherever American servicemen face danger, there you'll find members of the Chaplain's Corps. Captain Arthur E. Mills is the first member of his corps to come back from Korea for hospitalization in the United States. He was wounded twice in frontline action. Now there could be no more fitting invocation for an occasion like this than a prayer offered by a brave man, Chaplain Mills.

After Mills' prayer, Jimmy continues.

STEWART: To those of us who know him best, Bing Crosby is more than just an entertainer. We respect him as a conscientious, responsible American citizen. Recently, Bing came up with some ideas on the subject of Independence Day which we thought he should repeat on this program. Here he is.

Bing presents his thoughts and then Jimmy comes back.

STEWART: This morning, 17,000 clergymen announced from their pulpits that at noon on Independence Day all the church bells will ring out across the land and the Committee to Proclaim Liberty earnestly hopes that you will follow your minister's suggestion that this should be a moment of thanksgiving to God. And now, Mr. Lionel Barrymore reads the Preamble to the Declaration of Independence.

As you would expect, Barrymore gives a very dramatic reading of the document.

STEWART: From Ralph Bradford's narrative poem, *Heritage*, Roland Bradley has selected verses and set them to music as a chorale. Here is baritone Steven Camalian with our choir in a work composed especially for our broadcast — "Heritage."

After the performance concludes, Stewart continues.

STEWART: A few weeks ago, a special resolution was passed in the Congress of the United States granting citizenship to a courageous woman. Most of you will remember how a couple of years ago Oksana Kasenkina jumped from the third-story window of the Russian Consulate in New York. Well, tonight, a great America actress, Gloria Swanson, is waiting to introduce her to you.

Swanson talks more about Oksana's story before introducing her. Oksana also makes a short statement.

STEWART: It isn't very often that we Americans have a chance to hear directly from one of our military commanders speaking from his post of duty. And tonight the committee to Proclaim Liberty is fortunate in being able to bring you from Tokyo, the voice of General Matthew B. Ridgway.

Ridgway delivers a rather lengthy statement and then we hear a bit more of "Heritage" before Stewart ends the show.

STEWART: This broadcast and other activities of the Committee to Proclaim Liberty during this week in which we celebrate the 175th anniversary of our independence is to remind every American of his birthright. Remember that freedom is God's gift. Without His help we cannot save it for ourselves or our children. Our soloist tonight was Steven Camalian. The choir was conducted by Dr. Charles Hurt of the University of Southern California. Irving Talbot conducted the orchestra. If you wish to obtain a copy of General Ridgway's talk, just send your request to Liberty, care of Postmaster, Los Angeles, and it'll be sent to you without charge. This is Jimmy Stewart saying goodnight for the Committee to Proclaim Liberty.

The program then ends with the playing of the "National Anthem."

Fun for All
This quiz-style program was hosted by Arlene Francis and Bill Cullen. Stewart's one and only appearance was on Saturday, June 27, 1953. On CKRC, the program aired from noon until 12:30 pm. The show is not available for listening.

The General Electric Show
See *The Bing Crosby Show*.

The Gift of Christmas
Salvation Army KM 11576 (1983)
The record's label reads: "Christmas Greetings from The Salvation Army 'Army of Stars' Presents *The Christmas Story* featuring James Stewart and the Roger Wagner Chorale." Stewart is only involved on side one of the record. Stewart acts as both the narrator and as one of the Bible readers on the disc. The discs were sent to radio stations and could be played on the air as a 25-minute program. The actual playing time was 19:30, allowing for the station to add commercials and news to fill out the half-hour. The album was also packaged and sold to the general public.

Stewart introduces *The Christmas Story* with, "Merry Christmas everyone, my name's Jimmy Stewart and I'm here on behalf of the Salvation Army with an army of stars to tell you a story." Then we hear a series of Christmas songs interspersed with readings from the book of Luke. The music, by the Roger Wagner Chorale and Sinfonia Orchestra, and readings include:
"We Three Kings"
Orson Welles (Luke 2:1-5)
"What Child Is This"
William Conrad and Orson Welles (Luke 2:6-9)
"O Little Town of Bethlehem"
William Conrad (Luke 2:10-12)
"Gesu Bambino"
Orson Welles (Luke 2:13-14)
"Angels We Have Heard on High"
James Stewart (Luke 2:15-16)
"Virgin's Slumbering Song"
William Conrad (Luke 2:17-20)
"Joy to the World"

At the end, Stewart comes back to say, "Well, that's our story for Christmas, except for one last thought. More than 19 long centuries have come and gone since the birthday of the man whose anniversary we celebrate each Christmas. Yet, I'm sure I'm well within the mark when I say that all the armies that ever marched, all the rockets ever built, and all the parliaments that ever sat, and all the kings that ever reigned, put together, have nowhere near affected the life of man upon this earth as much and as powerfully as that one solitary life; and to all of you, the merriest Christmas ever."

The director and producer for the project was Dr. Robert Docter, Chuck Britz was the engineer and Robert Bearchell was the coordinator. Dileen Marsh is responsible for the cover art. Thanked in addition to the stars appearing on the disc are Commissioner Will Pratt, the American Federation of Radio and Television Artists and the American Federation of Musicians.

Gisele of Canada
NETWORK: Syndicated
SPONSOR: Sustaining
ANNOUNCER: Rupert Lucas

A 15-minute show was produced for the U.S., despite the references to Canada. The show starred Gisele MacKenzie, born Gisele Marie-Louise Marguerite LaFleche in Winnipeg, Manitoba, on January 10, 1927 (she died September 5, 2003). Her musical training includes piano, violin, and voice. Her first radio show was *Meet Gisele*, for the Canadian Broadcasting Corporation in 1946. To fans of early TV she is best remembered for her singing on *Your Hit Parade* from 1953-1957. She also appeared regularly on *The Jack Benny Show* and later on her own show, *The Gisele MacKenzie Show*. In later years, she acted in such shows as *Boy Meets World*, *Crazy like a Fox*, *MacGyver*, and *Murder, She Wrote*. Judging from the interviews conducted by Rupert Lucas (known best as one of the directors of *Duffy's Tavern*), the show was designed to point out the similarities between the U.S. and Canada, promote cooperation and establish a trading partnership between the two neighboring countries. According to *The Era*, a Bradford, PA, newspaper, the show aired there on October 24, 1950, at 11:15 a.m.

The show begins with Gisele singing two songs — "A Trout No Doubt" and a French cowboy song which incorporates parts of "Oh! Susanna."

Stewart is then interviewed by Rupert Lucas.

LUCAS: Today, our guest is James Stewart, and if I were to say anything about his screen work, I'd just be telling you what you already know. But I can also report for some Canadian bomber pilots who served with him in England and who remember him as a very right guy.

STEWART: I remember those Canadians, Rupert. Our Air Force and theirs clicked from the very start. They're natural born fliers.

LUCAS: Well, they have to be, Jimmy. They've built up a very big chunk of their country by air. Ever meet any of the ex-bush pilots from the north?

STEWART: Oh yes, and heard plenty about that North Country, pretty fascinating stuff.

LUCAS: Yeah, the last frontier, huh.

STEWART: Well, maybe so, it's a whale of a lot different from any other frontier. For one thing, it's crossed by nearly every principle airlines in the world and it's webbed with airlines of its own. The way I get it, there's hardly a place in the north that isn't within a few hours flying time of one of the big cities.

LUCAS: That's true and there's an enormous traffic back and forth in passengers and air freight.

STEWART: Certainly must be different than old-time frontier life; none of that feeling of remoteness. You know, there's…there's another thing about this frontier that interests me as a flyer.

LUCAS: Go on, I'm learning things.

STEWART: Well, that North Country is really a buffer between two very different worlds. In fact, between two ways of thinking that just don't mix at all; with Russia on one side and the rest of Canada and ourselves on the other.

LUCAS: If I were up there, I'd think I'd acquired a little too much strategic importance to feel comfortable.

STEWART: Yes, perhaps. Where could you go today to feel comfortable? But I suppose that's why the defense of the north takes such a big place in the joint military planning between Canada and the States. Let's hope that sort of thing is just fire insurance we'll never have to collect on.

LUCAS: Well, I'm with you there.

STEWART: One of the most comfortable thoughts for me is that the Canadian north has become a stamping ground for pretty nearly every kind of scientist you could name. Isn't that a fact, Rupert?

LUCAS: Oh sure…Weathermen, radar men, geographers, topographers, and the boys who study geophysics and terrestrial magnetism and the mechanics of snow and ice and how you live and what you eat in cold climates.

STEWART: Mm…hum, and big scale, long-range development work on the greatest storehouse of minerals and metals and strategic ores in the world. It's all work that takes specialists to carry out.

LUCAS: They tell me there are a lot of American scientists there, too.

STEWART: And what's all this I hear about new snowmobiles and such?

LUCAS: Oh, they're developing new types that buzz across the country in the winter the way the old Model T Ford used to do down here in the days of our dirt roads. We've been talking about the Canadian north, ice and snow; as though that was the one…that was the whole country.

STEWART: I know what you mean, but…but I imagine most Americans know about the bustling, modern, southern part of Canada. Enough of us travel up there, but it's…it's the north and its growth that really gets me. What's going on up there is sort of a 1950 version of the same kind of pioneering job that built our west.

LUCAS: Yes, the last and biggest of the pioneer jobs in North America.

STEWART: Mm…hum, and from what I've heard and seen of Canadians, Rupert, I'd say it was in pretty good hands. A mighty comfortable thing for us to know considering the stake we have in it.

LUCAS: It is, Jimmy. It is that. And many thanks for visiting us.

Gisele sings one final song to end the show — "Lili Marlene."

The Glenn Miller Era

This documentary, a Special Tribute to Glenn Miller, was broadcast over NBC.

Sunday, October 17, 1954 (6:30-8 p.m.)

Stewart, whose film *The Glenn Miller Story* had opened about 10 months earlier, was interviewed for the show. According to various newspaper articles of the day, the guests included Jimmy Stewart, Ray Anthony, Louis Armstrong, Doris Day, Dave Garroway (the show's host), Marion Hutton, Billy May, Frank Sinatra and Jack Webb.

The Glenn Miller Story *Premiere*

Thursday, December 10, 1953 (11:30 p.m.–midnight)
NETWORK: NBC
HOSTS: Eddie King, Shirley Towers
DIRECTOR: Art Jacobson
SUPERVISOR: Harry Bubeck

NBC marks the premiere of Stewart's new film with a live broadcast from the lobby of the Pantages Theater in Hollywood. Eddy King and Shirley Towers (NBC's Hollywood correspondent) take turns talking to various stars as they enter the theater. Stars included in the program are (the name in parentheses is the interviewer):

Valentine Davies — writer of *The Glenn Miller Story* (Towers)
The Modernaires' Paula Kelly (King)
Rock Hudson (Towers)
Julia Adams (King)
Jeffrey Hunter (Towers)
Barbara Rush (King)
Lori Nelson (described as having just been voted most popular new star) (Towers)
Spike Jones (King)
Debbie Reynolds and her escort Dick Anderson (Towers)
Marilyn Maxwell and Jeff Chandler (King)
Jimmy Durante (Towers)
Jane Powell (Towers)
Ben Pollack (drummer for the Miller band who plays himself in the film) and Doris Robbins, his wife (King)
Ronald Reagan and Nancy Davis (Towers)
Hugh O'Brian and Nina "Honeybear" Warren (King)

At this point, Jimmy Stewart enters the lobby and Towers began to interview him.

TOWERS: ...this is quite a big occasion, isn't it?

STEWART: It certainly is...it certainly is.

TOWERS: What was your first reaction when you learned you'd been cast in the role of Glenn Miller?

STEWART: Well, it was just sort of a...sort of a challenge, I suppose. I just hope we've...we've approached making a picture worthy of Glenn Miller...that's all I hope.

TOWERS: Did you ever know him personally, Jimmy?

STEWART: No, never...never...loved his music.

TOWERS: When you're doing a biographical character, and if I remember you've done a couple of them, haven't you?

STEWART: Um-hum, yeah I did...

TOWERS: How closely do you try to stay to the actual true life story of the people in your impersonation of them?

STEWART: I...I...I...you try to...ah...try to stay to the facts pretty much, I think...let's get the facts, kid. No, you really do. You try to stay to the facts. As far as actually...actually getting every movement and everything, I don't think you do that.

TOWERS: And in your character Monty Stratton in *The Stratton Story*, did you do a great deal of research on that, too, Jimmy?

STEWART: Well, I wouldn't call it research...I'd just say practice. I tried to get a little the way Monty moved just like I did...ah...I tried to get a little the way Glenn handled a trombone and...

TOWERS: Did you play the trombone yourself on the screen?

STEWART: Well, I didn't play it, but I...I sort of handled the trombone.

TOWERS: Well, you go through all the motions. Believe me, no one would even possibly detect you're not playing. Jimmy Stewart, congratulations on this very wonderful evening.

STEWART: Thank you very much.

King says that the film is about to begin and Towers goes into the theater. She describes the scene there, says hello to Jimmy and Gloria as they enter and signs off as the film begins.

Shirley Thomas also had her own show and Stewart appeared on it several time. See the *Shirley Thomas Show* for more information.

This program is not in general circulation, but is part of the NBC Collection in the Library of Congress.

About a month after this program aired, Stewart and his wife embarked on a nation-wide tour to promote the film, with a "heavy schedule" of radio interviews at each stop. Few of these have been documented.

The Golden Days of Radio
   NETWORK: Syndicated
   HOST: Frank Bresse

Occasionally, this program had a "blooper" segment, featuring some of radio's top stars, including William Conrad, Al Jolson, Jimmy Stewart and Orson Welles. At least two of *The Golden Days of Radio* shows featured Jimmy Stewart. One was broadcast Sunday, December 24, 1967, and the broadcast date of the second is not known. Although copies of both shows appear to be in existence, listening copies have not been located. It is quite possible that what was played was either the complete or a part of the *Presenting James Stewart & Jane Wyman in "Blow-Ups" from Magic Town* disc (See entry for this disc in Chapter 3).

Good News
   NETWORK: NBC
   SPONSOR: Maxwell House Coffee
   ANNOUNCER: Ted Pearson/Warren Hull
   MUSIC: Meredith Willson & Orchestra
   THEME MUSIC: *Always and Always* (Edward Ward/Robert Wright/Chet Forrest) and *Good News* (Ray Henderson/Buddy DeSylva/Lew Brown)

The show was also known as *Good News of 1938*, *Good News of 1939*, *The Maxwell House M-G-M Hour*, *Film Stars on Parade* and *Maxwell House Coffee Hour*. It was broadcast from Studio 30 at M-G-M. Some shows even went into other studios on the lot. The listeners were treated to an inside look at the glitz and glamour of Hollywood. M-G-M produced the show itself and very often used it as a vehicle to launch new films. Maxwell House plunked down $25,000 per weekly one-hour show, the largest amount paid by a sponsor at that time. Each week the listeners were told, "Your ticket of admission is just your loyalty to Maxwell House Coffee."

   SHOWS FEATURING JIMMY STEWART:

(1) Thursday, November 18, 1937 (9-10 p.m.)
Allan Jones was the show's M.C. Bill Bacher produced. Featured were Jimmy Stewart, Robert Young, Tom Brown, and Florence Rice in excerpts from the film *Navy Blue and Gold*. Others listed as guests were: opera singer Igor Gorin, Betty Jaynes, Judy Garland, Luise Rainer, and Ted Healy. This show is not available for listening.

(2) Thursday, November 25, 1937 (9-10 p.m.)

Allan Jones was the master of ceremonies for this show. The guests included Stewart, Rosalind Russell, Betty Jayne, Doug McPhail, Helen Troy, Mickey Rooney, Judy Garland, Sigmund Romberg, C. Aubrey Smith, Ronald Sinclair, and Max Terr's chorus. According to an article in the December 1, 1937, edition of *Variety*, Russell and Stewart perform a skit "wherein an actress rewrites an author's script from the viewpoint of a spotlight hugger."

This show is not available for listening.

(3) Thursday, December 16, 1937 (9-10 p.m.)

This program is not in general circulation, but is available as part of the NBC Collection at the Library of Congress. The first few minutes of the show are missing due to a break in the transcription disc. Possibly in this missing section is a skit featuring Baby Snooks, since at the end of the program it is announced that Hanley Stafford appeared as Baby Snooks' father, but no such skit appears in the recording. The available program begins near the end of a sketch starring Frank Morgan as Paul Revere.

At the conclusion of the sketch, Jimmy Stewart, the host for the evening, thanks Morgan and says that he will be back later in the program. He then introduces Douglas McPhail and Betty Jaynes. After a short conversation with them, they perform one song.

"Indian Love Call"

Next up is a Fanny Brice sketch which also features Jimmy Stewart. They talk a little bit about Jimmy's film, *Navy Blue and Gold*, and how much she liked it. Possibly because he starred in this film with Florence Rice, Jimmy calls Miss Brice, Rice. She quickly corrects him. Fanny asks Jimmy to do a scene from her new show with her. It's a love scene and requires Jimmy to kiss her. He excuses himself and says he must leave to do a love scene with Greta Garbo. The skit was written especially for Brice by Harry Ruby and Bert Kalmar.

Stewart next does a commercial for Maxwell House Coffee and breaks for a station I.D.

When the show returns, Stewart introduces a sketch, "Small Town Christmas Carol," featuring Spencer Tracy and Freddie Bartholomew. Tracy sees Bartholomew looking into a store window and asks him if he's hoping for one of the toys for Christmas. Bartholomew tells him that his parents are dead and he won't be getting anything, so he's just pretending he had a toy. Tracy suggests that he's going to pretend he's rich and asks the boy what he'd like in the window. He wants the hobby horse. Inside the store, he tells the boy to look around for anything else he'd like. While the boy is away, Tracy tells the sales lady that he's not pretending. He's really going to buy the hobby horse and up to $100 worth of anything else that he wants. He tells her to have them delivered to the boy the following morning. It turns out that Tracy is a gangster and two men are looking to kill him. He sees them pull their car up to the front of the store. He pays the lady and leaves the store where he's picked up by the men.

Stewart next introduces a song by Meredith Willson.

After the song, Jimmy introduces a sketch about feminine psychology. It's titled "If Men Played Cards the Way Women Do" and was written by George S. Kaufman. Starring as the card players are Frank Morgan, Meredith Willson, Spencer Tracy and Jimmy Stewart. Tracy is the first to arrive at the Morgan home and they gossip about Jimmy Stewart — he looks older, how he and his wife are getting along, Jimmy's wife. Then Jimmy enters and Tracy tells him that he's never seen him looking so young. Jimmy adds more gossip and tells Morgan that the room is adorable. Willson is the last to enter and Stewart tells him that he likes his vest. When Morgan leaves the room, they all gossip about him and his house. The four men have an argument about what to play for — 1/40 of a cent or 1/80 of a cent. When Jack Benny calls and tells them that he's going to be a father, they plan to go over to his house and throw him a shower.

Following the sketch, Stewart and Ted Pearson do another commercial for Maxwell House Coffee.

Next, Jimmy says that it's time for the M-G-M Concert Hall. Meredith Willson presents the #8 song on the list of the public's 10 favorite melodies — Franz Shubert's "Unfinished Symphony" (in abbreviated form). Joining him in the performance are Douglas McPhail, Betty Jaynes and Gilbert Russell.

Stewart reminds everyone to listen again next week for the party to celebrate the completion of the film *Rosalie* and special guest Louis B. Mayer.

(4) Thursday, December 23, 1937

On this week's show, the listeners are the guests at a party for the completion of the motion picture *Rosalie*. The guests on the show are the stars of the film, including Nelson Eddy, Eleanor Powell, Frank Morgan, Ray Bolger and Ilona Massey. The regulars included Fanny Brice as Baby Snooks, Hanley Stafford as her father and Meredith Willson and his Orchestra. The host for the show was Jimmy Stewart. The show begins with a dialog between Stewart and Willson.

This show is available from Radio Spirits as a Cassette (2218). It was released in 1998.

It is also on the mp3 only set, *Jimmy Stewart the Ultimate Radio Collection Vol. 3* (Master Classics Records, 2011).

STEWART: Hello, everybody. Ah…well, can I…Hello, Meredith.
WILLSON: Hello, Jimmy.
STEWART: Well, Ah…what have you got to start us off with tonight?
WILLSON: Well, Jimmy, tonight we have an arrangement of *Who*. It's a sort of a concert swing arrangement and…
STEWART: Great…that's great…that's perfect.
WILLSON: Yeah.
STEWART: Yeah. Now, listen, I've got a great idea to make this first number really stand out, Meredith. Now it'll give you a chance to do something distinctive, you know?
WILLSON: Well, we've been doing our best, Jimmy, but what's on your mind?
STEWART: Well, now, ah…how about making this first number a concerto?
WILLSON: A concerto?
STEWART: Yeah, yeah, concerto. You know, it's where one instrument plays the solo through the whole number, you know, and the orchestra's sort of an accompaniment.
WILLSON: Oh…oh, you mean you want me to play the number as a piano concerto.
STEWART: No, no, I…ah…the idea I had was more along the line of a…ah…the…well, Meredith, you know I play the accordion and I…ah…
WILLSON: Oh, well, I don't think it'll work with this number, Jimmy.
STEWART: No? Sure it'll work now…you…I've got a great accordion arrangement to "Who" and it'll make the band sound good, you know.
WILLSON: Well, the arrangement we've got won't fit an accordion solo, Jimmy.
STEWART: Why not?
WILLSON: Well…ah…the accordion's in B-flat and the arrangement's in E-flat.
STEWART: E-flat? Well, how many men do you have here tonight?
WILLSON: Forty.
STEWART: Well, 40, well, with all those musicians, you can fake it.
WILLSON: Fake it?
STEWART: Well, yes, what's a little transposition?

WILLSON: No, Jimmy, no, we can't do it.
STEWART: Now, listen, my accordion's right outside in the car and I can get it in just a few minutes.
WILLSON: Oh…oh you can, eh?
STEWART: Yeah, yeah, I'll be right back.
WILLSON: Take your time, Jimmy.
STEWART: No, I'll hurry right back.
WILLSON: Come on, boys, let's get the number over quick before he gets back.

"Who"
After the number, their conversation continues.

STEWART: Well, it sounded pretty good without me.
WILLSON: Well, thanks, Jimmy. Where's your accordion?
STEWART: Well, the doorman wouldn't let me bring it in.
WILLSON: Oh, a music critic.
STEWART: Yeah…yeah, a music critic. Well…ah…ladies and gentlemen…ah…I wanna present that implausible little girl we're all so crazy about on our Maxwell House show. I mean Fanny Brice's nightmare creation, Baby Snooks.

Baby Snooks skit — Baby Snooks shops for a new hat (with Hanley Stafford as Lancelot "Daddy" Higgins)
After their skit, Jimmy continues:

STEWART: Well, here's Ted Pearson with a word to the wise about good coffee.

Ted Pearson then does a commercial for Maxwell House Coffee with a little help from Jimmy Stewart. Actually, Jimmy has just one line. After Pearson mentions the term "roaster fresh," Jimmy says, "Roaster fresh, roaster fresh, what is that? Explain that, Ted."
When the commercial is completed, Jimmy continues.

STEWART: And now…now we're gonna move over to Stage 28, right across the way, next door to the replica of old Maxwell House we build right here on the lot, where the *Rosalie* party's going full blast. (There is a short interlude here while the scene changes) Hello, everybody. How are you? All right, now, everybody listen. Now I want to introduce the host of our party. The Vice President in charge of Metro-Goldwyn-Mayer Productions; a leader to whom the motion picture industry turns in times of stress. But to us at the studio, he's…well, he's more than that. Busy as he is, he's always ready to listen to our trials and tribulations, give us his kindly, sympathetic advice and guide us over rocky paths. And, in keeping with the spirit of the season, we've asked him to attend our little party tonight. And it's just like him to lay aside all business so that he'd be able to grant our wish. So, I'm happy to introduce not Mr. Louie B. Mayer, famous motion picture executive, but Louie Mayer, our daddy over at M-G-M.

Mayer then introduces a song by Nelson Eddy.

"The Caissons Go Rolling Along" (Anchors Aweigh) — Nelson Eddy

Next, Mayer tells Baby Snooks the story of *Rosalie* and introduces another musical number.

"In The Still Of The Night" — Ilona Massey

Next comes a comedy routine featuring Ray Bolger, Frank Morgan and Jimmy Stewart. The three quickly confuse the audience and maybe even themselves.

BOLGER: Say, Frank, by the way, are you any relation to the Pete Morgans in Pittsburgh?

MORGAN: Ah…no, Ray, I don't know them. But I know some Donnellys in Pittsburgh. They're awfully nice people.

BOLGER: Mmm…That so…well, I don't know any other people in Pittsburgh, except the Morgans. Funny you don't know them.

STEWART: Say, I know some Donnellys.

MORGAN: Oh, you do, Jimmy? Are they from Pittsburgh?

STEWART: No, he's from Atlanta.

MORGAN: Oh.

STEWART: Great place, Atlanta.

BOLGER: Oh yes…yes, a great place. I had an aunt who was born there.

MORGAN: Oh well.

STEWART: Really? She still live there?

BOLGER: No, she's dead, poor soul; died of a heart attack.

MORGAN: Well, you know, that's very odd. I had an aunt who died of a heart attack, too. How old was your aunt?

BOLGER: Ah…53.

STEWART: Funny, I had an uncle who was 53, the same as your aunt.

BOLGER: Not dead, eh?

STEWART: No, no, he's alive.

MORGAN: 53, that's a funny age, isn't it?

BOLGER: Yes, it's very funny.

STEWART: Sort of in between 52 and 54.

MORGAN: That's just what I was getting to.

BOLGER: Talking about 54 reminds me I have the most peculiar telephone number — 54…54, get it.

STEWART: Strange about telephone numbers, isn't it? Some of them are easy to remember and then some of them aren't easy at all.

MORGAN: You know, I have a cousin who works for the telephone company. She says they are very nice to her.

STEWART: You know, I'll bet it's a quarter till the hour or a quarter after, you know.

BOLGER: Why?

STEWART: There's always a lull at a quarter to or a quarter after.

BOLGER: Well, it's just 27 after.

STEWART: Well, you see…see, it was pretty close, 12 minutes away.

BOLGER: Where do you live, Frank?

MORGAN: Oh, me…ah…I live over near the Terrace Garden. You know where that is?

BOLGER: Let me see now…ah…is that the big white building past Sunset in the direction of Santa Monica from Hollywood?

MORGAN: No…no…no…no…no…I know what you're thinking. That's the Chinese Villa.

BOLGER: Oh, isn't that a beautiful building? I pass it every day and I never get tired of it.

MORGAN: Well, I really don't know it very well. I've just seen it a few times.

STEWART: Say, did you ever notice that building up on 5th and Mulberry? You know, the one with the…the red one with the shiny roof on it.

BOLGER: Sure, I've seen that. Frank, weren't you with me one day when I pointed out that building?

MORGAN: Well, yes come to think of it, I think I was.

(All three begin to talk at one time)

BOLGER: What were you going to say, Frank?

MORGAN: Oh no, you go right ahead, Ray. I was…it wasn't very important.

BOLGER: Jimmy?

STEWART: No, mine can wait. You go ahead.

BOLGER: Well, I was going to say…you remember the day the banks were closed?

MORGAN: Do I remember?

BOLGER: Well, the day before that, I was walking along Wilshire, right in front of my bank, when I tripped and fell. Isn't that odd? The very next day all the banks were closed.

STEWART: Must have been a warning of some kind.

BOLGER: That's what I mean.

MORGAN: Yes…do you believe in telepathy?

BOLGER: In a way, yes.

MORGAN: Well, I do. Last winter I was down south and my wife was living in the house up north. One day I remembered we forgot to lay in a supply of coal. So, I wrote a letter and told her to buy the coal. And, you know, when I came home, she said she was thinking of it even before I wrote. Now you know that just can't be accidental.

STEWART: No, no, there's something to it. I don't think it's developed yet, but…

BOLGER: You know, speaking of people, the trouble with some people is that…well, they're narrow minded.

MORGAN: Oh, I…I…you talking about me?

BOLGER: Well, if the shoe fits, wear it.

MORGAN: I'm narrow minded, huh? You know what you are, you…

STEWART: Now, wait. This has been a very interesting conversation, so don't spoil it with an argument.

MORGAN: Well, I know, but he says I'm narrow minded and I can't let him get away with that.

STEWART: I know, but everybody's entitled to their own opinion, Frank.

MORGAN: Yeah, but not about me they're not. Go away…I'm nobody's fool.

STEWART: All right, now why don't you two fellas make up? It's silly to argue. No, come on, Frank,…Frank…come on.

MORGAN: Well, all right. I'm sorry, Ray.

BOLGER: Me, too, Frank. You know sometimes these discussions get pretty heated, I guess.

STEWART: Say…ah…why don't we…why don't we all have lunch at my place tomorrow and continue this conversation.

MORGAN: Well, that's all right with me.

BOLGER: I'd love to come, Jimmy, but I've got to entertain some relatives from out of town; the Browns from Altoona. Terrible bores, babble on for hours about nothing.

STEWART: Yeah, well, you've got to expect that sort of thing from some people, I guess.

MORGAN: Oh yes, sure, you can't…

STEWART: Well, if we can't get together tomorrow, we'll make it sometime real soon, you know. So long fellas, this has been real interesting.

BOLGER: Well, so long, Jimmy.

STEWART: Goodbye.

MORGAN: Well, goodbye, Ray…

This is followed by another musical number introduced by Mayer.
"I've a Strange New Rhythm in My Heart" — Eleanor Powell
After the number, Jimmy continues.

STEWART: After tomorrow, they'll be just exactly no more shopping days till Christmas. So, I'd like to take just a second to extend the Season's Greetings to everyone listening in. And, I suggest that, as a part of the celebration, a steaming, fragrant cup of Maxwell House Coffee…and I hope it'll make your Christmas Merrier. And, while we're enjoying our coffee, Meredith…ah…I'll bring you a cup of coffee if you'll give us a tune.

At this point, there's a station break and a short bit with Mayer and Baby Snooks, then there's another song.
"Who Knows?" — Nelson Eddy
After the song, Jimmy introduces another sketch.

STEWART: Say, Frank…Frank.

MORGAN: Yes, Jimmy.

STEWART: Ray Bolger said he couldn't tell jokes because you were the wonderful joke man. How about giving us a little joke, huh?

MORGAN: Oh no, I don't want to do anything, Jimmy. I've been having such a good time here at the party, why should I work?

STEWART: Well, I think you oughta do something, Frank. If you wanna sing, I'd be glad to play the accordion for you.

MORGAN: The accordion…oh no…no…no.

STEWART: I could play for a little dance. Do you wanna do that?

MORGAN: No, no, no, I'd rather…

STEWART: You can't let your public down, you know.

MORGAN: No, well, that's right, I can't. I can tell you what happened at my broker's office the other day.

STEWART: Oh, you've been dabbling in the market again.

MORGAN: Well, I'd say it was me that was dabbled. You see, it was this way. I was working in a picture at the time…

(Goes into a skit with Hanley Stafford as his stockbroker.)

After the sketch, Mayer talks to Nelson Eddy and introduce his final song.

"Rosalie" — Nelson Eddy (after beginning the song, Eddy is joined by Eleanor Powell, who tap dances while he sings.)

As the song is completed, Jimmy talks to Eleanor Powell.

STEWART: Eleanor, Eleanor, come here. Eleanor, come here, come here now, don't go away.
POWELL: All right, Jimmy, what is it?
STEWART: Well…ah…Eleanor, gee, you look pretty tonight.
POWELL: Well, thanks, Jimmy.
STEWART: Ah…Eleanor, you've played and danced a lot in movies, musical comedies and nightclubs…
POWELL: Yes, that's right, Jimmy. I started my career in a nightclub. That was my first engagement. You see, Gus Edwards saw me dancing an acrobatic dance on the beach at Atlantic City. He gave me a job in the Ritz Grill. I was 13 years old.
STEWART: Acrobatic dancing…but I thought tap dancing…
POWELL: Oh no, I didn't tap dance in those days. But they told me I'd have to learn if I wanted to work in New York.
STEWART: Oh, so you learned so well you became the world's greatest woman tap dancer, huh. Well, I can imagine you played just about everything, but Eleanor have you ever played in a commercial?
POWELL: Have I ever played in what?
STEWART: A commercial.
POWELL: Oh no, Jimmy, I haven't. Is it fun? I'd like to try.
STEWART: All right…ah…Ted…Ted Pearson. I…I've fixed it for you. This is…Eleanor, this is Ted Pearson.
POWELL: How do you do?
PEARSON: Hello, Eleanor.
STEWART: This is your leading man.
POWELL: Well, thank you, Jimmy.
PEARSON: Grand…*(Pearson and Powell do a commercial for Maxwell House Coffee.)*

Jimmy is back again after the spot.

STEWART: And as a fitting conclusion to our *Rosalie* party, Meredith Willson is gonna play a composition that was not in *Rosalie*, but is most suitable to the Christmas spirit and to the M-G-M concert hall. Meredith, tell us about it.

WILLSON: Yeah, Jimmy, it's #7 in our series of the world's 10 favorite melodies — Handel's immortal "Hallelujah Chorus" from *The Messiah*.

"Hallelujah Chorus" — Meredith Willson Orchestra and Chorus
After the song, Mayer wishes everyone a Happy Christmas and New Year and then Jimmy closes the show.

STEWART: Well, we hope you'll all be with us again next Thursday because…oh…because listen who's gonna be here, fellas, Myrna Loy, newly crowned "Queen of the Movies," Fanny Brice will be here again, Wally Beery, Frank Morgan and a host of others; and, of course, Meredith Willson and his Orchestra. And, remember, your ticket of admission is just your loyalty to Maxwell House Coffee. That's the coffee that's good to the last drop. So we'll see you next week and, in the meantime, go to the movies and enjoy yourself. Good night, everybody. Merry Christmas.

(5) Thursday, December 30, 1937 (9-10 p.m.)
Jimmy Stewart hosts the show from M-G-M Studio 30, where scenes from the new film *Test Pilot*, starring Myrna Loy, had been shot that day. First up is a Frank Morgan-Jimmy Stewart skit about their plans for New Year's Eve.

STEWART: Hello, everybody. Well, I guess you got it from Ted Pearson's opening remarks that tonight's program is…ah…really something. And, ah, right now I wanna present the first…

MORGAN: Ah…excuse me, James.

STEWART: Frank Morgan, hey…

MORGAN: Eh, you said Frank…

STEWART: Yeah, Frank, yes.

MORGAN: That's me, isn't it. Well, Jimmy, I just wanted to wish you a Merry Christmas.

STEWART: Oh, thanks, Frank. That's…Christmas was last week, but…

MORGAN: Eh, oh, was it? Well, that's funny and here it is again. Well, my, time certainly does fly, doesn't it?

STEWART: Well, Frank, I think you're just a little bit confused. New Year's Day is the next big holiday on the schedule, you see, that's the day after tomorrow.

MORGAN: Oh, oh, of course, certainly, that's, well, that's what I wanted to do, wish you a Happy New Year.

STEWART: Oh well, thank you. Frank, I'd like to wish you the same.

MORGAN: Well, thank you and, by the way, where are you going to spend New Year's Eve?

STEWART: Oh, I just…little party at home. I'm having in some friends.

MORGAN: Yeah, well, I guess I'll go over to Meredith Willson's house. He usually has a little gathering on New Year's Eve and I…I…

STEWART: Oh, he does, does he? Did…ah…Meredith invite you?

MORGAN: Eh, did he invite…well, no, not exactly. But…eh…well, we've been friends for a long time and if he's having a party, I know I'll be more than welcome.

STEWART: Hmmm…well, I don't know, Frank, I've always been a little leery of breaking in on a party uninvited, you know.

MORGAN: Oh, I can see how you feel…

STEWART: Oh, I see.

MORGAN: …but with Meredith and me, it's different. I…we…why he'd probably feel hurt if I didn't show up at his party. I've always been there. He'll no doubt ask me before the program's over tonight. Of course, he'll invite me. It's…it's…it's…it's…my wife and his wife are the best of friends, too. Eh, I…well…I wonder why he hasn't ask me already?

STEWART: I don't know.

MORGAN: I've…ah…well, he'll invite me. It's absurd to think of it as being any other way, certainly, but…ah…say…I…I…supposing he doesn't invite me. Oh, but he will, of course. I…I remember the time I loaned him $200 to get him out of…well, there's no reason why he shouldn't invite me. Oh, sure he will. I don't…ah…say, come to think of it, he'd have a lot of nerve not to invite me. Who does he think he is anyway after all I've done for him? Having a party and not inviting his old pal Morgan. He can't do that to me.

WILLSON: Oh hello, Frank.

MORGAN: Well, now just get this, Mr. Willson. I wouldn't come to your party if you were going to play run sheep run and post office. You…you've got a lot…friends, you are, you're a fine…

WILLSON: Hey, what's he talking about, Jimmy?

STEWART: Well, I…I…ah…this story's funny. I think he just talked himself in and out of your New Year's Eve party.

WILLSON: My party? Why just this afternoon he invited me to spend New Year's Eve at his house.

STEWART: Oh, at his house, huh? Well, I don't know what all of this is about. Meredith, sing something, will ya? Sing...
WILLSON: Me, sing something?
STEWART: Yeah, sing or play something. Morgan's got me all mixed up here. Play...

After a Meredith Willson song, Jimmy introduces a Fanny Brice/Baby Snooks skit — "Daniel in the Lion's Den," with Hanley Stafford as Lancelot "Daddy" Higgins.

STEWART: Boy, you really did that up in ribbons, Meredith.
WILLSON: Well, thanks a whole lot, Jimmy.
STEWART: And, now, here's that little girl you're all waiting to hear. That amazing, alarming, maddening creation of Fanny Brice, Baby Snooks.

Next, Jimmy talks to 13-year-old singing sensation Freda Starr from Brooklyn, NY.

STEWART: And now I want you to hear a success story. The story of a little girl who was discovered in the east by an M-G-M talent scout and is now in Hollywood. Hey...ah...Freda, Freda Starr, come on...come on up here. Hey...stand up on here. Boy, you're little, aren't ya? Now, Freda, we'd like to know a little something about you. Now...ah...where'd you come from?
STARR: I come from Brooklyn.
STEWART: Oh, I see. And how old are you, Freda?
STARR: Thirteen.
STEWART: Thirteen. How'd you happen to take up singing?
STARR: The teacher at school heard me singing in the hall one day.
STEWART: Uh-huh.
STARR: And she said I ought to study voice and so I did.
STEWART: Oh, you did, huh? Well, tell me, Freda, how did the M-G-M talent scout happen to discover you?
STARR: On account of Brooklyn, I guess.
STEWART: Ah...how on account of Brooklyn?
STARR: I sang at the school in Brooklyn and somebody was in the audience that had a friend, and the friend had a cousin that knew Mr. Altman.
STEWART: Oh...Mr. Altman, that...ah...M-G-M talent scout, huh?
STARR: Yes, sir.
STEWART: And that's what brought you here, huh?

STARR: Mm...hum, that's right.
STEWART: Well, ladies and gentlemen, Freda Starr will sing...

Next up is the night's special guest, Myrna Loy.

STEWART: A few weeks ago, one of our guests on the Maxwell House program was the most gracious and charming lady, who has been crowned queen of the screen. We're very happy to have her with us again tonight... Miss Myrna Loy.
LOY: Thank you, Jimmy.
STEWART: Now, Miss Loy's going to play a part of Nancy Turner in a sketch called *Sweet Mystery*, written for her by George Oppenheimer.
LOY: Yes, and Jimmy Stewart plays the part of Alan Turner, Nancy's husband.
STEWART: Oh, yeah...Miss Loy, I just wanna take a little time here before we start this sketch to tell you that you've always been my dream girl, Miss Loy. I just wanted to tell you.
LOY: Thank you, Jimmy.
STEWART: Well, I just wanted to get that in here. Well, anyway, the scene is Nancy's house and we look in on a wedding ceremony.

Nancy and Alan are being married after knowing each other only two weeks. As they are driving and talking after the ceremony, they find that they may not be as compatible as they thought. After the sketch, Jimmy makes a short comment.

STEWART: Thank you, thank you, Myrna Loy. And now, Ted Pearson.

Ted and Frances Edwards, head of the commissary at M-G-M, talk about the number of cups of Maxwell House Coffee served there each day. After the commercial, Jimmy comes back once again.

STEWART: Meredith Willson continues our *Good News of 1938* with one of the best tunes from the Jeanette McDonald-Allan Jones musical, *The Firefly*...it's "Donkey Serenade."

"Donkey Serenade" — Meredith Willson & Orchestra
Next, Jimmy introduces Wallace Beery and they talk about Beery's new film, *The Bad Man of Brimstone*.

STEWART: Thank you, Meredith. You know, there are lots of stars here on Stage 30 tonight, but there's one star who was here before any of them. He's made a picture with all of them, I guess, and there's not one single one of them who hasn't learned something from him. Tomorrow his latest picture, *The Bad Man of Brimstone*, will open in your favorite theater, and he's here tonight to tell us a little about it — Wally Beery.

BEERY: Thank you, thank you, Jimmy. Thank you, Jimmy.

STEWART: Say, they tell me *Brimstone* turned out great, Wally. What kind of a part do you play in it?

BEERY: Well, let me see. I guess I play one of those tough guys.

STEWART: Yeah, well, how tough are you?

BEERY: Well, I was tough enough to shoot myself in the leg. Ah, they call me "Trigger Bill." That's when the picture starts, but along comes a young fellow named Jeff Burton that's going to clean me up and who do you think he turns out to be?

STEWART: Who?

BEERY: Well, my own son.

STEWART: Oh, I see.

BEERY: So, I can't be tough with him. Can't shoot my own kid, even though he's aiming to ruin me and my gang.

STEWART: Well, that's quite a situation.

BEERY: Yeah, that's a great spot. The boy doesn't know I'm his pa, so he beats me up and I can't do anything about it. The worst part of it is that I've gotten on the side of law and order just to help him. Well, I finally become a sort of a mayor and in one of the big scenes of the picture, where he's trying to arrest a crooked sheriff, "Blackjack" McCreedy. Both of them, my kid Jeff and "Blackjack" are standing in front of a bar about to pull their guns on each other, so here we go...

(A scene from the film is played.)

STEWART: That was mighty fine, partner.

BEERY: Well, thanks, tenderfoot. How long would you say it took that scene to play?

STEWART: Well, about three minutes, I guess.

BEERY: Well, you know, Jimmy, it's not right. Nobody's ever seen those people who work behind the scenes. Nobody ever hears about them, but without them, no picture could be made.

STEWART: Yeah, that's true, but I guess there's not much you can do about it.

BEERY: Yes, there is. We can at least give the public a chance to meet 'em.

STEWART: Yeah, well, I think that's a swell idea, Wally.

At this point Beery introduces the art director at M-G-M, Cedric Gibbons. They talk about the set designs for the film.

Ted and Jimmy do a short commercial.

STEWART: Ted Pearson, there's that good old smell of coffee again; must be coming from that old Maxwell House right across the street.

PEARSON: Um-hum. Sure is appetizing, isn't it, Jimmy? Let's invite the folks in, shall we, to have a steaming cup of Maxwell House Coffee.

STEWART: That's a swell idea, Ted. Yeah, let's…let's all go over and enjoy again our favorite custom, a cheery, friendly cup of Maxwell House Coffee. And while we're at it, this…this is a good chance to say Happy New Year to everybody. May the year 1938 bring you health and happiness and prosperity and…Meredith, while we're in for a cup of Maxwell House, how about a tune?

While Willson and his orchestra play, there is a break for station identification, then Jimmy comes back.

STEWART: This is Jimmy Stewart again and we're continuing our *Good News of 1938* with Wally Beery, Myrna Loy, Frank Morgan and, right now, you're gonna hear from Fanny Brice. Imagine a small apartment in New York City. At home, Mr. and Mrs. Sam Garfinkel and…ah…they're worried about money.

The Brice skit is titled "The Sweepstakes Ticket."

Next, Jimmy introduces Eadie Adams [not the later Broadway actress/singer, Edie Adams]. She sings her way through a medley of songs with "moon" in the lyrics. Jimmy talks his way through the same medley.

STEWART: Well, Eadie Adams, what's on your mind?

ADAMS: Listen, Jimmy, look up yonder. Way up in the sky before I start to ponder for a little thing for me.

STEWART: Okay, Eadie, now I'm looking up in the sky, but I don't see anything up there.

ADAMS: What's the matter, are you blind? Come on skipper; tell me what you see up there beside the big dipper. Hurry, tell me what you see.

STEWART: Well, really, Eadie, I don't see anything up there in the sky, except maybe the moon.

ADAMS: Well, of course, that's what I'm talking about.

(song)

STEWART: Now, listen, Eadie, you should know the moon's really not to blame. It's all your fault and you forgot to play the wishing game.

ADAMS: What wishing game?

STEWART: Well, Eadie, it's the new moon up there and you can make a wish to anybody, anywhere.

ADAMS: Well, Jimmy, just for fun, I'm going to try that wishing scheme.

STEWART: Oh, you are, huh?

ADAMS: Here I go.

(song)

STEWART: Thank you, Eadie…I…you know…have you ever been in New York City on a kind of…ah…well, you know…one of those nights you don't know exactly what to do to have a little fun. And you finally… you finally dropped into a ticket broker's office to find out what good shows there are in town. Well, if you have, you'll appreciate this George S. Kaufman-Mark Conley skit we're gonna present now, with Frank Morgan as the customer and Hanley Stafford as the broker. Now the scene is a ticket…ah…agency and it's on Broadway opposite the Lowes State Theater and the ticket broker is behind his desk and his telephone has just started to ring.

After the skit, Jimmy introduces Ted Pearson by saying, "And here's some more good news about coffee." Pearson does a spot for Maxwell House.

When the commercial is over, the show resumes with:

STEWART: And now we come to the M-G-M Concert Hall. An institution which is becoming one of the most outstanding features in our Good News program, thanks to Meredith Willson's presentation of his list of the world's ten favorite melodies.

WILLSON: Excuse me, Jimmy, but it's not my list. These 10 compositions were chosen by music critics, composers, editors, teachers of music, and the public. In the opinion of this representative group, these 10 melodies are the most popular in the whole field of fine music. Tonight is #6, the famous "Londonderry Aire."

"Londonderry Aire" (a.k.a. Danny Boy)

Next, Ted announces a Maxwell House Coffee contest to name a new M-G-M film starring Walter Huston, Beulah Bondi, and Jimmy Stewart and directed by Clarence Brown. The winner of the contest will win $5000 and a trip to Hollywood. Lionel Barrymore is there to tell the audience a little about the film. He says that the original title of the story was *Benefits for God* and it's about a man named Ethan Wilkins. To enter the contest, you must not only give the film a title, but must also give a reason, in 50 words or less, why your title is best. (The film in question would be released with the title *Of Human Hearts*.) This segment, and the show, closes with Stewart saying:

STEWART: ...and you'll hear the rest of the details tomorrow. Next week, you'll hear Fanny Brice, Frank Morgan, Lionel Barrymore and Robert Taylor. Sounds like a great show. And remember, your ticket of admission is just your loyalty to Maxwell House Coffee. So, tune in next Thursday and enjoy *Good News of 1938*. And, in the meantime, go to the movies and enjoy yourself. Good night everybody; Happy New Year.

An eight and a half minute segment of this show featuring the Myrna Loy and Jimmy Stewart sketch, has been issued on the mp3 only set, *Myrna Loy The Ultimate Radio Collection* (Master Classics Records, 2011).

Very early in 1938, Ed Gardner was brought in to replace Bill Bacher as the producer of *Good News*. According to an article in the January 18, 1938 edition of the Ironwood Daily Globe, Ironwood, MI, Gardner wanted to establish one person as the regular master-of-ceremonies and Jimmy Stewart was in the lead for that position.

(6) Thursday, February 10, 1938 (9-10 p.m.)

The format of this show is the same as previous shows — musical numbers, comedy sketches, etc. However, Robert Taylor is the host and Jimmy Stewart is a guest. Stewart appears in only one segment of the show. The segment is spotlighting the new M-G-M film, which listeners to this show had named, *Of Human Hearts*. It's also in honor of Abraham Lincoln's birthday in two days. Jimmy Stewart plays Jason, a medical officer in the Union Army who has been summoned to the Capitol by Lincoln, played here, as in the film, by John Carradine. The scene involves Lincoln having Jason sent to his office. While there, he tells him that his mother believes that he is dead because he hasn't written to her in two years. Lincoln makes him sit at his desk and write to her. He also has him promise to continue to write to her every week. When the scene is completed, the following takes place.

TAYLOR: Jimmy Stewart, John Carradine, that's a wonderful scene.
STEWART: Thank you, Bob.
TAYLOR: If I may say so, I think you played it beautifully.

STEWART: Thank you.

CARRADINE: Thank you. Actually the fella that ought to be taking the bows is director Clarence Brown.

TAYLOR: Well, he's right here and I think I'll ask him to say something... Clarence.

BROWN: Well, Bob, we had a great cast and a great script. You know, I don't believe there was ever an actor that came closer to really being Lincoln than John Carradine.

STEWART: Yes, that's a fact, Mr. Brown. I was really startled the first time I saw him on the set.

This is the last we hear from Stewart on the show.

(7) Thursday, June 23, 1938 (9-10 p.m.)
This show is not available for listening, but from newspaper articles of the time, the following information about the broadcast can be gleaned. Regulars Meredith Willson, singer Douglas McPhail, Fanny Brice, Hanley Stafford and Frank Morgan were on the show, as was world-ranked tennis player, Ellsworth Vines. Stewart appears in a sketch titled "The Morning After," in which he plays a bachelor. Barnett Parker is his valet. Vines is given advice on his tennis game by Frank Morgan. Mary Martin sings "Little Lady Make Believe" and Una Merkel presents another of her famous magazine interviews, this time one on the "real James Stewart."

(8) Thursday, June 30, 1938 (9-10 p.m.)
Margaret Sullavan, Walter Pidgeon and Stewart appear in excerpts from their film, *The Shopworn Angel*. This show is not available for listening.

(9) Thursday, March 2, 1939 (9-10 p.m.)
Robert Young hosts this evening's show dedicated to the Hollywood preview of *The Ice Follies of 1939*, a new film starring Jimmy Stewart, Lew Ayres, and Joan Crawford. The preview will be presented at the Westwood Village Theater right after this broadcast. Other guests included Frank Morgan, Fanny Brice, Gertrude Niesen and Miliza Korjus. The basic format of the show has not changed, but the announcer has. Gone is Ted Pearson who has been replaced by Warren Hull.

Stewart appears several times during the show. Near the beginning, he and Lew Ayres talk to Robert Young about the story of the film. After Young talks to Ayres about the film, the following takes place.

AYRES: Why don't you ask Jimmy Stewart for a synopsis?
STEWART: Sure, I'm a bit of a raconteur in a boring sort of way.
YOUNG: Hello, Jimmy. Can you give us the *Ice Follies of 1939* in ten words?
STEWART: I can give it to you in two.
YOUNG: Two words? Let's hear 'em.
STEWART: Te…rific!
YOUNG: Oh, now come on, boys, give us some idea of what the story's about.
AYRES: Well, Jim and I have an ice skating act and we're supposed to be sensational.
STEWART: Sure, and then I get an idea to make the act even better. I discover Joan Crawford selling cigarettes somewhere and I hire her and put her in the act.
AYRES: That ruins everything.
STEWART: Now, wait a minute…wait a minute, now, she…she's Te…rific!
AYRES: Yeah, then why were we cancelled three days after she joined the act?
STEWART: Well, the manager had no vision. Now you can't imagine a better act for an ice rink. Now think of it; Lew and I play a property horse on skates.
YOUNG: Property horse?
STEWART: Yeah…yeah, and Joan goes along with the act and sings. Now you can't top that.
AYRES: Mmm…hum, where did it get us?
STEWART: Well, Joan was lucky.
YOUNG: How was she lucky?
STEWART: Well, when the act was cancelled, she married the front part of the horse…that's me.
AYRES: I guess you can see where I wound up.
YOUNG: Well, boys, that sounds great. But don't tell me any more, I want to be surprised when I see it. Now, we'll give you boys a treat.
STEWART: What's that, Bob?

Robert Young now introduces a song from Gertrude Niesen.
At about the halfway point in the show, Jimmy makes another appearance.

YOUNG: Say, Jimmy Stewart, you haven't forgotten that familiar Thursday evening custom of ours have you?

STEWART: Not at all, Bob, after all Maxwell House and I are old friends. You know I used to be on this show myself. As a matter of fact, I held down your job a couple of times, you remember?

YOUNG: I certainly do, Jimmy. And just for old time's sake, I think you oughta do the honors for this evening.

STEWART: Swell, thanks, Bob. Well, pull up your chairs, everybody, it's time right now for that grand Thursday evening custom; a moment of relaxation over a steaming, fragrant cup of Maxwell House Coffee. And, as usual, we're inviting you all, wherever you are, to join us in your own home. All set, Warren?

Warren Hull finishes the spot and breaks for station identification.

After the I.D., Jimmy Stewart, Joan Crawford and Lew Ayres act out scenes from the film. The first scene is when the three find themselves fired from their jobs because they have a singer (Crawford) in their act. Ice skating acts don't need singers. Stewart's character says that he wants to produce musical ice skating shows — the Ice Follies. Next, Stewart and Crawford have gotten married and are telling Lew Ayers what they have done. After the last scene is completed, there's a short exchange between Young, Crawford and Stewart.

YOUNG: ...Joan, will you save me a seat at the preview?
CRAWFORD: Right next to me, darling.
YOUNG: Good.
STEWART: Now wait a minute...now wait a minute...ah...here... Lew's on one side of you and I'm on the other. Where are we gonna put Young?
CRAWFORD: Oh, he can sit on my lap.

Young lets out a scream and then introduces another song by Gertrude Niesen.

At the end of the show, most of the cast take part in a musical number where they mostly speak the lyrics to a song about going to the preview. Stewart has one line, saying, "Oh, now, Frank [Morgan] don't be discouraged. For a gentleman of your age, all the girls are just a little bit too gorgeous." Finally, Robert Young also announces that the world premiere of the film will take place at the Palace Theater in Superior, WI, next Saturday.

In 2011, it was issued in mp3 only format on *Jimmy Stewart the Ultimate Radio Collection Vol. 1* (Master Classics Records).

Guest Star

Guest Star was produced by the U.S. Treasury Department as a public service. The purpose of the 15-minute show was to promote the sales of savings bonds. The shows aired from 1947 to 1962. Stewart appeared on just one show.

Show #23 (1947)

ANNOUNCER: Win Elliot

The guests on the show were singer Mary Small and Jimmy Stewart. The show opened with Win Elliot introducing a song by The Three Singing Dollars backed by the Savings Bond Orchestra under the direction of Denes Agay.

"Goody Goody"

Next came a short skit featuring Elliott and Mary Small. She is very anxious to meet Jimmy Stewart right away, but Elliott says that she has to sing first. She does two numbers.

"Begin the Beguine"

"Mama Tell Me Do I Gotta"

Jimmy finally joins them and the following scene takes place.

STEWART: Ah, excuse me, Mr. Elliott, but...ah...ah...
SMALL: Mr. Elliott's busy, buddy. You...you can't talk to him now, sorry.
STEWART: But, ah...but...ah...
SMALL: All right, Win, introduce me to Jimmy Stewart.
ELLIOT: But, that's...
STEWART: Ah...ah...you see that...
SMALL: Look, buddy, beat it, will ya. I'm supposed to meet Jimmy Stewart now and I can't wait for the first glimpse of his face, the first sound of his voice...ohh....I'll bet I'll just naturally swoon.
ELLIOT: You lose...no swoon.
SMALL: How do you know, Mr. Smart Guy?
ELLIOT: Because...this guy shooing you away is Jimmy Stewart, yes sir.
SMALL: Oh...oh gosh, Mr. Stewart, isn't it wonderful, you and I being together on the same Savings Bond show?
STEWART: Wonderful's the very word for United States Savings Bonds, Mary. Just imagine, in 10 years you get back four bucks for every three bucks you invest. I'd call that real pretty pickings. As a matter of fact...
SMALL: Oh. He talks so sweet. I think I will swoon...ah...hmmm.
ELLIOT: Ah...now we can talk, Jimmy.

STEWART: Well...well I wanna talk about how easy it is to save regularly by purchasing United States Savings Bonds.

ELLIOT: For folks on a regular salary, there's the payroll savings plan.

STEWART: It works very easy. All you do is simply tell the cashier or the boss at your place of business how much you want to set aside each week toward purchasing United States Savings Bonds. The boss takes care of the rest. Every week, automatically, a part of your pay is invested in United States Savings Bonds.

ELLIOT: That's all there is to it. It's easy, automatic, it's regular and so is the bond-a-month plan.

STEWART: Yes sir, all you do is tell your bank to buy a bond every month, of any denomination you want. The bank buys the bond in your name and charges it to your checking account.

ELLIOT: Payroll savings or bond-a-month plan...they're both easy, automatic, and regular.

The Three Singing Dollars with the Savings Bond Orchestra under the direction of Denes Agay then sing one final song.

"There's No Business Like Show Business"

After the song, Jimmy tells us that he buys saving bonds:

STEWART: This is Jimmy Stewart again. I just got something I wanna say about buying United States Savings Bonds. Now don't get me wrong, I'm not gonna tell you you should buy them, or why you should buy them, that's up to you. I just want to tell you why I buy them. You see, the way I look at it, investing in United States Savings Bonds is buying insurance for my future. Now, it's gonna sound funny mentioning profit, but we Americans are a bunch of horse traders at heart and I never heard of a horse trader yet who wouldn't swap three of anything for four of them. And that's what I do every time I buy a United States Savings Bonds. I buy United States Savings Bonds, buy 'em plenty and I buy 'em plenty regular.

Win signs off after thanking Mary Small and Jimmy Stewart.

The show was released in mp3 only format on *Jimmy Stewart the Ultimate Radio Collection Vol. 1* (Master Classics Records, 2011).

Hallmark Hall of Fame

The *Hallmark Hall of Fame* was a spinoff of the *Hallmark Playhouse*. It aired from February 8, 1953, until March 27, 1955. Its directors were William Gay and William Froug. In 30 minutes each week the series told the true stories of many historic figures, including Benjamin Franklin, George Gershwin, Sam Houston, Tom Mix, Sacajawea and Mark Twain. The show's host was Lionel Barrymore. When Barrymore died on November 15, 1954, a special show, in tribute to him, was aired just days later, on November 21. Jimmy Stewart was a guest on that show. Stewart and Barrymore had been in the films *You Can't Take It With You* and *It's a Wonderful Life* together. They also had both appeared on the radio show *We Hold These Truths*.

Sunday November 21, 1954 (6:30-7 p.m.)
NETWORK: CBS
SPONSOR: Hallmark Cards
HOST: Edward Arnold
ANNOUNCER: Frank Goss
WRITER: James Poe
THEME: "Hallmark Hall of Fame Theme" (Bernard Green)

The program begins with Frank Goss announcing that Barrymore had died just six short days ago and that this is a "special program transcribed in memory of Lionel Barrymore." He then introduces Edward Arnold as the host of the show. Arnold says that "many of his friends are here to reminisce" and introduces the first speaker, Gene Fowler.

Next up are Jimmy Stewart and Helen Hayes, who read Lionel's own description of his first stage appearance from his book, *We Barrymores*, which had been published in 1951.

STEWART: Well, let me read you Lionel's own description of his first appearance on stage.

Stewart reads Lionel's part and Hayes reads the letter which Lionel's grandmother had written to him. After the reading, Arnold thanks them both and this short exchange takes place.

STEWART: Think of the courage it must have taken to continue his acting career after a letter like that.

HAYES: And what's wonderful about Lionel is that this letter meant so much more to him than the hundreds, even thousands, of rave notices he was to receive in later years.

ARNOLD: Well, I've got a different kind of review, Helen. Bing Crosby will read it later on. Any other actor would have burned it, but Lionel cherished it.

STEWART: I remember hearing about that review. It was probably the worst panning an actor ever took.

Helen Hayes makes a few more remarks and then Arnold introduces a short play based on Barrymore's 1953 novel, *Mr. Cantonwine*. Gene Fowler narrates the sketch and Louis Calhern plays Mr. Cantonwine. Mr. and Mrs Randall are played by Parley Baer and Virginia Gregg.

Next up were Dore Schary of M-G-M, Bing Crosby and J.C. Hall, president of Hallmark Cards Inc. Arnold then introduces two scenes featuring Barrymore. The first is from *Mayor of the Town* and featured Barrymore and Agnes Moorehead, while the second was a scene from *Dr. Kildare*, which also featured Lew Ayres. The final speaking guest, Dr. Norman Vincent Peale, is then introduced.

After Peale's comments, the tone poem, *In Memoriam*, composed by Barrymore and dedicated to his brother John, is performed by Eugene Ormandy and the Philadelphia Orchestra.

Finally, there is a short, recorded segment by Barrymore himself, reading from *Hamlet*.

Hazel Markel Show

Markel's show was broadcast on WWDC radio in Washington, D.C., from 12:30 to 12:45 weekday afternoons. On September 2, 1952, her guest was Jimmy Stewart. Markel's show was part of the Mutual Network. The program is not available for listening.

Hi Jinx (Meet Tex and Jinx, Tex and Jinx)

The husband and wife team of Eugenia Lincoln "Jinx" Falkenburg and John Reagan "Tex" McCrary had their own radio talk show program for many years under various titles.

Falkenburg was born in Barcelona, Spain, and raised in Chile. After moving to the U.S., she became a top model. She also appeared in many films and television shows.

McCrary, a Medal of Honor winner for his services in World War II, was a journalist, political strategist and public relations specialist. They first met when McCrary, who was working for *The Daily Mirror*, was sent to interview her for a story. They were married in 1945.

Many of their shows were broadcast from WNBC in New York City. They were on the air weekdays with the length of their shows varying from 30 to 60 minutes. Stewart appeared on several shows, only one of which is available for listening. Show #8, *New York Close-Up*, is a part of the NBC Collection in the Library of Congress.

NETWORK: NBC

THEME: Manhattan (Richard Rodgers-Lorenz Hart)

(1) Friday, January 17, 1947 — *Hi Jinx*
WNBC 8:30-9:00 a.m.
It is possible that Stewart talked about the film *It's a Wonderful Life*, which had been released just 10 days before this show took place.

(2) Wednesday, July 9, 1947 — *Meet Tex and Jinx*
WNBC 8:30-9:00 a.m.
SPONSOR: Bristol Myers for Ipana Toothpaste
PRODUCER: Wesley McKee
ANNOUNCER: Danny Seymour
WRITER: Tex McCrary
MUSIC: Johnny Guarnieri and Orchestra
This was the first of a series of evening shows for Tex and Jinx, as they replaced *Duffy's Tavern* for the summer. To mark the occasion, Stewart, who had just replaced Frank Fay in Broadway's *Harvey*, was their guest. Also on the show this morning was Mel Torme.

(3) Sunday, March 28, 1948 — *Hi Jinx*
WNBC 12-12:30 p.m.
Stewart was on the show this day to talk about his return to Broadway as Elwood P. Dowd in *Harvey*. Stewart had replaced Frank Fay in the leading role.

(4) Tuesday, April 6, 1948 — *Hi Jinx*
WNBC 8:30-9:00 a.m.
This was a special Army Day broadcast and Stewart, a reservist himself, was there to talk about the role of the reservists and their part in national security.

(5) Tuesday, May 17, 1949 — *Hi Jinx*
WNBC 8:30-9:00 a.m.
This show was apparently broadcast on WNBC only and not over the network.

(6) Thursday, December 28, 1950 — *Tex and Jinx*
WNBC 8:30-9:30 a.m.
This 60-minute show was broadcast from the WNBC studios in Manhasset, New York, and featured a segment on some of the year's headliners, including Jimmy Stewart, William "Hopalong Cassidy" Boyd, Ethel Merman, Margaret O'Brien and Elizabeth Taylor. Recordings of

all these stars were used on the program and none were actually in the studio for the broadcast. The in-studio guest was Josephine Hull, who was currently co-starring with Stewart in the film *Harvey*.

(7) Monday, February 11, 1952 — *Tex and Jinx*
WNBC 8:30-9 a.m.

(8) Tuesday, May 19, 1953 — *New York Close-Up*
WNBC 8:30-9:30 a.m.

The main sponsor for today's show was Saverin Coffee. After their Front Page news segment, Stewart was introduced. By his and Jinx's own estimation, this was his 12th or 13th visit to the show, only eight of which have been documented here.

Jinx says that Jimmy is there because of the world premiere that night of his new film, *Thunder Bay*. Jinx has a quiz for Jimmy. She's going to name some of his film titles and he must give the name of the character he played in that film. Stewart has quite a bit of trouble doing this.

First up is his latest film, *Thunder Bay*. He knows that his first name is Steve, but he has a problem remembering that his last name was Martin, although he does finally remember.

Next, is the film *Murder Man*. He easily remembers that his name was Shorty. It had been kind of a joke that a 6-foot-4-inch man had the name Shorty, so this was easy for him to recall.

When Jinx asks about *The Philadelphia Story*, Jimmy draws a blank. Jinx had not done her own homework and didn't prepare any of the names in advance and she couldn't think of his name in this film either. (Macaulay Connor was his name.)

Stewart has no trouble remembering that he played Elwood P. Dowd in *Harvey*, but can't come up with his last name in *It's a Wonderful Life*. He knows that his first name was George, but can't recall Bailey as his last name.

He doesn't have any better luck with *Magic Town*, recalling that his first name was Bill, but failing to come up with the last name. (Actually his name was Rip Smith.)

He is positive that his name was Glen McClintic in *Winchester '73*. (He was close…it was Lin McAdam.) He doesn't do as well with *The Naked Spur* when he can't think of any name at all.

He finally comes up with several correct names at the end of the quiz. First, he remembers his name was Buttons the Clown in *The Greatest Show on Earth* and Jefferson Smith in *Mr. Smith Goes to Washington*.

This first segment with Stewart ends with him telling Jinx that his Oscar is still on the knife counter at his father's hardware store in Indiana, PA.

After commercials and news, Tex and Jinx return with another quiz for Stewart. This time they play recordings of songs and people and Jimmy tries to identify each of them. He gets all of these correct.

First, they play the "Princeton Fight Song." Jimmy remembers this well and even sings and recites several lines of the song. He also talks about being a cheerleader at Princeton during his junior and senior years.

The next voice is that of Josh Logan. He was a year ahead of Jimmy at Princeton and was president of the Triangle Club. He wrote plays and music for the group. Stewart especially remembers the song "On a Sunday Evening," but he declines the invitation to sing a bit of it.

Then comes the voice of Jose Ferrer. Ferrer was a year behind Jimmy at Princeton and they both were architecture majors.

The final voice was that of Leland Hayward. Stewart talked about the fact that Josh Logan and Leland Hayward owned the rights to a story called *Rear Window*. They have talked Alfred Hitchcock into making a film of the story and Jimmy was set to be the star. Stewart also mentions three other films that he will be making in the coming months, including *The Glenn Miller Story*, *Alder's Gulch* (title changed to *The Far Country*) and *Strategic Air Command*.

After a break for more commercials, Jimmy is back, this time to talk about his marriage and four children. Jimmy says that he talks more since his marriage, but that it is probably out of self-defense. Jinx suggests that he may have gotten some training at being a father from some of his film roles and they try to figure out in which films he had played the role of a father. Mentioned are *It's a Wonderful Life*, *Made for Each Other* (Jinx tells him that she was in this film in one of the crowd scenes), *Carbine Williams*, and *The Stratton Story*. Jinx breaks in with a news flash — someone has handed her a piece of paper saying that Stewart's character's name in *The Naked Spur* was Howard Kemp.

The conversation switches to Stewart's involvement with scouting; he is a member of the Los Angeles Council. He mentions that there will be a scout jamboree at Urbine Ranch, near Santa Ana on July 16 and that 55,000 scouts are expected to attend. He plans to be there. (Note: In fact, Stewart hosts a radio show from the Jamboree on July 23 — see Chapter 3.)

The show ends with Stewart telling Jinx that his twin daughters are now two years old and are almost talking and walking. He asks if she has ever heard the old wives' tale about estimating a child's adult height. Jinx says that she hasn't, so Jimmy tells her about it. It seems that if you take a child's height at age two and double it, you will get the height they will be as an adult. According to this estimate, Judy will be 6'1" and Kelly will be 5'10". Jimmy doesn't like the idea of his daughters being that tall.

Hollywood Byline

This special program was broadcast by WMAL-AM 630, Washington, D.C., on Thursday, September 21, 1950, from 10-10:30 pm. It was pieced together from press conferences from the previous year. Besides Jimmy Stewart, listeners got to hear Humphrey Bogart, Gary Cooper, Charles Laughton and Gloria Swanson. The program is not available for listening. Also see WMAL-AM entry.

Hollywood Hotel

Hollywood Hotel was the first major network show to be broadcast from the west coast. The 60-minute variety show originated in Hollywood and featured celebrity hosts and Louella Parsons interviewing stars. The costs to produce shows on the west coast were very high due to AT&T charges for line usage. Because of Miss Parsons' influence, she was able to have stars appear on the show free, thus helping to keep the costs down.

The show's credits for the first two Stewart appearances included:

NETWORK: CBS
SPONSOR: Campbell Soup
MASTER OF CEREMONIES: Dick Powell
HOSTESS: Louella Parsons
ANNOUNCER: Ken Niles
VOCALIST: Frances Langford
SHOWS FEATURING JIMMY STEWART:

(1) Friday January 17, 1936 (9:00-10:00 p.m.) — *Next Time We Love*
Stewart and Margaret Sullavan, the stars of the film, recreate their roles (Christopher and Cicely) for the show. The show is not available for listening.

(2) Friday, November 13, 1936 (9:00-10:00 p.m.) — *Born to Dance*
Stewart, Eleanor Powell, Buddy Ebsen and Una Merkel, all of whom were in the film, appear on the show. Also on this evening's show were Clark Gable, Allan Jones, Jean Harlow, Myrna Loy and Robert Taylor. A portion of this show (less than half) is available.

(3) Friday, December 18, 1936 (10:00-11:00 p.m.) — *One in a Million*
NETWORK: CBS
SPONSOR: Campbell Soup
MASTER OF CEREMONIES: Dick Powell
HOSTESS: Louella Parsons
DIRECTOR: George MacGarret
ANNOUNCER: Ken Murray
ORCHESTRA LEADER: Raymond Paige
FEATURED SINGER: Frances Langford
WRITER: Wyllis Cooper
THEME SONG: "Blue Moon" (Richard Rodgers/Lorenz Hart)

Stewart made the briefest of appearances on this evening's show, hosted by Dick Powell. He's on less than two minutes into the show when Louella Parsons asks him, "Jimmy, will you say a word?" His reply is "Not too loud with my name, Louella. I'm playing hooky from the *Seventh Heaven* set." Parsons also talks with Tyrone Power, Jean Hersholt, Loretta Young, Michael Whelan and Dixie Dunbar, among others. About halfway through the show, they stop by the set of *Seventh Heaven* and hear director Henry King talking with songwriters Lou Pollack and Sydney Mitchell about the film's theme song. Tony Martin sings it for them. Jimmy Stewart doesn't appear in this scene.

This entire show can be found on the album, *Dick Powell in Hollywood Hotel* (Medallion ML 301).

The album was produced by Tony Thomas, who also wrote the liner notes. The recording was mastered by Richard Simpson.

Hollywood Personality Parade

Hollywood Personality Parade was produced for radio syndication by Selznick Productions as radio trailers for his films. The 15-minute show was hosted by Gayne Whitman. Whitman began the show with, "From behind the scenes in Hollywood, California, we present news, reviews and gossip about the stars and pictures you'll see on the screen of your favorite theater."

1939 — *Made For Each Other*

The film was released on February 10, 1939, so this program would have been broadcast at about the same time. The show begins with "Short notes from a Hollywood reporter's notebook." This features several short, quick-hitting news stories, including four about the stars of *Made for Each Other*. Included were:

Jimmy Stewart is the first motion picture star to cooperate with the U.S. government's new plan to train 20,000 civilian airplane pilots per year as an arm of our country's national defense. Jimmy won his pilot's license only a few months ago and is now practicing advanced flying so he can join the Reserve Air Corps. That patriotic stance should win many new friends for Stewart, who already is one of the screen's most popular stars.

One of the most unusual occupations in Hollywood is that of the fog salesman, who actually sells fog to the studios for use in motion pictures. His name is W.S. Shilliam, who represents a large oil company, and he sells a special type of oil, which when shot out of a vaporizer under high pressure remains suspended in the air like actual fog. Fifty drums of such material were used in David O. Selznick picture, Made for Each Other, starring Carole Lombard and James Stewart.

Speaking of Carole Lombard reminds me of a peculiar problem that arose on the set during the shooting of her latest picture. If you'd happened to be on the set at the time, you'd have seen Carole, Jimmy Stewart and director John Cromwell gathered in a huddle talking it over. "I'll tell you," said Cromwell, "You've got to fold them like this." Carole and Jimmy watched him, then Carole moved in and said, "No, John, that's all wrong. You've got to fold them pear-shaped, like this; wider at the top than at the bottom." Jimmy scratched his head for a moment and then said in his drawling manner, "Well, I don't pose as an expert on the subject, but I hear you fold them in triangles, let me try it once." As you may have guessed, the wheels of motion picture production were being held up while two stars and a director argued about the correct way to fold a baby's diaper. The baby, only 10 days old, appears in the Lombard picture and his costume, by the way, is pear-shaped.

Carole Lombard has jumped the track and surprised everyone. Hollywood is buzzing with the question, why has she forsaken comedy, in which she scored so heavily, to go in for serious dramatics? Out of the guesses, the theories, the hypotheses, comes Carole's own answer given to your reporter just an hour ago. She told us why she goes serious in the hit production, Made for Each Other. "It isn't a question of being typed in comedy," Carole told us, "for I don't think one can be typed in anything so broad. But, I seriously believe the best pictures of the next two years will be those with human qualities that touch a responsive chord in us all.

Gayne Whitman introduces the next segment with, "Our preview at this time is the David O. Selznick film, *Made for Each Other*, starring Carole Lombard and James Stewart. As a special treat, we have the stars with us to play for you scenes from the picture itself…"

Scene #1: Johnny Mason (Stewart) has just returned home from a class reunion. He feels he is not as successful as some of his classmates. He's still struggling to make a future for himself as a lawyer. He has not achieved material success. His wife Jane (Lombard) tries to tell him how to get ahead in his job.

Scene #2: Johnny, dejected once again, returns home early in the morning. Jane tells him that she ran into his boss, Judge Doolittle, that day and that she knows that he didn't get the promotion or the raise that he had hoped he would receive.

Scene #3: Jane has taken all the insults she can handle from her mother-in-law, Harriet Mason (Lucile Watson), and tells her so. Johnny tries to calm them both down.

Scene #4: Johnny is at his wits' end and goes to plead with Judge Doolittle (Charles Coburn) for the $5,000 he needs to have special medicine flown through stormy weather to save his infant son. We hear reports as the plane flies across the country and a doctor trying to calm Jane.

Hollywood Star Playhouse

Most old-time radio experts consider this to be a well-written and performed series. It presented many original plays, performed by some of the top names in Hollywood, including Dick Powell, Ronald Colman, Joan Crawford, Vincent Price, Eve Arden and Jimmy Stewart.

> Monday, April 24, 1950 (8-8:30 p.m.) — *Nor Gloom of Night*
> NETWORK: CBS
> SPONSOR: Bromo Seltzer
> HOST/NARRATOR: Herb Rawlinson
> ANNOUNCER: Norman Brokenshire
> DIRECTOR: Jack Johnstone
> WRITERS: Robert Libbott, Frank Burt
> ORCHESTRA: Jeff Alexander

This is the program's first show as a replacement for *Inner Sanctum*. Although the show is not available for review, it was remade and broadcast on April 27, 1952, with Alan Young as the star. It is reasonable to assume that the same script, or a very similar one, was used. Any changes would undoubtedly be minor, such as using different names for the characters.

Stewart would have played the same role as Young, Ernie, a small-town mail carrier who has a propensity to exaggerate the stories he tells. While making his deliveries one day, Ernie gets a piece of mail meant for Mr. Whitney in with Mrs. Whitcomb's stack. Before she realizes it, she opens the letter and begins to read it out loud. The letter mentions a property at Third and Parkway and 7:30 on Thursday evening. Realizing the mistake, Ernie puts the letter back in the envelope and tries to make it look as if it had not been opened. When he delivers the letter to Whitcomb, the man doesn't seem to notice the tampering.

The following day, while reading the local newspaper, Ernie reads that Mrs. Whitney had been killed by a hit-and-run driver the night before. The accident had taken place at Third and Parkway at 7:30. Ernie heads directly to police Chief Gordon and tells him all he knows. But, because of his tendency to exaggerate, the chief doesn't believe him. When Ernie has the Chief ask Mrs. Whitcomb about the letter, she denies ever having opened it, adding that that would be illegal. Thinking that he might be able to get some information from Mr. Whitney himself, Ernie asks him if he had decided to buy the property at Third and Parkway. Whitney asks Ernie if he has been reading his mail and tells him that could get him into trouble.

Later, Ernie spots another envelope exactly like the one that had caused all the problems. Convinced that this means someone else is about to be killed, he mixes the letter in with Mrs. Whitcomb's, hoping that she will open it. But this time, she spots the mistake and gives the letter back to Ernie. When he tries to deliver the letter to Mr. Whitney, he finds a change of address card saying that Whitney had moved to New York City.

Ernie is carrying the letter in his hand when a dog attacks him, grabs the letter and chews on it. He gets the letter back and as he walks along, he tries to get it back into the envelope. Without really trying to read the letter, he sees these words, "Dear Friend, new arrangements are satisfactory. We can stay the appointed courier at 4:30, corner of Westside and 11th. He's never late." But this time the courier — Ernie — was late because of his struggle with the dog. He arrives at the intersection just in time to see a grey car crash into a telephone pole.

The program was also broadcast by the AFN (Armed Forces Network) and received a small write-up in the European Stars and Stripe on September 14, 1951.

Sunday April 13, 1952 (5:30-6 p.m.) — *The Six Shooter*
NETWORK: NBC
SPONSOR: American Baker's Association
HOST: Wendell Niles
DIRECTOR: Jack Johnstone
WRITER: Frank Burt
MUSIC: Basil Adlam
THEME: "Hollywood Star Playhouse" (Basil Adlam-Jay Milton-Henry Russell)

The same script would be used for the NBC audition show, which aired Wednesday, July 15, 1953. The script was used again on Sunday 11/1/1953, in a show called *Ben Scofield*.

See *The Six Shooter* in Chapter 1 for more complete synopsis of this show.

House Party

This long-running radio series was also known as *Art Linkletter's House Party*. This show was on radio from 1945 until 1967 and on television from 1952 until 1969. Linkletter was well known for his interviews of young children, but also talked with many stars, including Jimmy Stewart.

Wednesday, November 30, 1955 (3-3:30 p.m.)
NETWORK: CBS
SPONSOR: Lever Brothers
PRODUCER: John Guedel
DIRECTOR/WRITER: Marty Hill
THEME SONG: "You (Gee But You're Wonderful)" (Walter Donaldson/Harold Adamson)

Stewart appeared on just this one show and that program is not available for review.

I Speak for Democracy
RCA D8MM-1107 (1947) (16-inch, 33 1/3 RPM)

This show was syndicated to radio stations in 1947 by the National Association of Broadcasters and released in conjunction with National Radio Week. The recording consisted of five short (4-5 minutes each) speeches. Jimmy Stewart is first, speaking about a "Platform for Democracy." The remaining speeches are by Major General Luther Miller (Chief of Chaplains, U.S. Army) on "Freedom of Worship," Dr. John W. Studebaker (Commissioner of Education) on "Education for Democracy," Judge Justin Miller (former president of the Association of Broadcasters) on "Freedom of Expression" and Paul Bagwell (National President of the Jaycees) on "Democracy at Work."

As a radio show, this was meant mainly for high-school students and possibly their parents and teachers. Each speaker talks about the contest and its importance. The contest itself was sponsored by the United States Junior Chamber of Commerce, the National Association of Broadcasters and the Radio Manufacturers Association. It was also endorsed by the United States Office of Education. As seen in the radio ad below, many stations ran the segments as five separate 5-minute programs.

Stewart's speech was as follows:

> *I imagine most of you know about this contest for high-school students. It was quite a success last year, the first year it was sponsored by the NAB, the RMA and the Jaycees, with the endorsement of the United States Office of Education. I was one of the judges and I got a real lift out of listening to some of the things you said about democracy and our form of government. The four girls who won the contest last year had to be very good to win over the contestants who entered…and they were good. They felt something I think and they felt deeply about their subject and the result was they wrote well about it. They spoke with conviction. Now, I'm not an expert on government; I don't even pretend to know the facts. If you ask me the date of the Battle of Brandywine, I'm sure I'd have to look it up, but there are some fundamental facts that nobody can forget, facts nobody has to look up in history books. Now, I'm as much of an expert on those facts as any historian –and so are you. They're the facts you're going to base your broadcast scripts on, because they're the basis of the way you live, the way all of us live. They're…well, you might say that they're…they're the planks in a kind of a platform for democracy. Have you…have you read the Constitution lately? I hadn't until the sponsor of this contest asked me to talk about it and then I thought it would be a pretty good idea to brush up on it a little, even though I live every day under its protection, and you know, I rediscovered some very interesting things in it. Maybe the most interesting thing of all is the way it starts out; "We the people" it says, "We the people." That's the whole thing in three words. Those…those three words are the most powerful words in the world. They mean, to me at least and to every American who understands them, they mean that this is a government designed to serve its citizens — not just to rule them or govern them. Now I'm not going into detail about how it sets up our government, you know those things better than I do, and the branches of the government and the powers and duties*

of the branches...you know all that. I think there's a more interesting big fact in the Constitution. It's a fact that it's a platform written by the people to ensure that they'll get government by the people and for the people. Well, you don't have any...you don't have to have any diagrams to understand how different that is from government of the people. Any dictator can govern people if he has enough strength, but it takes a strong people with pride in their heritage and their freedom to govern themselves. That's the big point in the Constitution and it explains why it's still working as a platform for democracy. It's something to be proud of you know. It's something to keep working at, too. Somewhere else in the Constitution it says that this great platform has been designed to secure the blessings of liberty to ourselves and our posterity. Take a good look at that word secure. Now it doesn't mean the same thing we mean when we say secure nowadays. When our forefathers wrote it, it meant to keep safe, to guard and protect. It didn't merely mean to get or win. They won those liberties and freedoms. And the words of the Constitution mean that it's our job to guard them, to keep them secure and safe. It's an everyday job, not just one for the bad years when it's necessary to fight for them. As somebody once said, "This liberty will look easy by and by when nobody dies to get it." Now, you think about that when you write your scripts about democracy. It's the everyday job of keeping liberty that keeps the Constitution alive — a living platform for American democracy.

Parts of Stewart's speech were used again for the 1949-1950 Voice of Democracy contest. See that entry for more details.

Ice Follies of 1953

This special program was broadcast in the New York City area on Friday, September 5, 1952, between 9:30-10 p.m. The following display ad and preview appeared in the Long Beach Press-Telegram, Long Beach, CA, where the show aired on September 4th.

The program is not available for review

Information Please

Information Please was an intellectual quiz program created by Dan Golenpaul. It aired original shows on NBC, and later CBS and Mutual, for 10 years (1938-1948). The show's moderator was Clifton Fadiman. Regular panelists were Franklin P. Adams, *New York Tribune* columnist ("The Conning Tower"), *New York Times* sportswriter John Kieran and musician, author and comedian Oscar Levant. Levant was not on every show and, in fact, was not on the program that featured Jimmy Stewart. The fourth spot on the panel was usually occupied by a celebrity, writer, comedian, sports figure, or a politician. The panel would attempt to answer questions sent in by listeners. If the panel was stumped, the person sending in the question would receive a monetary prize, plus a complete set of the *Encyclopedia Britannica*.

Stewart appeared just once on the program, that coming on January 22, 1947 (CBS — 10:30-11 p.m.). Frank Capra, director of *It's a Wonderful Life*, which had opened in New York City on December 20, 1946, and the remainder of the U.S. on January 7, 1947, was the other guest panelist. The show is not available for review.

It Pays to be Ignorant

This very popular spoof of other radio quiz shows was actually more of a comedy show than a quiz show. The panelists were asked ridiculous questions and then spent much time giving even more ridiculous answers. Stewart appeared on one show which is unavailable for review.

Friday, January 24, 1947 (10-10:30 p.m.)
NETWORK: CBS
HOST-QUIZ MASTER: Tom Howard
PANELISTS: George Shelton, Henry McNaughton, Lulu McConnell
CREATORS-WRITERS: Bob Howell, Ruth Howell
DIRECTOR: Herb Polesie
ANNOUNCER: Ken Roberts
SPONSOR: Philip Morris, Revelation Pipe Tobacco
COMMERCIAL SPOKESMAN: Johnny Roventini
MUSIC: Harry Salter, with vocals by the Esquire Quartet and Al Madru
THEME: "It Pays to Be Ignorant" (Tom Howard-Bob Howell, sung by Al Madru)

The big news for this show was that regular panelist Lulu McConnell was ill and had to be replaced by Kate Smith.

At about the halfway point of the show, coming from a commercial break, Tom Howard asks Ken Roberts, "Who's our first contestant this evening?" To which Ken replies, "Well, we have a very nice young man coming to the microphone Mr. Howard, a Mr. Stewart." There's much applause and whistling from the audience and then the fun starts.

HOWARD: Good evening Mr. Stewart and thank you for coming up. How are you this evening?

STEWART: Fine, thank you.

HOWARD: Where are you from…would you care to tell us?

STEWART: Indiana, Pennsylvania.

HOWARD: Indianna…

SHELTON: Indiana, Pennsylvania! Well make me a politician and call me influence. I…I used…I used…I used to work in that town.

HOWARD: Look out, you'll crack a tonsil. Just ignore him Mr. Stewart.

SHELTON: I was a farmer in a candy factory.

MCNAUGHTON: You…ah…you were a farmer in a candy factory?

SHELTON: I used to milk chocolates.

HOWARD: All right, please. So, you're from Indiana, Pennsylvania Mr. Stewart, is that right?

STEWART: Yes, yes I am Tom.

HOWARD: Strangely, I know some people that lived in Indiana. I knew a man by the name of Stewart that used to run a hardware store. Did you know him?

STEWART: Ah…a hardware store…yes.

HOWARD: Yes, you knew him?

STEWART: Yes, I was related to him by marriage.

HOWARD: Oh, you were; brother-in-law or something?

STEWART: No, he was my father.

HOWARD: Oh gee, well isn't that a coincidence, a blood relation.

STEWART: Blood relation.

SHELTON: Why don't you try to borrow some?

HOWARD: I…thank you Mr. Shelton.

SHELTON: That's all right, not at all.

HOWARD: I see, you know I thought your face looked familiar, Mr. Stewart. So you're old Alex Stewart's son?

STEWART: That's right.

HOWARD: Isn't that marvelous. Well, give Alex my regards the next time you see him, will you?

STEWART: I sure will, thanks very much.

HOWARD: Yes, I'll appreciate that. It certainly is…what do you work at? Are you in the hardware business Mr. Stewart? What do you do? What do you work at?

STEWART: I'm an actor.

HOWARD: Oh, an actor.

STEWART: Um-hum.

HOWARD: You mean like in the theater or the movies or…

STEWART: No, no, I work in the movies.

HOWARD: Of yes, have you ever made any pictures?

STEWART: A few.

SMITH: Well of all the blockheads. Mr. Howard, that's Jimmy Stewart.

HOWARD: I know that. Alex Stewart's son…I know that. Know him well, know his father.

SMITH: Mr. Howard, everybody knows Jimmy Stewart.

SHELTON: Certainly, I even know him. I've seen him in the movies.

SMITH: Sure.

SHELTON: That's the fellow that says to the girl, "I love you."

STEWART: Thank…thank…thank you Harry.

SHELTON: "Come to the Casbah."

HOWARD: Wait a minute. "Come to the Casbah," you're wrong Mr. Shelton. You're thinking about Spencer Tracy.

SMITH: Mr. McNaughton, certainly you've seen Jimmy Stewart in the movies haven't you?

MCNAUGHTON: I'm afraid not Miss Smith, no, you see I never go to the cinema.

SHELTON: But he's not in the cinema, he's in the movies.

SMITH: Jimmy, what in the world are you doing on this program?

STEWART: You know, I was sort of wondering the same thing about you.

HOWARD: Miss Smith is just slumming, Mr. Stewart.

STEWART: Well, I…I sort of saw a sign out the theater reading "It Pays to Be Ignorant," so I thought I'd come in and see how…how much it pays. If it pays to be ignorant, I should clean up some dough around here.

HOWARD: Tell me, have you heard this program in Hollywood Mr. Stewart?

STEWART: Oh yes, I have and that's another reason why I stopped in. I wanted to see if…if your board of experts had heads. I…I…

HOWARD: Yes, yes, they have, yes…

MCNAUGHTON: Why how dare you Mr. Stewart, how dare you sir, how dare you…

STEWART: Well, I'm sorry. I just wondered about…

MCNAUGHTON: Why how dare you, you padded cell, you straight jacket, you cross word puzzle, you jigsaw puzzle…

HOWARD: Wait, what are you saying Mr. McNaughton?

MCNAUGHTON: I'm putting him in his place.

SHELTON: You know, I'm thinking about shipping out to Hollywood and going into pictures myself.

STEWART: Uh-huh, what is that? I thought there was a law against shipping dope.

HOWARD: You're right, you're right.

SMITH: Oh George…

SHELTON: No, that's alright. Mr. Howard isn't going with me.

HOWARD: All right.

SMITH: Say Jimmy, I want to tell you that we're mighty proud of the great job you did with the Army Air Force.

STEWART: Thanks, Kate, thanks.

MCNAUGHTON: Yes, yes indeed, Jimmy. May I offer my congratulations? You know, I used to be in the Air Force. I flew a Burlington Zephyr.

STEWART: Burlington Zephyr, that's a railroad train, isn't it?

MCNAUGHTON: It is? No wonder I couldn't get it off the ground.

KATE: Oh Harry.

SHELTON: Say, is it true Mr. Stewart that some actors in Hollywood make $5000 a week?

MCNAUGHTON: $5000 a week?

SHELTON: Yeah.

MCNAUGHTON: Sometimes I have to work all day for that.

HOWARD: Well, Mr. Stewart, it's needless for me to say that we are certainly honored by this visit. And I mean that sincerely.

STEWART: Well Tom, I'm serious too when I say that this has been my favorite program. I made up my mind that when I got here the next time to New York, I was certainly going to see it. You know Tom, you have a lot of fans out on the coast, so keep up the good work because we all enjoy a good laugh out there and you fellows certainly hand them out.

HOWARD: Well that's wonderful Jimmy to tell us that. It's very encouraging. Now Jimmy, will you reach into Johnny's cap and pick out a quistion…a question, not a quistion…a question for us please and will you read the question if you don't mind? Just take your time and read it.

STEWART: Six and 7/8's.

HOWARD: Six…Six and 7/8's. Wait a minute, what is this?

JOHNNY: Mr. Howard, he took the lining out of my cap.

HOWARD: What…

STEWART: I'm very sorry.

HOWARD: That's all right Jimmy, but it's on a slip of paper there…just a slip of paper.

STEWART: Oh, I see, I see.

HOWARD: Just read the slip of paper if you don't mind.

STEWART: Ah…ah…oh, how many families live in a four family house?

HOWARD: How many families live in a four family house?

Tom, George, Harry and Kate then go into a silly routine to try to answer the question. When the comedy session ends, we hear:

HOWARD: Ken, please will you step in here and give our good friend Mr. Stewart $24.70 for helping us out.
KEN: Certainly Tom. Here you are Mr. Stewart.
HOWARD: And Jimmy that I might say (Jimmy apparently begins to count the money he has been given) that's right James, count it. That's right James, you count it because no mistakes are rectified after you leave the mic. And that is all for you.
STEWART: No, not all of it. I gotta pay 10% to my agent.
HOWARD: Oh, I see.
JOHNNY: And Mr. Howard, I'd like to give Jimmy 202 Philip Morris cigarettes.

Stewart was a winner on the show and pocketed a grand total of $24.70. According to newspaper articles of the time, he dutifully made out a check for $2.47 and mailed it off to the Music Corporation of America, the agency which represented him.

The Jack Benny Show
The Jack Benny Show ran on radio from 1932 until 1955 on NBC and CBS. The main premise running through the show all those years was Jack's cheapness. The major characters on the show were Mary Livingstone, Jack's girlfriend (in real life, his wife), Phil Harris, his band leader, Dennis Day, who added a singing touch to the show, Eddie Anderson, Benny's valet-chauffeur Rochester van Jones, and Jack's announcer Don Wilson. Mel Blanc also appeared on the show supplying several voices and the sound of Benny's Maxwell, his ancient car. A singing group, The Sportsmen, also appeared on many shows. Benny was born Benjamin Kubelsky on February 14, 1894 and died December 26, 1974.
SHOWS FEATURING JIMMY STEWART:

(1) Sunday, January 9, 1949 — *Lunch at the Brown Derby* (7:00-7:30 p.m.)
NETWORK: CBS
ANNOUNCER: Don Wilson
SPONSOR: Lucky Strike
MUSIC: Phil Harris
THEME MUSIC: "Love in Bloom" (Leo Robin/Ralph Rainger)

Those in the cast of the show were: Mary Livingstone, Dennis Day, Phil Harris, Eddie "Rochester" Anderson.

The sketch starts with Don Wilson saying, "We are going back to yesterday afternoon at the Brown Derby restaurant." All the tables are occupied when Jack and Mary enter, but Jack spies Jimmy Stewart sitting alone at a table. He and Mary join him. Their waiter, Chilius, is played by Mel Blanc. Mary mentions Jimmy's latest picture, *You Gotta Stay Happy*. Jack says that he's producing pictures now and says he'd like to have Jimmy in his next film. Jimmy tries to get out of it by saying he has other commitments, but promises to stop by Jack's radio show rehearsal later that night to talk to Jack. Jack himself balks when Jimmy tells him he usually gets $200,000 to make a picture. Jack tries a series of tricks to keep Jimmy coming back to him and talking, but none seem to work. Among these tricks are borrowing Jimmy's pen and then not giving it back, stealing Jimmy's shoes and socks and taking a filling from Jimmy's tooth. As the show ends, the listeners are left on their own to decide what has happened.

At one point during the show, Jimmy runs into Rochester in a parking lot trying to start Benny's Maxwell. During the course of their conversation, Rochester mentions Stewart's birthday as May 8, 1911, and Stewart agrees. Of course, his birthday is actually May 20, 1908.

Jack's writers during the two times that Stewart appeared on the show included George Balzer, Sam Perrin, Milt Josefsberg and John Tackaberry.

The show can be found on the six-cassette set, *The Jack Benny Program Volume 2* (Radio Spirits 4104) released in 1995. It is the second show on tape #5.

(2) Sunday, April 27, 1952 — *Bend of the River* (7:00-7:30 p.m.)
NETWORK: CBS
ANNOUNCER: Don Wilson
SPONSOR: Lucky Strike
MUSIC: Phil Harris

Those in the cast of the show were: Mary Livingstone, Dennis Day, Phil Harris, Eddie "Rochester" Anderson, The Sportsmen Quartet.

The show opens with a short sketch. Don Wilson has hired a replacement announcer (Mel Blanc does the voice) because he doesn't want to introduce Jack as a great concert violinist. Jack also talks with Phil Harris and his piano player. Several times during the opening, Benny's TV show is also mentioned. Then, we get a song.

"Be Anything (But Be Mine)" — Dennis Day

Then the cast starts its own version of *Bend of the River*. Playing roles are:

Kate	Mary Livingstone
Buck Benny	Jack Benny
Dobbin (the horse)	Mel Blanc
Jimmy Stewart	Jimmy Stewart
Chief Thunder Storm	Don Wilson
Little White Cloud That Cried	Dennis Day
Curley Hair	Phil Harris

It's 1867 and Buck Benny is taking a wagon full of food to Oregon. One night, Jimmy Stewart (that's his character's name, too) comes riding into Buck's camp and soon takes over as leader. When they are taken into an Indian tribe and become honorary Indians, Jimmy, Buck, and the Sportsmen Quartet sing:

"I'm An Indian, Too"

Stewart has two lines in the song — (1) Like the Seminole, Navajo, Kickapoo; like the Cherokee, I'm an Indian too (2) I'll wear moccasins, wampum belts, feather hats — both of which he flubs. This causes Benny to change one of his lines. Instead of singing "I'm an Indian too," Jack sings "You don't know your song."

They meet up with a gold miner named Curley Hair. He wants to buy their food and pay for it with gold. Buck wants to sell, Jimmy doesn't. There's a gunfight and Jimmy wins. They bury Buck in a gold mine so that he can be eternally happy. Stewart continues on until he reaches the settlement in Oregon at the bend of the river.

There were two running gags in this show, one revolving around Mel Blanc's willingness to be the show's announcer for $1.25 and the other involving Phil Harris' piano player, Bagby, driving off in his piano. Jack and Jimmy were to get one final laugh from the latter at the end of the show, but the timing was off and they ran out of time. All Jack could say was "we're a little late, so goodnight folks." Had there been enough time, Jack was to thank Jimmy for being on the show and his appearance the following night on *Lux Radio Theatre* when Stewart would star in *No Highway in the Sky*. Then would come the following exchange crossed out on the original script.

(sound: phone rings)
JACK: Get that, will you, Jimmy?
(sound: receiver up)

JIMMY: hello…uh huh…Uh huh…I don't know what you're talking about, but I'll give him the message.
(sound: receiver down)
JACK: What is it, Jimmy?
JIMMY: It was a policeman. He called to say there's a piano parked in front of the California Bank with it's motor running.
JACK: I knew Bagby couldn't stay out of trouble…Goodnight, folks.

This show can be found on the 10-CD (Radio Spirits 4334)/cassette (Radio Spirits 4333) set, The Jack Benny program, issued in 2004.

It is also included as part of an 8-cassette box titled *Radio's Greatest Comedies* (Great American Audio Corp. #48005), which was released in 1992. The cassette with this show is numbered 40369.

The program can also be found on the single cassette, *Jack Benny Volume II* (Radio Classics PN # 7217JC).

In 2011, it was released in mp3 only format on *Jimmy Stewart the Ultimate Radio Collection Vol. 1* (Master Classics Records).

The program was also issued by the Armed Forces Radio Services (AFRS 316).

Jimmy Stewart: It's a Thankful Life

This two-hour Mutual Network and Westwood One syndicated special was scheduled to air anytime between November 22-25, 1990, as part of the Thanksgiving weekend. Judging from the nature of the show, most stations probably aired it on the 22nd, Thanksgiving Day. This would be Jimmy Stewart's final new recordings for radio, coming a little more than 56 years after his first appearance on May 3, 1934. The show was sponsored nationally by Fisherman's Friend (the extra strong cough lozenge), AT&T and Sears Brand Central. The show was issued to radio stations transcribed on three 12-inch vinyl discs, with the second side of the third disc being blank. Each disc was marked JS '90 and had the appropriate side number. In all, there were nine segments, plus a 40-second promo, to the show.

The show's credits included:
WRITER/PRODUCER: Marsha Richardson
PRODUCTION & ENGINEERING: Fred Lindgren
ASSOCIATE PRODUCER: Ron Steffen
EXECUTIVE PRODUCER: Norm Pattiz
SPECIAL THANKS TO: John Strauss, Jimmy Stewart

The show begins with "What A Wonderful World" by Louis Armstrong

STEWART: Ah…I was wonderin', do you have room for one more at your Thanksgiving dinner? I'm…I'm Jimmy Stewart and I'd like to help you celebrate. I'll bring the music and some memories and an extra pumpkin pie. So set another place, I'll be there by halftime.

"I Want To Be Happy" — Judy Garland

STEWART: Thanksgiving is the day filled with food, family, friends, football and more food. Should we thank the Pilgrims for this holiday? They celebrated the first American Thanksgiving in 1621. They invited 90 of their new Indian friends who arrived covered in ceremonial bear grease. Well, we're having…ah…less than 90 at our house and…ah…I think Gloria would prefer if you forgot about the bear grease, but bring some flowers instead.

"Having a Wonderful Time" — Tommy Dorsey

STEWART: The Pilgrims had a lot of good ideas about how to celebrate their harvest. It was a custom to put five grains of corn on every empty plate before dinner was served. And then, before they carved the turkey, everyone would name five things they were thankful for. The corn ritual was to remind them of the hardships of their ancestors. The first Pilgrims were rationed just five grains of corn per person each day. Five things we're thankful for; let's put music on the list today.

"Get Happy" — Benny Goodman

STEWART: Cranberry sauce, now that's something to be thankful for; and phone calls from a friend, sneakers, now we have to thank the person who invented sneakers; and golden retriever puppies. There's a lot to celebrate this Thanksgiving and I'm glad to be here to help. I'm Jimmy Stewart and I'll be right back.

The show's second segment begins with Jimmy asking, "That turkey almost finished? I'm Jimmy Stewart here to celebrate Thanksgiving with you."

"(If I Could Be With You) One Hour Tonight" — Benny Goodman

STEWART: Who should we thank for thanksgiving? The Pilgrims celebrated the first American feast in 1621. But, this holiday has been around for centuries. Over a thousand years ago, English farmers believed that a spirit, the corn spirit, lived in their crops to make them grow. They even had magic rituals to keep the corn spirit happy. Well, we don't want any unhappy spirits around the house on Thanksgiving, so here's a little musical magic.

"Old Black Magic" — Glenn Miller

STEWART: Thanksgiving may be the purest holiday we have. It's a weekday, but we don't have to work and we can watch football and have two helpings of dessert, all with no guilt. No wonder the day starts with a parade.

"MacNamara's Band" — Bing Crosby

STEWART: You know…ah…Benjamin Franklin wanted the turkey to be our National bird. He thought that bald eagle had a bad moral character. Mr. Franklin thought the turkey was more respectable. Well, it's definitely more tasty. You know, we roast 600 million pounds of the bird every Thanksgiving.

"Ac-cent-tchu-ate The Positive"

STEWART: The sound of a crackling fire, the way fresh snow crunches under your boots, morning dew on a rose bush, there's a lot to be thankful for everyday. I'm Jimmy Stewart and I'll be right back with our celebration of Thanksgiving.

The next segment begins with Stewart saying, "Cranberry ice cream? Now I…I think that's going a little too far. Pumpkin pie has been Thanksgiving dessert for more than 300 years for a reason…it's always good. Now I hope you're saving some. I'm Jimmy Stewart and I'm here to celebrate Thanksgiving with you."

"Sentimental Journey" — Les Brown

STEWART: For the air we breathe and the water we drink, for a soul and a mind with which to think, for food that comes from fertile sod, for these and many things I'm thankful to my God. That was written by Danny Thomas when he was in the sixth grade. His father made all the children come up with a poem of thanks before one spoonful of mashed potatoes was served. That's a tradition worth borrowing.

"They Can't Take That Away From Me" – Fred Astaire

STEWART: All over America today we're all having the same dinner, turkey. But we can't take credit for making the bird the main course. The ancient Mayans celebrated their harvest with turkey and squash feast. The Pilgrims followed the custom mainly because there were so many turkeys running wild. And, since they can't fly, they run very slowly and they're easy target. Plus, the turkey feathers were very much in demand by fashionable women that wanted them for their hats.

"Hey! Look Me Over" — Peggy Lee
"That's My Style" — Peggy Lee

STEWART: Thanksgiving, it's the only day that all of America sits down for dinner at the same time…halftime. I'm Jimmy Stewart and I'll be right back to help you celebrate Thanksgiving.

Jimmy begins segment four with, "Your first kiss, that's a memory to be thankful for."
"It's Been a Long Long Time" — Bing Crosby
"Something to Remember You By" — Helen Forrest and Dick Haymes

STEWART: Thanksgiving, every year on the fourth Thursday of November, we take some time to give thanks and celebrate with friends and family. It was President Lincoln who proclaimed the first nationwide Thanksgiving, the last Thursday of November, 1863. The Civil War was still raging. Lincoln wanted the day to be a celebration, not of any military victories, but to honor a year filled with the blessings of healthful skies and fruitful fields. And in the battlefields, both the Confederate and Yankee troops marked the day with, well, what else, football games. However, if you look at pictures of their games, it seems that the rules were pretty loose. So to score a touchdown, you had to be fast and fearless and could tackle, trip, punch the quarterback; no wonder they were low-scoring games.

'Tain't What Cha Do — Jimmie Lunceford
He Ain't Got Rhythm — Benny Goodman

STEWART: Snoopy weighs 343 pounds and they still get him to float in Macy's parade. Have some more pie and we'll be right back with our Thanksgiving celebration.

Jimmy begins segment five by saying, "Thanksgiving, the only day it's okay to put marshmallows on your sweet potatoes. That's a reason to celebrate."

"Thanks for the Memory" — Martha Tilton

STEWART: 1924, that's the first year that Macy's celebrated the Thanksgiving and the beginning of Christmas shopping season with a parade. Donald Duck, Snoopy, Mickey Mouse, Betty Boop, Garfield, the Pink Panther, if you're a cartoon character, floating in the Macy's parade is just like getting a star on the Hollywood Walk of Fame. One year, Macy's released the balloons at the end of the parade and then they offered a reward to anyone who brought one back to the store. I guess there are no science buffs at Macy's. You see, helium expands at high altitudes, sort of like your worst nightmares about indigestion.

March From the River Kwai — Mitch Miller
Something's Gotta Give — Ella Fitzgerald

STEWART: We gather together to ask the Lord's blessing, we hasten and chasten his will to make known. Yeah, I've always wondered about that chasten part, how about you?

"Someone to Watch Over Me" — Linda Ronstadt

STEWART: I'll be right back to help you carve that turkey.

Jimmy begins segment six by saying, "Turkeys and Lions, you can't have Thanksgiving without them. I'm Jimmy Stewart, back to help you celebrate Joe Montana's favorite day."

"May You Always" — McGuire Sisters

STEWART: The Detroit Lions have been playing football on Thanksgiving Day since 1934, and in 1956 they took the game to television, making halftime to the exact moment when the turkey is done; more reliable than a meat thermometer.

"String of Pearls" — Glenn Miller
"Runnin' Wild" — Glenn Miller

STEWART: In the spirit of Thanksgiving, we'd like to give Texas the opportunity to claim the day as their own. On Highway 25, just outside of Anjou, Texas, there's a sign that reads, "The site of the first Thanksgiving in 1541, proclaimed by Padre Padilla." Leave it to Texas, it's bigger, better and first.

"Yellow Rose of Texas" — Mitch Miller

STEWART: Your favorite song on radio, a rainbow, the way your best girl's face looks in the morning — there's a lot to give thanks for every day, so we're celebrating, and I'll be right back.

"When You Wish Upon a Star" — Linda Ronstadt

STEWART: How would you like to celebrate Thanksgiving twice? It happened a couple of times in the '30s and '40s. Politicians couldn't agree on which Thursday was the best Thursday. In 1939, President Franklin Roosevelt moved the holiday up a week to lengthen the Christmas…the shopping season. Well, political cartoonists went to work and they called November 23rd the Democratic Thanksgiving and November 30th the Republican Thanksgiving. The mayor of Atlantic City had it all figured out, though. He proclaimed the 23rd Franksgiving and the 30th Thanksgiving. What about it, do you think he named it after Franklin Roosevelt or Frank Sinatra?

"Dream" — Frank Sinatra
"I'll Be Seeing You" — Frank Sinatra

STEWART: Rice on the church step after a wedding, seeing your favorite movie again, watching your grandson slide into home plate; every day can be Thanksgiving, even without the turkey. I'm Jimmy Stewart and I'll be right back.

STEWART: (to begin segment 8) Faded snapshots and crinkled memories, we can pull out all the boxes of both today and be thankful for them. I'm Jimmy Stewart here to help you finish that pumpkin pie and celebrate Thanksgiving.

"Through the Years" — Eydie Gorme and Steve Lawrence
"Our Love Is Here to Stay" — Toni Tennille

Segment eight ends cold and segment nine begins with a song. Stewart's voice and stories seem to have suddenly disappeared, but he will return with one final reading from the Bible

"Blue Skies" — Bing Crosby

STEWART: Make a joyful noise unto the Lord all ye lands. Serve the Lord with gladness; come before His presence with singing. We are his people and the sheep of His pasture, enter into His gates with thanksgiving and into His courts with praise; be thankful unto Him, and bless His name. For the Lord is good; His mercy is everlasting; and His truth endures to all generations.

"Count Your Blessings" — Eddie Fisher

The 40-second promo featured Stewart talking over a bed of "Sentimental Journey" and saying:

STEWART: Do you have room for one more at that Thanksgiving dinner? I'm Jimmy Stewart and I'd like to help you celebrate. I'll bring the music and some memories and an extra pumpkin pie, so set another place. I'll be there by halftime.

John Conte Show

NETWORK: AFN
MUSIC: Charlie Magnante Trio

The program was first announced in the August 1, 1954, edition of the European Stars and Stripes. On the first Tuesday after this date, August 3, the program in that time slot was listed as Songs of the Islands. However in the August 10th listings places John Conte in this time slot, so it is likely that this is the date on which Stewart was a guest.

The Charlie Magnante Trio at one time featured Magnante on accordion, Tony Mottola on guitar and George Wright on organ. The latter two may or may not have been with him at this point in time.

This program is not available for listening.

Keep 'Em Rolling

Keep 'Em Rolling was broadcast live on Sundays from 10:30-11:00 p.m. There were only 28 shows in the series (November 9, 1941-May 17, 1942) and most, including Jimmy Stewart's, are not available. The show was very patriotic in nature.

NETWORK: Mutual

SPONSOR: Office of Emergency Management
HOST: George S. Kaufman
PRODUCER: Arthur Kurlan
MUSIC: Morton Gould & His Orchestra
THEME MUSIC: "The Flame of Freedom is Burning" (Richard Rodgers/Lorenz Hart)

Sunday, February 22, 1942 (9:30-9:45 p.m.)

Stewart and Claude Rains appear in a short played entitled *Valley Forge*, written by Maxwell Anderson. Mary Jane Walsh also appeared on the show.

Kraft Music Hall
See *The Bing Crosby Show*.

The Larry King Show
NETWORK: Mutual

This show, which was previewed on *The Best of Larry King*, was originally aired in 1986 just after MCA had released home videos of five Stewart films — *The Glenn Miller Story, Rare Breed, The Bend of the River, Thunder Bay,* and *Winchester '73*. King was in Washington, DC, while Stewart was at the Westwood One Studios in Los Angeles.

King starts the show by asking Jimmy if there was ever a chance that he was going to be an architect. Stewart replies that he thinks so. When he graduated from Princeton, he had a scholarship to go to graduate school to get his master's degree in architecture. King then asks if he looks at a building and thinks about how he would have designed it. Stewart says no, but his education has made him a critic and he will spot the good and bad things in a design.

Next, they discuss the home video revolution and Stewart sees it as a natural extension of the movie industry. King asks if he played the instrument in *The Glenn Miller Story*. Stewart admits that he didn't and relates the story of how he at least learned the proper movements to simulate playing from trombonist Joe Eukel. King mentions that the video version of the film has stereo sound and asks if Jimmy has heard it. Jimmy tells him that the original film had a stereo track. Most theaters at the time were not equipped for stereo sound and the cost of making them would have been prohibitive, so the film was released in mono. When they did the video, the stereo soundtrack could not be found. It was finally located in the Decca Records vault in Chicago. It had been given to them so they could produce stereo albums.

Next, King asked what it was like to work with Frank Capra. Stewart tells him that Frank is his favorite person and that he admires him more than he can say. He adds that he has great values and could get them onto the screen without preaching. King asks about Hitchcock and Stewart says that he was about as near to genius as you can get.

At this point, King begins taking phone-in questions from listeners. The first is from a man who had sent a photo to Stewart. Jimmy had signed it and returned it to him. He asks if fan mail comes directly to Stewart and if he answers the letters personally. Jimmy says that the letters actually go to his office, but that he does answer each one personally. The next caller doesn't ask a question, but says that he had had his picture taken with Stewart during the filming of *Strategic Air Command*.

The next caller asks how he feels about the colorization of *It's a Wonderful Life*. Jimmy says that it is his favorite picture and that he doesn't like the idea of colorization at all. Black-and-white films should be left just the way they are. The next question comes from a man who wants to know Stewart's favorite actresses to work with and what it was like working with Bette Davis. Jimmy says that this is a dangerous question to answer. He does say that it was great to work with Davis and mentions several other actresses, including Donna Reed, Ginger Rogers, and June Allyson. The next caller wants to know his feeling toward censorship. Jimmy says that there was censorship in the 1930s when he started in films. He said that he didn't think it caused any problems and that he thinks that censorship has a value.

King throws in his own question, asking for Jimmy's thoughts on Mr. Reagan's actions in Libya. Jimmy says that he thinks it was the right thing to do and that he supports him 100%. The next caller asks how he got started working with Frank Capra and how many movies he had made with him. Jimmy says that it started with *You Can't Take it with You*, and then they did *Mr. Smith Goes to Washington* and *It's a Wonderful Life*. Jimmy adds that he was under contract to M-G-M which loaned him to Capra, who worked at Columbia.

The next listener wanted to know what it was like working with Katharine Hepburn. Stewart answered that she was a great woman and a wonderful person. The next caller said that Jimmy was his father's favorite actor. His father was about to celebrate his 70th birthday and he asked Jimmy to wish him a happy birthday, which Stewart did. The next listener said that he and his wife had recently been in a foreign country and heard the soundtrack only for a Stewart film on the radio. He had been impressed with how compelling his voice was and asked if he had ever been on the radio. Jimmy says that he loves radio. He mentions *Lux Radio Theatre* dramatizing films and his own show, *The Six Shooter*. He relates a story about sending the script for *Winchester '73* to *Lux* and them sending it back saying they couldn't use it because nobody says anything. (*Lux* must have eventually changed its mind because the show was produced.)

The next caller wanted to know if it were true that when Jimmy had tried to join the Army Air Corps, he didn't make the minimum weight requirement and that he talked the recruiter into taking him anyway. Jimmy said that he told the recruiter that if he let him join, then for the rest of the time he was in the Army he just wouldn't get weighed. Next came a question about movie heroes and if they have changed over the years. Yes, they have changed, said Jimmy. The movie business is made up of trends. These trends bring changes which lead from one thing to another. The follow-up caller mentions that *Cheyenne Social Club* was his favorite film and then asks what it was like working with Henry Travers who had played Clarence Oddbody III in *It's A Wonderful Life*. Jimmy says that he was one of his favorite actors and that he couldn't have been cast better.

The next woman asked if Jimmy remembered making a film at Westover Air Force Base. He said that he did and the woman said that her husband had been the bus driver who drove the cast around. Jimmy said, "Well, good for him," and asked that she say hello to him. The next caller wants to know what he thinks of the golden age films compared to those of today. Jimmy says that as more time goes by, there are more and more things about which films can be made, so films are bound to change with time.

Larry King then asks Jimmy what he thinks of the work of Robert De Niro and Jimmy replies that it is excellent. The next caller ask about his favorite recent films and also if he would consider working with Steven Spielberg. Stewart doesn't name any films, but does say that he would certainly like to work with Spielberg. The next caller wants to know how Jimmy feels about theatrical training in schools. Jimmy says that it's okay as long as it doesn't interfere with your regular education. Get your education first. Experience on the stage is more important than drama school.

Next was a question about the children in *It's a Wonderful Life*. Whatever happened to them? Jimmy says that he's often wondered that himself and that he really doesn't know what happened to them. The next caller says that she thinks she saw him on Broadway in *Harvey* and asks if that's possible. Jimmy says that it's quite possible since he did the show two times on Broadway and once in London. The follow-up caller wanted to know if Jimmy had played the harmonica himself in *Pot 'O Gold*. Jimmy said that someone else was behind him playing. Larry King asks if Jimmy had ever been cast as a villain. Jimmy said that he had in *After the Thin Man*. The next caller thanked him for visiting troops in Vietnam. The final question was about the film *Mr. Smith Goes to Washington*. Was there any controversy in Washington when the film came out? Jimmy said that when the film opened in Washington, some senators were there and so was Frank Capra. When the film broke, Capra went into the projection booth to help fix it. When he returned to his seat, many of the senators had gone.

At this point, King thanks Jimmy for appearing on the show and the program ends. A portion of this show was later used on the cassette release, *Larry King: Legends* (Simon and Schuster Audioworks 87953-7), issued in 1993. The cassette is subtitled *The Best of the Larry King Show Volume 2*. Side 2 of the cassette begins with just under eight minutes from Stewart's appearance on a 1986 show. Only one of the listener phone calls from the original show was used here and the question involved the film *Mr. Smith Goes to Washington*.

Wednesday December 6, 1989

Stewart is on the show mainly to talk about his book, *Jimmy Stewart and His Poems*. He also tries to answer questions phoned in by listeners.

Sunday November 5, 1990

Jimmy talks about his upcoming Thanksgiving radio special (see *It's a Thankful Life*) and also answers phone calls from listeners.

Leo Is On the Air

These 15-minute shows were produced by M-G-M as radio trailers for new films. It was their way of promoting new and upcoming films. After the success of this show, other film studios also produced shows for their movies.

SHOWS FEATURING JIMMY STEWART:

(1) *Born to Dance* (1936)

None of the stars of the new M-G-M film actually appeared on the show. Instead, songs from the Cole Porter score were played. Jimmy Stewart was featured in one song. Played were:

"I've Got You Under My Skin" — Frances Langford

"Easy To Love" — Eleanor Powell

"Love Me, Love My Pekinese" — Virginia Bruce & Raymond Walburn
"Rollin' Home" — Buddy Ebsen & Jimmy Stewart
"Swingin' the Jinx Away" — Frances Langford & Cast

Heard on all songs was the Metro-Goldwyn-Mayer Orchestra under the direction of Alfred Newman.

(2) *Navy Blue and Gold* (1937)

This disc would appear to have been issued for a re-release of the film since the label carries this information: For Release July 1, 1941.

The show begins with the announcer saying, "Leo is on the air…this is your Hollywood radio reporter coming to you from the Little Theater at Metro-Goldwyn-Mayer, bringing you James Stewart, Robert Young, Florence Rice and Tom Brown in several scenes from the motion picture *Navy Blue and Gold*." The listener is then treated to four scenes from the film.

Recruits being sworn in as midshipmen

"Truck" (Stewart), Roger (Young) and Dick (Brown) meeting each other and deciding to room together

"Truck" defends his father's honor by telling the true story of what had really happened the night his ship had run aground and sunk.

Waiting to hear if "Truck" will be dismissed. (He is found guilty and dismissed, but is given clemency and allowed to remain at the Academy.) His father is also reinstated at his previous rank. Florence Rice also appears in this scene.

(3) *The Shopworn Angel* (1938) — M-G-M 21470

The announcer begins the show by saying, "Leo is on the air…from Hollywood, where the blue bloods of the screen compete with the blue Pacific in beauty and brilliance. Metro-Goldwyn-Mayer brings you a quarter hour with the stars in music and song and dramatic highlight for the new success — *The Shopworn Angel* — starring Margaret Sullavan and James Stewart with Walter Pidgeon." He then introduces two musical pieces.

Medley of songs from the era of the film (1917) — Metro-Goldwyn-Mayer Orchestra under the direction of Edward Ward

"Let's Pretend It's True" (the film's theme) — Metro-Goldwyn-Mayer Orchestra under the direction of Edward Ward

Two scenes from the film are then played.

Bill (Stewart) and Daisy (Sullavan) in Central Park, talking and finding that they love each other.

Bill, Daisy and Sam (Pidgeon) discussing their strange situation.

One final song closes the show.

"Pack Up Your Troubles In Your Old Kit Bag (And Smile, Smile, Smile)" — M-G-M Orchestra, Chorus and the entire cast of the film with Edward Ward conducting

Let Freedom Ring

Let Freedom Ring was a 13-week series that aired between April 6 and June 29, 1948. Stewart appeared on the series' premiere. The subject of the first show was *The Fabulous Frontier, the Story of Steel*. The series was produced with the co-operation of the U.S. Chamber of Commerce.

Tuesday, April 6, 1948 (10:30-11 p.m.)

The show is not available for review.

Let's Talk Hollywood

Stewart appeared just once on this NBC show which served as the summer replacement for *The Jack Benny Show*. The show is not generally available, but is in the NBC Collection at the Library of Congress.

Sunday, July 4, 1948 (7-7:30 p.m.)

SPONSOR: Lucky Strikes

ANNOUNCER: Hy Averback

This quiz program was hosted by George Murphy, with Eddie Bracken and film columnist Edith Gwynn as regular panelists. On this, the very first show for the summer replacement for *The Jack Benny Program*, Jimmy Stewart and David Butler, a Warner Bros. director, were the guest panelists. The premise for the show was simple. Listeners would send in questions about movie stars and films and the panel would try its best to answer them. Those whose questions were used on the air would receive a prize of a five-year subscription to *Photoplay* and, if their question stumped the panel, they would receive a free movie pass good for one year at their favorite theater and an RCA-TV set with a one-year service agreement. If they didn't want the TV, they could take an RCA Crestwood radio-phono and $100 worth of RCA records instead. In addition, Lucky Strike would send thousands of its cigarettes to a Veterans Administration Hospital in the name of the winner.

The first question was from Cecil Wilson. Jimmy Stewart was not involved in answering any of the three parts, but since all three parts were answered correctly by the other panel members, Wilson did not win the big prize.

The next question came from Mrs. Earl O'Callahan. Each of the four panelists was given a card with some dialogue and the name of a famous star. The panelist was to read the dialogue in the style of the star. The others then had to identify the star. Butler was the first to go and Jimmy correctly guessed that he was doing Lauren Bacall. Gwynn is next and again Jimmy guesses correctly when he says that she was impersonating Edward G. Robinson. Eddie Bracken had to imitate Jimmy Stewart. Stewart didn't recognize himself, but Edith Gwynn did. Jimmy was the last to go and he had to impersonate Al Jolson. His impression wasn't that good, but when he sang a bit of "April Showers," his identity was guessed. Since all four were identified, O'Callahan was not a winner.

The third question was sent in by Louise Martin. This one required singing by Marion Morgan and piano playing by Harry Seutman. Gwynn answered the first part correctly. The second question was in three parts. Seutman played three different themes and the panelist had to identify what would be going on in the film when that type of music was played. Again, Gwynn answered the first part and was right. Jimmy answered the second part by saying, "Where the leading lady comes back to her lover or vice versa," which was considered the proper answer. Gwynn then gives the right answer for part three. For the third question, Morgan sang "By the Light of the Silvery Moon" and the panelists were asked to name the composer. Jimmy asks if they want "who's singing it or who wrote it?" After some clarification from Murphy, he says, "So the same fella who wrote it is singing it?" But, before he gets a chance to answer, Butler makes an accurate guess. For the third time in a row, there is no winner.

The next four-part question was sent in by Alona Lesley. This time, a statement from a film ad was given and the film's title had to be guessed. Gwynn and Bracken answer three of the four parts correctly, but Jimmy guesses "If You Were Mildred Pierce," which was not the right answer (the right answer was Nora Prentiss). Since none of the other panelists knew the answer either, Lesley was declared a winner.

Virginia Drake of Reading, PA, sent in the next question that involved identifying a film from the sound effects which was played. The panelists did not do well with this one at all, only getting two of the four parts right. One of the sound effects was three numbers being dialed on a rotary phone. Stewart guessed "Sorry, Wrong Number," which was wrong. He asked to hear the clue again and changed his answer to "Call Northside 777," one of his own films. This time he was right. On the next question, Stewart again asks to hear the sound effect a second time. This time a second listen doesn't help as he incorrectly guesses "Behind the Closed Door." The final sound effect was very long and complicated. Jimmy says, "Could you repeat that, please?" His question draws a good laugh from the audience, but not from the sound effects man. Drake became the show's second winner of the evening.

Ward Baker, the next questioner, wanted to know how some murders were committed in films. The first question was how they killed Charles Laughton in *The Big Clock*. Jimmy says, "You mean he got killed?" Murphy says, "Yes, but how?" Stewart's response is, "How'd they do that, David?" David didn't know and neither did anyone else, so Baker was already a winner. The next part was to explain how the killers planned to collect double indemnity in the film of the same name. Jimmy takes the long way around to get to the correct answer to this one. Everyone involved seemed to be confused.

> STEWART: Well, they killed him and then faked an accident…falling…
> MURPHY: Remember how?
> STEWART: Well, somebody…they faked a fella with a broken leg, with crutches on a…
> MURPHY: No…that's right…you're on the right track.
> STEWART: …and he was on a train and…ah…and then they killed the fella before-hand and they put him on the track…
> MURPHY: That's right!

The third part of the question wanted to know how Edward G. Robinson got away with a murder in *Woman in the Window*. This time Jimmy's answer was a little more direct and understandable when he said, "Oh, I know…because it was a dream." The final part of the question asked how Robert Taylor was killed in *Undercurrent*. Jimmy's "kicked in the head with [sic] a horse, wasn't he?" was judged a correct answer.

The final question of the evening was sent in by Andrew Gallison. The four-part question involved spirits in motion pictures. Stewart was only involved with the second question — in the film *Blithe Spirit*, they started with one spirit. How many spirits did it end with? Stewart said, "Two, isn't it?" This was the wrong answer, but Eddie Bracken knew it was three.

Louella Parsons

Louella Parsons wrote a Hollywood gossip column for the Hearst chain and her work appeared in more than 400 newspapers. She had the power to make or break a career and so performers seldom said no to her. On her various radio shows, she also dispensed Hollywood gossip to her listeners and had an occasional guest. Stewart's appearances on her program are not available for listening.

Parsons had also been the hostess of *Hollywood Hotel* and had talked with Stewart on that show. See that entry for more details.

Some newspapers referred to the show as the *Jergens-Woodbury Journal* or the *Woodbury Hollywood News*.

(1) Sunday, January 5, 1947 (9:15-9:30 p.m.)
NETWORK: ABC
SPONSOR: Jergens Lotion

(2) Sunday, February 6, 1949 (9:15-9:30 p.m.)
NETWORK: ABC
SPONSOR: Jergens Lotion

Luncheon with Maggi McNellis and Herb Sheldon

In June of 1948, Stewart was interviewed by Maggi McNellis (Maggi Newhouse). Jimmy had just finished work on Alfred Hitchcock's *Rope*, which was scheduled to be released by Warner Bros. in about two months on August 28. "Luncheon with Maggi and Herb," was heard Monday through Saturday via WJZ (ABC) in New York City. Newspaper listings from the time show that the program aired from 2:00-2:30 p.m. (1:00-1:30 p.m. on Saturday). Unfortunately, the listings do not include the names of the guests appearing on the show. The interview is not available for review.

Also see *Maggie's Private Wire*.

Lux Radio Theatre

Perhaps radio's premiere show of all time, *Lux Radio Theatre* was on the air from 1934 to 1955 and broadcast 927 shows. At first, the show adapted Broadway plays for its one-hour broadcasts, but then switched to films. As much as possible the stars of the original film were used in the radio adaptation. Often these stars were paid $5,000 to appear. Adding some authenticity to the show was the fact that Cecil B. DeMille himself served as host from June of 1936 until January 22, 1945. In 1943, *Lux* won the prestigious George Foster Peabody Award for Outstanding Entertainment in Drama. The Peabody Awards had first been presented in 1941 for shows broadcast during 1940. The awards were given for distinguished achievement and meritorious service by radio and television networks, stations, producing organizations and individuals. Stewart did not appear on the show during this award-winning year, due to previous commitments with the Army Air Corps. The *Lux Radio Theatre* was inducted into the Radio Hall of Fame in 1989. The show's famous opening line is "Lux…presents Hollywood."

SHOWS FEATURING JIMMY STEWART:

(1) Monday, June 14, 1937 — *Madame X* (9:00-10:00 p.m.)
NETWORK: CBS
SPONSOR: Lux Flakes
SEASON: Second
BROADCAST LOCATION: Music Box Theatre, Hollywood (called the Lux Radio Theatre in the show's opening)
PRODUCER/HOST: Cecil B. DeMille
DIRECTOR: Frank Woodruff
From the play *La Femme X* by Alexandre Bisson
ADAPTED FOR RADIO BY: John Raphael
ANNOUNCER: Melville Ruick
OPENING ANNOUNCER: Frank Nelson (also plays role of Harry in play)
COMMERCIAL SPOKESPERSONS: Hilda Heywood and Frank Coghlan, Jr.
Helen Wills Moody (Tennis player) — Intermission Guest (after Act 2)
Richard Mear & his Mother (a real-life Madame X) — Intermission Guests (after Act 3)
MUSICAL DIRECTOR: Lou Silvers
SOUND EFFECTS: Charles Forsyth
THEME MUSIC: "Lux Theatre Theme" (Robert Armbruster)
BETWEEN-THE-ACTS THEME: "Interlude" (Louis Silvers/Rudy Schrager)

Among the sound-effects people working for *Lux Radio Theatre* through the years were David Light, Walter Pierson, Max Uhlig and Charlie Forsyth.

In his introduction to the show, DeMille mentions that Jimmy was on the track team and studied architecture at Princeton. He also was a magician's assistant, but that there is no truth to the rumor that he became a lady killer by sawing a woman in half.

Young Raymond Cartwright (Jimmy Stewart) follows in his father Alan's footsteps by becoming a lawyer. Ray doesn't know that his mother is alive because his father had told him that she had died when he was very young. But, Jacqueline, his mother, is very much alive and living in San Francisco. Tony Phillips, her employer, has seen all the newspaper clippings she has carefully saved about Alan and Raymond. He calls a friend in New York City and has him check on the pair and finds out that Jackie is the wife and mother of the pair. He goes to New York with plans to blackmail them. Jackie follows and kills him.

She refuses to tell the police anything about her or the crime. She tells them her name is Laura Williams, but tells them it's not her real name. She is assigned a lawyer — Raymond Cartwright. She doesn't learn his name until just before the trial is set to begin.

At the trial, Alan and Sr. Chesney, a friend, see the woman for the first time and realize that it's Jacqueline. Ray's entire defense is based on the fact that she is remaining silent in order to protect someone close to her. He calls only one witness, Joe Harper. Harper testifies that Phillips had ask him to gather information on….but, before he can finish, Jackie breaks in and says that it is her son and husband that she is trying to protect. The jury acquits her.

The guest during the mid-break in the show was tennis champion Helen Wills Moody. She says that she is now designing clothes, painting, and has just finished a book, *15 to 30*. During the final break, a real-life Madame X and her son, Raymond, tell their story. At the show's end, DeMille talks to Ann Harding and Jimmy Stewart.

DEMILLE: Back to our microphone come Ann Harding and James Stewart, Giving us, among other things, a chance to learn from Miss Harding her impressions of the stage and screen in England.

HARDING: Well, I'm afraid I'm hardly the right person to ask about English pictures, Mr. DeMille. I did make a picture in England, but an American produced it, an American directed it and the cameraman was an American.

STEWART: Well, then, how about the English stage, Miss Harding?

HARDING: Ah, well now, it isn't safe to start me on that subject. Playing on the English stage was a marvelous experience.

DEMILLE: Isn't it rather strange that George Bernard Shaw's play *Candida* wasn't given a major production in London for 37 years? In fact, not till you went over to star in it.

HARDING: Well, I could hardly believe it when they told me that. It was pretty exciting to find that it was such a success. What have you been doing, Mr. Stewart? When I left Hollywood a year ago, everyone was talking about that amazing young actor who lived with Henry Fonda, owned 30 cats and played the accordion.

KEIGHLEY: We know Henry Fonda married, but what happened to the cats and the accordion?

STEWART: I don't know whatever attracted the cats in the first place, I don't know. They just seemed to come around. They haven't caught up with me yet. Every night I play the accordion to sort of discourage them.

KEIGHLEY: Are the neighbors in sympathy?

STEWART: Well, I...ah...I just ask them which they'd prefer, an accordion or a troop of 30 yeowing cats. I guess it's a case of the lesser of two evils.

KEIGHLEY: Well, what do they say to that?

STEWART: Well, sir, I hardly ever get a civil answer. But, Mr. DeMille, I meant to ask you about this. In case you need an accordion player for *The Buccaneer*, you remember Stewart's name.

KEIGHLEY: Thanks, Jimmy, but after all, even a pirate can endure just so much. Good night, Jimmy, you're a very remarkable fellow.

The show's cast consisted of:

Jimmy Stewart	*Raymond Cartwright*
Ann Harding	*Jacqueline Cartwright*
Conway Tearle	*Alan Cartwright*
Wheaton Chambers	*Dr. Perry Chesney*
Leora Thatcher	*Bessie*
Joe DuVal	*Dean*
Edward Marr	*Tony Phillips*
David Kerman	*Nick*
Lou Merrill	*Keene*
Forrest Taylor	*Murphy*
I. Stanford Jolley	*First judge (Gerald M. Desseck)*
Galan Galt	*Stone*
Frank Nelson	*Harry*
Victor Rodman	*Joe Harper*
Marjorie Norton	*Myrtle*
Ross Forrester	*Flynn*
Justina Wayne	*woman*
Gil Patric	*man*

Madame X can be found on *Lux Classics Presents the Best of Lux Radio Theatre* (Radio Spirits 40162), a 10-CD set released in 2006 and *Vintage Radio Collection Jimmy Stewart* (Stardust) a special downloadable set made available in 2008.

(2) Monday, February 10, 1941 — *The Moon's Our Home* (9:00-10:00 p.m.)

NETWORK: CBS
SPONSOR: Lux Flakes
SEASON: Sixth

BROADCAST LOCATION: Music Box Theatre, Hollywood
PRODUCER/HOST: Cecil B. DeMille
DIRECTOR: Sanford H. Barnett
ADAPTED FOR RADIO BY: George Wells
Based on the screenplay by Isabel Dawn and Boyce DeGaw, based on the Faith Baldwin novel
ANNOUNCER: Melville Ruick
COMMERCIAL SPOKESPERSONS: Julie Bannon and Duane Thompson
MUSICAL DIRECTOR: Lou Silvers
SOUND EFFECTS: Charles Forsyth
THEME MUSIC: "Lux Theatre Theme" (Robert Armbruster)
BETWEEN-THE-ACTS THEME: "Interlude" (Louis Silvers/Rudy Schrager)

The story opens with movie star Cherry Chester and Boyce arguing over whether or not they are going to go to New York City to visit Cherry's grandmother, Lucy. When a telegram arrives saying that Lucy is ill, the argument stops and they head for the train station. There's a large crowd at the train station, but they aren't there to see Cherry. Instead, they want to see famous author/explorer Anthony Amberton (Jimmy Stewart).

Cherry is not fond of his type and he's not fond of hers. When they arrive in New York there's another crowd waiting for the train. This time they are there to see Cherry, not Amberton.

In New York, Cherry finds that her grandmother is not ill. She just pretended so that Cherry would come. Her grandmother wants her to marry Horace, her third cousin. She doesn't want any part of it and leaves in a carriage to get away from everything. Anthony, who's in the middle of a book signing, has also had enough and runs out and begs a ride in her carriage. They find out that they both want to be left alone. Neither knows who the other is. He gives her a card and asks her to meet her there in Moonsocket, New Hampshire.

They both wind up at Simpson's in Moonsocket. They are registered under their real names — Sara Brown and Samuel Smith. They fall in love and are married by a Justice of the Peace. But, there's a problem; she has on Cherry Blossom perfume and it makes him sick. She thinks he's trying to get rid of her and goes back to New York. Once in New York, her grandmother again pushes for her to marry Horace. Cherry tells her that she's already married. That doesn't stop her grandmother. There's to be a party at Horace's club where the engagement will be announced. Horace invites one of his friends, Anthony Amberton. When they meet, Sam explains that the perfume really does make him sick and all seems well. But then they find out each other's other identity. Several misunderstandings and arguments later, all ends well.

During the closing, Jimmy and Carole Lombard are interviewed by DeMille.

DEMILLE: Once more the spotlight turns to Carole Lombard and Jimmy Stewart as they come back to this microphone.

STEWART: Thank you, Mr. DeMille. You know the thing I like about the *Lux Radio Theater* is the way everything runs so perfectly, never a miss anywhere.

LOMBARD: Say, you're not going to play the accordion now are you, Jimmy?

STEWART: Oh, no…I didn't bring it tonight. I…ah…should have been applause there. No…ah…this is no place for my accordion. Why even the boys and girls that collect autographs at the door won't take just anything. For instance, there was that girl who stopped me on the way in tonight.

DEMILLE: You…ah…you surely didn't disappoint her, Jimmy.

STEWART: Oh no, I signed. And then, I asked her what she was going to do with it and she said, "Well, if I can get Carole Lombard when the show's over, why…ah…I know where I can trade both of you for Clark Gable."

LOMBARD: I'll have to speak to her; she can't make a bad bargain like that.

STEWART: Oh, now be polite, Carole…I might have to take back my autograph.

LOMBARD: Seriously, Mr. DeMille, I have enjoyed very much coming back to *Lux Radio Theater*. In the past few months I think you've really taken on a new assignment here. All entertainment is a premium now and anything that lifts us out of the everyday routine for an hour or so is what we need at a time like this. America must be strong and we must keep it free by making it stronger still. While we're all working toward that end to the limit of our strength, we need the emotional outlet that a theater like this provides.

DEMILLE: Let me show you a little of our mail sometime, Carole, and you'll understand why we think of this as a national theater.

STEWART: Well, what's going on it next week, Mr. DeMille?

DEMILLE: (Tells of next week's show and stars)

STEWART: Well, that's a great story, Mr. DeMille, and you have a swell cast. Goodnight.

LOMBARD: Goodnight.

It is also announced that Stewart can currently be seen in the M-G-M production *Come Live With Me*.

The cast included:

Jimmy Stewart	Anthony Amberton/Samuel Smith
Carole Lombard	Cherry Chester/Sara Brown
Clara Blandick	Lucy
Verna Felton	Boyce (also does a public service announcement for War Bonds)
Hans Conried	Horace
Lou Merrill	Holbrook
Charles Seel	Justice of the Peace/Conductor
Rolfe Sedan	Abner
Stanley Farrar	Higgins, a coachman/Cop
Gloria Blondell	Hilda
James Eagles	Hotel Clerk/Newsboy
Jack Carr	Porter
Celeste Rush	Miss Manning
Noreen Gammill	Mrs. Simpson

The show is available on two different mp3 only sets: *Vintage Radio Collection Jimmy Stewart* (Stardust, 2008), and *Jimmy Stewart the Ultimate Radio Collection* (Master Classics Records, 2011).

(3) Monday, July 20, 1942 — *The Philadelphia Story* (9:00-10:00 p.m.)
NETWORK: CBS
SPONSOR: The United States Government
SEASON: Between 7th and 8th
PRODUCER/HOST: Cecil B. DeMille
DIRECTOR: Sanford H. Barnett
ADAPTED FOR RADIO BY: George Wells
Based on the screenplay by Donald Ogden Stewart, based on the Philip Barry play.
ANNOUNCER: John Milton Kennedy
MUSICAL DIRECTOR: Lou Silvers
SOUND EFFECTS: Charles Forsyth
THEME MUSIC: "Lux Theatre Theme" (Robert Armbruster)
BETWEEN-THE-ACTS THEME: "Interlude" (Louis Silvers/Rudy Schrager)
This is actually the first program from *Victory Theater*, a summer replacement in 1942 for the *Lux Radio Theatre* but, because it is a Lux production,

is included here. At the beginning of the show, this announcement was made, "The United States of America presents *The Victory Theatre*." Mr. DeMille says:

> This is a great moment in the American theater. The opening night of a great new Theater, dedicated to those principles for which people are now fighting on the battlefields of the world; dedicated above all to victory. Each Monday night, a popular Columbia Network program will donate an extra performance in the service of the United States. Speaking for the sponsor and staff of our Theater, which you've heard on Mondays at this same time for many years, and speaking for myself, we are highly honored that the government has asked us to produce this first program.

DeMille adds, "Incidentally, we used to borrow Jimmy Stewart from his picture studio. Tonight, he was assigned to us by Uncle Sam. As you know, he's now a lieutenant in the United States Army Air Forces."

Tracy Lord is about to be married to George, her second husband, and *Spy* magazine wants the story and pictures. Mike Connor (Jimmy Stewart) is to write the article and Elizabeth Imbrie will take the photos. To make sure they get into the wedding, C.K. Dexter Haven, Tracy's first husband, is also on hand. Dexter tries to pass them off as friends of Tracy's brother Junius, but she doesn't fall for it and figures out that they are from *Spy*. Dexter uses blackmail to force her into letting them cover the wedding. He tells her that the *Spy* has a story and photos of her father with a New York dancer. Mike would later give Dexter some dirt on the *Spy*'s editor that he can use to stop the story from ever being run.

Mike and Tracy begin to fall for each other. While swimming, she gets very drunk and passes out. Mike carries her to her room. Dexter and George see this and jump to the wrong conclusions. (Jimmy Stewart, not known for his singing voice, sings a bit of "Over the Rainbow" during this scene.)

During a break in the show, cast member Verna Felton appears in an ad for War Bonds.

On her wedding day, George announces that he won't marry her. Mike proposes, but she turns him down. But, he can be the best man as Tracy marries Dexter.

Stewart, Grant and Hepburn, along with Ruth Hussey and Virginia Weidler, are all cast in their original film roles.

At show's end, DeMille talks to the stars of the play and has this short conversation with Jimmy Stewart.

DEMILLE: Jimmy Stew...I mean Lt. Stewart, what's your personal slant on our part in the war?

STEWART: Well, sir, in the Army, we'd like to see everyone stop criticizing our Allies in England. So the next time, stop before you talk and ask yourself, what have I done that gives me the right to criticize people who have fought for three years as bravely as England?

DEMILLE: You wouldn't have to bring that up, Jimmy, if everyone realized that, above all, the enemy wants to see our side divided.

Later, after all the other main stars have spoken, Jimmy adds:

STEWART: It's been a very great privilege for me to have a part on the first *Victory Theater* program, Mr. DeMille. Goodnight.

The cast included:
> Jimmy Stewart.. Mike Conner
> Katharine Hepburn.. Tracy Lord
> Cary Grant.. C.K. Dexter Haven
> Ruth Hussey .... Elizabeth Imbrie
> Virginia Weidler .... Dinah Lord
> Nicholas Joy .... Seth Lord
> Janet Beecher.. Margaret
> Gale Gordon .... George Kittredge
> Verna Felton .... Librarian
> Sandra Coles.. Mother
> Leo Cleary, Charles Seel, Norman Field, Bruce Payne

This show was issued in mp3 only format in 2001 by Master Classics Records on *Jimmy Stewart the Ultimate Radio Collection Vol. 1*.

(4) Monday, November 5, 1945 — *Destry Rides Again* (9:00-10:00 p.m.)
NETWORK: CBS
SPONSOR: Lux
SEASON: 11th
BROADCAST LOCATION: Vine Street Playhouse, Hollywood
PRODUCER/HOST: William Keighley (his first show as the permanent new host)
DIRECTOR: Fredric MacKaye
ADAPTED FOR RADIO BY: Sanford H. Barnett

Based on the screenplay by Felix Jackson, Gertrude Purcell, and Henry Myers, based on a novel by Max Brand

ANNOUNCER: John Milton Kennedy
SECOND ANNOUNCER: Thomas Hanlon
COMMERCIAL SPOKESWOMEN: Doris Singleton (as Libby) and Truda Marson (as Merle Oberon)
INTERMISSION GUEST: Nancy Gates, RKO starlet
MUSICAL DIRECTOR: Louis Silvers
SOUND EFFECTS: Charles Forsyth
THEME MUSIC: "Lux Theatre Theme" (Robert Armbruster)
BETWEEN-THE-ACTS THEME: "Interlude" (Louis Silvers/Rudy Schrager)

The Sheriff of Bottleneck has just been killed and the mayor wants to name Wash Dimsdale, the town drunk, as the new sheriff. Wash had been a deputy for Tom Destry years before and now plans on getting his son, also named Tom, to come be his deputy. Tom has some trouble getting any respect when he says that he doesn't carry a gun. When Tom has a run-in with Bugsy, he asks to see Bugsy's gun. He uses the gun to shoot several small knobs off a sign down the street. That somewhat calms things down and earns him a little respect.

Johnny Kent, who runs the town's saloon, has won the Claggett ranch in a crooked card game. All the cattle in the area have to pass across the Claggett ranch too and Kent plans on charging ranchers 25¢ per head to pass. Claggett and his wife are trying to prevent him from taking over the ranch. When Wash and Tom arrive, Kent shows Tom the paper that Claggett had signed and everything looks legal. Tom tells the Claggetts that they will have to leave, but adds that if Sam can prove he was cheated, he will get the ranch back. Sam tells Tom that Frenchy, who works for Kent, spilled coffee in his lap and while he was getting cleaned up, his cards were switched. Tom lets Frenchy know that he knows that she is part of the problem.

Tom makes Kent think that he knows where Sheriff Watson's body is and Kent sends Gyp Miller to check. Gyp is caught with the body and is arrested for murder. Frenchy gets Tom to her room and tells him that she is planning on leaving town and going back to New Orleans. While Tom's there, Kent and his men break Gyp out of jail and kill Wash. Kent and his men are held up in the saloon and Tom and the men of the town are set to shoot it out with them. Frenchy organizes the women and they march down the street between the two groups of men. Everyone is captured except Kent. Tom goes in after him and kills him, but not before Kent kills Frenchy.

At the end of the show the following conversation takes place.

KEIGHLEY: With that well-deserved applause, our thanks to Jimmy Stewart and Joan Blondell who come to the footlights for their curtain call. And Jimmy, I hardly need to say how happy we are to welcome you back to the *Radio Theater*.
STEWART: Well, thank you, Bill, and I'm mighty glad you had Joan Blondell in the receiving line.
BLONDELL: And we're happy to hear that the welcome mat is out for you, too, Bill.
STEWART: I'd say you have everything it takes, Bill. You've been an actor, director and producer. I don't know of anyone in Hollywood who's better fitted for the job.
KEIGHLEY: Well, thanks for the kind words, both of you.
STEWART: Goodnight.
BLONDELL: Goodnight, Bill.
KEIGHLEY: Goodnight, and come back again soon.

The cast included:

Jimmy Stewart	Tom Destry (in his original film role)
Joan Blondell	Frenchy
Frances Robinson	Janice Tindall
Leo Cleary	Washington "Wash" Dinsdale
Ken Christy	Mayor Slade
Noreen Gammill	Lily Belle
Tommy Cook	Eli Whitney Claggett
Charles Seel	Sam Claggett/Turner
Dorothy Scott	Mrs. Claggett
Joe DuVal	Gyp Hiller
Ruby Dandridge	Clara
Tyler McVey	Creepy
Franklyn Parker	Bugsy
Doris Singleton	Frenchy's singing voice (and Libby, in commercials)

A rehearsal of this show, probably recorded November 4, also exists. The main difference between this and the show as aired occurs at the beginning and end. At the beginning of the rehearsal, William Keighley is introduced as the new regular producer and host of *Lux Radio Theatre*. Keighley then says how happy he is to welcome back Jimmy Stewart after a nearly five-year absence. The rehearsal itself goes very well. One noticeable mistake takes place at the beginning of act two when Keighley begins his announcement a little too early over the music. After a few seconds, a voice says "now" and Keighley begins his introduction again. Stewart himself makes a mistake at about the 41:30 mark of the rehearsal when he says "Federal John" and then quickly corrects John to Judge. This seems to throw off his concentration and he makes several other small mistakes over the next minute or two. He also reads, rather than acts, several of his lines.

At the end of the rehearsal, Jimmy, Joan Blondell, and Keighley do a public service announcement for War Bonds. On the night of the broadcast, the play evidently went a little long and the War Bond announcement had to be dropped.

KEIGHLEY: With that well-deserved applause our thanks to Jimmy Stewart and Joan Blondell who come to the footlights for their curtain call. And, Jimmy, I hardly need say how happy we are to welcome you back to the *Lux Radio Theatre*.

STEWART: Thank you, Bill, and I'm mighty glad you had Joan Blondell on the receiving line.

BLONDELL: And we're happy to hear that the welcome mat is out for you, too, Bill, as the regular producer of the *Lux Radio Theatre*.

KEIGHLEY: Well, I'm looking forward to the job, Joan. Right now it seems a big responsibility.

STEWART: I'd say you have everything it takes, Bill. You've been an actor, director and producer. I don't know anyone in Hollywood who's better fitted for the job.

KEIGHLEY: Well, thanks for the kind words, both of you. And I'm happy to see from that smooth complexion, Joan, that you've been faithful to the real producers of this theater, Lux Toilet Soap.

BLONDELL: I've always used Lux Toilet Soap and its wonderful complexion care.

STEWART: What's Lux producing next week, Bill?

KEIGHLEY: (Tells of next week's show)

STEWART: Well, *Guest in the House* should fill the house, Bill, congratulations.

KEIGHLEY: And while we're reminding our listeners to join us, there's another important reminder for this coming week.

STEWART: You mean a little matter of…ah…11 billion dollars, Bill, huh?

BLONDELL: A little matter of 11 billion dollars?

KEIGHLEY: Well, it depends on how you look at it. Eleven billion dollars is a lot of money, of course, but it's little when compared to the debt America owes to the men who fought and won the war.

BLONDELL: I guess you're right, Bill, and America was never a country to welch on debts.

STEWART: Of course, a lot of people may feel that, with the war over, there's no need to go on buying bonds. They feel that the job is done so the debt stops. And yet the job isn't done for thousands of men we're leaving overseas to keep the peace while we enjoy it. They're counting on us for food and shelter and supplies...

BLONDELL: And how about the cost of bringing so many thousands of our troops home?

STEWART: Well, just about the biggest, costliest transportation move in history. When we've got them home, another job begins. And we... we've been calling it rehabilitation. What it really means is that giving those men a break. Give them a chance to learn a trade, get an education, everything that was promised them while they were fighting.

KEIGHLEY: And, of course, some of those boys we'll never be able to repay.

STEWART: No, I'm afraid not. Oh, we can never repay the men who died in this war, but we can see that their families are cared for. And we can see that thousands of wounded in our hospitals will have the best medical care and the best possible chance to get back on their feet again.

BLONDELL: You know they're having a bond drive in Canada, too, and with many of these same purposes in mind.

KEIGHLEY: That's right, Joan. And in both countries, bonds are the safest and best investment you can find. How else, in the United States, can you get four dollars back for three and guarantee your future and your country's future at the same time? You know, if everybody in our audience tonight were to buy one extra $100 war bond this week, we'd have more than a quarter of the total loan subscribed.

STEWART: Well, that's quite a challenge to your audience, Bill. Or perhaps I should say quite an opportunity. Now, here's hoping with all our hearts they take it. Goodnight.

BLONDELL: Goodnight, Bill.

KEIGHLEY: Goodnight. Come back again soon.

The broadcast show has been released as *AMC Movies to Go: She Wore a Yellow Ribbon/Destry Rides Again* (AMC 51498) in 1999. The 2-cassette set was issued by American Movie Classics with the radio shows being provided by Radio Spirits. AMC's Jeffrey Lyons introduces the show and then returns after the show with some biographical information about Stewart. Lyons tells how Stewart met Joshua Logan while studying architecture at Princeton University. Later, Stewart, Logan, Henry Fonda and Margaret Sullavan joined a summer stock troop in Falmouth, MA. Later, Hedda Hopper was instrumental in getting Jimmy his screen test for M-G-M.

The show can also be found on the 3-CD set, *The Best of The West* (Radio Spirits 40152, 2006).

It has also been issued on two different mp3 only sets: *Vintage Radio Collection Jimmy Stewart* (Stardust, 2008), and *Jimmy Stewart the Ultimate Radio Collection Vol. 3* (Master Classics Records, 2011).

(5) Monday, December 17, 1945 — *Made for Each Other* (9:00-10:00 p.m.)
NETWORK: CBS
SPONSOR: Lux
SEASON: 11th
BROADCAST LOCATION: Vine Street Playhouse, Hollywood
PRODUCER/HOST: William Keighley
DIRECTOR: Fredric MacKaye
ADAPTED FOR RADIO BY: Sanford H. Barnett
Based on the screenplay by Jo Swerling, from a story suggested by Rose Franken
ANNOUNCER: John Milton Kennedy
SECOND ANNOUNCER: Thomas Hanlon
INTERMISSION GUEST: Jane Nigh, 20th Century-Fox starlet
COMMERCIAL SPOKESWOMEN: Julie Bannon (as Julie), Helen Andrews (as housewife), Betty Jean Hainey (as girl), Vivian Carter (as Nancy), Beverly Brown (as Betty)
MUSICAL DIRECTOR: Louis Silvers
SOUND EFFECTS: Charles Forsyth
THEME MUSIC: "Lux Theatre Theme" (Robert Armbruster)
BETWEEN-THE-ACTS THEME: "Interlude" (Louis Silvers/Rudy Schrager)
While in Boston taking a deposition for a case he is handling for his law firm, Johnny Mason meets, courts and marries Jane. Upon their return to New York, he asks his boss, Judge Doolittle, for a month off so that he and Jane can take a cruise to Bermuda. The Judge gives him 10 days. But, before their ship can sail, Carter from the office comes and tells them that they must get off the ship. Johnny's case, Higgins against Higgins,

is set to go to trial the next week. Johnny wins the case, but instead of being made a junior partner in the firm as he had expected, Carter gets the promotion.

When a son is born to Johnny and Jane, Judge Doolittle sends $10 as a gift. Jane thinks that Doolittle is taking Johnny for granted and insists that he ask for a raise. But before he gets a chance to ask, Doolittle tells him that things are tight and asks him to take a 25% pay cut.

Marsha Hunt and Jimmy Stewart delivering their lines at the Lux–CBS microphone.

The baby develops pneumonia and is near death in the hospital. There is a serum that will cure him, but it has to come from Salt Lake City and storms there are keeping all planes on the ground. Johnny finally finds a pilot, Conway, who is willing to make the flight, but he wants $5,000 to do so. Johnny goes to Doolittle and he agrees to advance the money. When they don't hear from Conway for hours, they lose hope. But Conway does make it through and Doolittle himself drives the serum to the hospital in time to save the baby. Johnny and Jane get a gift from Doolittle, too.

The intermission guest after the first act was Jane Nigh, who was currently in the 20th Century-Fox production of *State Fair*.

The post-performance conversation this evening began with William Keighley introducing the stars.

KEIGHLEY: Once more the spotlight turns on Jimmy Stewart and Marsha Hunt as they come back to the microphone for a well-deserved curtain call.
STEWART: Thank you, Bill.
KEIGHLEY: Jimmy, I understand that as soon as this program's over, you're packing to go home for Christmas.
STEWART: That's right, Bill, back to Pennsylvania...town where I was born and raised.
KEIGHLEY: How about you, Marsha, what's your hometown?
HUNT: Well, I was born in Chicago and raised in New York. I guess I'm strictly a city girl.
KEIGHLEY: Well, I can back you both up. I come from Pennsylvania and from the city...Philadelphia.
HUNT: Did you get your start in acting there, Mr. Keighley?
KEIGHLEY: Yes, our football team needed uniforms so we put on a play. I was 16 and played an old man of 60. I must have been pretty awful. You started your acting career in high school, didn't you, Jim?
STEWART: That's right, Bill. The senior class was having what they call *The Comedy* each year.
HUNT: Was that pretty high-class humor, Jim?
STEWART: Oh, yeah, yeah. Well, as I remember, one line in which an old henpecked character says to his wife...he says...ah..."Oh how I miss the old spittoon now that it's gone."
KEIGHLEY: And she says...ah...
STEWART: She says...she says, "You've always missed it. That's why it's gone."
KEIGHLEY: (laughing) Well, that answers Marsha's question.
HUNT: And a question for you now, Mr. Keighley. What is Lux presenting next week in this theater?
KEIGHLEY: (talks about the following week's play and stars)
STEWART: Well, it oughta make a great play for you, Bill. Goodnight.
HUNT: Goodnight.
KEIGHLEY: Goodnight and happy holidays.

It is also announced that Jimmy Stewart will next be seen in Liberty Film's Frank Capra production, *It's a Wonderful Life*.

The cast consisted of:

Jimmy Stewart....	Johnny Mason (a reprise of his film role)
Marsha Hunt	Jane Mason
Verna Felton	Mrs. Mason
Lou Merrill	Judge Doolittle
Guy Kingsford	Carter/Denver
Kathleen Fitz	Eunice Doolittle/2nd Nurse
Griff Barnett	Dr. Healy
Eddie Marr	Allentown/Boy
Ernestine Wade	Annie
Tyler McVey	Conway/Man
Ed Emerson	Hatton/Waiter
Alexander Gerry	Simon the Butler/Man
Dorothy Scott	3rd Nurse
Leone Le Doux	Baby Cry/Girl

Two *Lux Radio Theatre* shows are available on the 6-CD/4-cassette set, *The Best of Old Time Radio Starring Jimmy Stewart* (Radio Spirits 5035 (CDs)/5034 (cassettes), released in 2002. Found on this source are (cassettes are marked SJSC and CDs are SJSD; both are followed by the number of the cassette or CD on which the show appears): *Made for Each Other* (SJSC3/SJSD4), *Winchester '73* (SJSC2/SJSD3).

Radio Spirits also issued this show as an audiobook, *Made for Each Other: Classic Movies on the Radio*, in 2003.

(6) Monday, March 10, 1947 — *It's a Wonderful Life* (9:00-10:00 p.m.)
NETWORK: CBS
SPONSOR: Lux
SEASON: 12th
BROADCAST LOCATION: Vine Street Playhouse, Hollywood
PRODUCER/HOST: William Keighley
DIRECTOR: Fredric MacKaye
ADAPTED FOR RADIO BY: Sanford H. Barnett from a story, *The Greatest Gift* by Philip Van Doren Stern
Based on the screenplay by Frances Goodrich, Albert Hackett, Frank Capra, Jo Swerling and Michael Wilson
ANNOUNCER: John Milton Kennedy
COMMERCIAL SPOKESWOMAN: Doris Singleton (as Libby)
INTERMISSION GUEST: Susan Blanchard, 20th Century-Fox starlet
MUSICAL DIRECTOR: Louis Silvers

SOUND EFFECTS: Charles Forsyth
THEME MUSIC: "Lux Theatre Theme" (Robert Armbruster)
BETWEEN-THE-ACTS THEME: "Interlude" (Louis Silvers/Rudy Schrager)

Joseph, the Superintendent of Angels, is filling Clarence Oddbody, Angel Second Class, in on the life of George Bailey so that Clarence can help him. Saving his brother's life, preventing Mr. Gower from filing a prescription with poison, and meeting Mary Hatch are all skipped over very quickly (however, we do hear a bit of Stewart and Reed singing "Buffalo Gals"). Clarence learns that George's trip to Europe was cancelled because of his father's death and how Harry went to college on the money meant for George when George took over the Savings and Loan. He watched as George and Mary were married and then prevented from going on their honeymoon by a run on the Savings and Loan; a run which they stopped by using their honeymoon money. He listened as Uncle Billy lost $8,000 meant to pay a loan and to see a very distraught George Bailey find out that he was worth more dead than alive.

With George Bailey standing on a bridge thinking about committing suicide, it was finally time for Clarence to leap into action. And jump he did, right into the river. George jumped in and saved him, which was Clarence's plan from the beginning. George tells Clarence that he wishes he had never been born. Clarence makes it so and then takes George on a tour of Bedford Falls to show him what it would be like if he had never been born. George doesn't like what he sees and asks Clarence to be alive again. Back at home, Mary shows George a basket full of money that the townspeople have donated. He has the $8,000 he needs. And as Zuzu hangs her tinkling bell on the Christmas tree, Clarence gets his wings.

The intermission guest, appearing after the second act, was the up-and-coming 20th Century-Fox star, Susan Blanchard.

At the end of the show, Keighley talks with all three main stars.

KEIGHLEY: It's a wonderful life so long as we can have such fine performances as we enjoyed tonight from Jimmy Stewart, Donna Reed and Victor Moore. Jimmy, I'd like to thank whatever guardian angel whisked you back from Texas for our show this evening.

STEWART: Well, that guardian angel was an airlines wing…ah…Bill.

REED: You were in Texas for the premiere of this picture, weren't you, Jimmy?

STEWART: Yeah, Frank Capra and I went down for five openings in as many nights; pretty good down there in Texas.

KEIGHLEY: All of them in Texas, Jimmy?

STEWART: Yeah, every one of them. There were five premieres over Texas…you know it's a pretty big state…it takes that many to do it.

KEIGHLEY: Jimmy, I'm sure your fans were proud to read that you received an honorary degree from Princeton just the other week.

REED: Yes, how about that, Jimmy. Do we call you professor now?

STEWART: No…No…No…No, it's just an M.A.

KEIGHLEY: Master of Arts?

STEWART: Well, I…it might have been. It might be for Murdering Architecture — that's what I studied at Princeton.

KEIGHLEY: Well, you know, Donna has an honorary degree to her credit, too. LLC.

MOORE: What's that, Bill?

KEIGHLEY: LLC? Well, you can see for yourself…a lovely Lux complexion.

REED: Well, thank you, Bill. Or, should I thank Lux toilet soap? It's a wonderful complexion care. I use it faithfully.

KEIGHLEY: With wonderful results, I see.

STEWART: What's happening next Monday night on Lux, Bill?

KEIGHLEY: *(Talks about next week's show and stars.)*

MOORE: Now that ought to make great listening, Bill.

REED: I wouldn't miss it for anything.

STEWART/REED/MOORE: Goodnight.

KEIGHLEY: Goodnight and thanks a million.

It's also announced that Jimmy will soon be seen in RKO's *Magic Town*. The cast included:

Jimmy Stewart	*George Bailey*
Donna Reed	*Mary Hatch*
Victor Moore	*Clarence Oddbody*
Bill Johnstone	*Mr. Bailey*
John McIntire	*Joseph*
Leo Cleary	*Uncle Billy*
Edwin Maxwell	*Potter*
Janet Scott	*Mother*
Noreen Gammill	*voice of Mary's mother*
Cliff Clark	*Man*
Norma Jean Nilsson	*Baby*

Eddie Marr, Norman Field, Franklyn Parker, Ann Carter, Charles Seel

Stewart and Reed are in their original film roles.

By far one of the most popular of Stewart films and radio shows; this one has been legitimately released more than any of his other radio shows. It has been released as a single cassette (Radio Spirits 4159) and CD (Radio Spirits 7012) in 2000.

The show was released in a normal CD case which, in turn, was packaged in a cardboard case. The same CD, minus the cardboard case, was

Stewart, Donna Reed and Victor Moore check over the script for the show."

also issued as one of the three CDs in the *Favorite Holiday Stories* set.

The show was also issued as part of a 2-cassette set.

AMC Audio Movies to Go: It's a Wonderful Life/The Miracle of the Bells (AMC 60144) in 1999.

AMC's Jeffrey Lyons introduces the show and then returns after the show with some interesting historical information about the film. According to Lyons, the story had its beginnings in 1939 when author Philip Van Doren Stern wrote a two-page outline for a story he called *The Greatest Gift*. He had 200 copies printed and used them as Christmas cards to his family and friends. Somehow, actor Cary Grant came into possession of one of the cards and took it to RKO. They bought the film rights for $10,000. Grant was set to star in the film, but after several failed attempts at a screenplay, they sold the rights to Frank Capra and Liberty Films. Right from the start, Capra wanted Stewart in the film, but his first choice for the female lead was Jean Arthur. When she couldn't commit, Ginger Rogers and Olivia de Havilland were considered. The part finally went to Donna Reed. Filming was begun on April 16, 1946, and it premiered at New York's Globe Theater on December 20, 1946. Although the film was a critical success, garnering five Academy Award nominations, it wasn't a huge success with moviegoers. Then, in 1974, the copyright holder failed to renew and the film entered into public domain. Many television stations began to show the film because they didn't have to pay any royalties. It wasn't long before the film gained classic status.

The show can be found on *Favorite Holiday Stories*, a 3-CD set (Radio Spirits 48212), *Hollywood Stars on Radio* (Radio Spirits 40022 [CD]/40024 [cassette]) released in 2003, *Old Time Radio Dramas* (The Mind's Eye), released in 1984, *Old Time Radio Shows* (Metacom) (Adventures in Cassettes) 9133J130/AB130), a 6-cassette set released in 1998, and *Radio's Greatest Christmas Shows* (Radio Spirits 47122), a 10-CD set issued in 2003. It has also been issued several times as a single cassette. One release was on Mind's Eye (0-88142-271-1) in 1984, on the "Voices of Hollywood" series from Radio Yesterdays (Volume 8) in 1991 and *It's a Wonderful Life* from J.C. Entertainment Company (JCC-112) in 1997.

It has also been issued in mp3 only format several times. In 2008, it was released on *The Best of Classic Christmas Radio Shows* (Stardust Records).

In 2010, Gargoyle Productions issued it as a solo item.

Also in 2010, it was issued by Orange Leisure.

The show's popularity transcended continents. In 2008, British newspapers, The *Daily Telegraph* and The *Sunday Telegraph*, offered a series of seven Lux shows featuring famous film stars to their readers. One of those shows was this one.

(7) Monday, December 15, 1947 — *Magic Town* (9:00-10:00 p.m.)
NETWORK: CBS
SPONSOR: Lux Flakes
SEASON: 13th
BROADCAST LOCATION: Vine Street Playhouse, Hollywood
PRODUCER/HOST: William Keighley
DIRECTOR: Fredric MacKaye
ADAPTED FOR RADIO BY: Sanford H. Barnett
Based on the screenplay by Robert Riskin and Joseph Krumgold
ANNOUNCER: John Milton Kennedy
COMMERCIAL SPOKESWOMAN: Dorothy Lovett, as Libby
INTERMISSION GUEST: Martha Hyer, new RKO star

MUSICAL DIRECTOR: Louis Silvers
SOUND EFFECTS: Charles Forsyth
THEME MUSIC: "Lux Theatre Theme" (Robert Armbruster)
BETWEEN-THE-ACTS THEME: "Interlude" (Louis Silvers/Rudy Schrager)

Rip's (Jimmy Stewart) public opinion poll business is about to go under — taking polls is too expensive. He's looking for a shortcut. His friend, Hoopendecker, finds the perfect town. He's living there now, teaching high school and coaching basketball. Grand View perfectly matches the normal, average U.S. town.

Rip and his team move there and set themselves up as an insurance agency. That way they can talk to people and get their opinions, without anyone knowing what they are doing. Rip is even going to help coach the basketball team. There is a problem. Mary Peterman is trying to talk the town into building a new civic center. The center would attract new people and businesses to Grand View and probably ruin the town for Rip. So, Rip talks them out of it.

Their first poll is on progressive education. When it's finished, Ike takes the results back to New York. Their results perfectly match the results of a much more expensive and time-consuming poll. When Ike calls Rip to let him know, Mary overhears. She also finds some of the survey papers in the office. She writes a front page story exposing Rip and his crew. Rip begs her not to print it. He warns her that it will change the town. She prints it anyhow.

Hundreds of people and businesses pour into the "typical American town." The mayor now plans for the town to take its own polls and sell the results. But, when they take a poll on how the average person feels about a woman president, they are completely opposite from another nationwide poll. A great exodus begins and soon all the newcomers and most of the town's money are gone. Rip comes back to try to save Grand View. He and Mary put out a story about how the town, broken as it is, will build a civic center, even if they have to build it themselves. The story gets national attention and the mayor and people of the town get their confidence back and decide to go ahead with the plan.

Host Bill Keighley was on the show that night, but from Washington, DC, not Hollywood, but he still talked with the stars after the show.

KEIGHLEY: If Rip Smith could poll you listeners on their reaction to tonight's *Lux Radio Theater* play, I'm sure he'd get enthusiastic answers. Thanks to the good work of our stars, Jimmy Stewart and Jane Wyman. I only wish that I could have been there to have watched you two in person.

STEWART: Well, we certainly missed you, Bill. It seems strange to see that producer's chair unoccupied.

KEIGHLEY: Well, thanks, Jimmy, but I don't know any way in which I could have added to your performance.

WYMAN: You say that you just started your new picture, Bill, *The Street with No Name*.

KEIGHLEY: Yes, we spent the day at the F.B.I. Academy in Quantico, getting some authentic scenes in their drive against crime.

STEWART: Well, it sounds like a very interesting, much-needed, picture, Bill. And you have two fine young stars in Mark Stevens and Richard Widmark.

KEIGHLEY: Yes, I certainly have. And I'm extremely grateful, too, for the cooperation that we're having in Washington.

WYMAN: When do you get back, Bill?

KEIGHLEY: Well, not for another 10 days, I'm afraid. But, incidentally Jimmy, before I left, I caught a preview of your latest picture, *Northside 777* (he, of course, meant *Call Northside 777*). I enjoyed it immensely.

STEWART: Thanks very much, Bill. Right after Christmas I go to work again on another one with Alfred Hitchcock. (He was alluding to the film, *Rope*)

WYMAN: Oh, and speaking of Christmas, I understand, Bill, that you have something very special coming up on *Lux* next week.

KEIGHLEY: (talks about next week's show, *Miracle on 34th Street*, and its stars)

STEWART: Well, you couldn't have a better play for Christmas, Bill.

KEIGHLEY: Yes, a prize Santa Claus package, because it concerns no less than Kris Kringle himself. Bringing that gentleman to life in a warm and human Christmas story that it should appeal especially to the children in your family. We hope they'll join us.

WYMAN: It sounds like a treat for young and old alike, Bill. We'll be listening. Goodnight.

STEWART: Goodnight.

KEIGHLEY: Goodnight and a very Merry Christmas to you.

The cast included:
Jimmy Stewart..*Rip Smith*
Jane Wyman ....*Mary Peterman*
Herbert Butterfield...................................... *Mayor Barnes*
Ira Grossel .... *Hoopendecker/voice*
  (*Jeff Chandler working under his birth name*)

Wally Maher..*Ike*
John McIntire...*Narrator*
Alex Carey..*Daley*
Jack Edwards, Sr.............................*Senator Wilton/man*
Norman Field..*Man*
Tommy Cook..*Mike*
Gil Stratton..*Junior*
Lois Corbett..*Woman*
Eddie Marr..*Man*
Marie Windsor..*Woman*
Charles Woolf..*Boy*
Robert Griffin..*Mr. Hodges*
Earl Lee

Stewart and Wyman reprise their roles from the film.

The show is available as a part of *Vintage Radio Collection Jimmy Stewart* (Stardust), a special downloadable set made available in 2008.

(8) Monday, January 17, 1949 — *You Gotta Stay Happy* (9:00-10:00 p.m.)
NETWORK: CBS
SPONSOR: Lux Flakes
SEASON: 14th
BROADCAST LOCATION: Vine Street Playhouse, Hollywood
PRODUCER/HOST: William Keighley
DIRECTOR: Fredric MacKaye
ADAPTED FOR RADIO BY: Sanford H. Barnett
Based on the screenplay by Karl Tunberg, based on Robert Carson's *Saturday Evening Post* serial
ANNOUNCER: John Milton Kennedy
INTERMISSION GUEST: Ann Pearce, a new Universal-International Star
MUSICAL DIRECTOR: Louis Silvers
SOUND EFFECTS: Charles Forsyth
THEME MUSIC: "Lux Theatre Theme" (Robert Armbruster)
BETWEEN-THE-ACTS THEME: "Interlude" (Louis Silvers/Rudy Schrager)
The cast included:
Jimmy Stewart..*Marv Payne*
Joan Fontaine ....*Dee Dee Dillwod*
Frank Albertson..*Bullets*

Joseph Kearns, Bill Johnstone, Willard Waterman. Jane Webb, Gil Stratton, Jr., Herb Butterfield, Jeff Chandler, George Neise, Cy Kendall, Regina Wallace, Eddie Marr, Gail Bonney, Ed Max

Fontaine and Stewart reprise their film roles.
The show is unavailable for review.

(9) Monday, August 29, 1949 — *June Bride* (9:00-10:00 p.m.)
NETWORK: CBS
SPONSOR: Lux
SEASON: 15th (1st show of the new season)
BROADCAST LOCATION: Vine Street Playhouse, Hollywood
PRODUCER/HOST: William Keighley
DIRECTOR: Fredric MacKaye
ADAPTED FOR RADIO BY: Sanford H. Barnett
Based on the screenplay by Ranald MacDougall, based on the play *Feature for June*, by Eileen Tighe and Graeme Lorimer.
ANNOUNCER: John Milton Kennedy
INTERMISSION GUEST: Nita Talbot, a Warner Bros. starlet
MUSICAL DIRECTOR: Louis Silvers
SOUND EFFECTS: Charles Forsyth
THEME MUSIC: "Lux Theatre Theme" (Robert Armbruster)
BETWEEN-THE-ACTS THEME: "Interlude" (Louis Silvers/Rudy Schrager)

Linda Gilman is the editor of *Home Life* magazine, which is published by the Allied Magazine Syndicate. Carey Jackson (Jimmy Stewart), a former foreign correspondent and boyfriend, has just been transferred to her magazine as a writer. It's only January, but they are working on a story for the June edition. The story will be called June Bride and will feature the Brinker family of Crestville, Indiana. Their daughter Jean will be marrying Bud Mitchell. Linda and Carey fly to Indiana to begin getting the house ready for the wedding and they start collecting pictures and information for the article.

"Boo," Jean's sister, tells Carey that Jean had been engaged to Bud's brother Jim before he joined the military and moved to Chicago. Carey thinks it would be a great trick to get Jim home for the wedding, but then decides it would be too dirty a trick. "Boo" thinks it's a good idea, too, and arranges everything. Jim shows up thinking that Carey has sent for him. Linda believes so, too. Jean and Jim have a tiff and Jim leaves, but Jean runs after him. Several days later, they have not returned home. Carey finds them in Indianapolis — they have gotten married. When he tells Linda, she thinks their story has been ruined and that it is Carey's fault, but Jim thinks they still have a great story to tell. Linda fires him.

"Boo" loves Bud and Carey helps her to attract his attention. Carey pretends that he's in love with her. Bud falls for the trick and "Boo." He proposes to her and they plan to get married right away. The story is back on. Linda re-hires Carey and their love affair is also rekindled.

The cast included:

Jimmy Stewart	Carey Jackson
Bette Davis	Linda Gilman
Betty Lynn	"Boo"
Raymond Roe	Bud
Rhoda Williams	Jean
Eleanor Audley	Paula
Bill Johnstone	Mr. Brinker
Ruth Perrott	Mrs. Brinker
Herbert Butterfield	Carlton
Eddie Marr	Scotty

Holland Morris, Charlotte Lawrence, Noreen Gammill, Donald Randolph, Jane Webb, Joy Terry

Bette Davis, Betty Lynn and Raymond Roe reprise their film roles in the radio play. Stewart's role had been played by Robert Montgomery in the film.

(10) Monday, February 13, 1950 — *The Stratton Story* (9:00-10:00 p.m.)

NETWORK: CBS
SPONSOR: Lux
SEASON: 15th
BROADCAST LOCATION: Vine Street Playhouse, Hollywood
PRODUCER/HOST: William Keighley
DIRECTOR: Fredric MacKaye
ADAPTED FOR RADIO BY: Sanford H. Barnett
Based on the screenplay by Douglas Morrow and Guy Trosper
ANNOUNCER: John Milton Kennedy
COMMERCIAL SPOKESWOMAN: Dorothy Lovett
INTERMISSION GUEST: Pamela Britton, a new M-G-M star
MUSICAL DIRECTOR: Louis Silvers
SOUND EFFECTS: Charles Forsyth
THEME MUSIC: "Lux Theatre Theme" (Robert Armbruster)
BETWEEN-THE-ACTS THEME: "Interlude" (Louis Silvers/Rudy Schrager)

Traveling through Texas, ex-big leaguer Barney Wile sees Monty Stratton pitch and likes what he sees. He stays on at Monty's farm all winter, teaching him everything he knows about baseball. In the spring, he takes Monty to California to try out for Jimmy Dykes and the Chicago White Sox. While training with the Sox, Monty meets his future wife, Ethel. His first pitching assignment is against the Yankees and he doesn't do well. He's sent down to a minor league team in Omaha. He pitches well there, winning all six of his games. He also wins Ethel and they are married. He goes back up to Chicago, and as luck would have it, pitches his first game against the Yankees. This time he wins. He pitches well that season and does even better the next.

Then, on his farm for the winter, Monty is climbing over a fence with a rifle while hunting. The rifle fires and the bullet hits Monty's leg. The leg has to be amputated. Monty is very bitter and refuses to try his artificial leg, preferring to walk on crutches. As he watches his son struggle to learn how to walk, Monty comes around and straps on the leg. He and his son learn to walk together. Monty also begins to pitch again and Ethel serves as his catcher.

Barney is sent to Houston to scout players in an all-star game. When he walks into the locker room, there's Monty and he's in uniform. Monty has talked the coach into giving him a chance to see what he can do in a real ball game. After a shaky start, with the other team scoring a run, Monty settles in and pitches well. He hits the ball well, too, but while running to first base, he falls and is thrown out. When he comes to bat again with the bases loaded, he's sure the coach will pinch hit for him. But the players want Monty to bat so the coach lets him in the game. He gets a hit and two runs score, putting his team ahead. When the other team comes to bat they try a new strategy, but it doesn't work and Monty wins the game.

The cast included:

Jimmy Stewart	*Monty Stratton*
June Allyson	*Ethel*
John McIntire	*Barney Wile*
Helen Irwin	*Ma*
Cliff Clark	*Jimmy Dykes*
Herb Ellis	*Umpire*
Leo Cleary	*Waiter/Josh Higgins*
Bill Johnstone	*Conductor/Doctor*
Glen Durning	*Eddie Dibson*
Lawrence Dobkin	*Ted Lyons*
Charlotte Lawrence	*Woman*

George Neise	Bill Dicky
Willard Waterman	Manager/Umpire
Shepard Menken	Milliken
Eddie Firestone	Public Address Announcer
Eddie Marr	Taxi Driver/Player
Leone Le Doux	Dottie/Baby
Robert Bruce	Umpire

and the part of Hap, Monty's hunting dog

Stewart and Allyson reprise their film roles for Lux. Cliff Clark had also been in the film, but played a different role (Josh Higgins). At the end of the show, William Keighley talks to the two stars.

KEIGHLEY: After tonight's performance, it's easy for all of us to understand why *The Stratton Story* was voted America's favorite picture of the year. And, here are two of the reasons…Jimmy Stewart and June Allyson.

STEWART: Thank you very much, Bill. I think June and I'd like to tell the audience that we feel very complimented by the selection of *The Stratton Story* for *Photoplay* Gold Medal Award.

ALLYSON: Oh, yes indeed. We're very grateful to the moviegoers of America.

KEIGHLEY: You know, it's wonderful to have you back with us, June, and, as for you, Jimmy, there's just one question that I'd like…

STEWART: Yeah, well Bill, I feel fine, the honeymoon was wonderful, married life is great, I…ah…hope we have six children, preferably boys and girls and my wife said to be sure and bring home Lux Flakes.

KEIGHLEY: Well, Jimmy, that answers everything and you and June will find a supply of Lux Flakes waiting for you.

ALLYSON: Well, thank you, Bill. Say, Jimmy, I hear…ah…M-G-M has starred you in a fine new picture…*Malaya*. And there's a…there's another actor in it; I can't think of his name. What is it?

STEWART: Ah, yeah, a fellow by the name of Tracy…Spencer Tracy.

ALLYSON: Yes.

STEWART: Wonderful actor.

ALLYSON: Very good actor.

KEIGHLEY: Well, that seems like a very happy combination. But right now, we want to congratulate you, Jimmy, on receiving the *Photoplay* Award for being the actor of the year, whose performance was most enjoyed by the fans.

STEWART: I...I'm really grateful, Bill, and I'd like...I'd like to point out...(laughs). I'd like to point out that there's a very beautiful girl named June Allyson who is also receiving a citation tonight for her work during the year.

ALLYSON: Thank you, Jimmy. Of course, everyone's been wonderful. By the way, shouldn't we be leaving for the Beverly Hills Hotel?

STEWART: Um...hum.

KEIGHLEY: Yes, right after the broadcast you'll both receive your awards at the gala dinner there. George Murphy will be presiding as the Master of Ceremonies.

STEWART: Well, before we leave, Bill, what's the play for next week?

KEIGHLEY: Jimmy, it's one of the most unique comedies to come out of Hollywood this season, the intriguing drama, *A Letter to Three Wives*. And, we'll have two original stars from the 20th Century-Fox picture — beautiful Linda Darnell and a brilliant new star, making his first appearance on this stage, Paul Douglas.

ALLYSON: Oh, that's wonderful entertainment, Bill.

STEWART: You know, there's just one more thing I'd like to say. There's a fellow down in Texas who gets my award for courage and well, what ball players call "moxie"...he's got it...Monty Stratton. Good luck, Monty. Goodnight, Bill.

ALLYSON: Goodnight.

KEIGHLEY: Goodnight, and all our thanks for a memorable evening.

The Stratton Story is available from several sources. First, it is available as a single cassette as *AMC Audio Movies to Go: The Stratton Story* (AMC 6030), issued in 1999.

AMC's Jeffrey Lyons introduces the show and then comes back at the end to talk about all the films that have had a baseball theme. He also goes into some Stewart history, including his military and film careers. He does the same for June Allyson.

The show is also available on the sets — *Hollywood Stars on Radio* (Radio Spirits 40022 [CD]/40024 [cassette]), which was released in 2003, and Yogi *Berra's Favorite Baseball Shows* (Radio Spirits 40092 [CD]/40094 [Cassette]), released in 2004.

Radio Spirits also issued this show as an audiobook, *The Stratton Story: Classic Movies on the Radio*, in 2006.

Finally, it was released in mp3 only format twice by Master Classics Records in 2011: *June Allyson the Vintage Radio Shows* and *Jimmy Stewart the Ultimate Radio Collection Vol. 1*.

(11) Monday, February 26, 1951 — *When Willie Comes Marching Home* (9:00-10:00 p.m.)
NETWORK: CBS
SPONSOR: Lux
SEASON: 16th
BROADCAST LOCATION: Vine Street Playhouse, Hollywood
PRODUCER/HOST: William Keighley
DIRECTOR: Earl Ebi
ADAPTED FOR RADIO BY: Sanford H. Barnett
Based on the screenplay by Mary Loos and Richard Sale, based on a story by Sy Gomberg
ANNOUNCER: John Milton Kennedy
INTERMISSION GUEST: Helene Stanley, a new actress at 20th Century-Fox
MUSICAL DIRECTOR: Rudy Schrager
SOUND EFFECTS: Charles Forsyth
THEME MUSIC: "Lux Theatre Theme" (Robert Armbruster)
BETWEEN-THE-ACTS THEME: "Interlude" (Louis Silvers/Rudy Schrager)

The program is not available for review, although the newspaper column, *Today's Radio*, gives a good synopsis of the story. Like so many others since, even some newspapers of the time got the title of the program wrong.

The cast included:

Jimmy Stewart.. Bill Kluggs
William Demarest................... Pop (reprising his film role)
Joanne Dru..Marge
Gladys Holland... Yvonne
Eddie Firestone, Jr.. Charlie

Ruth Perrott, Wally Maher, Dan Riss, Bill Conrad, Bill Johnstone, Herb Butterfield, Ed Begley, Bob Griffin, Harald Dyrenforth, Larry Dobkin, Paul Dubov, Rye Billsbury, Howard McNear, Herb Ellis, George Neise, Charles Lung, Eddie Marr, Truda Marson, Charlotte Lawrence, David Light

Finally, it is part of *Vintage Radio Collection Jimmy Stewart* (Stardust), a special downloadable set made available in 2008.

(12) Monday, November 12, 1951 — *Winchester '73* (9:00-10:00 p.m.)
NETWORK: CBS
SPONSOR: Lux Flakes
SEASON: 17th
BROADCAST LOCATION: Vine Street Playhouse, Hollywood
PRODUCER/HOST: William Keighley

DIRECTOR: Earl Ebi
ADAPTED FOR RADIO BY: Sanford H. Barnett
Based on the screenplay by Robert L. Richards and Borden Chase, based on a Stuart N. Lake story
ANNOUNCER: John Milton Kennedy
COMMERCIAL SPOKESWOMAN: Dorothy Lovett
INTERMISSION GUEST: Suzan Ball
MUSICAL DIRECTOR: Rudy Schrager
SOUND EFFECTS: Charles Forsyth
THEME MUSIC: "Lux Theatre Theme " (Robert Armbruster)
BETWEEN-THE-ACTS THEME: "Interlude" (Louis Silvers/Rudy Schrager)

It's July 4, 1876, and Marshal Wyatt Earp is sponsoring a shooting contest in Dodge City, Kansas. The contest comes down to two men, Lin McAdam (Jimmy Stewart) and Dutch Henry Brown. Lola, a singer at the hotel, has been asked by Wyatt to leave town. She acts as the narrator for the story as well as acting in many scenes. Lin has come to town looking for Dutch and Dutch knows why. Lin wins the contest and the top prize of a brand-new Winchester '73, but Dutch and his men wait for him in his hotel room and steal it from him. Dutch and his men leave town in such a hurry, that they don't get their guns from Marshal Earp, so they try to buy some from a dealer named Lamont. His guns are very expensive and they can't afford them. Dutch accepts an offer to sell Lamont the Winchester '73 for $300. Lamont throws in some six-guns and ammo.

Lamont heads out to sell guns to Young Bull, an Indian. Young Bull doesn't like the guns he's offered, but he does like Lamont's Winchester '73. He kills Lamont and takes the rifle. Young Bull and his braves herd Lin, his partner High Spade, Lola, Steve (her boyfriend) and several Calvary men together. When the Indians attack them, they managed to drive them off. After the battle, Lin and High Spade leave for Tascosa to try to catch up to Dutch. After they leave, a soldier finds the Winchester '73 on the battlefield. The sergeant gives the rifle to Steve.

Steve and Lola ride on to meet with Waco. Waco sees the rifle and wants it. He kills Steve and takes it. Waco also takes Lola and heads for Tascosa to meet Dutch. Dutch sees Waco has the rifle and demands to have it back. They plan to rob the bank in Tascosa when the stagecoach brings in the money the next day. Waco is to wait at the bar across the street in case there's any trouble. While he and Lola are in the bar, Lin and High Spade come in. Lin tries to get Waco to take him to Dutch. Shots are fired. The stage driver hears the shots and doesn't stop, thus ruining the robbery attempt. Dutch heads for the hills and Lin follows closely behind. We find that Dutch's real name is Matthew McAdam and that he is Lin's brother. Lin is after him because he killed their father. Lin winds up with both the Winchester '73 and Lola.

At the end of the show, Keighley talks with the three stars.

KEIGHLEY: And here they are coming forward for a well-deserved curtain call — James Stewart, Stephen McNally and Julia Adams. Welcome to the *Lux Radio Theater*, Julia.

ADAMS: Thank you, Mr. Keighley. I'm delighted to be here.

MCNALLY: You know, Bill, Julia was starred in her first picture and here she is starring in her first appearance on the *Lux Theater*.

STEWART: Yeah, well ah, Julia believes in starting at the top and working her way up.

ADAMS: Well, I have to go some to catch up with you, Jimmy. You've appeared on this stage ten times already.

KEIGHLEY: Why don't you take a tip from Steve? Tonight he's making his second appearance of the season.

STEWART: Yeah, at this rate, he'll pass me by next April.

MCNALLY: Oh no. I…I haven't got room in my house for all that soap. Anyhow…ah…Julia's doing okay. Isn't she co-starring with you in your latest Universal-International Technicolor picture?

STEWART: That's right, *The Bend of the River*. It's the story of people who brave the northwest frontier back when it was called the Oregon Territory. I play the part of a pioneer guide.

KEIGHLEY: And Julia plays your sweetheart.

ADAMS: Yes, Mr. Keighley, but I don't see how any girl got her man in those days. After bouncing around in a covered wagon, I was anything but a glamour girl and I ate dust by the ton.

STEWART: Well, don't forget that women were scarce in those days, Julia…at least on wagon trains.

ADAMS: Well, I'm certainly glad Lux Flakes weren't scarce on our wagon train. I always insist on Lux Flakes for my personal wardrobe.

KEIGHLEY: Good for you, Julia. You know we have a supply for each of you to take home. Now let's see, with Jimmy's four children and Stephen's six, ah, excuse me while I order another truckload.

MCNALLY: Just a minute, Bill, we want to hear about next week's show.

KEIGHLEY: (Keighley talks about the next show, *Samson and Delilah*, and its stars, Hedy Lamarr and Victor Mature.)

STEWART: Wow, that'll be a great show, Bill. Goodnight.

ADAMS: Goodnight.

MCNALLY: Goodnight, Bill.
KEIGHLEY: Goodnight and hurry back.

The cast included:

Jimmy Stewart	Lin McAdam
Stephen McNally	Dutch Henry Brown (Matthew McAdam)
Julia Adams	Lola
Dan Riss	High Spade (Frankie Wilson)
Herb Butterfield	Wyatt Earp
Wally Maher	Waco Johnny Dean
Tim Graham	Sgt. Wilkes
Stephen Dunne	Steve Miller
Bill Johnstone	Joe Lamont
Bill Conrad	Westley
Bob Griffin	Noonan
Charles Lung	Wheeler
Jack Mather	Young Bull
Joe DuVal	Riker
James Best	Coates
June Whitley	Mrs. Jamison
Earl Browne	
Eddie Marr	Boone, bar keeper

Stewart and McNally reprise their roles from the film.

Winchester '73 is available on the 6-CD/4-cassette set, *The Best of Old Time Radio Starring Jimmy Stewart*. See *Made for Each Other* (#5 above) for complete details on this set.

Radio Spirits also issued this show as an audiobook, *Winchester '73: Classic Movies on the Radio*, in 2003.

In 2011, it was also issued on the mp3 only set, *Jimmy Stewart the Ultimate Radio Collection Vol. 3* (Master Classics Records).

(13) Monday, April 28, 1952 — *No Highway in the Sky* (9:00-10:00 p.m.)
NETWORK: CBS
SPONSOR: Lux Toilet Soap
SEASON: 17th
BROADCAST LOCATION: Vine Street Playhouse, Hollywood

PRODUCER/HOST: William Keighley
DIRECTOR: Earl Ebi
ADAPTED FOR RADIO BY: Sanford H. Barnett
Based on the screenplay by R.C. Sheriff, Oscar Millard and Alec Coppel, based on the Nevil Shute novel, *No Highway*
ANNOUNCER: John Milton Kennedy
COMMERCIAL SPOKESWOMAN: Dorothy Lovett
INTERMISSION GUEST: Virginia McGuire, a new 20th Century-Fox star
MUSICAL DIRECTOR: Rudy Schrager
SOUND EFFECTS: Charles Forsyth
THEME MUSIC: "Lux Theatre Theme" (Robert Armbruster)
BETWEEN-THE-ACTS THEME: "Interlude" (Louis Silvers/Rudy Schrager)

Theodore Honey (Jimmy Stewart) is studying the British Reindeer aircraft. He believes that engine vibrations will cause the tail assembly to fall off the planes after 1440 hours of flying. One of the planes has recently crashed in Labrador and the tail section was not found. The factory owners, Sir David and Sir John, sent Honey to investigate. He finds himself flying in a Reindeer which has spent 1422 hours in the air. He tells the pilot about his research and theory and asks him to turn back, but he doesn't. Monica Teasdale, an actress whom Honey's deceased wife was very fond of, is also on the plane. He tells her what might happen and tells her to sit on the floor of the men's room if the plane should start to crash. It is the most secure spot in the plane. She is half asleep and doesn't take much notice of his warning. Marjorie Corder, the stewardess, has been told by the pilot what is happening. She asks Honey not to tell any of the other passengers.

When she wakes from her nap, Miss Teasdale comes and sits beside Honey and they talk about the possibility of the plane crashing, why the men's room floor is the best place to be, and why he picked her to try to save. She's believes what he tells her.

The plane lands safely in Newfoundland. The pilot wants the plane completely inspected before he flies on. He also refuses to allow Honey back on his plane. The plane is found to be safe, but Honey tries to prevent its takeoff. Due to a faulty landing gear lock, he succeeds.

Miss Teasdale gets back to England before Honey and visits Sir John. She tells him that she is sure that Honey is sincere in what he believes. She wants to make sure that the company will stand by him. They say they will, but he will need to pass a psychological test.

When Honey gets home, he finds Marjorie there taking care of his daughter. She tells him that Miss Teasdale has also been there. He makes his visit to the psychiatrist and then goes back to the plant to continue his vibration study. The test plane passes the 1440-hour mark and the tail doesn't fall off. But, the next day, back in his laboratory, he is told that the tail assembly of the plane that crashed in Labrador has been found and that it had broken off the plane while in flight. Also, the plane that he had grounded in Newfoundland had been repaired and flew on to Montreal. While it was being taxied off the runway, its tail fell off also. As they are standing there talking, the tail falls off the test plane.

After the second act, Keighley talked with the special Intermission Guest, 20th Century-Fox starlet, Virginia McGuire.

The stars come back at the end of the show to talk with William Keighley.

KEIGHLEY: And here they are, coming forward to acknowledge your applause — Jimmy Stewart and Marlene Dietrich. Well, Marlene, what are you doing these days?

DIETRICH: Right now I am looking for a baseball game.

STEWART: Any particular one?

DIETRICH: Yes. I've just seen Dan Dailey as Dizzy Dean in the 20th Century-Fox picture, *The Pride of St. Louis*, and now I wish to see Mr. Dean pitch.

STEWART: Well Dean...Dean doesn't pitch anymore, Marlene. But... ah...instead why don't you see *Deadline U.S.A.* starring Humphrey Bogart and you can go looking for gangsters.

DIETRICH: All right, Jimmy, I shall look for the picture as soon as I return to New York.

KEIGHLEY: And by the way, don't miss the magnificent new Lever House, which has its formal opening this week.

STEWART: Well, isn't that the building I recently saw in a magazine almost entirely made of glass?

KEIGHLEY: Yes, Jimmy, that's because it has 1404 windows and no window sills. So it looks just like a shining block of glass 21 stories high. I have a wonderful view of my New York apartment...*(the available tape ends here)*.

The cast included:

Jimmy Stewart	*Theodore Honey*
Marlene Dietrich	*Monica Teasdale*
Evelynne Eaton	*Marjorie Corder*
Herbert Butterfield	*Sir David*

> *Leo Britt*... *Sir John*
> *Carleton Young* .... *Scott*

Stewart and Dietrich reprise their film roles.

The show is part of two different mp3 only sets: *Vintage Radio Collection Jimmy Stewart* (Stardust, 2008), and *Jimmy Stewart the Ultimate Radio Collection Vol. 3* (Master Classics Records).

In 2009, it was issued on the download only set, *Marlene Dietrich The Vintage Radio Shows* (Master Classics). With nineteen parts at 99 cents each, this was certainly no bargain to buy.

NOTES

Although Jimmy Stewart appeared in 13 *Lux Radio Theatre* productions, he was not featured in several shows based on his movies. Whether due to illness, previous commitments, or military service, Jimmy missed out on the following shows.

(A) *Next Time We Love* (November 7, 1938)
   Jimmy's film role went to Joel McCrea.
(B) *You Can't Take It with You* (October 2, 1939)
   Robert Cummings takes on Jimmy's role.
(C) *Made for Each Other* (February 19, 1940)
   Fred MacMurray is in Jimmy's role. Jimmy would play Johnny Mason, his film role, in the December 17, 1945, version for Lux.
(D) *Vivacious Lady* (January 6, 1941)
   Jimmy's film role was played here by Don Ameche.
(E) *The Shop Around the Corner* (June 23, 1941)
   Once again Don Ameche has Jimmy's role.
(F) *The Philadelphia Story* (June 14, 1943)
   Jimmy had played his film role in the original Lux production, but Robert Young played Mike here.
(G) *Broken Arrow* (January 22, 1951)
   Jimmy was set to play Tom Jeffords in this production, but became ill and had to be replaced by Burt Lancaster.

In introducing the cast, host William Keighley says, "...Burt Lancaster, who was kind enough to step in and play the role when James Stewart suddenly became ill." At the end of the show, when Keighley thanks Burt for stepping in, this short dialogue takes place.

LANCASTER: Thank you, I was glad to do it, Bill. And, Jimmy, to you, hurry up and recover. You did such a great job of Tom Jeffords in the picture that I hated to follow you…you can have the part back now. But, I'm going to keep your Lux Flakes.
KEIGHLEY: That's okay, Burt, but, confidentially, we're going to send Jimmy a double supply. We understand that he may become the papa of twins.
LANCASTER: Don't tell me that's why he collapsed.
KEIGHLEY: No, no, Burt, just a case of that old virus "x."

Stewart would finally get to reprise his film role on radio on September 7, 1951, on *Screen Directors' Playhouse*.

(H) *Carbine Williams* (March 22, 1954)
Jimmy's film role is played by Ronald Reagan.

In addition, the very first broadcast on *Lux Radio Theatre* was *Seventh Heaven* on October 14, 1934. Jimmy would star in the 1937 film version.

Maggi's Private Wire
Stewart made an appearance on Maggi's 15-minute NBC show on January 23, 1947 (12:30-12:45 p.m.). The show is unavailable for review. Stewart's film *It's a Wonderful Life* had just been released, so it's very possible that they chatted about that film. Also see *Luncheon with Maggi McNellis and Herb Sheldon*.

Man from Laramie Interviews
Jimmy Stewart traveled to Texas in July of 1955 for the premiere of his new film, *The Man from Laramie*. That event took place at the Majestic Theater in San Antonio on July 13th. An article appearing in the *San Antonio Light* on July 10th indicated that there would be radio interviews done the night of the premiere.
A newspaper article appearing on July 14th also says that the stars of the film had been interviewed, not only for radio, but also for TV and newspapers.
No listings of radio stations call letters or broadcast times have been located. It is possible that these were just short interview clips which were placed in newscasts.
Stewart's tour of Texas also took him to Houston, Dallas and Fort Worth. No documentation indicating that he did radio interviews in any of those cities has been located.

Also appearing in the newspaper was an ad telling readers they could "talk to Jimmy Stewart" by calling the number given. Similar ads appeared in newspapers around the country. Some of these ads more correctly stated that the actor would "talk to you." After dialing the number, the dialer would hear Stewart talking about his new film.

Martha Deane Show

There really was no Martha Deane. WOR (710 a.m.), the Manhattan radio station that broadcast the show, owned the name. Several different women broadcast under the name over the years. The first was Mary Margaret McBride, who headlined the show from 1934 until 1940. Marian Young Taylor, who took over the Martha Deane name in 1941, held that position for 32 years. She was the hostess when Jimmy Stewart made his three appearances on the program. George Hogan was her announcer. None of the programs is available for listening.

(1) Friday, January 24, 1947 (3-3:30 a.m.)

It is likely that at least one of the topics discussed this day was *It's a Wonderful Life*, which had had its New York City premiere on December 20, just days before the broadcast.

(2) Thursday, April 1, 1948 (10:15-11 a.m.)

It is possible that they talked about the film, *Call Northside 777*, which had only been showing for about two months at the time of this program.

(3) Thursday, May 19, 1949 (10:15-11 a.m.)

One topic of discussion was most likely *The Stratton Story*, which had premiered the previous week.

Martin and Lewis Show

Dean Martin and Jerry Lewis had been making a name for themselves as a nightclub act for several years when they were offered their own NBC radio program in 1949. Stewart appeared on the show just once and that show is unavailable for listening.

Tuesday, September 30, 1952 (9-9:30 p.m.)
NETWORK: NBC
SPONSOR: Sustaining
HOSTS: Dean Martin, Jerry Lewis
DIRECTOR: Dick Mack
WRITERS: Ed Simmons, Norman Lear

One newspaper ad of the time stated that Stewart would be a participant in a prison variety show sketch with the stars of the show.

There were two other regulars on the show at the time Stewart made his appearance — Sheldon Leonard (he had appeared as Nick in *It's a Wonderful Life*) and Ben Alexander (best remembered by fans of early TV as Officer Frank Smith on *Dragnet*).

Mary Margaret McBride

McBride hosted a talk/interview show broadcast from WABC in New York City. For most of its run, the show aired weekdays at 1 p.m. An ancillary show, *Saturday Digest*, aired on Saturdays. Her show was one of the most popular of its type and she was well respected among her colleagues. Although they are not in general circulation, all three programs are available as part of the NBC Collection at the Library of Congress.

NETWORK: ABC
PRODUCER: Stella Karn
ANNOUNCER: Vincent Connolly

(1) Friday, March 6, 1953 — *Mary Margaret McBride*
McBride talks with Stewart for the first half of the day's show and touches on many different topics.

MCBRIDE: ...once stuffed yourself just to gain weight.
STEWART: Oh yes, I remember it very well myself. As a matter of fact, I've done it almost all my life. I'm getting a little smug about it.
MCBRIDE: You seem to be a little heavier than the last time I saw you.
STEWART: Yes, I've gained about three pounds in the last seven years. That's pretty good for me.
MCBRIDE: ...I can put on ten pounds in a week without trying.
STEWART: When I gain weight it just sort of fills out those holes in my cheeks.
MCBRIDE: ...I think having twins agrees with you.
STEWART: Yes, I think the family life is for me...to coin a phrase.
MCBRIDE: ...remember your bachelor life?
STEWART: But don't undersell that now, Mary Margaret...that has its place.
MCBRIDE: It does?
STEWART: Yes...we don't want to be too unkind to the bachelor.
MCBRIDE: Well, all of them got married, didn't they?

STEWART: Well, it's getting a little rough…the club is dwindling.

MCBRIDE: …think you were the very last one.

STEWART: No…I was…I was way down the list.

MCBRIDE: …you went to a party and there was this girl.

STEWART: Yes…now there wasn't anything out of the ordinary about it. I just…I met this girl and thought she was fine and before I knew it I was walking down the aisle; just like it happens to all we men.

MCBRIDE: …knew a lot of tricks, but it all evaporated when the right girl came along.

STEWART: Yes, it wasn't a whirlwind thing; it was just sort of a natural course of events.

MCBRIDE: …never heard of anyone having twins unless there were twins somewhere in the family.

STEWART: Yes, I thought that, too. There aren't twins in either Gloria or my family. And I was a little surprised when I heard that we were gonna have twins…a little surprised he said. That's an understatement if I ever heard one. The doctor says that there's nothing unusual about this. He says it just has to start sometime. Now, the two girls…from now on, the two girls…they'll…they'll have twins probably…they're…the thing's started now.

MCBRIDE: …not the same peaceful atmosphere you had as a bachelor.

STEWART: No, it happened…when you come to think of it, I…years ago I had a sort of a bungalow and I had a dog named Bud and my father sent me a canary whose name was George, who didn't sing, and I had a housekeeper name of Daisy Dooley and that was sort of the set-up as far as my living place was concerned. And then a year and a half later I'm the father of four in a house with a police dog and a couple of cats…every once in a while it brings me up with quite a start.

MCBRIDE: Quick work.

STEWART: Yes, yes, rather hasty.

MCBRIDE: …stopped the habit of bringing home stray dogs and cats.

STEWART: Of necessity we had to stop this, yes. It's pretty crowded around our house now.

MCBRIDE: Are you a good disciplinarian?

STEWART: Oh, I don't think exceptional. I think I get by with it.

MCBRIDE: I'll bet you don't discipline worth a darn.

STEWART: No, I spare the rod and spoil the child…I believe that.

MCBRIDE: You do?

STEWART: Un-hum.

MCBRIDE: Were you disciplined when you were young?

STEWART: Yes, indeed…yes, indeed.

MCBRIDE: Well, you turned out okay.

STEWART: Yeah, I think it's a good thing…

MCBRIDE: Have you ever wished you had several lives, so that when you get tired of talking about one of them, you could switch to another?

STEWART: Yes, well, sometimes you…why don't you just try elaborating a little. My wife accuses me of exaggeration.

MCBRIDE: She does? You're the last man I'd pick for that.

STEWART: I always thought that, too.

MCBRIDE: In what way?

STEWART: The only way I can explain it to you is something that happened just the other day. We did this radio broadcast down from Constitution Hall and I was talking on the phone to somebody about it and I said that the show went very well and it was very thrilling to see all these 8,000 people in Constitution Hall. Well, actually, there were just 4,000. My wife caught me on it right away. But I thought 8,000 sounded so much better and I didn't think I was talking to anybody that was gonna to check up on me.

MCBRIDE: But you forgot you had a wife.

STEWART: Yes, it was twice too many.

MCBRIDE: I guess now she'll be a little suspicious.

STEWART: No, she's not a very suspicious girl.

MCBRIDE: She isn't?

STEWART: Very nice girl.

MCBRIDE: Can she cook?

STEWART: No, can't cook anything. Neither can I.

MCBRIDE: Hope you have a good cook then.

STEWART: You bet we do.

MCBRIDE: Was the Daisy you mentioned a while ago the one who used to censor your phone calls?

STEWART: Yes, Daisy never liked me very much, I'm afraid. I don't think that was because she liked me. I don't think Daisy liked many people at all.

MCBRIDE: …didn't like you to act in a picture unless she approved of the picture.

STEWART: No, but she didn't approve of pictures.

MCBRIDE: At all?

STEWART: No.

MCBRIDE: How long was that?

STEWART: Let's see, I had her about five years…about four years and then I went into the Army. Lots of people accused me of going into the Army to get away from Daisy.

MCBRIDE: And when you came out Daisy was…

STEWART: Yes, I thought, as a matter of fact, Daisy would sort of forget, but Daisy was the first one to call after I got out of the Army and I was so touched that I took her back…and that was a mistake because instead of mellowing over the years, Daisy had hardened up a little sort of like tungsten steel. And, ah, gee, I hope she's not listening in.

MCBRIDE: Ever take any interest now in architecture?

STEWART: No, no, I sort of…several years ago I was thinking about maybe designing a house, but I'm very sorry that I haven't gone on with it. I think maybe, perhaps later on I might get back to it. I hope so.

MCBRIDE: Did you take a whole course in it?

STEWART: Well, I majored in it in college and that's two years and I got a Bachelor of Science degree in it.

MCBRIDE: What diverted you?

STEWART: Well, I went up to a stock company the summer after I got out of college and got bit by the bug and been in show business ever since.

MCBRIDE: …first review…two lines and howls of laughter…

STEWART: In *Goodbye Again*, yeah, I wish I could find a part like that again.

MCBRIDE: …the words didn't sound so funny.

STEWART: Well, the part was spotted in the play very well. When they used to have vaudeville, you know, the spot of the act on the bill was a very important thing. And this part had absolutely nothing to do with the play. You could cut the thing out…had nothing to do with the characters or anything in the play, but it was just spotted as a sort of a wait between the introduction of the main characters of the play. As a matter of fact, I remember I used to stay and take the first curtain call after the play and people would wonder who it was because I hadn't been there since the first act. Yeah, it was the part of a chauffeur. I imagine people thought it was somebody's chauffeur who'd got lost and ended up on the stage.

MCBRIDE: …reviewer said, never before in history had a man spent so little time on stage and gotten so much laughter.

STEWART: Is that right?

MCBRIDE: …keep for your scrapbook, or don't you keep one?

STEWART: Yeah, my mother keeps one.

MCBRIDE: I guess you're not very vain.

STEWART: Well, I don't know…I don't think I'm particularly vain.

MCBRIDE: If you'd become an architect, you might never have been so famous.

STEWART: Never have been able to play a clown…never been able to be a cowboy, be brave and conquer the northwest.

MCBRIDE: Is the clown the nicest thing you've ever played?

STEWART: Well, it was really exciting.

MCBRIDE: It was?

STEWART: Oh dear, it was lovely.

MCBRIDE: Tell me about it.

STEWART: Well, I think everybody…I think everybody at one time or another in their life has wanted to run away and join the circus and has wanted to play a clown. The thing about a clown's makeup that they all say…all the clowns, all the real clowns in the circus…Emmett Kelly and all…they say that the minute you get the makeup on then your…then all your inhibitions, all self-consciousness that you have at some time or another…all actual stage fright that almost everybody in the business has, goes because you're another fella and you can do anything and it's all right.

MCBRIDE: Did you feel that?

STEWART: Yeah, very definitely. It's a wonderful experience.

MCBRIDE: Were you ever self-conscious?

STEWART: Oh yes. I think that's the thing in acting that you have to overcome and that you can't actually give true characterizations until you do overcome it. Stage fright is another thing. I think that just naturally happens to everybody.

MCBRIDE: What's the difference between the two? Stage fright…

STEWART: You're scared to death.

MCBRIDE: …and the other thing?

STEWART: The other thing is to let yourself not be conscious of anything except just the character that you're playing or what you're doing or who you're listening to. A lot of people, I think, you see a performance or you hear something on the radio and you get the feeling that the person that isn't talking at the moment isn't listening and that's just as important as talking in a conversation. You see it all the time in conversation around the dinner table. Somebody that won't listen is a very annoying person.

MCBRIDE: …I wish we could do something about people like that.

STEWART: Yeah, there ought to be a home for them or something.

MCBRIDE: Limbo.

STEWART: Yes, yes, I'd settle for that.

MCBRIDE: When did you begin to get over being self-conscious?

STEWART: Oh, I don't know. I think it's just a part of the experience in show business. I think it comes gradually. It doesn't come all at once and it depends on your experience. The only way to get over it is work, work at your craft.

MCBRIDE: Who discovered you?

STEWART: Gee, I don't know. Bill Grady…Bill Grady is a casting director for Metro-Goldwyn-Mayer, has been for 30 years, and I think maybe he had more to do with it than anyone else. I was in a play here in New York and he saw it and I took a test here. I think he was responsible for it.

MCBRIDE: Are those tests different now?

STEWART: They don't make them anymore very much.

MCBRIDE: …because they can tell without them.

STEWART: Pretty much, yes. Actually, they don't do much good. I mean it's a…they do it to the girls so that they can get the best way to photograph her and everything, but actually as far as acting is concerned… for knowing whether a person can play a part or not…they're of very little value. Well, another thing…it's a very expensive thing. They've had to economize and wisely so. So they've cut out a lot of that. It's an added expense that isn't necessary.

MCBRIDE: How does Hollywood feel about three dimensions and television?

STEWART: Well, it's all very exciting out there now. Everybody's…I don't know much about the three dimension…four dimensions…I don't know, but I think the thing will level off and they'll have some new kind of thing — probably a combination of Cinerama and three dimension. But it's very exhilarating now because the movie business is much better than it was. And this boogie man, television that everybody was talking about, I think actually has helped the movies. I think that people in the east and in different parts of the country have had whole new avenues of entertainment opened up to them by the movies. By seeing outdoor pictures in the western-type of movies on television, I think it's been a…it's given them the desire to see more of them on bigger screens, in color and to see more adventure-type movies; so that I think, actually, it's helped us.

MCBRIDE: …have a different opinion than most.

STEWART: Well, Hollywood is an emotional place, you know. Everybody's up in the clouds or we'll have something just…if something happens out there, it happens much more violently than anywhere else because, you know, it's a sort of an emotional place. We deal in emotions, so it's sort of natural that it happens that way.

MCBRIDE: What are you working on now?

STEWART: I've finished two. One is in release now, but will be here a little later, this month, I think, called *The Naked Spur*, the Western we did up in Colorado. Then I finished one called *Thunder Bay* that I did down in Louisiana. It's about the off-shore oil drilling thing down off the coast of Louisiana. We did the whole picture down there. It's in color. It's an adventure story with a sort of a broad, wide scope. Then I'm going to do the life story of Glenn Miller, the orchestra leader, in March. Then I'm gonna do a picture with Hitchcock; a murder mystery. And then I'm gonna do another Western. They call this one *Alder's Gulch* and we call this a wet Western. It starts on a boat out to sea. This is so you don't have to spend the whole picture on your horse, you see.

[Note: The title *Alder's Gulch*, was changed to *The Far Country* before the film's release.]

MCBRIDE: I love you, James Stewart.
STEWART: Well, bless your heart.
MCBRIDE: And give my love to the twins and your nice wife.
STEWART: I certainly will.
MCBRIDE: …recommend marriage to all bachelors out there.
STEWART: Well, I'm gonna tell my wife what you said.

(2) Saturday March 7, 1953 — *Saturday Digest* (1-2 p.m.)
Saturday Digest featured the best parts of some of the interviews done during the previous week on McBride's weekday show. Part of Stewart's interview from the day before was included, as well as interviews with writer Ed Reid and opera singer Nadine Conner.

(3) Monday March 23, 1953 — *Mary Margaret McBride* (2-3 p.m.)
This is the same show as the March 6 program, except with different commercials for the Chicago-area broadcast.

Meet Tex and Jinx
See *Hi Jinx*.

Merry Christmas from Merv
Merry Christmas from Merv was a 12-hour radio show produced by Merv Griffin Productions and hosted by Griffin himself. It first aired during the 1980 Christmas season. Besides featuring music of the season, Griffin also interviewed many celebrities, focusing on their personal memories and feelings about Christmas. In addition to Stewart many other stars including Bob Hope, Johnny Mathis, Phyllis Diller, Robbie

Benson, Gene Autry, Merle Haggard, Mel Torme, Norman Mailer, Pat Boone and Jackie Gleason appeared on the program.

Stewart's segment appeared during the first hour. Griffin introduced Stewart by saying there was a new Christmas favorite this year in *Mr. Krueger's Christmas* starring Jimmy Stewart. He mentioned that in a dream sequence in the made for TV film, Stewart dreamed that he was conducting the Mormon Tabernacle Choir. In a phone interview, Stewart then says:

> Well, it's one of the most wonderful experiences I've ever had. I've been a great fan of the Tabernacle Choir for years and years and to suddenly find myself up there on the platform facing the choir and leading them in a song is something I'll never forget.

Gerald Ottley, the director of the Mormon Tabernacle Choir, then added that their experience in filming *Mr. Krueger's Christmas* with Jimmy Stewart brings them great joy every time they perform *Sleigh Ride*. The song *Sleigh Ride* is then played.

Miracle Over Main Street
Monday, September 1, 1947 (10:30-11 p.m.)
NETWORK: NBC

This program is not generally available, but is part of the NBC Collection in the Library of Congress.

Tex McCrary (see *Hi Jinx*) introduces this as a special program coming at the end of Labor Day and on the eve of the second anniversary of Japan's surrender. With that short introduction, the program begins.

STEWART: Did you ever see a miracle? A war correspondent I know claims he did once; aboard the battleship *Missouri* when the Japs surrendered two years ago. Remember the scene on deck? American generals, British admirals, Russian generals…and, some forlorn Japs, all standing stiff as boards inhaling the history in the air…and then something happened. Suddenly, in the midst of all that war famous brass, a strange character showed up, just wandered in and stood there for a moment. It was a…a plain American soldier, a G.I., with an open collar; the sort of guy who can't stop looking like a civilian. Boy, on a battleship, he looked lost and bewildered. It was like he walked out on a stage where he didn't belong. Well, none of the big shots noticed him, but this war correspondent did and tried to get his name, but the G.I. shook his head and disappeared. He, ah…he just disappeared. Now, the newspaper man two years later, he's not so sure what he saw. The G.I., I mean, whether he was real flesh and blood or whether he was an apparition. Maybe he was a ghost of some soldier or someone trying to say something...something like...

In his mind, the G.I. is trying to make plans for a peace that will last.

STEWART: Now, my name is James Stewart and I'd like to sort of talk a little bit about peace and pieces of paper. You know, two years ago the most important piece of paper in the world was that surrender document signed aboard the *Missouri*. It was easy to talk about, it was exciting...it was historic...quite a piece of paper. It's probably under glass somewhere, part of the archives. But, it isn't the most important document in the world now. There's another document that's much more important...only a lot of people don't realize it. As a matter of fact, I've got one of them right here in my pocket. A two-by-six slip of green paper...it's a buck...a buck...an American dollar bill and it's the cornerstone of something called the Marshall Approach. Now, if you don't know what this is, don't be alarmed, you're in good company — right now you are. Because during the summer, as a topic of conversation, the Marshall Plan had a little too much competition from a lot more interesting subjects.

In this portion of the skit, men talk about golf, gambling, baseball and more.

STEWART: Well, those were the topics of conversation...not peace, but golf, long skirts, baseball; things we've wanted to talk about for a long time. And, as a matter of fact, maybe talking about a peace plan is sort of boring compared to a world series. And nobody knows that better than the State Department and General Marshall. All summer long they've been trying to figure out how to explain his plan for the rehabilitation of Europe to the American people. But, instead of listening or watching the main event, even Washington seemed much more interested of the fight in the grandstand. Well, sure, why not? It had...it had color.

The skit now focuses on a courtroom scene during a recent Washington probe.

STEWART: Well, that...ah...real-life drama was a little too much competition for any peace plan. You know, a hot Washington probe is always front page stuff. But, the Marshall Plan, about all it rates is a dry editorial. But I heard about one young guy, he used to be a bombardier out in the Pacific, now he works for a paper near here and, it's funny, the other day he thought he had the story of the year. And he wanted it run on the front page on the anniversary of the big surrender. But he had an editor who straightened him out.

In the skit, the news writer tries to sell the Marshall Plan story, but his editor won't go for it. The reporter says that he went out and asked 50 people if they support the Marshall Plan. Out of the 50, 20 said yes, 11 said no and 19 didn't know what the Marshall Plan was. It was those 19 that he wanted his story to reach. Still, the editor said no…the story would be dull reading.

STEWART: Dull reading — well, now, we've got a tricky sort of a situation here. We've got an editor, and a lot of others like him, who believes that you don't want to hear an explanation of a peace plan. He figures you're gonna be bored. So, you don't get the explanation. You just hear that we're spending millions of dollars abroad and you start saying to yourself, why don't we spend our own dough here…on ourselves, we need it. Charity begins at home. So, you begin to mistrust the Marshall Plan and Congress reacts the way you feel and what happens; they might refuse to give out with the money to help the other nations. It's that buck again. Right now, where are we? Well, I'll tell you…we're out for ourselves. That's the old ostrich of isolation rearing its ugly head and then ramming it right back in the sand again. That's us…because we weren't informed. You know, out where I work…out in Hollywood, there are a lot of men who learned how to use the movies for propaganda; for teaching guys how to fight during war. And a lot of them would still like to try to use the movies for explaining an idea like the Marshall Plan. But I…I guess out in Hollywood, we're just like everybody else; we think we know what people want and that's what we give 'em, maybe a little less to be safe, but, well, that is what happens most of the time.

In the next skit, an author doesn't like the way his story has been revised for a film. When he complains, he's told that his story won't draw people to the theater.

STEWART: Well, it looks pretty hopeless, doesn't it? Nobody seems to want to tackle the job of explaining a peace plan to us. Well, maybe… maybe it would take somebody really higher up to figure out a way to get it across. Some voice that would make us see this thing clearly. Someone who wants to tell us…someone we'd listen to. Oh, but I suppose I'm asking for a miracle to happen and miracles are only born in heaven.

Here, there's a burst of dramatic music.

STEWART: In heaven, say…say, you know, up there I'll bet there are a lot of men who'd know what to say. All the guys whose number came up in the last war; all the Yanks and the British Tommies and the Chinese and the Russians. Of course, we don't know what they'd do up there. I wonder…I wonder whether they just look down at us and watch, or maybe they're having a life all of their own up there. But, maybe even breaking off into foursomes and playing golf on a sort of green pasture. I wonder, maybe…maybe at this minute four of them are teeing off on a cloud…on a white fairway…four of them up there, speaking the same language.

In the skit, one member of the foursome, Joe Smith, tells the others that he has been drafted to become the Unknown Soldier for the Second World War. Joe isn't happy with the assignment. He'd rather go back to Earth and tell everyone of the need for peace. His superior tells him that he must find a "live" person to do that kind of work. Joe recommends Harold Russell. Russell had been a soldier in the war and had had both of his hands blown off in an explosion. His lost hands were replaced by hooks. He later was cast in the film, *The Best Years of Our Lives*, where he played Homer Parrish, a sailor who lost both hands in the war. Joe knows that people will believe Russell.

Next, we hear a voice saying, "We interrupt all those programs in progress to bring you…Harold Russell." Russell explains the Marshall Plan in terms of his own life, ending by saying that Europe needs rehabilitation, peace insurance…not charity.

STEWART: Well, I guess you'd say that this sort of thing couldn't happen; the voice of the Unknown Soldier whispering down Main Street, USA. Well, maybe that's what we need…a miracle like that; a miracle over Main Street. And, you know, that would be a pretty good way to celebrate the end of the war. Fix it up so that our second Unknown Soldier could help us understand the way to stop the next war before it starts. And, if the assignment angel likes the idea, I hope they work it out. Maybe…maybe, Joe down there in Arlington will try to get through tonight. You never know about miracles.

The available tape ends very abruptly at this point. No credits are given.

Mobilization for Human Needs
See *Community Chest*.

Monitor

In 1955, NBC President Sylvester P. Weaver, Jr. created a new show which he called *Monitor*. He hoped that the show would attract listeners who had been leaving radio by the thousands for television...and it did. *Monitor* had a little bit of everything, including news, comedy, sports, celebrity interviews, music, and remotes from anywhere in the world where something interesting or newsworthy might be happening. During its run on the air, *Monitor* was heard for as many as 40 hours on a typical weekend. Stewart made three appearances on the program, none of which is available for review. The show's theme music was "Night Flight to Madrid" (Kermit Leslie/Walter Leslie). The Stewart interviews, as were most of the celebrity interviews, were short, ranging in length from 3-5 minutes.

(1) Sunday, July 17, 1955 (2:45 p.m. segment)
According to a newspaper report, Stewart was interviewed by Barclay Russell. The interview had taken place in San Antonio, TX, two days earlier while Stewart was in town for the premiere of his new film, *The Man from Laramie*.

(2) Saturday, February 4, 1956 (10-11 a.m. segment)
The hosts during this segment of time were Frank Blair and Don Russell. The show's executive producer was Al Capstaff.

(3) Sunday, June 10, 1956 (7-8 p.m. segment)
The Sunday evening hosts were Dave Garroway and Don Russell. According to one newspaper listing, it was Garroway who interviewed Stewart. The interview is not available for listening.

(4) Sunday, August 26, 1956 (5-6 p.m. segment)
The late Sunday afternoon hosts were Frank Gallup and Gordon Fraser. Al Capstaff was the show's executive producer. Stewart was visiting an Air Force Convention.

(5) Sunday, May 26, 1957 (9:30-10 p.m. segment)
The Sunday evening hosts were Dave Garroway and Don Russell. Al Capsatff was still the executive producer of the show.

(6) Saturday, February 6, 1960 (8:05 p.m.)

In 1960, the Saturday evening hosts of Monitor were Monty Hall and Morgan Beatty.

(7) Saturday, May 22, 1965

By the mid-sixties, Bob Maurer had become the executive director of *Monitor*. The weekend hosts included David Wayne, Ed McMahon, Gene Rayburn, Barry Nelson and Frank Blair. This interview was conducted by *Monitor* reporter Hobart Lewis on location for Stewart's new film, *The Flight of the Phoenix*, near Yuma, Arizona.

LEWIS: Jimmy, let's talk some about *Shenandoah*. Do you feel another Oscar in the air with *Shenandoah*?

STEWART: *Shenandoah* is a story of the Civil War. An original story by James Barrett; I think a very good story. We're all very high on the result of the picture.

LEWIS: I understand your Oscar, which you acquired in 1940, was on display in your father's hardware store window in your hometown, Indiana, Pennsylvania, for ten years.

STEWART: That's right, that's right. He called me the night I won it and ask me what I was gonna do with it and I didn't have a direct answer for him, so, he said, well, send it back and I'll put it above the knife counter in the hardware store, which is what I did and it stayed there for ten years.

LEWIS: Real fine. Getting a bit more personal, Jimmy, you have been flying airplanes a long time. You are a Brigadier General in the Air Force Reserve and you have your own plane, right?

STEWART: Right.

LEWIS: Can you explain why you're so fascinated by flying? Was this flying an ambition of yours that you'd had since childhood or what?

STEWART: Yes, I think so. And I think…ah…you ask anybody that's been flying for a long time; I think they'll say the same thing to you. I think flying is a bug that bites you and gets into you. Strangely enough, I think, it's like the acting bug. I think the acting bug bites you and you're hooked. I think that pilots and actors can sit around and talk longer about just one thing — acting and airplanes — than probably any other group of people in the world.

LEWIS: I understand you and your wife, Gloria, are big game hunters. We'll change the subject there for a little bit.

STEWART: Yes, we sure did.

LEWIS: Okay, but I did want to ask you…didn't you bag a tiger in India at one time?

STEWART: Yes, in 1958.

LEWIS: Did you ever think about…ah…let's change the subject again, shall we?

STEWART: Okay.

LEWIS: I mean, safaris and all this sort of thing but, did you ever think of getting out of the acting profession and, perhaps, spending your life flying your plane and going on safaris and this sort of thing?

STEWART: No, I haven't…not so far. I feel…I feel that I have…this is my profession, the acting profession. I feel that this is my job. I like to have a job. I like my work and I'll keep at it as long as people want me.

LEWIS: Well, I'm sure that's gonna be for a long time. Well, James Stewart, thank you so much for talking with us on *Monitor*. You haven't visited with us in some time and it's been a real pleasure.

(8) Saturday, November 4, 1967

In 1967, the executive director of *Monitor* was still Bob Maurer, but the hosts had changed somewhat. Gene Rayburn and Ed McMahon were still there, joined now by Ted Steele, Henry Morgan and Brad Crandell.

Here, Stewart is interviewed by *Monitor* reporter Jay Miller on the set of the movie *Bandolero!* in southern Utah. In the introduction to this segment, it is mentioned that Stewart was retired from the Air Force Reserve in May and this is the topic of the first of Miller's questions.

MILLER: James Stewart, what would you like to do in the future? Would you like to be an advisor to the Air Force? Could you possibly get a consultant role?

STEWART: Well, I hope that I'll be able to make some kind of a contribution from…from here on. I don't know exactly what it'll be. I…I…I'll be in the retired United States Air Force.

MILLER: Um-hum. Well, it certainly won't mean the severing of your interest or connection with aviation. I believe you fly now, don't you?

STEWART: Well, I…I've sort of phased out of that, too.

MILLER: Have you really?

STEWART: Yeah.

MILLER: Oh, I thought that you had a twin-engine plane that you sort of got around the country in.

STEWART: Oh yes, I've had an airplane for a long time. I got my first airplane in 1937, and then after the war I've had several airplanes, but, it's become a pretty demanding business and when you don't have too much time to put to it to keep current…ah…I figure it was a pretty good time to get out of it.

MILLER: Now, you've made a number of Western pictures. Have you ever added up how many Westerns you've made?

STEWART: Oh gee, I don't know…I made 20…25…30.

MILLER: And you've made several pictures about aviation. One of the ones that most clearly stands out in everybody's mind, of course, is the Lindbergh story. What sort of pictures — aviation or Westerns — gives you the most enjoyment…or, is the answer really a good script?

STEWART: Well, I like the movies. I enjoy the work. I still think there's a great magic to the movies; to everything connected to the business of making motion pictures and I enjoy it. I look forward to getting on the set. I look forward to starting another picture and I'm one of the people that think that the movies are here to stay.

MILLER: The Air Force may retire you, but Hollywood is not.

STEWART: (laughing) I hope not.

MILLER: How about your university connection? You're a Princetonian. You were on the board of trustees at the University for four years. Are you still active in University affairs?

STEWART: No, I wish…I wish I had more time to do that, but those four years were wonderful. I…it gave me a chance to really get back to the University and to really see the new problems that all universities, all higher education, have today and it was a wonderful experience.

MILLER: It's certainly a fascinating expansion of the University. The universities today now seem to be concentrating on graduate school so heavily that a bachelor's degree is just like a high-school diploma, it seems, and I imagine that the pressure on trustees for discussions nowadays in this area must be very severe.

STEWART: It is, and it's a wonderful thing to see in a university like Princeton. The number of topnotch people, people that are really at the top of their field, men from the east, men from New York, the amount of time that they devote to Princeton and to the development of Princeton.

MILLER: Well, of course, what's true for Princeton would be true for many another university in the country, too.

STEWART: Yes, it certainly…it certainly is, but this was sort of the first time I'd had this firsthand look at it and it was very inspiring; very, very…ah…interesting.

MILLER: Well, now, one final question. Another Brigadier General in the Air Force of note, I think, has just retired — Barry Goldwater. Did you get to serve with General Goldwater at some time?

STEWART: No. I know of General Goldwater and I remember...I remember when he was retired. Our paths never crossed in the military, though.

MILLER: I think that would be a very interesting occasion when General James Stewart and General Barry Goldwater might be serving together in the Air Force.

STEWART: Well, who knows, maybe they might call us out of retirement and here we go.

MILLER: Well, we certainly hope that Hollywood never lets you get into retirement and thank you very much for being *Monitor*'s guest.

STEWART: Thank you very much.

(9) Sunday, March 1, 1970

Bob Maurer was still the executive producer for *Monitor* in 1970, but the show had been cut to just 16 hours each weekend. Gene Rayburn was the host on Saturday morning from 9 until noon, but since this show aired on a Sunday, it must have been pre-recorded for another segment of the show. Rayburn introduces the interview by mentioning that the play *Harvey* had just opened on Broadway the past week.

RAYBURN: Now, Jimmy, you starred in *Harvey* on Broadway once before and also in the movie version. What is there about the play that made you want to do it again?

STEWART: Well, I think...I've always loved the play and I think — and this isn't only my opinion — I think it's a beautifully constructed play and when I did it before, I didn't think I was right for it and I didn't think I did the part...I think I approached the part wrong and I just sort of secretly have wanted to do it ever since and I'm awful glad I had this chance, especially when Helen Hayes was in it with me.

RAYBURN: Yeah, she's great. Jimmy Stewart, do you have any offstage pets? Are you an animal lover?

STEWART: Yes, yes, I think I started being a real animal lover when I married Gloria. We've had wall-to-wall dogs in our house ever since. We even have a bushbaby, which Gloria and the twin girls brought home from Africa...six...yes, it's six years ago.

RAYBURN: What's a bushbaby?

STEWART: Well, a bushbaby is...the...the...sort of the scientific name for it is a Galago. It's actually before the monkey. It's a tiny little thing with great big eyes, sort of has a head a little like a bear and a long tail and big, sort of kangaroo-like legs and can jump 15…20 feet and is a nocturnal animal; sleeps all day, jumps around all night…an ideal pet.

RAYBURN: A lot of laughs in your house there…

STEWART: Yeah, a lot of laughs. But everybody…when they brought it home, everybody said, well, I think it's terrible that you'd take this beautiful little animal out of the jungle and he'll die immediately…ah…that was six and a half years ago. I…I built a big cage so he could jump…I think he's gonna outlive us all.

RAYBURN: What does he eat?

STEWART: Pabulum, and ah…

RAYBURN: You're putting me on, aren't you?

STEWART: No…I catch moths for him and he eats moths. He takes the wings off first…he doesn't like wings.

RAYBURN: I think Elwood P. Dowd is gotten a hold of you here…

STEWART: I…I…scout's honor.

RAYBURN: Jimmy, you and your wife have been big game hunters, haven't you?

STEWART: Yes, we've gone the whole circle, I think. We've hunted the tiger in India; we've hunted in Kenya four or five times. We've been back and slowly we've gotten away from the hunting part and now we go and take pictures of the animals. We've both become arch conservationalists and…but, by the same token, I wouldn't have missed the hunting experience.

RAYBURN: But the idea of getting pictures of them can be just as exciting and thrilling I…

STEWART: Well, it can…it…it…my theory on that is it can be if you…if you can do the thing the same as you do when you hunt. In other words, when you hunt you go into the animals' domain, you track him; you outsmart him to get close enough to him to kill him. Then the idea of having a record of that and then seeing the animal go off into his domain again is a tremendously thrilling thing.

RAYBURN: Our guest here on *Monitor* has been a man who's a legend in his own lifetime, James Stewart, now starring on Broadway in a marvelous play — *Harvey*; thank you, Jimmy.

(10) Saturday, April 11, 1970

Once again, Gene Rayburn conducts the interview. This time, it is aired on Saturday, so it most likely was broadcast between 9 and noon that morning.

RAYBURN: Jimmy, like Cary Grant, you're primarily considered as the good guy type. I don't recall you ever playing a heavy in your long career.

STEWART: Well, I did. I played...

RAYBURN: What'd you play?

STEWART: I played the murderer in the second *Thin Man* picture with Bill Powell and Myrna Loy. I was...of course in those Hammett stories, you know the real murderer is the fella that you least expect and I was the fella that you least expected. Now, I'd done it and they caught me and threw me out the window and killed me.

RAYBURN: Hmmm...so you're a bad guy...one time shot kind of bad guy, huh?

STEWART: Yes, I...I...I didn't care too much for the part.

RAYBURN: You won an Oscar nomination for your role as a protester in *Mr. Smith Goes to Washington*. How do you feel about the current-day protesters?

STEWART: Well, I give that example that you just stated there a lot of times when some of the protesters come to me and say, why are you establishment and why are you always making movies and saying things that are sort of pro-establishment?

RAYBURN: But Mr. Smith was...

STEWART: Mr. Smith was anti-establishment.

RAYBURN: No question about it.

STEWART: And I've made several of those. I made a picture...ah...later than that, a picture called *It's a Wonderful Life*. I was anti-establishment. I was against the banker in town and against the real estate developers and I was anti-establishment there. I was for the little fella.

RAYBURN: One of your most successful films, *Anatomy of a Murder*, was a forerunner to all the permissiveness in the movies...remember, they had trouble getting a seal for the film. They used words like...words that had never been used before...rape and so forth. If you'd known you were contributing to this trend, would you have appeared in that film?

STEWART: Yes...I really never felt that...that it contributed to a trend like that. I admit that Otto Preminger convinced me of this. But I felt that the story, the essence of that drama...ah...was good enough to necessitate a lot of the things that we said, a lot of the material that it was about. I don't think that stuff was dragged in; I think it was an integral part of the telling of the story and so I never...I never thought that was bad.

RAYBURN: Um-hum...

STEWART: I think that that's one of the big troubles today. I mean I...I...I think that if you...if you have a picture — whether it's doing well or not — if you have a picture and you have this tremendous shock thing in it...this sensationalism; if you take that out and don't have anything left, don't have any humor left, don't have anything of dignity, don't have any quality in the picture, then I don't think you're doing a good job. I think you're relying on a sort of a material, undramatic, really, thing and you're not doing a good job. You're not doing the right kind of job.

RAYBURN: Well, you've been doing the right kind of job throughout your career, Jimmy, and you'll be doing a lot of us a great favor if you'll just keep on making movies; our guest, Jimmy Stewart.

Moonlight, Memories and Miller

Jimmy Stewart and Jim Lang (*The Dating Game*) hosted this 3-hour Westwood One presentation which was originally broadcast during Thanksgiving weekend (November 27-30) of 1980. This is the first of three specials done for Westwood One by Stewart. The others being *Dancing With the Stars* (1988) and *It's a Thankful Life* (1990, his final radio broadcast).

The program opens with Glenn Miller's theme song...

"Moonlight Serenade" (over opening introduction)

Over Moonlight Serenade, Stewart says (this same Stewart segment would also be used again near the end of the show):

STEWART: I think the idea that the big band has survived all these years with all the different types of music that have come in and swept over the country and everything and the big band is still here and doing very well. This in itself is a very comforting thought and makes you very proud really. Makes you feel very lucky, the fact, that you were around and remember it very well when the big band was the thing.

"I'm Stepping out with a Memory Tonight"

STEWART: I was one of the first kids in town that had radio, I mean talking radio not the crystal set that you could get Arlington time signals on; and,...and...ah, my father helped me. I had aerials all over the house, bless his heart; my mother, they , they...ah...they let me bore holes through windows so I could put aerial wires down and I...but I...I...whenever KDKA, Pittsburgh started, a lot of the stuff they...they...ah...broadcast, was music and, of course, the big band was there. And...ah...it was a great thing in the early...in the early parts of radio.

Introduction, by Glenn Miller, for the *Chesterfield Playhouse*

"The Woodpecker Song" — Marion Hutton vocal
"Question and Answer Time" from an old radio show. Glenn Miller questions Ray Eberle
"To You" — Ray Eberle vocal

STEWART: I think it was in college. He was at one of the proms. I can't remember what…which…which prom it was or what…what year it was, God, but I think it was…ah…in Princeton when I…as I remember, there…there were…ah…a lot of the big bands come down for…for the proms and I think all of them did…did a lot of that all over the country, which just added to their popularity because they…you get all the college…all that age group and you got all the older people that have their dance in the cities of the country and so on. You get all them behind it, well it…it…ah…you just had something that was very popular with the whole nation.

"Tuxedo Junction"
After a break, Jimmy is back with another story.

STEWART: When you go dancing, in college when there wa a dance, lots of the times as you'd enter the dance floor…gosh, I remember this was when I was in training in the war and I just came back here on a three day pass and…ah…Glenn Miller was playing down at the Palladium…used to be a dance hall down in Hollywood…and he…ah…he was playing and I asked Dinah Shore, who was in town at the time, and we went down dancing. Well, we went into that place and there wasn't anybody dancing. They were all crowded around the stand and they were…I mean they all had their girls on their arms and they were all swaying…ah…at the same time, but the Modernaires were singing and the music was very quiet but had that great beat to it and everything, and…ah…this…this is a part of the big band thing. The idea that dancing and jumping around like everybody has to have so many square feet to do this without hitting somebody in the head with their foot, and…ah…so that…it's sort of a…it's not too quiet, I mean it seems a little confusing, but the big band, the band itself and the beat and the sound was always very important.

"Moonlight Becomes You"

STEWART: There used to be a place in Pennsylvania between my hometown, Indiana, and Pittsburgh and it was in a park and it was open…I mean it had a roof over it, but…and it was a dance hall. Paul Whiteman played several times...I heard Paul...this was when he had...had Bing Crosby and the Rhythm Boys — I think that's what they were called — but this was the same thing. Course people danced and loved it, but a lot of the time most of the people on the floor were right up standing...standing around the band.

"Make Believe Ballroom Time"

After a break, Jim Lang introduces the show's second half hour over Miller's "Polka Dots and Moonbeams":

"Sunrise Serenade" (Part of a broadcast from May 17, 1939, from the Glen Island Casino, New York, where Miller and his orchestra were beginning a three-month engagement. Miller talks with the show's announcer, Hugh James, before the music begins.)

STEWART: Glen Island was...I remember being there many times. A couple of times while I was in college, but then the three years I was in New York on the stage...oh, five or six times we went to Glen Island.

"Stairway to the Stars"

STEWART: It was always a party atmosphere, but it was subdued. It wasn't...people didn't jump around all the time and snap their fingers and...ah...and turn around and kick their legs, because #1, it wasn't that kind of music and #2, you were too impressed with the music itself to do all those things. You just sort of...if you were in a dance hall and if you were...as you did so many times...you're just standing in front of the orchestra and listening to...so many of the...Modernaires or so many of the vocalists. Frank Sinatra when he was with Dorsey...it wasn't the jump and...ah...holler type music that you see so much of now. It was very quiet, easy going, but had tremendous...as far as rhythm was concerned, the rhythm was there 100%.

"Here We Go Again" (Another live broadcast of the Miller Orchestra from the Steel Pier in Atlantic City, NJ.)

STEWART: I've got more memories and Miller coming up in just a minute. I'm Jimmy Stewart.

After the break, Jim Lang says that in 1940, Americans paid $50 million to listen to Glenn Miller records on the jukebox.

STEWART: I don't doubt it for a minute. That was right at the height, 1940, that was right at the height and I think that there were a few, you know, the Dorseys and Glen Gray, but Miller had the…it just meant that he…Miller had this certain something that made…made the orchestra, the whole idea of the Miller Orchestra, very popular.

"In the Mood"

After a break there are several more songs broken by comments from Jim Lang.

"Stardust"

This segment of the show ends with a short Stewart speech from *The Glenn Miller Story*:

> *I have one idea up here in my head. To me music is more than just one instrument. It's a whole orchestra playing together…see. And the only way I can express myself is to work out an arrangement.*

STEWART: *(In response to Jim Lang saying that around his house most people thought that Miller looked a lot like Jimmy Stewart).* Well, Glenn's mother would disagree with that…ah…she saw *The Glenn Miller Story*, oh, quite a while ago, but…and, I got this from…ah…Helen Miller's sister. And…ah…she said that mother liked it…she said it was a very nice picture, but Stewart sure didn't have the good looks that my Glenn had.

"Fools Rush In" (Where Angels Fear to Tread)

STEWART: In a way, you worry about as you approach every part, you're concerned about it and worried about it and sort of…ah…go… over the thing in your mind and sort of see, well now, how close do I… Do I want to makeup myself to look exactly like Miller and I decided against that. I…I think most of the time when you're picking out…ah… or when you do characters that are….are real…have been real characters, I always go back to a thing that Laurence Olivier said. He said… somebody said…ah…don't you get tired playing Laurence Olivier all the time? And he said, No, I…he said…ah…when I…ah…when I go for a part, I…I play Laurence Olivier with deference to the character. And this is when you're…when you're…ah…approaching a part like this, what…what you want to do is to fit in…fit into the picture, and… ah…fit in to the story.

"Elmer's Tune"

STEWART: The main problem with this was that Glenn Miller was a trombone player and...ah...he wouldn't be Glenn Miller unless the trombone was around. So, that was my problem to...whether I go off and take 2-3-4 years to learn to play the trombone, which wasn't in the cards, or, find a means, and there are a lot of means in the movie business, of convincing the audience that I was playing the trombone; at least doing it so that it doesn't draw attention away from the tune that I'm playing and so on. And this...we worked this out.

"Anvil Chorus"

STEWART: They got Joe Yukl...and Joe had been here in...very fine trombone player...and played in...ah...for...music for the pictures and special music for the movie musicals. And he jumped at the chance and we started and he said, now we're gonna have a fine time here because you...you can work up for the picture and while you're doing that you can learn to play the...ah...trombone, because it's...it's...ah...quite easy. We'd been working on it for about three days and...ah...on the morning of the fourth day, he came up and he said...I'm afraid I'm gonna have to quit. I said what...Joe, what's the matter? And he said, Well, the sounds that you make when you blow the trombone have upset...upset me so that I...I...I...I kicked my dog last night; I've never kicked my dog in my life. said, why...why don't we put a cork in the mouthpiece so that... that...and then you just teach me the positions on the...because that was...that was one thing about the instrument that was a little easier to fake than...ah...say a trumpet, because the trumpet...that's hand work on...on...the...and this is pretty easy to detect. But the...the...the positions on the...the trombone were very definite and made it easier. And... ah...Joe invented sort of like a piece of music only instead of the notes in the music, the notes weren't notes of music, they were positions that the trombone should be when the note was coming...ah...vocally. And it worked very well...and it worked...they had this above the camera. Joe was playing his trombone off...off screen. It took a lot of practice, but... ah...I had some pretty good reports from...from trombone people. They say I...I was watching very closely and I...you made a couple of mistakes, but overall I thought you faked it very well (laughs).

"That Old Black Magic"

STEWART: *(In response to Lang's question that after all that practice if he didn't remove the cork to see what he sounded like.)* Never, never; I didn't want Joe Yukl to have any more trouble in the family. I felt sorry for that dog.

"Indian Summer"

STEWART: We're gonna take a break now, but we'll have more music from Glenn Miller in just a few minutes. I'm Jimmy Stewart.

A scene is played from *The Glenn Miller Story* where Stewart as Miller calls June Allyson, as Helen, for a date after not having communicated with her, except for one card, in two years.
"Cinderella" (Stay In My Arms)
Another scene from the film is played here, this one having Miller showing up at Helen's house for a date. It's very late and she doesn't expect him. He has a gift for her…a string of pearls; they're not real.
"A String of Pearls"
The scene continues a year later with Miller phoning Helen and asking her to come to New York right away and marry him. She is to call him so he can meet the train. His number is Pennsylvania 6-5000.
"Pennsylvania 6-5000"
In the next scene, Glenn tells Helen that he's going to have a band of his own someday, with his own special sound.
After a break in the show, another scene is played from *The Glenn Miller Story*. This time Glenn is telling Helen that he hasn't found the right sound from his band yet. Then Jim Lang sets up a story from Stewart about how Helen Miller wasn't sure she wanted a film made about her husband.

STEWART: I think she wasn't sure about it. I…when…they approached her quite a while before it was even considered. I think she was a little concerned because Glenn Miller had just…well I don't know how long before the picture starting shooting…seems to me it was a year or two, that Glenn Miller was officially declared dead. Up until then been missing in action and at first she was very concerned about whether we would get on screen the real idea of the band…the real, sort of way Glenn…ah…developed the band from almost a very, very small start to one of the big ones in the country. Ah…I…I…I…I don't…I don't think she was sure this could be done in a movie. And, it was decided…it was decided because Helen Miller absolutely insisted on it…that she spend every minute of the shooting of the picture on the set, and that she had approval...at the end of a scene...she had approval of the scene. And everybody was a little worried about that at first, because that...that...that's giving pretty broad authority to...ah...someone, but we started out with that and it turned out that...ah...she was a tremendous help. And actually, she was a sort of guiding light to everybody working on the film.

"Moonlight Cocktail"
After a break:
"Jukebox Saturday Night" (Live broadcast with Harry James playing trumpet. After the song, Miller announces that James will be taking over his regular radios spots since Glenn has joined the Army.)

STEWART: He visited a base I was...I was stationed at...ah...once; and he was there during the day and I was on a mission and I didn't get back...and I didn't get to meet him. But he really did his job with touring, touring the different bases. He did a wonderful, wonderful job.

"(I've Got a Gal In) Kalamazoo"
A clip from the film with Stewart, as Miller, broadcasting from England is played here.
"Don't Sit Under the Apple Tree (With Anyone Else But Me)"

STEWART: All right, now's your chance to grab a turkey sandwich. We'll be back with more Moonlight, Memories and Miller right after this. I'm Jimmy Stewart.

After the break:
"Lights Out, Hold Me Tight"
An old radio program segment is played with Miller describing the full schedule of shows that the band is performing in England.
"Little Brown Jug"
Lang does a short segment on the loss of Miller's plane.
"Spring Will Be So Sad (When She Comes This Year)"
Another scene from the film is played at this spot. In the scene, Helen and some of the band members talk about the band going on even without Glenn.
"There'll Be Bluebirds Over (The White Cliffs of Dover)"

STEWART: I hope you're enjoying *Moonlight, Memories and Miller*. I'll be back with more music right after this. I'm Jimmy Stewart.

After the break, Stewart returns.

STEWART: I was in Tokyo. And I was over plugging Glenn Miller and some Hitchcock pictures. And Tokyo was one stop and…ah…I noticed it very much because they had an orchestra…ah…when we got off the airplane the orchestra was out in front of the airport playing Glenn Miller. But I…a fellow stopped me and he said…he turned out to be one of the leaders of the…I think there are now four or five Glenn Miller Orchestras in the country, but this fella, he said I…the Japanese asked me to come over and…ah…to do a concert in Tokyo…ah…do it for a week. And we were…we were traveling all over the United States, but I made it…we changed our schedule a little and I…I went over to Tokyo and we did… we did the week here. Well, we've been over here for seven months. I mean these people love the music. I've toured the whole country. These people love the Miller music.

"I Dreamt I Dwelt in Harlem"
"St. Louis Blues March"
So what made Miller so special? Jimmy Stewart has his own ideas on that subject.

STEWART: I think after you hear *Moonlight Serenade*, which I think was…ah…it was approached in a different way, as far as a band was concerned. I mean they usually had the trumpets leading the melody and so on. I think he got more out of that arrangement where with the clarinets sort of at the leading with the melody and the backup seemed more effective. I think this made the orchestra…it made it something different and…ah…something that was very easy to distinguish, to sort of set Miller sort of apart from other bands because I think the other big bands in those days had their sound too and then they had their way of projecting the sound, a way of presenting it, which is one of the things that I think made that such a great time and I think one of the things that has made the big band survive.

"A Nightingale Sang In Berkeley Square"

STEWART: I've got more memories and Miller coming up in just a minute. I'm Jimmy Stewart.
Jim Lang summarizes and talks of the staying power of the Miller Orchestra.

"American Patrol"

STEWART: I think the idea that the big band has survived all these years with all the different types of music that have come in and swept over the country and everything and the big band is still here and doing very well...this in itself is a very comforting thought and it makes you very proud really. It makes you feel very lucky, the fact that you were around and remember it very well when the big band was the thing.

"Chattanooga Choo Choo"

STEWART: I think he was just a...he was a very quiet...he was an excellent musician...but very quiet. I think there was a certain determination, but I think the determination was a little...had a little tendency to back away, and there's where Helen came in. And...ah...I...I really think he was a dreamer, but I think his dreams were just a...the fact that his dreams came true says a good deal for Glenn Miller himself, because he had this wonderful encouragement from Helen and from a lot of people but the fact that he...he made the dream come true and this speaks a great deal about Glenn Miller.

"Moonlight Serenade"
Original sign-off by Glenn Miller for a *Moonlight Serenade* radio program.
The show's credits include:
Writer/Producer.. Marsha Richardson
Production & Engineering .... Bill Levy
Executive Producer .... Norm Pattiz
Special Thanks to John Strauss, Jimmy Stewart, Paul Lindenschmit and Universal Pictures for excerpts from *The Glenn Miller Story*.

Stewart also recorded a special promo for the program. It is found at the end of record three, side two. Over a medley of Miller favorites, Stewart says:

> Hi, this is Jimmy Stewart. If you're a big band fan, you'll want to join me for Moonlight, Memories and Miller. It's three hours filled with the great music of Glenn Miller, plus a few of my favorite memories of the band leader. You get to supply the moonlight.

Music Parade
See *The Bing Crosby Show* of November 6, 1952.

Nancy Craig Program

This is a New York City program, broadcast on ABC, aired weekdays from 1:15-1:45 pm. The show is not available for review. Stewart's appearance was on Wednesday, May 11, 1949. Since Stewart's film *The Stratton Story* was going to open in New York City the following day, it was likely that the interview centered on that film.

National Air Races

On Labor Day, September 6, 1937, the National Air Races were held in Cleveland, Ohio. Jimmy Stewart made the trip from Hollywood to start one of the races.

While there, he also made a brief radio appearance which may or may not have been a part of the national broadcast of the races. If not national, it was at least heard in the Cleveland area. Unfortunately, the broadcast is not available. Radio stations around the country carried the race. Some carried it in its entirety, while others covered only the beginning and/or end.

National Defense Week

In the New York City area, this program was broadcast on Saturday, May 19, 1951, from 10:30-11 pm, although it may have been aired in different cities on other dates and times. The show is not available for listening and review.

Stewart portrays The Unknown Soldier. Also appearing are Bob Hope, Edward Arnold, Dick Haymes, J. Carrol Naish and General Omar Bradley.

NBC Weekend: Cover Story

Stewart was interviewed on this NBC news program on Sunday January 30, 1955. The show is not available for listening.

New York Close-up
See *Hi Jinx*.

New York Film Critics' Circle Awards
NETWORK: NBC
Sunday, January 7, 1940 (6:30-7 p.m.)

The awards had been announced to the public on December 27, 1939, and the broadcast of the 5th annual awards came a little more than a week later from the Rainbow Room, NBC Radio City, Manhattan. Kate Cameron, film critic for the *New York Daily News* and chairman of the New York Film Critics, introduces New York City Mayor Fiorello La Guardia. The mayor then announces the winners:

  Best Picture of 1939 — *Wuthering Heights*
  Best Male Performance — James Stewart in *Mr. Smith Goes to Washington*

Laurence Olivier, Vivien Leigh and Jimmy Stewart at the award ceremony in Hollywood.

Best Female Performance — Vivien Leigh in *Gone With the Wind*
Best Direction — John Ford for *Stagecoach*

Next, Mayor La Guardia introduces Samuel Goldwyn, who receives the award for Best Picture of the year and makes a short speech. With the New York City portion of the show completed, La Guardia says, "We take you now to Hollywood."

In Hollywood, Ken Carpenter introduces Vivien Leigh, who accepts her award and makes a short speech. Next, Carpenter introduces Stewart who accepts his award and makes this speech:

> Ladies and gentlemen, it's a great thrill to me to realize that, through Mr. Frank Capra, I have been able to do something on the screen which you, the New York Film Critics, consider worthy of this award. I'm very grateful. And now, with your permission, we would like to do again a scene which was one of Mr. Capra's favorites. Miss Anne Stone will play the part of Saunders.

Ken Carpenter does an introduction for the scene in which Stewart's character talks about liberty being a very precious thing that boys should be taught. He wants to build a camp for boys in his home state where this would be part of the training. The scene runs approximately five minutes.

Next, Carpenter introduces Walter Wanger, the executive producer of *Stagecoach*, who accepts the award for John Ford, who could not attend the ceremonies.

Finally, William Wyler, the director of *Wuthering Heights*, presents live scenes from the film. The players include the film's stars, Merle Oberon and Laurence Olivier.

This program is part of the NBC Collection at the Library of Congress.

Personal Angle with Kathy Godfrey
NETWORK: CBS
ANNOUNCER: Bob Hite
MUSIC: Norman Leyden and Orchestra

The hostess of *Personal Angle*, Kathy Godfrey was the sister of famous radio-TV star Arthur Godfrey. Her 25-minute show was broadcast daily on WCBS, New York. Stewart appeared on the Saturday, March 2, 1957 show along with Eartha Kitt.

Philco Radio Time
See *The Bing Crosby Show*.

Photoplay *11th Annual Gold Medal Awards Dinner*
  NETWORK: ABC
  SPONSOR: Sustaining
  PRODUCER: Sylvia Wallace
  DIRECTOR: Dwight Hauser
  HOSTS: Dick Powell, Sheilah Graham
  BROADCAST DATE: February 10, 1955 (9:30-9:55 p.m.)

The show was transcribed from Hollywood and began with several movie fans being asked what was their favorite film of 1954. Among the answers were *White Christmas, Seven Brides for Seven Brothers, The Glenn Miller Story, Magnificent Obsession, The High and the Mighty, The Barefoot Contessa, A Star Is Born, On the Waterfront, The Egyptian,* and *Susan Slept Here.*

Dick Powell is then introduced as the emcee for the night. He introduces his co-host, Sheilah Graham, a Hollywood gossip columnist, whose job it was to describe the scene inside the Crystal Room of the Beverly Hills Hotel for the listening audience. She describes the two-level room and its hanging crystal chandeliers, as well as telling who she can see from her vantage point. The list is a Who's Who of Hollywood at the time and includes Mr. & Mrs. Jack Lemmon, Kim Novak with Kerwin Mathews, Mr. & Mrs. Aldo Ray, Mr. & Mrs. Tony Owen (Donna Reed), Jane Powell with her new husband Pat Nerney, Mona Freeman, Anne Francis, Mr. & Mrs. Edmund O'Brien, George Nader with Barbara Rush, Jeff Chandler, Mr. & Mrs. Jerry Lewis, Mr. & Mrs. Gower Champion, Mr. & Mrs. Rory Calhoun, Jeanne Crain and her husband Paul Brinkman, Edmund Purdom, Mr. & Mrs. Howard Keel, Pier Angeli and her new husband Vic Damone, Mr. & Mrs. Gordon MacRae, Mr. & Mrs. Robert Mitchum, Jane Russell and hubby Bob Waterfield, and Mr. & Mrs. Dean Martin.

Adolph Zukor, winner of the first *Photoplay* award in 1920 for the film *Humoresque,* describes how he had won the award 35 years ago and the thrill it gave him.

Powell then began announcing the awards, beginning with the Special Achievement Awards, the first of which was for VistaVision. Accepting for Paramount was Y. Frank Freeman. Next, Danny Kaye accepted his award for his work as Ambassador at Large for the United Nation's Children's Emergency Fund. Van Johnson was up next for his outstanding performances in *The Caine Mutiny* and *The Last Time I Saw Paris.* The final of these special awards went to Otto Preminger for bringing the vast motion picture audience the classic Carmen in his production *Carmen Jones.*

Now, Powell moved to the Gold Medal Certificates, which were being awarded to the ten best films of the year as voted by the fans. Actually, only nine were mentioned at this point with the top film saved for the end of the show. The awards went to Warner Bros./Wayne-Fellows for *The High and the Mighty*, RKO for *Susan Slept Here*, Columbia Pictures for *On The Waterfront*, United Artists for *The Barefoot Contessa*, Universal-International for *The Glenn Miller Story*, and 20th Century-Fox for *The Egyptian*. At this point, Powell introduced Ann Higgenbotham, the editor of *Photoplay* magazine, who had special greetings for those in attendance and the listeners. The awards for the top-10 films then continued with M-G-M for *Seven Brides for Seven Brothers*, Paramount for *White Christmas*, and Warner Bros. for *A Star Is Born*.

Powell now moved on to hand out three of the five awards for the top five actresses of 1954. Each was presented with a *Photoplay* Gold Medal Certificate and each made an acceptance speech. The winners were Ann Blyth for her performance in *Rose Marie* and *The Student Prince*, Jane Wyman for her performance in *Magnificent Obsession*, and Debbie Reynolds for her performances in *Susan Slept Here*, *Athena* and *Give a Girl a Break*.

Next, Powell presented the *Photoplay* Gold Medal Certificates to the top actors of 1954. The first went to Rock Hudson for his work in *Magnificent Obsession* and *Bengal Brigade*. The second award went to Jimmy Stewart for *The Glenn Miller Story*. Stewart could not attend the ceremonies, but gave his acceptance speech from Hong Kong, China. He had these comments to make:

> Hello, Dick, and hello everybody in the Crystal Room. I'm very, very honored and very grateful to Photoplay and its readers for this award. And, although Gloria and I are some 6,000 miles away, we feel very close to all of you tonight.

The final award went to Tony Curtis for his performances in *Forbidden*, *Johnny Dark* and *The Black Shield of Falworth*.

Powell then announced that Gold Medal Certificates would also be going to two actors who couldn't be at the ceremonies — Marlon Brando and Judy Garland.

Now, it was time to announce the night's three biggest awards. First, the best actress award went to June Allyson for her performances in *The Glenn Miller Story*, *Executive Suite*, and *Woman's World*. The best actor award went to William Holden for *Sabrina*, *Executive Suite* and

The Country Girl. Holden made his acceptance speech from Hong Kong. Finally, *Magnificent Obsession* was named the best film of 1954. Accepting the award was Edward Mull, Vice President in Charge of Production for Universal-International Films.

Plays for Americans
    NETWORK: NBC
    SPONSOR: Sustained
    WRITER/PRODUCER/DIRECTOR: Arch Oboler

This was a wartime series whose main objective was to stir the souls of Americans, steeling them for the hardships of war. The series ran from February 1, 1942, through July 5, 1942. Only three shows from the series, including Stewart's, seem to have survived to the present day and there is some debate as to exactly how many shows there were. Stewart appeared on just one show.

A Letter At Midnight
Sunday, March 15, 1942 (4:30-5:00 p.m.)
Stewart's show, the seventh in the series, seems to have survived from a rebroadcast sometime after he retired from the Air Force as a general. The very end of the show also appears to be missing. The show begins:

> *The National Broadcasting Company presents Plays for Americans by Arch Oboler. As a further contribution to the war effort, NBC brings you a special series of new plays dedicated to people of goodwill everywhere who believe in the inherent dignity of man, who fight together now for a better world for all. This is a war of men and ideas and these are the plays of the men and ideas that make up our America and our world of today.*

As the play begins, an older man starts to read a letter from his son. His voice transforms into that of his son, Tom Greer III (Jimmy Stewart). He begins by trying to answer a question his father had asked in his last letter. The question was simply, "Son, why did you do it?" Tom goes back to college and to the year 1939 to begin his answer. Tom was all for keeping America out of the war and he was in an organization promoting that idea. A new girl appeared on campus and he began to fall in love with her. Her name was Lisa Edling and she was a refugee. Tom had a very hard time getting her to talk to him. One day, during a peace rally, Lisa interrupts a speaker, calling him a fool. He insists that she tell him why she had done this. He takes her to the Statue of Liberty, and while there, she says that the Nazis came into her town in Austria and killed her father and sister and tells him that the Nazis are out to change his world as well.

The next day, he learns that she has quit school to return to Europe and join a "Free Austria" group. Later, his friends want him to picket the Air Corps recruiters who are on campus. Instead, he signs up. He tells

Stewart and his co-star, Mercedes McCambridge posing in front of an NBC microphone.

his father that his safe world had allowed evil to develop and that he was going to help stop it. Then the voice transforms back to his father's saying, "That is the letter from my son dated December 7, Pearl Harbor."

The other actors appearing in the play were:

Mercedes McCambridge (Lisa Edling), Byron Kane, Gloria Blondell (Judy), Lou Merrill, and Byron Palmer.

The special musical score was composed by Meredith Willson. The orchestra was conducted by Charles Dant.

In Arch Oboler's book, *Oboler Omnibus* (Duell, Sloan & Pearce, New York, 1945), he writes, "...my favorite of the series was the play I did a month later with Jimmy Stewart, then a lieutenant in the Army Air Forces. Jimmy actually flew his pursuit ship through fog and rain to reach the studio just in time to go on the air in *Letter at Midnight*, a play which said something that I had wanted to say for a long time." Unfortunately, the script included in this book is the five-minute sketch which was broadcast January 24, 1942, on the NBC Blue and Mutual networks on a program entitled *Hollywood's Salute to the President*. That version starred Elliott Lewis. The full script for *Letter at Midnight* can be found in the book *Plays for Americas Thirteen New Non-royalty Radio Plays* by Arch Oboler (1942, Farrar & Rinehart, Inc., New York). There also is a section of "Production Notes," including a warning about casting someone as Tom Greer simply because he looks like Jimmy Stewart behind a microphone.

This program is available on two different cassette sets. The first set, *Arch Oboler's Yesterday, Today & Tomorrow* (Metacom YT-699) was released in 1987. This is a special 6-cassette set featuring twelve original shows written by Arch Oboler. The cassette case adds, "12 prophetic plays (rediscovered after 45 years) starring the greatest of theater and motion picture stars."

The back of the case adds, "Arch Oboler, winner of radio's greatest awards, looked into a prophetic crystal ball 45 years ago and wrote and directed these amazing productions. Amazing because they anticipated a war, and a madman, and a precarious peace at a time when there were some who tried to hide from reality in dark caves of wishful-thinking. A group of America's greatest performing artists, excited with the content of the Oboler plays, volunteered their time and talents, rejecting tremendous fees for commercial appearances which might interfere with the individual broadcasts."

The second set is titled *Arch Oboler Remembers WWII* (Adventures in Cassettes [a division of Metacom]) and was issued ten years later in 1997 as a 6-cassette set.

In 2011, it was released on the mp3 only set, *Jimmy Stewart the Ultimate Radio Collection Vol. 1* (Master Classics Records).

Presenting Alfred Hitchcock

This is a 25-minute documentary presented by NBC Radio on Wednesday January 25, 1956. Hitchcock himself explains, using clips from his films, how he achieves his unique brand of suspense. Stewart, who had appeared in several Hitchcock films, appears in a few of these clips. The show is not available for listening.

The Prudential Family Hour of Stars

The program began life as *The Prudential Family Hour* and featured concert music and the occasional short sketch of the lives of famous composers and how some of their best-known music was written. These shows were broadcast from August 31, 1941, until September 26, 1948. With its listenership declining, those in charge decided to change to a dramatic format. The title was also changed to *The Prudential Family Hour of Stars*, to reflect the new format. These new shows began October 3, 1948, and continued through the end of the series on February 26, 1950.

Six Hollywood stars served as the "Prudential Family" — Humphrey Bogart, Bette Davis, Gregory Peck, Ginger Rogers, Barbara Stanwyck, and Robert Taylor. During the first several months of the series (October 1948-May, 1949), one of these stars usually was the lead. By the time of Stewart's broadcast, the stars in the repertory group were being announced as Dana Andrews, Kirk Douglas, Irene Dunne, James Stewart, Jane Wyman and Loretta Young. In all, these twelve starred in 40 of the 74 shows broadcast. Other Hollywood stars, including Joan Bennett, Ronald Colman, Joseph Cotten, Van Johnson, Victor Jory, Joan Crawford, John Lund, Ray Milland, and Jane Powell were also cast in roles on the program.

An article in *Billboard* magazine on January 21, 1950, stated that Stewart had just signed a contract to replace Ronald Colman as one of the stars of the show. It stated that his first show would be broadcast on January 29. As it turned out, this would also be the only show on which he appeared since the show stopped broadcasting just three shows after that appearance.

The Short, Happy Life of Francis Macomber
Sunday, January 29, 1950 (6-6:30 p.m.)
NETWORK: CBS
SPONSOR: Prudential Insurance Company
PRODUCER: Ken Burton
DIRECTOR: Jack Johnstone
WRITER: Ernest Hemingway
ADAPTED FOR RADIO BY: Charles Tazewell
ANNOUNCER: Frank Goss
MUSIC: Carmen Dragon Orchestra
The cast included:
  Jimmy Stewart.. *Robert Wilson*
  Ted Osborne.. *Francis Macomber*
  Betty Lou Gerson.................................... *Margo Macomber*

In this Hemingway short story, Francis and Margo Macomber are on an African safari. Their guide is Robert Wilson. On the first day of the hunt, Macomber wounds a lion, but runs away, fearing for his life. He and Wilson go into the brush to kill the beast. Wilson is left to finish off the lion. Margo is happy that her husband is a coward, because she knows he will never have the nerve to leave her. Francis knows that she will never let him forget his cowardice. That night, she openly flirts with Wilson, remaining in his tent until two o'clock in the morning.

The next day, Wilson takes the Macombers to hunt water buffalo. Francis shoots three buffalo and begins to regain his confidence and bravery. Margo gets Wilson to admit that it is illegal to kill three buffalo and Francis warns him that she now has something to hold over his head as well. A gun bearer returns and tells them that one of the buffalo has not been killed, so they return to finish the job. When the wounded buffalo charges, Francis stands his ground and fires the final, killing shot. But, his wife also shoots. Her shot strikes Macomber in the back, killing him. Was it an accident?

At the end of the show, Stewart comes back to say:

> I'd just like to say my thanks to our cast, Betty Lou Gerson, who played Margo, and Ted Osborne, who was Francis. They were wonderful. Next week one of the Prudential family will be here to do a memorable play, The Night Must Fall, so don't miss it. Its star will be Kirk Douglas. Thank you and good afternoon.

Goss also announces that "James Stewart is currently being seen in the M-G-M production, *The Stratton Story*."

Quiz Kids

Not only were the kids on this popular show precocious, but they could also spell the word and give an exact definition for it. Each week five children, usually between the ages of six and 16, were the contestants on the show. For their appearance, all were given a $100 savings bond. The show originated from Studio E in NBC's Merchandise Mart, Chicago. Joe Kelly, a veteran of NBC's *National Barn Dance*, was the show's quizmaster. The show's researcher, Eliza Hickok, also wrote a book titled *The Quiz Kids* (Houghton Mifflin Company, Boston, MA, 1947).

Sunday, October 12, 1947 (4:00-4:30 p.m.).
NETWORK: NBC
SPONSOR: Alka Seltzer (Miles Laboratories)

HOST/QUIZMASTER: Joe Kelly
PRODUCER/WRITER: John Lewellen
WRITER/SCOREKEEPER: Maggie O'Flaherty
RESEARCH: Eliza Hickok
ANNOUNCERS: Fort Pearson, Roger Krupp
CREATOR: Louis G. Cowan
THEME: "School Days" (Gus Edwards-Will D. Cobb)

Although the show is not available for listening, it is believed that Stewart acted as guest quizmaster.

Radie Harris Show

Harris was a writer for *The Hollywood Reporter*. She was based in New York and her column was called "Broadway Ballyhoo." She had many friends among both Broadway and Hollywood stars. Because of these friendships, she was also able to sustain a radio interview show for both the Mutual and CBS networks. Jimmy Stewart was her guest on April 5, 1948. The program is not available for listening.

Two Stewart films had just been released — *Call Northside 777* (February 1) and *On Our Merry Way* (February 2). He also had finished a film with Alfred Hitchcock (*Rope*), which was scheduled to be released in August. It's possible that he was on the show to talk about one or more of these films.

On March 21, 1985, Stewart was one of many actors to attend the Radie Harris celebrity roast and tribute dinner at the Beverly Hills Hotel, Beverly Hills, CA. Others in attendance to pay tribute to Harris were Julie Andrews, Drew Barrymore, Milton Berle, Carol Channing, Phyllis Diller, Eva Gabor, Dorothy Lamour, Jack Lemmon, Mary Martin, Pamela Mason, Roddy McDowall, Gregory Peck, Robert Preston, Vanessa Redgrave, Alexis Smith, Robert Stack and Franco Zefferelli.

Radio Reader's Digest

The stories for many of the radio plays were adapted from the pages of *Reader's Digest* magazine. The show aired from 1942 through June 3, 1948, when it became known as *The Hallmark Playhouse* and continued on until February 1, 1953.

One Way to Broadway
Thursday, March 18, 1948 (10:00-10:30 p.m.)
NETWORK: CBS
SPONSOR: Hallmark Cards
ANNOUNCER: Jay Jackson

DIRECTOR: Marx Loeb

ADAPTED FOR RADIO BY: Robert Sloan, based on the story entitled *The Juggler* by Arthur Stringer as it appeared in the *Reader's Digest* (December 1938, Volume 33, Number 200), America's favorite magazine. (At least one newspaper had it listed under its original title.)

MUSIC: Jack Miller

THEME MUSIC: "Radio Reader's Digest Theme" (Nathan Lang Van Cleave)

Starring:
> Jimmy Stewart...Steven Spotswood
> Mercedes McCambridge ....Ally Spotswood

Before the play begins, Jay Jackson talks with Jimmy and they do a commercial for Hallmark.

JACKSON: And one way to introduce our star is to tell you he's a tall, lanky fellow from Pennsylvania, who happens to be a topflight actor, an Academy Award winner and one of the most likable people you've ever met, Jimmy Stewart. It's a pleasure to have you on our Hallmark show, Jimmy.

STEWART: Well, thank you, Jay. It's a great story you got for tonight.

JACKSON: Oh, tell me, when you first read it, did you have any idea how it would turn out?

STEWART: No...no, that's what I like about these Hallmark stories; you never figure them out in advance.

JACKSON: Ah...but there is one thing you can always count on, Jimmy.

STEWART: Ah...what's that?

JACKSON: Our asking a question about how to make certain of getting the finest greeting card.

STEWART: Now, I'm all ready for you, Jay. You just turn the card over and look on the back for those three identifying words — A Hallmark Card.

JACKSON: Good. And, of course, you know those three identifying words tell your friends you cared enough to send the very best. Now, shall we take our audience behind the scenes on Broadway, where there's no glamour, no glitter, just hungry, hard-working people desperately hoping for that one-in-a-million chance for fame. Steven Spotswood is one of those. The makers of Hallmark Greeting Cards bring you his strange story on the *Radio Digest* Radio Edition as you hear *One Way to Broadway*, starring Jimmy Stewart.

Steven Spotswood and his new wife Ally move to New York City, where Steven hopes to become a playwright. He writes a series of plays, including *Half a League Onward*, *The Last Straw*, *One Man's Poison*, *Never Say Die*, *Seven Pillars*, and *Flow the High Winds*. They are all offered to a Mr. Lee Grundy, but he doesn't buy any of them. When Steve talks to Grundy, he learns that all of the plays had something good in them, but that they just weren't good enough as a whole to work. In what he says will be his final attempt at selling a play, Steve gets the idea to take the best parts of each of the plays and combine them into one winner. Because they are so poor that they barely have enough money to eat, Ally gets a job to help support them while he writes the play. But, she begins to fall for Jim, her boss. Mr. Grundy buys the play, but when Steven returns home he finds a note from Ally saying that she has run away with Jim and plans to divorce him. Steve then plans to commit suicide by turning on the gas in his apartment. He gets two lucky breaks. First, Ally has a change of heart and returns to him and second…

At the end of the program, Jay and Jimmy have the following short conversation.

JACKSON: …and here's Jimmy Stewart again. Thank you, Jimmy, for one of the finest performances we've had.

STEWART: Thank you very much, Jay. Now, tell me, what's on the boards next week for the Hallmark program?

JACKSON: Well, are you a deepwater man?

STEWART: Well…who me? From Pennsylvania. No…No, I'm strictly an armchair admiral; I…ah…but I always like a good salty yarn, though.

JACKSON: Oh, we've got one — a story from real life called *Deep Water Captain*, one of the saltiest citizens who ever weighed an anchor or bossed a crew.

STEWART: Oh, who plays it?

JACKSON: Louie Calhern.

STEWART: Oh, that sounds like a fine show.

JACKSON: It is, so join us next Thursday, Jimmy, for the wonderful true story, *Deep Water Captain*, starring Louie Calhern, and presented by the makers of Hallmark Greeting Cards.

Jay later adds, "Jimmy Stewart can currently be seen in the 20th Century-Fox production *Call Northside 777*. Starting March 29, he will appear in the Broadway play *Harvey*."

One Way to Broadway is commercially available as a part of the 6-CD set, *American Icons* (Radio Spirits 43622). Also included are shows starring Kirk Douglas, Douglas Fairbanks, Jr., Clark Gable, Betty Grable, Cary Grant, Bob Hope, and Gene Kelly.

In 2011, it was issued on the mp3 only set, *Jimmy Stewart the Ultimate Radio Collection Vol. 3* (Master Classics Records).

Radio Week

This small notice appeared in the Sunday, November 14, 1948, edition of *The Wisconsin State Journal:*

> Miscellaneous
> 5:15 p.m. — Radio Week (WIBA) with Jimmy Stewart.

No other references to this show have been uncovered and the program is not available for listening. Because of this, it is not known what Stewart's involvement may have been.

Salute of Champions
NETWORK: NBC
DATE: Monday, September 22, 1941

The title of this radio special varies somewhat from source to source and may also be seen listed as *Salute to Champions, Salute of the Champions* and *Salute to the Champions.* This show is not available for review. Newspaper listings report this to be a tribute to the Army and Navy by stars of radio, sports, stage and screen. Compiled from several newspaper listings, those appearing with Stewart were: Lawrence Brown, Patsy Clark, Bill Cunningham, Dizzy Dean, Joe DiMaggio, Jack Dempsey, Leo Durocher, Betty Grable, Hank Greenberg, Rita Hayworth, Sonja Henie, John Kieran, Swede Larson, Joe Louis, Edmund Lowe, Alice Marble, Victor McLaglen, Bo McMillan, Pat O'Brien, Grantland Rice, Paul Robeson, Ann Sheridan, Albert Spalding, Gene Tunney, Lana Turner, Ted Williams and others.

Salute to Glenn Miller

On January 13, 1954, in Glenn Miller's hometown of Clarinda, Iowa, Jimmy Stewart was on hand for the premiere of his film, *The Glenn Miller Story* (the film had had its Hollywood premiere on December 10, 1953, and would premiere in New York City on February 10, 1954). Stewart, along with Miller's mother Mattie Lou, visited the house where Glenn was born, the school where Mrs. Miller taught and the family church. Iowa Governor William S. Beardsley was also there to dedicate the new Glenn Miller National Guard Armory. A half-hour radio program with highlights of the day's events was later broadcast on January 16, 1954.

This particular show was not broadcast nationally and, in fact, may have only been broadcast on this one Wisconsin station (WISC), or, at best, the upper Midwest area. According to an article in the *Waterloo Daily Courier*, Waterloo, Iowa, Stewart attended a "long list of receptions, a dinner and special radio programs before the night premiere." The number of programs, stations, content and Stewart involvement in any of these shows is not known.

Salute to the Reserves
NETWORK: ABC
DATE: February 19, 1949

Stewart himself was a member of the Air Force Reserve, so who better to be on a program to honor the reserves. Bob Hope, Gordon MacRae and Maureen O'Hara were also guests. According to newspaper reports of the time, Stewart and O'Hara were to appear in a dramatization based on the story of Nathan Hale. The story was written by Jean Holloway. Vice President Barkley was on hand with a speech. The show is not available for review.

Salute to You
See American Red Cross #5, April 25, 1957.

Same Time, Same Station

Same Time, Same Station was the brainchild of twin brothers John and Larry Gassman. It aired Sunday evenings between 5 and 7 p.m. from KPCC-FM, the Southern California Public Radio station. The brothers were the hosts, producers and engineers for the program. During the show, they talked about and played vintage radio shows from the '30s, '40s and '50s, as well as conducting interviews with radio personalities of that period.

On July 6, 1997, their show was a tribute to Jimmy Stewart, who had passed away four days earlier. That evening they played *The Jack Benny Show* from January 9, 1949, on which Stewart was a guest. They also played *The Six Shooter* from the April 13, 1952, edition of *Hollywood Star Playhouse*. The third program played was also the most interesting for Stewart fans. Titled *Flight 101*, the play had first been performed by

Stewart and Harry Bartell at an Airline Pilots Association Convention on March 14, 1958. At that time, it was not broadcast, but only performed for those in attendance. Its first public airing came on this program, 39 years later.

The script was written and produced by Jack Johnstone. Johnstone had worked with Stewart many times before in radio, directing all of *The Six Shooter* shows, as well as both Stewart's appearances on the *Hollywood Star Playhouse* and his appearance in *The Short Happy Life of Francis Macomber* on *The Prudential Family Hour of Stars*.

Shortly after Stewart's performance, the same storyline was used for an episode of *Yours Truly, Johnny Dollar*, titled *The Midnight Sky Matter*. It aired May 25, 1958.

In the play, Stewart plays the part of a man who must fly and land a plane in Alaska after the pilot is stricken with appendicitis. However, there is a catch. The plane's cargo is TNT, which will be used to change the course of a glacier that is threatening to cover up a gold mine. To further complicate matters, the plane's landing gear will not deploy, forcing a belly landing. The emergency landing comes off without a hitch and the TNT saves the mine. All in all, the perfect play for a group of pilots.

Screen Directors' Playhouse

The show began life as *NBC Theater — Screen Directors' Guild Assignment* on January 9, 1949. After only eight shows, the "Guild" was dropped from the title. Beginning on July 1, 1949, the title changed again, this time to *Screen Directors' Playhouse*. This title would remain through the programs final show on September 28, 1951. The show's stock-in-trade was to turn popular films into radio recreations. The catch was that the directors of the films were featured on the show. The director would usually introduce the show and then come back at the end of the show to discuss the film with the star(s).

SHOWS FEATURING JIMMY STEWART:

(1) Sunday, May 8, 1949 — *It's A Wonderful Life* (9-9:30 p.m.) (*NBC Theater, Screen Directors' Assignment*)
NETWORK: NBC
SPONSOR: Sustaining
GUEST DIRECTOR: Frank Capra
ADAPTED FOR RADIO BY: Milton Geiger from the screenplay by Frank Capra, Frances Goodrich and Albert Hackett, based on the story *The Greatest Gift* by Philip Van Doren Stern

ORIGINAL MUSIC COMPOSED AND CONDUCTED BY: Henry Russell (born Henry Russell Olson)

Production Under the Supervision of Howard Wylie

ASSOCIATE PRODUCER/DIRECTOR: Bill Cairn

ANNOUNCER: Frank Barton

Among the sound effects persons working for the program were Bob Conlan and Bob Grapperhaus.

THEME: "NBC Theater/Screen Directors' Guild Theme" (Henry Russell)

The cast included:

Jimmy Stewart..George Bailey
Arthur Q. Bryan .... Clarence Oddbody, Angel Second Class
(Bryan was the voice of Elmer Fudd
and you can hear some of Fudd's voice
in his portrayal of Clarence)
Joseph Granby... "Doc" Gower
Hans Conried .... Mr. Potter
Irene Tedrow .... Mrs. Bailey, George's mother
Georgia Backus .... Mrs. Chase, Mary's mother
Herb Butterfield... Uncle Billy
Barbara Eiler.. Mary Chase

Before the radio play begins, Frank Capra is introduced and talks about how the film was conceived.

The story begins with Clarence Oddbody, Angel Second Class, applying for a promotion to Angel First Class for helping George Bailey. As in the film, Clarence jumps into the freezing river so that George would save him at the same time as Clarence was keeping George from committing suicide. George then tells him his life story, complete with acted-out scenes, up to that point in his life.

Now, with $8,000 dollars missing from the loan company, and no way to replace it, George wishes that he had never been born. His wish is granted and Clarence shows him what life in Bedford Falls would have been like without him. George doesn't like what he sees and asks Clarence to help him get his life back again. George comes back to reality to find Mary, his wife, searching for him. She tells him that the people of the town have taken up a collection and have donated more than the $8,000 needed.

In this version of the story, it's musical chimes, not bells, that signal that an angel has gotten his wings.

To end the show, Jimmy Stewart has a question for Frank Capra.

STEWART: Say...ah...Frank, do you mind if I ask you a professional question?

CAPRA: Not at all, Jimmy.

STEWART: How do you...how do you turn out so many wonderful pictures? What's the secret anyway?

CAPRA: Do you really want to know?

STEWART: Yeah, I really do.

CAPRA: Clarence.

STEWART: Huh?

CAPRA: Clarence...the angel.

STEWART: Well...well you mean the character in the story?

CAPRA: Sure, he's been around for years. He stands behind my right shoulder and tells me what to do when I'm in trouble. He practically directs all my pictures.

STEWART: Eh...huh...well, Clarence, Huh? On a movie set.

CAPRA: Yeah, well, it was a little difficult at first.

STEWART: Yeah, I can imagine.

CAPRA: He didn't have a Screen Directors' Guild card.

STEWART: Oh, well, tell me, Frank...ah...if Clarence is so smart, how come we had to shoot the last scene of *It's a Wonderful Life* five times?

CAPRA: Oh, that, well, you see, Jimmy, that...ah...

BRYAN: (as Clarence) Hey, Capra, quit while you're even. Say goodnight and let's get out of here.

CAPRA: Okay, Clarence. See how he keeps me out of trouble. Goodnight, everyone.

STEWART: Goodnight, fellas.

It is also announced that *It's A Wonderful Life* has been presented through the courtesy of Paramount Pictures and that Jimmy Stewart can currently be seen in the M-G-M production, *The Stratton Story*.

This program can be found on the 6-CD/4-cassette set, *The Best of Old Time Radio Starring Jimmy Stewart* (Radio Spirits 5035 [CDs]/5034 [cassettes]) issued in 2002. It is found on the first CD or cassette in each set. See *Lux Radio Theatre — Made for Each Other* for further information on this set. It can also be found on the single cassette *It's a Wonderful Life — Bing Crosby* (Metacom GT220), released in 1991. The *Bing Crosby Show* is from December 14, 1949. It's also found on the Radio Spirits set, *The Best of Old Time Radio Starring Jimmy Stewart* (5034-cassette/5035-CD). It can be found on cassette #1 (SJSC1) and CD #1 (SJSD1). See *Lux Radio Theatre, Made for Each Other* for complete details on this set. It was issued as a single cassette, *"It's a Wonderful Life" Starring Jimmy Stewart*, Metacom RR639, in 1991.

Metacam also issued it as part of a specially packaged 4-cassette set for Christmas in 1991. The cassettes came housed in a wooden "Antiques & Collectibles" box which was made to look like a building decorated for the season.

In 2011, it was issued in mp3 only format on *Jimmy Stewart the Ultimate Radio Collection Vol. 1* (Master Classics Records).

(2) Friday, December 9, 1949 — *Call Northside 777* (10-10:30 p.m.) (*Screen Directors' Playhouse*)
    NETWORK: NBC
    SPONSOR: Pabst Blue Ribbon Beer
    GUEST DIRECTOR: Henry Hathaway
    PRODUCER: Howard Wylie
    DRAMATIC DIRECTOR: Bill Cairn
    ADAPTED FOR RADIO BY: Bob Wright
    ORIGINAL MUSIC COMPOSED AND CONDUCTED BY: Henry Russell
    ANNOUNCER: Jimmy Wallington
    THEME: "NBC Theater/Screen Directors' Guild Theme" (Henry Russell)
The cast included:
    Jimmy Stewart..P.J. McNeal
    William Conrad..................................... Brian Kelly/Boris
    Stacy Harris........................ Tillie Wiecek/Wanda Skutnik
And in the other roles: Peggy Webber, Paul Frees, Anne Stone, Rita Lynn, Ken Christy, Jim Nusser, Tyler McVey, Dan Riss

Police officer John Bundy is killed in Wanda Skutnik's speakeasy on Ashland Drive in Chicago. On her testimony, two men, Tomek Zaleska and Frank Wiecek, are convicted of the murder and sentenced to 99 years at Stateville prison.

Eleven years later, a small ad is placed in the *Chicago Times* offering a reward of $5,000 for the killers of officer Bundy — Call Northside 777. The paper's editor, Brian Kelly, assigns P.J. McNeal to find out what is behind the ad. He visits Tillie Wiecek, Frank's mother. She had placed the ad. He also goes to see Frank and finds out that Wanda had said two times that he wasn't the other man involved, but then at the trial said that he was. McNeal does a series of stories, but when he starts to involve Wiecek's ex-wife and son, Frank asks him to back off. McNeal agrees, but now, more than ever, wants to find the truth. Weicek passes a lie detector test and McNeal uncovers some political corruption. His stories are starting to create heat for the newspaper, which makes a deal. There will be a special meeting of the parole board. If the paper can prove its point, Frank will be pardoned. But, if it can't, it will completely drop the matter. When McNeal finds Wanda and she refuses to change her story, things look glum, but then some technology saves the day.

This same story, with a different script, had also been done by Stewart the previous year for *Screen Guild Theater*.

At the end of the play, Wallington introduces Jimmy Stewart.

STEWART: Thank you, thank you very much. As you heard in the beginning of *Call Northside 777*, the story's a true one. And, for us on the set in Hollywood, the attempt to recreate reality was focused on our director, whose fine talent has brought you such films as *The House on 92nd Street* and *Kiss of Death*. No man is more fit to answer the one question which our story, at the time it was filmed, did not answer. Ladies and gentlemen, meet Henry Hathaway.

HATHAWAY: Thank you, Jimmy. As for the question, it's what happened to Tomek Zaleska, the man who was arrested with Frank Wiecek?

STEWART: Well, he was sentenced to 99 years, too, wasn't he, Henry?

HATHAWAY: He was. And McNeal, the reporter, and his newspaper never gave up the fight to have Zaleska's case reviewed also.

STEWART: Yeah, I knew they were workin' on it.

HATHAWAY: Well, McNeal has wired me that after five years, they've finally secured enough evidence to re-open the case and right now the fight for Zaleska's freedom is taking place in the Chicago courtroom. So, that answers the question of what happened to the other man.

STEWART: Yeah, you think there might be another story in it, Henry?

HATHAWAY: We'll have to wait and see.

STEWART: Well, if there is and you need a reporter, I know an actor who's mighty anxious to work under your direction again…a fellow by the name of Stewart.

HATHAWAY: Okay, Jimmy, You're the first on my list. Goodnight.

STEWART: Goodnight, Henry. Goodnight, everybody.

At the end of the show, Wallington also announces that Stewart is currently starring in the title role of the M-G-M picture, *The Stratton Story*.

This show can be found on the 6-cassette set: *Mystery Superstars Vol. 2* Metacom BB429 (1977).

The set also includes episodes of *The Shadow, Sherlock Holmes, Cape Cod Mystery Theater* and *Alfred Hitchcock*. The Stewart show is on side 1 of the cassette, while *The Killers*, with Burt Lancaster, is on side 2.

The program is also to be found on *Screen Directors' Playhouse* (Radio Spirits 44812), which was issued in 2011.

Finally, it is part of two different mp3 only sets: *Vintage Radio Collection Jimmy Stewart* (Stardust, 2008), and *Jimmy Stewart the Ultimate Radio Collection Vol. 3* (Master Classics Records).

(3) Friday, January 6, 1950 — *Magic Town* (9-9:30 p.m.) (*Screen Directors' Playhouse*)
    NETWORK: NBC
    SPONSOR: RCA Victor
    GUEST DIRECTOR: William Wellman
    ADAPTED FOR RADIO BY: Richard Alan Simmons
    ORIGINAL MUSIC COMPOSED AND CONDUCTED BY: William Lava
    PRODUCER: Howard Wylie
    DRAMATIC DIRECTOR: Bill Cairn
    ANNOUNCER: Jimmy Wallington
    THEME: "NBC Theater/Screen Directors' Guild Theme" (Henry Russell)

The cast included:

Jimmy Stewart .... *Rip Smith*
Virginia Gregg .... *Mary Peterman*
Eddie Marr .... *Ike Sloan*
Hans Conried .... *Mayor of Grandville*
Sam Haye .... *Sam Hayes*
Gail Bonney, Jerry Hausner, Frank Barton
George Marshall .... *Guest President of the Screen Directors' Guild*

Rip Smith owns a public opinion poll business, but it is about to go under because of a bad forecast. Then, he and his partner discover a small town, Grandville, which exactly fits the national averages on everything. One town, that when surveyed, would make the perfect poll, a magic town.

Rip and Ike Sloan, his partner, set up an insurance agency there to camouflage their true purpose. But, there's a problem. Mary Peterson wants to change the town. She wants to build a civic center which would attract new people. Rip sets out to change her mind, while Ike handles the survey. But, when she finds public opinion forms in his "insurance" office, she runs the story in the newspaper. The average town is suddenly inundated with people moving in. The mayor tells Rip that the town is going to take its own surveys and sell them. Rip warns them they will fail and they do. A great exodus from the town begins.

Rip decides to take one final poll with the question being, how does the average American act when he has made a mistake? The 100% answer is he comes back fighting and tries to set things right again. The town does just that.

After the performance, Jimmy Stewart and Jimmy Wallington do a commercial for the RCA 45 record system.

> **WALLINGTON**: Now, here again is tonight's star, Jimmy Stewart. Well, Jimmy, how about some musical shoptalk?
> **STEWART**: Oh, that'd be fine, Jimmy. Ah…Jimmy, don't you have some other name, just for now?
> **WALLINGTON**: Well, my mother always called me James.
> **STEWART**: Oh well, so will I then.
> **WALLINGTON**: All right.
> **STEWART**: All right, now, James…ah…where were we?
> **WALLINGTON**: Well, Jimmy, I was just about to ask your personal opinion of the greatest advance in the 50-year history of recorded music; RCA Victor's new 45 RPM system.
> **STEWART**: Oh, I think it's wonderful, James. For one thing, that four… that 45 record changer's so handy to carry around.
> **WALLINGTON**: All over the house you mean?
> **STEWART**: That's right. Before, when I had my great big phonograph, I had to take my choice…now I just take my 45…see.
> **WALLINGTON**: Yes, the 45 automatic record changer is certainly a honey that way. Less than a cubic-foot big and it plugs into any radio or phonograph, anywhere.
> **STEWART**: And the 45 records are so tiny I can carry a whole symphony in my coat pocket.
> **WALLINGTON**: Yes, with the 45 you can really have music wherever you go.
> **STEWART**: You're so right, portable and practical.
> **WALLINGTON**: And the 45 record library includes every kind of music by the world's greatest artists and the stars who make the hits, all recorded with the finest tonal quality ever achieved; More than 2,000 wonderful titles.
> **STEWART**: And you certainly save dough on them.

WALLINGTON: Not to mention the dough you save on the original purchase. The 45 is far and away the least expensive automatic record changer ever made — only 12 dollars and 95 cents. The finest, smallest, handiest automatic record changer ever invented. Get yours soon at your RCA Victor dealer and be like Jimmy Stewart. Have the music you want, when you want it, wherever you go.

(Musical interlude)

STEWART: Well, ladies and gentlemen, this is the time that every guest of the *Screen Directors' Playhouse* looks forward to; our opportunity to introduce you to our directors, the men whose experience and guidance have made our careers possible. The director of *Magic Town* was William Wellman, but on this very special program, the first to be sponsored by RCA Victor, we have a guest who speaks for all the directors; one of Hollywood's true pioneers, the President of the Screen Directors' Guild, George Marshall.

MARSHALL: Thank you, Jimmy. You know, it was just a year ago today that the *Screen Directors' Playhouse* made its first broadcast.

STEWART: Oh, that was a mighty important date for the actors.

MARSHALL: What'd you mean by that?

STEWART: Well…eh…it's given us a chance to get you directors out in front of a microphone, shove a script in your hand and then…ah…

MARSHALL: Then…

STEWART: And…ah…just stand there and watch you suffer. Sorry. You know…now you guys know how we feel when we can't get that line right.

MARSHALL: I wish I had a 45, and I don't mean my record changer. Well, we've learned, Jimmy, and now this marks the beginning of our second year in radio; the beginning of our association with RCA Victor. So, speaking for all the screen directors, I'd like to express our thanks to the radio audience for making it possible. We hope you'll continue to listen and enjoy listening at this new time, one hour earlier. In the weeks to come you'll be hearing such stars as Fred Allen, Alan Ladd, Gary Cooper, Ray Milland, Rosalind Russell, Burt Lancaster and Douglas Fairbanks, Jr.; all on *Screen Directors' Playhouse*.

STEWART: And, now, I speak for the actors, George, in wishing you a lot of happy radio birthdays to come.

MARSHALL: Thanks, Jimmy, and goodnight to you all.

STEWART: Goodnight, George; good night, everybody.

MARSHALL: Goodnight now.

Magic Town was presented through the courtesy of Robert Riskin, the writer of the story.

Instead of the film's director appearing, the guest director is George Marshall, president of the Screen Directors' Guild.

At the end of the show, it is announced that Jimmy Stewart can currently be seen in the M-G-M production *The Stratton Story*.

In 2011, this program was issued on the mp3 only set, *Jimmy Stewart the Ultimate Radio Collection Vol. 3* (Master Classics Records).

(4) Friday, March 29, 1951 — *Next Time We Love* (10-11 p.m.)
(This and the remaining shows are one-hour in length, instead of 30 minutes)
NETWORK: NBC
SPONSOR: RCA Victor
GUEST DIRECTOR: E.H. Griffith
PRODUCER: Howard Wylie
DRAMATIC DIRECTOR: Bill Cairn
ADAPTED FOR RADIO BY: Jack Rubin
ANNOUNCER: Jimmy Wallington
THEME: "NBC Theater/Screen Directors' Guild Theme" (Henry Russell)
The cast included:
   James Stewart .... *Chris Tyler*
   Eleanor Parker .... *Cicely Tyler*
   Gerald Mohr .... *Tommy Abbott*
   Leone Le Doux .... *Baby Kit*
Bruce Cannon, Stanley Farrar, Joel Nessler

At the beginning of the show, after Jimmy Wallington introduces them, this short exchange takes place.

PARKER: Jimmy...Jimmy, since you created the original role of Chris in the motion picture *Next Time We Love*, I think it's only fitting that you tell the people a little about it.

STEWART: Well, thank you, Eleanor. *Next Time We Love* is the story of Chris and Cicely and what they did with their lives. It's sentimental, warm, tender and, above all, human. I assure you it'll live a long time in your memories. But, before we begin, here's Jimmy Wallington.

Cicely Tyler has suddenly retired at the height of her career. Tommy Abbott, her friend, tells her story...

Chris, a young newspaper reporter, marries Cicely. Tommy, their neighbor, is in the motion picture business. Tommy helps Cicely get a stage acting job to keep her busy while Chris is out writing his stories. Eventually, Chris becomes a foreign correspondent to England. Cicely doesn't go along because she doesn't want to leave her play. At least that's her story to Chris. Actually, she is pregnant, and she knows that if she tells Chris, he won't go. When Kit is born, Cicely becomes very ill and Chris has to rush home, losing his job in the process.

Tommy offers to lend Cicely some money so that she can land another acting job. Then Cicely gets Chris his foreign correspondent job back — this time in China. Chris and Cicely see each other only a few times a year and they seem to be growing apart. Chris resigns his job and moves to Switzerland to write a book. This time it's his turn to lie...he's not really writing a book. Instead, he has picked up a fatal disease while working in China and doesn't have long to live. When Cicely visits him for what may be the final time, Chris tries to run away on a train. Cicely tracks him down and learns his secret.

At the end of the program, Wallington again introduces the two stars.

WALLINGTON: Now, here are our two Academy nominees, Jimmy Stewart and Eleanor Parker.
STEWART: Eleanor...ah...would you mind if I...ah...sort of carry the ball here, so to speak, and say a few words about a very good friend of mine?
PARKER: Go right ahead, Jimmy; and I don't have to be a mind reader to know that you're referring to Mr. E.H. Griffith, the distinguished director of *Next Time We Love*.
STEWART: That's absolutely right, Eleanor; in my book, Ned Griffith rates with the best of motion picture direction. And, well, as I know I'll take him on my team any time. Ladies and gentlemen, I'm proud to present Mr. E. H. Griffith.

Griffith delivers a short speech and says goodnight.

STEWART: Thank you and goodnight, Ned.
PARKER: Goodnight , everyone.

When delivering the closing credits, Wallington says that Jimmy Stewart is now appearing in the Universal-International production *Harvey*.

In the early 1980's, Golden Age Radio Theatre, Inc., based in Fountain Hills, AZ, began syndicating old time radio shows to stations around the country on 12-inch discs. There were no set broadcast dates for these programs. Each show was hosted by Victor Ives. At least two Screen

Directors' Playhouse shows featuring Jimmy Stewart were used in this series — *Next Time We Love* and *Jackpot*.

Next Time We Love was program #188 in the series.

The show was included on the 2008 set, *Radio Legends Screen Directors' Playhouse*, issued by Radio Archives ((RA128). The 10-CD set features ten programs, all from the first half of 1951.

(5) Thursday, April 26, 1951 — *Jackpot* (10-11 p.m.)
NETWORK: NBC
SPONSOR: RCA Victor, Anacin, Chesterfield cigarettes
GUEST DIRECTOR: Walter Lang
PRODUCER: Howard Wylie
DIRECTOR: Bill Cairn
ADAPTED FOR RADIO BY: Jack Rubin from the screen play by Henry and Phoebe Ephron and an original story by John McNulty
ANNOUNCER: Jimmy Wallington
THEME: "NBC Theater/Screen Directors' Guild Theme" (Henry Russell)
The cast included:

James Stewart..Bill Lawrence
Margaret TrumanAmy Lawrence (Barbara Hale's film role)
Dawn Bender..Phyllis Lawrence
Jeffrey Silver... Tommy Lawrence
Jim Backus........................... Leslie of Harrington Interiors

Anne Diamond, Eddie Marr, Jerry Housner, Bill Bouchey, Betty Lou Gerson, Sidney Miller, Ed Max, Stan Waxman

According to an Associated Press story dated April 26, 1951, Margaret Truman took considerable pains to see that nothing got into the script that could have in any way reflected on her father, President Harry S Truman.

One of the film's characters had been named Harry, but she had that changed for the radio adaptation. A gag which involved General Douglas MacArthur was removed.

Director Bill Cairn also reported that Miss Truman asked to have one radio scene changed. In the scene, Stewart (who plays her husband) was to pull her out of bed in the morning. Miss Truman thought this was too suggestive, so it was altered.

Before the show begins, Jimmy Wallington announces that it is the 100th broadcast of the series and introduces the stars, saying:"...and here are our stars, Miss Margaret Truman and Mr. James Stewart."

TRUMAN: Good evening, ladies and gentlemen.

STEWART: Good evening. Tonight's story, *Jackpot*, is a comedy that deals with the trials and tribulations of the Lawrence family. It's a satire on the many "giveaway" programs offering thousands of dollars, fabulous amounts, to the average American family. Winning one is an adventure that is rather unforgettable, as we will soon see. But, before we begin, here's Jimmy Wallington.

The story involves the Lawrence family of Glenville, IN — Bill (Jimmy Stewart), his wife Amy, and their children Phyllis and Tommy. Bill gets a call from the Federal Broadcasting System in New York, saying that his phone number has been selected to be called during that evening's contest to name the mystery husband. The show will be on from 9-10 and Bill is told to keep his phone clear and be ready for the call. Since the prize is $24,000, Bill tries to find out who the mystery husband is.

(Bing Crosby and Bob Hope do a spot for Chesterfield cigarettes.)

While waiting for the call, Mr. Woodruff, Bill's boss, calls and invites them over to his house. Bill is rather rude to him. Then Tommy gets his head caught between two rails on the banister. While trying to extract Tommy, the phone rings. In his haste to answer it, Bill trips on a phone book and knocks himself out. Some water was thrown in his face and he's on the phone ready for the contest. His guess is Harry James and it's the right answer. They not only win the money, but many other gifts.

Bill is in an important meeting with Mr. Woodruff and Amy keeps calling him with problems. Bill doesn't get the vice presidency he was hoping for. The problems just keep coming. Leslie, an interior decorator, disrupts their household. Hilda Jones, an artist and a very beautiful woman, is there to paint a portrait of Bill. And then there are the taxes. A consultant tells them they owe $7,000 and they only have $400 in the bank. Bill begins to sell items they've won to raise money to pay the taxes. When Bill goes on a buying trip to Chicago, he goes into an illegal betting parlor trying to sell a diamond ring to Flick Morgan. But the police raid the place and Bill is arrested while Flick gets away with the ring still on his finger. Bill can only avoid going to jail if he can get Mr. Woodruff to vouch for him. But it's not a good time to call Woodruff because he's just found out that Bill was selling watches he had won in the store. He tells the police that no Bill Lawrence works there. (During this scene, there's a reference to *Harvey*. One of the characters says that Bill looks like somebody who would talk to rabbits…the six-foot kind.)

Amy is very jealous of Hilda Jones. Bill spends a lot of time at her apartment getting a portrait painted. But what Amy doesn't know is that she's painting a portrait of her, not Bill. Hilda brings the portrait over and Amy is very surprised. Mr. Pritchett, a lawyer for Flick Morgan, is also at the house. He says that Flick lost the ring and sent him with a check for $5,000 to cover the ring's cost. Mr. Woodruff even gives Bill his job back and makes him a vice president. Everything seems to be back to normal, and then the phone rings.

At the end of the show, Jimmy Wallington introduces the stars.

WALLINGTON: And now, here again are tonight's stars, Miss Margaret Truman and James Stewart.

TRUMAN: Jimmy, you starred in the motion picture *Jackpot* and are familiar with all its creators. How about telling us something about its director, Walter Lang?

STEWART: Well, that'll be a great pleasure, Margaret. One of the happiest experiences of my career was working with Walter Lang. And, as a matter of fact, I guess everyone else who worked on the picture had the same happy time. We really hit the jackpot when we drew him as our director. Walter is a combination of warmth and understanding and has an extraordinary sense of humor. Ladies and gentlemen, a very great director, Mr. Walter Lang.

LANG: Thank you, Margaret and Jimmy. Personally, I've gotten a great thrill out of listening to both of your performances, and I'll wager there are a great many more people who feel just the same way. On behalf of the *Screen Directors' Playhouse*, I'd like to extend an invitation to both of you to come back anytime; we hope real soon. Thanks again and goodnight.

STEWART: Goodnight, Walter.

TRUMAN: Goodnight, everybody.

Wallington also announces that Jimmy will soon be seen in the Cecil B. DeMille production *The Greatest Show on Earth*.

Jackpot was also used on the Golden Age Radio Theatre in the early 1980's. See *Next Time We Love* for more information on this program. The show was #204 in the series.

Jackpot is available as a single CD titled *Screen Directors' Playhouse* (Radio Spirits 2648).

Radio Spirits also issued this show as an audiobook, *Jackpot: Classic Movies on the Radio*, in 2006.

(6) **Friday, September 7, 1951** — *Broken Arrow* (8-9 p.m.)
NETWORK: NBC
SPONSOR: RCA Victor, Anacin
GUEST DIRECTOR: Delmer Daves
PRODUCTION SUPERVISOR: Howard Wylie
DIRECTOR: Bill Cairn
ADAPTED FOR RADIO BY: Richard Allen Simmons
ANNOUNCER: Jimmy Wallington
THEME: "NBC Theater/Screen Directors' Guild Theme" (Henry Russell)
The cast included:

Jimmy Stewart...Tom Jeffords
Jeff Chandler...Cochise
Debra Paget............................Sonseeahry (Morningstar)
Jerry Farber...Machogee

Ralph Moody, Byron Kane, Rye Billsbury, Jan Arvan, Paul Dubov, Herbert Butterfield, Tom Holland, John Stevenson

Tom Jeffords has been asked to come to Fort Grant to talk with Col. Bernall about scouting for the Army in their war with the Apaches. Before leaving his camp, he finds a young Indian boy, Machogee, who has been shot. He takes care of him and treats his wounds. He is rewarded with his life when the boy's father and another Apache find them.

Jeffords doesn't want anything to do with the war. He asks Juan, a "tame" Apache, to teach him the language so that he can talk to Cochise. Machogee is there when he rides into the Indian camp. Machogee tells Cochise that Jeffords is a different kind of white man and Cochise agrees to talk with him. Tom wants Cochise to allow the mail carriers to pass through his territory without killing them. Cochise agrees and they part friends. While at the Indian camp, Tom meets Sonseeahray and they begin to fall in love.

Back in town, Tom is about to be lynched by a group of men who think he is nothing but an Indian lover. He's saved by General Howard. The General tells him that he has been sent by the President to make peace with Cochise and that he needs Tom's help. Tom goes back to the Indian camp to see if Cochise will meet with the General. While there, Sonseeahray's parents agree to allow him to marry their daughter.

Tom brings the General to Cochise's camp to negotiate peace. Cochise agrees to try the treaty for a three-month period to see if it works. He breaks an arrow to signify peace.

Tom returns to the camp at the next full moon and he and Sonseeahray are married. Slade, one of the townsmen who hates Indians, shows up saying that an Indian has stolen his horse. But, when he gets close enough, he shoots and kills Sonseeahray and wounds Tom. But, the peace holds.

At the end of the show, Wallington introduces the show's three stars.

WALLINGTON: ...and now here again are tonight's stars, James Stewart, Jeff Chandler and Debra Paget.

STEWART: Debra, Jeff...well, this looks like a real *Broken Arrow* reunion. The gang's all here, isn't it?

PAGET: All except the horses...

CHANDLER: ...and the director.

STEWART: Well, the soundman's already gone home, so we can't do much about the horses.

PAGET: But, we can bring out the director, so ladies and gentlemen, Jimmy and Jeff and I would like to introduce the very talented motion picture artist who guides us through *Broken Arrow*...

CHANDLER: ...and directed *Bird of Paradise*, *Task Force*, *Destination Tokyo*...

STEWART: ...and so many other pictures that bear the name Delmar Daves.

DAVES: Thank you, Jeff, James, Debra. You all know the idea and the ideal that prompted us to make *Broken Arrow*. And the audience, after tonight's excellent performance, you'll also know that the picture is more than just a fascinating story. Through several decades of filmmaking, the camera seldom focused clearly on the American Indian. All too often, he was photographed as a purposeless, murdering savage. If that was motion picture's error, then motion pictures start to correct it with *Broken Arrow*, and restore the birthright of honor to a brave and proud people. Thank you and goodnight, everyone.

It is announced that Jimmy Stewart will soon be seen in the 20th Century-Fox production, *No Highway in the Sky*.

Screen Guild Theater

The Screen Guild Theater premiered on CBS on January 8, 1939, as the *Gulf Screen Guild Theater*. The sponsor was Gulf Oil. It aired under this title until October 19, 1942, when the sponsorship was taken over by Lady Esther and the show became known as *The Lady Esther Screen Guild Theater*. On October 6, 1947, Camel cigarettes became the regular sponsor and "Camel" was substituted for "Lady Esther" in the show's title. The show was sustained during its final two seasons. The final show was broadcast on June 29, 1952. The shows were a half-hour in length, except for the 1950-51 season when it was expanded to one hour. The show also changed networks several times, starting at CBS (January, 1939-June, 1948), NBC (October, 1948-June, 1950), ABC (September, 1950-May, 1951), and then back to CBS for the final season (March, 1952-June, 1952).

The star actors (they were backed by the Screen Guild Players) who participated in these shows, for the most part, donated their salaries to the Motion Picture Relief Fund. The fund was set up in 1921 to help actors in need. In 1938, Jean Hersholt, a Screen Actors Guild (SAG) member and president of the Motion Picture Relief Fund, said that the radio program's main purpose was "to raise enough money to build and maintain a home for the aged and needy who have given years of service to the motion picture industry." *The Screen Guild Theater* raised more than $5.3 million for the fund during its 13 years on the air.

The sound effects people working on *Screen Guild Playhouse* included Keene Crockett and Harry Essman.

Five *Screen Guild* shows appear on the 4-cassette (Radio Spirits 5034)/6-CD (Radio Spirits 5035) sets released in 2002. Found on this source are (cassettes are marked SJSC and CDs are SJSD; both are followed by the number of the cassette or CD on which the show appears):

Tailored By Toni (SJSC1/SJSD2)
Shop Around the Corner (SJSC3/SJSD5)
Vivacious Lady (SJSC4/SJSD6)
The Philadelphia Story (SJSC1/SJSD2)
Call Northside 777 (SJSC4/SJSD5)

See *Lux Radio Theatre — Made for Each* other for more information on this set.

SHOWS FEATURING JIMMY STEWART:

(1) Sunday, March 12, 1939 — *Tailored By Toni* (7:30-8 p.m.) (*The Gulf Screen Guild Theater*)
NETWORK: CBS
SPONSOR: Gulf Oil
ANNOUNCER: John Conte
MASTER OF CEREMONIES: George Murphy
DIRECTOR: Dorothy Arzner
WRITER: Connie Lee

MUSIC: Oscar Bradley and the Gulf Orchestra conducted by Frank Tours
THEME: "Romeo and Juliet" (*Fantasy Overture*) (Piort Ilyich Tchaikovsky; Oscar Bradley, arranger)

The cast included:

James Stewart	Peter Graham, a Greenwich Village author
Carole Lombard	Toni Warren, a designer of men's clothing
Spring Byington	Mrs. Warren, Toni's mother
Edward Everett Horton	Kenneth Pickles, Toni's business manager
Frank Nelson	gossip reporter

A competing men's clothing maker says that no real man would ever let a woman design his wardrobe. Toni decides to prove him wrong. She, her mother, and her business manager go to Greenwich Village to someone whom she can turn into both a well-dressed man and a successful man. She finds her man in Peter Graham. In no time they are married and living in New York City so that both can pursue their career. Now better dressed, Peter, who had not had much previous luck, now has a play in production and he seems to be spending a lot of time with the play's star, Ann Prentiss. Peter and Toni look like they are going to divorce, but they decide to try again, this time in Vermont.

After the play, this exchange of dialog takes place between Murphy and the stars.

MURPHY: Thank you, Oscar Bradley, and thank you, John Conte. And special thanks to Spring Byington, Edward Everett Horton, Carole Lombard and Jimmy Stewart for your swell performances here tonight.

HORTON: Well thank you very much and good night, George.

MURPHY: Goodnight, Eddie.

BYINGTON: Goodnight, George.

MURPHY: Goodnight, Spring

STEWART: Goodnight, and so long, too, George, it was a lot of fun. You know, George, I wish I could look like one of those Arrow collar fellas, you know. But, ah…my clothes just don't seem to hang right on me.

MURPHY: Oh, you're just self-conscious, Jimmy.

STEWART: No, no, not at all. Now look…look at this. Now that's a good piece of material, now feel it, it's okay. But there's just something wrong with it, you know.

LOMBARD: Oh, you don't like it, huh?
STEWART: No.
LOMBARD: Well, I think I can fix it for you.
STEWART: Oh, no, you don't…oh…wait a minute. (Lombard over Jimmy — Come back here. I won't do anything, I promise you.) No…oh no, I'm not taking any chances. Come on. So long, George.
MURPHY: So long, Jimmy. Now there, look what you've done, Carole, you've scared Jimmy away.
LOMBARD: Well, George, as I was saying…
MURPHY: Oh, no…no…no…no, you don't. No, I like my suit fine. It's wonderful, it's paid for, free and clear, no liens. There's nothing wrong with it. I like it.
LOMBARD: No, George…what I really wanted to say is that you've been a grand host.
MURPHY: Ah…thank you, Carole.
LOMBARD: Speaking for the rest of the cast, we've loved working just as much as we've loved listening to your Sunday evening…Sunday evenings to our friends on other *Screen Guild* shows.
MURPHY: Thank you, Carole, and it was swell of you to be here — grand show.

At the end of the show, it is announced that Jimmy Stewart has just finished a new picture, *The Ice Follies of 1939*.

Tailored by Toni can be found on the Radio Spirits set, *The Best of Old Time Radio Starring Jimmy Stewart* (5034-cassette/5035-CD). It can be found on cassette #2 (SKSC2) and CD #2 (SJSD2). See *Lux Radio Theatre, Made for Each Other* for complete details on this set. Finally, it was released in mp3 only format on *Vintage Radio Collection Jimmy Stewart* (Stardust, 2008) and *Jimmy Stewart the Ultimate Radio Collection Vol. 1* (Master Classics Records, 2011).

Radio Spirits also issued this show as an audiobook, *Tailored by Toni: Classic Movies on the Radio*, in 2006.

(2) Sunday, November 5, 1939 — *Going My Way* (7:30-8 p.m.) (*The Gulf Screen Guild Theater*)
NETWORK: CBS
SPONSOR: Gulf Oil
ANNOUNCER: John Conte
MUSIC: Oscar Bradley and the Gulf Orchestra, conducted by Frank Tours
HOST: Roger Pryor (the director of *Screen Guild Theater*)

THEME: "Romeo and Juliet" (*Fantasy Overture*) (Piort Ilyich Tchaikovsky; Oscar Bradley, arranger)

The cast included:

Loretta Young	Nancy Conway
Jimmy Stewart	Lewis Conway, her husband
Edward Arnold	J.P. Hampton
Fuzzy Knight	*elevator operator*
Roger Pryor	Don Hampton, J.P.'s son

The comedy is adapted from an original screenplay by Allan Scott and W. W. Watson.

Before the show begins, Pryor makes these comments about Stewart:

Jimmy Stewart is about a step and a half behind himself these days. It seems he hopes to open his own candid camera exhibit in about three weeks and so after working all day at the studio, he's been rushing madly home to spend the evening dividing his time between a roll of film, a pan of developer and a rather bedraggled sandwich for dinner.

Nancy is very upset with Lewis and threatens to divorce him. He works too much — he hasn't been home for several days. She's even taking back her maiden name, French. Unfortunately, J.P. Hampton, the owner of the department store where Lewis works, doesn't like divorce. If a man gets divorced, he also gets fired. Don, the boss's son, hires Nancy. He doesn't know that she is Lewis' wife because she is using the name French. Don and Nancy become very friendly. One night Don announces to Lewis that he and Nancy are engaged and that they want him to be the best man.

Later, Lewis runs into Nancy and she says that she hasn't agreed to marry Don. He asked her, but she hasn't said yes.

J.P. Hampton returns from Chicago with a list of promotions. He tells the married men to call their wives and ask them to come to the store's auditorium. When he talks to Nancy, she tells him that she can't marry Don until she's divorced. J.P. says that she can't marry Don at all and that she is fired. Lewis speaks to Hampton on her behalf, but Nancy comes in and says that Lewis is her husband. J.P. fires them both. About that time, Don enters with a telegram from his mother. She's in Reno and is going to divorce J.P.

One of the features of the *Gulf Screen Guild Theater* this season was that Roger Pryor would ask each of the stars a question at the end of the show. If the star couldn't answer correctly, he or she had to pay any forfeit that he then asks of them. The available tape for this show skips at the end and some parts are missing. Here is the best reconstruction of the Stewart section that could be assembled.

PRYOR: ...and here's a question for James Stewart, whose next M-G-M picture will be *The Shop Around the Corner*. Come on, Jimmy, you ready?
(The question is missing from the tape, but from the other information available, Pryor most likely asks him if Charlie Ruggles was in the 1935 film Ruggles of Red Gap.*)*
STEWART: No, no, Charlie Ruggles didn't play in that.
PRYOR: Well, I'm sorry, but he did.
STEWART: He did?
PRYOR: Yes, he did, Jimmy. Although Charles Laughton played the leading role...
STEWART: That's what I was thinking of...
PRYOR: ...and, incidentally, Charles Laughton will be here on the *Gulf Theater* next week with Elsa Lanchester, Jean Hersholt and Reginald Owen. And, now, Mr. James "You Can't Catch Me On That One" Stewart, here's the forfeit for you. You must play any little tune that comes to your mind on the sliding whistle.
(Another snippet is missing before Jimmy continues.)
STEWART: ...give me a pick-up...
Next we hear Jimmy playing a few bars of George Gershwin's *Someone to Watch Over Me* on the slide whistle.
PRYOR: Thank you, Jimmy...

(3) Sunday, February 11, 1940 — *Single Crossing* ((7:30-8 p.m.)(*The Gulf Screen Guild Theater*)
  NETWORK: CBS
  SPONSOR: Gulf Oil
  ANNOUNCER: John Conte
  MUSIC: Oscar Bradley and the Gulf Orchestra, conducted by Frank Tours
  HOST: Roger Pryor (the director of *Screen Guild Theater*)
  THEME: "Romeo and Juliet" (*Fantasy Overture*) (Piort Ilyich Tchaikovsky; Oscar Bradley, arranger)
  NOTE: William Powell was set to be the male lead in the show, but was confined to bed with the flu. When word got out, four actors called in to volunteer their services — Clark Gable, Cary Grant, Fred MacMurray and Jimmy Stewart. Stewart landed the role because he was the first to call. Because of this late replacement, Powell's name appears in the newspaper ads for the program.

The cast included:
Myrna Loy .... *Diana Hartley*
James Stewart .... *G. Alan Merrick*

The show is introduced as the radio preview of a new comedy by Robert Riley Crutcher from John McClain's *Cosmopolitan* story *Single Crossing*.

Alan Merrick is about to set sail for Honolulu to complete a merger with Egbert Eddington Williams. He gets a wire from Williams saying that his niece will also be on the ship and asks him to keep an eye on her. She also must approve of Merrick as a partner. He figures that she will be the worst looking girl on the ship, but when he gets a look at the only female Williams on board, she turns out to be just the opposite. But, because of another woman that he keeps running into, he never gets to meet Miss Williams.

The other woman is Diana Hartley. She first turns up in his stateroom suffering from sea sickness. When Alan learns that Miss Williams is in the pool, he goes to meet her. Instead, he finds Diana and he gets tied up with her as Williams leaves. Diana tries to help him make contact with Williams at a costume party. She dresses him as the devil and off he goes to the party. It turns out that the party is the next night.

When they finally arrive in Honolulu, it turns out that Williams' niece is his sister's daughter and her name is Diana Hartley. This results in a double merger.

The stars come back to talk to Roger Pryor at the end of the show.

PRYOR: Thank you, Myrna, and thank you, Jimmy. Don't go away, though; because in just a moment we're gonna bring on the Gulf question box.

STEWART: Say, Rog...ah...before you ask your questions, I'd like to ask you one.

PRYOR: All right, Jimmy, go right ahead.

STEWART: Well...ah...Rog, do you collect antiques?

PRYOR: Antiques? Well, what makes you ask a question like that?

STEWART: Well, let me see, I think it was Thursday night, I came... yes, it was Thursday night, I noticed an old-fashioned sort of a carriage in your driveway there.

PRYOR: Carriage?

STEWART: Carriage.

PRYOR: Oh, now, Jimmy, take it easy. That was Jack Benny's Maxwell.

STEWART: Oh, was it? My, how the automobile has changed.

PRYOR: Yes, and you're not fooling, Jimmy…(goes into a commercial for Gulf Oil).

PRYOR: And now for the Gulf Question Box. Remember, you must answer my question correctly or pay a forfeit. Ready? Our first question goes to Myrna Loy who will soon be seen with William Powell in M-G-M's forthcoming production, *I Love You Again*. Myrna, what movie star recently took a bow in Congress?

LOY: In Congress? Oh, I know, Olivia de Havilland.

PRYOR: That is absolutely correct. Olivia was in Washington for the birthday ball. She visited the Senate and was sitting in the gallery when a Senator noticed her and she was ask to take a bow. Incidentally, Olivia de Havilland will be here in the *Gulf Theater* next week with Jeffrey Lynn and that two-fisted star, Jimmy Cagney. Now, the next question is for Jimmy Stewart, who is currently appearing in M-G-M's *Shop Around the Corner*. Ah…Jimmy, come over here a second.

STEWART: Wait a minute…wait a minute. I'd like to ask you one.

PRYOR: You'd like to ask me one?

STEWART: Yeah.

PRYOR: Ah…all right…all right.

STEWART: A couple of weeks ago, I was listening to the program and you said something…that the first talking picture was…ah…*Lights in New York*.

PRYOR: *Lights of New York*.

STEWART: *Lights of New York*, with Antonio Moreno.

PRYOR: Um…hum…that's what I said.

STEWART: Yeah, well it was *Lights of New York* all right, but Antonio Moreno wasn't in it because I saw it. I wanted to check up on…

PRYOR: He wasn't in it?

STEWART: No. How about you paying a forfeit now. You…

PRYOR: Me? Paying a forfeit? Oh, I don't do forfeits; I give them to other people.

STEWART: No, no, you pay the forfeit. Here, I want you to recite this thing the way Rochester would do it…I'll fix him.

PRYOR: *(imitating Rochester)* To be or not to be, that is the question…

PRYOR: Thank you and goodnight, Jimmy, and goodnight, Myrna.

The show can be found on several mp3 only sets: *Vintage Radio Collection Jimmy Stewart* (Stardust, 2008), *Myrna Loy The Ultimate Radio Collection* (Master Classics Records, 2011) and *Jimmy Stewart the Ultimate Radio Collection Vol. 1* (Master Classics Records, 2011).

(4) Sunday, September 29, 1940 — *Shop Around the Corner* (7:30-8 p.m.) (*The Gulf Screen Guild Theater*)
   NETWORK: CBS
   SPONSOR: Gulf Oil
   ANNOUNCER: Bud Heistand (new announcer for the start of the third season)
   RADIO ADAPTATION BY: Norman Corwin
   MUSIC: Oscar Bradley and the Gulf Orchestra, conducted by Frank Tours
   HOST: Roger Pryor (the director of *Screen Guild Theater*)
   THEME: "Romeo and Juliet" (*Fantasy Overture*) (Piort Ilyich Tchaikovsky; Oscar Bradley, arranger)
   The cast included:
   Jimmy Stewart... Martin
   Margaret Sullavan .... Klara Novak
   Frank Morgan .... Hugo Matuschek

This is the first show of the new season for *The Gulf Screen Guild Theater*. All three actors are reprising their film roles for this radio play. However, for some reason, Stewart's character's name has been changed from Alfred Kralik in the film to simply Martin in the radio play. At times, Martin is used as if it was his first name and at other times he is referred to as Mr. Martin.

Before the show begins, Jean Hersholt, president of the Motion Picture Relief Fund, talks about the Home for the aged and needy who have given years of service to the motion picture industry which is about to begin construction. Much of the money raised for the community has come from this program.

Hugo Matuschek is the owner of Matuschek's Gift Shop in Budapest and the narrator of this story. Martin, his head clerk, is having some problems with Klara Novak, a new salesgirl. Nothing major, but they just don't seem to get along.

Martin has been writing letters back and forth with a woman whose ad he had seen in a newspaper. They had not exchanged names or pictures. But, they are about to meet for the first time in a coffee shop. Martin takes Pirovitch, another employee at Matuschek's, with him for support. Pirovitch looks through the window to find the girl. When he does, it turns out to be Miss Novak. Martin goes in and talks with her, but never tells her that he is the man she was to have met. Klara tells Martin that she could have easily fallen for him when she first started working at the shop.

In their letters, they arrange a second meeting at Klara's apartment. When she opens her door to answer a knock, there's Martin again. After some polite conversation, Martin tells her to get her key, open box 237 and read the letter waiting for her. For the first time, she realizes…

After the play, we hear the following:

PRYOR: Thank you, Margaret Sullavan, James Stewart and Frank Morgan, for a really grand performance and thank you, too, Norman Corwin, for your swell radio adaptation. And, now, on with the show. You know…

HEISTAND: Hey, Roger…Hey, Roger, remember me?

PRYOR: Oh, I'm sorry, Bud, I almost forgot to introduce you. Ladies and gentlemen, meet our new *Gulf Theater* announcer, Bud Heistand.

STEWART: Say…ah…say, haven't I seen you in pictures, Bud? Your face is familiar.

HEISTAND: Well, ah…I have done some work, Jimmy, but I'm usually just a face on the cutting room floor.

MORGAN: Oh yes…Well, don't fret, young man, we all start that way. Eh…I can remember when I first started in pictures, I was…ah yes, but that's another story. Besides, it's so glamorous I can sell it; why give it away? So, ah, you wanna be an actor? Well, I'm just the man to help you.

HEISTAND: Well, gee, that's swell, Mr. Morgan. Ah, right now, however, I'm busy learning to be an authority on gas…*(into a commercial for Gulf)*.

(After the commercial)

HEISTAND: James Stewart and Frank Morgan appear through the courtesy of Metro-Goldwyn-Mayer. Jimmy's latest picture is *The Philadelphia Story* and Frank Morgan will soon be seen in *Hullabaloo*.

This show can be found on the Radio Spirits set, *The Best of Old Time Radio Starring Jimmy Stewart* (5034-cassette/5035-CD). It can be found on cassette #3 (SJSC3) and CD #5 (SJSD5). See *Lux Radio Theatre, Made for Each Other* for complete details on this set.

In 2001, it was issued in mp3 only format on *Jimmy Stewart the Ultimate Radio Collection Vol. 1* (Master Classics Records).

Radio Spirits also issued this show as an audiobook, *The Shop Around the Corner: Classic Movies on the Radio*, in 2006.

(5) Monday, December 3, 1945 — *Vivacious Lady* (10-10:30 p.m.)
(*The Lady Esther Screen Guild Theater*)
NETWORK: CBS
SPONSOR: Lady Esther
PRODUCER: Bill Lawrence
ANNOUNCER: Truman Bradley
MUSIC: Wilbur Hatch (arranger and conductor)
The cast included:
   James Stewart .... Professor Peter Morgan
   Janet Blair .... Francey Brent Morgan
   Frank Nelson .... Keith Morgan
   Verna Felton .... Mrs. Martha Morgan

The show was adapted for radio from the 1938 RKO screenplay by P.J. Wolfson and Ernest Pagano, based on a story by I.A.R. Wylie. Stewart reprises his film role, while Blair replaces Ginger Rogers as Francey.

Peter Morgan is in a New York bar to find his cousin Keith and return him to Old Sharon College. But, when Peter spies Francey, the singer at the bar, he fall immediately in love with her. He takes her out and misses his train. They wind up getting married. When they return to Old Sharon, Helen meets them. Helen is engaged to Peter. Helen and Peter's father believe that Francey is with Keith and no one tells them any different.

Keith talks Francey into signing up for Peter's botany class. When she comes to class, Peter is flustered, but promises to tell his father that they are married. Needless to say, his father is very upset.

Keith shows up at Peter's class drunk and tells him that Francey is taking a train back to New York because she doesn't want to hurt his name. Peter begins drinking also. When his father turns up and finds them both drunk, he dismisses the class and takes Peter home. Peter's mother tells him that she thinks that Francey will be good for the family. Peter agrees and rushes off to stop the train.

The stars are not interviewed at the end of the play as they usually were. However, Truman Bradley announces that Jimmy's next project will be *It's a Wonderful Life* for Liberty Films, to be produced and directed by Frank Capra.

This show can be found on the Radio Spirits set, *The Best of Old Time Radio Starring Jimmy Stewart* (5034-cassette/5035-CD). It can be found on cassette #4 (SJSC4) and CD #6 (SJSD6). See *Lux Radio Theatre*, *Made for Each Other* for complete details on this set.

(6) Monday, March 17, 1947 — *The Philadelphia Story* (10-10:30 p.m.) (*The Lady Esther Screen Guild Theater*)

SPONSOR: Lady Esther
PRODUCER/DIRECTOR: Bill Lawrence
ANNOUNCER: Truman Bradley
RADIO ADAPTATION: Harry Kronman (from the screenplay by Donald Ogden Stewart, adapted from the play by Philip Barry)
MUSIC: Wilbur Hatch (arranger and conductor)
The cast includes:

Jimmy Stewart............................*McCauley "Mike" Connor*
Katharine Hepburn..*Tracy Lord*
Cary Grant...*C.K. Dexter Haven*
Lurene Tuttle..*Liz Imbrie*
Joan Banks– Margaret Lord
Gloria McMillan..*Dinah Lord*
Barney Phillips ....*Sidney Kidd*

Spy magazine wants an exclusive story, with photos, of Tracy Lord's wedding. Mr. Kidd, the editor, is sending Mike Connor to write the story and Liz Embry to take the photos. They are not invited and probably not wanted at the wedding, so Kidd brings in Dexter Haven, Tracy's first husband, to get them in. The ruse doesn't work, as Tracy deduces they are from *Spy*, but she doesn't care if they stay. Tracy falls for Mike and her fiancé, George, sees them kissing and sees Mike carry her to her room. He calls the wedding off. Mike quickly proposes, but she turns him down because she knows that he and Liz have something going. Through it all, Tracy and Dexter realize that there is something still between them. They never used their first marriage license because they eloped, so they decide to use it now.

Directly after the play, the following conversation takes place.

BRADLEY: Thank you, Jimmy Stewart, Cary Grant and Katharine Hepburn, for a most delightful half hour.
HEPBURN: Well, as a matter of fact, Mr. Bradley, there isn't an actor or actress in Hollywood who isn't eager to come here and take part in the great work this program does for the Motion Picture Relief Fund and its Country House. Am I right, boys?
GRANT: You are right, Kate.
STEWART: That's right…you can say that again.
HEPBURN: And now, before we tell you about next week's show, here's a word from one of America's best-known beauty authorities, Lady Esther.

After the commercial, Truman Bradley tells what films the three stars are now in, including saying, "James Stewart can now be seen in the Liberty Film's production of Frank Capra's *It's a Wonderful Life*."

The Philadelphia Story is available commercially as a single cassette, titled *Screen Guild Players* (Radio Spirits 1366).

Cary Grant and Stewart wearing skirts at a dress rehearsal.

It can also be found on the Radio Spirits set, *The Best of Old Time Radio Starring Jimmy Stewart* (5034-cassette/5035-CD). It can be found on cassette #1 (SJSC1) and CD #2 (SJSD2). See *Lux Radio Theatre, Made for Each Other* for complete details on this set.

(7) Monday, December 29, 1947 — *It's A Wonderful Life* (10:30-11 p.m.) (*The Camel Screen Guild Theater*)
NETWORK: CBS
SPONSOR: Camel Cigarettes
ANNOUNCER: Michael Roy
COMMERCIAL VOICES: Michael Roy, Ed Chandler
DIRECTOR: William Lawrence
ADAPTATIONS: Harry Kronman
SUPERVISOR: Don Bernard
SOUND: Harry Essman
MUSIC: Wilbur Hatch
THEME: "Camel Theme" (Freddie Rich)

It's a Wonderful Life was broadcast on three different occasions by Screen Guild Theater. The show of this date and the one for December 29, 1949, were both a half hour in length, while the show of March 15, 1951, was an hour long. None of the shows is available for listening, so it is not known if the two half hour shows were the same or different productions.

Although the audio for the 1947 show doesn't appear to have survived, the final script for the show is available. It lists the following actors as being heard (their roles are not supplied):
  James Stewart
  Donna Reed
  Victor Moore
  Joe Granby
  Bob Beban
  Ralph Moody
  Griff Bennett
  Lou Merrill
  Janet Scott
  Georgia Backus
  Joann Marlowe
Three other names also appear, but have been crossed out:
  Jenny Farber
  Howard Jeffrey (ad libs)
  Johnny McGovern (ad libs)

The script differs from all the other radio productions of *It's a Wonderful Life*, including those done for *Lux Radio Theatre*, *Screen Directors' Playhouse* and *Stars on the Air* in one important way. The story takes place on New Year's Eve, not Christmas Eve. It must have sounded very strange to hear Stewart shouting "Happy New Year" rather than "Merry Christmas" near the end of the play.

Even Stewart's remarks at the end of the show have been scripted. After Michael Roy tells the audience that the show supports the Motion Picture Relief Fund and its Country House, he introduces Stewart and says that he thinks he has a special message for the audience.

> *When you've been in a hospital a long time, anything that lightens the monotony is welcomed in a way that can hardly be understood by people on the outside. That's why it gives me real pleasure to tell you that the makers of Camels send free cigarettes each week to the men in servicemen's hospitals. This week, free Camels go to:*
>
> *U.S. Army Fitzsimmons General Hospital, Denver Colorado...*
> *U.S. Marine Hospital, Seattle, Washington...*
> *and Veterans' Hospital, Rutland Heights, Massachusetts.*
>
> *Goodnight, everybody. Happy New Year!*

This same basic script by Harry Kronman was also used for the December 13, 1951 production for *Stars in the Air*. There are a few minor variations, including the shift back to Christmas Eve, but most lines remain unchanged.

Radio Spirits also issued this show as an audiobook, *It's a Wonderful Life: Classic Movies on the Radio*, in 2006.

(8) Thursday, October 7, 1948 — *Call Northside 777* (10-10:30 p.m.) (*The Camel Screen Guild Theater*)
    NETWORK: NBC
    SPONSOR: Camel Cigarettes
    ANNOUNCER: Johnny Lang
    DIRECTOR: Bill Lawrence
    RADIO ADAPTATION: Harry Kronman from the screenplay by Cady and Jay Dratler, (which was based on a series of articles by James P. McGuire)
    THEME: "Camel Theme" (Freddie Rich)

The cast included:

Jimmy Stewart	*P.J. "Mack" McNeal*
Pat O'Brien	*Brian Kelly*
Richard Conte	*Frank Wiecek*
Howard McNear	*..Joe/Underwood, Wiecek's former lawyer*
Wally Maher	*bailiff/Mr. Soler*

This was the first show of the new season. Stewart and Conte appear in their original film roles. Jimmy prefaces the show with this statement:

Well, first of all, let's get one thing straight. I didn't just dream this story up. No, it's right off the record. It really happened. So, if the people in it resemble characters, living or dead, well, believe me, it's strictly intentional.

As Stewart says, this is a true story, based on the conviction of Joe Majczek and the Pulitzer Prize-winning articles of Jim McGuire from the *Chicago Times* which helped free him.

Mack is a reporter for the *Chicago Times*. His editor, Brian Kelly, spots an ad in the paper offering a reward of $5,000 for the killers of police officer Bundy, who had been murdered ten years earlier. He wants Mack to check it out to see if there might be a story. Mack tracks down Tillie Wiecek scrubbing floors in an office building. It was she who had placed the ad. Her son, Frank, was one of the men convicted of the murder and she thinks he is innocent. She has saved her money for 11 years in order to offer the reward. Mack writes the story, but then Kelly wants him to visit Wiecek in prison and get his story.

Wiecek also claims to be innocent. Mack believes him up to the point when he says that his wife had divorced him and then remarried. If she really loved him and believed him to be innocent, why did she get a divorce? He visits Wiecek's former wife and she tells him that it was Frank who forced her to get a divorce and remarry. He did it so that his son would have a chance at a life and a new name. After printing this story, Mack gets a call that Wiecek wants to see him at the prison. He tells Mack that he doesn't want him to write any more stories about his family. Mack agrees and tells him that he'll go after the truth now.

Wiecek takes a lie detector test and passes it. Mack finds the bailiff who was on duty at the trial and the bailiff tells him that the judge had told Wiecek that he was going to get him a new trial (the judge dies three weeks later). He also tells Mack that a truck driver who had been in the bar also says that he wasn't involved, but he was never called to testify during the trial. The real damaging testimony had come from Wanda Skutnik, who ran the speakeasy where the officer had been shot. She had claimed that she had not seen Wiecek from the time of the shooting until her testimony in court and she claimed that Wiecek was one of the men involved in the shooting. Mack can't find her, so he goes a different route. He tries to find any pictures that may have been taken at the time of the original trial. Sure enough, he finds a picture of Skutnik with Wiecek, which he believes was taken December 22, the day before the trial. But how can he prove when the picture had been taken?

During a chance talk with a taxi driver, he learns that there is now a machine that can be used to enlarge photos by as much as 1,000 times. Also in the picture he has found a newsboy with a stack of newspapers under his arm. He has the photo enlarged and sees that date on the paper is December 22, 1932. Wiecek is pardoned and Mack turns his attention to the other man convicted of the murder.

This exchange took place at the end of the show.

LANG: And, now, a final word of thanks to our stars, James Stewart, Pat O'Brien and Richard Conte. You know you fellas have gotten our program off to a terrific start.

STEWART: Now wait a minute, wait a minute. Let's not talk about us; we'd rather talk about the Motion Picture Relief Fund. That…ah…the country house and hospital.

CONTE: That's right, Jimmy. They're all supported by this program, so it's a real privilege to appear on the *Camel Show* with the Screen Guild Players.

O'BRIEN: Well, you fellas hold down 1st and 2nd, I'll cover 3rd. Namely, and to wit, a grand job by the makers of Camel cigarettes. They're going right on with this fine custom of sending free smokes each week to the men in servicemen's hospitals. Among other hospitals, free Camels are being sent this week to USAF Station Hospital, Mather Field, California, U.S. Marine Hospital, Chicago, Illinois and Veteran's Hospital, Chamblee, Georgia. This makes a total of more than 180 million cigarettes that the Camel people have sent to servicemen and veterans. Happy smokin', fellas, Happy smokin'.

Stewart would do this story again, with a different script, 14 months later, for *Screen Directors' Playhouse*. It's also mentioned that Jimmy can currently be seen in the Alfred Hitchcock film, *Rope*, presented by Warner Bros.

This show can be found on the album, *Call Northside 777* (Radiola Records MR-1137) (Crime series No. 16, Release No. 137), which was released in 1982. The show is on the B-side of the album. On the A-side is the *Screen Guild Theater* broadcast of *The Blue Dahlia*, starring Alan Ladd and Veronica Lake and broadcast on April 21, 1949.

It can also be found on the Radio Spirits set, *The Best of Old Time Radio Starring Jimmy Stewart* (5034-cassette/5035-CD). It can be found on cassette #4 (SJSC4) and CD #5 (SJSD5). See *Lux Radio Theatre, Made for Each Other* for complete details on this set. *Call Northside 777* can also be found on the 20-CD set, *Old Time Radio Shows with Famous Guest Stars* (Nostalgia Ventures 2016), which was released in 2005. This set features 40 different radio shows.

Radio Spirits also issued this show as an audiobook, *Call Northside 777: Classic Movies on the Radio*, in 2006.

In 2008, Saland Publishing also issued it as an audiobook.

(9) Thursday, December 29, 1949 — *It's A Wonderful Life* (9-9:30 p.m.) (*The Camel Screen Guild Theater*)
Not available for review.

(10) Thursday March 15, 1951 — *It's A Wonderful Life* (8-9 p.m.)
Not available for review.

Sealtest Variety Theater

The first incantation of this show aired from July 6, 1947, until September 28, 1947, as *Front and Center*. This show encouraged U.S. Army recruitment. After being off the air for a year, it came back as the *Sealtest Variety Theater*. There were a total of 41 shows broadcast from September 9, 1948, through July 7, 1949. Stewart was featured on just one show.

Thursday, May 26, 1949 (9:30-10:00 p.m.)
NETWORK: NBC
SPONSOR: Sealtest Ice Cream
ANNOUNCER: Hal Gibney
MASTER OF CEREMONIES: Frank Nelson
DIRECTOR: Glenhall Taylor
WRITERS: Howard Harris and Sydney Zalenka
MUSIC: Henry Russell Orchestra with the Crew Chiefs

Dorothy Lamour and Eddie Bracken are at the Brown Derby talking about this week's show. Dorothy wants Jimmy Stewart as a guest, but Eddie, who claims to know him well, says that he is out of town. But, Dorothy spots Jimmy sitting just a couple of tables away. Eddie goes over to talk to Jimmy and asks that he act friendly toward him. Eddie tells Dorothy that Jimmy will call her that night to talk about the guest spot.

"I'll String Along With You" — Dorothy Lamour

Back at the Brown Derby the next day, Dorothy tells Eddie that Stewart never called and he is angry. She's going to tell him what she thinks of him the next time she sees him. Eddie excuses himself under the pretense of going to buy a pack of cigarettes. While he's away, the head waiter asks Dorothy if Jimmy Stewart can sit at her table since the restaurant is full. She gets on Jimmy about not calling her. He has no idea what she is talking about. The head waiter brings her a phone saying there is a call for her. It turns out to be Eddie posing as Stewart. He tells her that he can't do the show. Dorothy says that there's a Jimmy Stewart fan at the table with her and she's going to put him on the phone. Eddie thinks his voice sounds familiar.

"Powder Your Face With Sunshine" — Dorothy Lamour

Now, Dorothy is upset with Eddie, so he goes to Stewart's house to apologize. Jimmy understands and says that he will do the show. Jimmy calls Dorothy to let her know, but she thinks that it's Eddie and hangs up on him. So Eddie calls her and in his Jimmy Stewart voice tells her that he will do the show. At rehearsal, Dorothy suggests that instead of doing a routine, they should just do the story of all that had happened. Jimmy gets a phone call and has to leave for New York to do retakes for this latest picture and he can't do the show after all. No problem says Eddie, I know…

At the show's end, Dorothy says, "Jimmy, your appearance contributes to a fine cause; the establishment of the American Federation of Radio Artists Welfare Insurance Fund."

Also mentioned is that Jimmy Stewart is currently starring in the M-G-M production, *The Stratton Story*.

In 2011, the program was issued on the mp3 only set, *Jimmy Stewart the Ultimate Radio Collection Vol. 3* (Master Classics Records).

Sealtest Village Store

This musical variety show was the successor to *The Rudy Vallee Show*. It first aired on July 8, 1943, and ended five years later. The cast underwent several changes with Jack Carson being the proprietor/host of the "Store" and Eve Arden being its manager when Stewart made his two appearances on the program.

NETWORK: NBC
SPONSOR: Sealtest
ANNOUNCER: Hy Averback
MUSIC: Frank DeVol

VOCALIST: Bob Stanton

THEME MUSIC: "On Wisconsin" (Carl Edwin Beck, Jr./W.T. Purdy) and "Great Day" (Vincent Youmans/William Rose/Edward Eliscu)

(1) Thursday, December 4, 1947 (9:30-10 p.m.)

This evening's program was dedicated to the commemoration of the Japanese attack on Pearl Harbor. Host Jack Carter and Jimmy Stewart urge listeners to support the Marshall Plan and also talk about their remembrances of December 7, 1941. The show is not available for listening.

(2) Thursday March 4, 1948 (9:30-10 p.m.)

Jimmy Stewart's blind date in one of the show's skits is "Bubbles" Coogenfeller, played by Eve Arden. The show is not available for listening.

Jimmy Stewart, Jack Carson and Eve Arden are having some fun during a rehearsal for Sealtest Village Store.

Shirley Thomas Hollywood

Shirley Thomas was the Hollywood reporter for NBC. She also had her own half-hour weekly program. The show was also sometimes known as *Shirley from Hollywood*. Stewart appeared on at least two shows, neither of which is available for listening.

(1) Sunday, July 26, 1953 (2:30-3:00 p.m.)
(2) Sunday, February 13, 1954 (1-1:30 p.m.)

Between these two programs, Thomas interviewed Stewart for the December 10, 1953, program, *The Glenn Miller Story Premiere*. See that entry for more details.

Silver Theater

Silver Theater, also known as *The 1947 Silver Theater*, was sponsored by the International Silver Company, makers of 1847 Roger Brothers silverware. It began broadcasting on October 3, 1937, with the final airing coming on August 17, 1947. During the 1946 and 1947 seasons, it ran only as a summer replacement for *The Ozzie & Harriett Show*, with eight shows the first two years and ten in the final year. The show aired on Sunday evenings from 5:00-5:30 p.m. for the first 13 shows and 6:00-6:30 p.m. thereafter. The program originated at Columbia Square, Hollywood.
SHOWS FEATURING JIMMY STEWART:

(1) Sunday, October 3, 1937 — *First Love Part 1* (5-5:30 p.m.)
NETWORK: CBS
SPONSOR: International Silver Company, 1947 Rogers Brothers Silverware
ANNOUNCER: John Conte
MASTER OF CEREMONIES: Conrad Nagel
DIRECTOR: Conrad Nagel
WRITER: Grover Jones
SOUND EFFECTS: David Light
ADAPTED FOR RADIO BY: True Broadman
MUSIC SCORED AND CONDUCTED BY: Felix Mills
The cast included:

Jimmy Stewart	Jimmy Parks
Rosalind Russell	Jean Wilson
Minerva Pious	Trista Lane
Cliff Arquette	Perry Burke

The series started out in a big way with a four-part show featuring Rosalind Russell and Jimmy Stewart. Each show began with John Conte introducing Conrad Nagel, who in turn talked briefly with Russell and Stewart. In the first show, it is announced that Stewart is in the forthcoming film *The Last Gangster*, starring Edward G. Robinson. Before each act, Nagel would say, "And now the lights are being dimmed and the silver curtain is rising…"

In Part 1, we are introduced to Jean Wilson who is on a cross-country train headed for Hollywood where a friend has arranged a screen test for her. Things go badly for her when there is no time to rehearse and everything is rushed. Her spirit is broken and she takes a job as a waitress in a diner across the street from Superbo Films.

Meanwhile, at Superbo, Jimmy Parks, a publicity man, and his helper Perry Burke are being fired. They go across the street to the diner where

Rosalind Russell and Stewart posing in front of the CBS microphone.

Jimmy yells at Jean to bring him coffee instead of the tea he had ordered. Feeling badly because of his behavior, he goes to her to apologize and winds up taking her to a Hollywood preview. At the preview, he introduces her as an international star who will soon be big in movies here. Jean isn't happy about that, but he convinces her that together they can pull it off. He will stick with her through everything.

1847 Rogers Brothers has created a new line of silverware just for the show. They claimed that it was named "First Love" by Rosalind Russell. As a special offer, listeners can buy a serving fork for just 45¢. The regular retail price is $1.45. The commercial for this sale will run through all four parts of this show.

At the end of the show, Conrad Nagel again talks briefly with the stars.

CONTE: Here come our stars, ladies and gentlemen. Conrad Nagel is bringing Rosalind Russell and Jimmy Stewart out in front of the curtain.

NAGEL: Well, Rosalind, how does it feel to have a first performance behind you?

RUSSELL: Oh, well, right now I'm scared to death, but I loved it. Thank you, everyone.

NAGEL: How about you, Jimmy?

STEWART: I hope I can get my knees to stop shaking by next week.

NAGEL: Well, I know you both want to get out and hear what your friends thought of the show, but before you go, let me thank you for two grand performances…

STEWART: So long, everybody.

(2) Sunday, October 10, 1937 — *First Love Part 2* (5-5:30 p.m.)

In Part 2, Jimmy puts his plan into action. He is going to sell Jean's contract to Martin Rickey, who had fired him from Superbo, for $1 million. He starts getting Jean the best of everything (penthouse, maid, clothes) by giving away a percentage of her first year's earnings. Perry tells Jimmy that he shouldn't sell Jean down the river that way and Jimmy agrees. He starts to tell her what he has done, but she is so excited that he backs off and decides to go through with the plan. That evening, at the Trocodero, he talks another film executive into pretending to be interested in signing Jean so that Rickey will up his bid for her. Jimmy has Jean sign a blank contract which he will fill in later. He also has her sign a contract making him her manager and giving him the standard 10%. Rickey does buy her contract, but Jean runs out crying because she thinks that all Jimmy wants is his 10% and he has done everything for money.

Conrad Nagel again talks to Russell and Stewart at the end of the show.

NAGEL: ...ladies and gentlemen, I'm sure you'd like a word from our stars, Rosalind Russell and James Stewart, before we ring down...hey... hey, wait a minute, you two. Where are you going?

RUSSELL: Well, you see, Conrad, I've just moved into a new house and I'm taking Jimmy home with me to help me shove the furniture around.

STEWART: Yeah, that's what she thinks. You know I've been making *Navy Blue and Gold* for M-G-M right now and for the past week I've been bounced around the Rose Bowl by a whole football team, so I couldn't move an ashtray 10 feet, Roz...

RUSSELL: Oh, you can't...eh...Jimmy. Well, you can try now, you can just try.

STEWART: Well, all right, so long everybody.

RUSSELL: Goodbye and thank you. Thank you, Conrad.

(3) Sunday, October 17, 1937 — *First Love Part 3* (5-5:30 p.m.)

In his opening remarks, Nagel mentions that they are trying something new with this show. Instead of having a narrator recap the story up to this point, the opening scene will tell everything that has already happened. This is accomplished by having a newspaperman named Barrett waiting for Jimmy. He tells Jimmy he knows everything and to prove it, he recounts all the important facts. Jimmy offers him money to keep his mouth shut. When that doesn't work, he threatens to beat him up.

Jimmy tells Jean that he had to be her manager so that he could make the deal with Rickey. He really wasn't interested in the money and he is going to stick by her. She tells him that she has a screen test that day and they begin to practice her lines. Jimmy realizes that the scene is from a movie Superbo's current female star, Trista, had made. Trista, of course, doesn't want a new female star to come in and take her place. Jimmy tells Jean that Trista has rigged the screen test against her. But, Trista's tricks backfire and Jean passes the test.

Barrett enters the picture once again as he tells Trista what Jimmy has done and sells her all the facts for $1,000.

Meanwhile, Jimmy once again tries to tell Jean what he has done, but she cuts him off before he has the chance. But, when they get back to her apartment, Trista is waiting for them and tells Jean the whole story.

(4) Sunday, October 24, 1937 — *First Love Part 4* (5-5:30 p.m.)

The final part opens with Jimmy and Perry searching all of Hollywood for Jean, with no luck.

Jean has gone to see Martin Rickey to tell him the truth. But, he already knows the story because Trista had told him also. He says it doesn't matter. He still plans to make movies with her. She had proven that she can act in the screen test. She begins work on a film titled *Cold Embers*, but Jean's acting isn't what it should be. They try several other scripts, but things don't go any better. All this time Jimmy continues to try to get in to see Mr. Rickey with no success. When he finally does get in, he says that he can write a story for her — her own story, the story of all that has happened to her in Hollywood. He knows that she has lost faith in herself and is sure this story will restore it. Rickey agrees. The story is called *Hollywood Girl* and it is written under the pen name of Ronald Hess. When the filming begins, Jean is at her best and everything is going fine until they shoot the closing scene. The scene ends with her throwing the guy out and that's not what she wants. She asks Perry to take her to Jimmy's apartment (she had long since known that he was the one writing the story). She sits at Jimmy's typewriter and, with him looking on, writes her own happy ending.

Conrad Nagel talks to Russell and Stewart at the end of the show.

NAGEL: Ladies and gentlemen, I feel that we're all a little sad right now for we've come to the end of our play, *First Love*, with Rosalind Russell and James Stewart. We hope you enjoyed it and we know you enjoyed our stars. I want to congratulate them on a grand job.

RUSSELL: Thank you, Conrad. I do know that I've enjoyed it.

STEWART: Me, too, Conrad.

RUSSELL: And I know everybody will be thrilled with Miriam Hopkins' play next week here on this program with her story *P.S. She Got the Job*. But, before I go, I would like to thank all of you for the wonderful way you've received our play. Your letters have meant so much to me. And I'd like to thank 1947 Rogers Brothers too…

NAGEL: …well, Jimmy, I guess it's onward for you, too, isn't it?

STEWART: Yeah, I guess it is, Conrad. I guess I'll pack up my "mic fright" and get back to Stage 8.

NAGEL: You've got a new M-G-M picture coming out soon, don't you, Jimmy?

STEWART: Yes, *The Last Gangster*, starring Edward G. Robinson.

NAGEL: Well, I know it'll be a big success and we also hope you'll do another play for us here on the *Silver Theater*.

STEWART: Well, maybe that's a date. And, what Rosalind said about your letters goes for me, too, and my most sincere thanks to 1847 Rogers Brothers for letting me do Jimmy Parks; so long, everybody.

RUSSELL: Goodbye…come along, Jimmy.

NAGEL: Goodbye, Rosalind; goodbye, Jimmy.

All four parts of *First Love* can be found on the mp3 only set, *Jimmy Stewart the Ultimate Radio Collection Vol. 3* (Master Classics Records, 2011).

(5) Sunday, October 23, 1938 — *Up From Darkness Part 1* (6-6:30 p.m.)
NETWORK: CBS
SPONSOR: International Silver Company, International Silver and 1847 Rogers Brothers Silverware
ANNOUNCER: John Conte
MASTER OF CEREMONIES: Conrad Nagel
DIRECTOR: Conrad Nagel
WRITER: Grover Jones
ADAPTED FOR RADIO BY: True Broadman
MUSIC SCORED AND CONDUCTED BY: Felix Mills

The story takes place in the coal-mining town of Middletown. Tim Barlow (Jimmy Stewart) is talking to his mother as the story begins. She tells him that Michael "Micki" Gargon (Rosalind Russell) is back in town from college. Tim tells his mother that his brother Joe is setting charges for the first time in the coal mine.

Michael and her father Mike, the mine's owner, are talking and she admits that she is afraid of going down in the mine and has been since she was a child. She knows that he is disappointed in her and that he had wanted a boy. That's why he gave her a boy's name.

When Tim and Micki meet, she tells him that she is surprised that he's still a miner. She thought that he would have found a better job and accomplished something by now. She asks him to take her down into the mine. There's still some blasting going on, but they go anyway. She's very afraid, but wants to stay down and see the mine. Her father Mike goes down into the mine as well to check on Joe since it's his first day on the new job. There's a blast and the mine collapses on them. Joe is killed, but Mike lives long enough to say his farewell to Michael. It's her mine now and she vows to make it safe.

At the end, it is announced that Jimmy Stewart can next be seen in the M-G-M production *Ice Follies*. The "of 1939" part of the title is not mentioned.

(6) Sunday, October 30, 1938 — *Up From Darkness Part 2* (6-6:30 p.m.)

It's now three months later. Mr. Melvin, the mine's head bookkeeper, is telling Michael that she's got to stop spending so much money on machinery. But, she's determined to make the mine safe at all costs. The men don't like the changes that she's making. They fear they will lose their jobs to the machines. Some even think that it's bad luck to have a woman

Adaptor True Broadman discusses script with Jimmy Stewart.

around a mine. Tim tries to tell them that they are wrong. Micki comes in and also tries to talk to them, but they all leave. Tim tells Micki that she's going about everything the wrong way and that she doesn't understand how the miners feel.

After finding out that the men have voted to strike for as long as Micki is in charge, Tim wants to leave. But, his mother talks him into staying and helping Micki as much as he can.

When the men fail to show up for work in the morning, Micki goes down into the mine to talk with her father's spirit. She tells him that she's let him down and that the men won't come to work. She hears her father's voice giving her two pieces of advice: *1. You've got to love the mine* and *2. If they call you by your first name, you're okay.*

Tim comes down and tells her that he loves her. She says she loves him, too. Jim tells her that her ideas are right. It's the way that she did it that the men don't like. She gets all the men together, let's them have it and promises them a fight. Then, she sets the mine on fire. The men scramble to put the fire out. One of them even calls her Mike.

At the end of the show, Nagel calls the stars back to the stage.

NAGEL: For two persons such as Rosalind Russell and James Stewart, there's only one thing we can do; Roz and Jimmy, here's the microphone and several millions of your fans.

STEWART: Go ahead, Roz, you start.

RUSSELL: Well, it's been very nice for both Jimmy and me returning together to the *Silver Theater*.

STEWART: Roz, you know this is a lot like the time we were on the *Silver Theater* last season. You know you'd just finished a new picture for Metro-Goldwyn-Mayer then and you've just finished *The Citadel* for them now.

RUSSELL: Well, you were all banged up from playing football for them last year…really banged up.

STEWART: Yeah…yeah, you know, it's happened again in the same place.

RUSSELL: Another football picture, Jimmy?

STEWART: No…no…no. Ice skating for *Ice Follies*, the picture M-G-M has me making now. I never knew ice could hit back so hard, you know.

RUSSELL: Now, Jimmy, there's one more thing; even nicer than a return engagement. Conrad has told me how much the people have liked *First Love* since we introduced it last season.

STEWART: Yeah, yeah…Roz, can I interrupt you again?

RUSSELL: I suppose so.

STEWART: I…ah…bought some silver last week, a whole lot of it; Enchantress and First Love, the pattern you named, you know, for my new house.

RUSSELL: Is that mansion of yours finished?

STEWART: No…no, the roof isn't on yet, but I thought I'd start furnishing it in the right way.

RUSSELL: Goodnight, everyone, and thank you.

STEWART: So long.

CONRAD: Goodnight, Rosalind Russell and Jimmy Stewart, we'll see you both again.

(7) Sunday, January 22, 1939 — *Misty Mountain Part 1* (6-6:30 p.m.)
NETWORK: CBS
SPONSOR: International Silver Company, International Silver and 1947 Rogers Brothers Silverware
ANNOUNCER: John Conte
MASTER OF CEREMONIES: Conrad Nagel
DIRECTOR: Conrad Nagel
WRITER: Grover Jones and True Broadman
MUSIC SCORED AND CONDUCTED BY: Felix Mills
In the cast are:
Jimmy Stewart... *Rusty Lane*
Jane Bryan.. *Mary Lou Masters*
John Gibson...*Elmer Sloan*

Rusty Lane and his co-pilot Elmer Sloan are about to take off in Flight 9 from Albuquerque to Los Angeles. They have to fly over Misty Mountain. Rusty switches radio frequencies and calls W6RX2, the call letters for Mary Lou Masters. She lives somewhere on the mountain and they have been talking via radio every time he passes over, even though it's against company policy and could get him fired.

When they get to Los Angeles, Helen Marshall and her father, owner of the airline, are there to meet him. Helen tells him that he's being sent east to help set up European flights. He'll be an executive now, and not a pilot. He and Helen are engaged and now they will be able to see more of each other. On the return flight, they are notified of a storm over Misty Mountain. Rusty calls Mary Lou and tells her that this is his next to last flight over the mountain. When he tells her this, she doesn't answer.

Rusty gets a mail run the following day. It's just Rusty, Elmer, and Millie Wexler, a stewardess on board — no passengers. As they approach Misty Mountain, he receives a call from Mary Lou. She needs help and tells him where there's a landing strip. Rusty spots a ranger station on the way down and heads there after landing. Mary Lou is there with her brother, Jack, who is a ranger. She tells Rusty that there is no emergency; she just wanted to see what he looked like. He's upset because he could get fired for landing while on a mail run. When he takes off again, Millie Wexler is on the ground and Mary Lou is in the plane.

At the end of Part 1 it is announced that Jimmy Stewart will soon be seen with Joan Crawford in the M-G-M production *Ice Follies of 1939*.

(8) Sunday, January 29, 1939 — *Misty Mountain Part 2* (6-6:30 p.m.)

Rusty says that he's going to tell the truth about what happened when they land. Elmer tells him that Mary Lou will probably get into trouble for faking the emergency if he does. So Rusty tells Mary Lou that when they land, she should get off the plane like a passenger and head for the lunch room. Rusty will go to Mr. Marshall and do all the talking. Helen runs into Elmer and Mary Lou in the lunchroom. Later, Mary Lou tells Helen the whole story.

When Mr. Marshall and Rusty come in, Helen announces that they will be leaving for New York in three days and that they can be married there. Rusty sees Mary Lou off on a train back to Misty Mountain.

When Rusty is flying Helen and her father back, he gets lost in a storm near Misty Mountain. He calls Mary Lou for help. She is to tell him when she hears the plane and this will help him get his bearings. A few days later, Rusty radios Mary Lou and tells her that he is about to land on Misty Mountain, kidnap her, and fly to Las Vegas to marry her.

At the end of the show, Conrad Nagel brings the stars back on stage for a short chat.

NAGEL: And here they are, James Stewart and Jane Bryan. Well, Jimmy and Jane, suppose you tell us something about yourselves. You, Jane, I understand you just finished *Hero for a Day* at Warner Bros.

BRYAN: Yes, that's right, Conrad.

NAGEL: And, you, Jimmy, how are you coming along with your flying?

STEWART: Oh swell. I've got quite a few hours in the air and it's a lot of fun. That's why I got a great kick out of playing pilot Rusty Lane.

NAGEL: Ever been grounded?

STEWART: Grounded? Ah…well, I…ah…just finished *Ice Follies of 1939* for Metro-Goldwyn-Mayer and I was grounded plenty in those skating scenes. I…ah…had to take the de-icer out of my plane and wear it in my pants for two weeks.

NAGEL: Maybe this will take your mind off all those spills. You know we're thinking of having a nice silver medal struck off for you.

BRYAN: Well, that's wonderful. For piloting?

NAGEL: No, for endurance.

STEWART: Endurance? Well, how come?

NAGEL: Well, Jimmy, you hold an all-time record for stars who've made *Silver Theater* appearances. You've chalked up eight broadcasts.

BRYAN: Oh, that's grand, isn't it, Jimmy? Ah…any chance of me piling up a record like that, Conrad?

NAGEL: Well, we'd love to have you, Jane.
BRYAN: But I wouldn't be satisfied with a Silver Medal when I do it.
NAGEL: No?
BRYAN: No, I'm going to hold out for a complete set of that lovely First Love pattern I've been hearing about.
NAGEL: Well, we'll try to do something about that. Now, I'm sorry to say that our time is about up and I'm afraid...
STEWART: Just one more thing, Conrad. I wanna get in a quick thanks for Johnny Gibson's work as Elmer, my co-pilot, in today's show. That guy's terrific.
BRYAN: And, thank the rest of the cast for us, too, will you, Conrad?
NAGEL: I'll do that gladly. Thanks a million, James Stewart and Jane Bryan. We hope you'll be back soon.

Both parts of "Misty Mountain" were issued in mp3 only format in 2011 on *Jimmy Stewart the Ultimate Radio Collection Vol. 1* (Master Classics Records).

(9) Sunday, January 5, 1941 — *Child, Save My Fireman*
Cast:
    Jimmy Stewart..Jimmy Morgan
    Marsha Hunt ....Molly Valentine
    Paula Winslowe.. Helen Martin

Although not generally available, this program can be heard at The Paley Center for Media, 25 West 52nd Street, New York, New York.

Stewart, playing the role of Jimmy Morgan, a volunteer fireman, arrives on the scene of a blaze to hear the cries of a woman begging the men to save her "baby." When Jimmy gets to the "baby," she turns out to be a beautiful young lady. He carries her from the burning building and then returns to help put out the fire. Although Jimmy is dating his boss's daughter, Helen Martin, he falls for the "baby," whose name he discovers is Molly Valentine.

All is not well between Helen and Jimmy. She wants him to take her to a fancy country club dance, but it's on the same day as a fireman's dance and Jimmy would rather attend the latter. When Helen refuses to go with him, Jimmy asks Molly and she agrees to go. But, Helen's not finished. She tells Jimmy that Mr. Briggs, the big boss of her father's company, will be at the country club and he wants to talk to Jimmy. So, he breaks his date with Molly to attend the other dance with Helen.

At the dance, Mr. Briggs tells Jimmy that he wants to promote him to assistant manager, but there's just one catch. Jimmy must outline for him, on the spot, his plans for the fall sales campaign. Just as Jimmy begins his plan, the fire alarm sounds and off he runs.

As the second act begins, three weeks have passed. Somehow, Helen has gotten Jimmy to marry her. But, before he can say "I do," the fire alarm sounds and off he goes, letting Helen standing alone at the altar. The "fire" is at Molly's house, but there is no fire. She has turned in a false alarm to stop the wedding. As Jimmy admonishes her for what she has done, another fire alarm is sounded. Jimmy and Molly head off on the fire engine to the fire. This time the fire is real. It's in a large chemical factory and it's threatening to burn down the entire town. When Molly hears that there's dynamite stored in the factory, she comes up with a plan to stop the fire. Her plan works and the fire is stopped. The factory owner is so happy that he offers Jimmy a job.

Helen shows up at the fire scene and tells Jimmy that she just can't marry him. On the spot, Jimmy asks Molly to marry him. She and Jimmy drive the fire truck to Judge Perkins' house to have him perform the ceremony. Believe it or not, before the ceremony can be completed, another alarm is sounded. But, this time it's only *Gang Breakers* on the radio. After the judge has his wife turn the volume down, Jimmy and Molly are married.

At the end of the show, host Conrad Nagel talks with Marsha Hunt and Stewart. He tells Marsha that Stewart was a volunteer fireman and gave them the idea for the show. Marsha asks if that's true and Jimmy says:

STEWART: Well, almost. See, back home in Indiana, Pennsylvania, my dad was a volunteer fireman. He used to drive a fire engine when I was a kid and he used to take me for a ride sometimes…boy, that was fun.

HUNT: As much fun as wrecking things with a fire ax?

STEWART: Oh no, no, they never did that; they didn't break things, they saved them. I can remember fellas rushing out of a burning house carrying furniture and paintings and family silver.

HUNT: Oh, so that's how you got all your beautiful silver.

STEWART: Wait a minute, why my silver is 1847 Rogers Brothers silver plate and I bought it…oh…oh…I just realized you were kidding. Hey, Marsha, you shouldn't do that here…you're too good an actress.

NAGEL: Well, say, I think you're both swell. I'd like to have you back again soon.

STEWART: Well, thanks, Conrad (a fire alarm sounds). I...I gotta go.
NAGEL: Don't tell me there's another fire.
STEWART: No, no, I...we've got a date and dinner with the soundman. Goodbye...come on...

Skyway to the Stars

Stewart was the guest on this CBS musical-variety program, hosted by Tex McCrary, on Sunday, September 26, 1948, from 4:30-5 pm. The short-lived show was only on the air for one season — September 12, 1948, until May 22, 1949. Stewart appeared on the third program in the series. Regulars on the show were Kay Armen and the Raymond Paige Orchestra. The 30-minute program was cut to about 15 minutes for rebroadcast by the Armed Forces Radio Service. On these broadcasts, Sgt. Russ Thompson acted as the announcer. The program is not available for review.

Sports Award Banquet of Los Angeles Times

The annual awards show was broadcast on Monday, December 27, 1948, on the Mutual Broadcasting System. The program was broadcast from the Ambassador Hotel in Los Angeles and was co-emceed by Bob Hope and Bing Crosby. At least one newspaper of the time, the *Newark Advocate* (Newark, OH) reported that Hope would be unable to attend and was being replaced by Danny Thomas. Others scheduled to be on the program were Dorothy Shay, Frankie Laine and Freddy Martin and his orchestra. Many top sports writers were also on hand for the fourth annual awards banquet. On the east coast it aired from 10:30-11 pm. The program is not available for listening.

Stars in the Air

Stars in the Air was basically an extension of *Screen Guild Theater*, which had ended its run of half-hour shows on May 31, 1951. Like *Screen Guild Theater*, the actors on *Stars in the Air* donated their salaries to the Motion Picture Relief Fund. On March 13, 1952, CBS brought back *Screen Guild Theater* to alternate with two of its other shows — *Stars in the Air* and *Hollywood Sound Stage*. Neither of these last two shows fared anywhere near as well as *Screen Guild Theater*, which ran for a total of 527 shows. *Stars in the Air* lasted for only 27 shows, while *Hollywood Sound Stage* would only be broadcast 16 times.

Stars in the Air opened with Jimmy Stewart and Donna Reed starring in *It's a Wonderful Life*. The shows all began with host John Jacobs uttering the line, "Hollywood's greatest stars, in Hollywood's greatest pictures." Stewart appeared on just this one show.

Thursday, December 13, 1951 (9:30-10:00) — *It's a Wonderful Life*
NETWORK: CBS
ANNOUNCER/HOST: John Jacobs
SPONSOR: Sustained
THEME MUSIC: *Stars in the Air* (Alexander Courage)
Cast:

> *Jimmy Stewart... George Bailey*
> *Donna Reed....................................... Mary Hatch Bailey*
> *Joseph Granby... Chief Angel*
> *Junius Matthews........................... Clarence Oddbody AS2*
> *(Angel Second Class)*

The story begins on Christmas Eve and we hear many people praying for George Bailey. We hear the Chief Angel telling Clarence about George Bailey's life. We find that he lost the hearing in one of his ears when he jumped into icy water to save his brother Harry's life. We hear George and Mary Hatch singing *Buffalo Gal* and throwing stones through the windows of the old Granville house for good luck. We hear of George's travel and college plans. And, we hear that George's father has had a stroke.

Next, Clarence hears George speaking out against Mr. Potter, while trying to save the Savings & Loan Company. The company is saved, but at George's expense. He must give up his own plans and run the Savings & Loan. Harry goes to college instead. Clarence is then shown George and Mary falling in love, Harry receiving the Congressional Medal of Honor, and Uncle Billy losing $8,000 of the Savings & Loan money. Finally, he is shown George standing on a bridge about to jump into the water and commit suicide.

Clarence heads for Earth and jumps into the river. George jumps in and saves him. When Clarence tries to tell him that he is his guardian angel, George gets even more despondent and wishes that he had never been born. Clarence grants his wish. George sees that Bedford Falls is known as Pottersville instead of Bedford Falls. Harry had died in 1919 instead of being saved. And Mary…Mary is an old maid librarian. George can't take what he is seeing and yells, "I want to live." Again, Clarence grants the wish. George heads for home saying, "Merry Christmas" to anyone and anything he sees. At home he finds that the townspeople have collected enough money to replace the lost $8,000. As all the town's church bells ring, Mary says that an angel has gotten his wings. George adds, "Atta boy, Clarence, atta boy."

After the play, Jimmy and Donna come back to talk with John Jacobs.

STEWART: Thank you. Thank you, very much.

JACOBS: Well, Jimmy, we're the ones who should be thankful to you and Donna taking the time out at this busy pre-Christmas season to come here and give us such a wonderful show.

STEWART: Well, we hoped you like it, of course, and look, about that "taking the time," there isn't an actor in Hollywood who wouldn't do the same thing. You know why? Because this is our show. This radio series helps support the Motion Picture Relief Fund and I'd like anyone to show me a better cause than that. Believe me, we're gonna make this the most exciting half hour of the radio week. Now, just for example, next Thursday night...

REED: Jimmy, excuse me, but haven't you forgotten something more important?

STEWART: More important? Now what could be more important than that? Oh...oh...oh that...oh...well, isn't it a little early?

REED: They always told me it's never too early.

STEWART: Oh, why by golly, you're right. Well, Merry Christmas, everybody...Merry Christmas.

REED: Merry Christmas. Goodnight.

As the show is ending, Jacobs announces that "Jimmy Stewart will soon be seen in Cecil B. DeMille's production for Paramount, *The Greatest Show on Earth*."

The Stars Review the Hits
RCA Victor SRH-104
HOST: Wayne Howell
PRODUCER/DIRECTOR: Leonard Raphael

This early fifties syndicated radio show featured interviews with Hollywood stars. As part of the show, the stars would give their opinions on new records, usually six per episode. Charlton Heston was the guest for show #104 and Jimmy Stewart is listed on the label as a special guest. Despite the lofty sound of "special guest," Stewart appears only via recording to present a public service announcement for the American Heart Association. It is the same announcement which appears on the 1953 Heart Fund recording (see Chapter 3 — Miscellaneous Recordings

Made for Radio) with one exception; at the end of the Howell recording, Stewart adds, "Remember, when you help the Heart Fund, you help your heart."

The program was scheduled to be aired anytime between February 16th and February 27, 1953.

Strengthen the Arm of Liberty
See *Boy Scout Jamboree*.

Suspense

"...a tale well calculated to keep you in...suspense." This simple opening line, along with some of the biggest names in Hollywood, was enough to keep *Suspense* on the air for twenty years — June 17, 1942, through September 30, 1962. A whopping 945 episodes were broadcast. The show advertised itself as, "Radio's outstanding theater of thrills." The show's main and end theme was the *Suspense Theme* (Bernard Herrmann), with an alternate ending march theme of *New Suspense Closing* (Lucien Alfred E. Moraweck).

CBS sound effects experts regularly working their magic on *Suspense* included Berne Surrey, Guz Bayz, Ray Kemper and David Light.

In 1946, *Suspense* was honored with the Peabody Award. The awards committee presented the trophy with these words, "The committee believes that there are too many whodunits for the good of radio; it also believes that in this overworked and melodramatic field there is one program which, for its casting, its music, and its suspense, is head and shoulders above the competition. A special citation therefore to *Suspense* of CBS and to William Spier, its producer and director."

SHOWS FEATURING JIMMY STEWART:

(1) Thursday, February 21, 1946 (8:00-8:30 p.m.) — *Consequence*
NETWORK: CBS
SPONSOR: Roma Wine
PRODUCED, EDITED & DIRECTED BY: William Spier
VOICE OF SUSPENSE: Joseph Kearns
STORY BY: Vladimir Pozner and George Sklar
ADAPTED FOR RADIO BY: Robert L. Richards
MUSIC COMPOSED BY: Lucian Moraweck
MUSIC CONDUCTED BY: Lud Gluskin
COMMERCIAL ANNOUNCER: Truman Bradley

The cast included:

Jimmy Stewart	Phil Martin
Cathy Lewis	Gwen Martin

Phil Martin, a doctor, attends a class reunion and brings an old friend, Ted Wolf, home for dinner which is prepared by his wife Gwen. Ted is about to leave for Ecuador to provide medical services. Ted thinks that Phil has it all until Phil tells him that he and Gwen hate each other.

Phil is having an affair with his secretary, Jo (Josephine Reynolds). Jo's father suspects and plans on going to the hospital board with the information, so she is about to leave for good. As Phil walks home from his encounter with Jo, he hears fire trucks. The fire is at his house. He arrives in time to see them carry a badly burned body from the fire — Ted's body. He knows they will think that's it's his body. He turns and runs back to his office to tell Jo that he is going with her — Dr. Phil Martin is dead.

Phil takes over Ted's identity. He goes to his hotel room, gathers his things and checks out. He turns in Ted's plane ticket for two train tickets to Los Angeles. In L.A., he marries Jo and gets a job as Ted Wolf in a hospital. All is well, but then one day he sees Gwen at the hospital. He and Jo go to their cabin at Caribou Lake. They let clues behind, so that if Gwen wants to find them, she will have no trouble doing so.

Gwen does follow them. She wants Phil back and if he won't come back, she will have him arrested for bigamy. Phil asks her to go outside so that he can talk it over privately with Jo. Instead, Phil and Jo plan Gwen's murder. Phil will go down the mountain to a store so he has an alibi. Jo will kill Gwen and then set the cabin on fire. Everyone will think the body that is found is Jo's. Then she'll hide in the back of Phil's car. The plan goes off without a hitch until Gwen rises from the back of Phil's car instead of Jo. And, the news gets even worse for Phil.

At the end of the show Stewart comes back and says:

> Hi, this is Jimmy Stewart again. Suspense *is a radio show that got its start just about the time I first found myself overseas. And with everybody it has always been one of the two or three top favorites. I've been looking forward for a long time to my appearance with the show tonight. And next Thursday, a very swell actor, Richard Greene, will be your star in his first broadcast since he joined the British Army four and a half years ago.*

(2) Thursday, May 19, 1949 (9:00-9:30 p.m.) — *Consequence*
NETWORK: CBS
SPONSOR: Auto-Lite
PRODUCER/DIRECTOR: Anton M. Leader
VOICE OF SUSPENSE: Paul Frees
COMMERCIAL ANNOUNCERS: William Johnstone, Harlow Wilcox
STORY BY: Vladimir Pozner and George Sklar
ADAPTED FOR RADIO BY: Robert L. Richards
MUSIC COMPOSED BY: Lucian Moraweck
MUSIC CONDUCTED BY: Leith Stevens

The same script was used for this show as the original show on February 21, 1946. Included in the supporting cast are:

    Paul Ford..*Mr. Dooley*
    Betty Lou Gerson .... *Gwen Martin, operator*

At the end of the show Jimmy comes back and makes these remarks:

Well, I wanna thank Mr. Tony Leader and his great cast of actors for making my Suspense visit so pleasant. I'm a great Suspense fan like all of you. I'm looking forward to next week's show, when Fredric March appears in Cornell Woolrich story, The Night Reveals, *another gripping study in...*

And Paul Frees adds, "Suspense."

It is announced at the end of the show that Jimmy Stewart can currently be seen in the M-G-M production *The Stratton Story*.

This 1949 version of *Consequence* can be found as a part of several commercial sets. The first is a 12-cassette set, featuring 24 *Suspense* shows — *The Best of Suspense!* (Greatapes), which was released in 1989.

It can also be found on the 6-CD/4-cassette set, *The Best of Old Time Radio Starring Jimmy Stewart* (Radio Spirits 5035 [CDs]/5034 [cassettes]), released in 2002 (see *Lux Radio Theatre — Made for Each Other* for complete information on this set). It can also be found on the Radio Spirits set, *The Best of Old Time Radio Starring Jimmy Stewart* (5034-cassette/5035-CD).

Hall Closet Tapes issued the 6-cassette set, *Stars on Suspense*, which also featured this version of the program.

Greatapes also issued a smaller, 4-cassette set in 1991 entitled *Tales of Mystery and Suspense Featuring Suspense 2*. This set was also issued on CD on May 10, 2001. The show is also a part of this set. Also, it can be found on cassette #4 (SJSC4) and CD #6 (SJSD6). See *Lux Radio Theatre, Made for Each Other* for complete details on this set.

Finally, it is part of *Vintage Radio Collection Jimmy Stewart* (Stardust), a special downloadable set made available in 2008.

(3) Thursday, December 1, 1949 (9:00-9:30 p.m.) — *Mission Completed*
NETWORK: CBS
SPONSOR: Auto-Lite
COMMERCIAL ANNOUNCER: Harlow Wilcox
VOICE OF SUSPENSE: Paul Frees
PRODUCER & EDITOR: William Spier
DIRECTOR: Norman MacDonnell
STORY BY: John R. Forrest
MUSIC COMPOSED BY: Lucian Moraweck
MUSIC CONDUCTED BY: Lud Gluskin
Also appearing in the cast were:
    John Dehner...Dr. Benson
    Herb Ellis.................................Murdock and patrolman
    Elliott Lewis...orderly
    Lurene Tuttle...Miss Rhodes

This program is also sometimes misnamed *Mission Accomplished*.

The program is introduced as "a special Pearl Harbor anniversary drama."

Tom Warner (James Stewart) has spent the last four years in a veteran's hospital in California. He is completely paralyzed and has been like that since he was liberated from a Japanese prisoner of war camp in 1945. He communicates with his doctors and nurses by blinking his eyes. But, his mind works just fine and we can hear everything he is thinking.

One day, while his nurse wheels him around the hospital, they happen to go by the flower shop. Through the window, Tom sees Suki, the leader of the prison camp where he had been held and so many of his friends had died. Tom resolves that he will get back to normal so that he can kill Suki. Every night, so that no one knows what he is doing, he practices at sitting, standing, and finally walking.

Tom calls the flower shop and asks that roses be delivered to his room at 9 o'clock that night. Then, he steals a gun from a hospital guard. When the door to his room opens, he fires all six shots and proclaims that he has killed Suki.

His doctor comes in assures him that he has killed Suki…in his mind…and now he is healed. The man he thought was Suki was actually Jimmy Kato and the gun, like all the guns carried by the guards, was loaded with blanks.

When Jimmy comes back out at the end of the show, there is a special guest, Gracie Allen. Their conversation is a strange one.

ALLEN: Oh, Mr. Wilcox…Mr. Wilcox.

WILCOX: Well, Gracie Allen, what are you doing here?

ALLEN: Well, I came to ask you and Jimmy Stewart if you can fix it with Auto-Lite for my husband, "Sugar Throat" Burns, to sing on *Suspense*. Our sponsor will hear it and realize how great George is and then he'll let him sing on our show Wednesday night.

STEWART: Well, ah…ah…look, Gracie, *Suspense* is all booked up for next week. Mickey Rooney…well, Mickey Rooney will be on.

ALLEN: Well, how about the week after that, Mr. Stewart?

STEWART: No, they're booked up for that week, too. Lana Turner will be here that week. As a matter of fact, they're booked up for the next 4,000 weeks.

ALLEN: Oh, 4,000 weeks would be about…ah…

STEWART: That's 80 years.

ALLEN: Oh…how about the week after that?

STEWART: Ah…well, I've got to leave, Gracie. Ah…tell George that he has all my condolences.

ALLEN: Oh, really? I'm surprised they fit him…you know, you're so tall.

At this point, Harlow Wilcox comes back in and he and Gracie do a commercial for Auto-Lite.

It is announced at the end of the show that Jimmy Stewart can currently be seen in the M-G-M production *The Stratton Story*.

There are several commercial sources for *Mission Completed*. The first is the 12-cassette set, *More Tales of Suspense* (Greatapes), which was issued in 1991.

Then came the 4-cassette set, *Tales of Mystery and Suspense Featuring Suspense 3* (Greatapes), in 1994.

The Best of Suspense (Radio Spirits 40682 [CD]/40684 [cassette]) was issued in 2002, and finally in 2004, *Listener's Choice* (Radio Spirits 30222 [CD]/30224 [cassette]) is released.

Finally, it is part of two different mp3 only sets: *Vintage Radio Collection Jimmy Stewart* (Stardust, 2008), and *Jimmy Stewart the Ultimate Radio Collection Vol. 3* (Master Classics Records, 2011).

(4) Thursday, April 19, 1951 (9:00-9:30 p.m.) — *The Rescue*
NETWORK: CBS
SPONSOR: Auto-Lite
ANNOUNCER: Harlow Wilcox
SPOKEMEN FOR AUTO-LITE: Harlow Wilcox, Kenneth Christy
VOICE OF SUSPENSE: Joseph Kearns
PRODUCER & DIRECTOR: Elliott Lewis
Adapted by John Meston from a story by Elizabeth Wilson
MUSIC COMPOSED BY: Lucian Moraweck
MUSIC CONDUCTED BY: Lud Gluskin
Also appearing in the cast were:

Sylvia Simms	Helen Sellers
Joyce McCluskey	Hilary
Lou Merrill	Dr. Radin
Joseph Kearns	Jack/Clerk
Peggy Webber	Nurse/Woman
Ted Osborne	Dr. Brune
Jack Kruschen	Lt. Rogers/Tailor
Sidney Miller	Poet

At the beginning of the show, Kearns tells the listener, "Tonight, Auto-Lite brings you a story of a man who tries to save a girl's life. A story we call, *The Rescue*, starring Mr. James Stewart."

Mr. Lee Atherton (Jimmy Stewart) hears a scream from outside the window of his 4th-floor public relations office at the Wardman Hotel in Washington, DC. A young lady, Hilary Sellers, is on the ledge outside. He tries to talk her back in, telling her that they'll help her. She says that they won't help, they'll kill her. She claims that the man claiming to be Dr. Brune is an imposter. Atherton talks to her and gets her to climb back inside where Dr. Brune, a nurse and an orderly are waiting for her. Atherton watches as Dr. Brune and the orderly carry a stretcher outside, place it in an ambulance and drive away.

Not satisfied, Atherton looks up Dr. Brune's phone number and calls his office. He's told that Dr. Brune is in the office and has been for some time. Lee talks to Dr. Brune and tells him that a man pretending to be him has just taken Sellers away in an ambulance. Hearing this, Brune tells his secretary to call the police. Brune then tells Lee that the man is probably Kirk Radin, an unlicensed doctor who had treated Hilary's mother. Brune believes that Radin had killed Hilary's mother by throwing her out a window of his office. Hilary believes that her mother had committed suicide. Brune had told the police his story and they had gone to arrest Radin, but he left his office before they got there. Now he's trying to kidnap and kill Hilary because he believes she knows what he had done.

On his way back to his office, Lee sees a woman sitting outside the elevator and he thinks he recognizes her. Back in his office, Lee receives a call from Lt. Rogers, who tells him that the police had found the ambulance in Georgetown. But, it was empty. Lee was still bothered by the woman he had seen downstairs, so he went back down to get another look at her. This time he recognizes her as the nurse who had been with Radin. And seated beside her was Radin. Atherton realizes that they must have lost Hilary somewhere in the hotel. The nurse had been the one on the stretcher when it left the building and the ambulance had been used to lay a false trail for the police. Now the two were back to find Hilary and kill her.

As he is about to call the police, Lee sees Radin and the nurse get up and start for the mezzanine. He quickly follows them. Going through the door they had gone through, Lee finds himself in some kind of party. He can't spot Hilary or Radin in the crowd, so he leaves through an exit door on the other side of the room. He goes through another door into a room where a poetry reading is in progress. He asks a woman if a man had recently come into the room. She says that he has and that he had gone out a door at the back. Lee goes out the same door and finds himself in a storage room full of decorations and furniture. From there he goes into another room where a string quartet is playing and it is here he finds Hilary standing as if hypnotized by the music. Hilary seems genuinely afraid when she sees him. He tries to explain to her that he knows the Dr. Brune chasing her is an impostor and that she is not insane, but she doesn't trust Lee at all.

Radin enters the room and spots them and the chase is on once again. Finally cornered by Radin, Lee knocks him out. Hilary grabs Radin's gun and points it at herself. Again, Lee tells her that she isn't insane and that her mother wasn't insane either, but had been killed by Radin. Still believing that Lee is a figment of her imagination, she tries to kill herself. Lee knocks the gun away, but during a struggle, his hand is nicked by a bullet. Seeing the blood pulls Hilary back to reality. This time, when Lee tells her that she is safe, she believes him.

Ten High
10th Anniversary Radio Salute to Continental Air Command 1948-1958

The show was issued to radio stations for airing in December 1958. It came in a gatefold album jacket with two discs. The second disc was only recorded on one side. Inside the album jacket is the story of

ConAC, from its inception on December 1, 1948, to the present. The show was produced through the Office of Information Services of the Continental Air Command. The show ran a total of 59 minutes. There are no commercials in the show, so the stations which ran it did so as a public service.

Heard in the show were: Frank Gallup (announcer), Dorothy Collins, Johnny Desmond, Skitch Henderson, Richard Hayman, Charlie Shavers, Honey Dreamers, Elliot Lawrence & His Orchestra

And special guests: Lt. General William E. Hall, James Stewart

The show opens with Frank Gallup introducing the Honey Dreamers singing a special song, whose lyrics mention all of the show's guests.

"On a Skyride" — Honey Dreamers
"I'll Remember April" — Johnny Desmond
"The Toy Trumpet" — Charlie Shavers

Frank Gallup introduces Stewart, and Jimmy says:

> *Thank you, Frank. Yes, I learned the fun of flying more than 20 years ago. But since then many new concepts have been added to this business of flying and certainly deepened our appreciation of that world of sky and space about us. I'm very grateful for this opportunity to join you because I like to be a part of whatever Continental Air Command and our air reserve forces are doing. It's a big job that was entrusted to Continental Air Command ten years ago. This training to be ready of more than half-a-million air reservists from cities and towns all across the country and to help them keep the skills they learned while in the service, and to improve them, this took time and it took work. It also took a great deal of dedication on the part of our citizen airmen. When the need arose, the air reservists rose to it. They served gallantly to secure our liberties. Not alone in Korea where they brought the sound of jet air power to Mig alley, but here at home where they leave their civilian pursuits to fly medical supplies and food to disaster areas, and where they serve on evenings and weekends to stay abreast of their fellowmen in the active air force... and where Air National Guardsmen stand 24-hour shifts on runway alerts in order to be airborne in seconds in any emergency. And then, too, there's Continental Air Command search-and-rescue activity, which has been responsible for saving over 700 lives in just the past year and a half. Now there are 700 birthday greetings that will certainly come from the heart. But, of course, the main business of all our air reserve forces is, and must be, instant readiness. Under Continental Air Command we have come a long way during ten difficult and dangerous years, and*

there are no grounds for belief that the next ten will be less difficult or less dangerous. Now I'm very proud to join my fellow citizen airmen across the nation in commemorating Continental Air Command's tenth anniversary.

This was Jimmy's only appearance on the show.

"Spring in Maine" — Dorothy Collins

Skit: Skitch Henderson, Dorothy Collins, Frank Gallup, Johnny Desmond, and Richard Hayman perform a short skit about two men eating the moon (you have to remember that the moon is made out of cheese, right).

"Things Are Looking Up" — Honey Dreamers

"Lover" — Skitch Henderson

"Get Happy" — Dorothy Collins

"All of You" — Johnny Desmond

"Blues In the Night" — Richard Hayman

"Around the World in 80 Days" — Richard Hayman

Next up is a medley of songs, sung by the Honey Dreams, except where noted, that have been popular during the 10 years ConAC has been in existence.

"Buttons and Bows"

"From This Moment On" — Elliot Lawrence

"Please, Mr. Sun"

"Hernando's Hideaway"

"I've Grown Accustomed to Her Face" — Elliot Lawrence

"Happy, Happy Birthday Baby"

"Volare"

Frank Gallup talks with Captain Skitch Henderson and introduces his next song.

"Body and Soul"

"Say Darling" — Johnny Desmond

Gallup announces that we are next going to Mitchell Air Force Base to hear from the commander of ConAC, Lt. General William E. Hall. Hall makes a short speech commemorating the 10th anniversary.

"I'll Be Home for Christmas" — Dorothy Collins

To close the show, Gallup again lists all those participating, including the two special guests.

Tex and Jinx
See *Hi Jinx*.

That Freedom May Live

This 30-minute radio drama was presented on behalf of Radio Free Europe and in cooperation with the Crusade for Freedom. Stewart stars in the presentation.

Thursday February 23, 1956 (9:30-10 p.m.)

The show is not available for listening.

Stewart and Leon Janney add some realism to their acting in Theatre Guild on the Air.

Theatre Guild on the Air

The show is also known as *The Theatre Guild Dramas* and *The United States Steel Hour*. Just as *Lux Radio Theatre* brought Hollywood films to the radio, *Theatre Guild* presented some of Broadway's best plays in the same fashion. They also presented films and original plays. Most of the shows were broadcast from the Belasco Theater in New York City. The show's theme music was *United States Steel March* (Bernard Green). The show also made the transition to television in 1953 and was broadcast on ABC and then CBS until 1963.

In 1947, *Theatre Guild on the Air* won The Peabody Award for drama. The presentation comments on the award's website reads:

> *This year, our award in drama goes unhesitatingly to Theatre Guild on the Air, American Broadcasting Company, which has done what every great company always dreamed of doing: it has brought the best of the Theatre, the finest plays of our time, right into every village and hamlet, right into every home. By the end of this season, more than one hundred plays will have been produced for an ever-increasing audience. For the admirable casting, for the unerring choice of plays, and for craftsmanship with which these plays are adapted, great credit is due to the supervisors, the director, the editor, the adaptors, and last, but not least, the actors.*

The sound effects department for the program included Keene Crockett, Bill McClintock, Wes Conart and Bob Graham.

SHOWS FEATURING JIMMY STEWART:

(1) Sunday, September 7, 1947 (10:00-11:00 p.m.) — *One Sunday Afternoon*
NETWORK: ABC
WRITER: James Hagen
This show is not available for listening. It was the opening show for the series' third season. Besides Stewart (as Biff Grimes), the cast included Haila Stoddard, Leon Janney, Agusta Dabney, Russell Collins.

Stewart also performed this play on the *Academy Award Theater*, on August 28, 1946. See that entry for the storyline.

(2) Sunday, April 4, 1948 (10:00-11:00 p.m.) — *The Philadelphia Story*
Although this show is not available for listening, a program for the show gives the following information:
NETWORK: ABC
SPONSOR: United States Steel Corporation
DIRECTOR: Homer Fickett
PRODUCTION EXECUTIVE: Carol Irwin
MUSICAL DIRECTOR: Harold Levey
RADIO ADAPTOR: Arthur Arent
EXECUTIVE DIRECTOR: Armina Marshall
MANAGING DIRECTOR: H. William Fitelson
EDITOR: S. Mark Smith
GENERAL SUPERVISION: Lawrence Langner, Theresa Helburn
NARRATOR: Roger Pryor
ANNOUNCER: Norman Brokenshire
REPORTING FOR U.S. STEEL: George Hicks

The cast for the performance included:

James Stewart	Macauley (Mike) Connor
John Conte	C.K. Dexter Haven
Joan Tetzel	Tracy Lord
Rosemary Rice	Dinah Lord
Vera Allen	Margaret Lord
Oliver Thorndike	Sandy Lord
Howard St. John	Seth Lord
Audrey Christie	Elizabeth Imbrie (Liz)
Don Briggs	George Kittredge

The program was broadcast from the Syria Mosque in Pittsburgh, PA, which was within easy driving distance of Stewart's hometown of Indiana, PA. Many from the town came to Pittsburgh to see the broadcast, including Stewart's parents, who were introduced to the audience before the play began. Before the show went on the air, Stewart was presented with two awards. First the town's Burgess, J.R. Maloney, made Jimmy honorary Chief of Police of Indiana Borough. Then Indiana's Chief of Police, John F. O'Mara, presented Jimmy with a membership in the Fraternal Order of Police. According to the article in the *Indiana Evening Gazette*, 30,000 requests were made for the 8,000 available tickets for the program and all tickets were gone within 24 hours of the announcement of the program.

Also according to the same article, Stewart visited with William Neff between the rehearsal and the broadcast. Neff and Stewart worked together as magicians while they were still in high school.

(3) Sunday, September 26, 1948 (10:00-11:00 p.m.) — *That's Gratitude*
This show is not available for listening.

(4) Sunday, February 17, 1952 (8:30-9:30 p.m.) — *The Meanest Man in the World*
NETWORK: NBC
Besides Stewart, the show also stars Coleen Gray, Kenny Delmar and Josephine Hull. The 1943 film of the same name starred Jack Benny and Priscilla Lane. Paddy Chayefsky, author of the original story, wrote the radio adaptation.
This show is not available for listening.

(5) Sunday, April 6, 1952 (8:30-9:30 p.m.) — *The Silver Whistle*
NETWORK: NBC
SPONSOR: United States Steel Corporation
ANNOUNCER: Norman Brokenshire
HOST: Elliott Reid
DIRECTOR: Homer Fickett
PRODUCER: George Kondolf
ADAPTED BY: Robert Anderson
WRITER OF ORIGINAL STORY: Robert E. McEnroe
ORIGINAL MUSIC COMPOSED AND CONDUCTED BY: Harold Levey
The cast included:
James Stewart, Diana Lynn, Parker Fennelly, Cameron Andrews, Kathleen Comegys, Frances Brandt, Doro Merande, Richard Bishop, Donald Bain, Nathaniel Frey, Eric Sinclair

Elliott Reid is introduced as "speaking for the Theatre Guild" and says to the listeners:

> *Good evening, ladies and gentlemen. Tonight, we bring you the radio premiere of a recent* Theatre Guild *comedy stage success,* The Silver Whistle, *by Robert E. McEnroe. James Stewart is on hand to play Oliver Erwenter and Diana Lynn will be heard as Miss Tripp. They will be supported by a fine cast, including members of the original New York stage company. So, with an appropriate toot, we raise the curtain on* The Silver Whistle, *adapted for us by Robert Anderson and directed by Homer Fickett.*

Wilfred and Emmett are a couple of hoboes working a shell game on some unsuspecting people when they are chased by the police. Hungry, Wilfred is going through trashcans looking for food when he finds a birth certificate. The certificate is for an Oliver T. Erwenter, who had been born in 1875, making him 77 years old now. Even though Wilfred is only 40 years old, he plans to use the birth certificate to get himself admitted to a nearby old people's home for some food and relaxation. His pet chicken, Omar, comes along with him.

No one at the home, especially Mr. John Watson, the supervisor, can believe that he is actually 77. Erwenter says that he can make everyone in the home younger by 25 years. He quotes a poem, reciting:

> *The old dog crawled away to die and hid amid the thistle.*
> *Then joy and youth came back to him on the note of a silver whistle.*

Wilfred also begins falling in love with Miss Harriett Tripp, a nurse at the facility. He wants her to act younger and get a life away from the home. He doesn't know that she and Mr. Watson are engaged. When he does find out, he says that he will marry her now and gives her a cigar band for an engagement ring.

Wilfred meets with Emmett, whom he has promised food, and tells him he wants to help the people at the home. He tells him that he has made a trip to the post office and prepared a package to take to the home. The package is marked as being from Tibet and contains a "potion" which will make the users younger. He also asks Emmett to get a few things for him and post signs saying there would be a bazaar at the home. He hopes to raise enough money so that everyone at the home can have what they need.

Erwenter gives Mr. Cherry and Mr. Beebe some of the "potion" and some whiskey to wash it down. They begin to feel better and even start singing *Mademoiselle from Armentières*, but Watson comes in and stops them. Erwenter spends much of the night planting flowers on the home's grounds.

Emmett brings all the things Erwenter had requested and they set them up for the bazaar. When he tells Emmett that he is engaged to Miss Tripp, Emmett threatens to expose him and informs him that the sheriff is also the director of the home.

When Sheriff Chandler shows up and tries to stop the bazaar, Watson tells him that it was his idea. Erwenter also lets him win at the shell game. The sheriff lets the bazaar go on and returns to his office to see if the description of Wilfred has arrived.

Miss Tripp tells Erwenter that she would rather be with Watson. When Emmett shows up, Wilfred tells her of his true identity as a tramp. He also tells her that he is only 40 years old, but asks her not to tell any of the residents. They have become younger acting and he doesn't want that to change.

The show is part of *Vintage Radio Collection Jimmy Stewart* (Stardust), a special downloadable set made available in 2008.

(6) Sunday, March 1, 1953 (8:30-9:30 p.m.) — *O'Halloran's Luck*

Tonight's program was moved from its usually Pittsburgh, PA, location to Constitution Hall, Washington, DC, to help with the nation-wide radio-TV kickoff for the 1953 Red Cross fund-raising drive. The program for the show outlined the problems of moving the entire show to a new location. There was also a separate portion of the show as well, which was aimed at raising funds for the American Red Cross. This included speeches by Clifford F. Hood, President of U.S. Steel, John

Clifford Folger, Chairman, District Red Cross, E. Rowland Harriman, President, National Red Cross and The Honorable Leverett Saltonstall, Senator from Massachusetts.

NETWORK: NBC
SPONSOR: United States Steel Corporation
ANNOUNCER: Norman Brokenshire
REPORTING FOR U.S. STEEL: Elliott Reid
DIRECTOR: Homer Fickett
EXECUTIVE PRODUCER: Armina Marshall
MANAGING DIRECTOR: H. William Fitelson
EDITOR: S. Mark Smith
ORIGINAL STORY BY: Stephen Vincent Benet
ADAPTED BY: Peter Berlinrut
ORIGINAL MUSIC COMPOSED AND CONDUCTED BY: Harold Levey
General Supervision by Lawrence Langer and Theresa Helbur
The cast included:

James Stewart	Mick the Fixer, a Leprechaun
John Lund	John Timothy O'Halloran, opening narrator
Gloria DeHaven	Molly Malone
Una O'Connor	Mrs. Malone
Norman Barrs	Kelly
Cameron Andrews	Atwood
George Mathews	Sullivan
Oliver Thorndike	O'Hagen
Tom Scott	folk singer

Playing the part of a leprechaun could only have been pulled off by the 6-foot-3-inch Stewart on a radio show. The Irish accent he uses may have come easy for him since he can trace his ancestry back to County Antrim, Ireland. This was actually Stewart's second role to require an Irish accent. He also needed one in the 1935 Broadway play, *Yellow Jack*. According to James Aswell's column, "My New York," of April 13, 1934, Stewart honed the accent by talking to a butcher, two bartenders and an elevator boy.

Molly Malone and her mother are about to leave Ireland for Boston. Molly's boyfriend, John Timothy O'Halloran, is planning on following them there and making his fortune working for the railroad. A leprechaun, who wants to escape from a curse placed on him by St. Patrick, is tricked into going to America on the same ship as the others.

Later, John is discouraged because he hasn't received any mail from Molly in quite some time. He knows that she has been seeing Aloysius Sullivan and worries that they may be getting closer. Molly, too, is worried because she hasn't heard from John either.

After a night of drinking and dancing, John is walking back to the railroad camp when he encounters what he thinks is a young boy and saves him from a wolf. The boy turns out to be a leprechaun known as Mick the Fixer (although at one point later in the show he is called Mixer the Fixer). The Fixer has lost his magical powers, but regains them when John believes in him. After finding out that John is worried about Molly, the Fixer has him look into the end of an empty bottle. John sees Molly, all right, but she's with Aloysius. John breaks the bottle.

O'Halloran passes Mick off as his Uncle Mike to the railroad foreman, and gets him a job as a water boy. One night, Mick tells John that he was a normal man until St. Patrick put a curse on him which changed him into a leprechaun. The curse says that he has to "serve the folks of Clonmelly 'til the day he serves the servant of a servant in the lands at world's end." He thinks that he has escaped from the curse in America, until O'Halloran tells him that he is from Clonmelly.

O'Halloran's fortunes on the railroad begin to change for the better when he gets help from the Fixer. First, the Fixer tells him that the tracks are about to be built over land with water under it and that the tracks will sink if built there. John tells the engineer who checks it out and finds it to be true. John is made a foreman. Next, the Fixer sees Thomas Alva Edison trying to patent a machine for laying tracks. He makes one himself and when O'Halloran shows it to his superiors, he's made a section superintendent.

The Fixer talks John into going to Boston to see Molly, who is now a servant scrubbing floors for others. Molly tells him that she's going to marry Aloysius. The two men fight and John wins the fight and Molly. After the fight, Molly tells John that he might as well get used to being a husband and asks him to pick up her mother's dishes. As he does so, the Fixer tells him his shoe is untied. John doesn't want to take the time to tie it himself and tells the Fixer to tie it. When the task is completed, the Fixer has served the servant of a servant and the curse is broken.

Benet's original story can be found in his book, *O'Halloran's Luck and Other Short Stories* (Penguin Books, New York, 1944). For some reason there are several name changes made between the story and the radio play. In the story, Molly's name is Kitty, there is no John in front of Timothy O'Halloran's name and instead of being passed off as Uncle Mike, the leprechaun is introduced as Tim's nephew, Rory.

Theater of Romance

The show began in New York City, but moved to Hollywood in 1945. It was on CBS for its entire radio run. The first show was broadcast on April 19, 1943. For the first season, the show was sustaining and aired on Monday evenings from 6:00-6:30 pm. From July 4, 1944, through August 27, 1946, it was sponsored by Colgate and Halo and aired Tuesday evenings from 5:30-6:00 pm. It came back on October 2, 1946, as a sustaining show heard Wednesdays from 5:30-6:00 pm. It went off the air permanently after its final show on December 11, 1946. In its first and last incarnations, the show was known simply as *Romance*. Jimmy Stewart was on the show just once.

Tuesday, November 20, 1945 — *No Time for Comedy* (8:30-9 p.m.)
NETWORK: CBS
SPONSOR: Colgate Tooth Powder and Halo Shampoo
HOST: Frank Graham
PRODUCER: Charles Vanda
COMMERCIAL ANNOUNCER: Joe Burton
WRITER: S.N. Behrman
ADAPTATION BY: Joel Malone and Stanley Rubin

Gaylord Esterbrook (Jimmy Stewart), Gay for short, a playwright, has always written comedies. But now, because of a new girlfriend, Amanda Swift, he wants to write a serious drama. The problem is that he still has a wife. Linda Esterbrook is an actress and believes that he should continue to write comedies. Gay is with Amanda in her apartment one day when her husband, Philo Swift (Lou Merrill), comes in with Linda. Gay tells her that he is going to marry Amanda. But, Linda has read his new play and thinks that he can do better if he would go back to writing comedy. She thinks that a romantic triangle between Gay, Amanda and herself would make a great comedy and Gay agrees.

At the end of the show, we hear:

GRAHAM: We're looking forward to your return to the screen in the Frank Capra/Liberty production, *It's a Wonderful Life*, Jim.

STEWART: Thank you, thank you very much. It was a pleasure to be on stage for the *Theater of Romance*. And it looks like your regular customers are in for a great holiday line-up. Next week, Bob Walker returns in *Penny Serenade*. Then, Bob Taylor makes his first appearance since his discharge from the Navy. He'll star in *Magnificent Obsession*. The week after that, one of my favorite friends, Susan Peters, joins up with Van Johnson in *The Love Affair*. Well, thanks again, see you soon. Goodnight. Good listening.

In 2011, this show was issued in mp3 only format on *Jimmy Stewart the Ultimate Radio Collection Vol. 1* (Master Classics Records).

This Is New York

Stewart made two appearances on this WCBS radio show, hosted by Bill Leonard. Neither appearance is available for listening.

(1) Monday, March 4, 1957 (11:10-11:30 p.m.)
It is highly likely that the topic of Stewart's interview was his soon-to-be-released (April 20) film, *The Spirit of St. Louis*. Leland Hayward, the producer of the film, was also a guest on the show.

(2) Friday, May 30, 1958 (9:30-10:30 p.m.)
Stewart's latest film, *Vertigo*, had just had its premiere and it is possible that this was the focus of today's interview.

This Is War

This 13-week series was on the air from February 14 until May 9, 1942, and was the brainchild of Norman Corwin. It was broadcast by all four major networks simultaneously. More than 600 stations in the U.S. carried the programs and they were broadcast around the world on short-wave. It was estimated at the time that approximately 20,000,000 people listened to each show. Keene Crockett was in charge of sound effects. The three aims of the show were *1. To inspire, 2. To frighten,* and *3. To inform.* The purpose of the series was to help keep up the morale of Americans and to show them how their enemies thought and plotted. Three shows — *Your Navy, Your Army* and *Your Air Forces* — planted the idea in the listener's minds that the Armed Forces belong to them, to all the people. The war effort was a total effort of all Americans and not just those in the military. Stewart appeared on just one of the shows — number 8 in the series. The script for all the shows, including this one, can be found in the following book for which Corwin served as editor: *This Is War! A Collection of Plays About America on the March* (Dodd, Mead & Company, 1942).

Saturday, April 4, 1942 (7:00-7:30 p.m.) — *Your Air Force*
NETWORKS: ABC, CBS, MBC, NBC
SPONSOR: Sustaining
NARRATOR: Lt. Jimmy Stewart, Army Air Forces
DIRECTOR: Glenhall Taylor

ASSOCIATE PRODUCER: Lt. Howard Nussbaum, Army Air Forces
WRITER: Ranald MacDougall
Original Music by Charles Dant

Also in the cast was Frank Albertson as the pilot. After the war, Albertson would play the role of Sam Wainwright in the film *It's a Wonderful Life*.

This show originated from Hollywood and promoted the Army, Navy, Marine and Coast Guard Air Forces. The entire production takes place over a backdrop of a bomber crew flying out to sink a Japanese battleship. Stewart narrates and describes the planning and teamwork that goes into such an attack. Most importantly, he emphasizes the fact that it takes all 135 million Americans for such a bombing run to work properly.

He starts with the swearing in of new recruits, their training, and how they work as a team — the pilot, the bombardier, the navigator, the radio man and the rear gunner. Stewart also describes what it took to design and build the aircraft, how our Air Force men were training our allies in Russia, China, Britain, Australia, and other countries to keep those planes flying. He visits an aircraft factory and gets a guarantee that there will be no strikes by workers during the war and sees how engines are developed to work well in all types of weather.

Finally, we hear the bombers' attack run on the Japanese battleship and experience the excitement of the crew as they sink same.

As *The Air Force Song* is played in the background, Stewart ends the show with this speech:

> Now this is your Air Force and it's really yours, you know. Now the day after tomorrow is Army Day. Air fields, other than those in strategic military areas, will be open tomorrow and the next day. Now, why don't you visit your air forces and get acquainted with the men and the machines that make the Air Force what it is. Well, I'll be seein' ya…and keep 'em flyin'.

NOTE: The script for this show, and those of the other 12 shows in the series, can be found in the following book for which Corwin served as editor: *This Is War! A Collection of Plays About America on the March* (Dodd, Mead & Company, 1942).

Tomorrow's America
See *Boy Scout Jamboree*.

Tony Awards Show
 NETWORK: Mutual
 SPONSOR: Sustaining
 PRODUCER: Paul Jonas
 ANNOUNCER: Jack Irish

The second annual Antoinette Perry "Tony" Awards Show was broadcast from the Grand Ballroom of the Waldorf Astoria Hotel in New York City on March 28, 1948. The show, as broadcast, runs just under 15 minutes. All acceptance speeches were kept to a minimum, with Jimmy Stewart's introduction of Henry Fonda being one of the longest. Bert Lytell gave a short introduction to the show and then handed things over to James E. Sauter, chairman of the entertainment committee, who thanks all the Stage Door Canteen workers. Sauter then introduced Brock Pemberton who announced the winners. The first five winners were:

Judith Anderson for *Medea*
Katharine Cornell for *Antony and Cleopatra* (Her award was
 accepted by her husband, Guthrie McClintic)
Jessica Tandy for *A Streetcar Named Desire*
Paul Kelly for *Command Decision*
Basil Rathbone for *The Heiress*

Pemberton then introduces Jimmy Stewart, who makes this short speech:

> *Ladies and gentlemen, I have to do this because...this is a very pleasant chore for me. The fact that this fellow is gonna be awarded an award for good acting is absolutely no surprise to me. This fellow has sort of approached this acting business with a great integrity and honesty. And the fact that he's done it in such a way, it's been a very inspiring thing to watch him all the time I've known him. We're very proud of you, Hank, come on...Mr. Roberts.*

Possibly because he was afraid some may not know the award winner, Pemberton breaks in to say, "The name is Fonda, Henry Fonda." Fonda himself adds, "Ahh...you're cute, Jimmy."
The show then continued with awards going to:
Paul and Grace Hartman for *Angel in the Wings*
Vera Allen (Special Award)
Mary Martin (Special Award accepted for her by Oscar
 Hammerstein II and Richard Rodgers)

Joe E. Brown (Special Award accepted for him by Mary Chase, writer of *Harvey*)

Thomas Heggen and Joshua Logan writers of *Mr. Roberts*

Leland Hayward — producer of *Mr. Roberts*, who accepted for himself, as well as Heggen and Logan

Because of time restraints, the awards for Scenic Designer (Horace Armistead), Costume Designer (Mary Percy), Choreography (Jerome Robbins) and Stage Technicians (George Gebhardt, George Pierce) were not included in the show. Also missing were several Special Awards (Paul Beisman, Robert Dowling, Rosamond Gilder, June Lockhart, Robert Porterfield, James Whitmore, Experimental Theatre, Inc.).

Tony Weitzel Interview

This interview was broadcast on WBBM-AM (780) in Racine, WI. The interview is not available for listening and the content of the interview is not known.

The Traitor Within
NETWORK: NBC
NARRATOR/HOST: Jimmy Stewart
PRODUCER/DIRECTOR: Harvey Divavek
PRODUCTION COORDINATOR: Jo Dickey
TECHNICAL CONSULTANT: Dr. Ian MacDonald
TECHNICIAN: Leon Frye
WRITER: Richard George Pedicini
Music Score Composed and Conducted by: Robert Armbruster

This 30-minute show was produced by NBC in cooperation with the American Cancer Society and broadcast on April 12, 1953. It consisted of several short sketches and speeches from experts, tied together by Jimmy Stewart's narration.

After some dramatic music, Stewart begins the program.

STEWART: Ladies and gentlemen, this is Jimmy Stewart speaking and before we begin this very special program, I'd like to issue a few words of caution. If you're easily frightened when confronted with the awful truth, well, then, you're not going to like this program. You see, words have different meanings for many people, but there's one word that means the same thing to all of us, no disguising it…and that word is cancer. We all know what cancer means. Cancer is the traitor within.

The NBC announcer then introduces the show and finishes with, "Ladies and gentlemen, your narrator for the next 30 minutes, Hollywood's Mr. James Stewart."

STEWART: I didn't mean to sound like an alarmist a few moments ago; I didn't mean to scare you; that isn't our intention, not at all. We personally don't intend to frighten any of you, but we think that truth of this matter will, and frankly we hope our story will do some good. Now we've got approximately 30 minutes in which to discuss a very vital subject with you. Thirty minutes is not nearly time enough, but that's all the time we've got. Now, we'll discuss the past, the present and a glimpse into the promise of tomorrow. In fact, it was only yesterday that this subject was sort of taboo in local society. Eh…ah…oh, excuse me. Did I say sort of? I mean definitely taboo. For some strange reason people just didn't dare discuss this subject among themselves. Now, recall to mind if you will you…you older folks, recall that way Aunt Ethel's death was usually hushed around the neighborhood. It went something like this if I'm not mistaken.

In the brief skit that followed Stewart's remarks, two women are discussing Ethel's death using such phrases as: "suffered a long time," "died of a lingering illness" and "Oh, the shame of it all."

STEWART: Shocking? Yes, it was shocking, but not for shame. Shocking because man, even with all his infinite wisdom, was helpless to do anything for Ethel. Lingering illness, yes, that was one polite way of revealing the reason of her death. There are other ways, too. Now this scene took place in the general store.

The two men discussing her death agree that she was "ailin' a long time." One, speaking in a whisper, says that the cause of her death was a malignant tumor.

STEWART: A malignant tumor, now I ask you, why did people try to disguise it? What were they afraid of? Well, we can only guess that it was because it was an unknown quantity…and cancer was certainly an unknown quantity.

At this point another voice adds, "Ladies and Gentlemen, cancer is still an unknown quantity."

STEWART: Well, that's the subject we're going to discuss and we're not going to try to disguise it…it's been disguised for too long a time. If you'll forgive me for the use of this timeworn term, we're gonna call a spade a spade and not something else. Okay, then the first order of business is to find out what cancer is. Well, there are a lot of good ideas floating around as to what it is. And just to give you a vague idea of what the men of science are up against, we've ask one of the country's leading cancer authorities to make a few brief remarks; ladies and gentlemen, Dr. Ian MacDonald, a member of the cancer committee of the American College of Surgeons.

Dr. MacDonald's remarks include the statement that cancer is a complex group of many diseases and that there are as many as 300 different types of cancer.

STEWART: Three hundred types of cancer…well, that's a frightening figure if I ever heard one. Not one disease, but many. Well, then it only stands to reason that there can't be any one cure for cancer. It's possible there may have to be many cures, as many cures as there are types of cancer. Well, now, what are we doing about this disease of cancer? A lot is being done about it. Some of the good that's being done you know or hear about and some of it you don't. What was done yesterday? What's being done today? How about tomorrow? Here's something I'll bet you never knew.

A voice tells listeners that Hippocrates knew about and studied cancer in 375 B.C.

STEWART: It's amazing, isn't it? Hippocrates knew about cancer. Now, here's a startling fact.

The voice tells us that surgery for breast cancer was performed as early as 38 A.D.

STEWART: Now that was 38 A.D. — one thousand nine hundred and fifteen years ago. Now, let me give you another fact. It was 38 A.D. when Celcus performed the first successful surgery of breast cancer, yet the next important development in the control of cancer didn't take place until 1824, one thousand seven hundred and eighty-six years later. Now, that is shocking. This very important development took place in Paris, France. It involved a man named Raspail.

In the short skit that follows, Raspail shows a group of doctors cancer cells under his newly invented microscope. He shows that cancer results from an abnormal multiplication of cells, so cancer is the result of cells gone wild.

STEWART: And the scientists learned something else after Raspail's discovery. They learned that the cancer cell never ages…it never dies as normal cells do. The cancer process has eternal youth…it's primitive, savage, it preys upon its useful neighbors, it invades tissue in greedy, grasping groups destroying as it advances.

Another voice adds that these cancer cells can then be carried to other parts of the body by the blood and lymphatic system.

STEWART: The traitor within…it's the only known, unwelcomed guest who commits suicide by destroying its host. Well, it was the turn of the century and the men of science were finally beginning to build a pyramid of defense against this deadly scourge called cancer. In 1933 another major step forward was taken. In Pittsburgh, a doctor James J. Gilmore, an obstetrician, developed a peculiar chest cough. He had x-rays of his chest taken and the results were positive…Dr. Gilmore had cancer of the left lung. As a medical man, he knew the only hope lay in immediate surgery. He wrote a letter to one of his former classmates in medical college, Dr. Evarts Graham, a noted chest surgeon practicing in the city of St. Louis, and a few weeks later, he went to see Dr. Graham personally.

In the short skit which follows, we learn that Dr. Graham has taken lungs from animals, but never from a human. Dr. Gilmore volunteers to be his human guinea pig.

STEWART: Without any loss of time, Dr. James Gilmore headed for surgery.

Another voice tells us that on April 5, 1933, the first cancerous lung is removed.

STEWART: Was the operation a success? Well, Dr. Gilmore lost one lung, but that was 20 years ago and he's alive today — still practicing medicine. Thus, in 1933, did the science of surgery prove that cancer in an organ formerly unapproachable, could be cured, but only if it was detected in an early stage. Early discovery is half the battle in the control.

Another voice then tells us that the number of patients surviving cancer surgery has increased in this century.

STEWART: That's a good thing, but not good enough.

A voice asks, "What about the 75 of 100 patients who still died?"

STEWART: Well, folks, that's a pretty vague idea of a couple of important things that happened in the past, but now it's time for us to examine the present — today. What's happening today that holds promise for a bright tomorrow? Now, in 30 short minutes, we couldn't possibly hope to tell you the whole story, but we'll give you a fragment. As of now, there are only three proven cures…

Another voice adds, "Surgery, x-ray, radium."

STEWART: Only three methods that can cure; thousands of chemicals have been screened against cancer in laboratory animals…only a few are of some value. Right now there's an important experiment being conducted at the University of Wisconsin.

A voice tells the listeners that a chemical has been found that will block cancer cell reproduction, but, it also damages the normal cells.

STEWART: In other words, many thousands of chemical compounds have been concocted in the hopes that one of them will be the right mixture, the right degree, the right cure. Now, listen to what they've learned at Alabama Polytechnic Institute.

An anonymous voice tells the listeners that diet can affect cancer. Well-fed animals get cancer more often.

STEWART: Then fat people have more cancer than skinny ones, huh?

The voice answers, "Yes, but thin people have cancer, too."

STEWART: Problems…millions of problems are posed for the scientists… listen to what's happening at Jefferson Medical College in Philadelphia.

A voice informs listeners that chromosomes also appear to be able to cause cancer.

STEWART: Probing into the very origins of our sex; is that where one solution of cancer control may exist?

The voice answers, "We don't know, but we'll keep on experimenting."

STEWART: Yes, the search goes on and on and on; experiment after experiment. Rewards? Sometimes, sometimes there are rewards.
VOICE: Oh, Mr. Stewart.
STEWART: Yeah.
VOICE: May I show you something?
STEWART: Yeah, yeah, of course.
VOICE: Right here in the lab.
STEWART: Oh, well, what is it?
VOICE: Well, this is what we affectionately call an atomic oven.
STEWART: Um, atomic bombs, tanks, toys, wrestlers and now ovens, huh, what won't they think of next? Well, what do you cook?
VOICE: Chemical compounds are cooked in this atomic oven until they carry a heavy charge of radioactivity.
STEWART: What for?
VOICE: Well, these compounds are fed or injected into the cancer patients or implanted directly into tumors.
STEWART: Well, what are some of them?
VOICE: Radioactive iodine is one. This usually settles into the tumor of about one-fifth of the patients who have thyroid cancer. And then there's cobalt. This substance, in many cases, can take the place of radium. It's cheaper than radium and carries a large range of radioactive charges. A golf ball-sized chunk of cobalt cooked for 18 months will actually deliver to deep-seated tumors, rays that are comparable to a two-million-volt x-ray machine.
STEWART: Well, are cobalt and iodine the only ones?
VOICE: No, no, there's sodium and potassium, sodium and bromine, tantalum and gold.
STEWART: Gold?

VOICE: Yes, the very inert property of gold makes it helpful in this approach to the disease.
STEWART: And that's the oven that does it, huh?
VOICE: Um-hum.
STEWART: You call it the atomic oven, huh?
VOICE: Yes, that's right.
STEWART: Yeah, well, what won't they think of next?

The voice informs listeners that the use of radioactivity has broadened.

STEWART: This next story is the story of a woman named Ruth Morris. She lives up in San Francisco. This incident took place between Ruth and her husband, Andy, in their home one Sunday afternoon.

In a short skit, the listener learns that Ruth is having some physical problems and that her husband asks her to call the doctor.

STEWART: Ruth Morris called her family physician and then the following Monday morning, she went to see him. He did a thorough examination…three days later she was back for the results.

In another short skit, the doctor tells Ruth that she has uterine cancer. He recommends that she undergo radiation treatment.

STEWART: Ruth Morris underwent extensive radiation treatment. Today, she's a healthy woman again.

After a short musical selection, a voice says that there is a growing awareness of cancer and that it can strike anyone.

STEWART: Well, we have a somewhat vague idea of what took place in the past. We know a little of what's going on now, but now what about the future? Well, the future holds promise…yes it does.

The anonymous voice now says, "Research, education and service to cancer patients.

STEWART: Research, education and service…is that it?
VOICE: That's right.
STEWART: Well, let's start with education…now what about education?

The voice informs us that the American Cancer Society spends millions each year to educate the public. The seven warning signs of cancer are then listed. Then the voice concludes by telling us that all too often people still try home remedies.

STEWART: Home remedies?

The voice gives a few examples.

STEWART: Yeah, I think I see what you mean.

The voice introduces a skit which informs the listeners that treating symptoms with home remedies hinders early diagnosis of cancer.

STEWART: Early diagnosis…I see.

The listeners are told that early diagnosis and treatment can save lives.

STEWART: Then cancer is curable provided it's treated in time?
VOICE: Yes…
STEWART: Well, then there is promise of a bright tomorrow.
VOICE: Definitely.
STEWART: And who is responsible for this promise?
VOICE: The people.
STEWART: Well, that's it, folks. It's as simple as that. This gentleman here says it's up to you, it's up to me, it's up to all of us to strike out this vicious disease. And, of course, the big question on everybody's mind is, "How do we do it?" How do we join ranks and wipe out this traitor within? Well, ladies and gentlemen, one of Hollywood's most distinguished citizens will answer that question for you. And, I'm honored and privileged to introduce him to you right now — Mr. Cecil B. DeMille.

DeMille reaffirms that we can all look forward to the day when cancer can be easily cured, but, to do so, the American Cancer Society needs your support — give generously. A skit presented as part of DeMille's portion of the program, has a woman in 1971 being told that she has cancer and that it can be cured simply by taking some pills.

STEWART: Thank you, Mr. DeMille. Well, folks, there isn't anything more to be said. You've heard what we had to say in just 30 minutes — you've heard what we had to say about cancer. I assure you these words were carefully chosen and there were a lot of people who had to do with bringing you these words. Our thanks to Dr. Ian MacDonald, who served as technical consultant, Miss Jo Dickey, who was production coordinator, Robert Armbruster, our musical director who composed a special musical score, Richard George Pedicini, writer, our technician, Leon Fry, and Harry Divavec, the producer-director. And, of course, a special note of thanks to NBC for giving us all the time to bring this to you. So long, folks.

Although none of the other actors appearing on the show were given, two voices did stand out — Parley Baer and Virginia Gregg.

A Tribute to Glenn Miller

A Tribute to Glenn Miller was a local program put together by Jack Cullen and broadcast over CKNW, Vancouver, British Columbia, Canada, in 1971. Cullen had a show called *Sunday Special* and this 90-minute program was a part of that show. Born in 1922, Cullen was a teen during most of Miller's career and obviously developed quite a love for the man and his music.

Many of Miller's most popular songs are played during the tribute, as well as a few rarities, including a live broadcast from the Café Rouge of the Hotel Pennsylvania in New York City and a broadcast of Miller with the Army Air Force Orchestra on the BBC. But by far the highlights of the program are the many interviews with those associated with Miller. Among those interviewed are Ben Pollack (Miller played in his band), Gene Norman, Frank Sinatra, Warren Reed (a Canadian Miller expert), Ray Eberle, Cleveland Amory, Dave Garroway, Hal Dickinson and his wife Paula Kelly (both of the Modernaires, who sang with the Miller Band), Benny Goodman, Guy Lombardo, Jerry Gray, Vernon Harris (who interviewed Miller on the BBC), June Allyson and Jimmy Stewart.

Two different Stewart interviews are used in the program. In the first, he talks about the ad-lib jam session featuring Louis Armstrong in the film, *The Glenn Miller Story*.

> Yeah, well, I think that's one of the reasons why it was so effective is because it was a completely impromptu thing. Believe me; the whole studio was over at the recording stage the morning that number was recorded. And, it was a big thrill for all of us, especially for the recording people because they had no idea what Armstrong was gonna play. They had no idea what piece of music or what number he was gonna play, so

when it all sort of took form and all sort of suddenly exploded into this wonderful Basin Street thing, it was quite a thrill.

Cullen then tells the listeners that he interviewed Stewart in August of 1953 at the Hotel Vancouver and plays part of the transcription.

STEWART: Well, I just finished a picture called *The Glenn Miller Story*.
CULLEN: I was waiting for that.
STEWART: Which is about an orchestra leader which I think you're acquainted with.
CULLEN: Let's have a talk about it, Jimmy. You play the part of Miller and, I believe, June Allyson is in this film, too.
STEWART: June Allyson plays Mrs. Miller.
CULLEN: Any other people we'd know?
STEWART: Ahh…June Allyson. Henry Morgan plays Chummy MacGregor, the ahh…
CULLEN: Piano boy.
STEWART: Piano boy and I think that's about all the people that you would recognize. We have several of the original Miller Orchestra in the Orchestra that we use in the picture. I don't know about the picture. I saw it the other night — a very rough cut.
CULLEN: Are you gonna be happy, do you think, with the finished picture?
STEWART: I have no idea. Funny thing, you do a picture and you get so close to it that when you suddenly see it all together and you see what you've been doing all boiled into an hour, what you've been doing for the last eight or ten weeks, it takes you quite a while to decide just exactly what you think about it.
CULLEN: This is a different sort of picture for you. Is your lip in good condition after blowing a trombone for, shall we say, a couple of months?
STEWART: Yes, it certainly is a different sort of picture. I had quite a problem with the trombone because the trombone, as you know, is a very difficult instrument. And, it's also a very awkward instrument. And, I don't know, there's something about sitting down at the piano and even if you've never seen a piano in your life, you could sort of do it gracefully.
CULLEN: You know the high notes are up here and the low notes are down there, but with a trombone, where are the low notes?
STEWART: With a trombone, even to pick a trombone up you know it's sort of like picking up a bicycle. So I had a little problem to become sort of at home when I had the trombone. I got a fella that certainly filled the bill and if I don't come across and if I don't convince people I sort of…

CULLEN: Felt it.

STEWART: Felt it, it isn't his fault, it's mine. His name's Joe Yukl and he's been a musician around the country for years and years. He was in the original Tommy Dorsey Band and he's been out in Hollywood playing for all the orchestras around the studios, and ah and all radio shows like Crosby's and Hope's and an excellent musician.

CULLEN: Musically, he is a big man. We've heard of him.

STEWART: Really. He ah…he's not only a…musically, he was wonderful for me because he's a very good teacher. And he had a problem with me because he had to do it in a matter of two months. And, he actually couldn't teach me how to play the trombone. It was more in teaching me how to handle the trombone and sort of how to make people think that I knew what I was doing.

CULLEN: Sort of like a person ghost singing as they do sometimes with somebody else's voice and to act the part of a singer and as it were, of course, you had to act the part of a musician and you sure came through with flying colors, although I haven't seen the picture, we've heard a lot of reviews and read a lot of reviews about the picture.

STEWART: Well, ah, this is, as you said, sort of a change of pace for me and it and it's sort of a different type of picture.

CULLEN: Ever had anything to do with a musical before? Not to my knowledge.

STEWART: A long time ago, long time ago.

CULLEN: Let's remember.

STEWART: I made a picture at M-G-M called *Born to Dance*.

CULLEN: Eleanor Powell, wasn't it?

STEWART: Eleanor Powell.

CULLEN: Was that 1936?

STEWART: 19…yes, it was, I think it was.

CULLEN: *Easy to Love* was the hit tune and *I've Got You Under My Skin*…

Because they had gotten off the subject of *The Glenn Miller Story*, Cullen ended the transcription playback here. Cullen admitted that portions of the show had been taken from many different sources and no general credits were given. Several credits from a BBC program he had used were given:

PRODUCTION, SCRIPT AND RESEARCH: Henry Wiston
ANNOUNCER: Ted Miller

Tusher in Hollywood

William Tusher, a writer for the *Daily Variety* and *Hollywood Reporter*, also hosted a 15-minute radio show. Jimmy Stewart was a guest of the program on Sunday, May 11, 1952 (7:15-7:30 p.m.). The program is not available for listening, so it is not known what topics were discussed.

25th Anniversary of the 'Air Force Song'

The Air Force Song was written by Robert Crawford and adopted in September 1939 (Labor Day weekend), as the official Air Corps anthem. Crawford, a captain in the Army Air Corps, wrote the song in response to a *Liberty* magazine contest, which offered a $1,000 prize to the writer of the best song. The contest drew 757 entries. They were judged by a committee of Air Corps wives, chaired by Mildred Yount. Crawford's song was judged best. The only change in the lyrics over the years came when the Army Air Corps became the U.S. Air Force. This show was issued to radio stations as a single 12-inch vinyl record (EXTV98320) in a special jacket, to be played during September 1964, to mark the anniversary of the song. The 25-minute show is on one side of the disc. On the other side are seven, 1:30 versions of *The National Anthem*, played by the U.S. Air Force Orchestra.

NARRATOR/HOST: Walt Tease
ANNOUNCER: Bob Dalton
GUESTS: U.S.A.F. Orchestra with the Singing Sergeants Airmen of Note
SPECIAL GUEST STAR: Jimmy Stewart

The show opens with:
"The Squadron Song" — Singing Sergeants

Tease then introduces Jimmy Stewart, who reads the poem *High Flight*, written by John G. Magee, who had been killed in an air battle on December 11, 1941, at the age of 19. After Stewart reads the poem, the Singing Sergeants sing a version which has been set to music by Sgt. Floyd Worley.

> *Oh! I have slipped the surly bonds of earth*
> *And danced the skies on laughter-silver wings;*
> *Sunward I've climbed, and joined the tumbling mirth*
> *Of sun-split clouds — and done a hundred things*
> *You have not dreamed of — wheeled and soared and swung*
> *High in the sunlit silence. Hov'ring there*
> *I've chased the shouting wind along, and flung*
> *My eager craft through footless halls of air.*
> *Up, up the long, delirious, burning blue*
> *I've topped the wind-swept heights with easy grace*

*Where never lark, nor even eagle flew –
And, while with silent lifting mind I've trod
The high untrespassed sanctity of space
Put out my hand and touched the face of God.*

In the first line, Stewarts substitutes "bounds" for "bonds."

Tease then looks back at the year 1939, mentioning, among other things, Stewart's film, *Mr. Smith Goes to Washington.* The show is completed with several musical numbers.

"Big Band Themes" — Airmen of Note
"I Didn't Know What Time It Was" — Sgt. Jerry Whitman
"Glenn Miller Medley" — Airmen of Note
"The Air Force Song" — Concert Orchestra and the Singing Sergeants

Twenty Questions

The concept was simple — one person would have something in mind and the rest of the panelists would ask him/her questions about that "thing" which could be answered yes or no. If they guessed the "thing" before all twenty questions were asked, they won…if not, they lost.

The radio show was created by Fred Van Deventer, who was a very popular newsman at radio station WOR in New York City. He kept the show in the family, making himself a regular panelist. Also on the panel were his wife Florence (she appeared using her maiden name, Florence Rinard), his son, Robert (known as Bobby McGuire on the program) and occasionally his daughter Nancy. The panel was rounded out by Herb Polesie, who doubled as the show's producer, as a guest. The Stewart show is not available for review.

Saturday, May 16, 1953 (8-8:30 p.m.)
NETWORK: Mutual
SPONSOR: Wildroot Cream Oil
PRODUCER: Herb Polesie
ANNOUNCER: Frank Waldecker
MODERATOR: Jay Jackson
THEME MUSIC: "Twenty Questions" (Bernard Green/Moe Jaffe/Dick Hardt)

Uncle Jay Jay's Playtime

Uncle Jay Jay's Playtime was a local Cedar Rapids, Iowa, program which aired on radio station KCRG from 1950 through 1952. Jimmy Stewart was advertised as appearing on the show just one time. The date of his appearance was Saturday, February 2, 1952 (9-9:30 a.m. Central time). That show is not available for listening.

Judging from the other "guests" who appeared on the program at about this same time — Roy Rogers and Gabby Hayes, Jimmy Durante, Hopalong Cassidy, Uncle Wiggley — it is more than likely that Jimmy was not actually in the studio with Uncle Jay Jay. Instead, it is likely that Uncle Jay Jay simply played selections from the Winnie the Pooh Upside-Down Storybooks which RCA Records had released several months earlier. All of his other "guests" also had children's records out at that time.

United We Stand

The main purpose of this show was to promote the USO and the work it would be doing. It is not in general circulation, but is a part of the NBC Collection at the Library of Congress.

Tuesday, June 3, 1941 (10:30-11 p.m.)
NETWORK: NBC Blue
ANNOUNCER: Bob Trout

The program begins with a short skit involving a new recruit and an Army old timer. The recruit is complaining that there is nothing to do in town.

Admiral Harold Stark and Chief of Staff General George Marshall talk about how widespread this type of problem is in both the Army and the Navy.

In the next skit, a sailor can't find his girlfriend in the mob at the dock. He looks all over town for her, but they never find one another. If only there were a place they could have gone to meet.

Admiral Stark and General Marshall are joined by Secretary of the Navy Frank Knox and more of the problem is outlined.

The next sketch is about the conditions in the small towns in which defense workers now have to live. Not being natives of the towns, they are reluctant to venture into the downtown area. When they do, they are treated badly. At a bowling alley they must wait three hours to bowl and then pay 25¢ per game, while townspeople only pay 10¢. They can't even buy ice cream or a soda as these are being held for townspeople only.

Assistant Secretary of War John J. McCloy speaks next, telling listeners that they have a common spirit as they are all working for the defense of the country. The announcer, Bob Trout, says that the USO has been formed to help the situation. The remainder of the show will outline the mission of the USO.

Mr. Walter Hoving, President of the USO, is the next to speak. He says that the USO has been around since World War I, but now many of the problems have been corrected. He also says that the other groups involved in the USO are the YMCA, YWCA, National Catholic Community Service, Salvation Army, Jewish Welfare Board and National Travelers Aid Association. He then introduces Charles P. Taft, Assistant Coordinator for Health, Welfare and Related Defense Activities of the Federal Security Administration. He says that the government will equip more than 250 USO clubs around the U.S., but that citizens must help to keep the clubs open and running well.

Bob Trout now introduces Thomas E. Dewey, National Campaign Chairman, for the USO. It will be his job to raise the $10,765,000 needed to do all of this. He asks for full cooperation from all Americans. He knows, "Every American will do his part."

In the skit that follows, we hear from the new recruit again. This time he has just returned from town and is telling his sergeant that the new USO will soon be opening and things will be much better.

Trout introduces Paul V. McNutt of the Federal Security Administration who reads a letter from President Roosevelt, who thanks all for the success of the USO campaign.

"My Country 'Tis of Thee" plays as the show comes to an end.

According to the records that accompany this show at the Library of Congress, the actors in the short skits were Jimmy Stewart and John McIntire. It would make sense that Stewart would appear in a show of this type, but none of the voices sound like his. Nor do any sound like McIntire. None of the newspaper ads of the time which have been located list either Stewart or McIntire as appearing on the program. So, at this point, there is a considerable doubt that Stewart actually appeared in the program.

U.S. Air Force Anniversary Program

The U.S. Air Force had been officially formed on September 18, 1947. This show was broadcast to mark the first anniversary of that event. The program is not generally available, but is part of the NBC Collection at the Library of Congress.

Thursday, September 16, 1948 (8-8:30 p.m.) — *Slim and the Colonel*
NETWORK: NBC
PRODUCER/DIRECTOR: Jack Lyman
ANNOUNCER: Hal Gibney
DIRECTOR OF CHORUS & ORCHESTRA: Henry Russell

The show's cast included:
Jimmy Stewart.. *Narrator*
Hanley Stafford.. *the Colonel*
Peter Leeds...*Slim*
Charlie Lung, Leo Cleary, Victor Perrin, Johnny McGovern

The show begins with the statement, "Air power is peace power." *The Air Force Song* (*Off We Go Into the Wild Blue Yonder*) is established and then Hal Gibney introduces the program with these remarks:

The President of the United States has decreed that September 18, 1948, shall be set aside to celebrate the first birthday of the new autonomous United States Air Force and the 41st anniversary of air power as a part of the American military establishment. Joining the nation-wide birthday festivities, the National Broadcasting Company, in cooperation with the Air Force Association, presents "Slim and the Colonel," a special dramatization with narration by James Stewart.

As the music ends, Stewart begins:

STEWART: Ladies and gentlemen, this is James Stewart. I'm going to act as narrator on this Air Force program. But if you think I'm going to do any bragging about what a great Air Force we have, I want to correct that impression right here and now; because between you and me, there isn't too much to brag about. It was just three years ago, three years and two weeks ago to be exact, that Japan surrendered. Germany had already quit, so that was the end of the war. At that time, we had the most powerful Air Force in the world; an Air Force that could fight and win on two fronts at the same time. We were genuinely proud of that Air Force, you and I…all of us. But what is that American Air Force like today? What is it going to be like tomorrow? What can we expect of it in case of an emergency? Well, let's try to find out by going back to the year 1945…to an Air Force base in Okinawa, near midnight of a night late in August.

As the play *Slim and the Colonel* begins, planes are about to take-off to test the enemy forces. But, before they can get into the air, the air raid sirens begin to wail. However, no attack is imminent. Instead, the sirens mark the end of the war. Although pilots and crews will be needed for the peace time Air Force, these men want out…they've put in their time.

STEWART: Does that attitude sound familiar? Well, it should and I'll tell you why. When Japan surrendered, the Air Force had nearly two-and-a-quarter-million men. Today, it has barely over 200,000. Now, think that over…our present Air Force strength is roughly only 10% of what we needed to win the last war. The reason? Well, I think it's largely a matter of the individual men themselves. The pilots, the gunners, bombardiers, the navigators, radiomen — they had a belly full…they wanted out. And they were mustered out at a rate of five to 11,000 a day. And, of course, the men who remained behind, they knew this wasn't so good. In case of an emergency, it could easily become a national catastrophe. So, they tried to build up the Air Force, but the fight was a losing battle.

We hear men being discharged. Slim is the last. The Colonel, Jocko, tries to talk Slim into remaining in the Air Force, but Slim will have no part of it.

STEWART: Yes. The men in the Air Force were streaming out of uniform, all right. But the men at the top realized something that perhaps has come to be a kind of corny phrase — that we had won the war, but that we were losing the peace. And that's why President Truman sent a special message to Congress.

The skit continues with a part of Truman's speech to Congress. He asks that the U.S. Air Force be an autonomous unit, independent of the Army and Navy.

STEWART: You all know what happened. Congress realized that the threat to this country was too big for them to worry about party lines, even with an election coming up. And so, on July 26, last year, Congress gave the Air Force autonomy as a military force separate from all other branches of the service. Well, now, that was fine as far as it went. The trouble was that outside the armed services, no one paid much attention to what was really going on. We'd won a war, we were at peace and you know how it was. The United States just wanted a long drift back into the soft, pleasant occupations of peacetime, just as if there's never been a war at all. Just as if there might never be another.

The Colonel runs into Slim, who is now operating an airplane ride for kids at a carnival. He tells Slim that times are bad and that the Air Force really needs men. He asks him to consider re-enlisting and Slim begins to weaken.

STEWART: How do you like those facts? I told you there wasn't much to brag about and there isn't. During the war we had around 250 combat groups, now we can't muster 55. What do you think would happen to those 55 undermanned air groups in case of a sudden attack? What do you think would happen to us? Of course, you hear a lot of people say, "Oh, we got plenty of planes…look at all the ones that were left over from the last war." Well, I don't have to tell you what's happening to most of them and what's happening to more and more of them every day.

Slim and another man are driving near Kingman, Arizona, when they see hundreds of World War II planes sitting in the desert. The planes are being broken apart and hauled away to be melted down to make new planes. They stop to watch. A lieutenant tells him that men are badly needed and about the new B-36. Suddenly, Slim spots his old plane, Big Belly Bertha, and sees her destroyed. This was the last straw; Slim Baker goes to see the Colonel and re-enlists.

STEWART: That's right…why not? Oh, I know exactly how he felt. That airplane meant something to him; it was almost like it had a soul. When he was flying it, he felt safe; he felt like he had something solid under him, something to fight for him, to protect him. But he kind of took that airplane for granted, the way the country takes the Air Force for granted, I guess. He didn't realize just how much that airplane meant to him until he saw them smashing it up for junk. That made it a personal matter and it hurt him way down deep inside. And, you know, it might be a good idea if the rest of us just kind of made the United States Air Force a personal matter, too. The Air Force is making new planes out of old ones and it'll build a new Air Force too, but it needs men…and they've got to have time.

The show ends with Gibney's credits and more of *The Air Force Song*.

U.S. Treasury Bond Independence Drive Show

A public service program, this show was used to kick off the annual campaign to purchase United States Treasury Department Savings Bonds. Although not in general circulation, the program is a part of the NBC Collection at the Library of Congress.

Monday, May 15, 1950 (10:30-11 p.m.)
NETWORK: All Networks
PRODUCER: William Wilkes
ANNOUNCER: Ken Carpenter

WRITER: Charles Isaacs
MUSIC: Robert Armbruster and His Orchestra

Some stations, Like WOR in New York City, recorded the program and broadcast it later. In this case on May 18th.

The guests on the show were President Harry S Truman, Secretary of the Treasury John Snyder, Jimmy Stewart, Jack Benny, Eddie Cantor, Eddie "Rochester" Anderson, Doris Day, Jack Kirkwood, Jane Wyman, Bob Hope and Bing Crosby. Stewart narrates the program, helping to tie together sketches and pitches for bond sales. After a short introduction, Stewart begins the show.

STEWART: Thank you, Ken Carpenter. Ladies and gentlemen, 174 years ago on July 8, the people of Philadelphia were summoned to Independence Hall by the incessant and joyous ringing of what we now call the Liberty Bell. There they heard Colonel John Nixon read these imperishable words (from the Declaration of Independence):

> *We, therefore, the representatives of the United States of America, in General Congress, assembled, appealing to the supreme judge of the world for the rectitude of the good people of these colonies, solemnly publish and declare, that these United Colonies are, and right ought to be free and independent states.*

And from that day on the very word independence has become synonymous with America. Today, this continued independence, both for you and for your country, can be furthered by your support of the Independence Drive for Savings Bonds. That spirit that carried our forefathers along the sometimes bloody trail to final liberty and independence still lives. And today, when freedom is on trial, we have only to turn for encouragement to the dramatic story of the stalwart pioneer, who with his wife, came to the barren wilderness of America only a few short years after Columbus had discovered the continent. In the tangled underbrush of the dark, unexplored forests, he made his bid for independence.

The first sketch stars:
Bob Hope as Daniel Boone Hope
Doris Day as his wife
Jack Kirkwood as the Indian Chief

The skit involves the settling of Chicago. Hope and Day sing a song to the tune of "If I Knew You Were Coming I'd a Baked a Cake," but with special lyrics about buying bonds.

STEWART: Thank you, Bob Hope, Doris Day and Jack Kirkwood. To misquote an old phrase, where there's laughter, there's Hope. And, where there's Hope, Bing Crosby can only be putting distance away. Now, a man who's been dealing in harmonious notes for years is jotting down a couple himself. It's a lyric with a pretty good moral, so listen closely.

Crosby makes a pitch for savings bonds and sings "Dear Hearts and Gentle People."

STEWART: Thank you, Bing Crosby. You know, we've spoken much of independence tonight. Well, have you ever stopped to think that women are more independent than men? It's true. Three men can show up at a party wearing the same suit and they don't mind a bit. But, let three women show up wearing the same dress and a cold war starts. Yeah, a woman wants to be individual, and what a woman wants, she usually gets, too; especially when she's as lovely as Jane Wyman.

Wyman speaks on behalf of bonds.

STEWART: Thank you, Jane Wyman. You know, a few days ago we received a call from the United States Treasury. They had a real tough nut to crack and they asked us if we could find a good bond salesman. Well, without a moment's hesitation, we recommended a man who we think is one of the foremost salesmen of United States Savings Bonds in the country. In San Francisco, during a 24-hour period, he sold 43 million dollars' worth of savings bonds. With a record such as this, we're certain that Eddie Cantor was the proper choice.

In a short sketch, Cantor comes to Jack Benny's house to try to sell him bonds. Rochester doesn't think he'll have much luck. Benny buys some bonds, but Cantor is charged for his drink.

STEWART: Thank you, Jack Benny, Eddie Cantor and Rochester. Part of our American heritage is political independence. But independence has other meanings, too. It can mean financial security, the chance to be free of worry and want. In America, we've learned that this freedom from want, freedom from worry…in another word, independence, is within reach. It takes effort, but independence has always taken effort. What we obtain too cheap, we esteem too lightly. These were the words of Thomas Paine back in the day when independence was being purchased in blood rather than bonds. Today, United States Savings Bonds are your key to an independent future. And now, just before we take you to Philadelphia for Secretary Snyder, who will introduce President Truman, we'd like you to hear the sound of liberty. In 1835 the crack appeared which muffled the voice of the Liberty Bell and it has not been heard in over 100 years. But this year, 52 full-scale replicas have been cast in the same process used to make the original and they'll be carried throughout the country so that everyone may see and hear them. They're exact duplicates of the first bell, even to the inscription from the Bible around the crown: "Proclaim liberty through all the land and to all the inhabitants thereof." For the first time since 1835, here is the true voice of the Liberty Bell.

One of the replica Liberty Bells is rung three times.

STEWART: Ladies and Gentlemen, the Honorable John W. Snyder, Secretary of the Treasury.

Snyder delivers a short speech on behalf of savings bonds. He then introduces President Harry Truman who does likewise, ending the show.

The Veteran Wants to Know
The Veteran Wants to Know came into existence after World War II to help veterans adjust to civilian life and get their lives back into order. The 15-minute public service program was broadcast weekly on Sundays. Times of broadcast varied from one station to another. The show remained on the air from 1946 until 1950. Many shows had guests and the topics discussed were varied. Among those appearing were AFL President William Green; Commissioner of Internal Revenue George J. Schoeneman; A.S. Fleming, the U.S. Civil Service Commissioner; Maurice Tobin, Secretary of Labor; and Dr. Paul Hawley speaking on the topic, "Are veterans being used as guinea pigs at veterans' hospitals?"

Jimmy Stewart appeared on the program on July 6, 1947. The reason for his appearance was not given in any newspaper ads of the time.

Victory Theater
See *Lux Radio Theatre*, July 20, 1942, *The Philadelphia Story*.

Voice of Democracy
RCA D9-QM-10597 (1949-1950) (16-inch, 33 1/3 RPM)

Stewart had appeared on the 1947 *I Speak for Democracy* contest disc. By 1949, the name of that contest had been changed to *Voice of Democracy*. The other difference is that the contest was now in conjunction with National Radio and Television Week, with TV viewing now on the rise. All the other sponsors and endorsements remained the same. As with the earlier disc, there are five short speeches (4-5 minutes each) on this disc. The big difference is that this year two of those speeches were made by the winners of the 1947 and 1948 contests. Appearing with Stewart on side 1 of the disc are Judge Justin Miller (President of the Association of Broadcasters) speaking on "Freedom of Expression" and Dr. Earl J. McGrath (Commissioner of Education) speaking on "Education for Democracy." On side 2 are the speeches of Janet Geister, a 1947 contest winner, and a 1948 winner, Charles Kuralt. Of course, Kuralt later became a very popular newscaster for CBS and host of the Peabody Award-winning *On the Road*.

Stewart's original 1947 speech is used here again, with some slight editing. The first paragraph has been completely edited out, except for the first sentence. See *I Speak for Democracy* for the text of the speech.

Voice of the Army

The 15-minute show was transcribed from Hollywood and sponsored by the U.S. Army and U.S. Air Force in cooperation with the broadcasting station.

Also in the cast were:

Sam Edwards	*Sgt. Karinsky*
Jeff Chandler	*Pilot*
Don Oreck	*Jake*
Bill Martell	*Jack*

The other credits given are:
MUSIC: Eddie Dunstedter
WRITER: Staff Sgt. Martin Lemmon
DIRECTOR: Major Hugh K. Murray
ANNOUNCER: Rye Billsbury

Jimmy Stewart appeared on just one show in the series—#448 (two other numbers can also be found on the label—RR-16473 and D-36548), *The Flying Dutchman*. The show was "Prepared by the Recruiting Publicity Bureau for the U.S. Army and U.S. Air Force Recruiting Service under direction of the Adjutant General, U.S. Army." The show was broadcast in 1949. Stewart is mainly the narrator, but also acts in the first scene. After the show's opening, Rye Billsbury says:

BILLSBURY: ...and now, Jimmy Stewart.

STEWART: Hello, everybody. Well, this is one of those stories that has become legend. The story is true, whether the legend is or not, well, that's up to you to decide. Many people believe in it and, perhaps, without realizing it, you do, too.

(Dramatic music)

STEWART: This was told to me by a veteran of the South Pacific and these are his words. I first learned this story as I sat in the operations hut of a troop carrier outfit on the island of New Guinea. It was in June 1943. We were waiting for the weather to lift before continuing on our journey to the Australian mainland for supplies. It was raining as only it can rain in the tropical South Pacific. Sgt. Karinsky, the operations clerk, and I have been talking when suddenly he paused…listening…and then he said…

Play: Sgt. Karinsky begins telling Stewart the story of The Flying Dutchman.

STEWART: For a moment I thought Sgt. Karinsky was kidding me, but the expression on his face and the sound of the airplane that couldn't be seen, convinced me of his sincerity. And he told me that in November of the previous year, his outfit was based at Seven Mile Strip, just outside Port Moresby, New Guinea. Their C-47's were kept busy providing airlift to the infantry across the Owen Stanley Mountain range. It was a…a routine job for the pilots, but a tough, dangerous trip, believe me. This mountain range, running down the center of New Guinea, sometimes reaches a height of 14,000 feet. It…it's so rugged that it formed the main barrier to the Japanese advance on Australia. Well, our pilots crossed these mountains by using a natural cleft in the range known as Cocoda Trail. Yeah, it's a mighty small bridge in the vastness of the Owen Stanley Mountains, and a mighty hard one to find in a sudden tropical rainstorm.

Play: The pilot is told that he will be carrying replacement troops across the mountains.

STEWART: Honest, that…that's the way those people in the Air Force talk. And…and, confidentially you know, that's what makes it so great. That's what makes it big enough for a legend like this. Everybody works together and it really works. Why the…the airplane that you see overhead today isn't flying solely because of the guy at the controls. Sure, he has something to do with it, but…but so have a lot of other guys. Gus like the sergeant who crewed The Flying Dutchman. He loved that ship. He pampered it. He believed in it. He babied it. He…why, he wrote a poem about it…and it's…well, I'll tell you about that later.

Play: The pilot prepares to take-off in a heavy rainstorm.

STEWART: There's the old Cocoda Trail across the Owen Stanley Range and the stories told about it are many and they're strange.

> *But the one that teases memory and the one that we'll relate*
> *is about The Flying Dutchman and the day she met her fate.*
> *Was the 10th of November in the year of '42*
> *when she revved up for take-off in a sky that wasn't blue.*
> *For the heavens gray and sullen, thick with heavy thundercloud*
> *had loosened on Earth their waters, hid the sunlight like a shroud.*

Play: The plane take-off.

STEWART: This is it. This is it. This is it. Half hour out of Moresby, in the worst of the thunderstorm…

Play: The plane loses its port engine. The troops and crew bail out and the pilot tries to crash land the plane in the jungle.

STEWART: Earth bound now in tropic land, she lies to rot away, airborne never more again. Yet there are some who say ad loosen on Earth their reign, the good ship Flying Dutchman cruises through the skies again.

> *The natives swear they've heard the sound of her motor's mighty roar*
> *High above the old Cocoda Trail where she once flew proud before.*
> *That her pilot's hand still guides her through the rain-swept tropic sky*
> *From the airport in Valhalla, where the brave came to die.*
> *And true this legend may well be for I've heard the sound in air*
> *During sudden tropic rainstorm of a plane that wasn't there.*
> *And perhaps The Flying Dutchman and her pilot proudly sail*
> *Somewhere through God's heavens high above Cocoda's Trail.*

(Music)

STEWART: Well, that's the story and the legend. The story's true. Now, whether the legend is or not, that's for you to decide. The man that told me the story, he believed it...and I...I kind of believe it, too.

As the show ends, Rye Billbury comes back and says:

BILLSBURY: Thank you, Jimmy Stewart, for your excellent narration of a little-known legend of our Air Force.

STEWART: Well, it was a great pleasure for me to appear before your *Voice of the Army* audience.

We Hold These Truths

December 15, 1941, marked the 150th anniversary of the ratification of the Bill of Rights. President Franklin Delano Roosevelt himself commissioned this radio broadcast to celebrate the occasion. Norman Corwin was asked to write and produce the program by the U.S. Office of Facts and Figures. As fate would have it, the broadcast date came just eight days after the Japanese attack on Pearl Harbor. The program was broadcast by the combined radio networks of the U.S. (CBS, NBC Red, NBC Blue, and Mutual). According to the Crosley Rating Service, the audience for the show was estimated to be 63 million people, about half the total population of the U.S. at that time. This was the largest audience in history for a dramatic performance.

The first 45 minutes of the show originated in Hollywood and told the story of the Bill of Rights. Corporal Jimmy Stewart, on loan from the Army Air Corps, acted as "a citizen" in the program, filling in gaps between the skits which dramatized the need for, the writing of, and the ratification of the Bill of Rights. Along the way, all ten of the amendments included in the Bill of Rights are outlined.

Corwin himself handpicked Stewart as the show's narrator and a special rehearsal for Stewart alone was held on Sunday, December 14, the day before the broadcast.

The credits for the Hollywood portion of the show include:
WRITER, PRODUCER, DIRECTOR: Norman Corwin
MUSIC COMPOSED AND DIRECTED BY: Bernard Herrmann

Another radio producer/director, Sterling Tracy, appears in a famous photo of the cast for *We Hold These Truths*. His involvement was as an assistant to Corwin in staging the production.

The actors involved included (in alphabetical order):
Edward Arnold — orator, bricklayer

Lionel Barrymore — After Walter Houston's short introduction, Barrymore continues by naming the writer and actors involved in the project. He also informs the listeners that President Roosevelt will deliver a short speech from Washington after the program has concluded and that Dr. Leopold Stokowski and a symphony orchestra would also be heard.

*This photo was taken during the broadcast. From left to right are Walter Huston, Edward G. Robinson, Edward Arnold, Walter Brennan and Jimmy Stewart (*Movie-Radio Guide *Vol. 11, No. 13, January 3-9, 1942).*

- Walter Brennan — friend (of the blacksmith)
- Bob Burns — farmer
- Dane Clark — Sam (the bricklayer's helper)
- Walter Huston — introduces the program, smith (blacksmith)
- Marjorie Main — widow
- Edward G. Robinson — prisoner
- Corporal James Stewart — citizen (narrator)
- Rudy Vallee — singer (sings a few lines from an old folk ballad titled *Jefferson and Liberty*)
- Orson Welles — narrator (second largest part after Stewart)

The full script for the Hollywood segment of the show can be found in the books: (1) *Best Broadcasts of 1940-41*, selected and edited by Max Wylie (Radio Department N.W. Ayer & Son, Inc.) and published in 1942 by Whittlesey House, New York, (2) *More By Corwin: 16 Radio Dramas*

(1944, Henry Holt, New York), and (3) *The Weaver Luther Technique of Radio Writing* (1948, Prentice-Hall, New York). After the completion of the Hollywood portion of the show, President Franklin Delano Roosevelt addressed the nation from the White House. He spoke about the importance of the Bill of Rights and spoke out against those in the world, Hitler in particular, who were trying to eradicate those basic principles.

Norman Corwin and Jimmy Stewart going over the script for the program.

The final element of the show was the playing the *The Star Spangled Banner* by the New York Philharmonic Orchestra, under the direction of Dr. Leopold Stokowski. This segment originated from New York City.

Following the printed script in the 1944 book, *More By Corwin*, Corwin adds two short sections. In the first, he tells of the lessons he learned from the experience of writing and producing the show. The second is a list of "Additional Notes." In the second of these 19 notes, Corwin describes what he considered the most serious mistake made during the broadcast. According to him, "…a mistake in the relaying of a signal caused Corporal Stewart to leave the isolation booth from which he had been speaking, and it was impossible for him to get back in time to deliver the line, 'No. There will be no speeches.'" Actually, Corwin and the others in the studio may have been the only ones to know that any mistake had been made at all. A close listen to the program, while following along in the script, will show that even Corwin himself remembers the mistake incorrectly. The omission occurs after the Constitution has been signed. Stewart's narration is leading to the fact that the people are going to be

*Stewart delivers his lines from an isolation booth (*Movie-Radio Guide *Vol. 11, No. 13, January 3-9, 1942).*

suspicious of the document. He asks that if when the delegates return to their homes, there will be bands playing. We hear the sound of a band playing and then Stewart says, "No. There will be no band." His next line is to be, "Will there be speeches." It is this line which he fails to deliver. Instead, the listener hears a speech being made. After this speech, Stewart does say the line, "No. There will be no speeches," and then continues on with the script. Most listeners probably never knew anything was wrong.

Norman Corwin was presented with a Peabody Award for his work on the program. In presenting the award, the Peabody committee said, "We wish to confer an award in drama upon Norman Corwin, whose program on The Bill of Rights demonstrated what patriotism and a fine dramatic sense could do seven days after Pearl Harbor. Here is a program which ought to be rebroadcast until it is familiar." Corwin did, in fact, update the program for the 200th anniversary of The Bill of Rights in 1991. Once again, the program was broadcast over every national public and commercial national radio network. Some of the actors in this new version included Richard Dysart, James Earl Jones, Lloyd Bridges, Jill Eikenberry, Esther Rolle, Edward Asner, Tom Bosley, Fess Parker, Ray Bradbury, Dan O'Herlihy, Stuart Whitman and many more.

The cast and crew of the program included (from the left) Orson Welles, Rudy Vallee, Dane Clark, Bernard Herrmann, Edward G. Robinson, Bob Burns, Lionel Barrymore (seated), Jimmy Stewart, Norman Corwin, Marjorie Main (seated), Walter Brennan, Edward Arnold and Walter Huston (seated).

The program was also selected for the 2004 National Recording Registry by the National Recording Preservation Board of the Library of Congress.

It was also made available to high schools, colleges and civic groups well up into the 1950s as evidenced by this entry in the *Catalog of Radio Recordings A Transcription Service for Schools*, issued by the Federal Radio Education Committee in 1950. Notice that you could purchase the program for just $2.50…try to find the discs for that price today!

Also, a special set of six two-sided, 12-inch 78 RPM discs was prepared for each of the performers on the program. The sets were made by Studio

& Artists Recorders of Hollywood. Each set came in an individual six-sleeve album stamped with the name of the recorders and, on the spine, the title *Bill of Rights*. Each of the six records was marked as having been recorded on December 17, 1941, two days after the broadcast. The matrix numbers on the discs ran from SA-108-1 through SA-119-12. The records were pressed so that side one was backed with side 12, side two with side 11, and so on. In this way, with two turntables, the show could be played in its entirety with no noticeable breaks. Needless to say, these sets are very difficult to locate today.

We Hold These Truths can be found commercially on several sets. It's on the 20-cassette set *America at War* (Radio Spirits 4561), issued in 2001.

It is also on the 10-CD set, *Norman Corwin Centennial* (Radio Spirits 44622), issued in 2010.

It is also available as a single CD titled *We Hold These Truths 1941* (Otherworld Media SKU CORW027).

Finally, it is part of the 2-cassette set, *World's Greatest Old-Time Radio Shows* (MediaBay 80964), released in 2004. Two cassettes are included in this final set — *Sherlock Holmes* and *We Hold These Truths*. The *We Hold These Truths* tape also has two other numbers on it–#143 and 28414. The set also included two collector cards — one on Tom Conway, who portrayed Sherlock Holmes on the radio, and the other on Norman Corwin. Stewart is mentioned and pictured on the card.

The program was re-broadcast in the New York City area, on Monday, July 5, 1948.

With the elimination of President Roosevelt's closing speech, the show now ran just 45 minutes.

We the People

We the People began as a sketch on *The Rudy Vallee Hour* during the 1936 season. It quickly became so popular that it was spun off as its own series beginning on October 4, 1936. It remained on the air through January 25, 1951. The program is usually categorized as a "human interest" show. It featured normal, everyday people who had suddenly had "their 15 minutes of fame" and were on the show to tell their own stories. Hollywood stars, sports figures and other famous people also appeared on the program, each with a story to tell about themselves. Stewart appeared just once on the program and that show is, unfortunately, not available for listening.

Tuesday, June 24, 1947 (9-9:30 p.m.)
NETWORK: CBS
SPONSOR: Gulf Oil

HOST: Milo Boulton
COMMERCIAL SPOKESMAN: Dan Seymour
HOLLYWOOD ANNOUNCER: Tom Hanlon
MUSIC: Oscar Bradley and his Orchestra
CREATOR: Phillips H. Lord

Many newspapers ran a special display ad for this show, but that ad did not mention Stewart as being a guest.

WEAM-AM, 1390, Arlington, VA

One very uninformative entry was found for this Washington, DC area station for Tuesday, September 2, 1947.

The program is listed as being broadcast from 10:15-10:30 am. Margaret Lockwood did interviews for the station, but her guests, when listed, were given in "Today's Radio Highlights" section and not listed with or above her name in the listings section. So, Stewart most likely was not interviewed by her that day. Just what his appearance may have consisted of is not known.

Welcome Travelers

What if you just walked up to people getting off a plane, bus or train in Chicago and interviewed them? What stories could they tell? Would anyone listen to them? These were the questions asked by Les Lear and Tommy Bartlett, the creators of radio's *Welcome Travelers*. Apparently, the answer was a resounding yes as the show was on the air from 1947 until 1954. All the interviewees were found as they exited buses and trains and even members of the audience, about 1,000 people for every show, were travelers on those same buses and trains. The show was broadcast five days a week from the College Inn Porterhouse of the Hotel Sherman, Chicago. Proctor & Gamble sponsored the program, pitching their products, including Cheer, Joy, Lava Soap, Prell, and Spic-N-Span. Director Bob Cunningham introduced each guest to Bartlett and also told him something about the guest so that he had an idea of what to ask. Cunningham sometimes asked a question or two himself.

Tuesday, February 5, 1952 (10-10:30 a.m.)
NETWORK: NBC
SPONSOR: Proctor & Gamble
HOST: Tommy Bartlett
ANNOUNCER: Ken Nordine
DIRECTOR: Bob Cunningham
This show in not available for listening.

WJJD-AM, Chicago

The radio section from the *Chicago Tribune* of July 22, 1948 shows that Jimmy Stewart would be appearing on WJJD-AM (1160) at 10:30 am. The name of the 15-minute program is not given and it is not available for listening. Since Stewart's film *Call Northside 777*, which takes place in Chicago, had just been released a few months earlier, it is possible that this was a topic of discussion.

WMAL-AM, 630, Washington, DC

Except for a short listing in *The Washington Post*, very little is known about these two interviews. The name(s) of the person(s) doing the interviews is not given and neither is the name(s) of the program(s). Neither interview is available for listening.

(1) Friday, August 24, 1951 (10:30 a.m.)
The only information about this first appearance is that Stewart would be talking about his role as the clown, Buttons, in the film *The Greatest Show on Earth*.
(2) Saturday, February 9, 1952 (11 a.m.)
There is even less information available about this appearance.

SPECIAL MENTION

Stewart did not make an appearance in any of the following productions. However, they are being listed because of their connections to Stewart.

Jack Benny Program
On the Jack Benny Program of March 23, 1952, Jack and Mary were attending the Academy Award Ceremonies. A radio announcer (played by Frank Nelson) was interviewing celebrities as they entered the Pantages Theatre. One of those interviewed was Mr. Stewart.
However, it wasn't Stewart who appeared on the show but rather someone (probably Dennis Day) imitating his voice.

Explotation Record:
Marlene Dietrich & James Stewart In "Destry Rides Again"
RCA PBS 042195
Although Stewart is mentioned on the record label and several times on the record itself, his voice is never heard. Instead, this record is simply to introduce to an audience the songs sung by Miss Dietrich in the film.

Favorite Story
    Syndicated
    HOST AND SOMETIME STAR: Ronald Colman
    MUSIC: Claude Sweeten
    PRODUCERS/WRITERS: Jerome Lawrence, Robert E. Lee
    SOUND EFFECTS: Jack Hayes

The show was originally broadcast on radio station KFI, Los Angeles, but then was syndicated nationally by Frederic W. Ziv Syndication. The premise was a simple one: Celebrities from many different professions (film, radio, sports, music, art, literature, etc.) were asked to name their favorite story. These stories were then dramatized in a half-hour radio format. For example, Robert Young chose *The Lady and the Lamp*, Clyde Beatty (animal trainer/circus owner) chose *Ben-Hur*. Bandleader Kay Kyser picked *The Time Machine* as his favorite story, while songwriter Irving Berlin selected *Alice in Wonderland*. *Les Miserables* was preferred by artist Rockwell Kent and Hall of Fame baseball player Tris Speaker named *Casey at the Bat* as his favorite story.

Now understand that none of these people actually appeared on the program. Colman simply stated that each had chosen the story to be presented that evening. So, when we see Jimmy Stewart listed for this series, it was simply because he had been asked to pick a favorite story. Stewart decided on *The Little Minister*, which had been a 1934 film starring Katharine Hepburn. His story was presented April 5, 1949 and was the third to last program in the series' run on the radio.

Hedda Hopper's Diary

Newspaper listings for *Hedda Hopper's Diary* are sporadic, but occur mostly from November 1945 through March 1946. The shows were 15 minutes in length. The ad for the Thursday, November 29, 1945 show mentions Stewart.

In the program, Hopper simply outlined Stewart's rise to fame for her audience and Stewart didn't actually make an appearance on the program.

Another Stewart appearance on Hopper's show was faked. In her syndicated column for December 20, 1951, Hedda told her listeners about it:

> During the war I wanted an actor to impersonate Jimmy Stewart on my radio show, but since Stewart was then a colonel commanding a bombing squadron in Europe, I had to get his consent. No one knew how to reach him. Case came up with the answer. He talked every other

day to Ed Murrow whon was stationed in London. Ed got to Jimmy, who said "tell Hedda she can do anything with my life, except make it mushy." I phoned Stewart's parents in Indiana, Pa., and asked them to listen to the show. They thought it was Jimmy on the air.

The date of this broadcast is not known.

Sig Sakowicz

Sakowicz was a very popular Chicago radio personality in the '50s and '60s. His programs were heard on a number of stations in that area. *Sig's Show*, on WGN, was one of his most popular programs. His claim to fame was interviewing famous personalities who were visiting the Chicago area. In early 2008, an autograph book went up for sale on eBay. According to the description, the book belonged to a woman who had worked for Sakowicz and contained the autographs of those whom he had interviewed on his show. One of the signatures included was that of Jimmy Stewart. A search of the Chicago newspapers has not turned up any reference to Stewart having appeared on his show. In fact, most listings do not give the name of his guests. Most likely, Stewart did appear on his program, but an exact date cannot be confirmed.

One Man's Destiny

One Man's Destiny was presented at a SPEDVAC (Society to Preserve and Encourage Radio Drama, Variety and Comedy) convention held November 10-11, 1989. It really wasn't a real radio broadcast, just a simulation. But, the story is about Jimmy Stewart and well worth a listen.

The 14:32 play simulated an old-time radio soap opera, complete with organ music to set the mood. The story begins with Earl Johnson, head of United Press, calling Harold Swisher, a United Press correspondent in Hollywood, and assigning him a story on Jimmy Stewart.

Swisher goes to Stewart's house on the day after he has won an Oscar for his role in *The Philadelphia Story*. He finds Stewart sitting and playing the accordion with his house guest, Henry Fonda. Swisher's interview deals with four distinct areas of Stewart's life.

They talk about Jimmy's time in Falmouth, MA, and acting in Joshua Logan's stock company. Margaret Sullavan and Fonda also appear in this segment, which ends with Jimmy getting an acting part in *Goodbye Again*.

Jimmy's first roles in Hollywood and getting his first leading man role in *Next Time We Love* opposite Margaret Sullavan.

The war years are discussed, with Jimmy as commander of a squad of Liberator bombers and his bombing missions over Germany. Stewart is made Wing Commander, in charge of 48 bombers.

Stewart's return to Indiana, PA after the war. His downplaying of the role of hero and, instead, going on a bass fishing trip with his childhood friend, Clyde Woodward.

CLOSE, BUT NO CIGAR

In the course of research for this book, several shows claiming to feature Jimmy Stewart came to light. However, no factual material could be found to substantiate the claim or, upon listening, Stewart's voice was nowhere to be heard.

Mobilization for Human Needs (Community Chest)
Gerard Molyneaux, in his book *James Stewart A Bio-Bibliography*, lists Stewart as being on this program on September 3rd, 1947. No record of such an appearance could be located. It is possible that it was confused with Stewart's appearance on the September 26, 1947, Community Chest program.

NBC University Theater of the Air — The Red Badge of Courage
This program, first broadcast on May 8, 1949, is found on nearly all .mp3 compilations of Stewart's radio work. However, Stewart is nowhere to be heard on any available recordings. The star of the show was John Agar and the other male actors were Parley Baer, Tom Charlesworth, John Dehner, Ted Von Eltz, Frank Gerstle, William Lally, Jack Lloyd and Lee Millar. The intermission commentator was Mark Van Doren. Nowhere in the credits is Stewart's name to be found. Likewise, Stewart cannot be heard on any commercials or promo spots in this program.

Exactly how this program has come to be associated with Stewart is not understood, but he definitely has nothing to do with the show.

RADIO RATINGS

Radio ratings were practically nonexistent until the 1930-31 season, when the Cooperative Analysis of Broadcasting (C.A.B.) began to sample Americans to find to which shows they were listening. The C.A.B.'s continued to monitor audience performances through the 1934-35 season.

For the 1935-36 season, C.E. Hooper, Inc. became the most popular radio rating service. Their supremacy continued for 14 seasons, lasting through the 1948-49 season. If you're listening to an old-time radio show, especially comedy or variety shows, you might hear someone ask, "How's your Hooper?" If you didn't know it before, now you know they're asking about the show's rating.

Between the 1948-49 and 1949-50 seasons, Hooper was bought out by the A.C. Nielsen Company. They rated shows until the end of the 1955-56 season, when the number of network radio shows dropped to such a low point that it was no longer profitable to continue to rate them. Nielsen, of course, continues to rate TV shows to the present time.

Eleven programs on which Stewart appeared were rated in the top-20 during the season(s) is which he was on that show. Ironically, Stewart's own critically acclaimed program, *The Six Shooter*, did not make the top-20 during its one season on the air.

Here is a short history of the rating success of shows on which Stewart appeared (chronologically, based on his first appearance on each program):

Fleischmann Hour
Stewart's appearance came on May 3, 1934, near the end of the 1933-34 season. The program was rated the #3 show for that season. This season of the *Fleischmann Hour* was also rated the #8 all-time show on NBC.

Hollywood Hotel
This program was rated #8 for the 1936-37 season. Stewart was a guest twice that season — November 13, 1936 and December 18, 1936.

Screen Guild Theater
This program was rated in C.E. Hooper's top-20 in four different seasons during which Stewart made an appearance.
  1938-39 — #18
  1940-41 — #18
  1945-46 — #7
  1946-47 — #6 (tied with *Lux Radio Theatre*, on which Jimmy also
     participated this season)
Two of these seasons also made the all-time top shows on CBS.
  1945-46 — #19
  1946-47 — #17 (again tied with the 1946-47 season of *Lux Radio
     Theatre*)

Chase and Sanborn Hour
(Charlie McCarthy Show, Edgar Bergen Show)

Like *Screen Guild Theater*, four different seasons of this show on which Jimmy appeared made the top-20.

1940-41 — #2
1941-42 — #1
1953-54 — #12
1955-56 — #2

The first two seasons were rated by Hooper, while the final two were by Neilsen. Two of these seasons also placed on the all-time most popular shows on the NBC (Red) Network.

1941-42 — #13
1940-41 — #21

Lux Radio Theatre

Stewart's first appearance on *Lux* during the 1936-37 season went unrated. After that, the show was rated in the top-20 a total of ten times during seasons in which Jimmy made an appearance.

1940-41 — #5
1941-42 — #7
1945-46 — #3
1946-47 — #6 (tied with *Screen Guild Theater*)
1947-48 — #7
1948-49 — #1

Up to this point, the Hooper ratings were in effect. From this point on, Nielsen ratings were used.

1949-50 — #2
1950-51 — #1
1951-52 — #3
1953-54 — #5

Seven of these seasons also made the all-time top shows for CBS.

1941-42 — #3
1948-49 — #5
1945-46 — #6
1940-41 — #8
1949-50 — #12
1946-47 — #17
1947-48 — #23

Bing Crosby Show

Stewart made appearances during four top-20 rated seasons of Bing Crosby's shows.

1947-48 — #20
1948-49 — #19
1949-50 — #19
1952-53 — #20 (tied with *Theatre Guild of America*)

The 1948-49 season is also rated #13 all-time for the ABC (Blue) Network.

Jack Benny Show

Stewart appeared on Benny's show during two seasons in which the show was rated in the top-20.

1948-49 — #3 (this season was also rated #9 on the all-time list of top shows for CBS)
1951-52 — #2

Suspense

Suspense was rated in the top-20 during the following seasons:
1948-49 — #15
1949-50 — #18

Stewart was a guest during both of these seasons.

Theatre Guild on the Air

Theatre Guild on the Air was #20 during the 1952-53 season, the same seasons Stewart appeared in *O'Halloran's Luck*.

Hallmark Hall of Fame

The series was rated #15 during the 1954-55 season, the only season during which Stewart made a guest appearance.

Bob Hope Show

Jimmy Stewart appeared as a guest during the 1954-55 season when the show was rated #20.

CHAPTER 3

Recordings Made for Radio

Stewart was also involved with the recording of many radio spot announcements, open-ended interviews, commercials and other short programs. These include public service announcements, drop-ins, commercials for films and film interviews. The majority of these recordings are only 10 seconds to 5 minutes in length, but a few extend to 15 and 30 minutes. They have been released in a variety of formats — 16-inch 33 1/3 RPM, 12-inch 78 RPM, 12-inch 33 1/3 RPM and 7-inch 45 RPM — some on colored vinyl. These discs have become highly collectable. Because of the rarity of these shows and the lack of available information about them, there may still be discs which have not been documented.

PUBLIC SERVICE ANNOUNCEMENTS

Stewart was involved in several public service campaigns over the years. In each case, he and other Hollywood stars, music and sports figures, recorded short announcements which were then pressed as discs and sent to radio stations. Stations could then air the announcements as they chose. Some of the announcements had a very specific time period during which they could be played, while others were open-ended.

A Moment for Thanksgiving
See *United Presbyterian Church: A Moment for Thanksgiving*.

American Cancer Society
(1) 101845A/B (1957)

The A-side of this 16-inch transcription disc features ten one-minute announcements. Each one is done by a different star, including Clark Gable, Henry Fonda, James Stewart, Claudette Colbert, Lauritz Melchoir, Bing Crosby, H.V. Kaltenborn, Jean Simmons, Ernie Kovacs and Jimmy Durante. Stewart's spot, which runs 56 seconds, is as follows:

ANNOUNCER: Each of us is affected in some way by the disease cancer. It's something we think about and talk about. Jimmy Stewart has a thought he would like to express.

STEWART: It seems criminal to me that in this day and age we're still losing so many people to a disease like cancer; especially those thousands who are dying needlessly. Each of us can do something about it. This American Cancer Society slogan tells it best, "Fight cancer with a checkup and a check." Having been active in the society for years, I know that regular medical checkups have often led to cures. Now, as to your check, well it's needed in vital cancer research. So when you're approached by a volunteer from your unit of the American Cancer Society, be generous.

ANNOUNCER: Thank you, Jimmy Stewart. Give generously when an American Cancer Society volunteer calls. Or, if you wish, mail your contribution now care to Cancer, care of your local post office.

The B-side has "This is…" announcements for that year's fund drive. There were 11 bands (approximately 20 seconds each) on the 33 1/3 RPM recording. Each band features three or four stars. Stewart, Yvonne De Carlo, Spencer Tracy and Esther Williams can be heard on band 6. The track lasts about 18 seconds and goes as follows:

This is Yvonne De Carlo. This is Spencer Tracy. This is Esther Williams. And, this is Jimmy Stewart. We all want you to fight cancer with a checkup and a check. Regular medical checkups are good cancer protection and your check to your unit of the American Cancer Society will help conquer cancer.

Also appearing in groups of three or four on this side were: Kirk Douglas, Janet Leigh, Fred MacMurray, Clark Gable; Joan Fontaine, Bing Crosby, Greer Garson, Henry Fonda; Danny Kaye, Jane Wyman, Burt Lancaster, Jean Simmons; Art Linkletter, Ralph Edwards, Bill Cullen,

Hal March; Gregory Peck, Barbara Stanwyck, Jose Ferrer, Claudette Colbert; Cecil B. DeMille, Bob Considine, H.V. Kaltenborn; Marian Anderson, Robert Merrill, Mimi Benzel, Lauritz Melchoir; Bing Crosby, Anne Baxter, Ray Bolger, Dinah Shore; Jimmy Durante, Steve Allen, Danny Kaye, Ernie Kovacs; and Jack Dempsey, Joe DiMaggio, Kirk Douglas, Hugh O'Brian. Stations could play the announcements as they wished for the month of April.

(2) 113042 — 1959 Crusade

Stewart appears only on the B-side of the 1959 disc. Like the 1957 disc, this side features "This is..." announcements. There are 12 bands, each about 20-seconds in length and feature the voices of three or four show business or sports stars. Stwart can be heard on the next to last band, along with Clark Gable, Jane Wyman and Betsy Palmer. The track goes as follows:

> *This is Clark Gable. This is Jane Wyman. This is Jimmy Stewart. And, this is Betsy Palmer. We want to pass along some lifesaving advice from the American Cancer Society. Guard your family with a checkup and a check. See your doctor for the checkup and send the check to your unit of the American Cancer Society.*

Gable, Wyman and Stewart just introduce themselves; it is Betsy Palmer who reads the announcement.

Others appearing on this side of the record are: Janet Leigh, Tony Curtis, Joanne Woodward (2 different spots), Paul Newman (2 different spots), Hoagy Carmichael (2 different spots), Oscar Hammerstein (2 different spots), Richard Rodgers (2 different spots), Jack Dempsey, Jersey Joe Wolcott, Floyd Patterson, Yul Brynner, Kim Novak, Tallulah Bankhead, Danny Kaye, Judy Holliday, Red Buttons (2 different spots), Barbara Stanwyck, Kirk Douglas, Joan Fontaine, Eddie Albert, Spencer Tracy, Greer Garson, Fredric March, Claudette Colbert, Jackie Gleason, Jimmy Durante, Sid Caesar, Bing Crosby, Esther Williams, Louis Jordan, Patrice Munsel, Joe DiMaggio, Ted Williams and Richie Ashburn.

(3) 1960 Cancer Crusade

Disc is unavailable for listening, but like so many other public service discs, his message may be the same as the one used in 1957 or 1959.

American Heart Association — Heart Fund

Stewart appeared on two different Heart Fund Drive discs during the fifties — 1953 and 1957. On both discs, he delivered a one-minute plea for donations.

(1) Gotham Recording Corporation GRC-2324

The 1953 Heart Fund drive took place during the month of February. A special two-sided, 16-inch transcription disc was prepared and sent to radio stations around the country. Side-A featured one-minute "Heart Fund" appeals from 10 famous persons, including Lowell Thomas (newsman, author), General G.E. Armstrong, Earle Stanley Gardner (author), Fanny Hurst (author), Bruce Barton (author), Bette Davis, Humphrey Bogart, James Stewart, Joseph Cotten and Bing Crosby. The eleventh track is titled *Turning the Tables on Heart Disease*. Side-B is a 15-minute musical program featuring music and interviews with Hoagy Carmichael and Victor Young. The songs included:

"Doctor, Lawyer, Indian Chief"
"Small Fry"
"When I Fall In Love"
"My Foolish Heart"

In Stewart's spot he says:

> *This is Jimmy Stewart. The other day I learned something from my Heart Association that just stopped me in my tracks, and it's this. More than 10 million Americans suffer from diseases of the heart and circulation. Ten Million! You know how many of them are kids in their teens and even younger; five hundred thousand. But, there's a bright side to this story. These kids have a far better chance to live normal, useful lives than ever before. And this is due to the marvelous work being done by medical science. The Heart Fund, with our dollars, can speed up that work. We've got to find out what causes hardening of the arteries and high blood pressure and rheumatic fever. Research has already created new drugs and perfected miraculous new heart operations that have made us all sit up and take notice. Well, it's time now to take notice of a need for money. The Heart Fund is America's investment in its own heart. Now, send your share to your Heart Association or simply to Heart, care of your local post office.*

(2) Gotham Recording Corporation GRC-4289

In 1957, the American Heart Association's Heart Fund enlisted the aid of many Hollywood stars, sports figures, and news reporters to record public service announcements for the Heart Fund. The spots were placed on 16-inch transcription discs and sent out to radio stations. The spots were scheduled to air during the month of February. The announcements are broken into several different categories.

(1) Group One — General One Minute
　Ann Blyth, Ernest Borgnine, Judy Garland, Rex Harrison, Boris Karloff, Hal March, Risë Stevens, Jimmy Stewart
(2) Group Two — "Flashes" 6-11 seconds
　Steve Allen, Bing Crosby, Bette Davis, Clark Gable, Jennifer Jones, Sugar Ray Robinson
(3) Group Three — Heart "Breaks" 6-11 seconds
　Ray Bolger, Eddie Cantor, Nanette Fabray, Bob Hope, Ida Lupino, Donna Reed
(4) "Heart Beats" Group One — 30 seconds
　Mel Allen, Red Barber, John Cameron Swayze, Lowell Thomas
(5) "Heart Beats" Group Two — 15 seconds
　Bill Corum, John Daly, Gabriel Heatter, Edward R. Morrow
(6) General Group Three — 30 seconds
　Katharine Cornell, Bob Feller, Glenn Ford, Audrey Hepburn, Grace Kelly, Burt Lancaster, Dr. Paul Dudley White
(7) General Group Four — 15 seconds
　Pier Angeli, Gertrude Berg, Jeff Chandler, Dan Dailey, Arlene Francis, Mickey Mantle, John Payne

Stewart's spot is the same one used on the 1953 disc.

American Legion

The American Legion had been organized in 1919 by veterans returning to the U.S. after World War I. It was headquartered in Indianapolis, IN. By 1969, membership in the group had been opened to any member of the armed services who had served during wartime. Stewart was involved with at least two of their radio campaigns.

(1) American Legion 50th Anniversary 1919–1969 Spot Radio — AAVP # 23427 (1969)

To mark the group's 50th anniversary, a 12-inch record album was released to radio stations. The album featured messages, ranging in length from 10 to 60 seconds, from film stars, television personalities and sports figures; most appeared on both sides of the disc with announcements of different lengths. Stewart delivered spots of 10 seconds and 30 seconds. His photo was even used on the back of the album cover. Others appearing include (numbers in parentheses are the length[s] of the spots): Commander William C. Doyle (:60/:60) — Doyle was the Commander of the American Legion for 1968 and 1969, Al Hirt (:10/:30/:60), Tom Harmon (:20/:60), Lawrence Welk (:15/:30), Bing Crosby (:10/:20), Mel Allen (:20/:60), Shirley Temple Black (:20), Ed Sullivan (:10), Johnny Unitas (:60/:20) and Bart Starr (:20).

Both of the Stewart spots are fully produced with a music bed. In the 30-second spot he says:

> Hello, this is Jimmy Stewart. I'm proud of our American form of government and I think we all have a responsibility to understand how good government works. Now the American Legion has a program, Boys' and Girls' State, which trains young people as good citizens by letting them participate in the functions of government. I salute the American Legion on its 50th anniversary. Keep up the good work.

The 10-second spot is as follows:

> This is Jimmy Stewart and I'm wishing a happy 50th anniversary to the American Legion, which is training our young people in good citizenship in its Boys' and Girls' State program.

(2) Reach Out the Future is in Your Hands (AAVP #27185/AAVP #27186)

This 12-inch 33 1/3 RPM record album was issued to radio stations in 1970. It featured twenty different public service announcements for stations to use. Making announcements besides Stewart were: Alfred P. Chamie (National Commander of the American Legion)(two 60-second spots), John Wayne (two 30-second spots), Robert Stack (a 30-second and a 40-second spot), Johnny Unitas, Martin Milner (a 30-second and a 40-second spot), Lawrence Welk, James Drury (three 30-second spots), Johnny Grant, Mel Allen, Bing Crosby, Macdonald Carey, Peter Graves, and Leif Erickson.

The first few sentences of Stewart's remarks are the same as his 30-second spot from 1969. He says:

> Hello, this is Jimmy Stewart. Like any other American citizen, I'm very proud of our Democratic form of government and I think we all have a responsibility to understand how good government functions. Now the American Legion has a wonderful program which teaches young people the principles of good government. The name of the program is Boys' State for young men and Girls' State run by the American Legion Auxiliary and available to teenage girls. Now this is a program where the kids learn by doing. Two outstanding boys and girls from each state are then invited to Boys' and Girls' Nation in Washington, where they elect a president and a senate and during the week they get a good look at the mechanics of Federal Government. Boys and Girls State and Nation give youngsters a terrific insight into American government and help train them as good citizens.

The spot is fully produced with music and Stewart's voice.

American Red Cross (Public Service)

Stewart has been documented as appearing on three Red Cross campaign programs. His interest in the Red Cross dates back to his school days in Indiana, PA. In 1923, when he was a student at Indiana Normal School's laboratory school for children, he wrote an essay about the Red Cross. This quote from that essay appears in his biography on the Medal of Freedom website:

The American Red Cross and its work in our midst is something that should appeal to every earnest citizen. During the past year, the Indiana chapter has been doing a great deal toward setting aright the tangled affairs of both ex-soldiers and civilians, be their troubles mental, physical or economic.

(1) HDB-MM-4062 (1948)

One side of the disc has 12 short spot announcements which were to be used anytime during the month of March. For his spot, Stewart says:

> *This is Jimmy Stewart. I'm not an accountant, but I know that eighteen million is a pretty large number, especially when that number refers to veterans. The Red Cross points out that the nation now has eighteen million war veterans, who with their families, comprise 32%*

of our population. That means the Red Cross has a big job to do in providing services to veterans. For instance, there are the many services provided in Veterans Administration hospitals supplementing the fine work of the doctors and nurses. Also claims services, expert help in securing government benefits, home service, counseling assistance with personal problems and financial aid. The Red Cross must have ample funds to continue these services for veterans and their families. Your support is necessary. So give generously to the Red Cross 1948 fund campaign.

Others appearing on this side of the record are: Lauren Bacall, Edward G. Robinson, Humphrey Bogart, Dorothy Lamour, Amos 'N' Andy, Eddie Cantor, Herbert Marshall, Rod O'Connor, Howard Petrie, Art Linkletter and Bud Hiestand. The other side has three 4:30 shows, one each by Ella Raines, William Bendix and Robert Montgomery.

(2) February 28, 1949
NETWORK: ABC
DIRECTOR: Homer Fickett
MUSIC: Wayne King and his Orchestra
This program was not available for review.

(3) 1954 (F-21390X)
One side of this disc has spot announcements from 14 different people. Besides Stewart, there are spots by E. Roland Harriman (chairman of the American Red Cross), Arthur Connell (National Commander of the American Legion), Wayne Richards (National Commander, Veterans of Foreign Wars), Henry J. Mahady (AMVETS National Commander), Howard Watts (past Commander, Disabled American Veterans), Bing Crosby (2 spots), Robert Stack, Dan Dailey, Claudette Colbert, Pat O'Brien, Mona Freeman, and Lizabeth Scott. On the other side of the record is a 15-minute version of *The Jack Benny Show*.

Stewart's segment is about 50 seconds in length and he says:

Hello everybody, this is Jimmy Stewart, speaking of something very close to all of us — the Red Cross. You know what the Red Cross is of course, it's people helping people. That means that when disaster strikes, a fire, flood or epidemic, we can be there through the Red Cross. There with shelter for the homeless and food for the hungry, medical care for the injured, comfort for a sick child and help in rebuilding homes and livelihoods. We can be there, too, when our servicemen need a bit of help, a word of cheer and a reminder that they're not forgotten. And we're there when blood is needed to save lives, whether it's a mother on the brink of death or a surgical patient or a wounded soldier. So when that Red Cross worker calls, open your heart and your pocketbook and join me in joining our American Red Cross.

(4) 1955 (F-41191 — Program 3)
ANNOUNCER: Bill Goodwin
MUSIC: Les Brown & His Orchestra

The 15-minute show features a sketch edited from the regular April 22, 1953, edition of the Bob Hope Show (see that entry for more details). Hope's regular announcer and orchestra appear on the show. Margaret Whiting, another regular on his show, also makes an uncredited appearance. This show was made possible through the cooperation of the Advertising Council, the American Federation of Musicians, James C. Petrillo, president, the American Federation of Radio and Television Artists, and the Hollywood Coordinating Committee.

The show is basically one skit with a break in the middle for a Red Cross announcement and another spot at the end. The skit has Bob with nothing to do. He tries to tagalong with Margaret Whiting, but she doesn't allow him to do so. He tries the same thing with Bill, but Goodwin is also too busy to bother with him. Bob stops by a grocery store and runs into Jimmy Stewart. Jimmy's doing the shopping because Gloria and the kids are away and he is having an important business dinner that evening with a Mr. Higgins. Jimmy tells Bob that he is going to have his cook, Hilda, make spare ribs. Bob volunteers to come over and make his famous Lamb Ragout Espanol. Jimmy thinks that he has him talked out of it, but then Bob shows up at his door. Again, Jimmy tries to talk Bob out of making dinner by telling him that he doesn't have any lamb or, any ragout. This doesn't discourage Bob, who finally makes his way into the kitchen and begins cooking.

During the show, Hope makes reference to Stewart's recent appearance on his show. Jimmy comments that he received the check for his appearance two times — once from Hope and once from the bank when it bounced.

At the end of the show, Hope's theme song, *Thanks for the Memory*, is played.

This program has been issued as an mp3 download as *The Bob Hope Collection Vol. 70* (Radio Library).

(5) April 25, 1957 (8–8:30 p.m.)

The program appears on the FEN-Okinawa schedule in the 8 pm time slot on a show that was actually called *Salute to You*.

Because this show is not available for listening, it is impossible to determine exactly what it is, but it is possible that it is simply a repeat of the 1955 Hope-Stewart show with additional material, including a statement from President Eisenhower added.

(6) 72-2 (1972)

This is a 7-inch disc which plays at 33 1/3 RPM. The spots could be used anytime during the year. Appearing on the disc, besides Stewart, are Martha Denny, Andy Maluke and Mary Ann Ryan. The text for Stewart's 60-second spot is as follows:

ANNOUNCER: Mr. James Stewart for the American Red Cross.

STEWART: On the early frontier, distances were great and winters were long and you could count on your neighbors to help you. Today things are different and when you need help, where is the neighbor you can really count on? Who pitches in when there's a catastrophe? Who gets the word to a young serviceman that his daughter has just been born? Who makes sure there's blood when it's needed? Who teaches blind kids to swim? Who does all those things that most other folks never seem to have time for? Well, there's one neighbor close by…your Red Cross volunteer. Now maybe you haven't got a lot of hours to give to the American Red Cross every month, but think, where do you fit in…neighbor?

The 30-second spot begins with the same announcer statement and then Stewart comes in with a very similar speech:

STEWART: On the early frontier you could count on your neighbors to help you. Today things are different. When you need help, who can you count on? Who does all those things that most other folks never seem to have time for? Well, there's one neighbor…your Red Cross volunteer. Now maybe you haven't got a lot of hours to give to the American Red Cross, but where do you fit in…neighbor?

Boy Scouts of America Radio PSAs

Jimmy Stewart has always been an advocate of scouting. Although not an Eagle Scout as many sources say, he did receive Scouting's highest award, the Silver Beaver. The Jimmy Stewart Museum in his hometown of Indiana, PA, even offers a special award to scouts called the James M. Stewart Good Citizenship Award.

If you are interested in learning more about the award and/or how to attain it, go to *www.jimmy.org/scoutaward* for complete details.

(1) DWP937A/DWP937B

The two-sided, 7-inch 45 RPM disc features many 30-second public service announcements for scouting. Side one ends with Stewart's spot, in which he says:

> *Have you ever felt lost, not sure of what you want to do? This is Jimmy Stewart with some good advice — check out the Boy Scouts. Scouting can be a big challenge. It takes toughness to paddle a canoe all day. It takes guts to be a leader and a doer. That's what the Boy Scouts teach — leadership, the outdoor life; it's fun and it's a challenge. So why don't you check out the Boy Scouts in the white pages of your phone book.*

Others heard on side one are: Jack Klugman, Michael Landon, Leslie Nielsen, Leonard Nimoy, Doug Gray (of the Marshall Tucker Band), "Mean" Joe Greene and Martin Balsam.

On the second side you can hear: Ricardo Montalban, Elliott Gould, Chuck Connors, Patrick Duffy, Tom T. Hall (reading the same script as Jimmy Stewart), James Brown, Nipsey Russell and Gerald Ford.

(2) CB557A/CB557B

This is a 7-inch, small-hole 33 1/3/ RPM record featuring 14 public service announcements for the Boy Scouts. The label reads, "Celebrity Endorsements, a local campaign produced by The Boy Scouts of America, North Brunswick, New Jersey 08902." The exact release date is not known, but since John Glenn wasn't elected to the senate until 1974 and Richard Boone died in 1981, it most likely dates from that seven-year period.

Stewart's endorsement is the first track of side one. Besides Stewart, other celebrities appearing on the disc were (all spots are 30 seconds, except for those marked otherwise): Danny Thomas, Captain Kangaroo, Bill Bradley, Richard Boone (:60), Cliff Robertson (:60), Senator John Glenn, Tim Conway, Kareem Abdul-Jabbar, Johnny Carson, Lloyd Bridges, James Whitmore (:60), Jack Lord (:60) and Casper the Friendly Ghost.

Stewart's 30-second spot is as follows:

> *This is Jimmy Stewart speaking for the Boy Scouts of America. You know when I was growing up back in Indiana, Pennsylvania, being a member of Scout Troop 3 meant a lot to me. I made new friends, learned how to get along with others, how to lead others and along the way I picked up a lot of good rules for living and growing up to be a responsible citizen. You can get the same start I did by joining the Scouts today. This is Jimmy Stewart, thank you.*

In the 1950s, Stewart recorded several Boy Scout PSAs at the C.P. MacGregor Studios in Los Angeles, CA. Besides recording, the MacGregor company also produced, transcribed and syndicated many old-time radio shows, including *Proudly We Hail*, *The La Rosa Hollywood Theatre of Stars*, *Heartbeat Theater* and *Obsession*. MacGregor himself often hosted these programs. Several master 7-inch reels of taped Stewart announcements have been documented and are described here.

(1) 1957

This first reel is dated March 22, 1957, and features several spots recorded by Stewart. This tape features the actual recording session, flubs and all.

The first spot to be recorded was one minute in length and Stewart did two takes, with the second being the better. He says:

> *This is Jimmy Stewart. I've been a member of the Boy Scouts of America for many years and I've seen first-hand how Scouting gives lively good times and valuable training to boys of all ages. For youngsters, Cub Scout games and projects teach cooperation and introduce them to the world we live in. Boy Scouts discover the out-of-doors, master physical and mental skills, and develop the fine American qualities of self-reliance, reliability, and love of God, home and country. Teenagers, as Explorers, test their abilities against land, sea and sky and preview their futures*

as adult citizens and wage earners. Such a comprehensive program is possible in your community only if your local Boy Scout Council has full financial support. Give generously to your Boy Scout fund drive.

Stewart's only notable mistake on the first take was to say "Boy Scout's fund drive" at the end, after which he immediately says, "Well, I'm gonna do that again."

The second spot was also taped in two takes, with the second being the keeper. Stewart's script is:

> This is Jimmy Stewart. Now for a long time I've been actively interested in the Boy Scouts of America. And I'm convinced that scouting is not only fine recreation for boys, but it's also performing an invaluable service for our country. How? Well, because the familiar scout motto, be prepared, is the very heart of the scout program. All of Scouting, from the simplest Cub Scout Indian game to Boy Scout camping to Explorer emergency service training, is preparing boys to meet life head on. The wide range of activities and requirements, plus the Scout code, develops boys into adults who are physically and mentally and morally equipped to be good citizens. Now what more can our nation ask? Now you can help Scouting prepare the boys of your town for manhood. Your local Boy Scout Council is right now conducting a finance campaign, so give generously to the Boy Scouts of today...men of tomorrow.

Stewart's first attempt ended on the word "motto," and he went immediately to take two.

The third spot is just over 20 seconds in length. He did fine on the first take, but said, "I'll retake on that," and started over again. The text of the spot is:

> This is Jimmy Stewart. The primary job of your Boy Scout Council is to equip our boys physically, mentally and morally for manhood. Now help scouting do that job in your community. For a strong Scout program reaching more boys, support your Boy Scout fund drive.

The only difference in the two spots comes in the third sentence. In take one he says "Now help scouting..." while in the second he says "So help scouting..."

The fourth spot is the shortest, but it took six takes to get it right. The first five barely got beyond the first several words. Stewart says:

> *This is Jimmy Stewart. Your Boy Scout Council needs money to keep Scouting running on all cylinders in your community; to organize Scout units, to train leaders, to maintain camps, to keep a good staff of professional Scouters. Prime scouting with your dollars — give generously to the Boy Scout fund drive.*

Two takes were required for the final spot. It is one minute in length and the second take was the better. The text for the spot is:

> *This is Jimmy Stewart. You know I hate to sound like a gloomy Gus, but no one today can help but wonder how black the future will be before it gets brighter. We parents are especially concerned. How can we best prepare our children to face the increasing complexities of living? Now one of our strongest partners is the Boy Scouts of America; today doubling its efforts to prepare our boys for the big job of manhood. Scouting, while still giving the boys the same good times it has for almost 50 years, is more than ever emphasizing physical and mental fitness, moral and spiritual values. It's stressing survival skills and emergency training, science, brotherhood, citizenship and leadership. So join forces with your local Boy Scout Council which needs money for the Scout program. Scouting is preparing your boys for life; well, put life in Scouting with your dollars.*

The first take breaks down on the word "forces" in the next to the last sentence.

It is presumed that all of these spots were used at one time or another, but only the second has been documented. It appears on the disc CPM-12-2168 (see next entry).

(2) 1958

The second tape is dated January 22, 1958, and is the master tape for a 12-inch album of Boy Scout radio spots. The album's matrix number is given on the tape box as CPM-12-2168. Side one features one-minute spots and side two has 30-second spots. Stewart appears on both sides. Also appearing on side one are: Danny Thomas, Walt Disney, Art Linkletter, Eddie Cantor and Glenn Ford. Joining Stewart on side two are: Walt Disney, Groucho Marx, Eddie Cantor, Glenn Ford and Danny Thomas.

The one-minute Stewart spot was recorded March 22, 1957, and was the second spot recorded that day. See above entry for the text of this message.

The 21-second spot is not from the same recording sessions and its origin is not known. The text of the message is:

> *This is Jimmy Stewart. The Boy Scouts of America are helping communities solve juvenile problems successfully, because scouting makes sense to boys and they readily adopt its activities and its code. So help scouting reach the boys of your town; support your Boy Scout Council with your dollars.*

Christmas Seals
See *National Tuberculosis Association*.

4-H Public Service Announcements
Released on a 12-inch 33 1/3 RPM disc in 1966, Stewart and others give announcements in support of the 4-H organization. Others appearing on the disc are: Vice President Hubert H. Humphrey, Bill Cosby and Miss America 1958 Marilyn Van Derbur.

International Fund for Animal Welfare
WR-1002

The International Fund for Animal Welfare was formed in 1969, and is still in operation today. The "Every Letter Counts" campaign on behalf of the baby harp seals was produced for them by Wormwood Projects.

Also appearing on the disc are Henry Fonda, Mary Tyler Moore, Brian Davies (IFAW Director), Donnie Osmond, Anne Baxter, Burgess Meredith, Hugh O'Brian, Bea Arthur, Gregory Peck, Zsa Zsa Gabor, Walter Pidgeon and Caesar Romero.

In Stewart's clip, he says:

> *Hello, this is Jimmy Stewart for the International Fund for Animal Welfare. This spring another brutal slaughter of those beautiful white coat baby harp seals is going to happen again. We know that they will be clubbed with hard wooden bats or steel hooks. We know that these seals die so that we might have trinkets and novelty fur products like slipper trims and stuffed animals. We know that the Canadian government continues to ignore seal quotas set by their own scientists. We know that even a majority of Canadians oppose the seal killing. Please, let the Canadian government know how you feel; every letter counts.*

Another voice then gives the address.

March of Dimes
Orthacoustic ND6-MM-3517 (1946)

James Stewart delivers a very dramatic appeal for the March of Dimes. By today's standards, his impassioned speech is far from politically correct in spots, but in 1946 that didn't seem to matter. The show, which runs just over 13:30, was set for broadcast between January 14 and 31, 1946, and served as the beginning of that year's collection period. Stewart was introduced by Basil O'Connor, the president of the National Foundation for Infantile Paralysis. Howard J. London was the radio director for the National Foundation for Infantile Paralysis. Stewart's plea is transcribed here. On the opposite side of the disc is a show titled *Music Fights Infantile Paralysis* with Dinah Shore, Harry Von Zell and Robert Emmett Dolan and His Orchestra.

Thank you, Mr. O'Connor. Ladies and gentlemen, I'm here on behalf of some people who are getting up a parade. It's the biggest parade in the world. It lasts for two weeks without stopping. The line of marchers extends from coast to coast and from the border of Canada to the border of Mexico. And there are more marchers in it than there are people in the United States. Yes sir, that's right. I kind of think it sounds a little crazy myself, but it's true. You see, the marchers aren't people — they're dimes. Little silver ten-cent pieces out of men's pockets, women's handbags, children's piggy banks...millions on millions of them join up in this parade. It's the annual March of Dimes, sponsored by your National Foundation for Infantile Paralysis. And, it isn't only the biggest parade in the world; it's the best...because it does the most good. Now I've got figures on that to prove it to you. But I won't start out by telling you that there were 13,000 infantile paralysis victims here in this country in 1945 and that it was the fourth worst epidemic in the recorded history of the disease. I'll just begin by talking about a kid. A kid, well, a kid likes to play and whoop and holler; make a nuisance out of himself banging around the house. When his folks want him downstairs, he's upstairs. When they want him in, he's out throwing a ball through somebody's window or something. And his folks get mad, you know. What wouldn't they give to be able to keep him still for a whole afternoon. And then there comes an afternoon when he is still. Yeah, yeah, he was all right yesterday, but this morning he couldn't get out of bed. The doctor said it was infantile paralysis. The kid's gonna keep still for an awful long time. His folks maybe don't say anything now. Dad sits in the corner with paper unfolded, but he isn't reading the paper. Mom just cries where nobody can see her. But they don't have to say what they'd give if the kid was up again playing, whoopin' and hollerin'. They'd give all the money they had, their house and their car and their lives thrown in. Only it's too late.

Well, now, I've said that, I'll tell you the rest of it. That kid didn't live in a house in 1945; he lived in more than 13,000 houses. He was more than 13,000 kids, none of them different until this thing happened. He was city kids, country kids, rich kids, poor kids, big kids, little kids. Your National Foundation for Infantile Paralysis doesn't care who or what or where a kid is. If he's in danger of death or being crippled for life and his folks need to call for help, your National Foundation will be at his side. In almost any case you know, they need to, because infantile paralysis costs such a lot. I've got figures on that too which I'll give to you in just a minute. And, when I do, remember the kid. They're for him... they're for infantile paralysis. Now it's a pretty bad financial problem to be sick anyhow for most people. President Truman has said this in his health message to Congress last November. He said, "The principle reason why people do not receive the care they need is that they cannot afford to pay for it on an individual basis at the time they need it." This is true not only for the needy persons, it is also true for a large proportion of normally self-supporting persons. They may be hit by sickness that calls for many times the average cost; in extreme cases, for more than their annual income. When this happens, they may come face-to-face with economic disaster. Many families, fearful of expense, delay calling the doctor long beyond the time when medical care would do the most good. Yes, but you delay calling the doctor for a kid with infantile paralysis and you're taking away the kid's one chance to grow up straight and useful and happy. You've got to get care for him quick, and go on getting care for him for a long time afterwards. And that's where my figures come in. Now I'll skip the cost of doctors and nurses and ordinary hospitalization because you all probably know something about that. I'll come down to just one thing — the special appliances used in the treatment of infantile paralysis. Listen to what they cost—a swimming pool for $35,000. Now that's not a Hollywood swimming pool, you understand, it's...it's a hospital or scientific institutions'. And, if you could see the little kids in it, getting back their strength and the use of their limbs, you'd know it was cheap at the price. But alone by yourself, well maybe you wouldn't have the price. A respirator for $1300 — that's for patients with paralyzed lungs. They can't live without it. Somebody's got to provide it for them while they need it. But you maybe, maybe you couldn't do it by yourself. The equipment for physical therapy, such as an electric cabinet for $520, *and a whirlpool bath for $385, and an ultraviolet ray machine for $200. A hot pack machine for $125. Oh, and there's some little stuff among the appliances, too. Stuff a lot easier on the pocketbook, like a leg brace for $40, a wheelchair for $35…but I wouldn't say those are easier on the heart. Especially if you knew they mightn't have to be bought at all if the kid could be cured by the big stuff. You've got to get him by the big stuff and you say there isn't that much money in the world. Well, sure there is. Here it comes across the country on parade…the March of Dimes. The millions on millions of little round ten-cent pieces jingling their music to march by…with dollars joining in because there's no law against it; dimes and dollars pouring out of all the houses to give a future to all the victims of infantile paralysis. Five million dollars' worth of them in 1945; spent for medical care and treatment for those victims hit by the fourth greatest infantile paralysis epidemic. Here they come now in 1946. By January the 30, the date which will always commemorate the birthday of Franklin D. Roosevelt, our great war president, there will be enough of them to support this tremendous work which he founded. There will be enough because you will open your doors and send your dimes and dollars out into the parade. Do it today, ladies and gentlemen. Join the March of Dimes and half of them will come marching back again and take care of your neighbor and your kid, if there should be need this year.*

At this point the announcer came back and reiterated a few of Stewart's more important points and closed the show.

National Cooperative Forest Fire Prevention Program
U.S. Forest Service Platter 26 (1969)

The U.S. Forest Service's 1969 campaign to prevent forest fires relied heavily on Hollywood stars, including Jimmy Stewart. There were songs — two different lengths (:60 and :30) of both "What a Piece of Work Is Man" from *Hair* and featuring Willie Weatherby and Ben Vereen and "America the Ugly" by Judy Collins. There are three different tracks simply titled "A Commercial for Squirrels" (:60, :30, :20) and a short comedy bit from Carol Burnett called "Take a Bear to Lunch." Tracks 3-4-5 on side two of the disc are titled "Guess Who?" (The longest track also says "…The Voices of Hollywood." The tracks are :60, :30 and :20 in length. According to the sleeve, these tracks are "for news/talk formats, or any station interested in intriguing an audience." It is possible that some stations may have used one of these tracks as part of a contest; identify the stars and win a prize. All the stars say the same thing, "all it takes is people to prevent forest fires." Carol Burnett drops the "all" from her statement. These are then edited together to make up the proper length commercial message.

Stewart's voice can be heard in all three spots. Appearing, in order, in the 60-second spot are: George Burns, Jim "Gomer Pyle" Nabors, Chet Huntley, Zsa Zsa Gabor, James Cagney, Fred MacMurray, Sammy Davis, Jr., Jack Benny, Eddie Albert, Pat Paulsen, Edward G. Robinson, Bill "Jose Jimenez" Dana, Jimmy Stewart and Carol Burnett.

The voices in the 30-second version are: George Burns, Jim Nabors, Zsa Zsa Gabor, Pat Paulsen, Jack Benny, Jimmy Stewart and Bill Dana.

The 20-second spot features George Burns, Jim Nabors, Zsa Zsa Gabor, Jimmy Stewart and Jack Benny.

National Tuberculosis Association

The National Tuberculosis Association and Christmas Seals have been around since the early 1900s. Its purpose has been to raise money for research and awareness of tuberculosis and, today, other lung diseases. Today, the organization is known as the Lung Association. As with many charitable organizations, entertainment stars often recorded messages to help promote the cause. Jimmy Stewart appears on at least three such promotional discs.

(1) Christmas Seal Campaign 1958
Stewart's message is as follows:

> *This is Jimmy Stewart. You know there's a very important sale going on all over America this holiday season. It's the annual Christmas Seal sale in the fight against our country's number one infectious killer, tuberculosis. There's no price tag, of course, on a human life. To save a life at any price is cheap enough, and that's why Christmas Seals are one of the best bargains we can buy. Everyone can be proud of having a part in this lifesaving effort. Now, won't you join with me and millions of Americans in buying and in using Christmas Seals to make all of us safer from TB? Answer your Christmas Seal letter today. Thank you.*

(2) Christmas Seal Campaign 1961 (RCA M8MR-9864/M8MR-9865)
This is a 12-inch disc playing at 33 1/3 RPM. Also appearing on the recording are Mel Allen and Charles O. Finley, Laurence Harvey, James Garner, Richard Widmark, William Bendix, Joanne Woodward, Paul Newman, Jack Webb, Jack Lemmon (2), Bing Crosby (2), Jack Benny, Robert Young, Susan Hayward (2), Tony Curtis, Frank Sinatra, Natalie Wood, Bob Hope (2), Ronald Reagan and Robert Stack.

Stewart appears on side 2 of the disc and his message is:

This is Jimmy Stewart. Do you know what shows the true colors of Christmas? Well, you can see those true colors in the Christmas Seals we use each holiday season. Because those bright patterns of Christmas Seal color on your cards and envelopes mean that we're lending a hand to those less fortunate. Because each Christmas Seal we use fights tuberculosis and helps save lives. Answer your Christmas Seal letter today.

Total running time is 28-and-a-half seconds.

(3) Christmas Seal Campaign 1963 (Decca MG 79610)
Other celebrities appearing with Stewart on this disc are: Charlton Heston, George Burns, Jimmy Durante, Richard Widmark, William Bendix, Jack Webb, Jack Lemmon, Lee Remick, Tony Curtis, Edgar Bergen, Jose Jimanez (Bill Dana), Gene Barry, Jack Benny, Bob Hope, Walter Brennan, Susan Oliver, Robert Stack, Fabian, Karl Malden, Dan Duryea, Rita Moreno, Fess Parker and Sal Mineo.
Stewart's message is the first on side 2 of the record. It is the same spot which appeared on the 1962 disc.

(4) Christmas Seal Campaign 1964 (Decca MG 79980/MG 79981)
Again, this is a 12-inch disc playing at 33 1/3 RPM. Other celebrities appearing on the record are Danny Kaye, Efrem Zimbalist Jr., Eva Marie Saint, Ernie Ford, Frank Sinatra, Gisele MacKenzie, Bob Hope, Bea Benaderet, Robert Young, George Maharis, Shirley MacLaine, Jack Lemmon, Tony Curtis, Bing Crosby, Lee Remick, Fred MacMurray, Jack Benny, Robert Stack, Stephen Boyd, Mitch Miller, Bobby Rydell, Bobby Vinton, Lena Horne, Connie Francis and Jimmy Dean.
Stewart's message, again appearing on side two, is the same message used on the 1961 disc. It has, however, been produced with the music of *The 12 Days of Christmas* running throughout, adding a short introduction and ending. As a result, the time is increased to 41-and-a-half seconds.

Project HOPE Radio Spots

Jimmy Stewart recorded several public service announcements in 1968 for Project HOPE and the S.S. HOPE. Project HOPE was founded in 1958 by William Walsh, M.D. The S.S. HOPE was the very first peacetime hospital ship and Project HOPE conducted medical training and health care education programs. The S.S. HOPE was retired in 1974.

A 7-inch vinyl record (RS 1968) containing five Jimmy Stewart spots was issued to radio stations to play as public service announcements. The disc featured one 60-second spot:

> *Take a drop of water. And, then another and another, then another, and pretty soon, if you work at it steadily, you have yourself an ocean. And that's the way it's done with Project Hope. Hope brings self-help medical aid and know-how to nations that are long on illness and disease, but short on medical staffs and facilities. Project Hope is an independent, nonprofit organization that relies on people like you for support. Individuals, each contributing to keep the hospital ship S.S. Hope sailing. So, Hope is a lot like a do-it-yourself ocean. Send your contribution. It's important, do it, do it today. Project Hope, Room A, Washington, DC.*

Two 30-second spots:

> *Take a drop of water. And, then another and another, and pretty soon, if you work at it steadily, you have yourself an ocean. That's the way it's done with Project Hope. Hope brings self-help medical aid to nations that are long on illness and disease, but short on medical staffs and facilities. So send your contributions. Do it today. Project Hope, Room A, Washington, DC. The hospital ship S.S. Hope brings self-help medical aid to countries that have illness and disease, but not enough medical staffs or facilities. Hope becomes a dockside hospital where volunteer professionals help train local medical people to treat the ill. Now Project Hope needs your help. Please give whatever you can. It's important. And do it today. Project Hope, Room A, Washington, DC.*

One 20-second spot:

> *Project Hope brings self-help medical aid and training to countries of medical staffs and facilities. Hope volunteers help treat the ill and teach modern medical techniques. Now you can help Hope. Send your contribution to Project Hope, Room A, Washington, DC.*

And one 10-second spot:

Project Hope brings medical training and treatment to developing nations, so send your contributions to Project Hope, Room A, Washington, DC.

The spots were prepared by Ron Stone & Company, Advertising.

Salvation Army Announcements

According to an article appearing in *European Stars and Stripes* on December 4, 1983, Jimmy Stewart had been named Chairman of the 1983 Salvation Army National Christmas Campaign.

One of his duties was to make both radio and TV announcements requesting donations for the organization. None of these announcements has been located for listening.

Stewart also appeared on the Salvation Army's *A Gift of Christmas* album and radio show issued this same year. For more information, see that entry in Chapter 2 of this book.

Toys for Tots

The U.S. Marine Corps Reserve began their Toys for Tots program in 1947 by Marine Major William Hendrick and a group of Los Angeles Marine reservists. The following year, the program was adopted by the Marine Corps. The mission of the program is to collect new, unwrapped toys to distribute as Christmas gifts to needy children in the communities where each campaign is conducted. Their goal is to "deliver a message of hope to these youngsters that will motivate them to grow into responsible, productive, patriotic citizens and community leaders."

The program was often advertised on the radio by the use of pre-recorded messages from music and entertainment stars. Since Bill Hendrick was, in his civilian life, the Director of Public Relations for Warner Bros. Studio, he was able to secure the services of many different celebrities, including Jimmy Stewart, to contribute to the project. And it was only natural that Warner Bros. Records would distribute the spots to radio stations.

(1) Warner Brothers PRO 119 — Voice Tracks US Marine Corps Toys for Tots (7-inch, 45 RPM)

This particular disc features messages from movie and TV stars, including Jack Webb, Natalie Wood, Connie Stevens, Will Hutchins, Bob Conrad and Clint Walker.

Stewart's track is the final track on side two of the disc and he says, "This is Jimmy Stewart wishing you all a very Merry Christmas and asking you to remember our less fortunate children by giving Toys for Tots. Yes, through your gifts of new toys or toys in good condition, you can help make happier holidays for the less fortunate children in your community. So join the Toys for Tots campaign of your hometown Marine Corps Reserve unit and the cooperating community organizations. Give Toys for Tots."

An edited version of this voice track was used on all of the remaining discs.

(2) Warner Bros. PRO 269 — Voice Tracks US Marine Corps Toys for Tots (7-inch, 45 RPM)

This particular disc features messages from movie and TV stars, including Danny Thomas, Phyllis Diller, Jim Backus, Dale Robertson, John Wayne, Efrem Zimbalist Jr., Jack Webb, Joan Crawford, Jimmy Durante, Greer Garson, Charlton Heston, Ben Alexander, Yvonne Craig and Dean Jones. Since Yvonne Craig introduces herself as Batgirl, the disc would most likely date from Christmastime 1967, when that character was a regular on the Batman TV series.

Stewart's track is the final track on side two of the disc and he says, "This is Jimmy Stewart wishing you all a very Merry Christmas and asking you to remember our less fortunate children by giving Toys for Tots. So join the Toys for Tots campaign of your hometown Marine Corps Reserve unit; give Toys for Tots."

(3) Warner Bros. PRO 381 — Vocal Tracks U.S. Marine Corps. Toys for Tots (7-inch, 45 RPM)

The probable release date for this record is 1970. Appearing with Stewart are Efrem Zimbalist Jr., the U.S. Marine Corps Band, Karen Valentine, Natalie Wood, Leslie Nielsen, Glen Campbell, Leonard Nimoy, Clarence Williams, Charlton Heston, Danny Thomas, Phyllis Diller, John Wayne, Bing Crosby, Jack Webb and Jimmy Durante.

Stewart's message is track seven on side two of the disc and is the same as that used on PRO 269.

(4) Warner Bros. PRO 541 — Vocal Tracks U.S. Marine Corps Toys for Tots (7-inch, 45 RPM)

Besides Jimmy Stewart, this 1972 disc features Efrem Zimbalist, Jr. introducing the U.S. Marine Corps Band who play the *Toys for Tots March*, Karen Valentine, Chad Everett, Gary Owens, Glen Campbell, Florence

Henderson, Clarence Williams, Charlton Heston, Danny Thomas, Phyllis Diller, John Wayne, Bing Crosby, Jack Webb and Jimmy Durante.

Stewart's message is track seven on side two of the disc and is the same as that used on PRO 269.

(5) Warner Bros. PRO 774

This disc most likely dates from Christmas 1978. Like discs from the previous years, it has Efrem Zimbalist Jr. talking about Toys for Tots and introducing the Marine Corps Band playing the *Toys for Tots March*. Only one other track is on this side of the record. It features no talking at all and is the Martine Corps Band playing the *Marines' Hymn*. The other side of the disc features Stewart's message, plus spots from Frank Sinatra, Mike McDonald (of the Doobie Brothers), John Wayne, Ray Stevens, Susie Allanson, Pal Ricks and former Beatle George Harrison.

Stewart's message is track three on the second side of the disc and is the same as that used on all other discs.

United Jewish Appeal

In 1960, the United Jewish Appeal issued a special 7-inch vinyl disc to radio stations. On the disc, six Hollywood stars ask listeners to support the 1960 United Jewish Appeal and the UJA Special Fund. The 60-second spots were read by Jack Benny, Burt Lancaster, Jean Simmons, Jimmy Stewart, Robert Ryan and Cornel Wilde.

In Stewart's appeal, he says:

> *This is Jimmy Stewart. Drop by drop the rain comes through the canvas roof and the sagging walls. Drop by drop despair sinks into the hearts of thousands. Yes, through the United Jewish Appeal, we helped bring a million refugees to Israel. But one out of every three of those refugees is still unabsorbed. Sixty thousand live in canvas huts and tin shacks. They need decent housing. A hundred and thirty thousand live on farms without the tools or the means to really support themselves; another hundred and fifty thousand, young and old, need social and welfare aids of every kind. So help fight the despair that builds up drop by drop. Meet the unmet needs of Israel through the 1960 United Jewish Appeal and the UJA special fund.*

United Presbyterian Church: A Moment for Thanksgiving

When Stewart was a boy, his parents had been members of the Presbyterian Church in Indiana, PA. He remained with the Presbyterian

Church his entire life, with his funeral service held at the Presbyterian Church in Beverly Hills, CA.

In the early 1970s, the United Presbyterian Church organized a public service campaign called "A Moment for Thanksgiving" and promptly enlisted the aid of Jimmy Stewart to record a radio spot. The spot has special music, recorded by the Forest Hill Presbyterian Church Choir, Cleveland Heights, Ohio, Clair T. McElfresh director, at both the beginning and end. Stewart says:

> *This is Jimmy Stewart with a moment for Thanksgiving. You remember the man who said, I cursed God because I had no shoes until I saw a man who had no feet." Man's quite an ungrateful creature as a rule. It isn't easy to be thankful. Oh sure, we give thanks for little things — somebody opening a door for you, handing you your pencil or passing the salt. But, do we thank God with every breath we draw for the gift of life, for home, health, church and school, family and friends, our job and the privilege of living in America? And, do we pay sufficient homage to the creator of all heaven and earth, you and me? The Psalmist says, "Praise the lord, praise him with trumpet sound, lute and harp, timbrel and dance, strings and pipe, sounding cymbals, loud clashing cymbals. Let everything that breathes praise the Lord." We have so much for which to be grateful and that's why I too give thanks on Thanksgiving.*

Unconfirmed Public Service Announcement

Word of mouth has it that Stewart was also involved in several other public service projects, but research has yet to turn up any information on these. The search for information and/or recordings for these unconfirmed projects continues.

(1) American Red Cross

Stewart may have participated in the 1948 campaign. To date, four 1948 Red Cross programs have been confirmed, but *The Bob Hope Show* (Program #1) and *The Bing Crosby Show* (Program #2) do not include Stewart. Another 1948 disc features three five-minute dramas, one each by Ella Raines, William Bendix and Robert Montgomery, but nothing by Stewart. Likewise, a flood relief program broadcast on June 13, 1948, did not include any contribution from Stewart.

It is also possible that he participated in the 1953 campaign, but not definite proof of this has been uncovered.

(2) Christmas Seals (National Tuberculosis Society)

To date only a few of these discs have been located. In all likelihood, Stewart appeared on more than the four which have been uncovered.

SPECIAL RADIO DROP-INS

These are short, usually under 30-second, recordings by film and TV stars, sports and music figures which radio stations could use to promote themselves or their programs and services.

The Big Sound

The Big Sound was a series of 12-inch 33 1/3 RPM records which radio stations could use to help promote their programs and specialties. Each disc featured a number of celebrities giving short promos. Radio station personalities could simply play a selection from the album on their show to make it sound as though a Hollywood, music or sports star were right there with them. Jimmy Stewart appears on at least two discs in this series. The discs were issued by Stars International, through its exclusive United States distributor, Richard H. Ullman, Inc. Both companies were divisions of The Peter Frank Organization, Inc., Hollywood and New York. There is no indication on the jackets or discs as to the year of release, but since Sam Cooke, who appears on the baseball record, was killed on December 11, 1964, they would have to have been produced before that date. All records were released in the same generic jacket.

Many of the Big Sound discs were also issued on records which needed to be played using a 78 RPM needle. These also had a different label design using the musical note with tape reel design featured on the V.I.P. labels (see V.I.P. Radio) on a red field.

(1) Baseball Coverage Promos (SB-1-R)

The LP contains 26 tracks by stars including Stewart, Bob Crosby, Bobby Rydell, Howard Duff, Ed Sullivan, Frankie Laine, Count Basie, Kirby Stone, Chuck Connors, Sam Cooke, Tony Bennett and Johnny Cash. The tracks on side one run between 16 and 24 seconds, while on side two they are shorter — 7 to 15 seconds. There also is a 13-second "Production Track" beginning each side. The same stars do one spot each on both sides of the record. This was the same musical jingle used for each spot so that the station could produce its own material.

All of the tracks on side one include a voice track with production music added. On this side, Jimmy simply says, "This is Jimmy Stewart and your dial is set for all the latest baseball scores, so leave it right where it is."

Side two has the same comment from Stewart, but without the production music.

(2) Big Sound Promos with Stars (B-1 R)

Side one of this album features 15 promos, each produced with a jingle in and out of the star's promo. Side two features the same star's promos, but without the jingle. Appearing besides Stewart are Pat Boone, Gogi Grant, Tony Bennett, Ed Sullivan, Carol Lawrence, Harry Belafonte, Rock Hudson, Peggy Lee, Milton Berle, Steve Allen, Carol Burnett, Tony Martin, Polly Bergen and Jerry Lewis.

In his promo Stewart says, "Hi, this is Jimmy Stewart reminding you that your dial is set to the Big Sound all year 'round."

(3) Christmas Greetings (XGT-1 R)

Appearing on this disc with Stewart were Pat Boone, Jayne Mansfield, Kay Starr, Fabian, Gogi Grant, Fred Astaire, Frankie Laine, Polly Bergen, Tommy Sands, Mitzi Gaynor, Ray Conniff, Tab Hunter, Jane Morgan, Milton Berle, Bob Hope, Jerry Lewis, Andre Previn, Vic Damone, Dodie Stevens, Tony Martin, Frankie Avalon, Carol Lawrence, Jack Lemmon, Rosemary Clooney, David Rose, Margaret Whiting, George Shearing, Bob Crosby and Art Linkletter. In addition, there is also a New Year's Eve track on the album which features many of the stars already mentioned, plus Steve Allen, Connie Francis, Tennessee Ernie Ford, Shelley Berman, Tony Bennett, Stan Freberg, Tony Curtis, Pearl Bailey, Bobby Darin, Sammy Davis Jr., Jim Backus, Frank Sinatra and Mel Blanc. This final track times out at 1:43.

All of the drop-ins are produced using the same musical jingle, making them all in the 20-30-second range, depending on how much spoken word is included. Stewart says, "Merry Christmas and Season's Greetings to all our listeners at this spot on the dial, from yours truly, Jimmy Stewart."

(4) Football Coverage Promos (SF-1 R)

There are 24 tracks on this album, 12 on each side. Joining Stewart are Bobby Darin, Tony Curtis, Steve Allen, Earl Grant, Robert Stack, Frankie Laine, Phil Harris, George Shearing, Milton Berle, Tommy Sands, Stan Freberg, Jimmie Rodgers, Pat Boone, Nelson Riddle, Stan Kenton, Ed Sullivan, Jack Lemmon, Jackie Cooper, Rock Hudson, Vincent Price, Tennessee Ernie Ford, Jimmy Durante and Tony Bennett. All tracks run from 14-26 seconds in length, with Stewart's lasting 15 seconds. Stewart's track is on side two of the record and is completely produced with music. He says, "This is Jimmy Stewart and your dial is set for all the latest football scores, so leave it right where it is, hmm." The only change from the baseball disc is, of course, substituting "football" for "baseball" and the little "hmm" at the end.

(5) Shopping Days Till Christmas (XSD-2 R)

This disc features 24 stars counting down the shopping days remaining until Christmas, beginning with 12 days remaining. Two different stars are available for each day. Stewart announces that there are three shopping days till Christmas. Milton Berle is the other star for three days remaining. Others appearing on the disc are Gogi Grant and Roger Williams (12 days), Jimmie Rodgers and the Mary Kaye Trio (Mary Kaye, Norman Kaye, Frankie Ross) (11 days), Jimmy Dean and Billy Eckstine (10 days), Jane Morgan and Connie Francis (9 days), Tony Bennett and the Everly Brothers (Don and Phil) (8 days), Maureen O'Hara and Tex Ritter (7 days), Hoagy Carmichael and Les Baxter (6 days), Phil Harris and Andre Previn (5 days), Four Freshmen (Ross Barbour, Don Barbour, Bob Flanigan, Ken Albers) and Martin Denny (4 days), Jerry Lewis and Mitzi Gaynor (2 days) and Ed Sullivan and Tennessee Ernie Ford (1 day).

When it's his turn, Stewart says: "Hi, this is Jimmy Stewart. Ah...I guess I'd better step in here to mention the fact that if you haven't finished your Christmas shopping yet, well you better hurry because there are only three more shopping days till Christmas."

Stewart, plus ten others from this disc also appear on V.I.P. Radio Disc 4, *Shopping Days Till Christmas*. See that entry.

(6) Station Break "Frames" (MF-2-R)

The fifteen spots on this disc are designed to "frame" the local DJ's insertion of name and station ID. There are two pauses in each to accommodate this.

Stewart's dialogue is as follows: "I'm Jimmy Stewart, actor. (Pause) Yeah, well, don't all these dials and gadgets ever confuse you? Ah, which, ah, which button do you press to tell the listeners where they're tuned? (Pause) Yeah, looks as bad as an instrument panel on a B-52."

The entire spot runs about 32 seconds and it is completely produced with music. The music continues through the pauses in Stewart's dialogue.

Also appearing on the disc are Billy Eckstine, Dagmar (Virginia Ruth Egnor), Shelley Berman, Dean Martin, Jo Stafford, Jack Lemmon, Lionel

Hampton, Joni James, Jerry Lewis, Mitzi Gaynor, Ed Sullivan, Hermione Gingold, Kay Starr and Stan Kenton.

Stewart's spot, as well as those of Jerry Lewis, Mitzi Gaynor, Ed Sullivan, Hermione Gingold and Kay Starr, can also be found on V.I.P. Radio disc 31-B (see that entry).

(7) Thought for the Day (TFD-2 R)

Included on the disc besides Stewart are Tony Martin, Jayne Mansfield, Ed Sullivan, Buddy Hackett, Lionel Hampton, Margaret Whiting, Lorne Greene, Jackie Cooper, Caesar Romero, Alan Young, David Rose, Vincent Price, Mitzi Gaynor and Tony Bennett.

Side 1 features fully-produced spots with special jingles in and out of the spoken word. Stewart says, "This is Jimmy Stewart with a thought for the day. When you're stopping to look back, it's a cinch that you can't see the opportunities that lie ahead." Side 2 has the vocal track of each star only, without any production.

(8) "Vote" Public Service (PS-2 R)

Included on this disc besides Stewart are Mitzi Gaynor, Fabian, Cesar Romero, David Rose, Tommy Sands, Jackie Cooper, Dwayne Hickman, Margaret Whiting, Tab Hunter, Billy Eckstine, Andre Previn, Tony Bennett, Joni James, Ed Sullivan and Shelley Berman (side 2 only). Side one is completely produced with music and sound effects, while side two is voice alone.

Stewart says, "This is Jimmy Stewart reminding everyone that a voting American is a good American, so be sure you get to the polls and cast your ballot."

(9) Who Am I Contest (CI-3 R)

Appearing on this disc with Stewart were Jerry Lewis, Gogi Grant, Ernie Ford, Connie Stevens, Andre Previn, Joni James, Fred MacMurray, Lionel Hampton, Debbie Reynolds, Craig Stevens, Martin Denny, Kay Starr, Earl Grant and Margaret Whiting. Side one is completely produced with music and sound effects, while side two is voice alone. Echo has been added to the voice tracks on both sides of the record to help disguise the famous voices.

Stations could use these spots for any kind of contests they wished. The person(s) guessing the celebrity voice would win.

On the produced side, Stewart says, "Who Am I? Have you seen me on television? On your movie screen? On the stage? Have you heard me on records? Who am I? Who am I?" On the unproduced side, the second "Who am I?" at the end is missing. All the stars say basically the same thing.

Flashback

Flashback is an ABC Radio program which features disc jockey Bill St. James playing rock 'n' roll hits. The theme for the first hour of show #683, whose air dates were January 31-February 6, 2000, was *Flashback's Wild Wild West*. Many clips from Western films, radio shows, TV shows and even cartoons were played during the hour. One of those clips was of Jimmy Stewart saying, "I had taken Horace Greeley's advice literally — 'Go west, young man, go west,'" from the film *The Man Who Shot Liberty Valance*. The quote appears twice on the 4-CD set; first in the opening sequence for the show's first hour (disc 1) and again as track #10 on disc 4. The latter time, Stewart's 9-second line stands alone, to be used by the disc jockey at the local station as a drop-in or promo for *Flashback*.

Hollywood Profiles

Hollywood Profiles were short (4-5 minutes) radio drop-ins hosted by Dick Strout. The program was based on his column in *Modern Screen* magazine and, at its peak, was broadcast on more than 800 radio stations. The premise of the show was simple. Listeners would send in questions that they wanted their favorite stars to answer. Strout would pose the chosen question of the day to the star and play back the answer on the program. Jimmy Stewart appeared on at least one of these programs.

Stewart's program appears on the Series 62-303 (#1159), which was issued on a 12-inch record playing at 33 1/3 RPM. It is Program 21, for broadcast on October 22, 1962. The program opens with Strout introducing himself and the program. He says that Connie Webster of Paradise, Kansas, has sent in a question for Jimmy Stewart. For her trouble, she will receive a transistor radio. He then announces that he'll be back with the question, and Stewart's answer, in a minute.

When Part 2 of the program begins, Strout tells the listeners that the question is "Why doesn't Jimmy Stewart do more Westerns?" Strout adds that he went to Stewart's Beverly Hills home for the answer. At this point, we get Stewart's reply.

> *I never did Westerns until after the war. I did one years ago that sort of was a…they called it Destry Rides Again, that sort of was a… not a Western in the true sense of the word. I got started in Westerns*

sort of not voluntarily, just because after the war, the sort of the kind of part that I'd been identified with, more or less, people just didn't seem to want to see that type of picture. It was a thing to hunt around and find out whether I could do another type or get out of the business. I like Westerns. I like the whole idea of the Western story because I think, ah... more than almost any other type of story, it adapts itself to the movies. I think that the simplicity of the west as it was is ideal for telling in the medium of motion pictures. I think frankly people have had a bellyful of just the run-of-the-mill Western. I think television has been harmful to the actual classic Western story...ah...because I think too many of them have been made and too many of them have been made in a shoddy manner and haven't been made well. However, I don't think that this has hurt the actual real, genuine Western story, but I do think that nowadays you have to present a story that isn't run of the mill, that has something different or else you're just not gonna get an audience.

Strout thanks both Stewart and Webster and, after about a 40-second musical interlude, gives the address to which listeners can send their questions.

V.I.P. Radio

Like the Big Sound series described earlier, this is a series of 12-inch, 33 1/3 RPM records which radio stations used to promote themselves on the air. Music, TV, radio and movie stars presented the short promos for stations to make use of as they chose. There are no dates on the discs to indicate when they may have been released, but because a 78 RPM needle was required to play them, they were most likely released in the 1950s. Jimmy Stewart appeared on several of the discs.

(1) Station Break "Frames" (31-B)(M(f) — 9)

Six "Station Break Frames" appear at the beginning of side 1 of this record. All other tracks on the disc are instrumental station breaks and themes. Besides Stewart, the others doing "Station Break Frames" are Jerry Lewis, Mitzi Gaynor, Ed Sullivan, Hermione Gingold and Kay Starr.

Stewart's dialogue is as follows: "I'm Jimmy Stewart, actor. (Pause) Yeah, well, don't all these dials and gadgets ever confuse you? Ah, which, ah, which button do you press to tell the listeners where they're tuned? (Pause) Yeah, looks as bad as an instrument panel on a B-52."

All of these can also be found on Big Sounds MF-2-R (see that entry for complete details).

(2) (V.I.P. Promos (32-AX)(VIP — 2)

All announcements range from 4-to-10 seconds in length.

Others reading announcements are Bob Crosby, Tony Bennett, Frank DeVol, Billy Eckstine, Mitzi Gaynor, Margaret Whiting, Hoagy Carmichael, Frankie Avalon, Billy Daniels, Jerry Wallace, The Lancers, Tony Pastor, Andre Previn, Tony Martin, Frankie Laine, Jerry Lewis, Ed Sullivan, Tab Hunter, Walter Brennan, Edward Byrnes, Jack Lemmon, Dwayne Hickman, Jackie Cooper, Edmond O'Brien, Gene Barry, Shelley Berman, Art Linkletter, Jay North and Eddie Cantor.

On Stewart's spot he says, "Hi there, I'm Jimmy Stewart reminding you that your radio dial is set for V.I.P. radio."

(3) Open End Station Breaks (33- A)(ID — 13)

Others appearing on the disc with Stewart are Tommy Sands, Annette, Tony Bennett, Kay Starr, Tony Pastor, Dodie Stevens, Alvino Ray, Dakota Staton, The Lancers (Jerry Meacham, Dick Burr, Bob Porter, Corky Lindgren), De Castro Sisters (Peggy, Cherie, Babette), Bob Crosby, Jo Stafford, Ed Sullivan, Art Linkletter, Shelley Berman, Cesar Romero, Edward Byrnes, Arthur Lyman, Bud & Travis (Bud Dashiell & Travis Edmonson), Jack Lemmon, Jackie Cooper, Edmond O'Brien and Tony Curtis.

Stewart's segment goes like this: "Oh, I, ah excuse me, I'm Jimmy Stewart. (Pause) Well you go right ahead and finish what you were doing. (Pause) Ah-ha, okay, well now that we have the details out of the way, ah, what's next on the program?" The pauses are several seconds in length and allowed the disc jockey to say whatever he wanted. The spot is not produced with any music, but is simply Stewart's voice.

(4) Shopping Days Till Christmas (DISC 4) (GR — 6)

Twenty-four stars, two for each day, count down the final 12 shopping days remaining before Christmas. Stewart and ten others on this disc also appear, saying the same things, on Big Sounds *Shopping Days Till Christmas* (XSD — 2 R): Andre Previn, Billy Eckstine, Ed Sullivan, Hoagy Carmichael, Jane Morgan, Jerry Lewis, Jimmie Rodgers, Les Baxter, Mitzi Gaynor and Tony Bennett. See the Big Sounds entry for more complete details.

New stars appearing on this disc are: Bud and Travis (Dashiell and Edmonson), David Rose, Debbie Reynolds, Dodie Stevens, Frank DeVol, Hope Holiday, Jackie Cooper, Jay North, Kay Starr, the Lancers (Jerry Meacham, Dick Burr, Bob Porter, Corky Lindgren), Margaret Whiting, Ronnie Burns and Sue Rainy.

RADIO SPOTS — FILM COMMERCIALS

First, let's look at the film commercials relating to Stewart. Once a film was ready to be released, it had to be advertised. In many cases, special discs were prepared and sent to radio stations with pre-produced commercial announcements for the film. These commercials often used dialogue from the films. No specially recorded Stewart material is used on any of the spots.

Anatomy of a Murder
This 1-sided twelve inch 33 1/3 RPM disc contains a total of ten radio spots for the film *Anatomy of a Murder*. It was issued at about the same time as the film which was released on July 1, 1959, in the U.S. There are four 60-second spots, three 30-second spots and three 20-second spots on the record. All spots were produced by Thaddeus Suski Productions (Radio Recording Division). Stewart's voice from the film can be heard on tracks 1-3 and six.

Bandolero
This is a one-sided 7-inch disc featuring two commercials for the film. Stewart's voice does not appear on either of the spots. The film was issued on June 1, 1968, and 20th Century-Fox released the record at about the same time.

The Cheyenne Social Club
This 10-inch, 1-sided, 33 1/3 RPM disc featured four radio spots for the film *The Cheyenne Social Club*. It was issued at about the same time as the film, which was released on June 12, 1970.
0:60 — *Humor*
0:30 — *Humor*
0:60 — *Action*
0:30 — *Action*
Stewart and co-star Henry Fonda can be heard singing *Rolling Stone* on tracks 1 and 2. A small bit of Stewart dialogue, from the film, can be heard on track 3. Stewart is not heard on track 4.

Dear Brigitte
This is a 12-inch, 1-sided, 33 1/3 RPM disc featuring two 60-second spots and three 30-second spots for the film. Stewart's voice is not heard on any of the spots.

Firecreek

Firecreek was released in the U.S. on January 24, 1968. This 12-inch disc (WBSA-4890) was issued by Warner Bros.-Seven Arts at the same time. It featured five tracks (two 60-second spots, two 30-second spots and a 10-second spot). Stewart's voice is not heard on any of the commercials.

The Flight of the Phoenix

This is a 1-sided, 12-inch, 33 1/3 RPM disc featuring three spots (one 60-second, one 30-second and one 20-second) for the Stewart film. It was issued at about the same time as the film, which was released December 15, 1965. Stewart's voice is not heard on any of the spots.

Fool's Parade

The film was released on August 18, 1981, and a one-sided 7-inch vinyl transcription disc (C-Fools) with four generic radio spots was issued at the same time by Columbia Pictures. The disc had just four spots — one of each length, 60-second, 30-second, 20-second, and 10-second. Jimmy Stewart's voice is not heard on any of the spots.

Glenn Miller Story

This 12-inch disc (SP — 1378) was issued for the 1959 re-release of the film. There are eleven different spots — four one minute in length, three 30-second spots and two which ran approximately 20-seconds each. Some of Stewart's film dialogue is used on five of the tracks.

The Greatest Show on Earth

This is a 1-sided, 12-inch, 33 1/3 RPM disc (Suski No. 32). It was issued at about the same time the film went into general release in May of 1952. Nine different spots appear on the disc. Stewart's voice is not on any of the spots, although Cecil B. DeMille himself voices three of them.

The Man Who Shot Liberty Valance

The Man Who Shot Liberty Valance was released in the United States on April 22, 1962. This 12-inch disc was issued at about the same time to be used by theater owners to place ads on local radio stations. There were a total of 12 spots on the one-sided record: three spots each at 60-seconds, 30-seconds, 20-seconds and 10-seconds. Stewart and co-star John Wayne are both heard in sound clips from the film on the second of the 60-second spots. Liberty Valance (Lee Marvin) is heard on the third 60-second spot. The first six spots feature clips of Gene Pitney's hit record, *The Man Who Shot Liberty Valance*.

Rare Breed

This 7-inch transcription disc (CPM 7-122) played at 45 RPM and was released at the same time as the film on April 13, 1966, by Universal Pictures. The disc was issued on red vinyl. It featured six radio spots for the film — two 60-second spots, two 30-second spots, and two 20-second spots. All of the spots featured Jimmy Stewart dialogue from the film.

Shenandoah

When *Shenandoah* was released on June 3, 1965, a special 7-inch transcription record (CPM 7-108) containing seven commercials advertising the film was also released by Universal Pictures. It was issued on red vinyl and played at 45 RPM. Most radio stations would then transfer a spot, or spots, to a tape cartridge to be played on the air. Some of the records have survived. The *Shenandoah* record contained four 60-second spots, two 30-second spots and one 20-second spot. All spots are generic and only the third 60-second spot has Jimmy Stewart on it in the form of some dialogue from the film.

RADIO COMMERCIALS FOR PRODUCTS

Stewart did very little work as far as radio commercials were concerned. He had done a promo for his own series, *The Six Shooter*, in 1954 (see *The Six Shooter* section for more details on this), but only two commercial spots have been verified.

Campbell's Soup Company

In 1988, Stewart became the spokesman for Campbell's "Home Cookin" Soups Campaign. The spots were produced by the Batten, Barton, Durstine and Osborn Advertising Company of New York City and, at first, were aired only on the radio. As the company received more and more calls for people asking if the spokesman was actually Jimmy Stewart, they decided to also produce TV spots. However, like the radio spots, Stewart was never seen; the viewers only heard his voice. Appearing in those TV commercials was child actress Thora Birch.

American Gas Association
Lennen & Newell, Inc. R1448 (1959)

In 1959, Gloria and Jimmy (Jimmie on the record label) recorded two commercials for the American Gas Association; one for Gold Star Ranges and one for gas refrigerators. Two copies of each commercial were pressed on 12-inch, 33 1/3 RPM records and mailed to radio stations for play during the Christmas season. In addition, Gloria and Jimmy also appeared in print ads for the Gas Association:

The Gold Star Range commercial went like this:

ANNOUNCER: In their home in Southern California, here are Gloria and James Stewart.

GLORIA: Hi there.

JIMMY: Hello. You know, I've just made an amazing discovery. I'm a pretty good cook.

GLORIA: A very good cook.

JIMMY: Well actually, the reason for my new talent is this gas range Gloria and I gave ourselves for Christmas.

GLORIA: It's one of those beautiful new gas ranges that does almost everything all by itself.

JIMMY: Yeah, well that's the secret of my success. This range is so automatic, I can't do anything wrong. Maybe you've seen the kind of range we're talking about; it has a Gold Star on it.

GLORIA: That means it's a gas range built to the new Gold Star standards, with at least 28 wonderful cooking conveniences.

JIMMY: Everything lights automatically. There's a top burner that controls flame so food can't burn. And this range has an automatic griddle, a meat thermometer and a rotisserie that bastes and well, it's just wonderful.

GLORIA: There are many gas ranges built to the new Gold Star standard...see them at your gas company or dealer.

JIMMY: It'll be the most wonderful Christmas present your family's ever had.

The gas refrigerator commercial had Gloria doing more of the talking.

ANNOUNCER: In their beautiful Southern California home, here are Gloria and James Stewart.

GLORIA: Hello.

JIMMY: Hi. It's fascinating, it's absolutely fascinating.

GLORIA: Jimmy's talking about the ice maker in our new RCA Whirlpool gas refrigerator.

JIMMY: It's just wonderful.

Print ad from the December 3, 1959, edition of the Forest Park Review, *Forest Park, IL.*

GLORIA: Wonderful because it's the reason we don't have any ice tray troubles anymore.

JIMMY: Gloria's right, in fact we don't even have any ice trays.

GLORIA: That's because our new refrigerator makes and serves ice cubes automatically, then stores them for us in a handy server.

JIMMY: Well you've just never seen anything like it. You take out a few cubes and before you know it, that RCA Whirlpool gas refrigerator has made you a new batch of cubes; even the water's supplied automatically. It's just fascinating.

GLORIA: I like its other virtues too; automatic defrost, permanent silence and a 10-year warranty on the cooling system.

JIMMY: Now you just can't beat a thing like that; and what a wonderful Christmas present.

GLORIA: An RCA Whirlpool gas refrigerator just like ours.

JIMMY: See your gas company or dealer right away. Give your family a wonderful Christmas present.

FILM INTERVIEWS

To help promote new films, Stewart often was interviewed. The interviews were then pressed onto records and sent to radio stations. The interviews could be one of two types. They could be regular interviews with someone asking questions and Stewart answering them. Or, they could be open-end interviews. Here only Stewart's answers were on the disc. A local disc jockey could then voice the questions (a script was usually provided with the discs), thus personalizing the interview and the station which was using it.

Bend of the River — Open-End Interview

This is a 12-inch 33 1/3 RPM red vinyl disc featuring an open-ended interview with Stewart to promote the film *Bend of the River*. The film was released February 13, 1952, and the interview was scheduled to be played no earlier than one week before the film opened. The interview ran about 6:25. The B-side of the record is blank. Here are Mr. Stewart's answers to the questions posed by the "interviewer."

OK, I'll be glad to.

Well, thanks a lot and believe me I'm very pleased. I guess I've been lucky in getting good roles in very well-written pictures.

Yeah, well it sounds like I've been pretty busy. I...I...I like keeping busy though. I feel that an actor is like anyone else...If his wares are put on the shelf they get a little rusty.

Well, personally, I like a good variety...more interesting and from a career standpoint, variety makes anyone more alert. I like comedy, a good love story, drama, whimsy, and I'd like to do one good Western a year like Bend of the River. I feel they have a great, universal appeal.

Well, starting with current events, the twins, Judy and Kelly. They really amaze me every day with their antics. They're not identical, you know, and their personalities are entirely different. Just enjoys everything and everybody, but Kelly takes a little convincing.

Well, they've been very manly about the whole thing. They...they're pleased that Gloria and I were considerate enough to ah...arrange that each one of them could have one sister.

Well, yes and no. But with Gloria I have a perfect golfing companion. She's...ah...almost as enthusiastic about it as I am. As a matter of fact, she usually gets a lower score than I do.

I give her a little handicap, of course. The accordion, that's in the garage and as for the piano, well, I play the same two songs...Ragtime Cowboy Joe.

A Technicolor picture for Universal-International entitled Bend of the River. And...ah...I sort of think folks are really gonna enjoy this one.

Well, there's Arthur Kennedy and lovely Julia Adams, newcomer Rock Hudson and loveable old-timer Stepin Fetchit. It's a really, really good cast.

You sure are right. About a hundred and fifty of us, accompanied by about twelve truckloads of equipment left Hollywood for about five weeks for Mount Hood, Oregon, and the Columbia River, in order to shoot the picture.

That's right, yes.

Fine, huh. Well, yes, in a way, but ah, in a way not. I don't...I'd... I'd say the role of the pioneer guide in Bend of the River was a very demanding one and...ah...well...I...I...I'd just say that we all worked very hard on this picture.

Well, let...let me give you a rough idea of some of the things Tony Mann had us do. Tony Mann, that's the director. Besides which, I spent two days fist fighting with a character actor 8,000 feet up on the side of a mountain. And let me tell you, it's mighty hard fighting in the air...

when the air gets…the air gets very thin up there. And then, I had to cross over the steep slopes of Mount Hood on horseback and wagon, crawl through the roaring rapids of the river and then had a knockdown drag-out battle right in the…right in the water with Arthur Kennedy. I, ah, I don't know…this was…this wasn't exactly a vacation. I wore out six pairs of trousers during the location shoot.

The picture relates the adventures of a group of pioneers who travel west along the famed Oregon Trail to settle in the unconquered portion of our country — he great northwest. I'm with the group as their leader and I help them reach their destination after fighting off Indians, renegade whites and the treacherous climate.

That's not the story, that's only the start of it. After we reach our destination, we discover that our food supplies have been held up in Portland. So I head that way to find out what the trouble is. Once there, I find it necessary to steal the supplies we paid for and to start heading toward our camp again only to run into more trouble than you can imagine. How I make the trip back is actually the story of Bend of the River.

Well, yes, with attractive Julia Adams in the cast, yes. But, ah…of course, not enough to ruin the picture for the men, you see.

Fine and thanks for letting me guest with you today, I've really enjoyed it.

Be glad to. So long.

The Glenn Miller Story — Open-End Interview

This interview was released to radio stations by Universal-International in two formats — a 12-inch 33 1/3 RPM red vinyl disc and a 7-inch 45 RPM red vinyl disc (DCLA 1337). Both discs carried a request to "Please hold for playing one week prior to picture release in your town." Side one is an open-end interview with Jimmy Stewart running just over 4-and-a-half minutes, while June Allyson appears on side two. The film went into general release in the U.S. on December 10, 1953. Stewart's answer bands are as follows.

The campaign booklet issued for the film even had a small ad telling that these discs were available.

Cue sheets were also issued with the discs. These had the questions for the local disc jockey to read and then play the record for Stewart's answer. The cue sheet also offered this bit of advice — "May we suggest that if time permits you rehearse this interview with earphones so that you secure the proper timing. Your cooperation is appreciated." Here's how the interview went.

ANNOUNCER: As our guest today we are privileged to talk with one of Hollywood's least talkative citizens — Jimmy Stewart. Few performers in Hollywood achieve stardom, fewer still achieve stature as well as stardom, and modest self-effacing Jimmy Stewart is one of them. Perhaps during this interview you will understand why Jimmy Stewart has remained on the Hollywood scene as one of the stars' favorite stars. Hello, Jimmy... and a real warm welcome.

STEWART: Thank you, it's a great pleasure to be here.

ANNOUNCER: Jimmy, I know one thing that's happened in that — well, twenty-five years, isn't it, since you first went to Hollywood?

STEWART: That's about it.

ANNOUNCER: Your billing is still James Stewart, but does anybody ever call you James — isn't it Jim or Jimmy pretty much all of the time?

STEWART: Yes, I don't know exactly how to answer when somebody says James to me. But I've noticed that lately, even on the billing, they usually change it to Jimmy. That's much better than an old school teacher of mine... she used to call me Jamie. I'm glad I didn't get tagged with that moniker.

ANNOUNCER: Well, we'll stick to Jimmy, and if I'm not mistaken, you started your film career in about 1935 with M-G-M. Do you remember the title of your first picture?

STEWART: *The Murder Man*, M-G-M. Spencer Tracy, Virginia Bruce. I played a newspaper man. If you winked, you missed me in that one. When I was brought out, the producer said well, of course, we can't use this man because the man that plays the part in the script is named "Shorty," and we can't have this tall, string bean playing it. Somebody suggested that they change the name in the script. Well this caused well sort of a disaster all through the office that they just didn't do it, they kept the name "Shorty" and I played the part and they called me "Shorty" which I guess is all right.

ANNOUNCER: I'm sure it was, Jimmy, because what happened to your career after that is motion picture history. We've heard some wonderful reports about your Technicolor picture, *The Glenn Miller Story*, in which you play the role of Glenn Miller, and June Allyson plays your wife. I noticed in your biography that you play the accordion and also the piano. How do you rate yourself as a musician?

STEWART: Well, now, there are several schools of thought on that.

ANNOUNCER: Well, let's hear about them.

STEWART: Well, the one school was sort of my school. I sort of used to fancy myself as an accordion player. I think probably it took a world war to convince me that I wasn't so hot as an accordion player because when I got back out of the Army, I found that I…shall we say, don't dig it anymore. But, it's still down in the basement and I try it out every once in a while for the kids, but I haven't been too successful. The piano is the same thing, as a matter of fact, my mother taught me a couple of tunes in the key of C when I was a very small boy and I've been getting away with that for quite a while.

ANNOUNCER: Well, those instruments weren't too much assistance in your portrayal of Glenn Miller.

STEWART: No, no, this is a trombone.

ANNOUNCER: When we see *The Glenn Miller Story*, Jimmy, will the sounds we hear issuing forth from the trombone be you playing the instrument?

STEWART: No, the sounds won't. The piece of music itself is recorded before the picture starts and then the orchestra plays to that playback. They got a very fine trombone player that could play the pieces of music that Glenn played. I'll play to the playback, but we found that it's…ah… much less nerve wracking if I just stop-up the mouthpiece of my trombone and just make like I'm playing.

ANNOUNCER: If that's the case, then I know you put a lot of time and effort into perfecting your movements to make the role convincing. Jimmy, there's just one more question before you leave — I watched you and your wife make your joint television debut on Jack Benny's program. I was wondering if Mrs. Stewart has any aspirations for a movie career?

STEWART: No, she loved doing that Jack Benny program and sort of fitted in so well, that I was very proud of her that day. As a matter of fact, it was sort of embarrassing because I remember right before we went on, I sort of got Gloria in a corner and I said now this is your first time and everything and there's a thing in acting we call timing. Now you have quite a problem here because it's a comedy show. So when I say the lines and the people laugh, I want you to keep quiet and not talk over the laugh. Well, it was rather embarrassing because I said the lines and nobody laughed. The only timing that has to be done was me stepping on the laughs Gloria got.

ANNOUNCER: Jimmy, that's a wonderful story to end this interview with, and we'll certainly be looking forward to seeing you and June Allyson co-starring in Universal-International's Technicolor biography of the great bandleader, *The Glenn Miller Story*. It was a real pleasure having you on the show, Jimmy Stewart.

STEWART: Thank you, thank very much.

Harvey Open-End Interview
UR-150616 (1950)

This 12-inch, 1-sided, 33 1/3 RPM, red vinyl disc was issued to radio stations by Universal-International. The disc carries a request to "Please hold for playing one week prior to picture release in your town." The film went into general release in the U.S. on October 13, 1950. Stewart's answer bands are as follows.

STEWART 1: (Knocking and door opening) Thank you, we will.

STEWART 2: Who's going to leave right now if you don't drop this mister business.

STEWART 3: Who, Harvey? No…no…no, he's not late. Why he's right here sitting next to me.

STEWART 4: He's right here with me.

STEWART 5: Uh huh…well, he's here.

STEWART 6: No, I'm afraid not. He's got a bad case of laryngitis right now and can't talk above a whisper.

STEWART 7: Well, why don't you ask me what you want to know and I'll do my best to give you the answers.

STEWART 8: Well, it was back in 1947, in the Broadway comedy hit which was named after him. And, Frank Fay, the leading man, decided to take a vacation for a few weeks and Harvey consented to my taking over the role of Elwood P. Dowd. I did the same thing for a few weeks in 1948 and after that I didn't see Harvey for quite a while, until he came out here to Hollywood to star in the motion picture version of the play.

STEWART 9: It sure is. Yes sir. I've been in films for some time now and no one has ever thought of making a film named Jimmy Stewart. But, then you have to realize that Harvey isn't like any other star. He's…he's…ah…he's quite unusual.

STEWART 10: Well, Harvey was born in the carrot patch section of St. Louis, Missouri.

STEWART 11: Well, ah…Harvey's quite a gourmet. Among his favorite foods are carrots and hearts of lettuce, Brussel sprouts a la Louis the

Sixteenth. His pet aversions are rabbit stew and people who carry rabbit's legs as good luck charms. He...he carries a chicken foot himself.

STEWART 12: Hmmmm...let me think now...just a minute, I'll...I'll ask him. Oh...oh...oh yeah well, oh well, that's right, Harvey, I almost forgot.

STEWART 13: Well, certainly, didn't you hear him?

STEWART 14: Well, he did. And he said his favorite hobbies are dancing the bunny hug, the cabbage patch stomp and the Lindy hop.

STEWART 15: He certainly does. Film town really gave him the red carpet treatment. After all, you...you have to remember that Harvey was quite a star in his own right even before he went to work for Universal-International Pictures. How many other personalities can you mention who have played on Broadway for more than five years and received more than 10 different awards, including the Pulitzer Prize? And, who's broken box-office records in New York City and San Francisco, Los Angeles, St. Louis, London, Spain, Peru, Ecuador, Brazil and is presently being besieged with offers to appear in Greece, Israel, France and Belgium.

STEWART 16: Well, they...they gave him his own dressing room, his own make-up artist, even reserved a chair for him in the studio commissary.

STEWART 17: Well, in a way...in a way. I'm...ah...I'm sure he won't mind me saying so, but Harvey is a great scene stealer. Well, no...no...no...yes you are, Harvey. Now...now...now, don't deny it.

STEWART 18: Well, as Elwood P. Dowd, I portray a man who a lot of people think has quite an imagination.

STEWART 19: Oh, Josephine Hull, Victoria Horne, Peggy Dow, Cecil Kellaway, Charles Drake.

STEWART 20: No...No, I don't think so.

STEWART 21: Oh, they claim that Harvey doesn't exist, that he's just in my imagination. Now...now, that's pretty silly, isn't it? You know as well as I do that Harvey exists because you can see him right here in this room, can't you?

STEWART 22: Well, well, you...well you can, can't you?

STEWART 23: He's six feet three and one half inches tall and with long ears and he's dressed in white fur.

STEWART 24: What...what do you mean, for what?

STEWART 25: He's dressed in white fur...f-u-r...rabbit fur.

STEWART 26: No, not exactly, he's a pookah.

STEWART 27: Well, it's...it's...ah...ah...oh...pardon me just a minute. Hum...Oh, ah...uh-hah...oh, all right, Harvey...ah...now? I see... uh-hah. I'm...I'm awfully sorry, but you'll have to excuse us. Harvey says he isn't feeling very well.

STEWART 28: Thank you, and on behalf of Harvey and myself, may I say the best to you and yours. Come on, Harvey.

Metro-Goldwyn-Mayer Air View — Carbine Williams
M-G-M — 12 — 45 (1952)

This is a 12-inch, 33 1/3 RPM transcribed interview disc, marked as being from Howard Strickling, Publicity Director of M-G-M Studios. Side one features questions posed by Dick Simmons and answered by Jimmy Stewart and David Marshall ("Carbine") Williams, the inventor of the rifle for which the film was named. Side two is an open-end interview, with Dick Simmons' questions left off. The local deejay could then ask the questions and play the answer tracks, making it appear that the interview was being done locally. The original disc came with a cue sheet so the local deejay would know what questions to ask and when the interviewee was finished answering that question. Here is the entire script.

SIMMONS: Hello, folks, this is your Hollywood reporter, Dick Simmons, again, bringing you today one of Hollywood's most popular celebrities. He's a tall, lanky fellow whom you've doubtlessly seen many times on screen. Such favorite pictures as *The Philadelphia Story*, *It's a Wonderful Life*, *The Stratton Story*, *Harvey* and *The Greatest Show on Earth*. And that adds up, of course, to Jimmy Stewart. Welcome, Jimmy.

STEWART: Thank you. Mighty glad you ask me along. Yeah, this is the first chance I've had to relax in weeks.

SIMMONS: Yes, I understand you've really been busy of late, Jimmy. Ah, but you must get time to relax around the house.

STEWART: Oh, you mean you haven't heard about my twin daughters, Judy and Kelly? Now, there's not much relaxing done around home these days.

SIMMONS: Well, Jimmy, we're glad to give you a chance to sit back and take it easy. That is, as long as you keep talking about yourself.

STEWART: Now, ah, wait a minute. I wasn't exactly aiming to talk about myself.

SIMMONS: No?

STEWART: No, I'd sorta like to tell you about another fellow. A fellow, I don't know, I'd say he's just about the most amazing man I've ever met.

SIMMONS: Who's that, Jimmy?

STEWART: A fellow named David Marshall Williams — probably one of the most famous gun inventors since Browning. I imagine you've heard about the Army carbine. That lightweight rifle our boys found so handy during World War II.

SIMMONS: Certainly. It's a mighty friendly weapon to the G.I.s in Korea right now, too.

STEWART: It sure is, and they can thank Marsh Williams for it. You see, among his inventions — he holds 68 U.S. patents — is one that became a basic principle of the carbine. But there's something more remarkable about Marsh than his success as an inventor. Something that goes much deeper — it has to do, well, I guess it has to do with what he has accomplished within himself.

SIMMONS: Well, just what do you mean, Jimmy?

STEWART: Well, today Marsh is a respected citizen. And it's very hard to believe that once he was convicted of killing a man.

SIMMONS: That is startling. When did it happen?

STEWART: Well, it was back in Prohibition days in North Carolina, where Marsh was born and raised. There was a law against it, but Marsh and a lot of other folks didn't seem to think that it was wrong to operate a still. The woods were full of them making moonshine whiskey. Well, one day there was a raid on Marsh's still and a federal agent was killed. Nobody knew who shot at what, but it was Marsh who was held responsible.

SIMMONS: And convicted?

STEWART: Yes, of second-degree murder. He was just 20 years old at the time. He was sentenced to 30 years — 30 of the best years of a man's life.

SIMMONS: I'm beginning to see what has impressed you so much. Almost any man would have been licked right there, but apparently he wasn't.

STEWART: No, he sure wasn't. Even in leg irons on a chain gang Marsh's character stood out. So much so, that a warden allowed him to design a revolutionary new gun, build it, and even test fire it while in prison. Now you know that warden must have had a tremendous faith in him.

SIMMONS: He certainly must have. But, tell me, did Williams stay in prison the full 30 years?

STEWART: No, he was granted a full pardon by the Governor of North Carolina after some eight years. The interest in his new gun unquestionably helped to gain his freedom, but he owes a lot to his wife, Maggie, too. She stuck loyally by him throughout all his trouble… never stopped fighting for a review of his case. Theirs, incidentally, is quite a love story.

SIMMONS: Sounds like it. Jimmy, maybe I should put in a word here to explain how it happens that you know so much about this man. The M-G-M Studios in Hollywood, it seems, were as impressed as you have been…and so now have just completed the motion picture *Carbine Williams*. Based on his own story and, of course, you were picked to portray him on the screen. You know, Jim, that must have been a strange experience for Mr. Williams watching you reenact events out of his life.

STEWART: Well, now, I kind of figured after you heard something about Marsh, you'd want to meet him and find out how he felt about it, so I took the liberty of asking him along. Marsh, come on in here. Folks, this is Marsh Williams.

WILLIAMS: Hello, Jimmy.

SIMMONS: Mr. Williams, we've been hearing part of your incredible story from Mr. Stewart. Must have seemed quite surprising to you to be in Hollywood watching it unfold again right in front of your eyes.

WILLIAMS: Well, I'll tell you…after a man does time, it gets so that there's very little surprises him. Of course, I'll have to admit it was satisfying.

SIMMONS: In what way, Mr. Williams?

WILLIAMS: I guess that goes back to why I wanted the picture made in the first place. You see, I have a son David, he's 13. I've made my mistakes in the past, but I don't want them to ever crop up in the boy's future. I can figure if everybody knows my whole story, there's nothing going to hurt the boy.

SIMMONS: Mr. Williams, it strikes me that not every man, particularly a man with a prison record in his past, would reveal his story as you have done…even with such a fine purpose. You're to be congratulated.

WILLIAMS: Well, like I said, I made my mistakes. But as long as a man is willing to try to make something of himself, he'll find there are people willing to help him…people who will have faith in him and be willing to let the present speak for itself. That's a great thing about this country we live in.

STEWART: Well, Marsh, that's a simple philosophy, but it's a pretty wonderful one. It should give heart to a lot of folks…the ones down on their luck and feeling the world's got them buffaloed.

SIMMONS: I'm sure it will — and, Jimmy Stewart, thanks for bringing Marsh Williams along with you. And thanks to both of you for a most interesting chat. You know I've heard, Jimmy, that you give another one of your top performances in Metro-Goldwyn-Mayer's *Carbine Williams*, as do Jean Hagen and Wendell Corey. We'll be looking forward to seeing it as a picture that promises something…well, really out of the ordinary. Thanks a lot, fellows and come back again, will you.

Metro-Goldwyn-Mayer Air View — The Stratton Story
M-G-M 27597/27598 (1949)

This 12-inch disc plays at 78 RPM. Side one features the Dick Simmons' questions and Stewart's answers. Side two has just Stewart's answers only, so that local DJs could ask the questions themselves and then play Jimmy's answers, thus making it sound as though they were doing the actual interview. The date, March 29, 1949, is etched into the run-off area of the record. The film wasn't released until early June of that year (late May in New York City), so the interview appears to have been done after the film was completed, but before it went into general release in the U.S.

SIMMONS: Hello, folks, this is your Hollywood reporter, Dick Simmons, back on an M-G-M soundstage once again. You know, if we were running one of those radio guessing games, we scarcely could hope to fool you with our guest today. His drawling voice is unmistakable. Likewise, is this description of him: He's the motion picture star who won an Academy Award in *The Philadelphia Story*. His latest is a picture we've heard called one the best of the year — Metro-Goldwyn-Mayer's *The Stratton Story*. It's a pleasure, Jimmy Stewart, to have you here, so come on, climb aboard, and tell us all about yourself.

STEWART: Well, you seem to have covered the subject pretty well.

SIMMONS: Oh no, there's plenty left to tell about Jimmy Stewart. Your experiences in the Air Force, your life in Hollywood, your work, anything, anything you'd like.

STEWART: Anything I like, huh, well that makes it easier. I'd like to tell you about a man, and I'd say it's talking about myself, too. I spent several months being this fella.

SIMMONS: Well, it sounds like you're running a guessing contest. Who is this man?

STEWART: Well, you mentioned *The Stratton Story* a moment ago. Well, it's about a man, a real-life living man named Monty Stratton. About as regular and courageous guy I've ever met.

SIMMONS: He was a Chicago White Sox baseball star, wasn't he?

STEWART: Yes, until fate struck him about as cruel a blow as could happen to an athlete. You'll probably remember how, back in 1938, a hunting accident took away his right leg. And, it probably cost him a chance at baseball's Hall of Fame, he was that good.

SIMMONS: And that's the story you put on the screen?

STEWART: Well, that's part of it. Monty's story goes way beyond that. You see, it really begins when he was a big, awkward Texas boy with one great love, baseball. It led him to give up the security of his farm and gamble with the strange life in the big city. That's one story about Monty. Now, there's another. This one's about his love for a girl. From the time they met on a blind date, she became his inspiration. She played a vital part in his remarkable comeback.

SIMMONS: Tell us about that comeback, you know, it sounds like a very dramatic story.

STEWART: It is. It's a story full of excitement and romance, too. Eight years after his accident, encouraged by the girl he loved, he came back to the game he loved.

SIMMONS: And I suppose that's when Hollywood discovered his story. You know, it must have been a thrilling one to make.

STEWART: Yes, and more so because Monty was right there on the set with us every day as our technical advisor.

SIMMONS: Ah...how about the love scenes with June Allyson? Did he advise you on those, too?

STEWART: (laughs) Ah...no...no. When June and I came to those, Monty just sort of disappeared. I asked him about it later, as a matter of fact, and he said he didn't figure he could be of any help in the romance department. But I'll tell you, I'll tell you where he did give me some advice — and I needed June's advice, too — even with the kidding she gave me about it.

SIMMONS: Where was that, Jim?

STEWART: Well, in the picture, we show the first of Monty's two sons, Monty Jr., when he was eight months old and then again when he was about 18 months old. Now that...that meant two babies in the picture and each one had a twin working as his stand-in, you see. Now a situation like that can be mighty rough on a bachelor, believe me. Between babies and baseball, I had my troubles. I think I made fewer errors on the diamond, though.

SIMMONS: Does that mean that maybe you'll be giving up acting for a career in the national pastime?

STEWART: Ahh...no. Gee, I still get nightmares every time I think of pitching to Bill Dickey. Now...now I know why Monty calls him the toughest man he ever pitched against in the majors. An then...and then there's another fella named Gene Bearden. You know, he's only the hero of last year's World Series. I had to bat against him.

SIMMONS: That sounds like a tough spot for an actor or a baseball player, how'd you make out?

STEWART: Hmmm...glad you ask that. Well, Dickey...Dickey...I ah...I struck Dickey out. Only took all afternoon to do it, but I struck him out. And...and Bearden, well, the game was hanging in the balance, the winning runs were on base and, well I just came up and got a clean hit. Of course I only missed a dozen pitches before I connected, but got a clean hit.

SIMMONS: Well, Jimmy, that sounds as though you had a lot of fun, plus an exciting and unusual experience in bringing Monty Stratton and his remarkable story to the screen. Now we'll be looking forward to seeing you and June Allyson in *The Stratton Story*. And, say, will you drop around again? The welcome sign is always out there swinging in the breeze for Jimmy Stewart.

STEWART: Thank you very much. It's been a pleasure.

Rare Breed — Interview
Universal Pictures 555 (1966)

The complete title is Universal Pictures Presents Interview-Specials with the Stars of *The Rare Breed*. This 10-inch disc plays at 33 1/3 RPM. One side of the record features Dick Strout, Hollywood Commentator, conducting two interviews — one with Stewart and one with Maureen O'Hara. The other side has the same two stars and their answers as open-end interviews. Their answers are on the disc, but not Strout's questions. Local announcers could thus make it sound as if they were doing the interviewing. A script with the questions for local announcers to ask was included with the disc.

STROUT: Universal Studios has brought to the screen a uniquely stirring drama of the old west, *The Rare Breed*, starring Jimmy Stewart and Maureen O'Hara. And we're honored today to have Mr. Stewart as our special in-person guest. Welcome to our mic. It's certainly a pleasure to have you here again.

STEWART: Thank you very much.

STROUT: You've seen Westerns and action pictures come and go for quite a few years now. I understand *The Rare Breed* stacks up with some of the best. Would you agree?

STEWART: Well, we think this is a good, big...ah...action picture. Ah, that's what we started out to make. Ah, sort of the theory...ah...a lot of people have about making...ah...Westerns, making the outdoor action picture, is to try to get a good, plausible story. The story can be rather an intimate story. And then to place this intimate story, a good personal story, in front of the big, massive background...ah...of the west...of the old west. And we think we've done that in *The Rare Breed*. Photography is very important in a picture like this and...ah...I think that you'll find that the photography in this picture is something special. Ah...as I say, we started to make a...a big, boisterous action Western and I think...ah...I think that's what we got.

STROUT: And you've got Maureen O'Hara, too, which is also something special. Is it true that you're wearing the same costume in this picture that you wore in *Winchester '73*, and in several Westerns since?

STEWART: Pretty much...pretty much the same outfit. I had to change hats this time. This wasn't voluntary...ah...but the reason I had to change hats is because the old hat, that I had worn in...in every Western I've been in for years and years, just started to come apart. Ah...it wasn't a very good hat to start with...ah...and it had seen a good bit of service before...ah...I started wearing it way back in *Winchester '73*, oh that's... mmm...10–12–15 years ago. Ah...so the poor thing just...ah...what with all the sweat, the beating and the stepping on that it took, it just...ah... threw in the sponge. As far as the chaps and the shirt and the boots... ah...they're the same.

STROUT: I know the story of *The Rare Breed* concerns the Hereford breed of cattle which came over from England. Now what about the ladies who came over from England with the Herefords...Maureen O'Hara and Juliet Mills...do they have as much impact on you as the cattle do in the picture?

STEWART: Yes, that's a part of the personal story, the intimate story that I was talking about a little bit ago. Maureen O'Hara and Haley Mills' sister, Juliet Mills, are...ah...mother and daughter. And they come over from England with a few of the Polled Herefords to introduce into this country. Now, this is founded on fact...ah...this actually happened right back several years after the Civil War, when the west was being...ah... settled and when there were these enormous...ah...cattle ranches in the southwest part of the country. And...ah...this is the story we...we try to tell here. These two very proper English women...ah...introducing Polled Hereford cattle to a bunch of wild cowboys...ah...and sort of getting subjected to the wild west as we know it.

STROUT: And you've got a couple of formidable antagonists in the picture: Brian Keith, the ranch baron who's got his eye on Maureen O'Hara, and Jack Elam, who is out to do you in if he can. Elam has tried to do away with you in several of your pictures, hasn't he?

STEWART: Yes, Jack's been out after me for quite a while. Ah…well back in 1953, there was one called *The Far Country* and another one called *Night Passage* a few years later than that. And, we've been in several other pictures. Jack is a wonderful heavy, has a great face and a…a great, sort of menace…ah…he's a…he's an awful good actor…awful good in…in the part of the Western bad man.

STROUT: As Jimmy Stewart continues to be awfully good in the part of the Western good guy…especially in *The Rare Breed*, which we're certainly going to see before the week is out. Mr. Stewart, our thanks to you for dropping by. As always, it's a pleasure, indeed, to have had you on our show.

STEWART: Thank you.

STROUT: James Stewart, star of Universal Studio's *The Rare Breed*. And this has been Dick Strout reporting from Hollywood, returning you to our main studios.

Universal Pictures Presents
"Interview-Specials" with the Stars of Shenandoah

Garrison System Ltd., Beverly Hills, CA, serving 2500 stations worldwide, released this special disc simultaneously with the release of the film. The 12-inch, 2-sided transcription disc (U-565-USA) played at 33 1/3 RPM. The record was pressed on red vinyl.

The A-side (375) featured complete interviews with three of the film's stars — James Stewart, Doug McClure and Rosemary Forsyth. Each was interviewed by Hollywood commentator, Dick Strout. The interviews run about 5 minutes each. Both Strout's questions and the star's answers can be heard.

The B-side (376) features open-end interviews with the same three stars. In other words, Dick Strout's voice has been edited from the interview. Scripts were provided with the disc so that a local commentator could read the questions and then the star's answer could be played, thus making it seem as if the local commentator was actually talking with the celebrity.

Here is a transcript of the Jimmy Stewart open-end interview.

ANNOUNCER: One of the all-time motion picture greats and a five-time Academy Award nominee, having won the coveted Oscar once, our special interview guest today is that fine actor and fine gentleman, Jimmy Stewart. Mr. Stewart, welcome to our microphone.

STEWART: Well, thank you very much. It's a great pleasure for me to be here.

ANNOUNCER: You have a wonderful new picture showing in theaters throughout the country. It's Universal Studios' fine Civil War adventure-drama, *Shenandoah*. And it's your 67th major movie, I understand! After 67 of them do you still enjoy making movies, or has it become a chore?

STEWART: No, I consider myself very fortunate. I still like my work. I always have. Making motion pictures has a tremendous fascination. I think it's a worthwhile profession. And I consider myself very fortunate to have been connected with it for the last 30 years.

ANNOUNCER: A real tribute to the industry and to the profession. Mr. Stewart, the critics are saying that your role in *Shenandoah* is one of the very finest roles, and one of the most moving character portrayals in many years. What's your own feeling about the picture?

STEWART: I think the story itself is a tremendous story. It might be interesting to the audience to know that it's an original story. It seems to me that in the last, oh, 5–10 years, the motion picture story has so many times not been original. It's been taken from a novel, from a book, but *Shenandoah* is an original by James Barrett, a young fellow. He sat down and wrote this story for the motion picture. I think this is a great asset and I hope that this can be a sort of a start of a trend toward more original motion picture stories.

ANNOUNCER: Well, certainly, the medium deserves original material. You've become noted for giving opportunity to young actors and actresses as well as to original and creative writers. And your movie, *Shenandoah*, is a case in point. You have some of Hollywood's younger generation in it, don't you?

STEWART: Yeah, we kept saying that this is sort of a father-son deal. Tim McIntire is one of my sons, who, of course, is the son of John McIntire, famous for the *Wagon Train* series. The director of the picture, Andrew McLagen, is the son of Victor McLagen, one of the all-time great stars. Pat Wayne, son of my very good friend Duke Wayne, is another one of my sons in the picture. Another young and very, very promising young woman Rosemary Forsyth, who had come out from New York, plays my daughter. A charming actress and I think has a tremendous future.

ANNOUNCER: After 67 pictures and 30 years, most of them as a top star, you've reached the very pinnacle of your profession. Where does a Jimmy Stewart go from here?

STEWART: I, I've never really looked at it that way. I've never really felt that this idea of arriving…I feel that this business is such that you really never arrive. The work is never done. This is a craft and I feel that my responsibility from here on out is to work at my craft and to do the best I can.

ANNOUNCER: What about the popular recognition that comes with stardom? I hear that on location for *Shenandoah* the townspeople showered you with gifts. Everything from blueberry pie to arrowheads.

STEWART: The whole idea of people coming up…maybe they don't have blueberry pie or arrowheads, maybe they just come up and say hello and say I don't know whether this means anything to you, but I've seen a lot of your pictures and I think that's fine. And I always say to them well I want to tell you how much it means to me. It means everything to me. And it does. This is one of the tremendously rewarding things about the picture business and about this business of being in the movies and being movie actors. I can't express what great satisfaction this gives me. What a tremendous thrill it is.

ANNOUNCER: Makes for a good feeling for us fans to know that our recognition has meaning for you. Jimmy Stewart, as always it's been a unique pleasure having you visit with us. Thank you so much for dropping by today, and we'll be looking forward to seeing you in *Shenandoah*.

STEWART: Thank you, it was a pleasure.

The final disc included here is not, strictly speaking, an interview recording, but is included here because it was recorded to help promote a film and is about the same length as most of the film interviews.

Presenting James Stewart & Jane Wyman in "Blow-Ups" from Magic Town HD7-MC-238 (1947)

This is a special, limited edition 12-inch, 78 RPM disc sent to radio stations in 1947 at the time of the film's release. It could be used as a "filler" by the stations and ran just under 5 minutes. The disc was also marked "Compliments of Robert Riskin," who had produced the film. The disc is one-sided, with the reverse side stamped with a large "RCA Victor" and the company's dog logo. The remaining space is filled with what look like cobwebs.

The disc begins with Riskin's own introduction:

> *When an actor blows up in his lines, it's not news. But, it is sometimes funny. I've had some blow-ups recorded and if they should fail to send you into convulsions, I hope at least you'll find them of academic interest.*

These are from scenes in Magic Town with Jimmy Stewart and Jane Wyman. My name is Robert Riskin and I wrote and produced Magic Town. Why I should be getting any amusement out of this, I don't know. Every time they muffed a line, it cost money. Oh well. The first few you'll hear are examples of the quiet, "what a dope I am" type of fluff.

Three blow-ups are presented in this section. The first ends with Stewart saying, "Up on your lines" and everyone laughing. In the second, Jane Wyman has a very dramatic reading, but then says, "Some damn thing." Again, everyone breaks into laughter. The third segment has Jimmy talking about firecrackers, but then suddenly adding, "Hello, firecrackers," causing everybody to laugh.

Riskin comes back at this point, saying, "The next two are of the explosive variety. The 'I could kick myself' type of blow-up."

The first has Stewart saying, "I'm all screwed up with this," while, in the second, he says, "What the hell is that line." In both cases, the rest of the cast and crew break into laughter.

Riskin introduces the final segment with "This last one is the longest ad-lib fluff in history."

In this one Jane Wyman tries to recite *Hiawatha* while Stewart is reciting *The Charge of the Light Brigade*. After the first breakdown and restart, Jimmy begins reciting a very distorted version of *The Three Bears* and *Hickory Dickory Dock*:

Once upon an island there were three bears, a mother bear, a father bear and they had 300 children, all boys. And one time they were going through the woods and they came to a great big bathtub full of spaghetti. And the mother bear said, "Children, be careful because whenever you come to a bathtub…hickory dickory dock, the mouse ran up the clock. The clock struck one…lunch."

This caused Wyman to laugh, ending the scene.

Riskin ends the disc by saying, "It can't be that funny. Good Grief, the time and film that was wasted. Now you know what a producer is up against."

This recording was also used, in a slightly edited form, on the album *Academy Award Winners on the Air* (Star-Tone Records ST-215), released in 1979. Also see that entry.

BIBLIOGRAPHY

Audio Classics® Archives *http://www.audio-classics.com*.

Bannerman, R. LeRoy. *On a Note of Triumph: Norman Corwin and the Golden Years of Radio*. New York: Carol Publishing Group, 1986.

BBC Radio 4 Desert Island Discs. *http://www.bbc.co.uk/radio4/features/desert-island-discs*

Benet, Stephen Vincent. *O'Hallorans Luck and Other Short Stories*. New York, Penguin Books, 1944.

Billips, Connie, and Arthur Pierce. *Lux Presents Hollywood*. Jefferson: McFarland & Company, Inc., Publishers, 1995.

Bloom, Ken. *The Complete Film and Musical Companion Volumes 1-2-3*. New York: Facts on File, 1995.

Broderick, Gertrude G. (Preparer). *Catalog of Radio Recordings A Transcription Service for Schools*. Washington, DC: The Federal Radio Education Committee, 1950.

Campbell, Robert. *The Golden Years of Broadcasting*. New York: Charles Scribner's Sons, 1976.

Corwin, Norman. *More by Corwin: 16 Radio Dramas by Norman Corwin*. New York: Henry Holt and Company, 1944.

Daane, Art M. *The Cappy Barra Story*. *http://www.geocities.com/jayvare/cb.pdf*. 2003.

DeLong, Thomas A. *The Mighty Music Box*. Los Angeles: Amber Crest Books, Inc., 1980.

Doolittle, John. *Don McNeill and his Breakfast Club*. Notre Dame, IN: University of Notre Dame Press, 2001.

Dunning, John. *On the Air: The Encyclopedia of Old-Time Radio*. New York: Oxford University Press, 1998.

Goldin, J. David. RadioGOLDINdex. *http://www.radiogoldindex.com*.

Grams, Jr., Martin. *Suspense: Twenty Years of Thrills and Chills*. Kearney: Morris Publishing, 1997.

Grams, Jr., Martin. *The History of the Cavalcade of America*. Kearney: Morris Publishing, 1998.

Grams, Jr., Martin. *Radio Drama*. Jefferson: McFarland & Company, Inc., Publishers, 2000.

Grams, Jr., Martin. "Keep 'Em Rolling: The Exclusive Story of an Obscure Patriotic Program." *Sperdvac Radiogram* 26.6 (August, 2000): 12-14.

Grams, Jr., Martin. *Information, Please*. Albany, GA: BearManor Media, 2003.

Grams, Jr., Martin. "The Edgar Bergen and Charlie McCarthy Show: An Episode Guide and Brief History." The Original Old Time Radio (OTR) WWW Pages. 1994-2007. *http://www.old-time.com*.

Hart, Dennis. *Monitor The Last Great Radio Show.* New York: Writers Club Press, 2002.

Hemingway, Ernest. *The Fifth Column and the First Forty-Nine Stories.* New York: Scribner, 1938.

Hickerson, Jay. *The 3rd Revised Ultimate History of Network Radio Programming and Guide to ALL Circulating Shows.* Hamden: Presto Print II, 2005.

Internet Movie Database (IMDb). *http://www.imdb.com.*

Jerry's Vintage Radio Logs *http://otrsite.com/radiolog/.*

JJ's Newspaper Radio Logs *http://www.jjonz.us/RadioLogs/.*

Lackman, Ron. *Same Time Same Station.* New York: Facts on File, Inc., 1996.

Lackman, Ron. *The Encyclopedia of American Radio.* New York: Facts on File, Inc., 2000.

Laird, Ross. "The Columbia 91000 and 170000 Personal Series." *The E-Discographer. http://www.hensteeth.com.*

Lyons, Leonard. "The Lyons Den." *Oakland Tribune.* 3 February, 1947: 5.

MacDougall, Ranald. "Your Air Forces." *This Is War!.* New York: Dodd, Mead & Company, 1942. 165-189.

McBride, Mary Margaret. *Out of the Air.* New York: Doubleday & Company, Inc., 1960.

MacKenzie, Harry. *Command Performance, USA!: A Discography.* Westport, CT: Greenwood Press, 1996.

MacKenzie, Harry. The Directory of the Armed Forces Radio Service Series. Westport, CT: Greenwood Press, 1999.

Meyers, Barlow. *The Restless Gun.* Racine. Whitman Publishing Company, 1959.

Monitor Tribute Pages <http://www.monitorbeacon.net>.

Mott, Robert L. *Radio Sound Effects.* Jefferson: McFarland & Company, Inc., Publishers, 1993.

Movie-Radio Guide. Vol. 11, No. 23. March 14-20, 1942, pg. 23

"Musical Sidelights from "The Glenn Miller Story." *Down Beat*, February 24, 1954, Vol. 21 — No. 4, pg. 3.

NewspaperARCHIVE.com. *http://www.newspaperarchive.com.*

Oboler, Arch. *Oboler Omnibus.* New York: Duell, Sloan & Pearce, 1945.

Old-Time Radio *http://www.old-time.com/.*

Old Time Radio Researchers Group *http://www.otrr.org/.*

Pairpoint, Lionel. "Bing Crosby — The Radio Directories." *BING Magazine. http://www.bing-magazine.co.uk/*

The Peabody Awards *http://www.peabody.uga.edu/.*

People Magazine. "Lookout: A Guide to the Up and Coming." January 8, 1979.

"The Personality." *Time* (June 30, 1947). *http://www.time.com, http://www.medaloffreedom.com/ JimmyStewart.htm.*

Radio Guide. Vol. 8, No. 22. March 18, 1939, pg. 4.

"Radio, The Personality." *Time.* June 30, 1947.

Scheuer, Steven R. "John Payne to Star in Western Series." *The Troy Record* (Troy, NY) 16 August, 1957: 25.

Settel, Irving. *A Pictorial History of Radio.* New York: Grosset & Dunlap, 1967.

Siegel, Susan and David S. *Radio Scripts in Print.* New York: Book Hunter Press, 2006.

Siegel, Susan and David S. *A Resource Guide to the Golden Age of Radio.* New York: Book Hunter Press, 2006.

Slide, Anthony. *Great Radio Personalities in Historic Photographs.* Vestal: The Vestal Press, Ltd., 1982.

Smart, James R. *Radio Broadcasts in the Library of Congress 1924-1941.* Washington, DC, 1982.

Sparta Old Time Radio. *http://spartaotr.com.*

Stewart, James. Interview. National Film Theatre. 1972. 31 Jan. 2008 *http://www.bfi.org.uk/.*

Stringer, Arthur. "The Juggler." *20 Best Short Stories in Ray Long's 20 Years as an Editor.* Ed. Ray Long. New York: Ray Long & Richard R. Smith, Inc., 1932.

Stringer, Arthur. "The Juggler." *Reader's Digest* December 1938: 129-132.

Terrace, Vincent. *Radio's Golden Years.* New York: A.S. Barnes & Company, Inc., 1981.

Tobacco Documents Online. *http://tobaccodocuments.org/.*

Variety. "People Magazine Tapped Ancier as 'Up and Comer, (Garth Ancier of 'Focus on Youth' Radio Program.")November 22, 1999.

The Walter J. Brown Media Archives & Peabody Awards Collection. 2006. University of Georgia, Athens Libraries. *http://www.libs.uga.edu/*

Waring, Virginia. *Fred Waring and the Pennsylvanians.* Chicago: University of Illinois Press, 1997.

Wylie, Max. *Best Broadcasts of 1940-41.* New York: Whittlesey House, 1942.

"Young Producer's Efforts Spawn Top Public Affairs Show." *Albuquerque Journal* 28 February, 1977: 13.

INDEX

Adlam, Basil 18, 31, 296
Abbott, Bud 229
Abdul-Jabbar, Kareem 520
Acuff, Edward 238
Adams, Eadie 278-9
Adams, Franklin P. 298
Adams, Julia 261, 352-3, 547-8
Adams, Wylie 238
Adamson, Harold 296
Ades, Hawley 253
After the This Man 194, 247, 316
Agay, Denes 284-5
Ager, Milton 229
Ahlert, Fred 107-8, 123, 152
Airmen of Note 482
Akst, Harry 228
Alberghetti, Anna Marie 85, 135, 139
Albers, Ken 536
Albert, Eddie 511, 527, 535
Albertson, Frank 344, 468
Alder's Gulch 290, 365
Alexander, Ben 358, 531
Alexander, Denise 192
Alexander, Jeff 294
Allanson, Susie 532
Allen, Fred 210, 408
Allen, Gracie 219, 454
Allen, Mel 513-4, 527
Allen, Steve 511, 513, 535
Allen, Vera 461, 469
Allman, Elvia 61
Allyson, June 13, 83, 85, 314, 347-9, 382, 390, 478-9, 548-9, 551, 557-8
Ameche, Don 211, 219, 231, 236, 356
Ameche, Jim 86
Amory, Cleveland 478
Anatomy of a Murder 376. 541
Ancier, Garth R. 239-42
Anderson, David 192

Anderson, Dick 261
Anderson, Eddie 303, 488
Anderson, Judith 469
Anderson, Marian Young 511
Anderson, Maxwell 247, 313
Anderson, Robert 462
Andrews, Cameron 462, 464
Andrews, Dana 394
Andrews, Helen 334
Andrews, Julie 396
Angeli, Pier 389, 513
Annette 540
Anthony, Ray 261
Arden, Eve 82, 294, 433-4
Arden, Toni 129, 134, 140
Arent, Arthur 460
Arlen, Harold 252
Armbruster, Robert 208, 322, 325, 327, 330, 334, 338, 342, 344-6, 350-1, 354, 470, 478, 488
Armen, Kay 447
Armistead, Horace 470
Armstrong, G.E. 512
Armstrong, Louis 221, 261, 306, 478
Arnold, Eddie 171
Arnold, Edward 225, 286, 386, 419, 494-4, 498
Arquette, Cliff 435
Arthur, Bea 523
Arthur, Jean 225, 340
Arvan, Jane 414
Arzner, Dorothy 416
Ashburn, Richie 511
Asner, Edward 498
Astaire, Fred 85, 216, 218, 309, 535
Aswell, James 464
Audley, Eleanor 43, 48, 53, 58, 62, 67, 74, 346
Autry, Gene 83, 366
Avalon, Frankie 535, 540

Averback, Hy 172, 318, 433
Ayres, Lew 224, 281, 283, 287
Babbitt, Harry 184-5
Baby Snooks 264-5, 267-8, 271, 275
Bacall, Lauren 516
Bacher, Bill 263, 280
Backus, Georgia 402, 428
Backus, Jim 411, 531, 535
Baer, Parley 32, 34, 38, 42, 43, 50, 54, 63, 66, 69, 75, 76, 287, 478, 504
Bagwell, Paul 296
Bailey, Pearl 535
Bain, Bob 72
Bain, Donald Ogden 462
Baker, Art 87-92
Baldwin, Bill 231
Baldwin, Faith 325
Ball, Suzan 351
Balsam, Martin 519
Balzer, George 304
Bandolero 372, 541
Bankhead, Tullulah 213, 511
Banks, Joan 426
Bannon, Julie 325, 334
Barber, Red 513
Barbour, Don 536
Barbour, Ross 536
Barkley, Vice President Alben 124, 400
Barnett, Griff 337
Barnett, Sanford H. 325, 327, 329, 334, 337, 341, 344-6, 350-1, 354
Barrett, James 561
Barrett, Michael Anne 36, 48
Barrett, Tony 39, 48, 52
Barron, Jack 49, 75
Barrow, Jack 38
Barrs, Norman 464
Barry, Dave 235
Barry, Gene 528, 540
Barry, Philip 327, 426
Barrymore, Drew 396
Barrymore, Ethel 128, 211
Barrymore, John 231
Barrymore, Lionel 93, 256, 279-80, 286, 495, 498
Bartell, Harry 35, 56, 66, 67, 401
Bartholomew, Freddie 264
Bartlett, Tommy 500
Barton, Bruce 512

Barton, Frank 402, 406
Barton, Greg 38
Basie, Count 534
Bates, Jean 237
Baxter, Anne 83-4, 511, 523
Baxter, Les 536, 540
Bayz, Guz 450
Beals, Richard "Dick" 48, 60
Bearchell, Robert 258
Bearden, Gene 558
Beardsley, William S. 400
Beatty, Clyde 502
Beatty, Morgan 371
Beban, Bob 428
Beck, Jr., Carl Edwin 434
Beckhard, Arthur J. 87
Beecher, Janet 329
Beery, Wallace 273, 276-8
Begley, Ed 350
Behrman, S.N. 466
Beisman, Paul 470
Belafonte, Harry 535
Bell, Greg 30
Benaderet, Bea 528
Bend of the River 32, 146, 148, 304-5, 313, 352, 546-8
Bender, Dawn 411
Bendix, William 516, 527-8, 533
Benet, Steven Vincent 464
Bennett, Bruce 206
Bennett, Connie 219
Bennett, Griff 428
Bennett, Joanne 394
Bennett, Tony 206, 534-537, 540
Bennington, William A. 83
Benny, Jack 13, 21, 78, 79, 82, 164, 214, 215, 259, 265, 303, 304, 305, 306, 318, 400, 421, 461, 488, 489, 501, 507, 516, 527, 528, 532, 550
Benson, Robbie 365
Benzel, Mimi 511
Berg, Gertrude 513
Bergen, Edgar 78, 84, 210-2, 214-5, 228-35, 506, 528, 535
Bergen, Polly 535
Berigan, Bunny 216
Berle, Milton 109, 174, 224, 396, 535-6
Berlin, Irving 230, 502
Berlinrut, Peter 464

Berman, Shelley 535-7, 540
Bernard, Don 428
Berner, Sara 203
Bernier, Daisy 251, 253
Bernstein, Elmer 49
Best, James 75, 353
Billsbury, Rye 350, 414, 491-2, 494
Birch, Thora 543
Bishop, Richard 462
Bisson, Alexandre 322
Bivens, Bill 246-7, 251
Blair, Frank 370-1
Blair, Janet 229, 425
Blanc, Mel 185, 214, 303-5, 535
Blanchard, Susan 337-8
Blandick, Clara 327
Bleyer, Archie 93
Bliss, Betty 223-4
Bliss, Ted 48
Blocker, Dan 27
Blondell, Gloria 327, 392
Blyth, Ann 83, 85, 206, 390, 513
Bogart, Humphrey 117, 291, 355, 394, 512, 516
Boland, Clay 253
Bolger, Ray 265, 268-71, 511, 513
Bonanova, Fortunio 107
Bond, Lyle 180, 184
Bond, Ward 93
Bondi, Beulah 38, 93, 237, 279
Bonney, Gail 345, 406
Boone, Pat 366, 535-536
Boone, Richard 520
Booth, Shirley 84
Borgnine, Ernest 85, 513
Born to Dance 78, 197, 248, 291, 316, 480
Bosley, Tom 498
Bouchey, Bill 411
Boulton, Milo 500
Bowe, Rosemarie 206
Bowes, Edward "Major" 210
Boy Meets Girl 251
Boyd, Stephen 528
Boyd, William "Hopalong Cassidy" 184, 288
Bracken, Eddie 318-20, 432
Brackett, Charles 83-4
Bradbury, Raymond 498
Bradford, Ralph 256
Bradley, Bill 520

Bradley, Omar 386
Bradley, Oscar 417-20, 423, 500
Bradley, Roland 256
Bradley, Truman 425-7, 450
Braga, Gaetano 86
Brand, Max 330
Brando, Marlon 390
Brandt, Frances 462
Brannum, Hugh "Uncle Lumpy" 251
Brennan, Walter 204, 206, 236, 495, 498, 528, 540
Bresse, Frank 263
Brewer, Teresa 202
Brice, Fanny 264-5, 267, 273, 275, 278, 280-1
Brickhouse, Jack 78, 192-201
Bridges, Lloyd 498, 520
Briggs, Don 461
Brill, Marty 25
Brinkman, Paul 389
Britt, Leora 355
Britton, Pamela 346
Britz, Chuck 258
Broadman, True 235-6, 435, 440-1, 443
Brodney, Oscar 38
Brokenshire, Norman 294, 460, 462, 464
Brown, Beverly 334
Brown, Clarence 279, 281
Brown, James 519
Brown, Joe E. 470
Brown, Lawrence 399
Brown, Les 172, 178-9, 308, 517
Brown, Lew 263
Brown, Tommy 263, 317
Browne, Earl 353
Brubeck, Dave 202, 227
Bruce, Robert 348
Bruce, Virginia 196, 198, 317, 549
Brundage, Hugh 80
Bryan, Arthur Q. 402
Bryan, Jane 443-5
Brynner, Yul 511
Bubeck, Harry 261
Bucholz, Betty 100
Bud & Travis 540
Burnett, Carol 526-7, 535
Burns, Bob 107, 495, 498
Burns, George 219, 527-8
Burns, Ronnie 540
Burr, Dick 540

Burt, Frank 18, 19, 26, 40, 48, 49, 60, 294, 296
Burton, Joe 466
Burton, Ken 394
Bush, Florence 38, 49, 75
Butler, David 318
Butterfield, Herbert "Herb" 343, 345-6, 350, 353, 355, 402, 414
Buttons, Red 85, 511
Buyeff, Lillian 54, 67
Byington, Spring 417
Byrnes, Edward 540
Caesar, Irving 243
Caesar, Sid 511
Cagney, James 81, 83, 422, 527
Cahn, Sammy 85
Cairn, Bill 402, 404, 406, 409, 411, 414
Calhern, Louis 287, 398
Calhoun, Rory 389
Call Northside 777 77, 253, 319, 343, 358, 396, 398, 404-5, 416, 429, 431-2, 501
Calvet, Corinne 204, 206
Camalian, Steven 256
Cameron, Don 171
Cameron, Kate 387
Campbell, Douglas 171
Campbell, Glen 531
Canfield, J. Gordon 87
Cannon, Bruce 409
Cannon, Frank 203
Cantor, Eddie 24, 41, 85, 112, 210, 488-9, 513, 516, 522, 540
Capra, Frank 81, 84, 90, 93, 210, 225, 230, 299, 314, 316, 336-8, 340, 388, 401-2, 425, 427, 466
Capstaff, Al 370
Captain Kangeroo 520
Carbine Williams 206, 290, 357, 553, 555
Carey, Alex 344
Carey, Macdonald 514
Carmer, Carlton 208
Carmichael, Hoagy 511-2, 536
Carpenter, Ken 82, 107-8, 112-6, 122-3, 126-9, 134-5, 140, 152, 158-63, 230, 388, 487-8
Carr, Jack 238, 327
Carradine, John 280-281
Carroll, Carole 210
Carroll, Madeleine 219
Carson, Jack 433-4

Carson, Johnny 520
Carson, Robert 344
Carter, Ann 339
Carter, Vivian 334
Carvell, Rich 192
Case, Daniel 240
Cash, Johnny 534
Cass County Boys 83
Cassidy, Hopalong "William Boyd" 483
Caton, Floyd 18, 21
Catrell, Clyde 243
Chambers, Reed 171
Chambers, Wheaton 324
Chamie, Alfred P. 514
Champion, Gower 75, 389
Chandler, Ed 428
Chandler, Jeff 261, 343, 345, 389, 414-5, 491, 513
Channing, Carol 396
Chaplin, Linn S. 229-30
Charisse, Cyd 85
Chase, Borden 26, 351
Chase, Mary 470
Chayefsky, Paddy 461
Chevalier, Maurice 85, 210
Christie, Audrey 461
Christy, Ken 46, 54, 331, 404, 455
Churchill, Stuart 246-7, 254
Churchill, Winston 171
Ciannelli, Eduardo 238
Clark, Buddy 158
Clark, Cliff 339, 347-8
Clark, Dane 23, 495, 498
Clark, Patsy 399
Cleary, Leo 329, 331, 339, 347, 485
Clinker, Zeno 230-1, 234
Clooney, Rosemary 158-60, 162-3, 535
Cobb, Will D. 396
Coburn, Charles 84, 294
Coghlan, Jr., Frank 322
Cohan, George M. 171
Colbert, Claudette 510-11, 516
Coles, Sandra 329
Collins, Dorothy 457-8
Collins, Joan 85
Collins, Judy 526
Collins, Russell 460
Collins, Tom 208, 210
Colman, Ronald 84, 213, 294, 394, 502

Colonna, Jerry 85
Comegys, Kathleen 462
Como, Perry 198
Compton, Francis 238
Conart, Wes 460
Conlan, Bob 402
Conley, Mark 279
Conlon, Jud 123, 152
Connell, Arthur 516
Connelly, Joe 86
Conner, Nadine 365
Conniff, Ray 535
Connolly, Vincent 359
Connors, Chuck 519, 534
Conrad, William "Bill" 23, 32, 34, 41, 42, 52, 53, 65, 258, 263, 350, 353, 404
Conried, Hans 327, 402, 406
Considine, Bob 251-2, 254, 511
Conte, John 312, 416-8, 420, 435, 440, 443, 461
Conte, Richard 430
Conway, Tim 520
Cook, Tommy 331, 344
Cooke, Sam 534
Cooper, Gary 81, 85, 291, 408
Cooper, Jackie 535, 537, 540
Cooper, Wyllis 292
Coppel, Alec 354
Corbett, Lois 344
Corey, Wendell 85, 556
Cornell, Katharine 469, 513
Correll, Charles 86
Corum, Bill 513
Corwin, Norman 423-4, 467-8, 494-9
Cosby, Bill 523
Costello, Lou 229
Cotten, Joseph 394, 512
Cowan, Louis 213, 396
Craig, Don 255
Craig, Nancy 386
Craig, Yvonne 531
Crain, Jeanne 82, 389
Crandell, Brad 372
Crane, Jr., Earl 38
Cranston, Joel 53, 66, 70
Crawford, Broderick 84
Crawford, Joan 14, 84, 281-3, 294, 443, 531
Crawford, Robert 481
Crisp, Donald 84

Crocker, Betty 100-1
Crockett, Keene 416, 460, 467
Croft, Mary Jane 208
Crosby, Bing 77, 78, 79, 106-58, 164-70, 172, 212, 219, 220, 253, 256, 257, 286, 287, 308, 309, 312, 313, 379, 386, 388, 403, 412, 447, 480, 488, 489, 507, 510, 511, 512, 513, 514, 516, 527, 528, 531, 532, 533
Crosby, Bob 534-5, 540
Crosby, Dixie Lee 109, 126, 158
Crosby, Gary 206
Crutcher, Robert Riley 421
Crutchfield, Les 19, 40
Cullen, Bill 257, 510
Cullen, Jack 478-80
Culley, Fred 243, 254
Culver, Howard 237
Cummings, Robert 356
Cunningham, Bill 399
Cunningham, Bob 500
Curtis, Kelly 237
Curtis, Tony 390, 511, 527-8, 535, 540
Dabney, Agusta 460
Dagmar 536
Dahl, Arlene 83, 206
Dailey, Dan 78, 355, 513, 516
Dakota Station 540
Dalton, Bob 481
Daly, John 513
Damone, Vic 85, 389, 535
Dana, Bill 527-8
Dandridge, Ruby 331
Daniels, Billy 84, 540
Daniels, William 49
Dant, Charles 392, 468
Darin, Bobby 535
Darwell, Jane 84
Dashiell, Bud 540
Daves, Delmer 414-5
Davies, Brian 523
Davies, Valentine 49, 261
Davis, Bette 85, 172, 314, 346, 394, 512-3
Davis, Glen 185
Davis, Nancy 261
Davis, Jr., Sammy 527, 535
Davis, Sylvia 192
Dawn, Isabel 325
Day, Dennis 303-5, 501
Day, Doris 85, 261, 488-9

De Carlo, Yvonne 510
De Castro, Babette 540
De Castro, Cherie 540
De Castro, Peggy 540
De Castro Sisters 540
de Corsia, Ted 65
de Havilland, Olivia 82-4, 341, 422
De Kruif, Paul 238
De Niro, Robert 315
Dean, Dizzy 399
Dean, Jimmy 528, 536
Deane, Martha 358
DeBona, Joe 200
Dee, Vincent 38, 49, 75
DeFoe, Daniel 227
DeGaw, Boyce 325
DeHaven, Gloria 464
Dehner, John 453
Dell, Alan 106
Delmar, Kenny 461
Demarest, William 350
DeMille, Cecil B. 84, 191, 321-9, 413, 449, 477, 511, 542
DeMille, Katherine 84
Dempsey, Jack 399, 511
Denny, Martha 518
Denny, Martin 536
DeRogers, Leo 214
Desmond, Johnny 457-8
DeSylva, Buddy 263
Deutsch, Adolph 83
DeVol, Frank 228, 433, 540
Dewey, Thomas E. 484
Diamond, Anne 411
Dickey, Bill 557
Dickey, Jo 470
Dickinson, Hal 478
Dietrich, Marlene 13, 355-6, 501
Dillard, Harrison 102-4
Diller, Phyllis 365, 396, 531-2
DiMaggio, Joe 399, 511
Disney, Walt 84, 522
Divavek, Harvey 470
Dobkin, Lawrence "Larry" 346, 350
Docter, Robert 258
Dodds, Gil 102-4
Dolan, Robert Emmett 82, 524
Dolph, John M. 243
Donaldson, Walter 296

Doobie Brothers 532
Doolittle, General Jimmy 87
Dorsey, Jimmy 198
Dorsey, Tommy 216, 220-2, 226, 307, 480
Dortort, David 27
Douglas, Kirk 85, 394-5, 399, 510-1
Douglas, Larry 171
Douglas, Paul 82, 349
Dow, Peggy 83, 552
Dowd, Elwood P. 98, 242, 288-9, 375, 551-2
Dowling, Robert 470
Doyle, William C. 514
Dragon, Carmen 394
Drake, Charles 552
Drake, Irvin 243
Dratler, Cady 429
Dratler, Jay 429
Dreyer, Dave 251
Drill, Helen 234
Driscoll, Bobby 84
Dru, Joanne 83, 350
Drury, James 514
Dubov, Paul 350, 414
Duff, Howard 534
Duffy, Patrick 519
Dunbar, Dixie 292
Duncan, John 215
Dunne, Stephen 353
Dunstedter, Eddie 85, 491
Durante, Jimmy 85, 210, 261, 483, 510-1, 528, 531-2, 535
Durning, Glen 346
Durocher, Leo 171, 399
Duryea, Dan 528
DuVal, Joe 324, 331, 353
Dyrenforth, Harald 350
Dysart, Richard 498
Eagles, James 327
Eaton, Evelynne 355
Ebb, Earl 230
Eberle, Ray 478
Eberly, Bert 198
Eberly, Bob 198
Ebi, Earl 350-1, 354
Ebsen, Buddy 78, 291, 317
Eckstine, Billy 206, 536-7, 540
Eddy, Nelson 211, 231, 234-5, 265, 268, 271-2
Edmonson, Travis 540
Edwards, Frances 276

Edwards, Gus 272, 396
Edwards, Jack 344
Edwards, Ralph 510
Edwards, Sam 43, 47, 48, 49, 56, 61, 71, 74, 491
Eikenberry, Jill 498
Eiler, Barbara 47, 71, 74, 402
Dwight Eisenhower, Dwight 518
Ekberg, Anita 85
Elam, Jack 560
Eliscu, Edward 434
Elliot, Win 100, 284-5
Ellis, Herb 36, 71, 347, 350, 453
Emerson, Ed 337
Englebach, Dee 81
Ephron, Henry 411
Ephron, Phoebe 411
Equire Quartet 299
Erickson, Leif 514
Essman, Harry 416
Evans, Dale 184, 213
Everett, Chad 531
Everly, Don 536
Everly, Phil 536
Everly Brothers 536
Eyer, Richard 49
Fabian 528, 535, 537
Fabray, Nanette 513
Fadiman, Clifton 298
Falkenburg, Jinx 78, 287-91, 365-6, 386, 458
Far Country, The 179, 204-6, 290, 365, 560
Farber, Jenny 428
Farber, Jerry 414
Farrar, Stanley 327, 409
Fay, Frank 288, 551
Faye, Alice 215, 217-21, 223-4
Feller, Bob 513
Felton, Verna 180, 183, 327-9, 337, 425
Fennelly, Parker 462
Ferrer, Jose 83, 290, 511
Fickett, Homer 460, 462, 464, 516
Field, Norman 329, 339, 344
Fields, Irving 243
Fields, W.C. 210, 231
Fine, Bernard 208
Finley, Charles O. 527
Firestone, Eddie 348, 350
Fisher, Eddie 312
Fitelson, H. William 460, 464

Fitz, Kathleen 337
Fitzgerald, Ella 217, 227, 310
Flanigan, Bob 536
Fleming, A.S. 490
Flight of the Phoenix, The 371, 542
Flippen, Jay C. 204
Flynn, Errol 102
Folger, John Clifford 464
Fonda, Henry "Hank" 78, 196, 216, 218, 227, 242, 323, 334, 469, 503, 510, 523, 541
Fontaine, Joan 83, 344, 510-1
Fonville, Chuck 102-4
Forbstein, Leo 82
Ford, Ernie 528, 535-7
Ford, Gerald 519
Ford, Glenn 513, 522
Ford, John 388
Ford, Paul 452
Forrest, Chet 263
Forrest, John R. 453
Forrester, Ross 324
Forsyth, Charles 322, 325, 327, 330, 334, 338, 342, 344-6, 350-1, 354
Forsyth, Rosemary 560
Foster, Royal 230
Four Aces 203
Four Freshmen 536
Fowler, Gene 286-7
Francis, Anne 389
Francis, Arlene 257, 513
Francis, Connie 528, 535-6
Frank, Peter 534
Franken, Rose 334
Fraser, Gordon 370
Fraser, Sally 49
Freberg, Stan 535
Freeman, Mona 389, 516
Freeman, Y. Frank 389
Frees, Paul 404, 452-3
Frey, Nathaniel 462
Fritz, Allen 184
Froug, William 285
Frye, Leon 470
Frye, William 38, 75
Gable, Clark 85, 211, 291, 326, 399, 420, 510-1, 513
Gabor, Eva 396
Gabor, Zsa Zsa 523, 526
Gallup, Frank 370, 457-8

Galt, Galan 324
Gammill, Noreen 327, 331, 339, 346
Gamse, Albert 243
Garbo, Greta 216-7, 264
Gardner, Earle Stanley 512
Gardner, Ed 280
Garland, Judy 220, 225, 263-4, 307, 390, 513
Garner, James 527
Garrett, Betty 83
Garrett, Joe 87
Garroway, Dave 261, 370, 478
Garson, Greer 84, 510-1, 531
Gassman, John 400
Gassman, Larry 400
Gates, Nancy 330
Gay, William 285
Gaynor, Janet 84
Gaynor, Mitzi 535-7, 539-40
Gearhart, Livingston 254-5
Gebhardt, George 470
Geiger, Milton 401
Geister, Janet 491
Gerard, Charles 238
Gerard, George 203
Gerry, Alexander 337
Gershwin, George 243, 247, 420
Gershwin, Ira 243, 248
Gerson, Betty Lou 394-5, 411, 452
Gerstle, Frank 43, 51, 53, 59, 73, 504
Gibbons, Cedric 83-4, 278
Gibbs, Georgia 85
Gibney, Hal 18, 20, 25, 44, 49, 51, 53, 54, 61, 432, 484, 485, 487
Gibson, John 443
Gilder, Rosamond 470
Gilmore, James 473
Gingold, Hermione 537, 539
Gleason, Jackie 366, 511
Glenn, John 520
Glenn Miller Story, The 44, 46-8, 50-63, 65-8, 70-4, 76, 206, 261, 290, 313, 380, 382, 385, 389, 390, 399, 435, 478-80, 542, 548-51
Gluskin, Lud 450, 453, 455
Goddard, Paulette 224
Godfrey, Arthur 93, 127, 171, 388
Godfrey, Kathy 388
Goldwater, Barry 374
Golenpaul, Dan 298
Gomberg, Sy 350

Goodlow, Walter 215
Goodman, Benny 216, 218-9, 223-6, 307, 309, 478
Goodrich, Frances 337, 401
Goodwin, Bill 172, 178-9, 517
Gordon, Anita 230
Gordon, Gale 329
Gordonairs 243
Gorin, Igor 263
Gorme, Eydie 311
Gosden, Freeman 86
Goss, Frank 286, 394
Gough, Lloyd 238
Gould, Elliott 519
Gould, Morton 313
Gould, Sandra 74
Grable, Betty 227, 399
Grady, Bill 364
Graham, Bob 460
Graham, Evarts 473
Graham, Frank 466
Graham, Sheilah 389
Graham, Tim 353
Grahame, Gloria 84
Granby, Joe 402, 428, 448
Grant, Cary 13, 85, 194, 329, 340, 376, 399, 420, 426-7
Grant, Earl 535, 537
Grant, Gogi 535-7
Grant, Johnny 514
Grapperhaus, Bob 402
Graves, Peter 514
Gray, Coleen 461
Gray, Doug 519
Gray, Glenn 389
Gray, Jerry 478
Greatest Show on Earth, The 191, 289, 413, 449, 501, 542, 553
Green, Bernard 286, 459, 482
Green, Johnny 82-3
Green, William 490
Greenberg, Hank 399
Greene, "Mean" Joe 519
Greene, Lorne 537
Greene, Richard 451
Gregg, Virginia 47, 50, 57, 58, 63, 65, 66, 67, 76, 287, 406, 478
Grever, Maria 243
Griffin, Merv 365-6

INDEX 579

Griffin, Robert "Bob" 38, 43, 50, 56, 57, 60, 63, 65, 344, 350, 353
Griffith, E.H. 409-10
Grimes, Jack 192
Grossel, Ira 343
Grubb, John C. 49
Guarnieri, Johnny 288
Guedel, John 296
Gwenn, Edmund 84
Gwynn, Edith 318-9
Hackett, Albert 337, 401
Hackett, Buddy 537
Hagen, James 460
Hagen, Jean 556
Hagen, Kevin 49
Haggard, Merle 366
Haight, George 87
Hainey, Betty Jean 334
Hale, Barbara 83, 411
Hale, Nathan Lang 400
Hall, J.C. 287
Hall, Monty 371
Hall, Porter 213
Hall, Tom T. 519
Hall, William E. 457-8
Hammerstein II, Oscar 469, 511
Hampton, Lionel 537
Handley, Alan 84
Hanlon, Thomas 330, 334, 500
Harding, Ann 14, 323-4
Hardt, Dick 482
Harlow, Jean 218, 221, 291
Harmon, Tom 514
Harriman, E. Rowland 464, 516
Harris, Howard 432
Harris, Phil 20, 303-5, 535-6
Harris, Radie 396
Harris, Stacy 404
Harris, Vernon 478
Harrison, George 532
Harrison, Rex 513
Hart, Lorenz 287, 292, 313
Hartman, Grace 469
Hartman, Paul 469
Harvey, Laurence 527
Harvey 94-5, 129, 172, 206, 241-2, 253-4, 288-9, 315, 374 5, 398, 410, 412, 470, 551, 553
Hatch, Wilbur 425-6, 428

Hathaway, Henry 404-5
Hauser, Dwight 389
Hausner, Jerry 146, 406
Hawley, Adelaide 100
Hawley, Paul 490
Haye, Sam 406
Hayes, Gabby 483
Hayes, Helen 171, 213, 286-7, 374
Hayes, Jack 180, 502
Hayman, Richard 457-8
Hayward, Leland 200, 290, 467, 470
Hayward, Susan 82, 527
Hayworth, Rita 156, 399
Head, Edith 202
Healey, Francis C. 229-30
Healy, Ted 263
Heatter, Gabriel 513
Heggen, Thomas 470
Heistand, Bud 423-4, 516
Helburn, Theresa 460, 464
Hemmingway, Ernest 77, 171, 394
Henderson, Florence 531
Henderson, Ray 263
Henderson, Skitch 457-8
Hendrick, William 530
Henie, Sonja 399
Hepburn, Audrey 513
Hepburn, Katharine 14, 314, 329, 426, 502
Herbert, Don 38
Herrmann, Bernard 494
Hersholt, Jean 84, 292, 416, 420, 423
Heston, Charlton 206, 449, 528, 531-2
Heywood, Hilda 322
Hickman, Dwayne 537, 540
Hickok, Eliza 395-6
Hicks, George 460
Hiestand, John 234-5
Higgenbotham, Ann 390
Hill, Marty 296
Hilton; James 83
Hirt, Al 514
Hitchcock, Alfred 105, 194-5, 202, 207, 290, 314, 321, 343, 365, 384, 393, 396, 406, 431
Hite, Ray 237
Hodges, General Courtney 87
Hodiak, John 83
Hoffat, Harold 238
Hogan, George 358
Holden, William 390

Holiday, Hope 540
Holiday, Johnny 202
Holland, Bert 32, 33, 41, 50, 56, 61, 67, 72
Holland, Gladys 350
Holland, Maury 214
Holland, Tom 414
Holliday, Judy 511
Holloway, Jean 400
Holm, Celeste 84
Holmes, Dennis 49
Holton, James L. 171
Honey Dreamers 457-8
Hood, Clifford F. 463
Hooper, C.E. 505
Hope, Bob 78, 82, 83, 84, 85, 140, 172-9, 184, 214-5, 219-20, 365, 386, 399-400, 412, 447, 488-9, 507, 513, 517, 527-8, 533, 535
Hope, Jack 172, 178
Hopper, Hedda 117, 221, 334, 502-3
Horne, Lena 528
Horne, Victoria 552
Horton, Edward Everett 417
Houghton, Amory 184
Hoving, Walter 484
Howard, Sidney 238
Howard, Tom 299-303
Howell, Bob 299
Howell, Cliff 86
Howell, Ruth 299
Howell, Wayne 449
Hoy, Johnny 219-20, 223, 225
Hubbard, Eddie 78, 192-201
Hudson, Rock 85, 261, 390, 535, 547
Hughes, Russell 208
Hull, Josephine 99, 289, 461, 552
Hull, Warren 263, 281, 283
Humphrey, Hubert H. 523
Hunt, Marsha 335-7, 445-6
Hunter, Colin 238
Hunter, Jeffrey 261
Hunter, Tab 85, 535, 537, 540
Huntley, Chet 527
Hurst, Fanny 512
Hurt, Charles 257
Hussey, Ruth 328-9
Huston, Walter 279, 495, 498
Hutchins, Will 530
Hutton, Marion 261, 378
Hyer, Martha 341

Ice Follies of 1939 14, 224, 281-2, 418, 443-4
Irish, Jack 469
Irwin, Carole 460
Irwin, Helen 346
Isaacs, Charles 488
It's a Wonderful Life 14, 77-8, 80-2, 88, 90, 93, 210, 230, 248, 286, 288-90, 314-5, 336-7, 340-1, 357-9, 376, 401, 403-4, 425, 427-9, 432, 447-8, 466, 468, 553
Iturbi, Jose 107
Ives, Victor 410
Jackpot 77, 129, 133, 411-3
Jackson, Felix 330
Jackson, Harry 208
Jackson, Jay 396-8, 482
Jacobs, John 448-9
Jacobson, Art 261
Jaffe, Moe 253, 482
Jagger, Dean 84
James, Harry 383, 412
James, Joni 537
James, Marquis 208
Janney, Leon 459-60
Jaynes, Betty 263-5
Jeffrey, Howard 428
Jenkins, Gordon 203, 227
Jessel, George 202
Johnson, Lamont 44, 56, 57, 67, 69
Johnson, Van 85, 389, 394, 466
Johnstone, Jack 18, 19, 20, 21, 60, 294, 296, 394, 401
Johnstone, William "Bill" 44, 47, 51, 52, 56, 58, 62, 67, 69, 70, 74, 172, 339, 345, 346, 347, 350, 353, 452
Jolley, I. Stanford 324
Jolson, Al 79, 263, 319
Jonas, Paul 469
Jones, Allan 263-4, 276, 291
Jones, Grover 435, 440, 443
Jones, James Earl 498
Jones, Jennifer 85, 513
Jones, Shirley 85
Jones, Spike 261
Jordan, Louis 511
Jory, Victor 394
Josefsberg, Milt 304
Joy, Nicholas 329
Jukes, Bernard 238
Julian, Joseph 208

Junkin, Harry W. 192
Kahn, Gus 243, 247
Kalmar, Bert 264
Kaltenborn, H.V. 510-1
Kane, Byron 392, 414
Kane, Whitford 238
Karloff, Boris 513
Karn, Stella 359
Katzman, Henry 243
Kaufman, George S. 265, 279, 313
Kaye, Danny 389, 510-1, 528
Kaye, Mary Jane 536
Kaye, Norman 536
Kearns, Joseph 215, 345, 455
Keaton, Buster 224
Keel, Howard 389
Keighley, William 323-4, 329, 331-4, 336-9, 341-6, 348-50, 352-7
Keith, Robert 238
Kellaway, Cecil 552
Kelly, Gene 237, 399
Kelly, Grace 194, 202, 513
Kelly, Joe 395-6
Kelly, Patsy 219
Kelly, Paul 469
Kelly, Paula 261, 478
Kemper, Ray 450
Kendall, Cy 345
Kennedy, Arthur 547-8
Kennedy, John Milton 327, 330, 334, 337, 341, 344-6, 350-1, 354
Kent, Rockwell 502
Kenton, Stan 535, 537
Kerman, David 324
Kern, Jerome 229
Kerr, Deborah 83
Kerr, Geoffrey 238
Kevy, Charles 184
Kibbee, Guy 225
Kieran, John 298, 399
Kilgallen, Dorothy 228
Kilgallen, Jim 171
King, Eddie 261
King, Harry 292
King, Larry 78, 313-6
King, Wayne 516
Kingsford, Guy 337
Kirkpatrick, Jess 35, 58
Kirkwood, Jack 172, 234-5, 488-9

Kitt, Eartha 388
Kline, Bill 237
Klugman, Jack 519
Knight, Fuzzy 419
Knight, Vick 214
Knox, Frank 483
Kondolf, George 462
Korjus, Miliza 281
Kovacs, Ernie 510-1
Kranendonk, Leon 247
Kronman, Harry 426, 428-9
Krumgold, Joseph 341
Krupp, Roger 396
Kruschen, Jack 455
Kuhl, Cal 214
Kuralt, Charles 491
Kurlan, Arthur 313
Kyser, Kay 502
La Franco, Tony 235, 237
La Guardia, Fiorello 387-8
Laine, Frankie 447, 534-5, 540
Lake, Stuart N. 351
Lamas, Fernando 206
Lamour, Dorothy 211, 214, 224, 396, 432-3, 516
Lancaster, Burt 85, 356-7, 406, 408, 510, 513, 532
Lancers, The 540
Lanchester, Elsa 420
Landon, Michael 27, 519
Lane, Priscilla 461
Lang, Jim 377, 379-80, 382-4
Lang, Johnny 429
Lang, Walter 411, 413
Lange, Hope 85
Langford, Frances 85, 291-2, 316-7
Langner, Lawrence 460, 464
Larson, Swede 399
Lasky, Ben 184
Last Gangster, The 435, 439
Laughton, Charles 211, 291, 320, 420
Laurie, Piper 84
Lava, William 406
Lawrence, Carol 535
Lawrence, Charlotte 346-7, 350
Lawrence, Elliot 457-8
Lawrence, Jerome 502
Lawrence, Mary 49
Lawrence, Steve 311
Lawrence, William "Bill" 425-6, 429

Lay, Bernie 202
Layne, Zella 100
Le Doux, Leone 40, 337, 348, 409
Leader, Anton M. 452
Lean, David 85
Lear, Les 500
Lear, Norman 358
Lebieg, Earl 243
Lee, Charles 179
Lee, Connie 416
Lee, Earl 344
Lee, Peggy 84, 122, 309, 535
Lee, R.E. 238
Lee, Robert E. 502
Leeds, Peter 485
Leigh, Janet 510-1
Leigh, Vivien 387-8
LeMay, General Curtis 203, 207
Lemmon, Jack 85, 227, 389, 396, 527-8, 535-6, 540
Lemmon, Martin 491
Leonard, Jack 215, 222
Leonard, Sheldon 358
Leonard, Sugar Ray 513
Lerner, Seth 240
LeRoy, Mervyn 82
Leslie, Kermit 370
Leslie, Walter 370
Levant, Oscar 298
Levene, Samuel 238
Levey, Harold 208, 460, 462, 464
Levy, Bill 385
Lewellen, John 396
Lewis, Cathy 451
Lewis, Ed 215, 223-4
Lewis, Elliott 393, 453, 455
Lewis, Forrest 43, 53, 56, 67
Lewis, Hobart 371-2
Lewis, Jerry 203, 358, 389, 535-7, 539-40
Lewis, Monica 171
Lewis, Sam 228
Lewis, Warren 180
Libbott, Robert 294
Light, David 322, 350, 435, 450
Lillie, Beatrice 85-6
Lindbergh, Charles 200-1, 207, 373
Lindenschmit, Paul 385
Linder, Eric 240
Lindgren, Corky 540
Lindgren, Fred 215, 306
Ling, Richie 239
Linkletter, Art 296, 510, 516, 522, 535, 540
Livingstone, Mary 303-5
Lockhart, June 470
Lockwood, Margaret 500
Loeb, Marx 397
Logan, Joshua "Josh" 240, 290, 334, 470, 503
Lombard, Carole 210, 219, 293-4, 326-7, 417-8
Lombardo, Guy 227, 478
London, Howard J. 524
Longenecker, Bob 235
Loos, Mary 350
Lord, Jack 520
Lord, Phillips H. 500
Loren, Sophia 85
Louis, Joe 399
Lovett, Dorothy 341, 346, 351, 354
Lowe, Edmund 399
Loy, Myrna 14, 195, 218, 273, 276, 278, 280, 291, 376, 421-2
Lubitsch, Ernst 197
Lucas, Rupert 258-60
Lunceford, Jimmie 309
Lund, John 83, 394, 464
Lung, Charles 350, 353, 485
Lupino, Ida 83, 513
Lyman, Arthur 540
Lyman, Jack 484
Lynn, Betty 346
Lynn, Diana 462
Lynn, Jeffrey 422
Lynn, Rita 404
Lyons, Jeffrey 334, 340, 349
Lytell, Bert 469
MacDonald, Ian 470
MacDonnell, Norman 453
MacDougall, Ranald 345, 468
MacGarret, George 292
MacGregor, C.P. 520
Mack, Dick 358
MacKaye, Fredric 329, 334, 337, 341, 344-6
MacKenzie, Gisele 78, 258-60, 520
MacKenzie, Murdo 108, 123, 152
MacLaine, Shirley 528
MacLane, Barton 239
MacMurray, Fred 356, 420, 510, 527-8, 537
MacRae, Gordon 159-63, 389, 400

Made for Each Other 77, 248, 290, 292-4, 334, 337, 353, 356, 403, 416, 418, 424-5, 428, 432, 452-3
Madru, Al 299
Maduro, Carlos 247
Magee, John G. 481
Magic Town 13, 77-8, 248-51, 263, 289, 339, 341, 406, 408, 562-3
Magnante, Charlie 312
Mahady, Henry J. 516
Maharis, George 528
Maher, Wally 344, 350, 353, 430
Mailer, Norman 239, 366
Main, Marjorie 495
Malden, Karl 528
Malone, Dorothy 85
Malone, Joel 466
Maloney, J.R. 461
Maluke, Andy 518
Man from Laramie, The 19, 357, 370
Mangrum, Lloyd 185
Mann, Tony 547
Mansfield, Jayne 535, 537
Mansfield, Joseph F. 237
Mantle, Mickey 513
Mapes, Ted 38
Marble, Alice 399
March, Fredric 82, 84, 452, 511
March, Hal 511, 513
Marine, Joe 243, 251
Markel, Hazel 287
Marks, Larry 172, 178
Marlowe, Joann 428
Marlowe, Mickey 203
Marr, Eddie 208, 324, 337, 339, 344-6, 348, 350, 353, 406, 411
Marsh, Dileen 258
Marshall, Armina 460, 464
Marshall, George 406, 408-9, 483
Marshall, Herbert 516
Marson, Truda 330, 350
Martell, Bill 491
Martin, Dean 83, 85, 358, 389, 536
Martin, Freddy 447
Martin, Mary 281, 396, 469
Martin, Tony 221, 292, 535, 537, 540
Lee Marvin, Lee 543
Marvin, Tony 93
Marx, Groucho 121, 224, 522

Mason, Pamela 396
Massey, Ilona 265, 268
Mather, Jack 353
Mathews, George 464
Mathews, Kerwin 389
Mathis, Johnny 85, 365
Matthews, Junius 70, 73, 448
Matwick, Millie 196
Maurer, Bob 371
Max, Ed 345, 411
Maxwell, Edwin 339
Maxwell, Marilyn 84, 172, 261
May, Billy 261
Mayer, Louis B. 265, 268, 272-273
Mayo, Virginia 213
McAdam, Michael 38, 49
McBride, Mary Margaret 358-65
McCall, Bill 185
McCallion, James "Jimmy" 37, 42, 46
McCambridge, Mercedes 392, 397
McCarthy, Charlie 78, 84, 210, 212, 214-5, 228-31, 234-5, 506
McClain, John 421
McClintic, Guthrie 238, 469
McClintock, Bill 460
McCloy, John J. 483
McClure, Doug 560
McCluskey, Joyce 455
McConnell, Lulu 299
McCormick, Myron 196, 239
McCrary, Tex 287-8, 366, 447
McCrea, Joel 356
McDonald, Mike 532
McDowell, Roddy 396
McElfresh, Clair T. 533
McEnroe, Robert E. 462
McFee, Jerry 208
McGarth, Earl J. 491
McGill, Ralph 171
McGovern, Johnny 428, 485
McGuire, Bobby 482
McGuire, James P. 429
McGuire, Virginia 354-5
McGuire Sisters 310
McIntire, John 49, 339, 344, 347, 484, 561
McIntire, Tim 561
McKee, Wesley 288
McKellar, Kenneth 227
McKennon, Dal 44, 73

McKeon, Jeannie 214
McLagen, Andrew 561
McLaglen, Victor 84, 399, 561
McLean, Gloria 126
McMahon, Ed 371
McManus, Kenny 234
McMillan, Bob 399
McMillan, Gloria 426
McNally, Stephen 352-3
McNamee, Graham 238
McNaughton, Henry 299-302
McNear, Howard 36, 46, 48, 51, 52, 56, 61, 69, 76, 350, 430
McNeill, Don 228
McNellis, Maggi 321, 357
McNulty, Dorothy 107
McNulty, John 411
McNutt, Paul V. 484
McPhail, Doug 264
McVey, Tyler 331, 337, 404
Meachan, Jerry 540
Mear, Richard 322
Meeham, John 49
Melchoir, Lauritz 510-11
Mellomen 235
Meltones 214
Menjou, Adolph 171, 210
Menken, Shepard 51, 348
Merande, Doro 462
Mercer, Johnny 84
Meredith, Burgess 523
Merkel, Una 281, 291
Merman, Ethel 288
Merrill, Lou 37, 67, 324, 327, 337, 392, 428, 455, 466
Merrill, Robert 511
Meston, John 455
Milland, Ray 83-4, 394, 408
Millard, Oscar 354
Miller, Glenn 44, 46-8, 50-63, 65-8, 70-4, 76, 206, 216, 221, 226-7, 261-2, 290, 308, 310, 313, 365, 377-82, 384-5, 389-90, 399-400, 435, 478-80, 482, 542, 548-51
Miller, Jay 372-4
Miller, Justin 296, 491
Miller, Luther 296
Miller, Marvin 48, 65
Miller, Mattie Lou 399
Miller, Mitch 310-1, 528

Miller, Sidney 208, 411, 455
Miller, Ted 480
Mills, Arthur E. 255-6
Mills, Felix 435, 440, 443
Mills, Haley 559
Mills, Juliet 559
Milner, Martin 514
Milo, George 49
Miltern, John 239
Milton, Jay 31, 296
Milton, Tommy 171
Mineo, Sal 528
Mitchell, Millard 239
Mitchell, Shirley 40, 60
Mitchell, Sydney 292
Mitchell, Thomas 93, 225
Mitchell Boy Choir 180, 183
Mitchum, Robert 389
Mohr, Gerald 69, 409
Molyneaux, Gerard 180, 504
Monaghan, Frank 208
Monroe, Marilyn 234
Monroe, Vaughan 227
Montalban, Ricardo 83, 519
Montgomery, Robert 78, 346, 516, 533
Moody, Helen Wills 322
Moody, Ralph 237, 414, 428
Moore, Garry 85
Moore, Mary Tyler 523
Moore, Victor 338-40, 428
Moorehead, Agnes 287
Morawcek, Lucian 450, 452-3, 455
Moreno, Antonio 422
Moreno, Rita 528
Morgan, Dennis 78, 81, 213
Morgan, Frank 264-5, 268-71, 273-4, 278-81, 423-4
Morgan, Henry 204, 372, 479
Morgan, Jane 535-6, 540
Morimer, Graeme 345
Morley, Virginia 254-5
Morris, Holland 346
Morrow, Bill 108, 123, 152
Morrow, Douglas 346
Mosher, Bob 86
Mottola, Tony 312
Mr. Krueger's Christmas 366
Mr. Smith Goes to Washington 90, 225-6, 247, 289, 314, 316, 376, 387, 482

Mudell, Gloria 245
Mull, Edward 391
Muni, Paul 84
Munro, Jock 239
Munsel, Patrice 511
Murder Man 247, 289, 549
Murphy, George 83-4, 318, 349, 416-8
Murphy, Horace 208
Murray, Arthur 168
Murray, Hugh K. 491
Murray, Kent 292
Murray, Ross 234
Murrow, Edward R. 85-86, 503, 513
Myers, Henry 330
Nabors, Jimmy 527
Nader, George 389
Nagel, Conrad 83, 85, 435, 437-40, 443-6
Naish, J. Carrol 386
Naked Spur, The 163-4, 178, 289-90, 365
Nash, George 239
Nash, Ogden 211
Navy Blue and Gold 197, 263-4, 317, 438
Neal, Patricia 83
Neilson, James 38
Neise, George 35, 345, 348, 350
Nelson, Barry 371
Nelson, Frank 322, 324, 417, 425, 432, 501
Nelson, John 87
Nelson, Lori 261
Nelton, Hugh 171
Nerney, Pat 389
Nessler, Joel 409
Newman, Alfred 84, 317
Newman, Paul 85, 511, 527
Newton, Ruth 192
Next Time We Love 77, 291, 356, 409-11, 413, 503
Nichols, Red 121, 146
Nicholson, James 49
Nielsen, A.C. 505
Nielsen, Leslie 519, 531
Niesen, Gertrude 281-3
Nigh, Jane 334-5
Niles, Wendell 31-2, 214, 291, 296
Nilsson, Norma Jean 339
Nimoy, Leonard 519, 531
Niven, David 85, 219
Nixon, John 488
Noble, Ray 227, 229-31, 234-35

Nolan, Jeanette 38, 43
Nordine, Ken 500
Norman, Gene 478
Norman, Loulie Jean 158
North, Jay 540
Norton, Marjorie 324
Novak, Kim 85, 193, 195, 389, 511
Nussbaum, Howard 468
Nusser, Jim 404
Oakie, Jack 211
Oberon, Merle 330, 388
Oboler, Arch 391-3
O'Brian, Hugh 511, 523
O'Brien, Edmund 389, 540
O'Brien, Margaret 115, 211, 214-5, 261, 288
O'Brien, Pat 121, 399, 430-1, 516
O'Connor, Basil 86, 524
O'Connor, Caroline 210
O'Connor, Donald 83
O'Connor, Rod 516
O'Connor, Una 464
Of Human Hearts 280
O'Flaherty, Maggie 396
Ogg, Sammy 39
O'Hara, Maureen 400, 536, 558-9
O'Herlihy, Dan 38, 47, 48, 498
O'Keefe, Walter 171
Oliver, Susan 528
Olivier, Laurence 380, 387-8
O'Malley, Pat 38
O'Mara, John F. 461
On Our Merry Way 396
Oppenheimer, George 276
Ordway, Fred 171
Oreck, Don 491
Ormandy, Eugene 287
Osborne, Ted 394-5, 455
O'Shea, Michael 213
Osmond, Donnie 523
Ottley, Gerald 366
Owen, Reginald 420
Owen, Tony 389
Owens, Gary 531
Pagano, Ernestine 425
Paget, Debra 414-5
Paige, Raymond 292, 447
Pallette, Eugene 225
Palmer, Betsy 511
Palmer, Byron 392

Palmer, Gretta 208
Paris Sisters 206
Parker, Barnett 281
Parker, Eleanor 409-10
Parker, Fess 498, 528
Parker, Franklyn 331, 339
Parsons, Louella 108, 117, 125, 133, 139, 224, 291-2, 320
Parton, Reggie 38
Pasquale, Charles 243
Pastor, Tony 540
Patric, Gil 324
Patrick, George 38
Patterson, Floyd 511
Patterson, William A. 198
Pattiz, Norm 215, 306, 395
Patton, Mel 185
Paul, Norman 231
Paulsen, Pat 527
Payne, Bruce 329
Payne, John 26, 513
Peale, Norman Vincent 213, 287
Pearce, Ann 344
Pearson, Fort 396
Pearson, Teddy 263, 265, 267, 272-3, 276, 278-9, 281
Peary, Hal 184
Peck, Gregory 85, 213, 394, 396, 511, 523
Pedicini, Richard George 470
Pemberton, Brock 469
Percy, Mary 470
Perkins, Jack 80
Perrin, Sam 304
Perrin, Victor 485
Perrott, Ruth 346, 350
Perry, Penny 245
Petrie, Howard 516
Petrillo, James C. 517
Peyton, Father Patrick 235, 237
Philadelphia Story, The 13-4, 77-8, 248, 289, 327, 356, 416, 424, 426-7, 460, 490, 503, 553, 556
Philips, George Harvard 235
Phillips, Barney 40, 43, 52, 59, 60, 66, 70, 72, 426
Pickford, Mary 84-5, 211
Pidgeon, Walter 281, 317, 523
Pied Pipers 227
Pierce, George 470

Pierce, Sam 86, 231, 234
Pierson, Walter 322
Pious, Minerva 435
Pitney, Gene 543
Plomley, Roy 227
Poe, James 286
Poleise, Herb 299, 482
Pollack, Ben 261, 478
Pollack, Lou 292
Pons, Lily 85
Porter, Bob 540
Porter, Cole 83, 162, 197, 316
Porterfield, Robert 470
Pot of Gold 247, 316
Powell, Dick 83, 217, 291-2, 294, 389
Powell, Eleanor 265, 271-2, 291, 316, 480
Powell, Jane 261, 389, 394
Powell, William 195, 420, 422
Power, Tyrone 292
Pozner, Vladimir 450, 452
Pratt, Will 258
Preminger, Otto 376, 389
Prentiss, Ed 179
Preston, Robert 396
Previn, Andre 535-537, 540
Price, Vincent 85, 294, 535, 537
Princie, Carl 235
Prinz, LeRoy 171
Pritchett, Florence 93, 413
Pryor, Roger 418-24, 460
Purcell, Gertrude 330
Purdom, Edmund 389
Purdy, W.T. 434
Quinn, Anthony 85
Quinn, Bill 192
Raft, George 41, 107, 219
Rainer, Luise 84, 263
Raines, Ella 516, 533
Rainger, Ralph 172, 178-9, 303
Rains, Claude 225, 313
Rainy, Sue 540
Randolph, Donald 346
Raphael, John 322
Raphael, Leonard 449
Rathbone, Basil 469
Rawlinson, Herb 294
Ray, Aldo 389
Rayburn, Gene 371-2, 374-7
Raye, Martha 224

Reagan, Ronald 38, 49, 82, 85, 87, 261, 357, 527
Rear Window 193-4, 202-3, 290
Redgrave, Vanessa 396
Reed, Alan 46
Reed, Donna 93, 214, 314, 338-41, 389, 428, 447-8, 513
Reed, Warren 478
Reid, Ed 365
Reid, Elliott 462, 464
Remick, Lee 528
Rene, Henri 202, 206
Rennaham, Ray 38
Reynolds, Betty 245
Reynolds, Debbie 85, 261, 390, 537, 540
Reynolds, James 171
Rhythmaires 108, 116, 122-3, 129, 135, 140, 152, 163, 170
Rice, Florence 263-4, 317
Rice, Glen 192
Rice, Grantland 399
Rice, Rosemary 461
Rich, Freddie 428
Richards, Carole 123, 128, 235
Richards, Paul 40, 59, 73
Richards, Robert L. 351, 450, 452
Richards, Wayne 516
Richardson, Marsha 215, 306, 385
Rickenbacker, Eddie 171
Ricks, Pal 532
Riddle, Nelson 535
Ridgway, Matthew B. 257
Rinard, Florence 482
Ringwald, Roy 243, 247, 251
Rippe, Bill 192
Riskin, Robert 249, 341, 408, 562-3
Riss, Dan 350, 353, 404
Ritter, Tex 84, 536
Ritzo, Marco 203
Robbins, Doris 261
Robbins, Jerome 470
Roberts, Kent 299
Robertson, Cliff 520
Robertson, Dale 531
Robeson, Chuck 38
Robeson, Paul 399
Robin, Leo 172, 178-9, 252, 303
Robinson, Edward G. 319-20, 435, 439, 495, 527

Robinson, Frances 331
Robson, Mark 83
Rockefeller, Lawrence 171
Rodgers, Jimmie 85, 535-6, 540
Rodgers, Richard 255, 287, 292, 313, 469, 511
Rodman, Victor 208, 324
Roe, Raymond 346
Rogers, Ginger 83-4, 216, 218, 314, 341, 394, 425
Rogers, Roy 29, 180-4, 213, 483
Rolle, Esther 498
Rollinson, Herb 237
Roman, Ruth 83, 204, 206
Romberg, Sigmund 264
Romero, Cesar 221, 523, 537, 540
Ronstadt, Linda 310
Rooney, Mickey 178, 264, 454
Roosevelt, Franklin D. 85, 171, 216, 311, 484, 494-6, 499, 526
Rope 105, 194, 321, 343, 396, 431
Rose, David 535, 537, 540
Rose, Hilda 234
Rose, Sy 231, 234
Rose, William 434
Ross, Frankie 536
Roventini, Johnny 299
Roy, Michael 428-9
Rubin, Jack 409, 411
Rubin, Stanley 466
Ruby, Harry 264
Ruby, Herman 251
Ruggles, Charlie 420
Ruick, Melville 322, 325
Rush, Barbara 261, 389
Rush, Celeste 327
Russell, Barclay 370
Russell, Connie 203
Russell, Don 370
Russell, Gilbert 265
Russell, Harold 369
Russell, Henry 31, 180-1, 213, 296, 402, 404, 406, 409, 411, 414, 432, 484
Russell, Jane 389
Russell, Nipsey 519
Russell, Rosalind 14, 85, 194, 210, 264, 408, 435-40, 442
Ruth, Babe 171
Ryan, Mary Ann 518
Ryan, Robert 85, 532

Rydell, Bobby 528, 534
Saint, Eva Marie 85, 528
Sakowicz, Sig 503
Sale, Richard 350
Saltonstall, Leverett 464
Sande, Walter 38
Sands, Tommy 85, 535, 537, 540
Sauter, James E. 469
Schary, Dore 84, 287
Scheff, Walter 247, 251
Schoeneman, George J. 490
Schrager, Rudy 322, 325, 327, 330, 334, 338, 342, 344-6, 350-1, 354
Schuck, Arthur A. 184, 188-189, 191
Scott, Allan 87, 419
Scott, Art 208
Scott, Dorothy 331, 337
Scott, Janet 339, 428
Scott, Lizabeth 516
Scott, Tom 464
Sedan, Rolfe 327
Seel, Charles 237, 327, 329, 331, 339
Semel, Mitch 239-43
Seventh Heaven 248, 292, 357
Seymour, Dan 85-6, 288, 500
Sharpe, Dolores 206
Shavers, Charlie 457
Shaw, Artie 219
Shaw, Robert 243
Shay, Dorothy 447
Shayne, Robert 239
Shearing, George 535
Sheldon, Herb 321, 357
Sheldon, Walt 213
Shelton, George 299-302
Sheridan, Ann 399
Sheriff, R.C. 354
Shirl, Jimmy 243
Shopworn Angel, The 248, 281, 317
Shore, Dinah 85, 163, 228, 378, 511, 524
Shore, Hannah 184
Shute, Nevil 354
Silver, Jeffrey 411
Silvers, Lou 322, 325, 327
Simeone, Harry 253
Simmons, Dick 553-8
Simmons, Ed 358
Simmons, Jean 85, 510, 532
Simmons, Richard Alan 406, 414
Simms, Sylvia 455
Sinatra, Frank 85-6, 213, 261, 311, 379, 478, 527-8, 532, 535
Sinclair, Eric 462
Sinclair, Ronald 264
Singing Sergeants 481-2
Singleton, Doris 330-1, 337
Singleton, Penny 107
Skelton, Red 83, 180-3
Sklar, George 450, 452
Slater, Harry 299
Sloan, Alfred P. 171
Sloan, Robert 397
Small, Mary 284-5
Smith, Alan 230
Smith, Alexis 396
Smith, C. Aubrey 264
Smith, C.R. 199
Smith, Darrell 253
Smith, Jack 83
Smith, Kate 90, 299, 301-2
Smith, Kent 196
Smith, S. Mark 460, 464
Snerd, Mortimer 211-2, 229-35
Snyder, John 488
Spaatz, General Carl A. 87
Spalding, Albert 399
Spiegel, Sam 85
Spielberg, Steven 315
Spier, William 450, 453
Spirit of St. Louis, The 200, 467
Sportsmen 79, 184, 303-5
St. James, Bill 538
St. John, Howard 461
Stack, Robert 206, 396, 514, 516, 527-8, 535
Stafford, Hanley 264-5, 267, 272, 275, 279, 281, 485
Stafford, Jo 227, 536, 540
Stanley, Don 101-2
Stanley, Helene 350
Stanton, Bob 434
Stanwyck, Barbara 394, 511
Stark, Harold 483
Starr, Bart 514
Starr, Freda 275-6
Starr, Kay 116, 122, 535, 537, 539-40
Steele, Ted 372
Steffen, Ron 306
Stenger, Dick 237

Stephenson, John 44
Stern, Bill 13, 101-2, 105-6
Stern, Philip Van Doren 337, 340, 401
Stevens, Connie 530, 537
Stevens, Craig 537
Stevens, Dodie 535, 540
Stevens, Leith 81, 452
Stevens, Mark 343
Stevens, Ray 532
Stevens, Rise 513
Stevenson, John 414
Stewart, Alex 300-1
Stewart, Donald Ogden 327, 426
Stewart, Gloria 123-8, 130-3, 135-7, 140-2, 145, 153, 156-7, 164, 166, 173, 175, 178, 262, 307, 360, 371, 374, 390, 517, 544-7, 550
Stewart, Judy 51, 291, 547, 553
Stewart, Kelly 6, 51, 291, 547, 553
Stoddard, Haila 460
Stokowski, Leopold 495
Stone, Anne 388, 404
Stone, Kirby 534
Stone, Ron 530
Stordahl, Axel 85, 222
Strategic Air Command 199, 202-3, 206-7, 290, 314
Stratton, Monty 262, 347, 349, 556, 558
Stratton, Jr., Gil 344-5
Stratton Story, The 13, 77, 105-6, 128, 206, 262, 290, 346, 348-9, 358, 386, 395, 403, 405, 409, 433, 452, 454, 553, 556, 558
Strauss, John 215, 306, 385
Strickling, Howard 553
Stringer, Arthur A. 397
Stringfellow, Frank 239
Strout, Dick 538, 558-60
Studebaker, John W. 296
Sullivan, Ed 514, 534-7, 539-40
Sullivan, Margaret 196-7, 281, 291, 317, 334, 423-4, 503
Sullivan, Norman 172, 178-9
Summers, Hope 49
Surrey, Berne 81, 450
Sutton, Daniel 210
Swanson, Gloria 256, 291
Swayze, John Cameron 513
Sweeten, Claude 502
Swerling, Jo 334, 337
Swingerettes 243

Tackaberry, John 304
Taft, Charles P. 484
Talbot, Irving 257
Talbot, Nita 345
Tandy, Jessica 469
Tatum, Jean 50
Taylor, Elizabeth 288
Taylor, Forrest 324
Taylor, Glenhall 432, 467
Taylor, Marian Young 358
Taylor, Paul 107
Taylor, Robert 14, 280, 291, 320, 394
Tazewell, Charles 237, 394
Tchaikovsky, Piort Ilyich 417, 419-20, 423
Tearle, Conway 324
Teasdale, Verree 210
Tease, Walt 481
Tedrow, Irene 402
Temple, Shirley 218, 514
Templeton, Alec 210
Tennille, Toni 311
Terr, Max 264
Terry, Joe 346
Tetzel, Joanne 461
Thatcher, Leora 324
Thomas, Danny 214, 308, 447, 520, 522, 531-2
Thomas, Lowell 513
Thomas, Shirley 262, 434
Thompson, Dee J. 35, 76
Thompson, Duane 325
Thompson, Russ 447
Thorndike, Oliver 461, 464
Thorsen, Russell 39
Three Singing Dollars 284-5
Thunder Bay -
  35-40, 42-3, 289, 313, 365
Tighe, Eileen 345
Tilton, Martha 224, 310
Tobias, Charles 247
Tobin, Maurice 490
Torme, Mel 243, 251, 288, 366
Tours, Frank 417-8, 420, 423
Towers, Shirley 261
Townsend, Colleen 213
Tracy, Spencer 218, 264-5, 301, 348, 510-11, 549
Tracy, Sterling 494
Travers, Henry 93, 315
Tremayne, Les 58

Trevor, Claire 83-4
Trosper, Guy 346
Trotter, John Scott 107-8, 123, 134, 152, 154, 159, 162
Trout, Bob 483
Troy, Helen 264
Truman, Harry S 215, 488, 490, 525
Truman, Margaret 411-3
Tunberg, Karl 344
Tunney, General Carl A. 399
Turk, Roy 107-8, 123, 152
Turner, Lana 85, 399, 454
Tusher, William 481
Tuttle, Lurene 426, 453
Twiss, Buddy 229
Uhlig, Max 322
Ullman, Richard H. 534
Umeki, Miyoshi 85
Uncle Wigley 483
Unitas, Johnny 514
Valentine, Karen 531
Vallee, Rudy 210, 229, 231, 238, 433, 495, 498-9
Van Cleave, Nathan Lang 397
Van Derbur, Marilyn 523
Van Deventer, Fred 482
Van Deventer, Nancy 482
Van Rooten, Luis 192
Vanda, Charles 466
Velez, Lupe 107
Venuti, Joe 159, 161-4
Vereen, Ben 526
Vertigo 193, 195, 467
Vigran, Herb 32, 34, 38, 42, 44, 47, 52, 54, 59, 70
Vines, Ellsworth 281
Vinton, Bobby 528
Von Zell, Harry 41, 184, 524
Vonn, Veola 135, 137-40, 143-6, 151-8, 164, 167-70
Wade, Ernestine 337
Wagner, Roger 257-258
Walburn, Raymond 197, 317
Wald, Jerry 84
Wald, John 18, 22, 53, 54, 60, 61, 64, 65, 66, 67, 71, 73, 74, 75, 76
Waldecker, Frank 482
Walker, Clint 530
Wallace, Jerry 540

Wallace, Regina 345
Wallace, Sylvia 389
Wallers, Clyde 239
Wallington, Jimmy 210, 404-15
Walsh, Mary Jane 313
Walsh, Pat 234
Walsh, William 528
Walters, James 38
Wanger, Walter 388
Ward, Edward 263, 317-8
Waring, Fred 7, 77, 243-54
Warren, Fran 79, 146, 151-2
Warren, Nina 261
Waterfield, Bob 389
Waterman, Willard 345, 348
Watson, Lucile 294
Watson, W.W. 419
Watts, Howard 516
Waxman, Stanley 411
Wayne, David 371
Wayne, Fredd 38
Wayne, John 84-5, 514, 531-2, 542
Wayne, Justina 324
Wayne, Pat 561
Weatherby, Willie 526
Weaver, Jr., Sylvester P. 370
Webb, Chick 216-7
Webb, Jack 261, 527-8, 530-2
Webb, Jane 345-6
Webber, Peggy 404, 455
Webster, Connie 538
Weems, Dave 242
Weidler, Virginia 328-9
Weihe, Fred 192
Weill, Kurt 247
Weissmuller, Johnny 219
Weitzel, Tony 470
Welch, Robert L. 83
Welk, Lawrence 514
Welles, Barbara 78, 93-100
Welles, Orson 258, 263, 495, 498
Wellman, William 406, 408
Wells, George 325, 327
Wells, Robert 243-4, 251
West, Mae 85, 139, 210
Wheatley, Joanne 245, 252
Wheaton, Glenn 214
Whelan, Michael 292
White, Paul Dudley 513

INDEX

Whiteman, Paul 85, 106, 378
Whitfield, Ann 237
Whiting, Margaret 172, 174, 178-9, 517, 535, 537, 540
Whitley, June 353
Whitman, Gayne 208-9, 292, 294
Whitman, Jerry 482
Whitman, Stuart 498
Whitmore, James 470, 520
Widmark, Richard 343, 527-8
Widom, Bud 201-7
Wilcox, Harlow 86, 452-5
Wilde, Cornel 532
Wilkes, William 487
Williams, Clarence 531-2
Williams, David Marshall 553, 555
Williams, Dean 38
Williams, Esther 83, 510-11
Williams, Ralph Vaughan 21
Williams, Rhoda 346
Williams, Roger 536
Williams, Ted 399, 511
Wills, Henry 38
Willson, Meredith 236, 263, 265-7, 272-6, 278-9, 281, 392
Wilson, Don 303-5
Wilson, Elizabeth 455
Wilson, Frank 81
Wilson, Jane 243, 245, 252-3
Wilson, Katherine 239
Wilson, Michael 337
Wilson, Morton 86
Wilson, Stanley 38, 49, 75
Wilson, Teddy 171
Winchell, Walter 83
Winchester '73 13, 77, 289, 313, 315, 337, 350-3, 559
Windsor, Marie 344
Windust, Bretaigne 196
Winnie the Pooh 483
Winslowe, Paula 445
Winterhalter, Hugo 206
Wissler, Rudy 235
Wiston, Henry 480
Wolcott, "Jersey Joe" 511
Wolfson, P.J. 425
Wood, Gloria 123
Wood, Natalie 527, 530-1
Woodruff, Frank 322
Woodward, Joanne 85, 511, 527
Woolf, Charles 344
Woolrich, Cornell 452
Work, Henry C. 229
Worley, Floyd 481
Wray, Richard G. 38, 49, 75
Wright, Ben 71, 72
Wright, Bob 404
Wright, Edythe 222
Wright, George 312
Wright, Howard 38
Wright, Robert 263
Wright, Teresa 84
Wright, Will 36, 38, 49, 54, 57, 61, 72
Wyler, William 388
Wylie, Howard 402, 404, 406, 409, 411, 414
Wylie, I.A.R. 425
Wyman, Jane 82-4, 263, 342-3, 390, 394, 488-9, 510-1, 562, 563
Wynter, Dana 85
Yellen, Jack 229
You Can't Take It With You 90, 99, 247, 286, 314, 356
Youmans, Vincent 434
Young, Alan 184, 213, 294, 537
Young, Carleton 73, 356
Young, Joe 228
Young, Loretta 13-4, 83-4, 219, 236, 292, 394, 419
Young, Robert 263, 281-3, 317, 356, 502, 527-8
Young, Victor 207, 512
Yount, Mildred 481
Yukl, Joe 381-2, 480
Zalenka, Sydney 432
Zefferelli, Franco 396
Zimbalist, Jr., Efrem 528, 531-532
Zimmerman, Harry 237
Ziv, Frederic W. 502
Zoller, Jack 208
Zukor, Adolph 389

Bear Manor Media

Classic Cinema.
Timeless TV.
Retro Radio.

WWW.BEARMANORMEDIA.COM

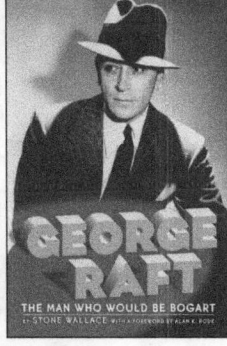

www.ingramcontent.com/pod-product-compliance
Lightning Source LLC
Chambersburg PA
CBHW071231300426
44116CB00008B/985